# Log on to IT for CSEC

Roland Birbal
Michele Taylor

Pearson Education Limited
Edinburgh Gate
Harlow
Essex CM20 2EJ
England
and Associated Companies throughout the World

www.longmancaribbean.com

Carlong Publishers (Caribbean) Limited
33 Second Street
Newport West
Kingston 13
Jamaica

Lexicon Trinidad Limited
LP# 48 Boundary Road
San Juan
Trinidad



Third impression 2009
ISBN 978-1-4058-2042-4

Prepared for publication by eMC Design

We are grateful to the following for permission to reproduce photographs:
Photos supplied courtesy of **Alamy Images**, **Getty Images**, **PunchStock Royalty Free Images**, **Arkeia Corporation**, **NASA/Galaxy**, **Ronald Grant Archive**, **Hewlett-Packard Company**, **Microsoft Corporation**, **PunchStock**, **Rex Features**, **Science Photo Library**, **Symantec(UK)Ltd**.

Every effort has been made to trace the copyright holders and we apologise in advance for any unintentional omissions. We would be pleased to insert the appropriate acknowledgement in any subsequent edition of this publication.

Picture Research by Francis Topp

Printed in China
GCC/03

Index compiled by Indexing Specialists (UK) Ltd.

# Contents


1 **Types of computers and their parts** 4
What is a computer?
Stages of processing
Types of computers
Generations of computers

2 **Input devices** 14
Data collection
Typical input devices
Scanning devices
Audio and video input devices
Other input devices

3 **Primary and secondary storage** 26
Primary storage
Units of storage
Secondary storage devices
Other storage media

4 **Output devices** 40
Soft copy output devices
Hard copy output devices
Robot and control systems

5 **Data storage and representation** 50
Number systems
Adding binary numbers
Representing signed integers
Data representation
Fixed point representation
Floating point numbers

6 **Software** 66
Applications software
System software
User interfaces
File management operations using Windows
Utilities

7 **Data communications, networks and the Internet** 81
Data communications
Networks
The Internet
Communication services
World Wide Web

8 **Programming** 107
Generations of computer languages
Program development – steps in algorithm development
Step 1 – defining the problem
Step 2 – analysing the problem
Step 3 – developing an algorithm
Step 4 – writing a computer program corresponding to the algorithm
Step 5 – testing and debugging the program
Step 6 – documenting the program

9 **System security and computer crimes** 138
Data integrity and security
Data privacy

10 **Word processing** 150
Starting Word
Editing and proofing text
Formatting
Page layout
Drawing a line
Mail merge
Newspaper columns
Tables
Inserting graphics
Inserting symbols and special characters

11 **Spreadsheets** 192
Starting Excel
Entering data
Formatting
Editing
Working with worksheets
Formulae
Functions
Absolute cell references
Sorting
Filtering records
Creating graphs and charts
The IF function
Finding a record in a list
Date function
Printing a worksheet

12 **Databases** 233
Manual databases
Computerised databases
Creating a database using Microsoft Access (Office XP)
Creating tables
Properties
Setting a primary key
Entering records into a table
Designing a database
Indexing and sorting data
Queries
Forms
Reports

13 **Integrating data** 271
Mail merge (using an Access or Excel table as the data source)
Integrating data and graphs from a spreadsheet into a word processing document
Integrating reports and tables from a database into a word processing document
Exporting a database object to a spreadsheet
Importing a spreadsheet to a database
Sample SBA project on data integration
A solution to the project

14 **Careers in computing** 299
Jobs in an ICT department
Other jobs within the computer industry
Other ICT jobs

15 **Applications and implications of IT** 312
Collecting, storing and sharing information
Computers in banking
Computers in business
Computers in education
Computers in engineering and manufacturing
Computers in Artificial Intelligence (AI)
Computers in law enforcement
Computers in medicine
Computers in entertainment
Computers in weather forecasting
Social effects of computers
The effects of computers on employee health

**Glossary** 343

**Index** 350

# 1 Types of computers and their parts

**OBJECTIVES**

At the end of this chapter you will be able to:

- Define the term computer
- Describe the difference between data and information
- State some of the reasons for using computers
- Explain the difference between hardware and software
- State the stages involved in computer processing
- Explain the functions of the Central Processing Unit, Control Unit, Arithmetic and Logic Unit, Registers, program counter and instruction register
- Classify computers as personal computers, minicomputers, mainframe computers, supercomputers and embedded computers
- Describe the different types of portable computers (laptops, notebooks, sub-notebooks, organisers and palmtops)
- Classify computers by generations

## What is a computer?

A computer is a programmable electronic device that processes data, following a set of instructions to produce information which it can output or store for future use. An electronic device uses tiny electric currents, flowing through circuits, to perform its operations.

### What is the difference between data and information?

Data is all the raw facts and figures that a computer processes by following a set of instructions called a program. Data by itself has no meaning; it can be in the form of letters (a, b, c, d... x, y, z, etc.), numbers (1, 2, 3, 15, 456, etc.), pictures, sounds or symbols. It is only when we attach meaning to data that we get information.

For example, if you collect the temperature of your classroom each day for a month, you have collected data. When you instruct a computer to arrange (sort) this data, you could get information such as the following:

- The highest temperature over the period
- The lowest temperature over the period
- The mean (average) temperature over the period.

This information may then be useful, for example, to determine whether a classroom is too hot or too cold for comfortable working. If the information were just raw data, it would not be easy to interpret. Hence, the computer has helped you look at a real-life situation or problem and make some sense of it.

### Why do we use computers?

- For their data-processing speed: computers are very fast; they can perform tens of millions of operations per second. With this speed comes the power to undertake many different tasks such as predicting weather forecasts, performing scientific research and producing thousands of bills for utility companies.
- For their data-processing accuracy: computers are very accurate. Errors occur only if there is an error in the way hardware and software have been set up, or if there are errors in the data that has been input. When errors occur it is therefore usually because of some human error. Computers can only do what they are set up and programmed to do.
- For storing large amounts of information in a small space: there are many types of computer storage media that can be used to store large volumes of data and information. For example, a single CD-ROM disk can hold the equivalent of a shelf of library books in electronic form.
- For their ability to work continuously: computers can work continuously for very long periods, only stopping for upgrading or maintenance checks. In fact, most modern computers can be left switched on all the time if desired, 24 hours per day and 7 days a week, continuously processing data.

## Hardware and software

A computer system consists of both hardware and software. **Hardware** is all the parts of the computer system you can see and touch. These devices, which are also called **peripherals**, include keyboards, printers, speakers, mouse and hard drives. **Software** is a set of instructions (called a **program** ) that a computer needs to carry out its tasks. For example, if you want to use the computer to type a letter, draw a picture or do some accounting work, you would need different types of software to accomplish these tasks. Some typical examples of software are word processors, spreadsheets, graphics packages and database packages. Both hardware and software are needed to process data.

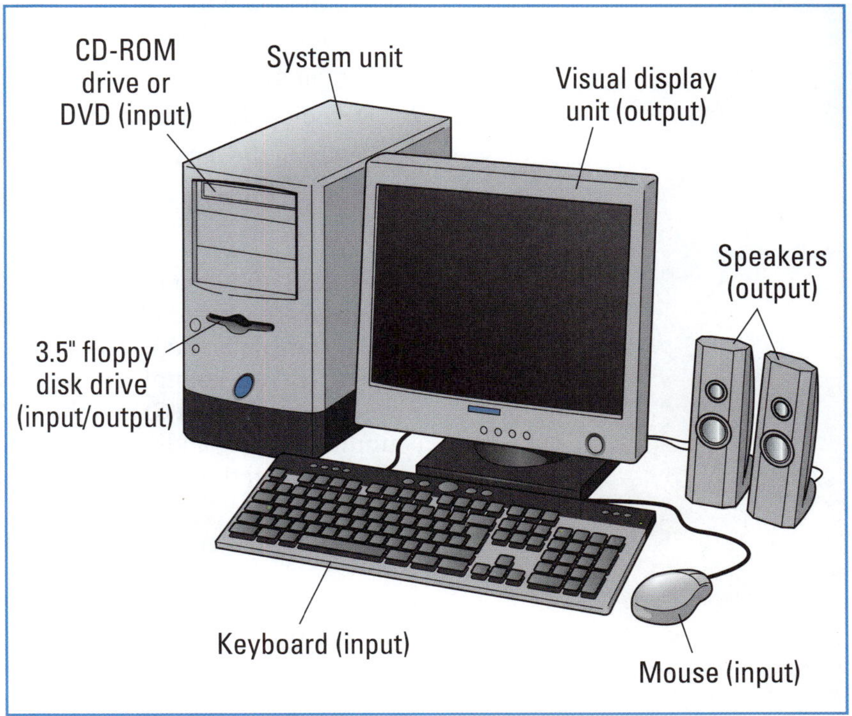


*Figure 1.1 The parts of a personal computer*

# Stages of processing

To accomplish its tasks a computer has to process data. Processing data to get information involves three stages: input, processing and output.

Input → Processing → Output

*Figure 1.2 Stages of processing*

Input devices are used to get the data and instructions into the computer for processing. The processing takes place in that part of the computer called the central processing unit (CPU). The CPU, also known as the **processor**, is the 'brain' of the computer. It takes raw data and, following a set of instructions (programs), converts it into information. The speed at which a CPU processes data to convert it is measured in megahertz (millions of machine cycles per second) or for newer machines in gigahertz (billions of machine cycles per second). A machine cycle is the sequence of instructions performed to execute one program instruction. Machine cycles are measured in nanoseconds (one billionth of a second) or picoseconds (one trillionth of a second). The CPU consists of two smaller units known as the Control Unit (CU) and the Arithmetic and Logic Unit (ALU).

### Did you know?

Did you know that the scientific unit of measure 'hertz' (Hz) is named in honour of the German physicist Heinrich Rudolf Hertz (1857–1894). Hertz did the groundwork for the development of the vacuum tube. He also discovered electromagnetic waves.

## Control unit

The control unit is the main part of the CPU. It directs and co-ordinates all the activities within the CPU. The control unit determines the sequence in which instructions are executed. It does not execute the instructions itself; instead it sends the data and instructions to the ALU for processing. The CPU is primarily responsible for movement of data and instructions from itself to the main memory and ALU and back. The CU executes an instruction by performing the following steps:

1. Fetching the instruction from memory
2. Decoding the instruction
3. Fetching the data required by the instruction from memory
4. Sending the data and instruction to the ALU for processing
5. Sending the data to the memory unit after processing

The control unit contains a number of registers. A **register** is a temporary storage location that holds a single instruction or data item. Registers are used to store data and instructions that are needed immediately and frequently. Two examples of registers found in the control unit are the **program counter** (PC) and the **instruction register** (IR). The program counter holds the address of the current instruction (the instruction being processed) and the instruction register holds the instruction itself.

## Arithmetic and Logic Unit

The Arithmetic and Logic Unit (ALU) performs all the arithmetic and logic functions in a computer. For example, if an instruction involves an arithmetic operation such as addition, subtraction, multiplication or division or the comparison of data, the control unit sends the data to the ALU for processing.

Some of the logic functions are comparisons, such as:

| | |
|---|---|
| equal to = | not equal to ≠ |
| less than < | greater than > |
| less than or equal to < = | greater than or equal to > = |

For example, using the 'equal to' logic function, the ALU compares two values to determine if they are equal.

Other logical operations performed by the ALU are AND, OR and NOT. You will learn more about these in Chapter 8.

*Figure 1.3*
*The components of a basic computer system*

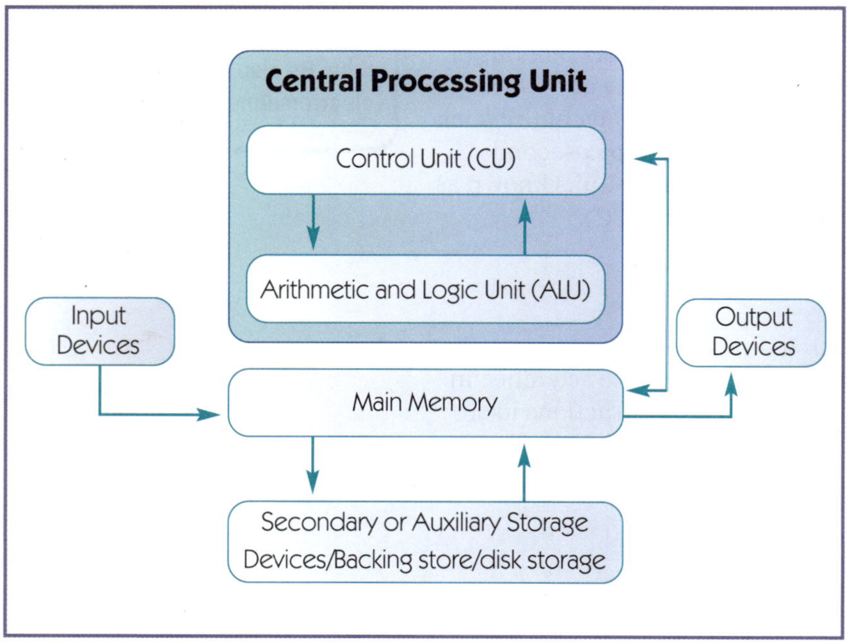


## The main memory

The **main memory**, which is directly accessible to the CPU, holds data and instructions that the computer is processing at the time. Therefore, the data collected in the example about the temperature of the classroom would be placed in main memory while it is being processed.

Output devices then translate information processed by the computer into a form which the user can understand. After processing, the data and information can be either stored in a secondary storage device, such as a disk, or sent to an output device such as a printer or a computer screen.

# Types of computer

Computer systems are classified on the basis of system performance, which in turn affects physical size and cost. Given the rapid pace at which computer technology is changing, classifying computers on this basis is often very difficult, since many of the newer, smaller systems can outperform the large models of a few years ago. Nevertheless, some broad categories can be defined, as follows.

## Personal computers (PCs)

Personal computers (PCs), also sometimes called microcomputers, are the most common type of computer. They come in many different shapes, sizes and colours, depending on the manufacturer. PCs are designed to be used by one person at a time and fit on an office desk, hence the other name given to them, 'desktop computers'. A PC consists of a system unit, a keyboard, a mouse and a display screen, and has all the functional elements found in any larger system. It is designed to perform the input, control, arithmetic/logic, output and storage functions mentioned earlier in the chapter, just like any other computer system would do. It can execute software program instructions to perform a very wide variety of tasks.

*Figure 1.4*
*A PC with VDU, system unit, speakers, mouse and keyboard*

## Laptops

A laptop computer is a portable version of a PC, equipped with a flat liquid crystal display (LCD) screen and weighing about one to four kilograms. The two principal types of laptop computers are notebooks and sub-notebooks.

A notebook computer is a portable computer that weighs two to four kilograms and is roughly the size of a large thick notebook, around 35 × 25 × 4 centimetres. They have a fairly large LCD colour screen (about 30 cm across) and a fairly large keyboard, usually with a small touch-sensitive pad which serves as a mouse. Notebook PCs can easily be tucked into a briefcase or backpack, or simply under your arm, and can use power from an electrical outlet or rechargeable batteries. Notebooks are usually just as powerful as a desktop PC but cost more than their equivalent desktop PC.

A sub-notebook computer weighs about half a kilogram and can fit in a large jacket pocket. It has a small screen, sometimes in colour, and a small keyboard without the mouse function. It can perform many of the functions of notebooks, but not to the same degree of complexity.

*Figure 1.5*
*A notebook computer*

## Minicomputers

Minicomputers have become outdated and are rarely used today. They were very popular in the 1960s. Their cost, storage and processing capabilities were somewhere between those of a PC and a mainframe computer. They were mainly used in small manufacturing plants, research labs and businesses. Mini systems were usually designed to handle simultaneously the processing needs of multiple users. They allowed many users to share access to central hardware through stations called terminals. Minis can support dozens of terminals. A typical terminal has a keyboard, a display screen and a wire that connects the terminal to the computer system.

*Figure 1.6*
*A mainframe computer*

## Mainframes

Mainframes are very powerful computers and are therefore very expensive. Mainframes are systems that offer faster processing speeds and greater storage capacity than a typical mini. A mainframe can handle more than a thousand users at a time. They are found in large organisations such as banks, government agencies, insurance companies and corporations where they perform tasks that require a lot of computational power: typically, bulk data processing such as censuses, industry/consumer statistics and bank transaction processing. The IBM zSeries 990 Model D32 is currently one of the most powerful mainframe computers available.

## Supercomputers ('monsters')

Supercomputers such as NEC's Earth Simulator and California Digital Corporation's Intel Itanium2 Tiger4 were two of the largest, fastest and most powerful computers in the the year 2004. They are typically used for 'number crunching' in scientific simulations, scientific research and developments in areas such as energy, space exploration, medicine and industry. Supercomputers are designed to process complex scientific applications. These systems are the most expensive computers in the world, often costing millions of dollars.

## Tablet PC

A tablet PC is a computer that looks like a notebook computer except that data can be entered through the use of a keyboard, touch screen or a digitising tablet. Data can be entered through the digitising tablet with the use of a special pen called a stylus.

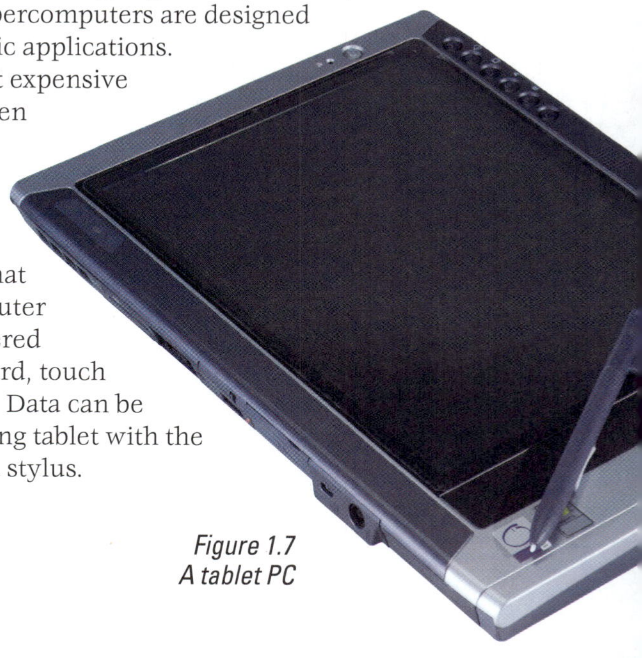

*Figure 1.7*
*A tablet PC*

## Electronic organisers and palmtop computers

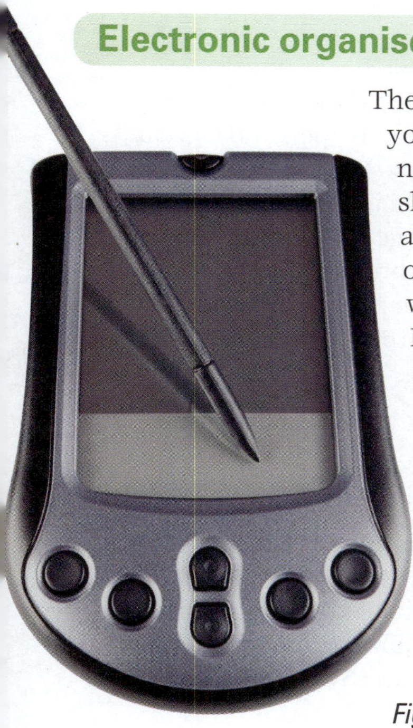

These are so-called because they fit in the palm of your hand and are therefore less powerful than notebooks and sub-notebooks. They can fit into a shirt pocket and weigh perhaps 300 grams on average. They might have a very small keyboard, or a palm-sized screen (sometimes in colour) which can be written on with a special pen. Electronic organisers are mainly used to store appointments, addresses, phone numbers and 'to do' lists.

Palmtop computers are more powerful than electronic organisers, and these days can even run some of the same software as sub-notebooks and notebooks. Some cellular phones are now powerful enough to act as very small personal organisers.

*Figure 1.8 A palmtop computer*

## Embedded computers

An embedded computer is a special-purpose computer used inside a device and is usually dedicated to specific functions. It is housed on a single microprocessor board with the programs stored in ROM. It is connected to sensors – devices which detect changes in the environment such as light, temperature or pressure – and actuators, hardware output devices that convert an electrical control signal into a physical action. They are commonly used in items such as washing machines, cameras, cars, motors, sewing machines, clocks and microwaves.

*Figure 1.9 The button panel of a microwave*

# Generations of computers

Computers can be broadly classified into five generations. These generations are based mainly on the basic electronic component that was used to build the computer.

## First generation (1945–1956)

The vacuum tube or valve was the main electronic component of first generation computers. This made the computers very large; they contained many kilometres of electrical wire, used a lot of electrical power and generated a lot of heat. Because vacuum tubes were blown so easily, processing was unreliable. Also, each computer had a different binary coded program called a 'machine language' that told it how to operate, and had to be programmed directly in this machine language. This made the computer difficult to program and limited its versatility and speed.

The Harvard Mark I (electromechanical) was the first computer in this generation. The ENIAC (Electronic Numerical Integrator and Calculator) produced in 1946 was the first computer to use electrical signals for calculating and storing results, with no mechanical operations involved. Other first generation computers include UNIVAC, Burroughs 220 and the IBM 700 series.

> **Did you know?**
>
> Did you know that the transistor is considered to be one of the greatest inventions of modern times? Without transistors, modern computers would not have been possible. The transistor was invented at Bell Laboratories in December 1947 by John Bardeen, Walter Houser Brattain and William Bradford Shockley. They were awarded the 1956 Nobel Prize in physics for their outstanding achievement.

## Second generation (1956–1963)

Transistors were invented in 1947 and these formed the basis for second generation computers. A transistor is a device used to open and close a circuit in computer processors and digital memory. Computers became smaller, faster, more reliable and more energy-efficient than their predecessors. The machine languages of the first generation computers were replaced by assembly language, allowing abbreviated programming codes to replace long, difficult binary codes. Some popular second generation computers include the IBM 1400 and 1600 series, UNIVAC III, NCR 300 series and the Burroughs B500 series.

## Third generation (1964–1970)

With the invention of the integrated circuit (IC), or chip, computers became even smaller, faster, more reliable, more energy-efficient and cheaper than their predecessors. Another third generation development was the invention and use of 'high-level' languages, which used English words and the base ten number system to program the computer. Some third generation computers include the IBM System 3 and System 7, UNIVAC 9000 series, NCR Century series and the Burroughs 6700.

## Fourth generation (1971–present)

Fourth generation computers are still based on the chip, but with many more components packed inside. First there was large-scale integration (LSI), where hundreds of components were placed on the chip. By the 1980s very large scale integration squeezed thousands of components onto a chip. Ultra large scale integration (ULSI) increased that number to millions of components. Computers became even smaller, cheaper and much more reliable; their processing capabilities increased accordingly. Some examples of fourth generation computers include the IBM System 3090 and RISC 6000, HP 9000 and the Cray 2 XMP, which were developed in 2002.

## Fifth generation (present–future)

Fifth generation computers will be able to mimic many of the things that so far have only been within the capacity of human beings to achieve, i.e. they will demonstrate a certain level of **artificial intelligence**. For example, fifth generation computers, including standard PCs, are starting to accept spoken word instructions (voice recognition) and can now assist doctors in making very specific diagnoses (expert systems).

Computers of this generation make use of parallel processing: they are capable of performing multiple, simultaneous operations using more than one microprocessing chip. This makes them especially powerful. The eventual goal of fifth generation computers is to develop devices that respond to natural language input and are capable of 'learning'. An artificial intelligence program would therefore eliminate the need for users to write programs, since they could communicate their orders to the computer via ordinary English.

# Summary

1 A computer system consists of both hardware and software.

2 Hardware is all the parts of the computer system you can see and touch, e.g. printers, keyboards, mouse, system unit.

3 Software is a set of instructions (program) that a computer needs to carry out its tasks.

4 Data is all the raw facts and figures that a computer processes by following a set of instructions (called a program) to produce information.

5 Input, processing and output are the three stages of processing.

6 Input devices are used to get data and instructions into the computer for processing.

7 The Central Processing Unit is the 'brain' of the computer. It consists of two smaller units known as the Control Unit (CU) and the Arithmetic and Logic Unit (ALU).

8 The control unit is the main part of the CPU. It directs and co-ordinates all the activities within the CPU.

9 A register is a temporary storage location that holds a single instruction or data item.

10 The program counter (PC) holds the address of the current instruction (the instruction being processed) and the instruction register (IR) holds the instruction itself.

11 The Arithmetic and Logic Unit (ALU) performs all the arithmetic and logic functions in a computer.

12 The main memory holds data and instructions that the computer is processing at the time.

13 Output devices translate information processed by the computer into a form which the user can understand.

14 Computers are used because of their great speed, accuracy, large storage capacity and ability to work continuously in solving a variety of problems that would otherwise require many human hours of work.

15 Computer systems may be classified as embedded computers, personal computers (PCs), minicomputers, mainframe computers and supercomputers ('monsters').

16 Personal computers (PCs), also called desktop or microcomputers, are the most common computers. PCs are designed to be used by one person at a time and can usually fit on an office desk. A PC consists of a system unit, a keyboard, a mouse and a display screen, and has all the functional elements found in any larger system.

17 Minicomputers have become outdated and are rarely used today. They were very popular in the 1960s. Their cost, storage and processing capabilities were between those of a PC and a mainframe. They were mainly used in small manufacturing plants, research labs and businesses.

18 Mainframes are very powerful computers and are very expensive. They offer faster processing speeds and greater storage capacity than a typical mini. A mainframe can handle more than a thousand users at a time. They are found in large organisations such as banks, government agencies and insurance companies where they perform tasks that require a lot of computational power – typically bulk data processing such as censuses and bank transaction processing.

19 Supercomputers are the largest, fastest and most powerful computers at present. They are typically used for 'number crunching' in scientific simulations, scientific research and development in areas such as energy, space exploration, medicine and industry.

20 Laptops, notebooks and sub-notebooks are all portable computers with flat LCD screens.

21 A tablet PC is a computer that looks like a notebook computer except that data is entered through the use of a digitising tablet or touch screen.

22 Electronic organisers are mainly used to store appointments, addresses, phone numbers and 'to do' lists. Palmtop computers are more powerful than electronic organisers, and can even run some of the same software as sub-notebooks and notebooks.

23 An embedded computer is a special purpose computer that is used inside a device and is usually dedicated to specific functions.

24 The vacuum tube or valve was the main electronic component of first generation computers.

25 Transistors were invented in 1948 and formed the basis for second generation computers. Computers became smaller, faster, more reliable and more energy-efficient than their predecessors.

26 The integrated circuit (IC) or chip formed the basis for third generation computers. The use of high level languages, which used English words and the base ten number system to program the computer, was a feature of this third generation.

27 Fourth generation computers are based on the chip but with many more components packed inside. Ultra large scale integration (ULSI) increased that number to millions of components.

28 Fifth generation computers will be able to mimic many of the things so far only achievable by human beings (artificial intelligence). These computers will be able to accept spoken word instruction (voice recognition) and assist doctors in making diagnoses (expert systems).

# Questions

## Copy and fill in the blanks

1 A set of instructions that a computer needs to carry out its tasks is known as ________.

2 ____________ is a set of raw facts and figures.

3 _________ are used to get the data and instructions into the computer for processing.

4 Processing takes place in that part of the computer known as the ______________.

5 ____________ computers will be able to mimic many of the things that so far can only be done by human beings.

6 The vacuum tube or valve was the main electronic component of _________ generation computers.

7 The ________________ directs and co-ordinates all the activities within the CPU.

8 An ___________computer is a special purpose computer that is used inside of a device and is usually dedicated to specific functions.

9 A _______ is a temporary storage location that holds a single instruction or data item.

10 The ______________ holds the address of the current instruction in the control unit.

11 The _____________ performs all the arithmetic and logic functions in a computer.

12 _________ holds data and instructions that the computer is processing at the time.

13 _____________ translate information processed by the computer into a form which the user can understand.

14 A computer system consists of both ______________ and ______________.

15 All the parts of the computer system you can see and touch is known as __________.

## True or False?

1 Data and Information are the same. T ❑ F ❑

2 The CPU is the main part of the computer. T ❑ F ❑

3 All the data is processed in the memory unit. T ❑ F ❑

4 The control unit sends data from the memory to the ALU for processing. T ❑ F ❑

5 Output devices translate information processed by the computer into a form which the user can understand. T ❑ F ❑

6 A modern mainframe has the same processing power of a very powerful PC. T ❑ F ❑

7 An embedded computer is housed on a single microprocessor board. T ❑ F ❑

8 First generation computers were based on the integrated circuit (IC) or chip. T ❑ F ❑

9 CRAY T3E 900 and GRAPE are examples of personal computers. T ❑ F ❑

10 The most popular computers today are mainframe computers. T ❑ F ❑

11 A register can hold data permanently. T ❑ F ❑

12 The program counter (PC) is found in the control unit. T ❑ F ❑

## Multiple choice

1 ENIAC was the first:

(a) Electromechanical computer
(b) Electronic computer
(c) Computer with integrated circuits
(d) Microcomputer

2 Which is not an example of a peripheral device?

(a) Keyboard
(b) Mouse
(c) Floppy disk
(d) Speakers

3 A program is a:

(a) Hardware device
(b) Memory device
(c) Set of instructions
(d) Register

4 Which device is not found in the CPU?

(a) ALU
(b) Control unit
(c) Instruction register
(d) Printer

5 The ALU processes data and stores it in:

(a) A diskette
(b) Main memory
(c) The instruction register
(d) The program counter

6 Which one of the following is not a function of the control unit?

(a) Fetch instructions from memory
(b) Decode instructions
(c) Process instructions
(d) Fetch data for required instructions

7 Complex scientific research is usually done using:

(a) Microcomputers
(b) Supercomputers
(c) Minicomputers
(d) Mainframe computers

8 The main component that formed the basis for second generation computers was:
(a) Vacuum tubes
(b) Registers
(c) Integrated circuits
(d) Transistors

9 Third generation computers were used during the period:
(a) 1933–1945
(b) 1945–1956
(c) 1956–1963
(d) 1964–1970

10 Which generation of computers used ultra large scale integration (ULSI)?
(a) First generation
(b) Second generation
(c) Third generation
(d) Fourth generation

## Short answer questions

1 Define the terms hardware and software.

2 Using examples, explain the difference between data and information.

3 Draw a diagram showing the three stages of processing.

4 (a) Draw a block diagram to illustrate the main components of a computer system.
(b) Describe the functions of the two main units found in the central processing unit.

5 Explain the purpose of the following devices:
(a) Input device
(b) Output device
(c) Main memory

6 State FOUR reasons why computers are used.

7 Describe the features of a personal computer (PC).

8 (a) Explain the difference between a mainframe computer and a supercomputer.
(b) State TWO reasons why a bank may want to purchase a mainframe computer.
(c) Differentiate between a notebook computer and a sub-notebook computer.
(d) What is an embedded computer?

9 (a) List the components that formed the basis of the first four generations of computers.
(b) What are some of the expected features of fifth generation computers?

10 Discuss with your classmates how a portable computer could assist these professionals with their work:
(a) A teacher
(b) A police officer
(c) A newspaper reporter
(d) A sales representative

## Crossword

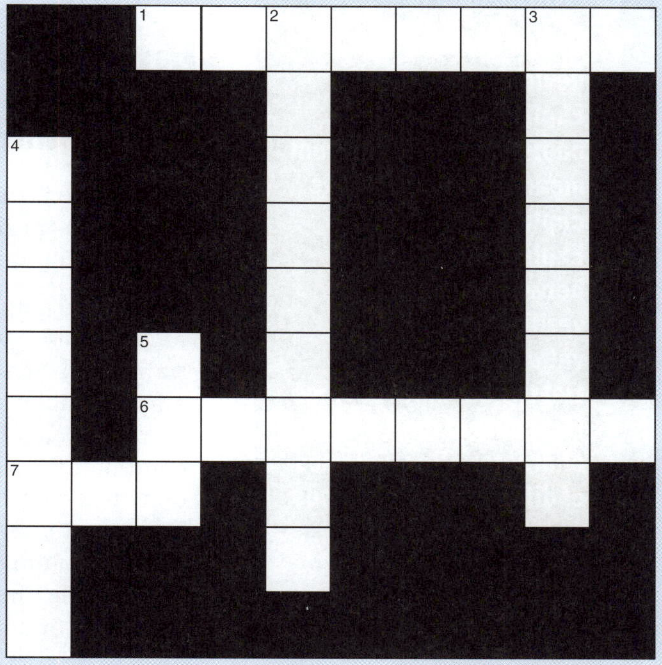


### Across

1 A device in the control unit that is used to store data and instructions that are needed immediately and frequently (8)

6 A type of processing that will be used in fifth generation computers (8)

7 Performs the logic functions in the computer (3)

### Down

2 It represents billions of machine cycles per second (9)

3 A special purpose computer that is used inside a device (8)

4 A set of instructions that the computer needs to carry out a task (8)

5 Also known as the brain of the computer (3)

# 2 Input devices

## OBJECTIVES

At the end of this chapter you will be able to:

- Define the term 'input device'
- Explain the term 'data capture' and the different means by which data is captured
- Explain the difference between data verification and validation
- List typical input devices
- List some of the characteristics and uses of different input devices

A computer needs input, output and storage devices so that it can accept data, process that data and produce useful output. All the input, output and storage devices connected to and dependent on a computer for operation are called peripherals. **Input devices** are pieces of equipment that are used to put data into the computer.

## Data collection

### Data capture

**Data capture** is the first stage of getting data into a computer. It is at this point that the various input devices are used to import data that the computer will process and/or store.

There are two main ways of inputting data:

- *Manual data input*: Data is entered directly into the computer one transaction at a time by hand. Keyboard, mouse, touch screen, light pen, graphics tablet and voice input devices are some of the devices used.
- *Automatic data input/data capture*: Data is entered directly into the computer from source documents. **Source documents** are documents on which data is first recorded before it is entered into the computer. Data entered from these documents is transferred directly from the document into the computer's memory. Data is captured at the source, for example directly from barcodes on supermarket items into the computer or directly from national lottery slips into the computer.

### Data verification and validation

The data captured or entered manually must be verified and validated by the computer before it is transferred to backing storage.

The process of **verification** is checking for accurate transcription or copying. A person copying the data may be required to type the data twice. Data typed in the second time is compared with that typed in first time. If there is a difference then it is considered that an error has occurred and has to be corrected by re-entering the data. For example, when you are asked to enter a password twice it is usually to verify that what you entered the first time is correct.

Once data has been entered into the computer, it is usually checked by the computer to see that it obeys the rules which apply to it; this is called **validation**. For example, you may be asked to enter your birthday according to the format mm/dd/yyyy. However, suppose you entered 21/10/1988 instead of 10/21/1988. There are only 12 months in a year, so the computer checks to see that you have entered a value within the correct limit: between 1 and 12 for months, between 1 and 31 for days of the month, and so on.

# Typical input devices

Typical input devices include the following peripherals. In this next section, we will look at each of these in turn.

| | |
|---|---|
| Keyboard | Optical Mark Reader (OMR) |
| Mouse | Barcodes |
| Joystick | RFID |
| Digitising tablet | Magnetic reader |
| Touch-sensitive screen | Smart cards |
| Light pen | Voice data entry |
| Digital stills camera | Sound capture |
| Magnetic Ink Character Recognition (MICR) | Video capture |
| Image scanner (OCR) | Biometric systems |
| Flatbed/drum scanners etc | Remote control |
| | Sensor |

## Keyboard

The most common input device is the keyboard. A digital code is sent to the computer when each key is pressed. For example, the code 01100001 is produced when the 'A' key is pressed. Keyboards play a pivotal role in the input of data into the computer. Their design is of critical importance for comfort and usability, since users may spend long periods of time entering data. Many keyboards are therefore designed with ergonomics in mind.

There are two types of keyboard: the alphanumeric keyboard and special-function keyboards. The alphanumeric keyboard contains letters, numbers and symbols in particular layouts. This keyboard is modelled on the typewriter keyboard, also known as a QWERTY keyboard (based on the sequence of letters at the top left). Keyboards may be attached to the computer by wires or they may be wireless.

Special-function keyboards are invented for a particular purpose. For example:

- *The Braille keyboard* has its keys marked with raised dots to aid the blind.
- *The concept keyboard* contains a flatbed of contact switches covered by a flexible membrane. Over each contact switch whole words, pictures or symbols are superimposed. The computer is then programmed to respond appropriately to these. These keyboards are used in education as an early-learning aid, in restaurants so the operator can visually add up the cost of standard menu items, and in messy places where a normal keyboard would be at risk.
- *The left-handed keyboard* is designed for the left-handed individual.
- *A virtual/projection keyboard* is projected onto any surface and touched. The keyboard can register your finger movement and hence translate that movement into a keystroke. An example is the touch-screen keyboard of the automatic teller machines (ATM) found in front of banks, etc.

## Pointing devices

Pointing devices are used by graphical operating systems such as Windows to show the motion of a pointer or cursor, and enable the control and selection of objects on the display.

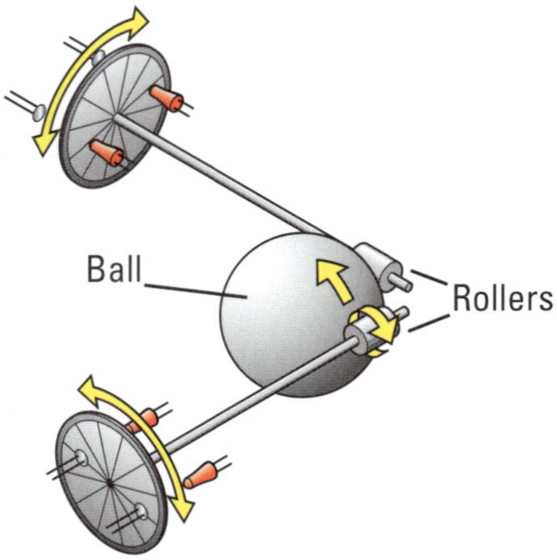


*Figure 2.1*
*Illustration of the mechanics inside a mouse*

## Mouse

The movement of the mouse over a flat surface is mirrored by a pointer on the monitor screen. Under the mouse is a ball which rolls and turns two shafts, one for each direction – left/right and up/down (Figure 2.1). Buttons on the mouse allow you to make selections from menus, move objects around the screen and paint or draw.

The ball can get dirty and transfer the dirt to the shafts. This can cause the mouse pointer to move erratically. The mouse therefore needs to be cleaned regularly.

Besides the regular mouse, there are other kinds of mouse: some designed for comfort and others a matter of preference:

- *The optical mouse* can slide over most surfaces since it does not have a ball. It emits a small beam of red light which bounces off the surface into a sensor. The sensor sends co-ordinates to the computer which in turn moves the cursor or pointer on the monitor screen, according to these co-ordinates. The advantage of this type of mouse is that you do not need to worry about dirt and cleaning, and it is very easy to manipulate. Since there are no moving parts the mouse is less likely to fail because there is less wear and tear. The disadvantage is perhaps that this type of mouse is more expensive than an ordinary mouse. A mouse can come with or without a wire attachment, hence we have the wireless mouse.
- *The trackball mouse* has a large ball on top rather than underneath. You can roll the ball with the palm of your hand or fingers. These are found mainly on laptop computers. Buttons placed close by allow you to select features on the screen.
- *The pointing stick mouse* found on laptop computers looks like a pencil eraser. It protrudes from the keyboard between the B, G and H keys. Pushing on the pointing stick with your finger will move the pointer around the screen. Once again, buttons placed close by allow for selection of features on the screen.
- *The touchpad mouse* contains a touch-sensitive pad and is normally found on laptops. It is a pressure- and motion-sensitive flat surface of about 5 cm × 5 cm, over which you move your fingers to control the cursor/pointer on the screen. Buttons placed close to this surface allow for selection of features on the screen.

**Did you know?**

Did you know that the measurement for the speed and movement direction of a computer mouse is called a mickey? One mickey is approximately 1/200 of an inch.

*Figure 2.2*
*An optical mouse*

## Joystick

A **joystick** is a device which lets you control the movement of an object on the screen by operating a small lever. It is used mainly for computer games such as flight simulators.

## Digitising tablet (graphics tablet)

To digitise data means to convert it from an analogue form (like a picture) to a digital form (binary numbers – see Chapter 5). A **digitising tablet** is a board which can detect the position of a pointing device such as a stylus or a puck on its surface. A **stylus** is a pen-like pointing device for a graphics/digitising tablet. A **puck** is a mouse-like device which is moved over the surface of the tablet. It has cross-hairs to position it accurately and a number of buttons for different actions. Drawings and sketches can be easily entered onto the computer using the digitising tablet.

## Touch-sensitive screen

This pointing device lets you interact with the computer by touching the screen. The pointer is the human finger. There are three forms of touch screen: pressure-sensitive, capacitive surface and light beam. These screens are used in bank ATM machines, for example. They allow you to perform actions on your bank account by following instructions and options on-screen, using your finger to choose the option you wish.

*Figure 2.3 A light pen*

## Light pen

This is shaped like a pen (Figure 2.3) and is connected to a VDU/monitor. It allows you to point and make selections more accurately on a screen. The tip of the light pen contains a light-sensitive element which, when placed against the screen, detects the light from the screen and enables the computer to identify the location of the pen on the screen. Making selections with a light pen is far more accurate than using your finger to make selections on a touch sensitive screen. Light pens also allow the user to draw directly on the screen. However, they are not as accurate as a digitising tablet and drawing can become uncomfortable.

## Exercise 1

**1** What is the most common input device?
(a) Mouse
(b) Printer
(c) Monitor
(d) Keyboard

**2** Which of the following is not a pointing device?
(a) Joystick
(b) MICR
(c) Light pen
(d) Mouse

**3** A device that enables the user to control the movement of objects on the screen by operating a small lever is a
(a) Touch-sensitive screen
(b) Joystick
(c) Puck
(d) Light pen

**4** Which of these has a ball positioned at the top?
(a) Optical mouse
(b) Pointing stick mouse
(c) Touchpad mouse
(d) Trackball mouse

**5** Which type of keyboard would most likely be used by a physically challenged person?
(a) Concept keyboard
(b) Alphanumeric keyboard
(c) Virtual keyboard
(d) Left-handed keyboard

# Scanning devices

## Scanners

*Figure 2.4*
*A flat-bed scanner*

**Scanners** were originally designed to scan pictures (image scanners) but now their use is extended, for example to scan text into a word processing program.

There are many types of scanners:

- *Flat-bed scanner*: The picture is placed on a flat scanning surface and the image is captured, similarly to how a photocopying machine works. Household versions are inexpensive, costing less than 100 US dollars.
- *Hand-held scanner*: The scanner reads in the picture while the user drags the scanner over it. The quality of the image provided by this scanner is poor, but it is useful for quick data capture.
- *Drum scanner*: These are normally used in the publishing industry (magazines, books) to capture images with high detail. These scanners tend to be expensive, costing perhaps thousands of US dollars.
- *Sheet-fed scanner*: The sheet that contains the image is fed through rollers and the picture is scanned as the paper passes through.

## Magnetic Ink Character Recognition (MICR)

MICR is mainly used in the banking industry to read cheques. Bank cheques have the following information encoded in them:

- The cheque number
- The bank branch number
- The customer's account number.
- After the customer has written a cheque, the bank also encodes the amount of money using a special magnetic ink which contains iron oxide.

The cheques can then be read by an MICR reader. As the document passes into the MICR reader the shapes of the characters can be recognised electronically. The characters have to be printed in a special font since the reader can only recognise a specific font and a limited number of characters: some readers can only recognise 14 characters.

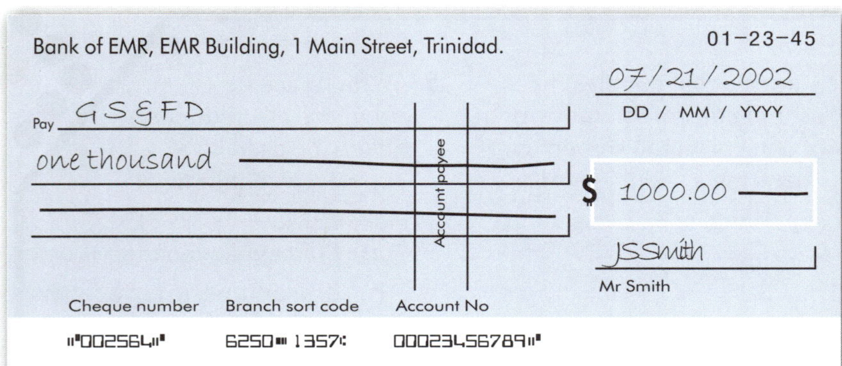


*Figure 2.5*
*Photo of a bank cheque*

### Advantages

- Documents are difficult to forge.
- Documents can still be read after being written on, folded, soiled etc.

### Disadvantages

- MICR readers and encoders are expensive.
- The system can accept only a few characters.

## Optical Mark Reader (OMR)

OMR detects the position of black marks on white paper. The documents to be read have empty boxes pre-printed on them. The user makes pencil or ink marks in the appropriate boxes. The intensity of the reflected light from these marks on the form is detected by the OMR. This is sometimes called mark sensing. The computer records the position of the marks and analyses it to determine the meaning of the data. OMRs are used mainly in assessing multiple-choice examinations or questionnaires given out by market researchers.

## Optical Character Recognition (OCR)

Optical character recognition is used for reading characters from paper, using special OCR readers. The reader includes an optical scanner for reading the text. The shapes of different characters are detected by shining light on them from a photo-electric device and sensing the patterns of reflected light. The reader looks at each pattern (say, a letter, like 'R') individually. Sophisticated software allows each pattern to be compared with a set of stored patterns until the closest match is found. This match is translated into electronic text in the computer, so it can be manipulated by the user.

### Advantages

- OCR is great for converting large volumes of printed data into a form that can then be manipulated on the computer, for example in a word processing program. It can therefore be used to create computer archives of old printed books and documents, preserving these in a searchable electronic form for the future.

### Disadvantages

- OCR has difficulty understanding handwritten text if the letters in that text are not formed properly. OCR also has difficulty recognising certain unusual fonts.

## Barcode readers

A **barcode** is a set of vertical lines of differing thickness with a string of numbers printed at the bottom. The barcode is read by a scanner in which a laser beam scans the barcode and the light is reflected back into the scanner. The information received by the scanner is sent to a computer for processing. The system gives fast and error-free data entry into the computer. Barcodes provide a quick method of recording the sale of items. You can see barcodes on items in supermarkets, books in libraries and on such things as magazines.

*Figure 2.6*
*A scanner being used to 'read' a barcode*

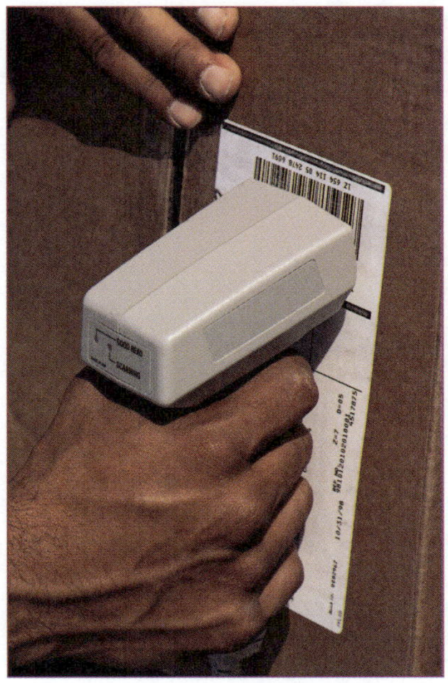

ISBN 0-582-83648-4

9 780582 836488

### *Point of sale (POS) system*

Barcodes form part of the POS system usually found at retail outlets. A terminal is connected to a central computer which records details after the barcode of an item has been scanned. The price of the product is displayed on a monitor at the point of sale. Meanwhile the central computer calculates the amount due, including VAT, and prints an itemised receipt. The information recorded can also be used for stock control and sales analysis.

### Advantages

- Customers get a quicker more accurate service, which improves efficiency.
- Supermarkets can get instant or continuous stock checks.
- Saves on paper work.

### Disadvantage

- Barcodes cannot be read by people.

## RFID (radio frequency identification)

**Radio frequency identification** (RFID) uses radio waves as a means of identifying animals, persons and objects. A chip connected to a small antenna makes up the RFID transponder or RFID tag. Information such as a serial number is transmitted to an RFID receiver that converts the radio waves to digital information so that it can be processed by the computer.

RFID chips are used for tracking animals, for example, as they can be embedded in the skin of the animal and the tag can be read once the animal is within range of the reader. Some stores are now tagging their merchandise with RFID tags to record POS information, and also as a means of security to reduce theft. Alarms can be raised when someone tries to exit a store without paying for an item. The disadvantage of RFID is that it is a lot more expensive than barcoding.

| **Barcodes** | **RFID** |
|---|---|
| Barcodes must be passed over a reader to be read. | RFID tags can be read once the items are within range of a reader. |
| Barcode labels can be ripped, soiled or removed making it difficult or impossible to read them. | RFID can be tagged on the surface or embedded in the object. Since radio waves can travel through non-metallic material, the RFID chip can be encased in plastic for further durability. |
| Barcodes do not identify single unique examples of a single product-type. For example, they distinguish between milk made by two different manufacturers, but cannot distinguish between two identical cartons with two different expiry dates from the same manufacturer. | RFID can distinguish between two identical cartons from one manufacturer with different expiry dates. |
| Barcodes are much cheaper than RFID and effective for certain tasks. | More expensive than barcodes but more effective for certain tasks. |
| Barcode tags cannot be reused | RFID tags can be reused again and again. |

*Table 1 Comparing barcodes to RFID*

## Magnetic strip codes

A magnetic strip is a short length of magnetic coated tape printed on the surface of or sealed into a ticket or card. It contains information to identify the ticket or card and its user.

The card is read by swiping it – moving the magnetic strip through a reader so that the strip can be read. Such strips are found on bank cards which identify the card holder's bank account, so that the card holder can perform banking transactions.

Cards with these magnetic strip codes can provide quick identification of people entering buildings, allowing access to the card holder. These cards are therefore used for security purposes too. Examples of other uses are in phone cards and debit cards for cell phones. The magnetic strip in this instance contains information about the amount of money left 'on' the card.

### Advantages

- They are easy and cheap to produce.
- The strip can store enough information for simple transactions.
- Cuts down on paperwork that would otherwise be involved in a transaction.

### Disadvantages

- The data can be changed, altered, forged or erased by magnetic fields.
- The strip can be damaged by scratching.
- The strip can store only a limited amount of information.

## Smart cards

In recent years, new means of storing data on cards have become available. 'Smart' cards with very thin gold-coloured memory chips sealed into them can store more information than magnetic strip cards. Data is stored on the memory chip embedded in the card, allowing a greater amount of information to be kept and updated on the card than would be the case with the old-style magnetic strip. The chips can hold information for cell phone use, debit and credit cards, and any prepaid services. Eventually, smart cards may store information about a person's driving history, their birth certificate or paper, and could even be imprinted with the holder's voice, fingerprints and retinal scans.

### Advantages

- The chip can store a good deal of information, including personal information, helping to confirm that the user of the card is also the owner of the card.

### Disadvantages

- The chip can potentially be damaged.
- The chip (and the machines that read it) are a little more expensive to produce than the old-style magnetic strip.

*Figure 2.7*
*Photo of a smart card chip in close-up*

### Exercise 2

**Across**

**3** Has difficulty translating hand written text to electronic text (3)

**4** Scanning device found in the publishing industry, to capture images of high detail (4)

**6** Scanned image must be fed through device containing rollers (2 words) (8)

**7** Type of scanner where the image is placed on a level surface (2 words) (7)

**Down**

**1** A set of vertical lines of various thickness (7)

**2** User drags scanner over image (2 words) (8)

**5** Used to read cheques (4)

# Audio and video input devices

## Voice data entry/voice recognition

Voice recognition systems require the use of a microphone. This system accepts the spoken word as input data or commands. Human speech is very complex, because it carries tones, inflections and emphasis of various parts of words and phrases. The computer is programmed to recognise certain patterns of speech. Using a microphone, human speech is coded into a sequence of electronic signals. These signals are compared to a set of stored patterns. If they match, the command or data being entered is accepted by the computer and is processed.

Simple commands can be used to control machines, or even 'type' letters in a word processor. Voice recognition has become important in many areas of our lives. It has made life easier for people with movement difficulties, such as the paralysed, who with suitable equipment can now operate a wheelchair, lighting and even open doors using voice commands.

### Advantages

- No typing is required.
- The system can be used remotely, e.g. by telephone.

### Disadvantages

- Recognition of words is still relatively slow.
- The system is not suitable for use in noisy places.
- You may need to train the system extensively to understand your particular voice patterns.

## Sound capture

All modern computers contain a built-in microphone for sound capture. This means that you can record your voice, for example, to make comments that are embedded in a word processing document. A sound card on your computer is required for recording voice or music. The sound card digitises the information into a form that the computer can understand.

## MIDI instruments

Electronic musical instruments can have a MIDI port (Musical Instrument Digital Interface) for input into the computer. The sounds are digitised and stored as a file, can be displayed on screen, edited and played back, using appropriate software.

## Digital cameras

Digital cameras capture an image and store it in memory within the camera. These cameras have a sensor that converts the light into electrical charges. The processor in the camera converts this information into digital data and stores it on a small diskette, flash memory or flash RAM card. The digital images can then be uploaded from the camera to a computer where they can be displayed, manipulated or printed. The memory can be erased so that more images can be captured. Unlike normal RAM memory (sometimes called temporary memory or volatile memory) where the information is lost when the computer is switched off, flash RAM is non-volatile. That is, the images are not lost when the camera is switched off. The resolution of the camera is measured in pixels. The larger the number of pixels the camera has, the clearer the image and the greater the detail captured.

*Figure 2.8*
*Digital camera*

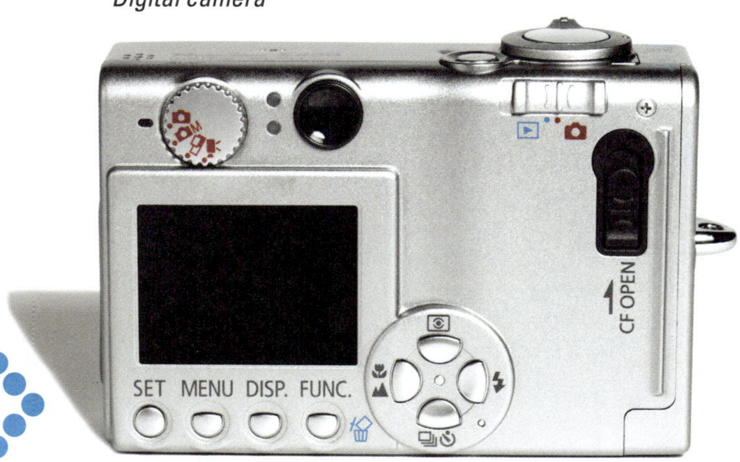


### Advantages

- Photos can be shown on a small screen on the camera, and resized and erased as you go along, so that you only store on the camera the images that you really want.

### Disadvantages

- The sharpness and colour balance of a digital camera may not always be as good as with a traditional film-based camera.
- It is relatively easy to lose or erase a digital camera's memory cards by, for example, accidentally passing the camera through an airport X-ray machine.

## Digital video camera

The digital video camera (also called a digital video camcorder or DVD camcorder) works in much the same way as a film camera, where light is focused onto a film treated with chemicals. The chemical reaction of the film to the light intensity forms the image on the film. Similarly, in a digital camera, light is focused onto an image sensor called a charge-coupled device which contains thousands of light-sensitive diodes called photosites. These detect the light intensity and record an image. The digital video camera/camcorder detects not only light intensity but also levels of colour to reproduce a coloured image. The camera takes many pictures per second to give an impression of movement.

# Other input devices

## Biometric systems

Biometrics refers to the science of identifying an individual through their body characteristics such as face geometry and hand geometry (e.g. fingerprints), iris or retinal scans, vein and voice patterns. All these forms of identifying an individual can be input into a computer system set up for security purposes. In the near future they may become common, for allowing access to buildings and bank accounts, for example.

Retinal scans use a ray of light directed into the eye to identify the distinct network of blood vessels at the back of the eye. Fingerprint readers scan the imprint made by the pattern of ridges on the finger and compare it to a set of patterns stored in memory. Fingerprints are considered unique, as no two individuals have the same fingerprint.

## Remote control

A remote control emits a beam of infra-red light that carries data signals. Commonly used for input to televisions, stereo systems, VCRs and DVD players, they are now being used by computers as a wireless means of communication.

## Sensors

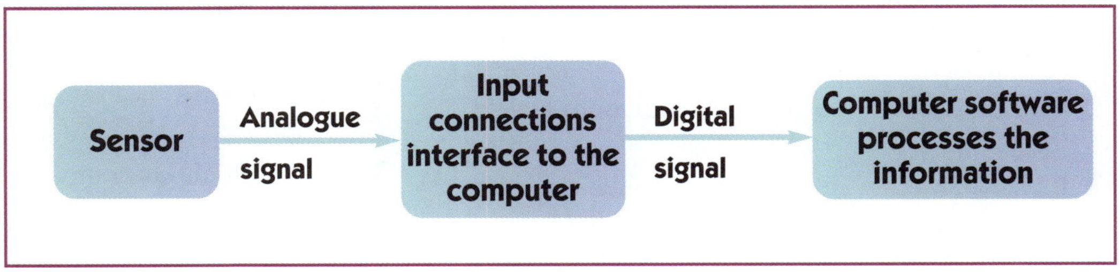


*Figure 2.9*
*How a sensor system works*

Chemical or physical changes in humans and their environment can be converted to electrical signals using sensors that pass information to a computer, where it is analysed, stored and manipulated by specialist software. These sensors are useful in the fields of medicine, environmental planning and preservation, weather reporting, and so on. A variety of sensors can be used to measure such things as heat, light, sound, pressure, strain, acidity (pH), oxygen concentration, humidity, pulse, water level, water flow, speed, tilt or even something like a door or a valve opening or closing.

## Summary

1 Input devices are pieces of equipment that are used to put data into a computer.

2 Data capture is the first stage of getting the data into the computer. The two main data input means are manual and automatic data input (or data capture).

3 Data verification is checking for accurate transcription, whilst data validation is the computer checking to see that the entered data obeys the rules already set up within the computer.

4 The most common input device is the keyboard of which there are two types: alphanumeric and special-function keyboards.

5 Pointing devices are used to move a pointer or cursor on the computer screen, and enable the control and selection of objects on the display. These devices include the mouse, digitising tablet, touch-sensitive screen, light pen and others.

6 Scanning devices use laser beams and reflected light to interpret and convert images, pictures and text into digital form.

7 Magnetic Ink Character Recognition (MICR) is used mainly to read cheques whose data is encoded with magnetic ink.

8 Optical mark readers (OMR) detect the position of black marks on white paper. They are used mainly in multiple-choice exam marking, and assessing market research questionnaires.

9 Optical character recognition (OCR) senses the patterns of reflected light off scanned text via a photo-electric device and compares it to the patterns in memory. The text is converted and stored in the computer, and can be manipulated by the user, e.g. in a word processing program.

10 A barcode is a set of vertical lines of differing thickness with a string of numbers printed at the bottom; it holds information about a product or item.

11 Radio frequency identification (RFID) is the use of embedded chips and radio waves to identify individual unique examples of animals, persons and objects.

12 Voice recognition system recognises certain patterns of speech and accepts it for processing by the computer.

13 Video input devices capture images and stores them in memory.

14 Biometrics refers to the science of identifying an individual through their body characteristics such as face geometry, fingerprint, hand geometry, iris, retina, vein and voice patterns.

15 Sensors can be used to measure heat, light, sound, pressure, strain, acidity (pH) and other changes in the environment.

## Questions

### Matching descriptions

Match each item in the first list to a description in the second list.

(1) MICR
(2) Braille keyboard
(3) Joystick
(4) Barcode reader
(5) OMR
(6) OCR
(7) Smart card

(a) Found on items in the supermarket
(b) For playing games
(c) A card containing a tiny memory chip
(d) Used to assess multiple choice exams
(e) Used by visually impaired persons
(f) Used to read bank cheques
(g) Translates text on paper into electronic text on the computer

### True or False?

1 RFID must be passed over a scanner. T ❑ F ❑

2 A smart card contains a microchip embedded in the card. T ❑ F ❑

3 Digital cameras do not require film. T ❑ F ❑

4 Biometric devices are less accurate than passwords. T ❑ F ❑

5 Remote controls are now used by computers as a wireless input communication device. T ❑ F ❑

6 OMR is used to read cheques. T ❑ F ❑

## Multiple choice

1 Checking for accurate copying of data is known as:
   (a) Validation
   (b) Verification
   (c) Source document
   (d) Data capture
2 Which one of the following is not an advantage of magnetic strip codes?
   (a) They are easy and cheap to produce.
   (b) The strip can store enough information for simple transactions.
   (c) The data can be changed, altered, forged or erased by magnetic fields.
   (d) Cuts down on paperwork that would otherwise be involved in a transaction.
3 Which of the following is *not* true about barcodes?
   (a) They are cheaper than RFID.
   (b) They can be reused again and again.
   (c) They can become difficult to read if they are ripped, soiled or removed.
   (d) They must be passed over a reader.
4 Sensors can be used to measure all of the following except:
   (a) Pulse
   (b) Temperature
   (c) Sound
   (d) OMR
5 OCR:
   (a) Detects marks on paper
   (b) Detects the unique ridges in a fingerprint
   (c) Understands and easily converts handwritten text
   (d) Detects the shape of characters
6 Which of the following is a scanning device?
   (a) Optical mark reader
   (b) Touch pad
   (c) Light pen
   (d) Remote control

## Short answer questions

1 You have been asked to select input devices that would be used by physically disabled persons in an organisation. List at least FOUR devices and explain the kind of person that would be able to use the device and why.
2 State TWO advantages and TWO disadvantages of the smart card over the magnetic strip card.
3 A pharmaceutical research company has decided to introduce biometric systems for security reasons. Consider TWO alternatives and discuss the advantages of using biometric systems over those systems.
4 List TWO advantages and TWO disadvantages of voice data entry systems.
5 Explain the difference between voice data entry and voice recognition systems.
6 List FOUR features of digital cameras that give them an advantage over regular cameras.
7 State TWO disadvantages of a digital camera or a digital video camera.
8 Explain how sensors work and list FOUR types of sensors.
9 What is RFID and how does it work?
10 List at least FOUR applications of RFID.

# 3 Primary and secondary storage

## OBJECTIVES

At the end of this chapter you will be able to:

- Define what primary and secondary storage are
- Explain the difference between primary and secondary storage
- Explain the functions of RAM and ROM
- Name the units of storage: bits, bytes, kilobytes, megabytes, gigabytes and terabytes
- List some characteristics of secondary storage media, such as magnetic tape, magnetic disk, optical disk, flash memory and USB drive

### Did you know?

Did you know that having more RAM may make a microcomputer operate faster and its software perform better? Most computers sold today come with 256 MB or 512 MB RAM as standard; extra RAM can easily be added, expanding the computer's capacity to 1 GB or more.

Storage refers to the media and devices used by a computer to keep data and instructions available for immediate or later use. Storage can be grouped into two categories: primary storage and secondary storage.

Primary storage, also called main memory or immediate access store (IMAS) is a group of chips that resides in the motherboard (main circuit board) of the computer. The distance the electrical signals have to travel from the CPU to primary storage or vice versa is much shorter than the distance between the CPU and secondary storage devices, which are connected to the motherboard via cables. This shorter distance, along with the design of the chips, allows for faster interchange of data and instructions. This speedy access is necessary since the CPU can only act on data and instructions held in primary storage. So for the computer to work fast, the primary storage must be as quickly accessible as possible.

## Primary Storage

Primary storage consists of two types of memory chips: **Random Access Memory (RAM)** and **Read Only Memory (ROM)** chips. A memory chip is an **integrated circuit** (IC) made up of millions of transistors and capacitors.

## Random Access Memory (RAM)

A computer uses RAM to hold data and instructions (programs) temporarily while processing is taking place using that data and program. It also holds the data that results from processing – data that is waiting to be output or stored in a secondary storage device. RAM is therefore also called working memory.

Programs and data stored in secondary storage must therefore first be loaded into RAM before they can be processed. For example, before a letter can be typed, or data for a spreadsheet entered, the CPU must first load the application programs – such as a word processing or spreadsheet program – into memory. These application programs, and whatever the user inputs using them, are held in RAM until the application is closed or the power is turned off.

If programs and data are not stored on a secondary storage device they will be lost when power is turned off. This is because the information in RAM is **volatile:** it is temporary and changeable. The information in RAM can also be accessed directly and easily, hence the term 'random access'. If the power is turned off or the computer is rebooted (started up again) all the information that is held in RAM will be lost. RAM chips are limited in storage capacity. RAM chips are also expensive and are a major determinant of the final price of a computer.

## Cache memory

Currently, processors can operate at speeds much greater than memory can supply the necessary data. In an effort to speed up processing, most microcomputers have **cache memory** (pronounced cash). Cache memory is very fast memory that the processor can access much more quickly than main memory or RAM. Usually there are two levels of cache, called L1 and L2. Newer computers have also included a third level called L3 cache. L1 cache is on the same chip as the microprocessor, while L2 cache is usually separate. When the microprocessor and motherboard both have L2 caches, the motherboard cache is designated L3, since it is further away. Cache is made of high-speed static RAM (SRAM) instead of the slower and cheaper dynamic RAM (DRAM) chip that is used for main memory.

Generally most programs access the same data or instruction over and over. By keeping as much of this information as possible in SRAM, the processor avoids accessing the slower DRAM. Cache memory works by attempting to predict which memory the processor is going to need next, loading that memory before the processor needs it, and saving the results after the processor is done with it. This speeds up processing.

## Read Only Memory (ROM)

ROM chips hold data and instructions necessary for starting up the computer when it is switched on. It is commonly used to store system-level programs such as the BIOS (Basic Input/Output System) program. ROM chips may also hold translators for high-level languages and operating systems.

These instructions are fixed at the time of manufacture and are sometimes described as being 'hard-wired'. This ensures that the instructions stored in ROM are always there, whether the power is on or not. ROM is therefore **non-volatile:** it cannot be easily changed, because it is 'read-only'. This is necessary since when the computer is first turned on, the system memory is empty and needs the instructions stored in ROM for the PC to boot up. ROM is also sometimes found in some input and output devices, such as scanners and printers.

ROM cannot easily be modified and therefore provides a measure of security against accidental or malicious changes to its contents. Users of a system cannot infect ROM chips with a virus. Variations of ROM chips namely PROM and EPROM, allowing some flexibility in storing data and instructions, are also available.

- **Programmable ROM (PROM):** This is a type of ROM that can be programmed using special equipment; it can be written to, but only once. This is useful for companies that want to make their own ROMs from software they write themselves: when they change their code they can create new PROMs without requiring a whole ROM manufacturing plant.
- **Erasable Programmable ROM (EPROM):** An EPROM is a ROM that can be erased and reprogrammed, which can make it more useful than an ordinary PROM, although EPROM chips do not last as long. This is done by exposing the chip to ultraviolet light of a specific frequency for a specified period of time. Reprogramming may become necessary if there are updates to the current data or instructions that are held in EPROM.
- **Electrically Erasable PROM (EEPROM):** This is a special type of ROM chip that can be erased and reprogrammed repeatedly by a user. A chip is erased by exposing it to an electrical charge, which erases the entire chip. Unlike EPROM chips, EEPROM chips do not have to be removed from the computer to be reprogrammed. EEPROM is non-volatile and can be used to hold data and instructions which need to be updated regularly. Flash memory is a type of EEPROM and is also used in a number of electronic devices such as CompactFlash cards known as 'electronic film' for digital cameras, memory cards and video game systems.

*Figure 3.1*
*RAM and ROM chips*

## Units of storage

The memories of all digital computers are two-state (bi-stable) devices. This means the components can be set to one of two states. On a disk or tape it is a magnetised spot or an unmagnetised spot. In a chip it is the presence or absence of an electrical charge, and in the case of optical disks, it is the presence or absence of the reflection when a laser beam hits the surface of the disk. The two states of all these devices are represented by the binary numbers 0 and 1 and are called a bit. A **bit** is the smallest unit of storage in a computer.

The amount of data and instructions that can be stored in the memory of a computer or secondary storage medium is measured in bytes. A **byte** is made up of a combination of eight bits and has the storage power to represent one character. A **character** can be a letter, a number, a symbol, a punctuation mark or a blank space. A **word** is the amount of bits the computer can process in one operation. **Word length** is the number of bits in a word.

| Name | Symbol | Binary measurement | Decimal measurement | Number of bytes | Equal to |
|---|---|---|---|---|---|
| kilobyte | KB | $2^{10}$ | $10^{3}$ | 1 024 | 1024 bytes |
| megabyte | MB | $2^{20}$ | $10^{6}$ | 1 048 576 | 1024 KB |
| gigabyte | GB | $2^{30}$ | $10^{9}$ | 1 073 741 824 | 1024 MB |
| terabyte | TB | $2^{40}$ | $10^{12}$ | 1 099 511 627 776 | 1024 GB |
| petabyte | PB | $2^{50}$ | $10^{15}$ | 1 125 899 906 842 624 | 1024 TB |
| exabyte | EB | $2^{60}$ | $10^{18}$ | 1 152 921 504 606 846 976 | 1024 PB |
| zettabyte | ZB | $2^{70}$ | $10^{21}$ | 1 180 591 620 717 411 303 424 | 1024 EB |
| yottabyte | YB | $2^{80}$ | $10^{24}$ | 1 208 925 819 614 629 174 706 176 | 1024 ZB |

*Table 1 Larger units of storage*

## Secondary storage devices

Secondary storage, also called auxiliary or backup storage, is used to store data and instructions when they are not being processed. Secondary storage is more permanent than main memory, since data and instructions are retained when the power is turned off. Secondary storage is also much cheaper than primary storage and is unlimited – you can have as much of it as you can afford.

A computer for home use will not need as much secondary storage as a computer used in a large organisation such as a bank, hospital or an insurance company. Because of this diverse range of storage needs, a number of secondary storage devices are available. Devices are chosen for a particular use based on their:

- Storage capacity (how much data the device can store)
- Access speed (the time needed to locate the data and transmit it to the CPU)
- Size (necessary for storage on shelves or portability)
- Portability (ability to be easily removed and used on another system)
- Cost.

The most commonly used secondary storage devices are magnetic storage (magnetic tapes and magnetic disks), optical storage (CD-ROM, CD-R, CD-RW, DVD-ROM, DVD-R and DVD-RW) and solid state memory (flash memory and USB drives).

## Magnetic tapes

Magnetic tape is a ribbon of plastic material coated with a metal oxide film on which data is recorded as magnetised or unmagnetised spots. The magnetic orientations of the magnetised and unmagnetised spots represent the binary digits 0 and 1. On mainframe computers the tape is stored on reels or cartridges. In microcomputers tapes are stored in cartridges similar to those used to store music, but of a much higher quality. Just like the tape in a tape recorder, data can be written to, or read from, the tape as it passes the magnetic heads.

Magnetic tape is not suitable for data files that are revised or updated often because it stores data **sequentially**. This means that data is retrieved in the order in which it was stored. Therefore accessing data is very slow as you cannot go directly to an item of data on the tape. It is necessary to start at the beginning of the tape and search for the data as the tape goes past the heads.

However, magnetic tapes are erasable, reusable and moderately durable, and are made to store large quantities of data inexpensively. For these reasons they are mainly used for emergency backup purposes.

### *Summary characteristics of magnetic tapes*

- Provide sequential access to data stored
- Easy to transport and store
- Cheaper than disk
- Mostly used for backups or archives (tertiary storage)
- Limited shelf-life (2 years)
- Must be stored in a suitable environment (smoke, dust, temperature and humidity must be carefully controlled)
- Difficult to update files (cannot make changes to a record without writing over the entire tape)

## Magnetic disks

Magnetic disks are one of the most widely used secondary storage media for computers. All magnetic disks provide **direct access** to data stored. This means that you can go directly to a specific piece of data without having to access any other data either before or after the data you want. The capacity and access speeds of magnetic disks vary with each device or medium. Magnetic disks include floppy disks (diskettes) and hard disks.

### *Floppy disks (diskettes)*

A 3.5-inch diskette or floppy disk is a removable, flexible plastic disk coated with a magnetisable material. The disk is contained in a hard plastic case to protect it from dust and grease. (The term 'floppy' refers back to the 5.25-inch diskettes that were used in the 1980s, and were actually soft and flexible. These are not used any more.)

Each disk surface contains a set of numbered concentric rings known as **tracks**. The tracks are also divided into wedge shaped (pizza slice) pieces known as **sectors**, which themselves are numbered. A sector is the amount of data that can be read from or written to a disk by the computer in one read/write operation. Data is stored as magnetised spots on the tracks.

Before a disk can be used to store data, it must be formatted. Formatting a disk means writing electronic information on the disk so that the computer can recognise the disk as a valid storage device and data can be stored. The formatting process sets up a method of assigning addresses to the different areas. It also sets up an area for keeping the list of addresses. Without formatting there would be no way to know what data is where. When a disk is formatted the following happens:

*Figure 3.2*
*A floppy disk*

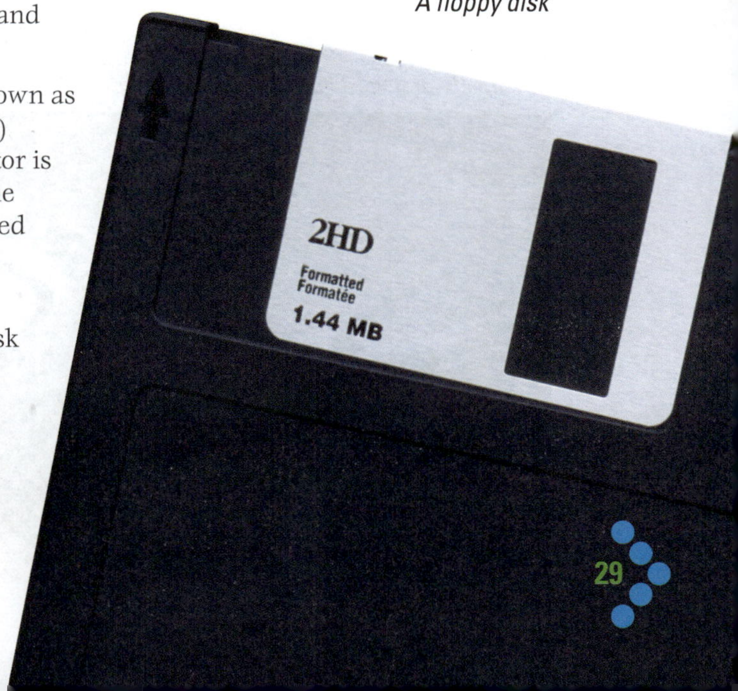

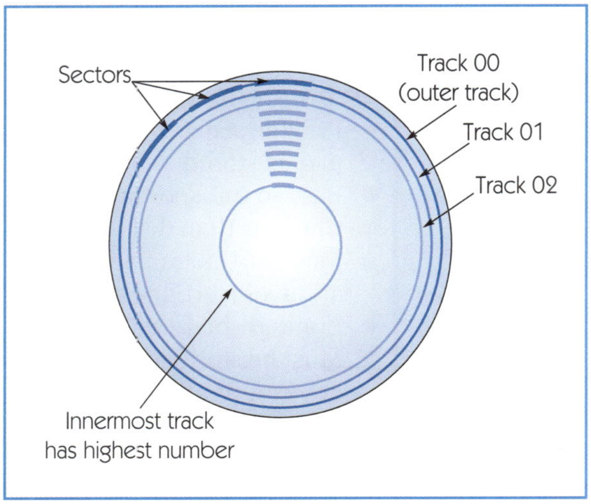


*Figure 3.3*
*How data is laid out on a disk*

1. All data in the disk is erased.
2. The surfaces of the disk are checked for any physical and magnetic defects.
3. A file allocation table (FAT) is created to record where data is stored.

Floppy disks are useful for transferring data between computers and for keeping a backup of small files. They are relatively slow to access because of their rotation speeds. Floppy disks hold 1.44 MB of information. This is plenty of space for most text documents (Word and Excel files), but for files containing graphics, a floppy's capacity may be insufficient.

Although generally PCs come with floppy drives, these are being replaced by CD drives, especially in most laptops. However, an external floppy drive can easily be attached via any of the USB ports available in modern computers. The present 3.5-inch floppy disk, like its predecessor, will nevertheless soon become obsolete as smaller devices with higher storage capacities become available.

### Summary characteristics of floppy disks

- Provide direct access to data stored
- Small and very portable (e.g. files can be transported from one computer to another)
- Suitable for backing up small files
- Data security (e.g. you can store small files that you don't want other computer users to see)
- Easy to store
- Limited shelf-life (2 years)

## Care of floppy disks

Taking care of your disks and handling them in the right way can prevent your data from being lost. Here are some simple precautions to protect the data on your disk:

- Keep your disks away from liquids, dampness, dust and dirt.
- Do not bend disks or handle them roughly.
- Do not touch exposed portions of a disk.
- Take care when inserting or removing a disk from a computer's disk drive.
- Keep your disks in a disk box, not loose in your pocket or inside a book.
- Do not leave the disk in the drive. If you do the read/write head remains resting on the disk surface.

## Hard disks

Hard disks as the name implies are thin but rigid, inflexible disks made of highly polished metal. The surface of each side of a disk (also called platters) is covered with a substance that can be magnetised, thereby allowing data to be stored on both sides as magnetised or unmagnetised spots.

*Figure 3.4*
*The inside of a hard disk*

The disks constantly rotate at a high speed and may have one read/write head per disk (moveable head) or, on more expensive disks, every track in each disk may have its own read/write head (fixed head). The combination of the disk, read/write head and the circuitry that goes with these is called the hard disk drive.

The access time (time to get data) from a spinning disk with one read/write head is a combination of:

- *Seek time* – how long it takes the head to get to the right track;
- *Rotational delay or latency time* – how long it takes for the data to rotate under the head; and
- *Transmission time* – the time taken to read the data and transmit it to the CPU.

For fixed-head disk drives, where each track has a read/write head, the time taken to access data and instructions is reduced, as the seek time is eliminated.

Hard disks are much slower than internal memory. To increase the speed at which data is written to and read from a hard disk, a cache, also often called a buffer, is included in most modern hard drives. The purpose of this cache is similar to other caches used in the PC, even though it is not normally thought of as L1, L2 or L3 cache. For hard disks, the cache is used to hold the results of recent reads from the disk, and also to 'predict' and hold data that is likely to be requested in the near future, for example, the data immediately after the one just requested. The use of cache improves performance of any hard disk, by reducing the number of physical accesses to the disk on repeated reads.

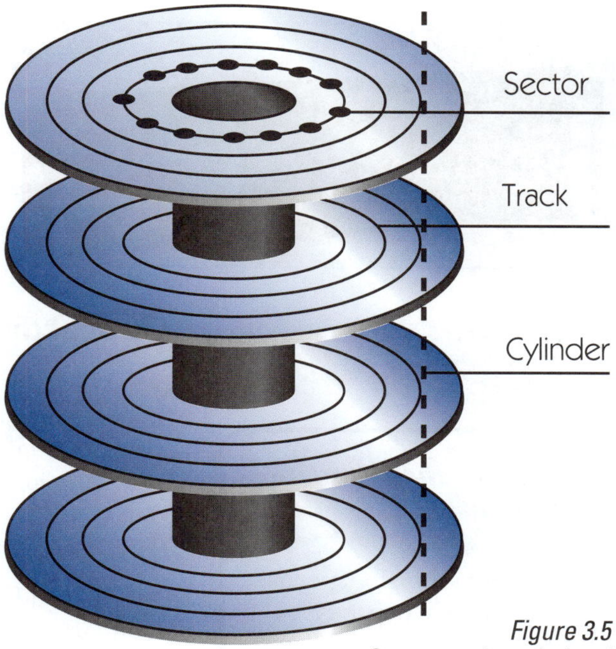


*Figure 3.5 Cross-section of a hard disk to show how it is arranged and divided into tracks, sectors and cylinders*

Like floppy disks, a hard disk must also be formatted before any data can be stored on it. Formatting sets up the tracks, sectors and cylinders. A **cylinder** is made up of all the tracks of the same number from all the metal disks that make up the hard disk, which can be read or written to at the same time. For example, if you start from the bottom of a stack of disks, track 5 of the second disk will be directly above track 5 of the first disk. Track 5 of the third disk will be directly above track 5 of the first and second disks and so on. If you put these all together on top of each other, you'd have something that looks like a tin can with no top or bottom – a cylinder.

The computer keeps track of what it has put where on a disk by recording the addresses of all the sectors used – a combination of the cylinder, track and sector numbers. Data is written down the disks on the same cylinder. This works quickly because each metal platter has a read/write head for each side and they all move together. So for one position of the read/write heads, the computer can put some data on all the platters.

Almost all PCs come with a hard drive that is housed inside the system unit and attached to the motherboard by a special cable. These hard drives are not removable and vary in storage capacity from around 20 GB to 120 GB and more. The hard drive usually stores applications software (word processor, database, spreadsheet, etc.) and the operating system. It is much faster than floppy disks because it rotates at a much faster speed.

Two additional types of hard drives that can be used with a PC are external hard drives and removable disk.

- *External hard drive*: An external hard drive can be used if there is no space in the system unit to house another hard drive. It may come with its own power source and is connected to the system unit via a special cable. External hard drives can be easily removed and connected to another computer, thereby giving them a certain amount of portability and flexibility of use.
  Examples of a removable hard disk are the Maxtor one touch 300 GB, Western Digital Dual Option 250 GB and the Seagate 200 GB models.

For 0larger computer systems hard disks consist mainly of removable hard disk packs, fixed disk drives and RAID storage systems.

- *Removable hard disk pack*: A removable hard disk pack may contain between 6 and 20 hard disks aligned one above the other in a sealed unit. The storage capacity is usually very large, in the terabyte range.
- *Fixed disk drives*: These are similar to those found in PCs. They have a high storage capacity and are more reliable than removable hard disks. A mainframe computer may have between 20 and 100 fixed disks housed in a single cabinet. Data is transmitted to the CPU using a single data path.

*Figure 3.6*
*RAID cabinet*

- *RAID storage system*: RAID stands for Redundant Array of Independent Disk. A RAID storage system consists of a cabinet which may contain a large number of disk drives (up to 100). Besides holding more data than a fixed disk, it stores multiple copies of data on different drives. If one drive fails, others can take over allowing the data to be recovered. Data is transmitted to the CPU using multiple data paths.

**Summary characteristics of hard disks**

- Direct access
- Fast data transfer speeds
- Vast storage capacity

## Optical disks

Optical disks are disks that are read by laser lights. The disk is made mainly of a type of plastic (polycarbonate). The data is stored on a layer inside the plastic. A metal coating (usually aluminium) reflects the laser light back to a sensor. The main types of optical disks are CDs and DVDs.

### CD-ROM (compact disk)

CD-ROM stands for Compact Disc–Read Only Memory. This means that you can only read (access) what is on the disk, but you cannot add or change anything. The data is encoded and read optically with a low intensity laser light. The data is represented as a series of pits and lands. A pit is a little depression formed by the laser burning into the data layer when the CD is created. The land is the part between the pits or the smooth surface. Reading a CD is done by shining a laser light at the disk and detecting changing reflecting patterns. When the laser beam reflects off the smooth surface (land) it is interpreted as a 1 bit. When the laser enters a pit there is no reflection, which is interpreted as a 0 bit.

*Figure 3.7*
*Compact disk*

The speed at which the data is accessed depends on how fast the disk spins. The faster the disk spins, the faster the data can be transferred to the computer's memory. The speed of a CD-ROM drive is indicated by a number followed by an 'X'. Typical CD-ROM drive speeds are 48X, 50X, etc. The higher the number the faster the disk spins, resulting in faster data access.

Because of their large storage capacity (up to 750 MB), CD-ROMs are used to store software packages for sale or distribution. They are particularly useful for storing multimedia (text, graphics, sound and videos) and application software packages such as encyclopedias, word processors, training programs, games and graphics packages.

### CD-R

CD-R stands for Compact Disc–Recordable. This disk allows you to write data onto the disk once only using a CD recorder (burner). The disk then becomes CD-ROM as the contents cannot be changed. It is ideal for storing large volumes of data that does not need to change. A typical use is to create music CDs. The storage capacity of CD-R, like all CDs, is around 750 to 800 MB maximum.

### CD-RW

CD-RW (Compact Disc–Re-Writable) is now a very common choice for backup storage. The data layer of these disks uses a phase-changing metal alloy film. By using a higher intensity laser light the film can be melted to level out the marks made by the laser burner when the data was stored, effectively erasing previously stored data. New data can then be recorded using a lower intensity laser light to burn the new data. In theory you can erase and write on these disks as many as 1000 times. It therefore makes it an ideal backup storage device for storing large volumes of data that change frequently.

### DVD disks

DVD stands for Digital Versatile Disk. The main types are DVD-ROM (read only), DVD-R (recordable) and DVD-RW (rewritable). They look similar to a CD-R disk but are capable of holding much more information. This is possible because:

- The tracks on a DVD are placed closer together as compared to a CD, thus allowing more tracks.
- The pits in which data is stored are much smaller in a DVD than a CD. This means many more pits will fit on the disk, allowing more information to be stored.
- Some DVDs are double-sided. This allows data to be stored on both sides and therefore dramatically increases the disk's capacity.

A typical DVD disk can hold between 4.7 GB and 17 GB of information. They are used mainly for storing movies. The quality of sound and video output is much superior to video tapes.

### Care of optical disks

CDs and DVDs are not indestructible, as they were made out to be when they first became popular. Although they are more reliable than diskettes, CDs must be handled with care otherwise data may be lost. Data loss results from:

- Physical damage (breaking, melting, scratching, etc.)
- Blocking of laser light by dirt, paint, ink and glue
- Corrosion of the reflecting layer.

The following are some guidelines for the proper handling of CDs and DVDs.

1. CDs and DVDs should be stored in their cases when not in use to prevent them from being scratched or getting dirty.
2. Avoid soiling the surface of a CD – hold it by the edge or centre hole.
3. Keep your CDs clean by gently wiping both sides with a clean damp cloth from the centre to the outer edge, *not* by wiping around the disk. Wiping in a circle can create a curved scratch, which can confuse the laser. For stubborn dirt, use isopropyl alcohol or methanol, or CD/DVD cleaning detergent.
4. Do not write on the top side of the CD with a ballpoint pen or other hard object as this can damage the data layer on the other side. Use a CD marker instead.
5. Don't write on the top side with a fine-point marker or with any solvent-based marker. (Solvent may dissolve the protective layer.)
6. Do not expose a CD to high temperature or humidity for an extended period of time, as the CD may warp.

#### Summary characteristics of optical disks

- Much sturdier and more durable than tapes or floppy disks
- Not usually sensitive to being casually touched, though they too can get dirty or scratched. Despite this they can be cleaned easily with a soft cloth
- Unaffected by magnetic fields
- Hold much more data than floppy disks
- Provide direct access to data stored

#### Did you know?

Did you know that many computers have a single drive to read and write to CD-R, CD-RW, DVD-R and DVD-RW?

## Other storage media

The modern computing industry is continually developing new products to assist the computer user.

### Flash memory

Flash memory technology is based on EEPROM (Electrically Erasable Programmable Read Only Memory) technology. Like EEPROM, flash memory is non-volatile. However, reading from and writing to flash memory is a lot faster than with EEPROM. This is because data in flash memory can be erased a block at a time instead of only a single byte at a time as is the case with EEPROM. Flash memory got its name because a block of memory cells is erased in a single action or 'flash'.

> **Summary characteristics of flash memory**
> - Physically very small
> - Highly portable
> - High data capacity, ranging from 16 MB to 2 GB, and even more
> - High data transfer speed to the device they are part of or attached to (camera, PC, etc)
> - Large storage capacity compared to diskettes

The compact nature of flash memory enables it to be incorporated into very small solid state (no moving parts) devices that are available in all shapes and forms. These devices are rapidly becoming an integral part of modern living. Flash memory is particularly well known today because of the popular flash memory cards used in digital still cameras. These include CompactFlash (CF), SmartMedia (SM), MultiMediaCard (MMC), Secure Digital (SD), Memory Stick (MS) and xD Picture cards.

*Figure 3.8 Different types of flash memory cards*

For example, the Sony Memory Stick is an extremely versatile storage card for digital images, music MP3 and more. This type of flash memory comes in the form of a card shaped like a stick of chewing gum, with dimensions of 21.5 × 50 × 2.8 mm and a storage capacity up to 2 GB. The Memory Stick weighs just 4 g and has a data-protection tag feature on the reverse which enables users to protect data written on the flash memory.

Flash memory is also used in many electronic devices including PCs, cell phones, PDAs, cable TV set-top boxes and video game consoles.

## USB drive

This new type of flash memory storage device does not yet have a generally accepted name. Each company calls it something different, including flash drive, flash pen, thumb drive, key drive and mini-USB drive. They often double as MP3 players, i.e. you can download music to them from your PC, plug in some headphones and listen to your favourite songs.

> **Summary characteristics of USB drives**
> - Easy to use
> - Convenient (small size – can be placed in a pocket or on a key chain)
> - Large storage capacity compared to diskettes
> - Highly compatible – 'plug and play' (no software needed)
> - Fast access
> - Password protection
> - Disk write protection switch (prevents data from being accidentally written over)

*Figure 3.9 USB drive*

All are small, about the size of your thumb or a large car key, and plug into a USB port on the computer. No additional software is needed for Windows XP, 2000 or ME. Plug it in and the computer notices that a new hard drive has been added, and will show it on your desktop.

These small flash drives can have storage capacities from 8 MB to 1 GB or more! Some flash drives include a password protection facility and the ability to run software directly off the USB drive.

| Storage device | Storage capacity | Advantages | Disadvantages |
|---|---|---|---|
| Magnetic tape | Usually 2–8 GB | • Easy to transport and store<br>• Cheap<br>• Mostly used for backups or archives | • Provides sequential access to data stored<br>• Limited shelf-life (2 years)<br>• Must be stored in a suitable environment (smoke, dust, temperature and humidity must be carefully controlled)<br>• Difficult to update files (cannot make changes to a record without writing over the entire tape) |
| Magnetic disk | 1.44 MB | • Provides direct access to data stored<br>• Small and very portable<br>• Easy to store<br>• Suitable for backing up small files<br>• Data security (e.g. you can store small files that you don't want other computer users to see) | • Small storage capacity (unsuitable for storing files containing graphics)<br>• Limited shelf-life (2 years)<br>• Slow read/write speeds |
| Fixed hard disks | 40–120 GB | • Direct access<br>• Fast data transfer speeds<br>• Vast storage capacity | • Not portable |
| Removable hard disks (Maxtor one touch 300 GB, Western Digital Dual Option 250 GB and the Seagate 200 GB) | Up to 2 GB | • Direct access<br>• Fast data transfer speeds<br>• Vast storage capacity compared to diskettes<br>• Portable | • Computer must have a USB port |
| Optical disks | CD – up to 800 MB<br>DVD – up to 17 GB | • Direct access<br>• Fast data transfer speeds<br>• Vast storage capacity compared to diskettes<br>• Portable<br>• Can be cleaned easily with a soft cloth<br>• Unaffected by magnetic fields | • Data on CD-ROMs cannot be changed<br>• Access times are slower than hard drives<br>• DVDs are still not widely used for storage because they have not been around very long. |

*Table 2 Advantages and disadvantages of secondary storage devices*

| Storage device | Storage capacity | Advantages | Disadvantages |
|---|---|---|---|
| Flash memory | Varies with devices; usually 16 MB to around 2 GB | • Physically very small<br>• Highly portable<br>• High data transfer speed to PCs<br>• Large storage capacity compared to diskettes<br>• Direct access | • May need special software to be used with PCs<br>• Limited storage compared to CD or DVD |
| USB drive | Up to 1 GB | • Easy to use<br>• Convenient (small size – can be placed in a pocket or on a key chain)<br>• Large storage capacity compared to diskettes<br>• Highly compatible – 'plug and play' (no software needed)<br>• Fast access, direct access<br>• Password protection<br>• Disk write protection switch (prevents data from being accidentally written over) | • May not be easily read with computers using Windows 98 or older operating systems.<br>• Limited storage compared to CD or DVD |

*Table 2 cont.* *Advantages and disadvantages of secondary storage devices*

# Summary

1 Storage refers to the media and devices used to keep data and instructions for immediate or later use.

2 Primary memory which resides on the main circuit board consists of RAM and ROM chips.

3 Random Access Memory (RAM) is immediately available to the processor and holds data and instructions temporarily, while processing takes place. It also holds processed data that is waiting to be output or stored in a secondary storage device. Data can be read from and written to RAM. RAM is volatile, limited and expensive.

4 Read Only Memory (ROM) chips hold data and instructions necessary for starting up the computer when it is switched on. Data can only be read from ROM chips. ROM is non-volatile.

5 PROM and EPROM are variations of the ROM chip which allow data to be added, once in the case of PROM and many times for EPROM.

6 A bit is the smallest unit of storage.

7 A byte is made up of a combination of eight bits, and has the storage power to represent one written character.

8 A word is the amount of bits a computer can process in one operation. The word length is the number of bits in a word.

9 One kilobyte (KB) is approximately 1000 bytes, one megabyte (MB) is approximately one million bytes and one gigabyte (GB) is approximately one billion bytes.

10 Secondary storage devices store data and instructions permanently, to be used when required.

11 Storage is chosen for a particular use based on its storage capacity, access speed, size, portability and cost.

12 Magnetic tape, magnetic disk (floppy disk and hard disk), optical disk (CD-ROM, CD-R, CD-RW and DVD), USB drives and flash memory are secondary storage devices.

13 Magnetic tapes are erasable, reusable and inexpensive. They have large storage capacities but only allow sequential access. They are mostly used for emergency backup purposes.

14 Sequential access refers to the accessing of data in the order in which it was stored.

15 Magnetic disk provides direct access to data stored.

16 Direct access means that you can go directly to a specific piece of data without having to access any other data.

17 Hard disks are thin but rigid, inflexible disks made of highly polished metal with a storage capacity from around 20 GB to 120 GB and more. The hard drive usually stores applications software (word processor, database, spreadsheet, etc.), and the operating system.

18 External hard drives can be easily removed and connected to another computer.

19 RAID stands for redundant array of independent disk. A RAID storage system consists of a cabinet which may contain a large number of disk drives (up to 100).

20 Formatting a disk means writing electronic information on the disk so that the computer can recognise the disk as a valid storage device and data can be stored.

21 A floppy disk can be used to store small files and provides direct access to data stored. It has a capacity of 1.44 MB.

22 Optical disks include CD-ROM, CD-R, CD-RW and DVDs. They provide direct access to data stored.

23 Flash memory is non-volatile, solid state memory of up to 2 GB that is incorporated into small devices such as digital still cameras, cell phones, PDAs, cable TV set top boxes and video game consoles.

24 USB drives are a new type of flash memory device with storage capacities from 8 MB to 1 GB or more. They are small, and plug into a USB port on the computer. No additional software is needed for Windows XP, 2000 or ME.

# Questions

## Multiple choice

Choose the most appropriate answer for each question.

1 The acronym ROM stands for:
- (a) Random Only Memory
- (b) Read Only Memory
- (c) Read Optical Module
- (d) Random Organising Memory

2 Which device holds data and instructions when it is not in use?
- (a) Primary storage
- (b) System unit
- (c) Monitor
- (d) Secondary storage

3 The smallest unit of storage is a:
- (a) Byte
- (b) Bit
- (c) Megabyte
- (d) Terabyte

4 Which device has the largest storage capacity?
- (a) Diskette
- (b) CD-ROM
- (c) DVD
- (d) Hard disk

5 Another name for primary storage is:
- (a) Secondary storage
- (b) Immediate access storage
- (c) Magnetic tape
- (d) Hard disk

6 Where are data and instructions held so that they are available to the CPU for processing?
- (a) ROM
- (b) DVD
- (c) CD-ROM
- (d) RAM

7 When a disk is formatted, which of the following happens?
- (a) All data on the disk is erased
- (b) It becomes damaged
- (c) Data files are copied onto the disk
- (d) It contains files to boot up the computer

8 Magnetic tape is used to:
- (a) Hold data necessary for starting up the computer
- (b) Back up large amounts of data
- (c) Hold data that the computer is processing at the time
- (d) None of the above

## True or False ?

1 A 3.5-inch diskette is capable of holding a large amount of graphical data. T ❑ F ❑

2 Primary storage consists of RAM and ROM chips. T ❑ F ❑

3 A magnetic disk has a number of concentric circles called tracks. T ❑ F ❑

4 RAM chips hold data permanently. T ❑ F ❑

5 The user inputs data and instructions into a ROM chip. T ❑ F ❑

6 A byte has the capacity to represent one character. T ❑ F ❑

7 EPROM chips cannot be erased. T ❑ F ❑

8 Magnetic tapes allow direct access to data stored. T ❑ F ❑

9 Magnetic tape is difficult to update. T ❑ F ❑

10 Floppy disks provide direct access. T ❑ F ❑

11 Some CD-ROMs can hold more than 650 MB of data. T ❑ F ❑

12 DVDs are used to store movies. T ❑ F ❑

13 A USB drive cannot be easily removed from a system. T ❑ F ❑

14 A digital camera is one device that uses flash memory. T ❑ F ❑

## Fill in the blanks

Fill in the blanks with the most appropriate word.

1 A ____________________ can hold the code for one character.

2 A ______________ is the smallest unit of storage.

3 ______________ is the data access method used by magnetic disks.

4 A ____________________ is about 1 billion bytes.

5 Magnetic tapes are mainly used for ____________________.

6 Optical disks are read by ___________________.

7 The concentric circles in a disk are known as __________________.

8 The tracks with the same number in each disk in a disk pack are known as ______________.

9 All diskettes must be ________________ before they can store data.

## Short answer questions

1 Explain the functions of RAM and ROM.

2 Explain with the use of examples the difference between the terms 'storage device' and 'storage medium'.

3 What is the function of secondary storage?

4 List the criteria used in selecting a secondary storage device for a particular use.

5 What kinds of secondary storage devices do large computer systems use?

6 Explain, using examples, the terms 'serial access' and 'direct access'.

7 Define the following terms: bit, byte, word and word length.

8 Define the terms track, sector and cylinder.

9 Explain what happens to a disk when it is formatted.

10 Explain how data is accessed from a disk that has one read/write head.

11 Name an application in which a CD-ROM is used for storing information.

12 State the advantages and disadvantages of using CD-ROMs rather than diskettes.

13 Give one of the main uses of DVDs.

14 Explain, giving examples, THREE ways in which data may be lost in an optical disk.

15 List THREE precautions for the care of optical disks.

16 List THREE precautions for the care of floppy disks.

17 Give the similarities and differences between each of the following pairs:

(a) RAM and ROM

(b) Hard disk and floppy disk

(c) Hard disk and magnetic tape

(d) Primary storage and secondary storage

## Crossword

### Across

1 Memory device used in digital cameras and cell phones (5)

4 Holds data and instructions necessary for starting up the computer (3)

5 Stores movies with high quality sound and video (3)

6 This medium only provides serial access (4)

7 A type of storage which holds data on a permanent basis for later use (9)

### Down

1 Performing this operation on a disk erases all the information (10)

2 The number of bits the computer can process in one operation (4)

3 It contains millions of transistors and capacitors (4)

# 4 Output devices

## OBJECTIVES

At the end of this chapter you will be able to:

- Define the term 'output device'
- Distinguish between soft copy and hard copy
- Name typical output devices
- Describe some of the characteristics and uses of different output devices

Output devices are pieces of equipment that are used to get information or any other response *out* of a computer. If the output can be read by human beings it is said to be **human readable**. If the output cannot be understood by humans it is said to be **machine readable**.

There are two types of output. **Soft copy** output or temporary output refers to information displayed on a screen or in audio or voice form through speakers. This kind of output disappears when the computer is switched off. When the computer is off neither the screen nor the speakers work, because they are always linked to and driven by the computer. Then there is **hard copy** output or permanent output – this refers to output printed onto paper.

The main output devices you are likely to come across are:

- VDU or monitor
- Multimedia projector
- Voice response
- Speech synthesis
- Modem
- Impact printer
  - dot matrix
  - daisy wheel
  - drum, chain or band printer
- Non-impact printer
  - thermal
  - inkjet
  - laser
- Plotter
  - pen
  - inkjet
  - electrostatic
- Robot/control system
- Microfilm/microfiche

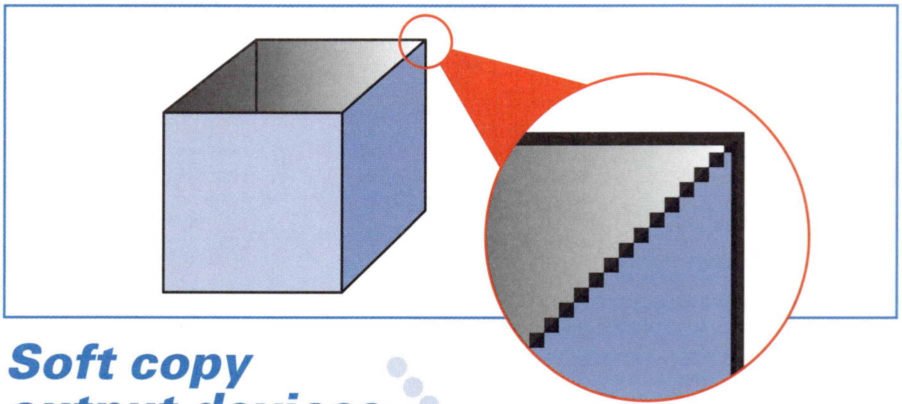

*Figure 4.1*
*Box with close-up view of corner showing pixels*

## Soft copy output devices

### Monitor/visual display unit (VDU)

The visual display unit (VDU) or monitor (also called simply 'the screen') can output still or moving pictures. The screen is similar in appearance to that of a television and helps the user to interface visually with the computer. Images and text are formed by many tiny dots of coloured light called **pixels** (short for **pic**ture **el**ement). A pixel is the smallest unit on the screen. It can be turned on or off or coloured in different shades. Pixels are so numerous that when placed together in certain patterns they appear to form a smooth image on the screen, be it a character in a word, a diagram or a photograph.

There are two types of monitors: cathode ray tube (CRT) and flat panel display.

## CRT

The most common type of display is the same as that of the standard television set. The inside of the screen is coated with phosphorescent material. An electron beam (a beam of charged particles) strikes this surface, exciting the phosphors and causing them to glow. A colour display has three different types of particles coating the inner surface of the screen. Each particle produces different colours: red, green and blue (RGB). These colours light the pixels on the screen. When viewed from a little distance away, the colours appear to blend, forming the full range of colours as required.

*Figure 4.2*
*Cathode ray tube (on the left) and a flat panel monitor*



## Flat panel display

There are two types:

- **LCD (liquid crystal display):** This display, as the name suggests, uses liquid crystals which change their appearance when an electric current is passed through them. It is small, light and flat with no moving parts, and uses much less power than the CRT display. It is therefore extensively used on laptop computers.
- **Plasma display:** In this display light is created by a plasma discharge from phosphors between two flat panels of glass.

### Did you know?

Did you know that the CRT was invented in 1897 by the German scientist Karl Braun? It was first used in the cathode ray oscilloscope, a scientific instrument used to display data about electric currents. Later, it became the basis of television. The first successful transmission of moving television images took place in 1925, by the Scottish inventor, John Logie Baird.

## Characteristics of monitors

A monitor's full capabilities depend on several factors:

1. The graphics/video card or adaptor being used
2. The monitor's size
3. Its resolution
4. Its 'image aspect ratio'
5. Its 'refresh rate'

Let us look at these:

- **Graphics/video card or adaptor:** This is an electronic link between the computer's processor and the monitor – it is a circuit board that connects the processor to the monitor. It determines the display resolution, the number of colours available and the refresh rate of the monitor. Both the type of monitor and the graphics card determine the resolution. The adaptor contains VRAM (video RAM memory) that will support a certain resolution. You cannot set a resolution higher than the adaptor can support. The more powerful the card is, the more capable the monitor will be in all these aspects.
- **Size:** This is the diagonal dimension of the screen. Common sizes include 15-inch, 17-inch and 19-inch monitors.
- **Resolution:** Resolution determines the clarity and sharpness of an image when displayed on the screen. The more pixels there are on a screen, the higher the resolution, and the greater the level of detail that can be shown in an image. Some common resolutions are:
  - VGA (Video Graphics Array) = 640 × 480 pixels
  - SVGA (Super Video Graphics Array) = 800 × 600 pixels
  - XGA/XVGA (Extended Graphics Array/Extended Video Graphics Array) = 1024 × 768 pixels
  - SXGA (Super Extended Graphics Array) = 1280 × 1024 pixels
  - UXGA (Ultra Extended Graphics Array) = 1600 × 1200 pixels

- **Image aspect ratio:** This refers to the ratio of width to height of an image on the screen. Most monitors have a 4:3 width to height ratio. Notice that all the pixel dimensions shown above can be reduced to this ratio mathematically.
- **Refresh rate:** This is the number of times the image is repainted or refreshed on the screen per second. We get the impression that, for example, a drawing on our screen is still, but in fact it is being repainted continuously. If this process is slow, the screen may appear to flicker.
  - The refresh rate is measured in hertz (cycles per second), e.g. 150 hertz (Hz) means the screen is refreshed 150 times a second.
  - The faster the refresh rate the less noticeable the flickering on the screen.
  - The higher the resolution the more lines need to be scanned across the screen, or repainted per second.

## Other visual output devices

### *Multimedia projector*

This device is used to create and deliver dynamic **multimedia** presentations (presentations in which sound, photos, video, text and other moving graphics may be combined to interesting effect). There are two types of multimedia projectors: LCD projector and LCD panel.

The **LCD projector** has its own built-in lenses and light source and connects directly to computer, television, video/DVD player and video camcorder. Images from these devices are projected through the LCD projector onto a screen or wall. Versions of the LCD projector now come with a digital video camera on an arm extension attached to it. This video camera allows real-time videos and pictures to be instantly projected through the LCD projector onto a screen. For example, the camera can be directed at a page in a book or at someone performing a demonstration; the video camera image is projected through the LCD projector onto a screen or wall.

The **LCD panel** is used with a normal overhead projector (OHP). This panel is the size of a notebook and is placed directly on the surface of the OHP. Like the LCD projector, the panel can be connected to devices such as computer, television, video/DVD player and video camcorder. The image displayed on the panel is projected onto a screen when the light of the OHP shines through it.

## Sound output

Sound output is another form of 'soft copy' output: it isn't permanent, as printing would be. Some of the devices involved are as follows:

### *Speakers*

A simple speaker will make a range of sounds available to the computer user. Computer-generated sound, music output, computer-synthesised voice and the normal speaking voice are now conventional output using a speaker. Sound cards need to be installed in microcomputers to obtain good sound quality for music or games.

### *Voice response systems*

The voice response system selects from a set of digitised prerecorded words, phrases, music, alarms or other sounds stored on disk. The system combines these prerecorded words into responses based on selections made by the user. For example, many phone banking systems use voice response systems. Based on the information given to them when a caller selects options on their telephone keypad, the bank computer outputs voice information to the caller. The sounds must be converted from digital format back to analogue before being output to the speaker.

### *Speech synthesis*

This system converts written text into computer generated speech ('text to speech'). It is used for computer-aided conversations by hearing- and speech-impaired persons, or for converting conversations/text from one language into another.

**Did you know?**

Did you know that speech synthesis can now be demonstrated on the Internet? Connect to the World Wide Web and see what speech synthesis web sites you can find.

## The modem

A **modem** (short for **mo**dulator/**dem**odulator) is a communication device that sends and receives data. Therefore it is both an input and an output device. It is used to convert digital data from the computer into analogue data that can be transmitted over the telephone line. When the data gets to the other end, another modem converts the analogue data back into digital data so that the computer at that end can process it. A modem is an extremely common device, often built into the computer. For example, it is used to read data from, and transmit data to, the Internet.

### Exercise 1

**1** Copy and fill in the blanks using A to E below.

(1) __________ = resolution
(2) __________ = pixel
(3) __________ = refresh rate
(4) __________ = speech synthesis
(5) __________ = voice response systems

A The smallest unit on the screen
B Converts written text into computer generated speech
C Selects and plays back prerecorded sounds
D Measured in hertz
E The clarity or sharpness of an image

**2** Copy and fill in the blanks:

Temporary output is also known as __________ output. Monitors are temporary output devices; __________ and __________ are the two types of monitors. The most common is the __________. The electronic link between the processor and the monitor is __________. Three characteristics that affect the capabilities of monitors are __________, __________ and __________.

# *Hard copy output devices*

You can print out information that is in the computer onto paper or film. By printing you create what is known as a 'hard copy'. It is tangible – you can hold it in your hands.

## Printers

Printers are used to present and store all kinds of information on paper, such as letters, legal documents, scientific data and graphs, photographs and advertising material. There are really no limits to the amount and type of information that can be printed on paper – just take a look at the paper-based material around you, in your classroom or in your home.

There are therefore many different kinds of printers, which vary in their speed and print quality, depending on the desired print output. One way of classifying printers is as:

- **Character printers:** These print one character at a time much like a typewriter. They are slow.
- **Line printers:** These are much faster; they print a line at a time, or so it appears as multiple hammer-like keys forming a line of text hit the page at one time. They are used with mainframe computers where high speed is vital for the large volume of printed output required. They print a limited number of characters and do not print graphics.
- **Page printers:** These print a whole page at a time. They are therefore even faster and deal with very large volumes of printed output.

The print quality will vary depending on the type of printer, and also the instructions you send to the printer as to the quality you require. For example, in a standard household or office printer, there is letter quality, near letter quality (NLQ), draft quality printing and photo quality.

Another more common way of classifying printers is as **impact printers** and **non-impact printers**. We will now look at these printers in detail.

## Impact printers

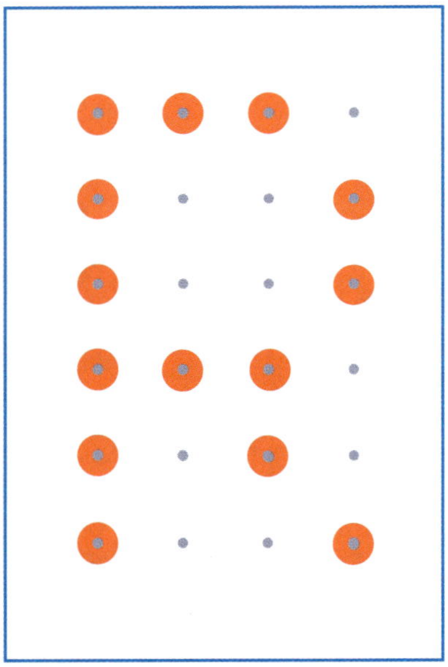

*Figure 4.4*
*Example of how a matrix printer constructs a character*

The print head of an impact printer contains a number of metal hammers which strike an inked ribbon placed between the print head and the paper. These hammers may contain complete characters; alternatively, they may contain 'dots' that are used to build up a character. The main types of impact printer are:

- Dot matrix printer
- Daisy wheel printer
- Drum, chain or band printer.

### *Dot matrix printers (character printers)*

Characteristics of these printers include:

- Characters are formed from a matrix of dots.
- The speed is usually 30–550 characters per second (cps).
- This is the noisiest of the printer family.
- These printers are relatively fast.
- The print obtained is usually poor. They are useful for low-quality carbon copy printing of text, or printing text on continuous sheets of paper.
- They are not good for printing shaded graphics or photographs.

### *Daisy wheel printers (character printers)*

Characteristics of these printers include:

- Moulded metal characters similar to typewriter keys are mounted on extension arms attached to a rotating wheel. Prints are made by a hammer-like action of the keys hitting the print ribbon.
- The process involves a lot of moving mechanical parts and is very noisy.
- Printing is slow (less than 90 cps).

- Printouts are similar to that produced by an electric typewriter.
- The text is generally crisp and clean – letter quality print.
- The size and font produced can only be changed by using a different wheel, as the characters on the wheel are fixed.

This printer is not used much any more: it is becoming obsolete, as laser printers are able to produce the same quality print as the daisy wheel printers and are much more versatile.

### *Drum, chain or band printer (line printers)*

These are line printers which contain characters on a drum, chain or band that rotates at constant speed; the keys strike the page as the required characters pass the print position. Characters do not get printed one at a time from left to right. Instead they are printed in the order in which they pass the head. They are high speed – 2500 lines per minute – and are used to print large volume of information.

## Non-impact printers

The print head of a non-impact printer does not strike the paper, so they are much quieter than impact printers. Most non-impact printers produce dot matrix patterns. Several technologies are now available and have been used to produce a variety of printers. The main types of non-impact printer are:

- Thermal printer
- Laser printer
- Ink-jet printer.

### *Thermal printers (character printers)*

There are two types of thermal printers.

- *Direct thermal printer*: This printer uses heated elements/pins to form the characters. These elements/pins come into contact with special heat-sensitive paper to form darkened dots where the elements have reached a critical temperature, thus shaping the characters. The pins actually burn the dots into the specially coated paper. Exposure to sunlight and heat tends to darken the thermal printer paper, which also tends to darken over time even at room temperature; the print quality produced by thermal printers is therefore poor.
- *Thermal wax transfer printer*: The print head of this printer melts a wax-based ink from a transfer ribbon onto the paper. This printer does not require special paper.

Thermal printers are widely used in battery-powered equipment such as portable calculators, fax machines and some ATMs (automated teller machines).

### *Laser printers (page printers)*

Laser printers use a process similar to that of a photocopying machine, and are very common in the modern office. A laser beam and dry powdered ink called toner produces a very fine dot matrix pattern. This pattern is transferred to the page and then fused onto it by heat and pressure. These printers can generate a large number of pages per minute depending on the specification and quality of the printer.

Colour laser printers use four different colour toners and work by printing four times – once with cyan toner, then with magenta toner, then yellow and then with black. The mix of these colours can produce all other colours, and the output quality is very good.

**Did you know?**

Did you know that the fastest black-and-white laser printers can produce around 40 fully printed pages per minute? The fastest colour laser printers are only slightly slower, producing around 30 pages per minute.

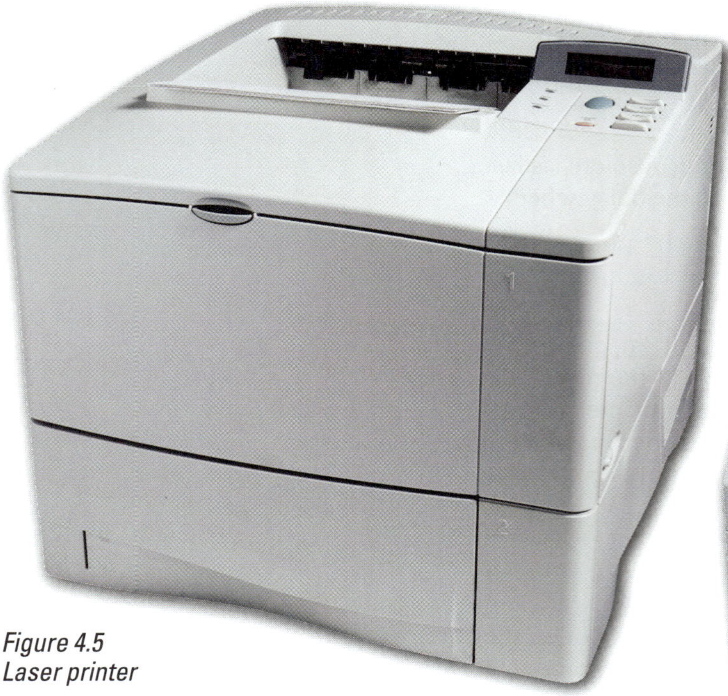

*Figure 4.5*
*Laser printer*

*Figure 4.6*
*Inkjet printer*

Compared to black-and-white laser printers, colour laser printers are a lot more expensive, sometimes thousands of dollars more than the black-and-white ones.

### Inkjet printers (line printers)

Inkjet printers produce an image by spraying ink onto the paper in a dot matrix pattern. Colour graphics can be produced by spraying cyan, magenta, yellow and black ink onto the page. Inkjet printers can print in both colour and black-and-white. They are very common for home use and the print quality is good, even very good, but not as good as laser printers. A typical printer of this type may cost around US$ 100, though the cost of continuously replacing ink should also be borne in mind.

#### Characteristics of non-impact printers

- Much quieter – useful in hospitals, busy offices, etc.
- Much faster printing speeds
- Sometimes require special paper
- Do not have multiple-copy facilities, that is they cannot produce multiple copies by printing on duplicating paper

#### Characteristics of impact printers

- Noisy
- Can produce multiple copies by printing on duplicating paper
- Used in many businesses

One other type of printer worth mentioning is the Braille printer. This is an impact printer which converts text into the Braille code, producing patterns of raised dots on paper for use by the blind.

## Plotters

A plotter is a peripheral used to draw high quality, high resolution graphics, charts, graphs, maps and vectors or co-ordinate graphics on large sheets of paper.

- Plotters are slow, but can draw continuous lines often in a variety of colours.
- They are useful for producing architectural drawings, building plans, maps and **CAD (computer aided design)** drawings, where precision is required.
- The paper is sometimes laid on a flat bed (flat-bed plotter) or on a rotating drum (drum plotter).

There are three main types of plotters: pen plotters, inkjet plotters and electrostatic plotters.

- Pen plotters use a mechanical arm or rail that holds a pen which can be moved across the page.
- Inkjet plotters work in the same way as inkjet printers by spraying ink onto the paper.
- Electrostatic plotters work in the same way as laser printers.

*Figure 4.7 Plotter*

## COM (computer output on microfilm/microfiche)

COM is a method that is used to store computer documents by reducing them in size to fit on very small photographic prints. They are therefore a physical output like printing, and are used to store large volumes of data. These prints can be read using a special magnifying machine. **Microfilm** is a roll of film and **microfiche** is a rectangular sheet of film on which many frames/pages of information can be stored.

# Robot and control systems

Computer processors can send signals to a robotic hardware device to produce a physical action. This is another type of output, therefore. Robotics is very common in the manufacture of high-tech goods such as cars, television sets and so on, in a complex factory production line process.

Control systems use sensors to measure physical quantities. Sensors send input to the processor of the controlling computer, which responds by sending an output signal to activate an item of hardware. An example sensor would be a smoke detector; once smoke is detected it can send a signal to the sprinklers in a building or to an alarm in a fire station.

## Summary

1. Output devices are pieces of equipment that are used to get information or any other response out of a computer.
2. Output can be human readable or machine readable.
3. Soft copy or temporary output disappears when the computer is switched off.
4. Hard copy or permanent output refers to output printed onto paper, microfiche or microfilm.
5. Monitors or VDUs are soft copy output devices. Types include CRT, LCD and plasma.
6. A pixel is the smallest unit on the screen that can be turned on or off or coloured in different shades.
7. A monitor's performance depends on the graphics/video card or adaptor, its size, resolution, image aspect ratio and refresh rate.
8. Sound is soft copy output. Computer-synthesised voice, computer-generated sound, music output and the speaking voice are output using a speaker.
9. Modems are both input and output devices, and are used to communicate information over a telephone line, e.g. to and from the Internet.
10. Printers are hard copy output devices and can be classified as character, line and page printers.
11. Printers can be divided into two broad categories: impact printers and non-impact printers.
12. Impact printers include dot matrix, daisy wheel and drum/chain/band printers.
13. Non-impact printers include thermal, laser and inkjet printers.
14. A plotter is used, e.g. in CAD, to draw high quality graphics, charts, graphs, maps and vectors or co-ordinate graphics on large sheets of paper.
15. Computer output on microfilm/microfiche (COM) is hard copy output used to store computer documents by vastly reducing them in size to fit on photographic prints.

## Questions

### Crossword

**Across**

3 Sound output (7)

5 The print head of this printer strikes the paper (6)

7 Clarity of an image (10)

**Down**

1 Sprays ink onto paper in a dot matrix pattern (6)

2 Permanent output (2 words) (8)

4 Specialised output device used to produce architectural drawings (7)

6 Smallest unit on the screen (5)

## Multiple choice

1 A monitor's capabilities depend on all except:
 (a) Resolution
 (b) Size
 (c) Refresh rate
 (d) Print quality

2 NQL refers to:
 (a) Refresh rate
 (b) The number of characters per second
 (c) Print quality
 (d) Type of monitor

3 All the following are non-impact printers except:
 (a) Chain
 (b) Thermal
 (c) Inkjet
 (d) Laser

4 Which is not a characteristic of laser printers?
 (a) They are quiet
 (b) They have high print speeds
 (c) Use toner similar to that found in photocopiers
 (d) Can produce multiple copies by printing on duplicating paper

5 Microfilm output is stored on:
 (a) Rectangular sheet of film
 (b) Photographic paper
 (c) Magnetic paper
 (d) A roll of film

## Short answer questions

1 Give TWO advantages and TWO disadvantages of a non-impact printer over an impact printer.

2 Explain the difference between a line printer and a character printer.

3 Explain the difference between microfilm and microfiche.

4 A number of output devices are used to assist the physically challenged person. Select TWO and explain how these devices work towards making things easier for the physically challenged.

5 Give ONE advantage of output on microfilm over that on printed paper.

6 There are a number of output devices that produce human readable as well as machine readable output. Explain what is the difference and list ONE of each type of device.

7 Describe how a robotic arm can be used in an assembly line.

8 You are a consultant to a small business that types documents and creates presentations for individuals. Select a suitable printer and explain to your client why you have chosen that printer for their business.

9 List TWO attributes of a monitor that affect its display and explain how the monitor is affected.

10 There are two types of flat screen monitors, LCD and plasma. Explain the difference between the two.

11 State what you would use to print the following documents: printer or plotter.
 (a) A resumé
 (b) A prenuptial agreement contract
 (c) A design for a new gown
 (d) A recipe
 (e) The redesign of a bathroom
 (f) A map to get from the centre of the town to your home

# 5 Data Storage and Representation

## OBJECTIVES

At the end of this chapter you will be able to:

- Explain the difference between discrete and continuous data and give examples of each
- Explain what a bistable device is
- Convert a decimal number to binary, and vice versa
- Add binary numbers
- Represent integers using sign and magnitude, one's complement, two's complement and binary coded decimal methods
- Perform subtraction using two's complement
- Explain the term character set
- Define the term parity bit and explain the difference between even and odd parity
- Represent real numbers using floating point representation
- Convert a binary fraction to decimal, and vice versa
- Understand how floating point numbers are stored

As you may recall, data is all the raw facts and figures that a computer processes by following a set of instructions called a program. The way in which data is stored and represented depends on the medium storing it and the type of data. Generally there are two types of data – discrete and continuous. **Discrete data** is data that can be counted; for example, the number of cars in a car park or the number of people that responded 'yes' or 'no' to a question. It has no value in between; for example, you cannot say two and a half students are present. On the other hand **continuous data** is data that can be measured and can be recorded at many different points. For example, the temperature of a liquid can be recorded as 35 degrees Celsius (°C). However, based on the accuracy of the instrument, the temperature may be recorded to greater levels of accuracy, such as 32.5 °C or 32.53 °C or 32.534 °C, and so on. Other examples of continuous data are length, temperature and volume (such as the volume of water or air). Discrete data is processed by digital computers while continuous data is processed by analogue computers.

A computer consists of a number of two-state (or bistable) devices that process and store data. A **bistable device** is one which can be set to one of two states at any one point in time. An example of a bistable device could be a light bulb. A light bulb can be either in the 'on' or 'off' state. A circuit can either pass a current or not pass a current through the bulb. The two states of a bistable device can be represented by the digits 0 and 1. In the case of the light bulb we can use 0 to represent the bulb being 'on' and 1 to represent it being 'off'. The **binary number system**, which consists of two digits 0 and 1, is used by computers to represent the two states. These two binary digits are also known as bits (short for **b**inary dig**its**).

A single bit can represent one of two values, 0 and 1. A group of two bits can be used to represent one of four ($2^2$) values:

00 01 10 11

These four values can represent four different symbols or characters. For example, the numbers 0, 1, 2, 3 could be assigned to the four bit patterns:

| | | | |
|---|---|---|---|
| 00 | 0 | 10 | 2 |
| 01 | 1 | 11 | 3 |

With three bits we can have 8 ($2^3$) bit patterns. This means we can now represent eight different characters (0 to 7):

| | | | |
|---|---|---|---|
| 000 | 0 | 100 | 4 |
| 001 | 1 | 101 | 5 |
| 010 | 2 | 110 | 6 |
| 011 | 3 | 111 | 7 |

With four bits we can represent 16 ($2^4$) characters, with eight bits we can represent 256 ($2^8$) characters, and so on. Therefore with '$n$' bits we will be able to represent $2^n$ characters.

# Number systems

The number system that you are most familiar with is the decimal (base 10) number system. This is the system that is used in everyday mathematical operations. However, since computers can only perform binary operations, you need to know how to perform calculations using the binary number system. The next section deals with converting numbers from binary (base 2) to decimal (base 10), and vice versa.

## Converting a binary number (base 2) to decimal (base 10)

Before converting a binary number to decimal we need to revise some basic concepts of the decimal number system. This system consists of ten digits (0, 1, 2, 3, 4, 5, 6, 7, 8, 9) and for this reason it is also referred to as the base 10 number system. The base of any number may be indicated as a subscript on the extreme right of the number (e.g. $455_{10}$ means '455 to the base 10'). These digits and their combinations are used to represent numbers in the decimal number system.

Each digit in the decimal number system has a value that depends on its position or place in the number. The place values start at $10^0$ for the digit of smallest value on the right. You know from your mathematics lessons that $10^0 = 1$, since any number raised to the power of 0 is 1. So $10^0$ is the 'ones place' or 'ones column'. Similarly, $10^1$ is the 'tens place'. The value of each place increases by a factor of 10 for each consecutive digit *moving right to left,* until the digit of greatest value is reached: the digit on the far left. Again, you will recall this from your mathematics lessons.

Let us look at the number 325. This number is made up of the sum (addition) of each digit multiplied by its place value. Table 1 shows the value of each digit in the number.

| **Hundreds (H)** | **Tens (T)** | **Ones (O)** |
|---|---|---|
| 3 represents 3 hundreds | 2 represents 2 tens | 5 represents 5 ones |
| $3 \times 100 = 300$ | $2 \times 10 = 20$ | $5 \times 1 = 5$ |
| Adding the totals together gives 325 | | |

*Table 1*

Another way of setting out the information in Table 1 is shown in Table 2.

| H ($10^2$) | T ($10^1$) | O ($10^0$) | |
|---|---|---|---|
| 100 | 10 | 1 | This row shows the value of each digit in that position: the 'place value'. |
| 3 | 2 | 5 | Each digit in this row is multiplied by its place value, above. |
| 300 | 20 | 5 | Sum the totals: |
| | | | The result is 325 |

*Table 2*
*Decimal number and place value*

Converting a binary number to decimal is very similar since each digit in a binary number also has a place value that depends on its position in the number. However, in this case the place value starts at $2^0$ for the least significant bit (LSB) and increases by a factor of 2 for each bit that follows, again *moving right to left*, as in the decimal example just given.

### Did you know?

Did you know that the *Voyager* space probe has binary messages for any intelligent life form it may encounter on its journey through space? Launched in 1977, *Voyager 1* and its twin, *Voyager 2*, were the first space probes to explore the outer planets of our solar system. *Voyager 1*'s primary mission ended in 1980 when it completed its observations of Saturn. Since then, it has been heading into deep space. *Voyager 1* and *2* both carry a so-called 'golden record' – a 12-inch gold-plated copper disk. The disk carries greetings and an overview of our culture for extraterrestrials who may one day stumble across one of these man-made craft. The record includes samples of music; natural sounds such as thunder, waves crashing, bird song; and greetings in multiple languages.

To convert a binary number to decimal, multiply each bit by its place value, starting from the least significant bit (LSB) on the right to the most significant bit (MSB) on the left, and then sum the totals. Example 1 illustrates how this can be done.

### Example 1

*Convert $1001_2$ to decimal.*

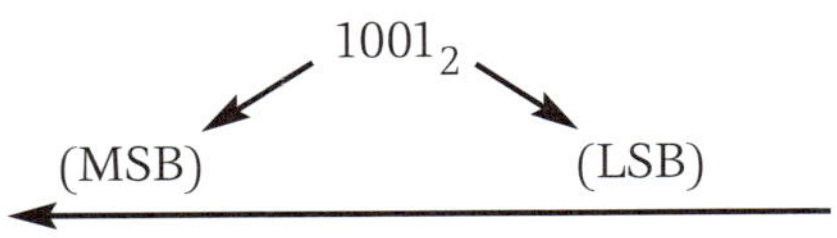


| $2^3$ | $2^2$ | $2^1$ | $2^0$ | |
|---|---|---|---|---|
| 8 | 4 | 2 | 1 | This row shows the value of each digit in that position: the 'place value'. |
| 1 | 0 | 0 | 1 | Each digit in this row is multiplied by its place value, above. |
| 8 | 0 | 0 | 1 | Sum the totals: |
| | | | | The result is 9 |

Therefore $1001_2 = 9_{10}$

### Example 2

*Convert $111001_2$ to decimal.*

| $2^5$ | $2^4$ | $2^3$ | $2^2$ | $2^1$ | $2^0$ | |
|---|---|---|---|---|---|---|
| 32 | 16 | 8 | 4 | 2 | 1 | This row shows the value of each digit in that position: the 'place value'. |
| 1 | 1 | 1 | 0 | 0 | 1 | Each digit in this row is multiplied by its place value, above. |
| 32 | 16 | 8 | 0 | 0 | 1 | Sum the totals: |
| | | | | | | The result is 57 |

Therefore $111001_2 = 57_{10}$

## Converting a decimal number (base 10) to binary (base 2)

Converting a decimal number (base 10) to binary (base 2) is a simple process. It involves dividing the decimal number by 2 and recording the remainder until the result is zero, then writing out the remainders starting from the last remainder to the first. The following example demonstrates how this can be accomplished.

### Example 3

*Convert the number $9_{10}$ to binary.*

| | | |
|---|---|---|
| 2 | 9 | a. Nine divided by 2 gives 4 remainder 1. |
| 2 | 4 R 1 | b. Four divided by 2 gives 2 remainder 0. |
| 2 | 2 R 0 | c. Two divided by 2 gives 1 remainder 0. |
| 2 | 1 R 0 | d. One divided by 2 gives 0 remainder 1. |
| | 0 R 1 | Write the remainders starting from the last remainder moving up to the first. This gives $1001_2$ |
| | Therefore $9_{10} = 1001_2$ | |

The process is the same for larger numbers.

### Example 4

*What is the binary equivalent of $225_{10}$?*

| | | |
|---|---|---|
| 2 | 225 | a. 225 divided by 2 gives 112 remainder 1. |
| 2 | 112 R 1 | b. 112 divided by 2 gives 56 remainder 0. |
| 2 | 56 R 0 | c. 56 divided by 2 gives 28 remainder 0. |
| 2 | 28 R 0 | d. 28 divided by 2 gives 14 remainder 0. |
| 2 | 14 R 0 | e. 14 divided by 2 gives 7 remainder 0. |
| 2 | 7 R 0 | f. 7 divided by 2 gives 3 remainder 1. |
| 2 | 3 R 1 | g. 3 divided by 2 gives 1 remainder 1. |
| 2 | 1 R 1 | h. One divided by 2 gives 0 remainder 1. |
| | 0 R 1 | Write the remainders starting from the last remainder moving up to the first. This gives $11100001_2$ |
| | Therefore $225_{10} = 11100001_2$ | |

## Adding binary numbers

To add two binary numbers you need to remember the following points. You should memorise these five sums, as they are a good basis for knowing how to add in binary.

1. $0_2 + 0_2 = 0_2$
2. $0_2 + 1_2 = 1_2$
3. $1_2 + 0_2 = 1_2$
4. $1_2 + 1_2 = 10_2$
5. $1_2 + 1_2 + 1_2 = 11_2$

To understand how the above calculations work, you can think of them as follows:

1. $0_2 + 0_2 = 0_2$. This is the same as:
   $(2^0 \times 0) + (2^0 \times 0) = (1 \times 0) + (1 \times 0) = 0 \times 0 = 0$.
   $0_{10}$ in base 2 is $\mathbf{0_2}$, hence the answer shown.

Similarly:

5. $1_2 + 1_2 + 1_2$ is the same as:
   $(2^0 \times 1) + (2^0 \times 1) + (2^0 \times 1) = 1 + 1 + 1 = 3$.
   $3_{10}$ in binary is the same as
   $(2^1 \times 1) + (2^0 \times 1) = 11_2$

You also need to remember always that when adding binary numbers $1 + 1 \neq 2$, because the digit 2 is not used in binary; similarly $1 + 1 + 1 \neq 3$.

Now let us look at adding in binary with a few examples.

### Example 5

*Add together the binary numbers 01 and 10.*

First, place the binary numbers one above the other, ensuring the bits with the same weighting are in the same columns. This gives:

```
  01
+ 10
```

**Step 1:** Starting from the column on the right add the digits: 1 + 0 = 1. Write the 1 in the same column.

```
  01
+ 10
----
   1
```

**Step 2:** Add the digits in the second column: 0 + 1 = 1. Write the 1 in the same column.

```
  01
+ 10
----
  11
```

Therefore $\mathbf{01_2} + \mathbf{10_2} = \mathbf{11_2}$

### Example 6

*Add together $011_2$ and $010_2$.*

```
(MSB) (LSB)
   0 1 1
 + 0 1 0
```

**Step 1:** Starting from the rightmost column (LSB) add the digits: 1 + 0 = 1. Write the 1 in the same column.

```
  0 1 1
+ 0 1 0
-------
      1
```

**Step 2:** Add the digits in the second column: 1 + 1 = 10. Write the 0 in the same column and carry the 1 to the next column.

```
(carry) 1
        0 1 1
      + 0 1 0
      -------
          0 1
```

**Step 3:** Add the digits in the third column: 1 (the carried bit) + 0 + 0 = 1

We now have:

```
  0 1 1
+ 0 1 0
-------
  1 0 1
```

Therefore $\mathbf{011_2} + \mathbf{010_2} = \mathbf{101_2}$

### Example 7

*Add together $1011_2$ and $0011_2$*

First place the binary numbers one above the other ensuring the bits with the same weighting are in the same columns.

```
(MSB)    (LSB)
  1 0 1 1
+ 0 0 1 1
```

**Step 1:** Add the digits in the rightmost (LSB) column: 1 + 1 = 10. Write the 0 in the column and carry the 1 to the next column:

```
        1
  1 0 1 1
+ 0 0 1 1
---------
        0
```

## Exercise 1

1 (a) Define data.
(b) What are the two types of data?
(c) Explain, giving examples, the difference between the two types of data.

2 Using an example, explain the term 'bistable device'.

3 Convert the following decimal numbers to binary:
(a) $7_{10}$ (b) $15_{10}$ (c) $25_{10}$
(d) $71_{10}$ (e) $205_{10}$

4 Convert the following binary numbers to decimal:
(a) $0011_2$
(b) $00110001_2$
(c) $10111001_2$
(d) $10110111_2$
(e) $11111111_2$

5 Add together the following binary numbers giving the answer in binary form.
(a) $101_2 + 110_2$
(b) $011_2 + 100_2$
(c) $01011_2 + 110_2$
(d) $011011_2 + 01011_2$
(e) $110101_2 + 01101_2$

**Step 2:** Add the digits in the second column, including the carry bit: 1 + 1 + 1 = 11. Write the 1 in the column and carry 1 to the next column.

```
    1 1
  1 0 1 1
+ 0 0 1 1
---------
      1 0
```

**Step 3:** Add the digits in the third column, including the carry bit: 1 + 0 + 0 = 1. Write the 1 in the column.

```
    1 1
  1 0 1 1
+ 0 0 1 1
---------
    1 1 0
```

**Step 4:** Add the digits in the fourth column:
1 + 0 = 1. Write the 1 in the column.

```
    1 1
  1 0 1 1
+ 0 0 1 1
---------
  1 1 1 0
```

Therefore $\mathbf{1011_2 + 0011_2 = 1110_2}$

# Representing signed integers

An integer is any whole number (positive or negative) that does not have a fractional part. So far, our discussion has focused on unsigned integers: integers we always assume to be positive. However, in practice we need both positive and negative integers, collectively called signed integers. In the decimal system the minus sign (–) is used to indicate that a value is negative and an optional plus sign (+) is used to indicate that a value is positive. In binary there are many different ways of representing signed numbers. In this chapter we will look at four of the more common methods: sign and magnitude, one's complement, two's complement and binary coded decimal (BCD).

## Sign and magnitude representation

In the decimal number system we can represent a negative number by placing the minus (–) sign in front of the number, for example, –3, –245. However, this is not possible in binary as we can only have binary numbers. In sign and magnitude representation the leftmost bit is used to represent the sign (positive or negative) and the remaining bits represent the magnitude. Usually a 0 sign bit indicates that the number is positive and a 1 sign bit indicates that the number is negative.

The four-bit binary representation '0001' in sign and magnitude representation is equivalent to the decimal number 'positive one' (+1), while '1001' is equivalent to the decimal number 'negative one' (–1). Table 3 below shows the sign bit and the bits that make up the magnitude.

| Sign bit | Magnitude | Decimal value |
|---|---|---|
| 0 | 0 0 1 | +1 |
| 1 | 0 0 1 | –1 |

*Table 3 Sign and magnitude representation*

Using four bits we can have 16 different combinations. Using the convention 0 sign bit for positive and 1 sign bit for negative, Table 4 shows the range of numbers that can be represented.

| | | | |
|---|---|---|---|
| 0000 | 0 | 1000 | 0 |
| 0001 | + 1 | 1001 | - 1 |
| 0010 | + 2 | 1010 | - 2 |
| 0011 | + 3 | 1011 | - 3 |
| 0100 | + 4 | 1100 | - 4 |
| 0101 | + 5 | 1101 | - 5 |
| 0110 | + 6 | 1110 | - 6 |
| 0111 | + 7 | 1111 | - 7 |

*Table 4*

The range of numbers that can be represented using four bits is –7 to + 7. From the table we can see that when the 0 sign bit of any number is replaced by a 1 sign bit (except for the numbers representing 0) we get the negative of the number. Example 8 describes how a signed integer may be represented using sign and magnitude representation.

### Example 8

*Give the eight-bit representation of –35 using sign and magnitude representation.*

First, find the binary representation of 35.

| ÷ | 35 | R |
|---|---|---|
| 2 | 17 | 1 |
| 2 | 8 | 1 |
| 2 | 4 | 0 |
| 2 | 2 | 0 |
| 2 | 1 | 0 |
| | 0 | 1 |

This gives $100011_2$

Notice the answer consists of only six bits. To make it an eight-bit number, we need add two zeroes to the left, which gives $00100011_2$. Note that adding the two zeroes to the left does not change the value of the binary string.

$+35 = \mathbf{0}0100011_2$

Sign bit magnitude

To get $-35$ we change the leftmost bit to 1.

$-35 = \mathbf{1}0100011_2$

Sign bit magnitude

From Table 4 we can see that there are two ways to represent the number 0, these are $0000_2$ and $1000_2$. Because of this drawback and a few others, computer scientists have developed other methods of representing numbers in the computer.

## One's complement

In one's complement notation, positive numbers are represented as usual in unsigned binary. However, negative numbers are represented by simply flipping all the digits. This means replacing all the zeroes by ones and all the ones by zeroes. For example, positive three ( + 3) in this system is written as $0011_2$. To get negative three (–3) we replace the zeroes by ones and the ones by zeroes, so that it becomes $1100_2$.

When converting a number to its one's complement the number of bits must be stated. It is therefore wrong to say, for example, 'find the one's complement of $100_2$'. You need to say, 'find the four-bit one's complement of $100_2$'.

This numeric representation system is not used very much today. It was common in older mainframe computers; the PDP-1 and UNIVAC 1100/2200 among many others.

### Example 9

*What is the seven-bit one's complement of 0110?*

1. Add three zeroes in front of the leftmost bit (MSB). This gives 0000110.
2. Flip the bits. This gives 1111001.

The seven bit one's complement of 0110 is therefore **1111001**. (The results do not need any further explanation. Students would not be required to discuss the decimal value of a one's complement number.)

### Example 10

*Using four bits give the one's complement representation of –6.*

1. Find the binary representation of 6, following the process in Example 3. This gives $110_2$, i.e. $(2^2 \times \mathbf{1}) + (2^1 \times \mathbf{1}) + (2^0 \times \mathbf{0})$
2. Add zero in front of the leftmost bit (MSB) to make it a four-bit number. This gives $0110_2$.
3. Flip the bits. This gives $1001_2$.

The four bit one's complement of –6 is therefore $\mathbf{1001_2}$.

## Two's complement

This is one of the most commonly used methods of representing signed (positive and negative) integers.

To represent a number in two's complement notation we begin by first finding the one's complement of the number, then add 1 to the result. The example below lists the steps involved.

### Example 11

*Find the two's complement of the seven-bit binary number 0011011.*

1. Find the one's complement.

   Binary number: 0011011

   One's complement: 1100100

2. Add one to the one's complement.

$$\begin{array}{r} 1100100 \\ +\quad 1 \\ \hline 1100101 \\ \hline \end{array}$$

The two's complement of 0011011 is therefore **1100101**.

Table 5 shows the two's complement representation of a four-bit binary number.

Notice, there is only one representation for zero: 0000. This is an improvement over one's complement because when performing arithmetic you don't need special circuits to deal with the two representations of zero.

| | |
|---|---|
| 7 | 0111 |
| 6 | 0110 |
| 5 | 0101 |
| 4 | 0100 |
| 3 | 0011 |
| 2 | 0010 |
| 1 | 0001 |
| 0 | 0000 |
| −1 | 1111 |
| −2 | 1110 |
| −3 | 1101 |
| −4 | 1100 |
| −5 | 1011 |
| −6 | 1010 |
| −7 | 1001 |
| −8 | 1000 |

*Table 5 Four-bit two's complement representation*

### Example 12

*Find the two's complement of the eight-bit binary number 00000000.*

1. Find the one's complement.

   Binary number: 00000000

   One's complement: 11111111

2. Add one to the one's complement.

$$\begin{array}{r} 11111111 \\ +\quad 1 \\ \hline \mathbf{1}00000000 \\ \hline \end{array}$$

(Discard the extra bit)

Note that we now have nine bits. Since we are working with eight bits we discard the leftmost bit. This discarding action (performed by the computer) is a convention used in two's complement notation to maintain the original number of bits specified, in this case eight. The answer is therefore 00000000, which is the same as what we started with.

The majority of modern computer systems use two's complement form to represent signed binary numbers. This is because there is only one representation of zero and addition and subtraction is made very simple. Using the two's complement system, the circuitry for addition and subtraction can be unified, otherwise they would have to be treated as separate operations.

### Example 13

*Using six bits find the two's complement representation of $-27_{10}$.*

1. Find the binary equivalent of 27. This gives $11011_2$.
2. Add a zero in front of the MSB to make it a six-bit number. This gives $011011_2$.
3. Find the one's complement of $011011_2$. This gives $100100_2$.
4. Add $1_2$ to $100100_2$. This gives $100101_2$.

−27 as a six-bit two's complement representation is therefore $\mathbf{100101_2}$.

From Example 13, $-27 = 100101_2$. This is possible because in two's complement coding the place value of all the bits are the same except the MSB which represents a negative number. Table 6 shows the two's complement binary representation of −27.

| $-(2^5)$ | $2^4$ | $2^3$ | $2^2$ | $2^1$ | $2^0$ | |
|---|---|---|---|---|---|---|
| −32 | 16 | 8 | 4 | 2 | 1 | This row shows the value of each digit in that position: the 'place value'. |
| 1 | 0 | 0 | 1 | 0 | 1 | Each digit in this row is multiplied by its place value, above. |
| −32 | 0 | 0 | 4 | 0 | 1 | Summing the totals together gives −27. |

*Table 6 The two's complement representation of −27*

### Example 14

*Find the value of $9_{10} - 6_{10}$ using four-bit two's complement binary.*

This could be written as $9_{10} + (-6_{10})$.

1. Convert 9 to its binary equivalent. This gives $1001_2$.
2. To find −6 we need to find the two's complement of 6. Convert 6 to its binary equivalent. This gives $0110_2$.

3 Find the one's complement of 0110. This gives $1001_2$.

4 Add 1 to get the two's complement. This gives $1010_2$ which is equal to −6.

5 Add $1001_2$ and $1010_2$.

$$\begin{array}{r} 1001 \\ +\quad 1010 \\ \hline 10011_2 \\ \hline \end{array}$$

We discard the extra bit because we are using four-bit. The answer is therefore $0011_2$.

### *Subtraction of binary numbers*

Two's complement can also help us deal with subtraction of binary numbers. Consider the following problem:

$1001_2 - 0110_2$

This could be written as $1001_2 + (-0110_2)$.

Instead of performing binary subtraction it is actually easier to find the two's complement of $0110_2$ (*not* $-0110_2$), and add it to $1001_2$. First we need to find the two's complement of $0110_2$:

1 Find the one's complement. This gives $1001_2$.

2 Add 1 to the one's complement. This gives $1010_2$.

3 Now add $1001_2$ and $1010_2$:

$$\begin{array}{r} 1001 \\ +\ 1010 \\ \hline 10011 \\ \hline \end{array}$$

(Discard the extra bit)

Since we are using only four bits we discard the extra (leftmost) bit. The answer is therefore **0011**.

Table 7 contains some examples of different binary representations of different decimal numbers:

| BINARY REPRESENTATION OF THE NUMBER | | | |
|---|---|---|---|
| **Decimal number** | **One's complement representation** | **Two's complement representation** | **Sign and magnitude representation** |
| 1 | 00000001 | 00000001 | 00000001 |
| −1 | 11111110 | 11111111 | 10000001 |
| 100 | 01100100 | 01100100 | 01100100 |
| −100 | 10011011 | 10011100 | 11100100 |

*Table 7*

## Binary coded decimal (BCD) representation

BCD representation is very common in electronic devices such as pocket calculators and microwave ovens where a numeric value is to be displayed. In BCD representation each digit of a number is represented as its four-bit binary code. For example, to store the decimal number 256 using BCD, means finding the four-bit binary equivalent of 2, 5 and 6:

$$256 = \underbrace{0010}_{2}\ \underbrace{0101}_{5}\ \underbrace{0110}_{6}$$

So $256_{10} = 001001010110_2$

This method can also be used to represent signed integers (+ and −). This system uses four bits to represent a number. We can therefore represent 16 different numbers (see page 50, where we saw how three bits can represent eight different numbers; logically, four bits allows 16). However, since we only need ten different codes to represent the digits 0 to 9, we can use any of the remaining six codes to represent positive (+) and negative (−). The most commonly used method represents positive (+) as 1010 and negative (−) as 1011.

Therefore the BCD representation of −256 would be:

$$\underbrace{1011}_{-}\ \underbrace{0010}_{2}\ \underbrace{0101}_{5}\ \underbrace{0110}_{6}$$

### Example 15

*What is the BCD representation of −325?*

1 Find the four-bit representation of each digit.

2 $\underbrace{0011}_{3}\ \underbrace{0010}_{2}\ \underbrace{0101}_{5}$

3 Place the BCD code for negative (1011) to the left of all the other bits.

$$\underbrace{1011}_{-}\ \underbrace{0011}_{3}\ \underbrace{0010}_{2}\ \underbrace{0101}_{5}$$

The BCD representation is therefore **1011 0011 0010 0101**.

# Data representation

Various codes have been developed to represent data in the computer and to enable it to be easily transmitted between systems. Data that is represented in computers is made up of characters. Characters include:

- Number characters (0 to 9)

- Alphabetic characters (lower case letters and upper case letters)
- Special characters (punctuation marks, $, /, etc)
- Control characters (backspace, delete, insert, etc).

All the characters that a computer can store and process are called the **character set** of that computer. Different types of computers may have slightly different character sets, depending on their operating system. Each character is represented by a code consisting of either seven or eight bits, called the character code.

Two of the most common codes used are Extended Binary Coded Decimal Interchange Code (EBCDIC pronounced 'Eb-see-dic') and the American Standard Code for Information Interchange (ASCII pronounced 'As-key'). EBCDIC uses eight bits to represent each character and is therefore able to represent 256 different characters (again, see page 50). ASCII on the other hand uses seven bits to represent each character plus an extra bit called a **parity bit** which is added to help ensure data integrity.

The standard ASCII code defines 128 character codes (from 0 to 127) of which the first 32 are deliberately defined as control codes. A control code is a non-printable code that is used to tell the computer to carry out a command such as 'skip a line' or 'start on a new page'. This is done by

| Char | 7 bit ASCII | Char | 7 bit ASCII | Char | 7 bit ASCII |
|---|---|---|---|---|---|
| A | 100 0001 | a | 110 0001 | 0 | 011 0000 |
| B | 100 0010 | b | 110 0010 | 1 | 011 0001 |
| C | 100 0011 | c | 110 0011 | 2 | 011 0010 |
| D | 100 0100 | d | 110 0100 | 3 | 011 0011 |
| E | 100 0101 | e | 110 0101 | 4 | 011 0100 |
| F | 100 0110 | f | 110 0110 | 5 | 011 0101 |
| G | 100 0111 | g | 110 0111 | 6 | 011 0110 |
| H | 100 1000 | h | 110 1000 | 7 | 011 0111 |
| I | 100 1001 | i | 110 1001 | 8 | 011 1000 |
| J | 100 1010 | j | 110 1010 | 9 | 011 1001 |
| K | 100 1011 | k | 110 1011 | blank | 010 0000 |
| L | 100 1100 | l | 110 1100 | . | 010 1110 |
| M | 100 1101 | m | 110 1101 | ( | 010 1000 |
| N | 100 1110 | n | 110 1110 | + | 010 1011 |
| O | 100 1111 | o | 110 1111 | $ | 010 0100 |
| P | 101 0000 | p | 111 0000 | * | 010 1010 |
| Q | 101 0001 | q | 111 0001 | ) | 010 1001 |
| R | 101 0010 | r | 111 0010 | - | 010 1101 |
| S | 101 0011 | s | 111 0011 | / | 010 1111 |
| T | 101 0100 | t | 111 0100 | , | 010 1100 |
| U | 101 0101 | u | 111 0101 | = | 011 1101 |
| V | 101 0110 | v | 111 0110 | RETURN | 000 1101 |
| W | 101 0111 | w | 111 0111 | LNFEED | 000 1010 |
| X | 101 1000 | x | 111 1000 | 0 | 011 0000 |
| Y | 101 1001 | y | 111 1001 | 0 | 011 0000 |
| Z | 101 1010 | z | 111 1010 | 0 | 011 0000 |

*Table 8 Characters and their ASCII code*

assigning one of the control codes to a command. Whenever the computer encounters the code it carries out the command. Control codes give programmers the opportunity to assign commands to actions that they may want to personalise in a particular computer. In many cases there are many unused control codes.

The remaining 96 character codes are representable (printable) characters (Table 8). ASCII code is mostly used in mini and PC computers while EBCDIC is mainly used on large IBM computing systems.

From Table 8 we can see that the codes increase by adding $1_2$ bit to the previous code. For example, the code for the letter A is $1000001_2$. To get the code for the letter B we add 1 to $1000001_2$, which gives $1000010_2$. This pattern is repeated for the entire character set. From this pattern we can determine the codes of other characters if we are given the code of any character in the set.

### Example 16

*The ASCII code for the letter A is 1000001. Determine the seven-bit ASCII code for the letter G.*

Let us look at two methods to solve this problem.

### *Method 1*

Since G is near the start of the alphabet, we can add 1 to the codes of the consecutive letters until we reach G.

The code for A is 100001; to get B we add 1 to the code of A, this gives 1000010; to get C we add 1 to the code for B, this gives 1000011: and so on. If we continue adding we will find that G is therefore **1000111**.

| | | | | | | | |
|---|---|---|---|---|---|---|---|
| A | 1000001 | C | 1000011 | E | 1000101 | G | 1000111 |
| B | 1000010 | D | 1000100 | F | 1000110 | | |

### *Method 2*

Here is another method which may be more efficient.

1 Convert the binary code for A (1000001) to its decimal equivalent.

   1000001 = 65

2 Find the decimal equivalent of the letter G. We know that A is represented by 65, B will be 66, C will be 67 and G will therefore be 71.

   Convert 71 to its binary equivalent.

   71 = 1000111

3 The ASCII code for G is therefore **1000111**.

## Exercise 2

1 Determine the BCD representation of $65_{10}$.

2 Explain the steps in converting an integer to binary using the BCD method.

3 What is the BCD representation of $-21_{10}$?

4 a. Convert the decimal number $45_{10}$ to binary.
   b. What is the one's complement representation of $-45_{10}$?
   c. What is the two's complement representation of $-45_{10}$?
   d. What is the BCD representation of $-45_{10}$?
   e. What is the sign and magnitude representation of $-45_{10}$?

5 The following eight-bit pattern represents the two's complement of an integer: 111001101. What is the decimal equivalent?

6 Subtract the binary number 0011011 from 11110010.

7 Explain the term 'parity bit'.

8 What is the one's complement of 1001 using (a) 4 bits? (b) 6 bits? (c) 8 bits?

9 Using 8 bits, give the two's complement representation of (a) −25 (b) 15 (c) −125.

10 What range of integers can be represented using two's complement with (a) 4 bits? (b) 6 bits? (c) 8 bits?

11 What is the decimal equivalent of the following BCD representations? The first four bits represent the sign (1011 for negative and 1010 for positive).
   a. 1011 1001 1000 0111
   b. 1010 0010 0101 0111
   c. 1010 0101 0111 0011 1001

12 What is the decimal equivalent of the following two's complement representations?
   a. 1001
   b. 1110
   c. 11100111
   d. 10010111

13 Give the ASCII representation of the following statement, 'Meet me at 6'. Do not include the quotes.

14 The ASCII representation for the letter 'F' is 01000110.
   (a) What is the ASCII representation of the letter 'K'?
   (b) What is the ASCII representation of the letter 'B'?

15 The ASCII code for the letter 'N' has a decimal equivalent of 78. What is the ASCII code for the letter 'R'?

## Parity bit

When data is copied from one part of the computer to another or transmitted from one computer to another, we must ensure that the data received is exactly the same as the data sent. One method of ensuring this is the use of a parity bit. A parity bit is an extra bit which is added to a byte to ensure data integrity. There are two types of parity: odd and even.

A computer only uses one of the two types. So, if a computer is using even parity, a 1 or a 0 is added to the bit string to ensure that the *number of ones in the bit string is always even*. In an eight-bit byte the leftmost bit would be changed to 0 or 1 to ensure that the number of ones is even.

For example, given the binary string 1100010, a one needs to be added to ensure that the number of ones is even. Therefore adding the parity bit would make this binary string **1**1100010. If the device receiving the data detects a string with odd parity, the data is rejected and an error is reported.

The process is similar for odd parity, but done in the opposite way.

# Fixed point representation

So far we have focused on representing integers (whole numbers) as binary numbers. We now need to consider how real numbers (numbers with decimal points such as 3.2, 6.375) are represented.

## Converting a binary fraction to decimal

To better understand converting binary fractions to decimals, we need to revise some facts about real numbers. Consider the number 3.257. This number is made up of the sum of each digit multiplied by its place value, as shown in Table 9. Notice that digits to the right of the decimal point are multiplied by negative powers of 10, starting with $10^{-1}$, $10^{-2}$, $10^{-3}$.

| | | |
|---|---|---|
| 3 | $3 \times 10^0$ | 3 |
| 2 | $2 \times 10^{-1}$ | .2 |
| 5 | $5 \times 10^{-2}$ | .05 |
| 7 | $7 \times 10^{-3}$ | .007 |
| | | 3.257 |

*Table 9*

Binary fractions operate in a similar way. Each digit to the right of the binary point has a weighting as shown in Table 10.

| **Binary** | **Place value** | **Decimal fraction** | **Decimal value** |
|---|---|---|---|
| First bit after the point .1 | $2^{-1}$ | $^1/_2$ | .5 |
| Second bit after the point .01 | $2^{-2}$ | $^1/_4$ | .25 |
| Third bit .001 | $2^{-3}$ | $^1/_8$ | .125 |
| Fourth bit .0001 | $2^{-4}$ | $^1/_{16}$ | .0625 |
| Fifth bit .00001 | $2^{-5}$ | $^1/_{32}$ | .03125 |

*Table 10*

Using the weighting for each digit in a binary fraction we can find the decimal equivalent. Let us look at an example.

### Example 17

*Convert the binary fraction $11.101_2$ to decimal.*

Starting from the left of the binary fraction, we record the digits down the table:

| **Binary** | **Weighting** | **Value** | |
|---|---|---|---|
| 1 | $2^1$ | $1 \times 2^1 =$ | 2 |
| 1 | $2^0$ | $1 \times 2^0 =$ | 1 |
| 1 | $2^{-1}$ | $1 \times 2^{-1} =$ | .5 |
| 0 | $2^{-2}$ | $0 \times 2^{-2} =$ | .00 |
| 1 | $2^{-3}$ | $1 \times 2^{-3} =$ | .125 |
| | | | $3.625_{10}$ |

**Or**

$(1 \times 2^1)+(1 \times 2^0)+(1 \times 2^{-1})+(0 \times 2^{-2})+(1 \times 2^{-3}) = 2+1+.5+.00+.125 = 3.625_{10}$

## Converting decimal fractions to binary

In a similar way to converting decimal numbers to binary numbers, where we used repeated division by 2, we can convert decimal fractions to binary fractions using repeated multiplication by 2. We repeatedly multiply the fractional part by 2 until the fractional part becomes zero, or until the pattern starts to repeat itself. We record the bit that is on the left of the decimal point in the result, placing it immediately to the right of the point in the binary number. The next binary digit is placed to the right of that one, and so on. The following example will help you understand this.

### Example 18

*Convert the decimal fraction 0.75 to binary.*

**Step 1:** $0.75 \times 2 = 1.50$, so the first bit is **1**, with 0.50 remaining

**Step 2:** $0.50 \times 2 = 1.00$, so the second bit is **1**.

Since all the digits after the decimal point are zero, we have no remainder, so we stop. Starting from the top of our series of calculations, we record the binary digits before the point.

Therefore $\mathbf{0.75_{10} = .11_2}$

### Example 19

*Convert* $.65_{10}$ *to binary.*

$0.65 \times 2 = 1.30$, so the first bit is **1**, remainder 0.30

$0.30 \times 2 = 0.60$, so the second bit is **0**; but we are still not finished, we need to multiply this remainder

$0.60 \times 2 = 1.20$, so the third bit is **1**, remainder 0.20

$0.20 \times 2 = 0.40$, so the fourth bit is **0**, remainder 0.40

$0.40 \times 2 = 0.80$, so the fifth bit is **0**, remainder 0.80

$0.80 \times 2 = 1.60$, so the sixth bit is **1**, remainder 0.60

$0.60 \times 2 = 1.20$, so the seventh bit is **1**, remainder 0.20

Carry on for a while, and you will soon notice that the pattern is now repeating itself, resulting in a very long string of numbers after the binary point. Depending on how many bits we want to store, we therefore truncate or round the result. Let us use five bits to store the value. If we truncate, the value would be 0.10100. If we round off we get 0.10101. The rounded version gives 0.65625 and the truncated version gives 0.625. We see that both versions are not very accurate ways to store real numbers.

In fact really large and really small numbers are hard to represent unless you're prepared to allocate very many bits of storage.

### Example 20

*Convert* $26.625_{10}$ *to binary.*

To convert $26.625_{10}$ to binary, we deal with the integer and fractional parts separately.

First, as we did earlier, we repeatedly divide by 2 to obtain $26_{10} = 11010_2$.

To convert $0.625_{10}$ to binary, repeatedly multiply by 2.

$0.625 \times 2 = 1.25$, so **1** remainder 0.25

$0.25 \times 2 = 0.50$, so **0** remainder 0.50

$0.50 \times 2 = 1.00$, so **1**

Since the fractional part is now 0, we stop. Starting from the top we record the digits.

$0.625_{10} = 101_2$

Therefore $\mathbf{26.625_{10} = 11010.101_2}$

The discussion pertaining to rounding and truncating is very complex. A further explanation will complicate matters and is not required at this level. The purpose of mentioning the rounding and truncating was to show that whenever we use a small number of bits to represent a number the accuracy of the numbers decreases.

## Exercise 3

1 Find the decimal equivalent of the following binary fractional numbers.
   (a) 0.1011
   (b) 0.1110
   (c) 0.0001
   (d) 1.0010
   (e) 11.11
   (f) 101.111

2 Find the binary equivalent of the following decimal numbers.
   (a) 0.25
   (b) 0.75
   (c) 0.375
   (d) 5.435
   (e) 9.875

# Floating point numbers

In many scientific and engineering applications very small or very large numbers have to be represented, from the sizes of atomic particles to intergalactic distances. To be able to accomplish this, many computers store numbers using the floating point format. This method is similar to the method of representing numbers in base 10 known as standard form. For example:

| The number 58 000 000 could be represented as: | The number 0.00000025 could be represented as: |
|---|---|
| $5\,800\,000 \times 10$ | $0.000\,0025 \times 10^{-1}$ |
| $580\,000 \times 10^2$ | $0.000\,025 \times 10^{-2}$ |
| $58\,000 \times 10^3$ | $0.000\,25 \times 10^{-3}$ |
| $5800 \times 10^4$ | $0.0025 \times 10^{-4}$ |
| $580 \times 10^5$ | $0.025 \times 10^{-5}$ |
| $58 \times 10^6$ | $0.25 \times 10^{-6}$ |
| $5.8 \times 10^7$ | $2.5 \times 10^{-7}$ |

In each of the numbers represented above the decimal points have been moved (or floated) along the digits. However, it is only the last representation of both numbers that is considered as standard form. This is where the decimal point is placed between the first and second non-zero most significant digits. There are four components to a standard form (floating point) representation.

Consider the decimal number $5.64367 \times 10^4$.

- The number is positive (sign).
- The fractional part (5.64367) is called the **mantissa**.
- The **base** is 10
- The power to which the base is raised is called the **exponent** (i.e. 4).

The number $5.64367 \times 10^4$ can therefore be represented as:

| **Sign** | **Exponent** | **Mantissa** |
|---|---|---|
| positive | 4 | 5. 64367 |

Binary fractions can be stored using a similar format of sign, exponent and mantissa (SEM). Computers use different amount of bits to store floating point numbers. Most computers use the IEEE standard which allocates 32 bits for single precision and 64 bits for double precision. This is more complicated than we need for our purposes at present, so in our examples we will use eight bits to represent a number using the following convention:

| Sign | Exponent | Mantissa |
|---|---|---|
| 1 bit | 3 bits | 4 bits |

Consider the binary number $11.11_2$.

This could be written as $.1111 \times 2^2$. The process of shifting the binary point and multiplying by a power of two is called **normalisation**. This is similar to writing a base 10 number in standard form. Generally when we shift a floating point number we shift the binary point so that it is *immediately to the left of the leading 1* (e.g. 11.11 becomes $.1111 \times 2^2$) unless the number stored is zero. This is done to ensure the maximum utilisation of the available memory space. We will also use the following convention for the sign bit: 0 for positive and 1 for negative. To represent positive and negative exponents, the exponent will be represented using sign and magnitude representation.

### Example 21

*Store $11.11_2$ using the SEM format.*

**Step 1:** *Normalise* the mantissa. This gives $.1111 \times 2^2$

**Step 2:** The exponent is 2, which is 010 in binary (using three bits to store the exponent)

**Step 3:** The number is positive. The sign bit is therefore 0.

$11.11_2$ in SEM format is therefore **00101111**.

### Example 22

*Represent $5.5_{10}$ using sign, exponent and mantissa.*

We can represent $5_{10}$ as $101_2$

.5 can be represented as .1 in binary fraction format, as you have already learned.

So $5.5_{10} = 101.1_2$

To represent $101.1_2$ in sign, exponent, mantissa format we need to normalise the mantissa. This gives
$.1011 \times 2^3$

Using our convention the sign bit will be 0 because the number is positive. The exponent is 3. Using sign and magnitude notation this will be 011.

Therefore $5.5_{10}$ is **0 011 1011** using SEM representation.

Let us look at another example.

### Example 23

*What is the decimal equivalent of 10111011?*

| Sign | Exponent | Mantissa |
|---|---|---|
| 1 | 011 | 1011 |

The sign is negative, and 011 means the exponent is 3, so:

$1011 \times 2^3 = 101.1$

$101_2 = 5_{10}$ and $.1_2 = .5_{10}$

Therefore $\mathbf{10111011_2 = -5.5_{10}}$

### Example 24

*What is the decimal equivalent of 11011011?*

| Sign | Exponent | Mantissa |
|---|---|---|
| 1 | 101 | 1011 |

The sign is negative, and 101 means the exponent is –1, so:

$.1011 \times 2^{-1} = 0.01011_2 = 0.343\ 75_{10}$

## Exercise 4

1 Represent the following numbers using sign, exponent and mantissa format. Use 1 bit for the sign, 3 bits for the exponent and 4 bits for the mantissa. The exponent is stored using sign and magnitude format.
   (a) 3.5
   (b) 2.75
   (c) .375
   (d) -3.75

2 What decimal numbers are represented by the following binary numbers – which are represented using sign, exponent and mantissa format? The exponent is stored using sign and magnitude format.
   (a) 00010101
   (b) 01010101
   (c) 10111101
   (d) 11101100
   (e) 00110011

## Summary

1 Data can be classified into two types: discrete and continuous. Discrete data is data that can be counted while continuous data is data that can be measured and can be recorded at many different points.

2 A decimal (base 10) number can be converted to binary by dividing the decimal number by 2 and recording the remainder until the quotient is zero and then writing out the remainders starting from the last remainder to the first.

3 A binary number can be converted to decimal by multiplying each digit by its place value starting from the least significant bit (LSB) on the right to the most significant bit (MSB) and summing the results. The place value is a factor of 2 starting from $2^0$ for the LSB and increasing by a factor of 2 for each consecutive bit.

4 Binary addition can be easily done by remembering the following rules:
$0_2+0_2 = 0_2$, $0_2+1_2 = 1_2$, $1_2+0_2 = 1_2$, $1_2+1_2 = 10_2$ and $1_2+1_2+1_2 = 11_2$

5 There are four main ways of representing negation inside the computer: sign and magnitude, one's complement, two's complement and binary coded decimal. In sign and magnitude, one's complement and two's complement, positive integers (whole numbers) are represented the same way as for unsigned binary numbers.

6 In sign and magnitude representation, the leftmost bit (MSB) is used to indicate the sign (+ or –) of a binary number. Usually '1' represents negative (–) and '0' represents positive (+). The remaining bits give the magnitude of the number.

7 Finding the one's complement of a number involves flipping the bits. This means changing the 1s to 0s and 0s to 1s.

8 Two's complement is found by adding 1 to the one's complement of the number.

9 The BCD system converts each digit of a decimal number into its four-bit binary code. Negative (–) is represented by 1011 and positive (+) is represented by 1010.

10 The character set of a computer consists of all the characters that a computer can store and process.

11 Characters (numbers, alphabetic characters, special characters and control characters) are represented by a code called the character code.

12 Two of the most common codes used to represent characters are the seven-bit American Standard Code for Information Interchange (ASCII) and the eight-bit Extended Binary Coded Decimal Interchange Code (EBCDIC).

13 To ensure that data transmitted from one part of a computer to another and from one computer to another is accurate a parity bit is used. There are two types of parity: odd and even parity. In an odd parity system, if the numbers of 1s in the original bit string (the bit string being sent) is even, then the parity bit is set to 1 to ensure that the total number of 1s is odd. The opposite applies for even parity.

14 To convert decimal fractions to binary fractions you have to repeatedly multiply the fractional part by 2 until the fractional part becomes zero, or until the pattern starts to repeat itself. Then starting from the top of the series of calculations, record the binary digits before the point to get the binary fraction.

15 To convert a binary fraction to decimal, multiply each digit by its weighting starting from $2^{-1}$ for the first digit after the binary point and then by $2^{-2}$, $2^{-3}$ and so on for each successive digit. The totals are then added together.

16 Floating point numbers are stored using the sign, exponent and mantissa format. All floating point numbers must be normalised before they can be stored.

17 Normalisation means shifting the binary point in a floating point number so that it is immediately to the left of the leading 1.

# Questions

**1** An 8-bit register stores integers using two's complement.

(a) What is the 8-bit representation of 65 and –65?

(b) Using binary addition find the value of –1–65.

(c) What is the decimal equivalent of 111.111?

**2** (a) Store the following bit strings using sign, exponent and mantissa format (SEM).

1 bit – sign, 3 bits – exponent,
4 bits – mantissa.

(i) 11.01 (ii) 01.11

(b) Represent the following decimal numbers using SEM format.

(i) 2.5 (ii) 3.75

**3** (a) Using examples, explain what is meant by 'normalising' the mantissa.

(b) Normalise the mantissa in the following :

(i) 1.1101 (ii) 111.001

**4** An eight-bit register is used to hold a floating-point number. The number is stored as follows:

1 bit for the sign

3 bits for the exponent

4 bits for the mantissa

The exponent is stored using two's complement.

(a) State the bit pattern of the largest and smallest numbers that can be represented.

(b) State the equivalent decimal value of the smallest and largest numbers that can be represented.

**5** (a) What is the decimal equivalent of 101011?

(b) The SX computer uses nine bits for storing a floating point number, one bit is used for the sign, three bits for the exponent (a power of 2, stored using two's complement) and five bits for the mantissa.

(i) Give the range of exponents (in decimal) which can be stored.

(ii) What is the largest decimal number that can be represented?

(iii) What decimal number is represented by the following bit patterns?

011011100

101110101

(iv) Give the nine-bit representation of 2.75.

# 6 Software: the power behind the machine

**OBJECTIVES**

**At the end of this chapter you will be able to:**

- **Distinguish between the two categories of software**
- **Define 'application software'**
- **Give examples of different types of application software**
- **Explain the terms general-purpose software, integrated software, specialised software, customised software, and custom-written software**
- **Define system software and operating systems**
- **Define the term 'booting'**
- **List different types of operating systems**
- **Explain the functions of the operating system**
- **Explain different types of operating system modes (real-time, batch and time-sharing)**
- **Explain the meaning of some of the icons found on the Windows desktop**
- **Perform file management functions such as naming files and creating folders**
- **Explain the term 'utility program'**
- **List the functions of some utility programs**
- **State the function of language translators**

Software is the general name given to all the programs (set of instructions) that computers use to perform different tasks. Software can be classified into two major types: application software and system software.

## Application software

These are programs developed to carry out specific tasks or solve particular problems. For example, if you want to type a letter, you would need to use a word processor. To create a highly decorated birthday card would require some type of graphics package. Word processors and graphics packages are examples of application software.

There are many different types of application software available these days. Each is designed for a particular type of activity. Selecting the right application software to perform a task makes it easier to accomplish the task, and will greatly improve the final outcome. When you purchase a new computer it is usually sold with systems software and some application software. However, depending on your needs, you may have to purchase additional application software. Application software includes entertainment software such as games, home or personal software such as CD-ROM encyclopaedias, productivity software such as word processing and spreadsheet packages, and specialist software such as desktop publishing and graphics packages. Application software can also be categorised as follows: general-purpose software, integrated software, customised software and custom-written (tailor-made) software packages.

### General-purpose software

This is software that is not written for any specific business or organisation but can be used or adapted to suit their specific needs. For example, a teacher can use a spreadsheet package to prepare students' end-of-term grades reports, and a word processing package to write letters to the parents. These same packages could also be used in a business to perform different tasks, such as accounting or memo-writing. General-purpose software packages, also called 'off the shelf" software, are usually well tested and relatively cheap.

### Integrated software

An integrated software package is a set of related programs combined in a unified package that allows data to be transferred easily between the programs. Examples include Microsoft Office, Microsoft Works, Lotus Smartsuite and the IWorks package used by Apple Macintosh computers.

A basic integrated package may contain word processor, spreadsheet, database, communications and graphics presentation programs. A major advantage of these packages is the ease with which data can be transferred from one component to another. For example, if you are working on a word processing document you can quickly incorporate a graph created in the package's spreadsheet component via a simple cut/copy-and-paste operation.

Some additional advantages of integrated software are:

- It takes up less disk space than individual applications.
- You can move much faster from one application to the next.
- It is usually easier to learn as the user interface for choosing commands is the same.
- It tends to be more powerful and versatile than individual applications.
- It is less likely to crash and contains fewer errors, since it has been widely tried and tested.
- The producers' after-sales service is often good (e.g. online help facilities); users can also get support from user groups and magazines.
- It is usually cheaper than purchasing the packages individually.

Some disadvantages of integrated software are:

- Not all the features of single applications are included.
- Some integrated packages do not contain all the applications that may be required to complete a task.

## Specialised software

Specialised software is software that is written for a specific task rather than for a broad application area. These programs provide facilities specifically for the purpose for which they were designed. For example, a payroll program will usually only be able to deal with all aspects of a company's payroll, i.e. for one very specific purpose. Other examples of specialised software are expert systems (software that operates like an expert in a particular field, e.g. medical expert systems), accounting programs such as ACCPAC, and theatre or airline booking systems.

## Customised software

This refers to general-purpose software which has been modified to meet the needs of an individual or organisation better. These packages are customised through the writing of code or **macros**. Macros are short programs written to automate several steps in software such as databases, spreadsheets and word processors. An instruction (usually a keystroke or keystroke combination) signals the computer to perform a predefined sequence of instructions. Macros are usually written by experienced end-users of the program once the program is complete. The core code of the program allows for these macros to be added.

## Custom-written (tailor-made) software

This is software written to meet the specific needs of a company. Every company is unique and may have unique needs, which is why a solution tailored to achieve a company's goals, based on their specialised requirements, offers many advantages when compared with general-purpose pre-packaged applications. Custom-written software may be written by programmers within the company, or it may be contracted out

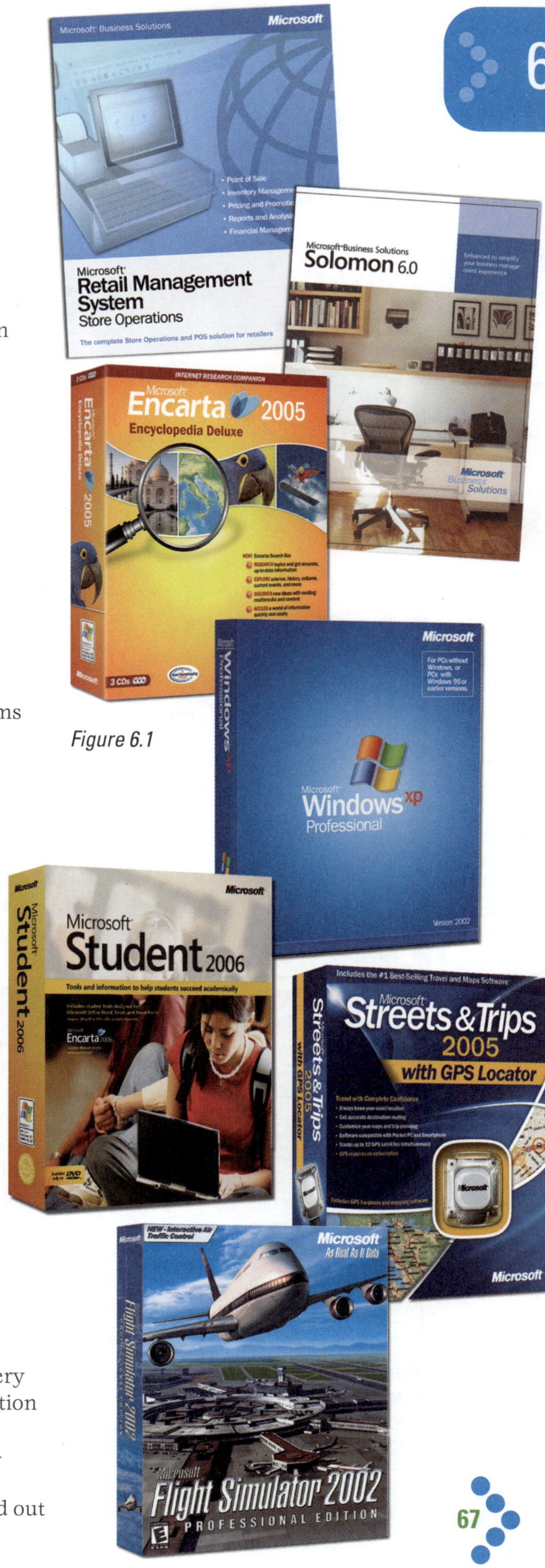


Figure 6.1

to a software house (a company that specialises in writing software). This may be necessary because there are no commercial applications or 'off the shelf" packages available.

The main advantage of custom-written software is that the solutions it offers give the greatest depth, breadth and flexibility possible in meeting the needs of the organisation, since the software product is tailored to the organisation's specifications. Also, the software developer delivers and installs the software and trains the end-users in the use of the new product.

Some additional advantages of custom written software are:

- It performs tasks that general-purpose software can't perform.
- The software can be quickly changed when the needs of the business change, since the source code belongs to the company.

Among the disadvantages are:

- *Cost*. The costs of developing the software, on-site installation, support and training are often high.
- *Lengthy development time*. It takes time to acquire the information necessary and write the code for the new software.
- *Increased probability of undetected error*. The probability of undetected error decreases not only with the length of time a product is in service, but also with the number and variety of users. Hence there are likely to be fewer errors in a long-established general-purpose package (possibly used all over the world) than in a custom-written package.

# System software

System software is software that manages and supports the resources and operations of a computer system. It enables the running of application software and the management of the system resources. Three major categories of system resources are the operating system, utility programs and language translators. System software acts as a buffer between the hardware and application software. Figure 2 shows a conceptual arrangement of hardware, system software, application software and the user.

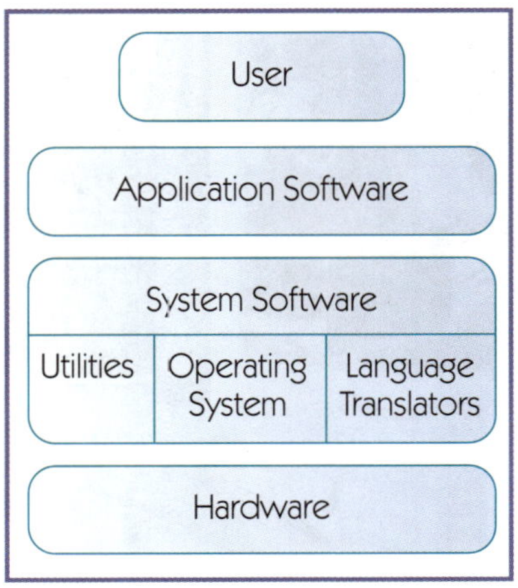


*Figure 6.2*
*Conceptual arrangement of hardware, system software, application software and the user*

## Operating system

An operating system is a set of programs that governs the operation of a computer. Without operating system software, the computer cannot function. In some hand-held computers such as PDAs and Palm pilots, the operating system is embedded on a ROM chip. However, for most PCs and larger computers the operating system is switched on as soon as you turn on, or 'boot', the computer. The term **booting** refers to the process of loading operating system software into a computer's main memory from disk. The operating system remains in main memory until you turn the computer off.

### Types of operating system

Some older operating systems that were used in PC computers include: MS-DOS, Windows 3.X, Windows 95. Some operating systems that are still in use today include: Windows 98, Windows ME (Millennium Edition), Windows 2000, Windows XP, Windows NT, Apple operating systems (e.g. OS9 and OSX), OS/2, Linux and Unix. There are Unix operating systems for PCs, mini and mainframe computers.

## Functions of the operating system

The functions of an operating system depend on the size and complexity of the computer system. It may also depend on whether the system is a single user system such as a PC or a **multi-access system** such as a mainframe or network. A multi-access system is one which allows a number of users with **online terminals** to interact with the same computer at the same time. An online system is one where the terminals and the computer are linked interactively. Although the operating systems of mainframes and networks are much more complex and perform a wider range of functions than those of PCs, the functions of most operating systems can be grouped under the headings discussed below.

> ### *Did you know?*
> Did you know that the Linux operating system was initially developed by a young University of Helsinki student by the name of Linus Torvalds? Linux was released with a General Public Licence and is example of 'open source' software. This means that anyone can copy, distribute and modify the software's code, thereby building on the source code written by Mr Torvalds. This source code is often used by other individuals to develop new, free programs. These individuals often share the same philosophy of cooperation and openness as the code's original inventor.

### *Managing computer resources*

Managing all the resources of the computer system is a large part of the operating system's function. The operating system allows application software or user programs such as word processing, spreadsheet and database packages to communicate with the computer's hardware. For example, if you are working in a document in Excel and you want to print the document, you simply access the 'Print' command or press the 'Print' button on the standard toolbar. Excel directs the operating system to select a printer (if there is more than one) to print the document. The operating system then notifies the computer to begin sending data and instructions to the appropriate program to get the document printed. Figure 6.3 shows how the operating system acts as an interface between application programs and the hardware.

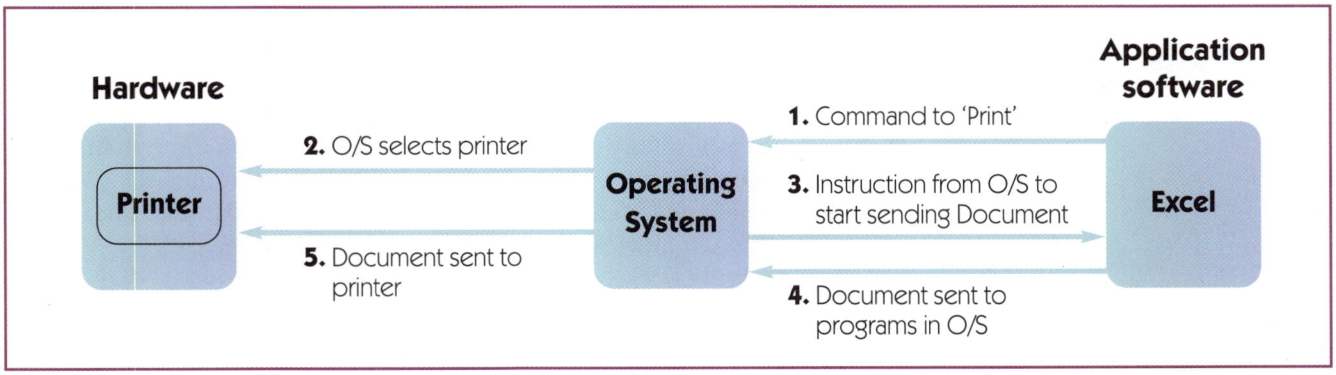


*Figure 6.3*
*The operating system is at the centre of operations, interfacing between software and hardware*

The operating system also manages the use of input and output devices. This is accomplished by the use of buffers. A **buffer** is an area of memory that temporarily holds data being transferred to be processed or output. Input buffers take data from a device (for example a keyboard) and hold the data, releasing it to the CPU at a rate the CPU can cope with. This function is especially important when a number of processes are running and taking up processor time. The operating system will instruct a buffer to continue taking input from the device, but to stop sending data to the CPU while the process using the input is suspended. Then, when the process which needs input is made active once again, the operating system will command the buffer to send data.

The operating system functions in much the same way with output buffers. An output buffer is used to store data waiting to be printed. For example, a program that has to use the printer will transfer whatever needs to be printed to the print buffer and continue processing. In this way the CPU does not have to be idle while the printer, which operates at a much slower speed, prints the document. The operating system also provides error messages to indicate devices that may not be working properly or not functioning at all.

### *Managing files and memory*

The operating system manages all the files on a computer. It keeps track of the locations where programs and data are stored in the computer's memory. For example, when you open a file that has been saved to your hard drive, you are first instructing the computer to find that file, and then open it. The operating system also allows you to easily find files stored in other secondary storage devices. Other file management functions include copying, erasing, renaming and backing-up files. In the case of mainframe computers, the operating system has to share storage between the many programs that may be running at the same time.

### *Maintaining security*

In networks and larger computers each user is given a username or ID and password to gain access to the computer system. The operating system keeps a register of all these names so that only persons with valid usernames or IDs and passwords can access the system. This prevents access by hackers and unauthorised persons. The operating system also keeps a log which records which users logged in, the length of time each user stayed on the system and what they did. Administrators can check the log for breaches and abuse of resources.

### *Managing tasks*

Early computers ran one process at a time. However, because of the fast speed of the CPU and the much slower speeds of input/output devices the CPU remained idle much of the time. To reduce the idle time of the CPU **multitasking** or **multiprogramming** operating systems were developed. Multitasking is the ability of the computer to appear to run more than one program at the same time, although at a specific instant in time the CPU is dealing with only one instruction for one of the active programs. The operating system manages which instruction to send to the CPU.

For example, many students like to listen to music on their computer while at the same time typing a document or playing a computer game. Another example of multitasking is a user typing an e-mail while another e-mail is being sent. These tasks appear to be happening simultaneously. Because computers are so fast, the operating system can switch the program executed in the CPU so quickly that the user cannot tell that, in reality, the music-playing and typing functions are performed at individual moments in time. Multitasking therefore accelerates the throughput of the system by using the CPU time efficiently. Processes running in a multitasked environment are called **concurrent processes**. In actuality, the CPU processes one instruction at a time, but can execute instructions from any active process.

### *Multiprocessing*

This refers to a computer system's ability to support more than one process (program) at the same time. Multiprocessing operating systems enable several programs to run concurrently. This is accomplished by linking two or more computers or processors which can then work on different programs or different parts of the same program simultaneously. This generally increases processing times.

Multiprocessing is much faster than multitasking/multiprogramming as more than one program is processed at the same time. This type of processing is used in real-time systems where fast processing speeds are very important.

### Processing modes

- *Time-sharing*: Time-sharing is one method that can be used in multi-access systems. It makes many users believe they have the undivided attention of the CPU. To accomplish this, the CPU allows each terminal in turn a small amount of processing time (time slice) before it goes on to the others. Each terminal is checked by polling to see if the CPU is required. The process happens so quickly that every user on the system thinks he/she has the continuous use of the CPU. The Unix operating system is used for multi-access time-sharing systems, for example in universities, where many students and professors may be connected to the central CPU at one time from different terminals.
- *Batch processing*: A batch processing system is one where programs and data are collected together in a batch queue before processing starts. Batch processing is normally done on large mainframe computers. Each piece of work the computer will do is called, simply, a job. Often a job consists of a program to be run and the data that will be manipulated by it. Batch jobs can be stored up during working hours and then executed whenever the computer is least in use (usually at night). Once a batch job starts, it continues until it is done or until an error occurs. There is no interaction with the user while the program is being run. Batch processing can be used for fairly automatic tasks, for example, weekly or monthly payroll processing, processing utility bills (water, electricity, etc) and credit card billing.
- *Real-time processing*: Real-time operating systems are designed to respond to an event within a predetermined time. As soon as the data is input it is processed and output immediately. In some applications the output is used to influence the input. These types of operating systems are found in environments where computers are responsible for controlling systems continuously; for example, robotics, manufacturing, interactive games, airline and theatre booking systems. In all these applications the computer is often a dedicated computer and runs the same program all the time.

### *Providing a user interface*

Many operating system functions are never apparent on the computer's display screen. What you do see, though, is the **user interface**. The user interface is the user-controllable part of the operating system which allows you to communicate, or interact, with it.

## User interfaces

There are three types of user interfaces, both for operating systems and applications software: command-driven, menu-driven and graphical.

### Command-driven interface

The command-driven interface is used in PCs that either operate exclusively with the MS-DOS operating system, or in PCs that are currently in MS-DOS mode rather than Windows mode. This interface requires you to enter a command by typing in codes or words. You have to type in the command at

*Figure 6.4*
*A computer screen in MS-DOS mode*

the prompt on the display screen. For example, at the C:\> prompt, where C:\ generally refers to the hard disk, you can type the following command:

C:\>delete *.*

This command tells the operating system to erase all the files on the hard disk. Figure 6.4 shows an example of a command user interface.

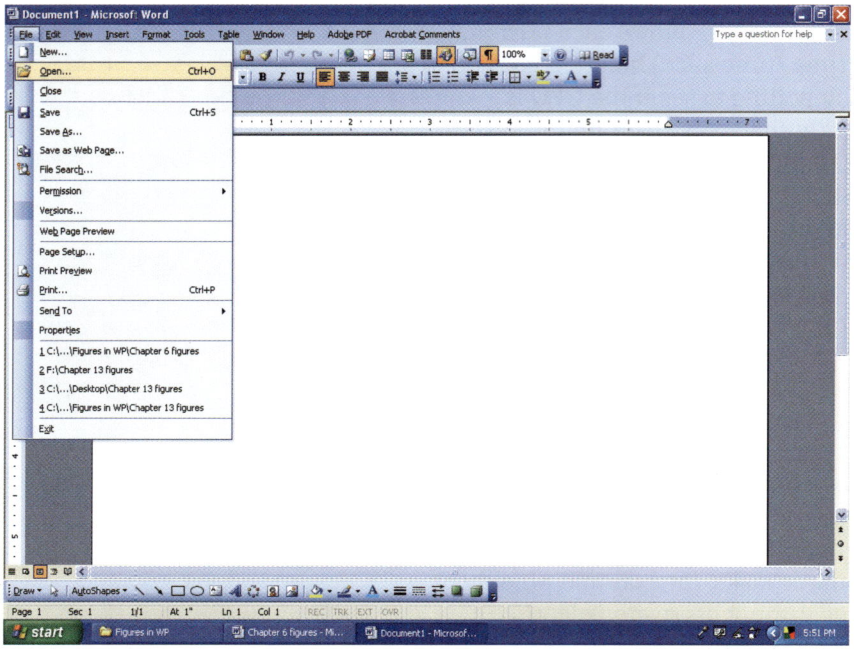


*Figure 6.5*
***File** pull-down menu in Word*

## Menu-driven interface

This type of interface allows you to use either a mouse or cursor-movement (arrow keys) to make a selection from a menu. Menus contain commands to Print, Save, Format and so on. Menus are easier to use than command-driven interfaces because you do not have to remember commands. You simply select from the lists provided. Figure 6.5 shows the options in the Microsoft Word **File** menu.

## Graphical user interface

The graphical user interface (GUI) (pronounced as 'goo-ee'), also called WIMP (windows, icons, menus and pointing devices), is the easiest device to use when interacting with the CPU. It allows you to use graphics (images), menus and keystrokes, to choose commands, start programs, see lists of files and other options. Some of these images take the form of icons. **Icons** are small pictorial figures that represent programs, folders, files, tasks, procedures and so on.

Another feature of the GUI is the use of windows. A **window** is a rectangular boxed area on a computer screen. (This is not to be confused with Windows, e.g. Windows XP, with a capital W, which is the Microsoft operating system.) The screen can show different windows at the same time, within which individual application programs may be running. Each window may show a different program, such as a word processing document in one window and a spreadsheet in another window. Or two windows may show two different documents being run by the same program. A window can also show other things, such as a directory of files on your hard drive. The windows appear over a common visual background known as the **desktop**. Figure 6.6 shows a Windows XP graphical user interface desktop, without any windows open.

## The Windows desktop

The Windows desktop is almost certain to be the starting place for your use of computers. From here you will perform tasks and functions such as:

- Interacting with the CPU and the hard drive
- Opening software programs
- Managing files, folders and directories
- Creating documents
- Printing photos
- Listening to music.

In this section of the chapter we will take you through some of the most basic and important features of this graphical user interface:

1. First you will look at some of the icons you need to be most familiar with.
2. You will then learn how to manage all your computer files.
3. Finally, you will learn about some of the key system utilities that will help you maintain your computer in good working order.

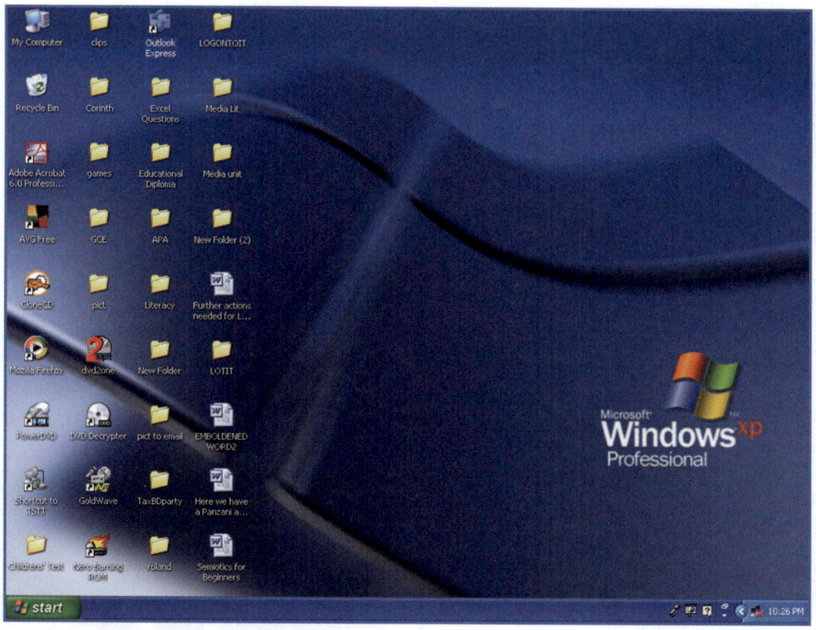


Figure 6.6
Components of a GUI desktop

After booting up a modern PC running Windows XP, the desktop appears as shown in Figure 6.6. If you are using Windows 98, ME, 2000 or NT, the desktop is likely to look very similar. You can think of the Windows desktop as being like the traditional office desk. Just as you can move things around on a real desk, putting away items in drawers, and adding and removing objects, you can do the same on your Windows desktop. The Windows desktop contains a number of shortcuts that allow you to access various processes available to you in the XP operating system. Some of the default icons contained on the Windows 98 desktop are described below.

## *My Computer*

When this icon is opened Windows 98 displays the icons which represent devices such as the hard drive (C:), 3.5-inch floppy drive (A:), CD drive (D:) and DVD drive (E:), as well as applications, folders, files and other items. In Windows XP, the 'My Computer' window shown in Figure 6.7 displays the different drives and folders, as well as other windows. One is a menu to select **System Tasks** such as adding and removing programs, viewing system information and changing a setting. Another titled **Other Places** gives the following options: 'My Network Places', 'My Documents', 'Shared Documents' and 'Control Panel'.

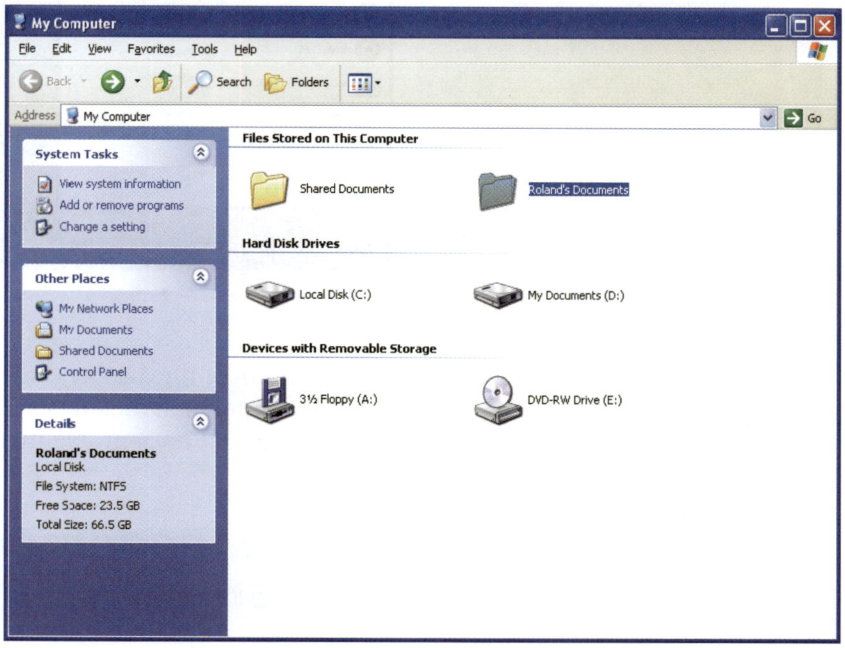


Figure 6.7
The Windows XP
'My Computer' window

## *Recycle bin*

This is where deleted objects (files, programs, etc.) are placed by the computer until you empty the bin. Items in the bin can be retrieved if you realise that you don't want to delete the item after all. However, once the bin is emptied items can no longer be retrieved. This icon functions the same for all versions of Windows (e.g. 98 and XP).

> **Did you know?**
>
> Did you know that there are Internet-based e-mail clients – such as Hotmail from MSN and Yahoo! mail – which can also be used to send and receive e-mail? You will learn more about these in Chapter 7.

> **Did you know?**
>
> Did you know that if you ever get stuck using Windows XP, there is a handy feature that can help you out? Simply click the **Start** menu button and select **Help and Support**. The 'Help and Support Center' window appears. Select from the options provided.

### Internet Explorer

If you have access to an Internet service provider you can use Internet Explorer to access the Internet.

### Outlook Express

This program allows you to send and receive e-mail. It is called an 'e-mail client'.

### Start button

Clicking the **Start** button displays a menu as shown in Figure 6.8, from which you can choose to open an application, open a document, customise Windows, find a file or folder, get help or shut down the computer.

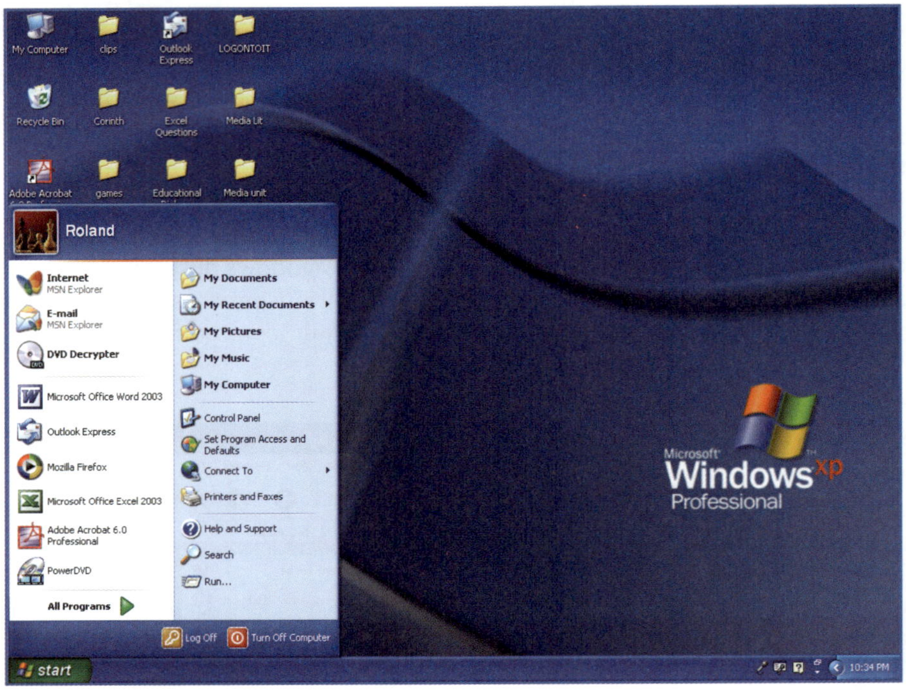


*Figure 6.8*
***Start** menu in Windows XP*

### Task bar

At the bottom of the display screen you will find the task bar. This contains the **Start** button and rectangles that represent any applications or windows that are active at present. Figure 6.8 shows the task bar.

# File management operations using Windows

## Naming a file

Each file on your computer has to be given a name to identify it. A file name in DOS can be no longer than eight characters; file names in later operating systems can be much longer. A file name usually consists of two parts: the name and the extension, separated by a dot. For example, the file name RESUME.DOC has RESUME as the name and DOC as the extension. The extension tells you and the computer what type of file it is, in this case, a DOCument. When you click on the file to open it, the computer then knows which application is needed. The RESUME.DOC file is opened by Microsoft Word (or another word processing package you have installed) since DOC is a common file extension for Word documents. Table 1 gives some extensions and their associations.

| Extension | Association |
|---|---|
| BAT | **BAT**ch files containing a series of DOS commands |
| COM | Executable **COM**mand files |
| EXE | **EXE**cutable command files |
| SYS | Various types of **SYS**tem files – usually drivers to control devices |
| DOC | **DOC**ument files created by e.g. Microsoft Word, the word processing program |
| XLS | A spreadsheet file created by e.g. Microsoft Excel, a spreadsheet program |
| WPD | **W**ord **P**erfect **D**ocuments (WordPerfect is another word processing program) |
| TXT | **T**e**XT** files – associated with the 'notepad' program |
| JPG or JPEG | A graphics file commonly used for photos and illustrations |
| BMP | **B**it**M**a**P**ped graphics, such as photos and illustrations |
| PDF | **P**ortable **D**ocument **F**ormat – a file type that displays finished text and graphics in an application such as Acrobat Reader. |

*Table 1 Some file extensions*

## Directories or folders

At first, a new disk will not have any folders on it: there is just the disk itself with a single base position called the **root drive** of the disk. The root drive will be C:\ for the hard disk, A:\ for the 3.5-inch floppy and D:\ for CD-ROM, CD-RW, etc. It is possible to store your documents, programs, music files and so on directly on one of these disks, with no arrangement into sections for the different types of files you are adding. But after a period of time continuously adding files, it will become very difficult to find specific files stored on the disk. You would need to look through all the individual files, in a long list, to find the one you want.

One way of keeping all files of a certain type together, so they can be easily viewed and accessed, is to store them in a **directory** or **folder**. Directories or folders are used to hold documents, programs, files and even further sub-directories and folders. There is no limit really to the sub-levels you could add. Directories allow you to group files that are in some way related, placing them in one location. For example, in your computer you may have assignment documents for the different subjects you are doing in school. These might be stored in drive C, in the 'My Documents' folder. You may have English documents, Social Studies documents and so on. Each type of document can be stored in an individual folder corresponding to a particular subject, as shown in Figure 6.9. For even easier reference, all the folders for the different

*Figure 6.9 Windows XP 'My Documents' window*

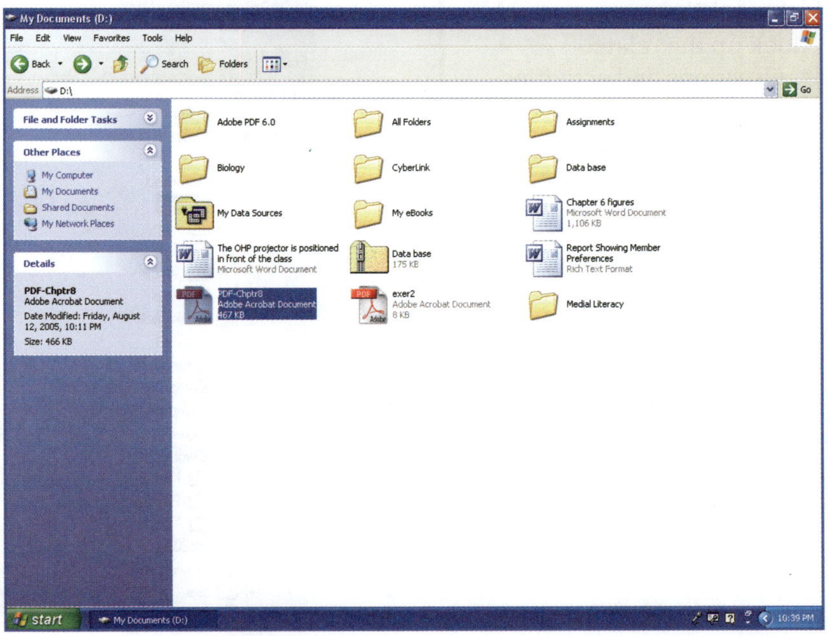

subjects could be placed in the one folder called 'Assignments', which is also shown in the figure. The name chosen by the user – 'Assignments' – is an 'umbrella' term for the all the sub-folders that would be found in that folder.

If this method is used, an English assignment document will therefore be stored in drive C, in the 'My Documents' folder, in the 'Assignments' folder and in the 'English' folder. This can be written as C:\My Documents\Assignments \English\DocumentName.doc. This hierarchical structure for storing files makes retrieval of files very easy: you simply click through the hierarchy of folders to find the file you want.

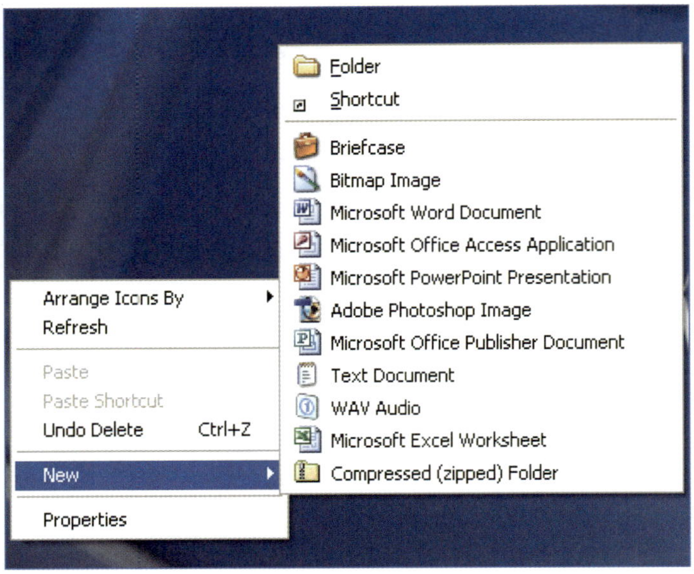


*Figure 6.10*
*Creating a folder on the desktop*

### Creating a folder

To create a folder on the desktop (e.g. Windows 98 or XP):

1. Right-click on any clear area on the desktop.
2. When the pop-up menu appears select **New**.
3. Select **Folder** from the menu that appears as shown in Figure 6.10.
4. A folder icon appears on the desktop and you can give it a name.

Folders can be created in a diskette or hard drive by selecting it, opening it and following the procedure outlined above, or by clicking the **File** menu and selecting **New** and **Folder**. Folders can also be created and stored within other folders.

## Windows Explorer

Windows Explorer is the utility used for file management functions in Windows operating systems. It can be used to move, copy, rename, duplicate and delete files, and to browse through the directory. Explorer displays the file structure in a hierarchical 'tree'.

If you want to find out more about this topic you could look up the related animations and activities on your companion CD-ROM.

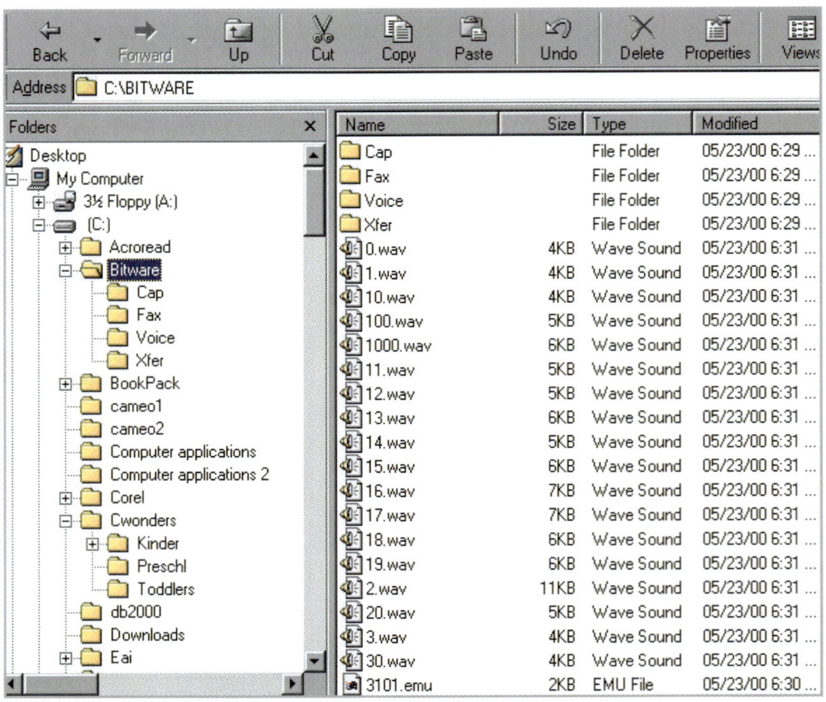


*Figure 6.11*
*Windows 98 Explorer window*

To launch Windows Explorer using Windows 98:

1. Click the **Start** menu.
2. Click on **Programs**.
3. Select **Windows Explorer**.

The Windows 98 Explorer window as shown in Figure 6.11 is displayed.

To launch Windows Explorer using Windows XP:

1. Click the **Start** menu.
2. Click on **All Programs**.
3. Click **Accessories**.
4. Select **Windows Explorer**.

The Windows XP Explorer window as shown in Figure 6.12 is displayed.

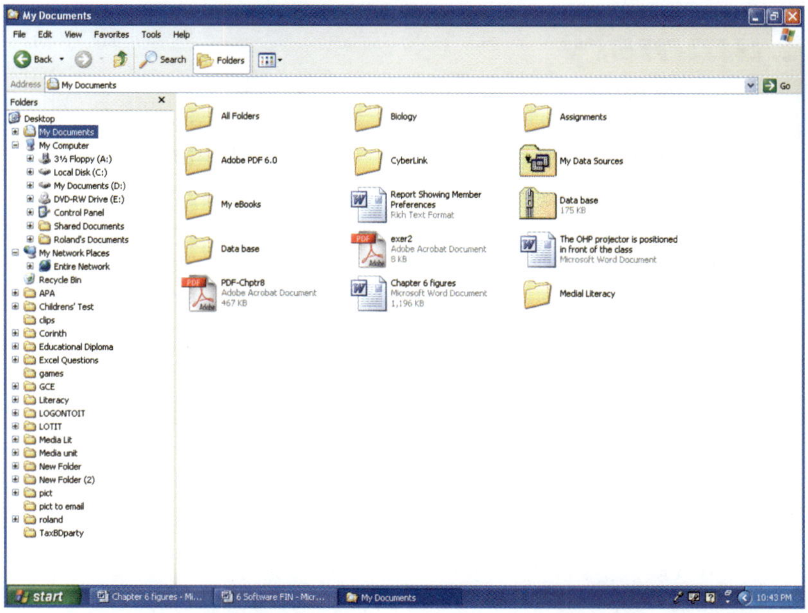


*Figure 6.12*
*Windows XP Explorer window*

The Windows Explorer window consists of two panes. The left-hand pane displays the location (e.g. desktop), device (e.g. 3.5-inch floppy (A:)), or folder where the data files are stored. The right-hand pane displays files or further folders within that location. As shown in Figure 6.12, devices or folders are displayed with a '+' sign or '–' sign in front of them. The + sign indicates that the folder or device contains other files or folders which are not displayed. The '–' sign indicates that all the files and folders are displayed. Clicking on a folder on the left-hand pane displays the contents in the right-hand pane.

## Utilities

Utility programs are system software programs which provide useful services, such as performing common tasks and 'housekeeping' routines. Some are included with the operating system (for example, disk repairing programs) while others are purchased separately by the user (for example, Norton Disk Doctor). Some of the functions performed by utility programs include:

- **Backup:** This utility allows you to make a duplicate copy of every file on your hard disk, which can be stored on CDs or diskettes.
- **File defragmentation:** When files are stored in a new computer or hard disk they are stored next to one another (contiguously). After using your computer for a while you will probably have deleted old files and added new ones. The computer fills free gaps with new files, including parts of files. After a while, the constituent parts of a typical file are scattered all over your hard disk – they are *fragmented*. This can considerably slow down your computer, as the operating system must first find all the parts of a file before they can be put back together and loaded. A defragmenter utility finds these fragmented files and organises them back in a contiguous manner.
- **Disk repair:** A disk repair utility scans a hard disk or floppy disk for bad sectors (defective areas) and either makes repairs to these sectors, or marks the defective area so that the operating system will not store any data in that location.
- **Virus protection:** Antivirus software programs are also utility programs. These are covered in Chapter 9.
- **Language translators:** Language translators (assemblers, compilers and interpreters) translate a program written by a programmer into machine language (the language the computer can understand).

# Summary

1 Software is the general name given to all the programs (sets of instructions) that computers use to perform different tasks; it can be classified into application software and system software.

2 Application software programs carry out specific tasks or solve particular problems and can be categorised as general-purpose software, integrated software, specialised software, customised software and custom-written (tailor-made) software packages.

3 General-purpose software is software that is not written for any specific business or organisation but can be used or adapted to suit anyone's specific needs, e.g. a word processing package.

4 An integrated software package is a set of related, specialised programs combined in a unified package that allows data to be transferred easily between each of the programs, e.g. Microsoft Office.

5 Specialised software is software that is written for a specific task rather than for a broad application area, e.g. accounting software.

6 Customised software is general-purpose software which has been modified to better meet the needs of an individual or organisation, for example, using macros.

7 Macros are short programs written to automate several steps in software, such as in database, spreadsheet and word processing programs. They are often written by end-users.

8 Custom-written (tailor-made) software is software written to meet the specific needs of a specific company or organisation; it is therefore expensive and highly specialised.

9 System software is software that manages and supports the resources and operations of a computer system; it includes the operating system, the user interface and utility programs.

10 An operating system is a set of programs that governs the operation of a computer. It manages computer resources, files, memory, tasks and maintains security.

11 A time-sharing processing system makes users in a multi-access environment believe they have the undivided attention of the CPU. It does this by giving each terminal in turn a small amount of processing time (a time slice) before going on to the others, then quickly returning to the first terminal again.

12 A batch-processing system is one where data is collected together in a sequenced batch queue before processing starts. The program is then run without interaction from the user.

13 Real-time operating systems are designed to respond to an event within a predetermined time. The response may in turn create a response in the user, e.g. in computer games, which are always in real-time mode.

14 The user interface is the user-controllable part of the operating system which allows you to communicate, or interact, with it. The three types are command-driven, menu-driven and graphical.

15 The command-driven interface requires you to enter a command by typing in codes or words. An example is MS-DOS.

16 Menu-driven interfaces allow you to use either a mouse or cursor-movement (arrow keys) to make a selection from a menu. An example is the pull-down menus in Microsoft Word.

17 The graphical user interface, also called WIMP (windows, icons, menus and pointing devices), allows the use of graphics (icons), menus and simple keystrokes to choose commands, start programs, see lists of files and many other options. The most popular example in use today is Windows.

18 Utility programs are system software programs which provide useful services by performing common tasks and 'housekeeping' routines, such as backup, disk defragmentation, disk repair, virus protection and language translation.

# Questions

## Fill in the blanks

1 ________________ software is written for a specific task rather than for a broad application area.

2 Software written to meet the specific needs of a company is known as ________________________.

3 Software that manages and supports the resources and operations of a computer system is known as ________________________.

4 Programs developed to carry out specific tasks or solve particular problems are called ________________.

5 ________________________ refers to a computer's ability to support more than one process at the same time.

6 A system where programs and data are collected together in a batch queue before processing starts is known as a ____________________.

7 The __________________ is a set of programs that governs the operations of a computer.

8 Software can be classified into two major types:____________________ and ____________________.

9 The ________________ is the user-controllable part of the operating system which allows a user to communicate or interact with it.

10 The processing of loading operating system software into a computer's main memory from disk is known as ________________.

11 The ability of a computer to appear to run more than one program at the same time, although at an instant the CPU is dealing with only one instruction for one of the active programs, is known as ____________________.

12 Command-driven, menu-driven and ________________ interface are the three types of user interface.

13 ______________ is the utility used for file management functions in Windows operating systems.

14 ____________________ operating systems are designed to respond to an event within a predetermined time.

15 A set of related, specialised programs combined in a unified package that allows data to be transferred easily between the programs is known as ____________________.

16 ______________ programs are system software which provide useful services by performing common tasks and 'housekeeping' routines.

## True or False?

1 Computer games are an example of application software. T❑ F❑

2 A word processor is an example of general-purpose software. T❑ F❑

3 Integrated software packages take up more storage space than individual applications. T❑ F❑

4 Specialised software is written for a broad application area. T❑ F❑

5 A payroll program is an example of specialised software. T❑ F❑

6 Customised software and custom-written software are the same. T❑ F❑

7 Custom-written software has an increased probability of undetected error. T❑ F❑

8 The operating system is one category of system software. T❑ F❑

9 The operating systems of palmtops and PDAs are embedded in a RAM chip. T❑ F❑

10 Maintaining system security is a function of an operating system. T❑ F❑

11 Multitasking means the computer is actually running more than one program at the same time. T❑ F❑

12 Multiprogramming and multiprocessing mean the same thing. T❑ F❑

13 Real-time systems are designed to respond to an event within a predetermined time. T❑ F❑

14 Batch processing can be used in airline booking systems. T❑ F❑

15 A command-driven interface is easier to use than a graphical user interface. T❑ F❑

16 Antivirus software is not an example of a utility program. T❑ F❑

17 Assemblers, compilers and interpreters are all language translators. T❑ F❑

## Multiple choice

1 Which of the following is not a utility program?
- (a) Disk repair program
- (b) Backup program
- (c) Spreadsheet program
- (d) File defragmentation program

2 Application software consists of:
- (a) Entertainment software
- (b) Productivity software
- (c) Speciality software
- (d) All of the above

3 An integrated software package:
- (a) Can transfer data from one component to another very easily
- (b) Costs less than individual applications
- (c) Takes up less disk space than individual applications
- (d) All of the above

4 Which of the following is not considered to be system software?
- (a) Graphics presentation software
- (b) Operating system
- (c) Utility program
- (d) Language translators

5 Which of the following is not a function of the operating system?
- (a) Managing files and memory
- (b) Managing tasks
- (c) Creating a document
- (d) Managing input and output devices

6 Batch processing can be used for:
(a) Payroll processing
(b) Processing utility bills
(c) Credit card billing
(d) All of the above

7 Real-time processing is used for:
(a) Interactive games
(b) Processing utility bills
(c) Credit card billing
(d) All of the above

8 Which of the following is not an operating system?
(a) Linux
(b) Unix
(c) Windows ME
(d) Language translator

9 A folder or directory can contain:
(a) Files
(b) Folders
(c) Programs
(d) All of the above

10 Operating system software that allows more than one user to access the same data is called:
(a) Multitasking operating system
(b) Multi-user operating system
(c) Single user operating system
(d) File managing operating system

## Short answer questions

1 (a) Define the term software.
(b) Define the term application software. Give THREE examples of application software.
(c) Explain the terms general-purpose software, integrated software, specialised software and customised software.

2 (a) Explain the term custom-written software.
(b) List the advantages and disadvantages of custom-written software.

3 Explain the difference between application software and system software.

4 Draw a diagram to represent the relationship between the operating system, the application software and the hardware.

5 What are the advantages and disadvantages of integrated software?

6 (a) Define the term operating system.
(b) List THREE types of operating systems.
(c) List FOUR functions of the operating system.

7 Explain the terms: time-sharing, batch processing and real-time processing.

8 Explain the difference between multiprogramming and multiprocessing.

9 (a) List THREE types of user interface.
(b) Explain how each type of user interface operates.

10 (a) Define the term utility program.
(b) Give the functions of any THREE utility programs.

## Crossword

### Across

2 Short programs written to automate several steps in software such as databases, spreadsheet and word processors. (6)

3 A processing system where programs and data are collected together in a queue before processing (5)

7 A pictorial representation of a file, folder or program (4)

8 Processes running in a multitasked environment (10)

### Down

1 The process of loading operating system software into a computer's main memory from disk (7)

4 System software programs which provide useful service by performing common tasks and 'housekeeping' routines (7)

5 A rectangular area that displays information on a computer screen (6)

6 An area of memory that temporarily holds data being transferred to be processed or output. (6)

# 7 Data Communications, Networks and the Internet

## OBJECTIVES

At the end of this chapter you will be able to:

- Define the term data communication
- Explain the terms bandwidth, narrowband, voice-band and broadband
- Define the terms simplex, duplex and half-duplex
- Understand the terms wireless communication, network, LAN and WAN
- Understand the terms Internet, ISP, TCP/IP, point-to-point protocol, hypertext and hypermedia
- Understand the different communications links used to connect to the Internet
- Appreciate the hardware and software needed to connect to the Internet
- Understand the terms e-mail, mail server, mail client, mailing list, chat, newsgroup, bulletin board, broadcasting, narrowcasting, webcast, webinar
- Create and send e-mail
- Understand World Wide Web, URL, etc
- Surf the web to find information using the directory in a home page, key words and known URLs
- Explain the terms intranet and extranet

## Data communications

Rapid advances in communications systems, computer use and multimedia technologies are changing the way people communicate and transmit data. **Data communication** can be broadly described as the transmission of data from one location to another for direct use or for further processing. A data communication system is made up of hardware, software and communications facilities. Communications systems may be set up to serve a small area; or they may be set up on a global scale. Data in any communications system is moved from one location to another via data communication channels or links. These channels are classified according to **bandwidth**. Bandwidth determines the volume of data that can be transmitted in a given time. The wider the bandwidth, the more data it can transmit. Bandwidths can be grouped into three classes of channels:

1. A **narrow-band** channel, which is almost obsolete, for example a telegraph system, can transmit data at slow speeds of between 10 and 30 characters per second (cps).
2. A **voice-band** channel can transmit data at the rate of 1000 to 8000 cps. A telephone line is voice-band, and is one of the most widely used methods of transferring data.
3. A **broadband** channel can transmit large volumes of data at speeds of over 100 000 cps. Coaxial cables, fibre optic cables, microwave links and communication satellites are commonly used to provide these channels. Microwave signals are very high frequency radio signals that can be transmitted through space. A communications satellite accepts signals beamed to it from a point on earth and then reflects the signals to another point as shown in Figure 7.1. Communication satellites can transmit data that includes text, voice, pictures and video.

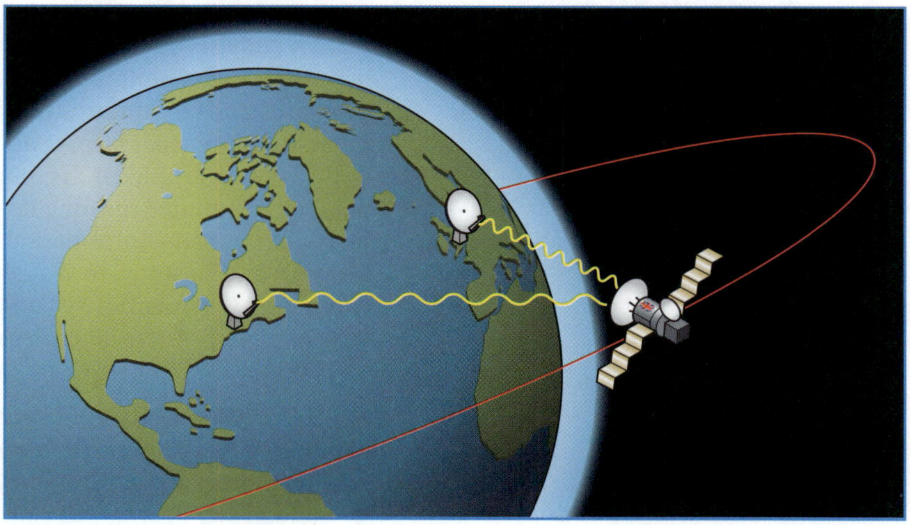

*Figure 7.1*

**Did you know?**

Did you know that there are currently over 2000 satellites orbiting the earth, many of which are used for communication?

The lines that transmit data can also be classified according to the direction in which data flows through them.

- A **simplex** line permits data to flow in only one direction. You can send data or receive data, but not both.
- A **half-duplex** line can alternately send and receive data. This means that at any particular time you can either send data but not receive it, or receive data but not send it.
- A **full-duplex** line can simultaneously send and receive data.

## Wireless communication

Wireless communications offer organisations and users many benefits, such as portability, flexibility, increased productivity and lower installation costs. Wireless technologies, in the simplest sense, enable one or more devices to communicate with each other without physical connections – without cabling. They use radio frequency transmissions as the means of transmitting data. Wireless communications range from complex systems, such as Wireless Local Area Networks (WLAN) and cell phones, to simple devices such as wireless headphones, microphones and other devices that do not process or store information. These devices include infra-red (IR) devices such as remote controls, some cordless computer keyboards and mouse, and wireless hi-fi stereo headsets, all of which require a direct line of sight between the transmitter and the receiver to close the link.

# Networks

Many businesses, organisations, universities and schools have networked computers. A **network** is a group of two or more computers linked together so that they can share resources (hardware, software and data) and can communicate with one another. Each computer network falls into one of the following groups:

- Local area networks (LANs)
- Wide area networks (WANs)
- The Internet
- Intranets
- Extranets

## Local area networks (LANs)

A **LAN** consists of a collection of microcomputers, such as in an office building, department or school that can share peripherals, files and programs and communicate with each other on the network. Each microcomputer that forms part of the network is connected either by cables or by a wireless link. Each computer can function both as an independent personal computer running its own software and as a workstation on the network accessing information from the network **server**. The server runs the networking software that allows resources to be shared with the other computers (called **clients** ) on the network. The devices shared by a LAN may include printers, hard drives, disk drives, optical drives (CD-ROM, CD-RW, DVD-ROM, DVD-RW), modems and fax machines.

A LAN's ability to share information and communicate with the devices and computers on the network has many benefits for its users:

- Hardware such as printers can be shared.
- Storage facilities can be shared.
- Software and data files can be shared by many users.

- It is usually cheaper to buy one copy of a software application and pay the licence fee for several machines, than to buy individual packages for each computer.
- Users can work together on a single document.
- Users can communicate using e-mail.

There are disadvantages, too:

- The initial set-up costs are high.
- There is an increased risk of data corruption. Since many users will be using the system, there is a greater chance of data being corrupted or tampered with.
- There is a greater risk from viruses, because they are easily spread between the computers that are part of the LAN.
- If the file server fails, all the workstations are affected and work stored on shared hard disk drives will not be accessible; nor will it be possible to use network printers, etc.
- Networks can be complicated to maintain and may require a network manager. Additional costs may therefore be incurred.

Before a PC can become part of a network it must be fitted with a **network interface card (NIC)**. This card fits into an expansion slot in the motherboard and enables the computers on the network to send and receive messages. The card has an external outlet into which one end of the network cable is plugged. The other end of the cable plugs into a connection based on the **configuration** of the network.

LANs can be divided into two categories based on how the computers communicate with one another: client/server networks and peer-to-peer networks.

1. A **client/server network** is one in which any computer on the network can be designated as the server, although most such networks will have a specially designed computer that operates as a **dedicated server** and has a faster processor, more RAM and a lot more storage space. A large LAN may have several servers to perform different tasks. For instance, a file server may look after the organisation of the files on the network, while a print server co-ordinates printing on the network and looks after the sending and receiving of faxes and e-mail. The server or servers contain the software that manages:
   - A shared hard disk
   - Requests from users
   - The protection of data
   - The security of the system.
2. A **peer-to-peer network** allows every computer to communicate with every other computer in the network. No computer is designated as a server. Instead, each computer can be considered as both a client and a server. This is because a user can access data from any computer on the network and vice versa. Peer-to-peer networks are limited to about ten machines, after which the performance drops and the system becomes cumbersome. They are used mainly in small businesses and departments.

### Cabled LAN

In a cabled LAN, all the computers and other peripheral devices on the network are attached to transmission cables. These cables fall into three types:

- **Twisted pair:** This is a convenient and cheap method of connecting computers and peripherals in a network. It is normally used for home networking or on small sites where the distances between devices are small and there is no great need for speed.

- **Coaxial cable:** Coaxial cable is more expensive than twisted pair because its transmission capabilities are higher; it is used to transmit voice, video and data. It is ideal for a medium-sized network.
- **Fibre optic:** Fibre optic cables are relatively expensive. They enable large volumes of digital data to be transmitted extremely fast and virtually error-free. A single strand of a fibre optic cable is a hair-thin piece of glass tubing. The inside of the tube acts as a mirror, allowing pulses of light to travel along it which carry data. A cable consists of thousands of these hair-thin strands.

## LAN topologies

How computers on a network are connected together determines its **topology** (or configuration). The most common topologies for a LAN are star, line or bus, and ring.

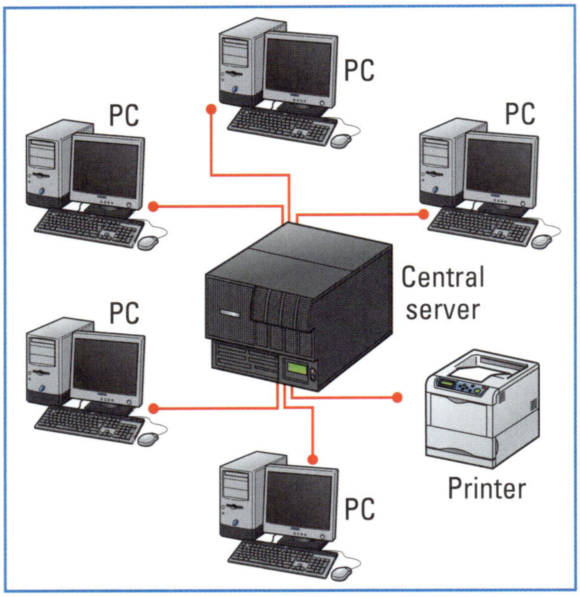


*Figure 7.2*
*A star network*

### *Star topology*

All the computers on the network are connected to one another through a central **hub** as shown in Figure 7.2. A hub is a hardware device to which a number of computers can be connected. Data is transmitted from one computer to the next by packets. A packet containing the addresses of the sender and receiver is first sent to the central hub, which then sends the packet to the designated computer.

#### Advantages of a star topology

- Adding new devices to the network is easy.
- If a computer stops working, the network is not affected.
- If one piece of cable is damaged, only one computer is affected.

#### Disadvantages

- It requires more cabling.
- If the central computer or server malfunctions, the entire network will fail.
- Only one computer on the network can send data at any particular time.

### *Line or bus topology*

This is a single line or cable (also called the **backbone**) with nodes at different points. Servers, computers and other devices can be connected to any of the nodes on the line, as shown in Figure 7.3. Data is sent down the line in any direction in packets. Each packet has the address of its sender and the address of the intended receiver. Each computer on the line examines each packet to determine for whom the packet is intended. If the packet is intended for this computer, it is retained for processing; otherwise it is sent on its way.

*Figure 7.3*
*A line or bus network*

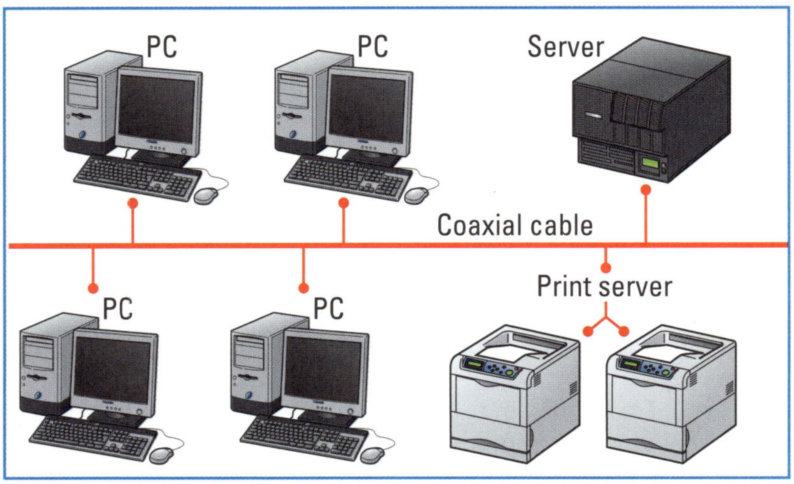


#### Advantages of a bus topology

- Extending the network is very easy. New equipment can be connected to it simply by tapping into the main cable.
- It requires less hardware to set up.
- It is easy to configure.

### Disadvantages

- Any problems with the main cable may cause the whole network to malfunction.
- Packets of data may collide, resulting in loss of information.

### *Ring topology*

Here the cable is connected to all the computers on the network. The ends of the cable are then connected together to form a loop or ring as shown in Figure 4. Data is passed from one computer to the next by means of a token (electronic signal), which is passed around the ring, giving each computer an opportunity to send data. A computer can send data only when it is in possession of the token.

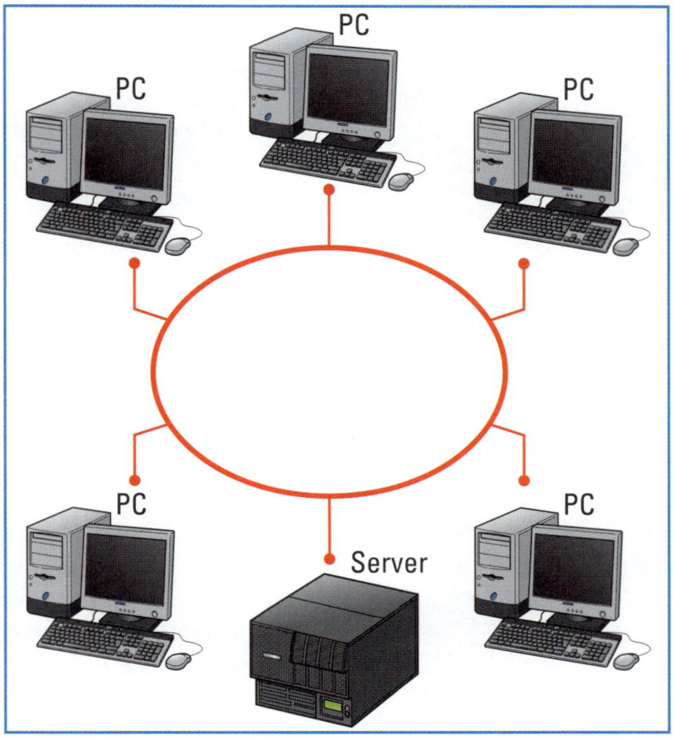


*Figure 7.4*
*A ring network*

### Advantages of a ring topology

- If a computer stops working, the other computers can continue to communicate.
- Communication is usually faster than with a line network.

### Disadvantages

- If the main cable is damaged, the entire network goes down.
- The entire network has to be shut down for any maintenance to be carried out.
- The network becomes very difficult to maintain if it gets very large.

## Wireless LAN (WLAN)

There are different ways of setting up a WLAN. One of the most common methods depends on two main sets of components: **access points** and NICs (network interface cards) with radio transmitters/receivers.

An access point is a device attached to a LAN network and contains a radio transmitter/receiver, encryption facility and communications software. It translates computer signals into wireless signals, which it broadcasts to wireless NICs on the network. NICs equipped for wireless communications receive these signals, and can transmit back. They have a fixed or detachable radio antenna in place of the usual coaxial cable.

The access point and the NIC communicate with one another using a 2.4 gigahertz (GHz) radio band. The access point performs its role in reverse when transferring signals from a wireless NIC to the conventional network: it translates wireless signals received from NICs into wired signals.

In 1999 the 11-Mbps 802.11b became the standard for access points on which products like the Cisco Aironet 350 series, Ericsson LAN 11 Mbps, and many others, are based.

'Mbps' is short for 'megabits per second', a megabit being just over a million bits.

A WLAN can be used where it may be difficult or impractical to use a cabled LAN – e.g. in homes, large offices, warehouses and lecture halls. A device can be as far as 300 feet from an access point and still be able to access the Internet. In a building with many rooms or large halls, a few access points may be needed. A user may take a laptop and walk from one room or from one end of a building to the next without losing network connectivity. This is because the laptop will lock on to the strongest signal from an access point and will transfer its link to another access point if the signal there is stronger.

A wireless LAN has the same features that are available in a wired LAN. It also provides more flexibility in acquiring information, as we have just seen. Less wiring also means greater flexibility, increased efficiency and reduced wiring costs. But, there are disadvantages. Besides the relatively slow speed at which a wireless LAN operates, there is also the problem of interference from other users or devices using the same 2.4 GHz band and the risk of illegal access to information. Interference can corrupt data and is therefore a major concern when installing a wireless LAN. Illegal access is also a big problem, since anyone with a compatible NIC can have access to the network. The need for encryption is therefore of the utmost importance.

### Bluetooth

The other emerging technology used to set up a WLAN is **Bluetooth** technology. Bluetooth is a standard developed by a group of electronics manufacturers that allows any sort of electronic equipment (computers, digital video cameras, cell phones, PDAs, keyboards, etc.) to automatically make their own connections without wires, cables or any direct action from a user. The manufacturers program a Bluetooth radio transmitter into each unit with an address that falls into a range of standard addresses established for a particular type of device. When a device is turned on, it sends radio signals asking for a response from any unit with an address within a particular range. For example, if a computer and a printer are turned on and their addresses are within the established range, they will respond to each other and a tiny network (piconet) is formed. Once the networks are established, the systems begin communicating amongst themselves. Note that this is different from a standard LAN: Bluetooth networks are formed, broken up and reformed all the time, simply by switching on Bluetooth-enabled devices when they are in close proximity to each other.

These 'ad hoc' networks, as they are called, allow data synchronisation with network systems and sharing of applications between devices. Bluetooth functionality also eliminates cables from scanners and other peripheral devices. Handheld devices such as personal digital assistants (PDA) and cell phones allow remote users to update personal databases, and provide them with access to network services such as wireless e-mail and Internet access. The Bluetooth method of wireless networking is already being used by many companies with great success. However, like any network, there are inherent risks. Some of these risks are similar to those of wired networks; some are the same as for other types of WLAN.

*Figure 7.5 WAN*

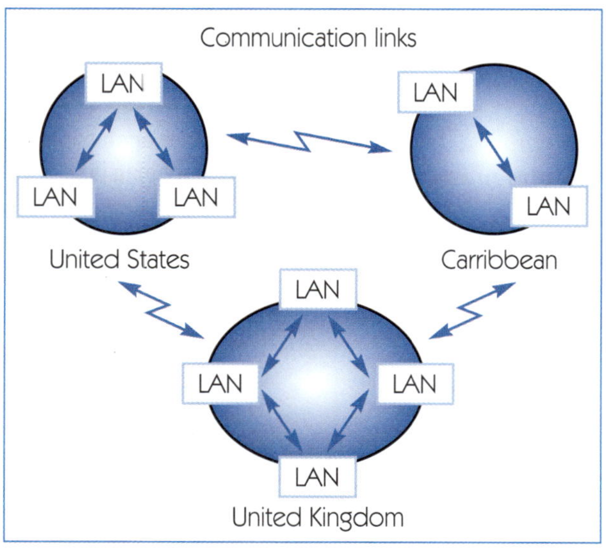


## Wide area networks (WANs)

A **WAN** can connect mainframes, LANs and PCs across a large geographical area such as a city, a state or a country. LANs are often connected to WANs using a special interface device called a **gateway**. A gateway is an interface that enables communication between two different networks. Information can be transmitted using special high-speed telephone lines, microwave links, satellite links or a combination of all three. WANs are used mainly by universities and research centres so that information can be shared, and by large organisations, companies and banks with branches in different countries, to share information and processing loads between the various branches. WANs can also be used to publish documents and distribute software. Figure 7.5 shows LANs in different countries connected together to form a WAN, using telecommunications links.

## Exercise 1

### Fill in the blanks

1 The three classes of bandwidth channels are broadband, voice-band and __________.

2 A ____________ line can simultaneously send and receive data.

3 Computers on a network can share software, data and ______________.

4 LANs can be divided into two categories: client/server and ____________.

5 LAN cables fall into three types: twisted pair, fibre optic and ____________.

6 A ___________ topology is a single line or cable with nodes at different points.

7 A LAN is able to connect to a WAN using an interface device known as a __________.

8 One of the most common methods of setting up a WLAN uses two main sets of components: access points and ____________.

9 Users can communicate in a LAN using ___________.

10 WANs are used by large organisations, companies and banks to share ________ and ___________ loads between the various branches.

### True or False?

1 A broadband channel can transmit between 1000 and 8000 cps. T ❑ F ❑

2 A half-duplex line can alternately send and receive data. T ❑ F ❑

3 Wireless communications use cables to transmit data. T ❑ F ❑

4 A LAN connects computers in a small geographical area like an office building or school. T ❑ F ❑

5 There is an increased risk of data corruption if computers are part of a LAN. T ❑ F ❑

6 The incidence of viruses is reduced if a computer is part of a LAN. T ❑ F ❑

7 A peer-to-peer network only has one computer designated as a server. T ❑ F ❑

8 In a star topology all the computers on the network are connected to one another through a central hub. T ❑ F ❑

9 Bluetooth technology can be used to create a wireless computer network. T ❑ F ❑

10 A WAN connects mainframes, LANs and PCs across a large geographical area such as a city or country. T ❑ F ❑

### Multiple choice

1 A simplex line permits data to flow:
(a) In one direction only
(b) Simultaneously in two directions
(c) In two directions but one at a time
(d) None of the above

2 The device that allows computers on a LAN to send and receive messages is known as a:
(a) Modem
(b) Network receiver
(c) Network interface card
(d) Network adapter

3 In a ring topology of a LAN all the computers are:
(a) Connected at different points in a cable
(b) Connected to one another through a central hub
(c) Connected to a central cable and the ends of the cable are connected together
(d) None of the above

### Short answer questions

1 A reliable data communication system is an important asset to any business organisation.
(a) What is data communication?
(b) What is meant by the term 'bandwidth' as it relates to data communication?
(c) Identify and explain the different types of bandwidth.

2 List and explain the three types of data transmission channels.

3 Define the following:
(a) Simplex
(b) Half-duplex
(c) Full-duplex

4 Many university campuses have established LANs.
(a) What is a LAN?
(b) What are the main reasons for establishing a LAN?
(c) State two methods used by computers to communicate using a LAN.
(d) State one difference between using a ring and a star LAN network.

## Exercise 1 cont.

5 Wireless LANs are now being used in many homes and offices.
   (a) Name two essential components of a wireless LAN that is not using Bluetooth technology.
   (b) Why would you choose to install a wireless LAN as opposed to a wired LAN?

6 Many small businesses have computer networks.
   (a) List THREE advantages of networking computers.
   (b) List TWO disadvantages of networking computers.

7 Many large companies use WANs to transact business.
   (a) What is a WAN?
   (b) Give two methods of communication that a WAN may use.
   (c) What are the advantages of using a WAN?
   (d) State two uses of a WAN.

# The Internet

## What is the Internet?

The Internet is a network of networks that connects computers worldwide via a huge set of telecommunications links. The individual networks may be owned by universities, research facilities, governmental organisations, business cooperations, non-profit organisations and private individuals. Being part of the network means you can access, share and exchange information.

## History of the Internet

The Internet began as ARPAnet, a United States Department of Defence project to create a nationwide computer network that would continue to function even if a large portion of it were destroyed in a nuclear war or natural disaster. The network was therefore decentralised, and originally consisted of four supercomputers.

ARPAnet was originally used by defence scientists and military researchers to log on and run programs from remote computers. In 1983 ARPAnet was split into two parts: MILnet, which was devoted entirely to the military, and ARPAnet, devoted to experimental research and development. In 1986 the success of networking and computer technology led the US National Science Foundation (NSF) to establish NSFNET, which connected users together with five supercomputers. This was then expanded to include regional and state wide networks that connected universities and research organisations. NSFNET eventually replaced ARPAnet and continuously linked more powerful supercomputers to the network.

The nature of the Internet changed in 1992, when the US government began pulling out of network management and commercial entities offered Internet access to the general public for the first time. This change in focus marked the beginning of the Internet's rapid expansion.

## Who owns the Internet?

The Internet does not have a central authority. There are organisations which develop technical aspects of the network and set standards for creating applications on it, but no one governing body or government is in control. The Internet therefore has very few rules and answers to no single organisation. It consists of independently maintained and administered networks. Each network on the Internet is responsible for formulating its own policies, procedures and rules. No one is in charge of the Internet. The Internet backbone, through which Internet traffic flows, is owned by private companies.

Some of the advantages and disadvantages of the Internet are as follows. We will look at these in more detail later in the chapter.

### Advantages of the Internet

- Vast volumes of information are available on virtually any topic.
- Information can be updated regularly.
- Much of the information is free.
- It allows people to 'telecommute', i.e. work from home using Internet facilities like e-mail, and keep in touch cheaply and quickly with friends and relatives.
- It is convenient for many common chores, e.g. booking flights, checking Internet bank balance.
- It is easily accessible: all you need is a PC with a modem and a phone line.

### Disadvantages of the Internet

- Lots of incorrect information is also available; there is no authority to check the accuracy of Internet documents, etc.
- It can be difficult to find exactly what you need because of the large volume of information available.
- Computer viruses can easily be downloaded without the user realising.
- There are lots of undesirable web sites on the Internet (pornography, racist propaganda, etc.).
- The security of computers and WAN/LAN systems connected to the Internet may be at risk from 'hackers'.

## How the Internet works

To connect to the Internet you need the following:

- Computer hardware – a personal computer and a modem
- Communications link – a phone line or cable or satellite dish
- An Internet Service Provider (ISP)
- Computer software – the facility to implement TCP/IP, and an Internet browser.

First, let's look at the hardware. You already know about the PC, so let's look in detail at some of the modems.

## Modems

A standard telephone line can transmit only analogue data, whereas data emitted from a computer is in digital form. A modem (short for '**mo**dulator/**dem**odulator') is a device used to convert the digital data emitted from the computer into analogue data that can be transmitted over a telephone line. When the data gets to the other end of the line, a modem converts the analogue data back into digital data for the computer at that end of the line to process. The data transmitted can be sound, pictures, video or text. Figure 7.6 shows how an external modem is used for data transmission over telephone lines.

*Figure 7.6*
*Transmission of data over a telephone line*

An internal modem performs the same function and is now a standard feature in most PCs. It is an interface card that fits into an expansion slot in the computer's motherboard. The modem has an external outlet for a telephone jack to be plugged into. Besides converting data signals, modern modems can also perform:

- Automatic dialling – a modem can dial a phone number.
- Automatic answering of remote computers – a modem can answer an incoming call.

### Integrated services digital network (ISDN)

An ISDN modem is a digital device which allows voice, video and data to be sent as digital signals over ordinary copper wire telephone lines or fibre optic lines. Since the device does not convert signals from analogue to digital and vice versa, it is not a modem in the true sense, but the name modem is still used. These devices are capable of transmitting data at 64 kbps for a single line and 128 kbps for a bonded dual line. This is twice the speed of the conventional 56 kbs modems. The relatively high speed and the ability to transmit voice, video and data over one line allow users to surf the Internet, make phone calls and receive faxes – all at the same time. With a standard modem, you can only perform one of these operations at a time. But despite these benefits ISDN systems are fast becoming obsolete due to the development of faster systems.

### Asymmetric digital subscriber line (ADSL)

The ADSL modem system uses a single regular telephone line to transmit digital data and make phone calls at the same time. ADSL is a type of digital subscriber line (DSL) where the downstream rate (the rate at which information is **downloaded** from the Internet) is much faster than the upstream rate (the rate at which information is **uploaded**). Data can be transmitted at speeds of between 384 kbps and 8 Mbps downstream, depending on the type of service, and 16 kbps to 640 kbps upstream.

An ADSL system requires both the user and the telephone company to have a special ADSL modem or adapter. It does not require a separate phone line and you are connected to the Internet all the time. This system has been available in many Caribbean islands on a limited scale since 2003. However, because of its higher cost and limited availability in some islands it is still mainly used by businesses and large organisations. Symmetric DSL (SDSL) is another type of DSL which does not allow you to use the phone at the same time, but the speed of receiving and sending data is the same. This kind of service might typically have a two-way transfer rate of 768 kbps.

### Cable modems

A cable modem is a modem that connects a cable-TV line to a PC. In some countries, such as the USA, TV cable companies install a single cable to provide both cable TV and Internet services to customers. A special cable box is needed to split the signal for the television and the PC. These cables are two-way, an improvement over the one-way cables used solely for cable TV. The new two-way cable enables the cable company to use a 6 MHz channel slot within the cable signal to deliver Internet service. The download speeds are phenomenal, reaching a maximum of 5 Mbps, with slower upload speeds of a little less than 1 Mbps. The actual transfer rate depends on the number of people in the area accessing the service at the same time. Data transfer rates drop drastically when the number of users increases. This type of connection provides continuous Internet service. It is not widely used.



## Internet connections/links

To get connected to the Internet with your modem, ISDN, cable or ADSL you need a connection between your computer and a host computer. The computers communicate with each other through these connections using protocols, which are like a recognised language for talking to each other. Some of the basic types of connections are:

- **SLIP/PPP:** Serial Line Internet Protocol/Point-to-Point Protocol. These are also referred to as a dial-in direct connection. It is the most common method used by individual users to access the Internet. You dial up an Internet service provider which gives you access to the Internet. A SLIP/PPP link enables you to import and export files directly between your computer and another.
- **Dedicated connection:** This means that you have a permanent connection and are part of the Internet at all times.
- **Remote network access:** Two-way satellite access is one of the most recent methods of providing remote access to the Internet. For this, you must have a satellite dish. You send data requests at speeds that vary from 300 kbps to 900 kbps, depending on the number of users on the system. These requests are transmitted to a satellite that reflects the signals to a satellite dish located at the satellite network operations centre. After the requests are processed, they are returned along the same route. The returned signals picked up by your dish are sent along a cable to a transceiver and then to your PC.

## Internet service provider (ISP)

An **Internet service provider (ISP)** is a company that has a direct connection to the Internet and gives users access to it, usually for a fee. The company usually has a small network that is linked via a high-speed communications link to a high-speed link that forms part of the Internet's backbone (supercomputers and other large networks that make up the Internet world wide).

## Software requirements for the Internet

You need the following software to connect to and access information or other services on the Internet:

- An implementation of **TCP/IP (Transmission Control Protocol/Internet Protocol)**
- A **browser**

### *TCP/IP*

All forms of communication, either electronic or other means, are based on some form of protocol. Computers connected to the Internet use a protocol called TCP/IP. This is a set of protocols used to transfer data from one computer to another over the Internet. A **protocol** is a set of rules that defines how computers interact or communicate with each other. TCP/IP is a non-proprietary protocol suite (it is not designed for any specific type of computer) that enables hardware and operating systems software from different computers to communicate. For example, an IBM (PC) compatible computer can communicate with an Apple or other computer.

TCP/IP is actually two protocols: the TCP portion divides the data that is to be transmitted into smaller pieces called **packets**. This allows data to travel more easily, and therefore quickly, along phone lines. Each packet is numbered so that the data can be reassembled when it arrives at the destination computer. The IP protocol sends each packet by specifying the address of both the sending and the receiving computers.

Each packet may take a different route depending on the amount of network traffic or on the location of the destination computer. The packets are sent along by **routers**. A router can be a specialised computer or a piece of electronic hardware designed specifically for routing. It chooses the best route to send data to its destination. Data arriving at the destination computer is reassembled. If a packet does not arrive or is corrupted, the entire file does not have to be re-sent – just the packet that was lost or corrupted.

### *Browser*

In order to navigate the World Wide Web (www), you need a web browser. A web browser is a program that resides in your computer and enables you to find, retrieve, view and send **hypertext** and **hypermedia** documents over the web. Popular browsers include Microsoft Internet Explorer, Netscape Navigator and Mozilla Firefox.

All web browsers operate in a very similar manner and have similar features. If you are using Microsoft Internet Explorer, the following are some of the things you can do or can control with associated software accessible through its 'toolbar':

- View hundreds of millions of web pages from all over the world.
- Send and receive e-mail: Outlook Express enables you to create and exchange e-mail globally.
- Participate in 'conferences': e.g. NetMeeting conferencing software in conjunction with a sound card, speakers and a microphone enables you to talk to and listen to other users in real time.
- Chat: the Chat program gives you the opportunity to join discussion groups and converse online.
- Develop web pages: you can build your own web pages by using the ActiveX controls software.
- View channels: a channel is a web site that automatically transmits information to your computer at the time you specify.
- Shop online: for books, CDs, clothes ... almost anything.
- See and hear recorded broadcasts: you can see and hear information as it is downloading; you do not have to wait until all of it has arrived.

## Internet Protocol (IP) addresses

Each computer on the Internet has a unique address that identifies it as a node so that information can be sent to it. This unique address is really a number called the **IP address (Internet Protocol address)**. It is a 32-bit address consisting of four sets of up to three digits each, separated by full stops, for example 196.361.232.4. The first part of the address specifies the network and the last two digits specify the host.

The IP address might be constant – that is, remain the same every time you connect to the Internet – or it could be a temporary address that changes each time you connect to the Internet. The IP address used by software is difficult to remember for humans, who prefer to use names.

To allow users to refer to hosts by names, the **Domain Name System (DNS)** was developed. This divides the Internet into a series of domains.

It uses a hierarchical naming system or tree structure to represent a host. A domain is divided into second-level domains, which further subdivide into third-level domains and so on. A host is therefore named for the largest domain to which it belongs, then for any sub-domains within the largest domain, and then finally for the unique host name. The DNS system allows an Internet host to find another Internet host, by translating the host name to the IP address of the computer.

At the top level there are domains corresponding to educational institutions (edu), commercial entities (com), public organisations (org), governmental bodies (gov) and the military (mil). Individual organisations each get their name at the second level of the naming hierarchy. For example, Microsoft has 'Microsoft.com' and the Association of Curriculum Developers has 'ASCD.org'. Departments within an organisation will be at the third level of the hierarchy, for example, 'shop.ASCD.org'. Sometimes a fourth level, which includes the unique host name, is included. For example, if your domain is 'fun.com' which points to your web site, you can create 'holiday.fun.com', which points to the holiday section of your web site. You may also have a 'Caribbean.holiday.fun.com' which now gives the name of the computer in the holiday section of the web site. The complete name of a host therefore includes: the unique host name, all sub-organisation units, the organisational name and the top level domain. Table 1 shows a list of the current top-level domains in the United States.

| Domain name | Purpose |
|---|---|
| .com | Commercial |
| .edu | Educational institutions |
| .gov | Government bodies |
| .mil | US military institutions |
| .net | Computer networks |
| .org | Other types of organisations, e.g. non-profit organisations |
| .rec | Recreational organisations |
| .store | Retailers on the Internet |
| .info | Distributors of information |
| .int | International bodies |

*Table 1 Current top-level domains in the United States*

## Internet applications

There are four main types of services available on the Internet:

- Terminal emulation services
- File access and transfer services
- Communication services
- The World Wide Web (www).

## Terminal emulation services (TES)

These services enable you to connect your computer to a remote host and use the services available as if your computer were a terminal of the remote host. This can give you access to specialist offerings like online databases, library catalogues and chat services.

### Did you know?

Did you know that many individuals in the Caribbean have pursued and are pursuing online degrees via the Internet from top universities in the UK and USA? This is called 'distance education' or 'distance learning'. It usually involves learning via web sites and e-mail contact between tutors and students, rather than face-to-face interaction. What do you think the advantages and disadvantages of this type of learning might be?

An important TES is **Telnet**, a special program that allows you to access data and programs from a Telnet server. When connected to a Telnet site, your computer becomes a 'dumb' terminal that can be used only to send text-based messages to the Telnet site and to view the results. The Telnet program provides a window into which you can type commands and access information from the host computer. Some browsers, such as CompuServe's, have built-in Telnet software, while others such as America Online (AOL) allow users to access the Telnet software but do not run it themselves.

## File access and transfer services

These services enable you to locate and use electronic files stored on computers across the Internet.

### *File transfer protocol (FTP)*

**File transfer protocol (FTP)** is a set of rules for communicating over the Internet. It enables you, through an FTP program, to find an electronic file stored on a computer somewhere else and download it (take a file from one computer on the Internet and copy it to a storage device on your computer). It also enables you to upload files (send files to other computers on the Internet). The electronic files are stored on what are termed FTP sites, which may be maintained by universities, government agencies and large organisations. Some of the sites are private, and you may have to pay to retrieve or store information on those sites.

The files in an FTP site are stored in directories. Each file has a name and an extension, the name labelling the contents of the file and the extension indicating the type of file – text, sound, program, image, video, etc.

# *Communication services*

## Electronic mail (e-mail)

If you want to find out more about this topic you could look up the related animations and activities on your companion CD-ROM.

**E-mail** is the most popular and widely used service on the Internet today. It enables users locally and world wide to send electronic messages (text, sound, video and graphics) to one individual or to a group of individuals, and to receive messages from others. A powerful feature of e-mails is the option to send attachments. For example, a document created in Microsoft Word can be attached to an e-mail message and received by the recipient with an e-mail program.

E-mail is much faster than mail delivered by the traditional postal system. An e-mail can be sent to an e-mail subscriber in any part of the world in a matter of seconds or minutes (depending on the 'traffic' on the Internet). Also, a subscriber can access his/her e-mail from any part of the world as long as Internet access is available. Apart from the fee that a subscriber has to pay to an ISP for Internet access, sending e-mail is free. You can send as many e-mails as you like at no additional charge and at your own convenience, any time of the day or night. This does not cause any problems for the person receiving it, who does not have to be present to receive the e-mail. They collect the e-mail (e.g. from their ISP) at a time convenient to them.

### *E-mail addresses*

To be able to send and/or receive e-mail, each user must have an **e-mail address** and an e-mail program such as Outlook Express. The address is unique to the user and consists of two parts separated by the @ ('at') symbol. The first part is the user name, which can be a real name, a shortened form of a real name or some made-up name. The second part is the domain name – the location of the e-mail account on the Internet, e.g. with your ISP. The general form of an e-mail address is as follows:

Username@Domainname

For example, an individual in Trinidad and Tobago who has an Internet account with the Telecommunications Service of Trinidad and Tobago (TSTT) may have an e-mail address like this:

brown@tstt.net.tt or Corinth@tstt.net.tt

Internet users can also use the free e-mail services offered by web sites such as Yahoo!, MSN and Excite. You simply fill out an online form to open an account and get an e-mail address. You access e-mail directly through the web site, rather than through an e-mail program resident on your computer. Examples of these addresses are:

pettipoo@yahoo.com

madd@hotmail.com

## *E-mail hardware and software requirements*

For an e-mail message to be sent and received, the following must be in place:

- **Mail server:** This is a computer on the Internet that operates like the traditional post office. The mail server receives incoming messages and delivers outgoing messages. It allocates a certain amount of storage to hold mail for registered users. The area of storage allocated to you is your **mailbox**. You can retrieve your mail by supplying your username and password. This is necessary to protect your e-mail from unauthorised access.
- **Mail client:** This is a program that enables you to read and compose e-mail messages, send e-mail and access e-mail from the server. If you are using Microsoft Office software, you may use the popular Outlook Express program as your mail client.

Figure 7.7 shows the Microsoft Outlook Express e-mail screen for creating a new message; the format for other e-mail software is quite similar.

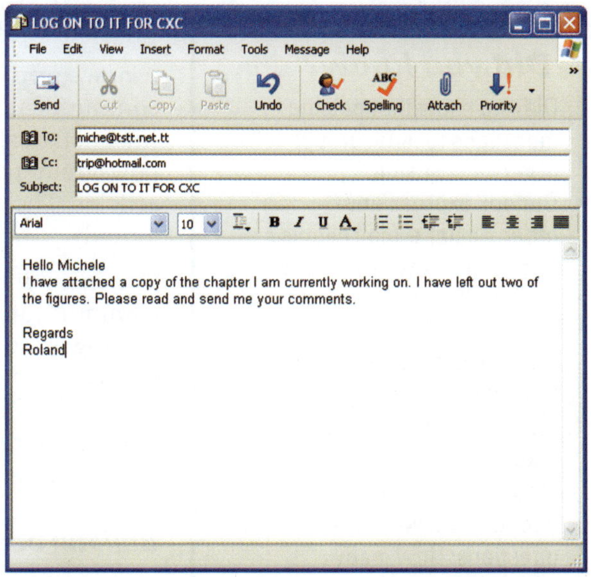


*Figure 7.7*
*An e-mail message*

## *Components of an e-mail*

To send an e-mail, in the 'To:' field fill in the e-mail address of the person to whom you want to send it. If you want to carbon-copy the e-mail (send the same e-mail for information to a number of other users), fill in the other addresses in the 'Cc' field. To give the receiver an idea of the contents of an e-mail before opening it, type a descriptive phrase in the 'Subject' field. Now move to the blank area and type the message.

You can also send attachments along with the original e-mail. An attachment can be a word processing file, a spreadsheet file, a database file or any other file that your computer can access. When a file is attached, a new field showing the name and size of the file is displayed below the 'Subject' field.

## Electronic discussion forums

Electronic discussion forums such as mailing lists, newsgroups, chats and bulletin boards are another very popular feature of the Internet.

### Mailing lists

An electronic **mailing list** is a group of people using e-mail to communicate their views on common issues or interests. You subscribe to become part of the group. Not all groups are open to everyone. Some might only allow professionals in a certain field. For example, a group discussing early childhood education may only want to include researchers in that field. A mailing list may therefore involve only a few people or thousands of people.

When you become a member of a group, you can send messages with your comments or views on some matter that is being discussed or to which you want an answer. A copy of your message is then sent to all subscribers on the mailing list. You can also simply read the contents of messages and not make a contribution. Some mailing lists only let subscribers receive messages but not send them. For example, there is a mailing list that sends a joke a day to its members, but the members cannot reply.

### Newsgroups

A **newsgroup** enables a group of people with common interests to communicate with each other. There are thousands of newsgroups on the Internet, dealing with almost every imaginable topic. A subscriber to a newsgroup posts a message, which can vary from a few lines to whole articles. The other subscribers read the message and may or may not choose to reply.

The main difference between newsgroups and mailing lists is the method of communication. Mailing lists use e-mail to communicate with subscribers. Messages are sent to a subscriber's e-mail address. Newsgroups post messages on the Internet for all the users to access. For you to be able to read and post messages to newsgroups, your computer must have **newsreader software**. For example, Microsoft's Outlook Express has a built-in newsreader.

> **Did you know?**
>
> Did you know that posting messages to newsgroups is very easy using Outlook Express and other similar e-mail clients? To set up a newsgroup account, click on 'Set up a newsgroups account...', displayed in the main Outlook Express window under the heading 'Newsgroups'. The Internet connection wizard will take you through the necessary steps. After setting up your account, answer these questions: How many newsgroups did you find? What topics were covered?

### Bulletin board system

A bulletin board system (BBS) is an Internet facility much like a newsgroup. It is dedicated to the exchange of messages. Most bulletin boards serve specific interest groups and are often free, although some may charge a membership or user fee. Everyone with access to the bulletin board can post and view messages on the topics covered by the board.

### Chats

Chatting on the Internet has become a favourite pastime for many users. A user can enter any one of the thousands of chat rooms that are present on the net. A **chat room** is a group of people with common interests communicating with one another interactively, in real time. There are chat rooms for specific topics, but many chat rooms discuss a range of subjects. For example, a chat room for unemployed Internet users at home might discuss things like their children's education or possible opportunities for work. Some of the different ways of chatting include:

- **Text-based chat:** This is the oldest and most common method of chatting. You enter a chat room and look at the comments posted about a topic. Everyone currently in the room is notified that a new person has entered the discussion. You are identified by a name, but many users prefer to use a **handle** or sobriquet (a name that they want to characterise their personality). You can see the comments made by other participants and can type out a reply on any of the comments to everyone connected, or, if you wish, only to selected people in the group. You may wish to start a topic of your own. Users can enter and leave a chat room as they wish. One popular chat program is ICQ.

- **Internet Relay Chat (IRC):** This is a real-time conference system that lets you talk with as many people as you like, grouped together on channels by topics, using text messages. Once you have accessed IRC, you can find out what topics are being discussed and how many users are involved. You can then search for a channel that suits your interest. IRC can be considered as a variety of text-based chat where each chat room (channel) is dedicated to a specific topic, and where users are not allowed to discuss topics unrelated to the channel's purpose.
- **Instant messaging:** This is a variation of IRC. With instant messaging, a user on the web can contact another user currently logged on and type a conversation. Chatting is therefore usually 'one-to-one'. Instant messaging is available from ICQ, MSN and Yahoo!; a very popular program to this end is MSN Messenger. The service is free as long as you have Internet service. You simply need to fill out an electronic form with some basic information and you can get started.
- **Multimedia chat:** Multimedia has created a new form in which users can communicate. With multimedia software, you can use the microphone in a computer to talk to another user anywhere in the world, as if you are on the phone. If you each have a small video camera (**webcam**) connected to your computer, you will also be able to see each other. However, in most countries at present the quality of video output is not very good, due to bandwidth issues, and users may have to wait many seconds for each video clip. For live video communication to function properly, the bandwidth of the present transmission channels will have to be increased.

### *Short message service (sms)*

There are currently a number of services that allow Internet users to send text messages from a computer to a mobile phone. For example, in Trinidad and Tobago there is an sms messaging service on the Internet which uses a gateway to allow text messages to be sent to mobile phones. You simply fill out the appropriate information in the boxes provided on the web page (as shown in Figure 7.8) and click 'Send'.

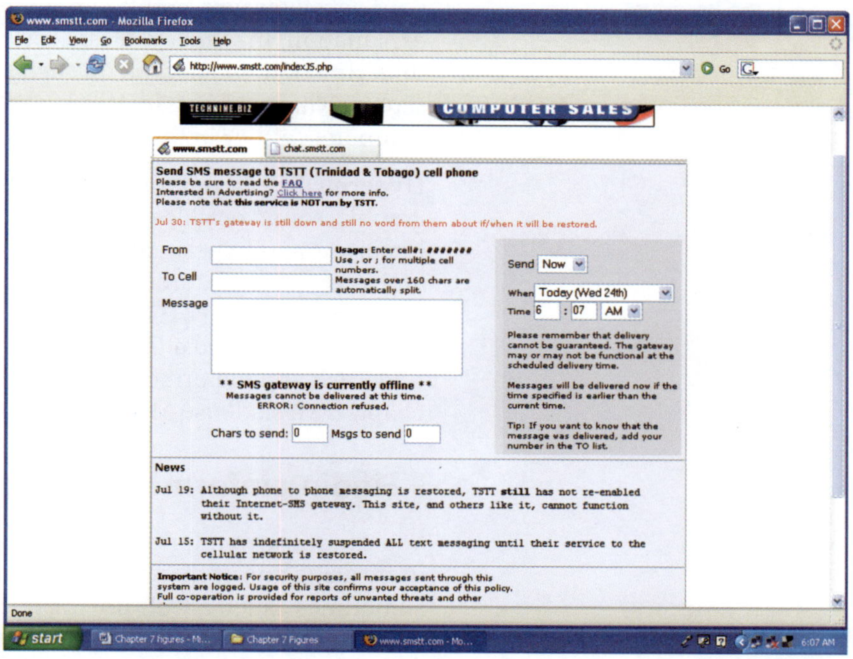


*Figure 7.8*
*The sms message box*

## Point-to-Point Protocol (PPP)

**Point-to-point protocol (PPP)** enables users to dial into a local Internet service provider to connect securely to their corporate network through the Internet. This is particularly useful for people who work from home or people who travel and need to access their corporate networks remotely, for example, to check e-mail.

## Broadcasting

Broadcasting refers to the distribution of information, programming or advertising content to everyone on a network. The sending of junk mail randomly to as many people as possible on the Internet is therefore an example of broadcasting.

## Narrowcasting

This is the opposite of broadcasting. It refers to the targeted distribution of information, programming or advertising content to specific individuals or venues. Narrowcasting ensures that its content is timely and relevant to its intended audience. It can therefore be used to select specific target groups and market products to them.

# World Wide Web

The web is a service offered on the Internet. It was originally developed to help physicists in Geneva, Switzerland, exchange data and research materials quickly with other scientists.

Many people believe the Internet and the World Wide Web (also called the Web, WWW or sometimes W3) to be one and the same, but this is not so. In fact the Web can be thought of as a large subset of the Internet. The Web consists of millions of web pages (hypertext and hypermedia) documents. A hypertext document is a document that contains a **hyperlink** to another document located on the same computer or on another computer in any part of the world. Hypertext allows you to move easily from one document to the next.

For example, if you have used the Help files in any of Microsoft Office's application programs, you have already encountered hypertext. You may have asked for help with a certain topic and been shown a displayed explanation, in which you saw certain words highlighted in blue and underlined. If you clicked on such a word, you would get an additional help screen. The word is associated with a hyperlink to somewhere else in the computer (either in the same file or in a different file).

Hypermedia is a general name for documents that contain links to text, graphic, sound or video files. A computer that stores and makes available hypertext and hypermedia documents is called a server (or **web server**), and a computer that requests such a document is called a client. **HyperText Transfer Protocol (HTTP)** is a set of rules that controls how data travels between server and client. In order to find, retrieve, display and send hypertext and hypermedia, you need a browser. In the examples in this chapter, we shall use Microsoft Internet Explorer.

## Finding information on the Web

You can retrieve information by clicking on a direct link using your browser, or by using one of the many **search engines**. A search engine, also sometimes called a **web portal**, is a web site that allow users to find information quickly and easily. Each search engine has its own database of web documents. Items are continually added to the site by a program called a **spider**, which searches the web looking for new pages to add to the database. In addition to giving access to information in its database, a search-engine site may also provide features such as a free e-mail service, chat rooms, news and facilities for **online shopping**. Some of the best-known search engines are Yahoo!, Excite, MSN, Hotbot and Google.

Access to web pages may be accomplished by:

- Searching through subject directories linked to organised collections of web pages.
- Entering an Internet address or URL and retrieving a page directly.
- Entering a key word or a search statement at a search engine to retrieve pages on the topic of your choice.
- Browsing through pages and selecting links to move from one page to another.

## Finding information using a directory service

Some search engines, for example Yahoo! and MSN, provide users with a directory on their home page containing a list of broad categories such as Education, Recreation and Sports, Arts and Humanities and many more, as shown in Figure 7.9. When you select a category, a list of sub-categories is displayed, and selecting a sub-category can result in further sub-categories. You keep selecting deeper and deeper until you see a description of a web site that you want to visit. This makes it easy to find information and is one of the features that have made Yahoo! a popular search engine. Figure 7.10 shows the results when the category 'computers' is selected, and Figure 7.11 displays the sites available when the topic 'Digital subscriber line (DSL)' is selected.

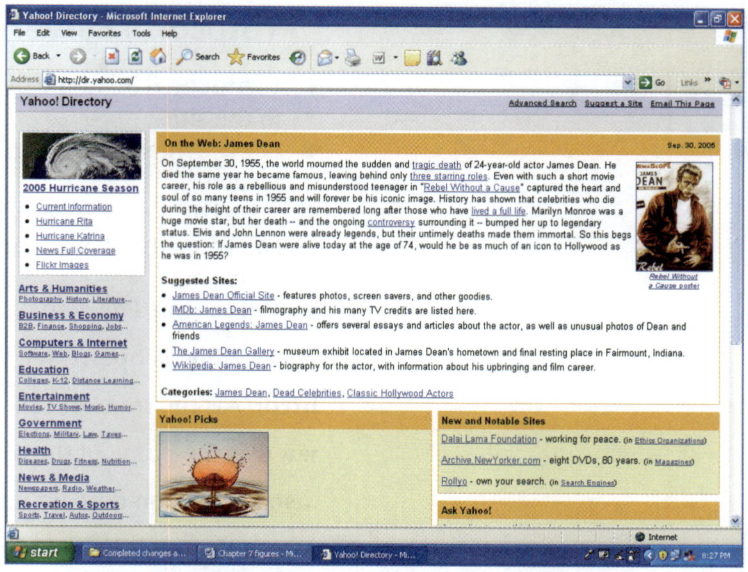

*Figure 7.9 Yahoo!'s home page, showing broad categories*

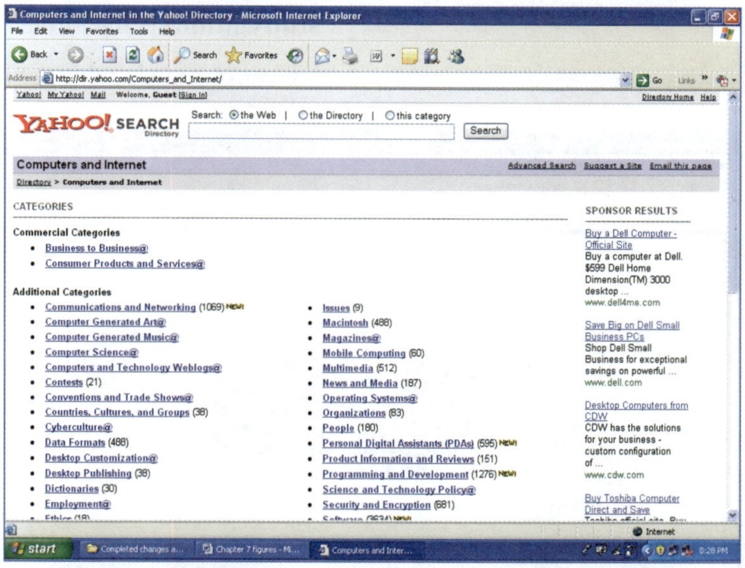

*Figure 7.10*
*Yahoo!'s listing of sub-categories of 'Computers and Internet'*

## Finding information using a Uniform Resource Locator (URL)

You can also find information by typing in a web site's direct address or **Uniform Resource Locator (URL)** into the 'Address' field, located at the top of the browser window, just below the menu bar. A uniform resource locator is the address of an Internet file, and usually is in this format, made up of four parts:

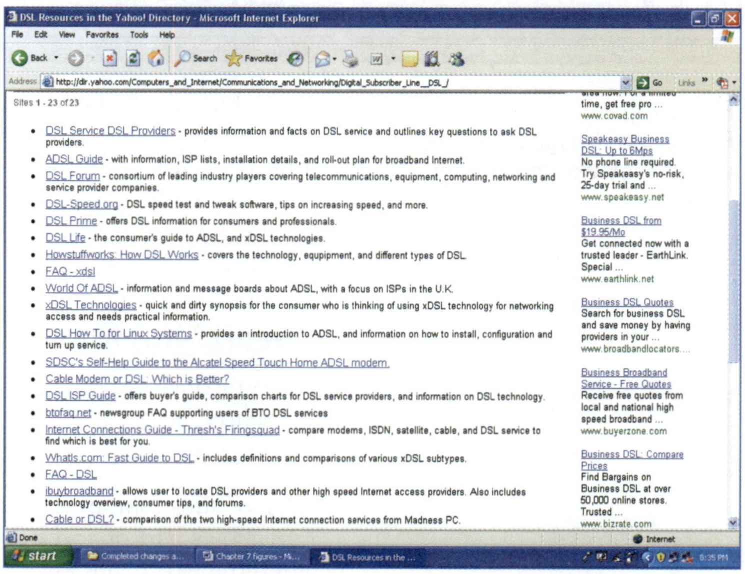

*Figure 7.11*
*The list of sites in Yahoo!'s sub-category for 'Digital subscriber line (DSL)'*

## Protocol://Server/Path/Filename

- **Protocol:** The name of the Internet protocol, usually 'http', giving access to the site.
- **Server** (host name, e.g. www): The computer on which the document is located.
- **Path** (directory hierarchy): The top-level directory and any lower-level sub-directories (separated by '/' characters) in which the required file is to be found.
- **Filename:** The actual file name of the document.

An example is **http://www.ascd.org/studyguides**

**http://** is the transfer protocol to be used

**www** is the name of the server computer

**.ascd** is the sub-domain name

**.org** is the top-level domain name (see page 93)

/ is a separator to indicate a change of directory in the servers' storage medium

**studyguides** is the name of the document

URLs are translated into numeric addresses using the Domain Name System (DNS).

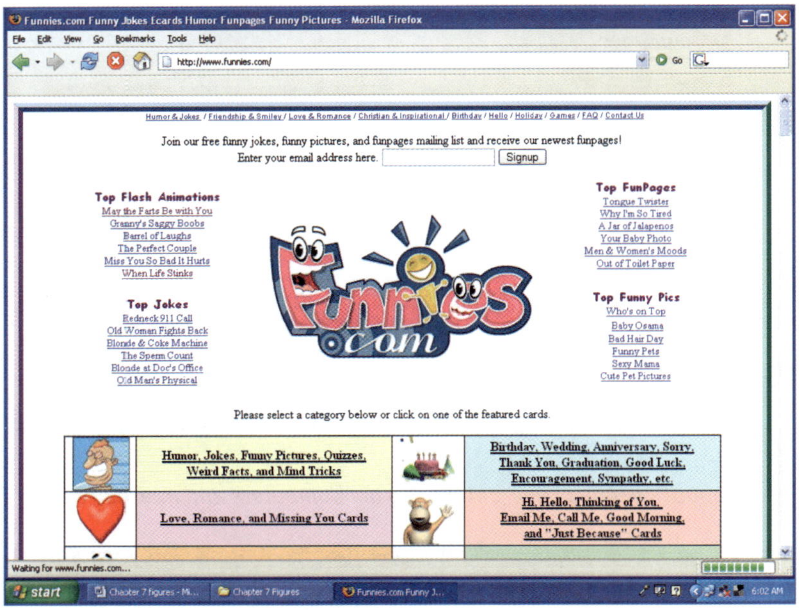


*Figure 7.12*
*Finding a web page with a known address – www.funnies.com*

### *Finding a web page with a known address (URL)*

1. Type the URL 'http://www.funnies.com' into the 'Address' field near the top of your browser window.
2. Click on **Go**.

Figure 7.12 shows the home page of the web site http://www.funnies.com.

## Finding information using key words or phrases

You can also find information by typing into a search-field one or more keywords or phrases that indicate the topic you would like to search for. The easiest way to start is by clicking the **Search** button on your browser toolbar. What happens after that will depend on which search engine is set as the default one for your browser to use. Typically, your browser window will split to include a new pane that enables you to type your search terms into a particular search engine. Of course, there are many search engines available, and you can use as many as you like until you find a site that you want to visit.

## Searching for a web site using keywords

1. Type one or more keywords or a phrase (e.g. 'Jamaica map') into the search box.
2. Click on the associated **Go** or **Search** button.

A list of sites that are related to the **search terms** will be displayed. Figure 7.13 shows part of a web page showing some of the web sites found by Google when the words 'Jamaica map' were typed in and the Search button clicked.

## Advanced search syntax

All search engines give you the option of an advanced syntax (rules of constructing searches) to narrow down searches, so that you can find specific information more quickly. The syntax used may differ between search engines, but here is some of the syntax used by Yahoo!:

- *Required and specific search words*: Placing a plus sign (+) in front of a word tells Yahoo! that the word *must* be included in all search results.
- Conversely, placing a minus sign (–) in front of a word specifies that the word *must not* be included in any of the search results.
- *Phrase-matching*: Placing double quotes ("...") around a string of words tells Yahoo! that all search results must contain the string in that exact sequence.

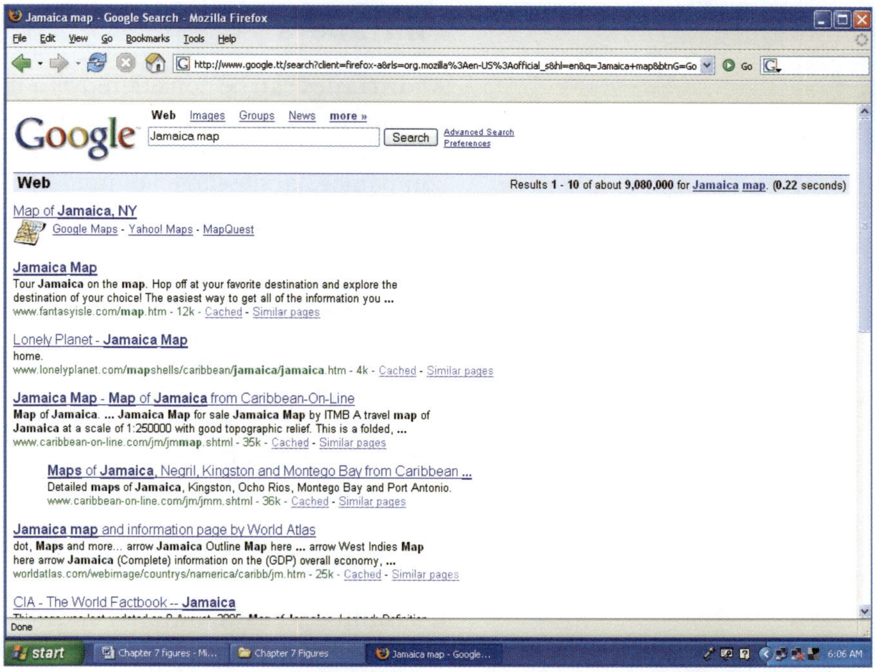


*Figure 7.13*
*Search using keywords*

## HyperText Markup Language (HTML)

**HTML** is a programming language that you can use to create web pages. It contains standard codes that are used to specify how a web page is structured and formatted. They determine the appearance of the web page when it is displayed by your browser. HTML also contains tags that are used to create hyperlinks to access related information on the web.

## New services offered using the World Wide Web

### *Webcasts*

The delivery of live or delayed sound or video broadcasts over the world wide web is called webcasting. The sound or video is captured by conventional video or audio systems. It is then digitised and 'streamed' on a web server. Live webcasting is commonly used to transmit radio. For example, if you are a student from St Lucia studying a long way from home in the United States, it might still be possible for you to listen live to your favourite radio station in Castries, using your computer's speakers and Internet connection. With delayed webcasting, individual web users can usually connect to the server via a web site to view/listen to the webcast at a time of their choosing. In both cases, the transmission is one-way, without any interaction between the presenter and the audience.

### *Webinars*

The term **webinar** is short for **web**-based sem**inar** and refers to conducting a seminar or lecture via the World Wide Web, using graphics (often slides), text, even live voice. Unlike webcasting, the audience is able to interact with the presenter, for example by 'asking' questions by sending an instant message. This interactive element allows the presenter and the audience to give, receive and discuss information.

## Intranets

An **intranet** can be considered as a micro-version of the Internet within a company or organisation. It offers the same features as the global Internet, but in a localised environment such as a factory site or an office. Many companies handle large volumes of information such as:

- Training manuals
- Company reports
- Job openings and descriptions
- Newsletters.

Authorised users within a company can use the company's intranet to find information easily and quickly. The documents in an intranet contain tags that provide links to other documents found in the company's network (or outside on the wider Internet). This is handled using the same browsers, other software and TCP/IP as used for the Internet.

## Extranet

If a company has an intranet and allows limited access to it by people outside the company, the intranet is referred to as an **extranet**. A company may set up an extranet, for example, to provide technical support information to its customers based on products it sells or services it provides.

# Summary

1 'Data communication' refers to the transmission of data from one location to another for direct use or for further processing.

2 The data communication channels used to carry data can be classified into narrow-band, voice-band and broadband, depending on the volume of data that can be transmitted.

3 The transmission lines that carry the data are classified according to the direction of data flow: simplex, half-duplex or full-duplex.

4 A local area network (LAN) is a collection of microcomputers connected within a small geographical area so that they can share information and peripherals, and also communicate with each other.

5 LANs can be divided into two categories: client/server networks and peer-to-peer networks.

6 The connection in a LAN can be through cables or wireless. Some typical configuration topologies of LANs are bus, star and ring.

7 A wide area network (WAN) can connect computers and peripherals across a large geographical area such as a city, a state or countries. Information is transmitted using special high-speed telephone lines, microwave links, satellite links or a combination of all three.

8 The Internet is a network of networks that connects computers across the globe. To connect to the Internet you need a personal computer or workstation, a modem, a communications link such as a telephone line, cable or satellite, and access to an Internet service provider (ISP).

9 A standard phone modem is a hardware device that converts analogue signals to digital signals and vice versa. Other types of modems that do not convert analogue to digital signals are ISDN modems and ADSL modems.

10 An ISP is a company that has a direct connection to the Internet and gives users access to it, usually for a fee.

11 To transfer data from one computer to the next, computers must follow a set of rules called protocols. The protocol used over the Internet is TCP/IP (Transfer Control Protocol/Internet Protocol), which allows operating systems software from different computers to communicate. Each computer on the Internet has a unique address called the IP address.

12 The four main types of service available on the Internet are:

- Communication services, including e-mail and electronic discussion forums (mailing lists, newsgroups, chat rooms and bulletin boards)
- File Transfer Protocol (FTP) services which enable you to locate and use electronic files stored on computers across the Internet
- Terminal emulation services such as Telnet which enable you to use your computer to connect to a remote host, as if your computer were a terminal of the host computer
- The World Wide Web (WWW).

13 A bulletin board system (BBS) is an Internet facility dedicated to the exchange of messages.

14 Broadcasting refers to the distribution of information, programming or advertising content to everyone on a network.

15 Narrowcasting refers to the targeted distribution of information, programming or advertising content to specific individuals or venues.

16 Point-to-point protocol (PPP) enables systems to dial into a local Internet service provider to connect securely to their corporate network through the Internet.

17 Webcast is the delivery of live or delayed sound or video broadcasts conducted over the World Wide Web.

18 Webinar is the conducting of a seminar or lecture via the World Wide Web.

19 The World Wide Web consists of hypertext and hypermedia documents. A hypertext document enables you to use hyperlinks to move from one document in a computer to another related document, either in the same computer or in another computer elsewhere.

20 HyperText Transfer Protocol (HTTP) is a set of rules governing how data travels between server and client computers on the Internet.

21 A web site consists of web pages built using specialised programming languages such as HyperText Markup Language (HTML). Each web page has a unique address called its Uniform Resource Locator (URL).

22 To find, retrieve, view and send hypertext and hypermedia documents over the web, you need a browser. Browsers also give you access to search engines such as Yahoo!, Google and MSN, enabling you to find information quickly by typing in keywords, a phrase or a web site address.

23 An intranet provides many of the features of the Internet within a company or organisation.

24 An extranet is similar to an intranet except that it allows limited access to individuals outside the company or organisation.

# Questions

## Fill in the blanks

1 The Internet is a ___________ that connects computers world wide via a huge set of telecommunications links.

2 A ___________ converts analogue signals to digital signals for transmission over telephone lines.

3 A(n) ________________ modem is a digital device which allows voice, video and data to be sent as digital signals over ordinary copper wire telephone lines or fibre optic cables.

4 Computers connected to the Internet use a protocol called ________________.

5 A ____________ is needed to navigate the WWW.

6 The ___________ address identifies a computer as a node on the Internet.

7 The _____________ system was developed to allow users to refer to hosts by names.

8 _____________ enable users to send electronic messages (text, sound, video and graphics) to one individual or to a group of individuals on the WWW.

9 The _________ is a computer on the Internet that operates like the traditional post office.

10 A _______ is a program that enables you to read and compose e-mail messages, send e-mail, and access e-mail from a server.

11 A(n) ________________ is a group of people using e-mail to communicate their views on common issues or interests.

12 With _____________ a user on the web can contact another user currently logged on and type a conversation.

13 ______________ means to take a file from one computer on the Internet and copy it to a storage device on your computer.

14 ______________ is a set of rules for communicating over the Internet.

15 ___________ is a general name for documents that contain links to texts, graphics, sound or video files.

16 A __________ allows users to find information quickly and easily on the web.

17 A web site's direct address is also known as ____________.

18 A ______________ can be considered as a micro-version of the Internet within a company or organisation.

## True or False?

1 The Internet is owned by the American government. T ❑ F ❑

2 The Internet is a world wide network of networks. T ❑ F ❑

3 All modems convert digital signals to analogue signals and vice versa. T ❑ F ❑

4 Some Internet connections allow users to have continuous Internet service. T ❑ F ❑

5 TCP/IP is a hardware device found on the motherboard of the computer. T ❑ F ❑

6 A browser is used to navigate the WWW. T ❑ F ❑

7 Yahoo! is a browser. T ❑ F ❑

8 Each computer has a unique IP address that identifies it on the Internet. T ❑ F ❑

9 The Internet and the WWW are the same. T ❑ F ❑

10 A document such as a Word file or Excel file can be attached to an e-mail to be sent to some one on the WWW. T ❑ F ❑

11 Terminal emulation is a service available on the Internet. T ❑ F ❑

12 HTTP is a set of rules that controls how data travels between a server and a client. T ❑ F ❑

13 Microsoft Internet Explorer is a search engine. T ❑ F ❑

14 A web site's URL can be typed into the search box of a search engine to access the information on the site. T ❑ F ❑

15 An extranet is a network that gives access to every one on the Internet. T ❑ F ❑

## Multiple choice

1 The Internet was started by:
(a) Universities around the world
(b) Large organisations in the USA
(c) The United States Department of Defence
(d) All of the above

2 The Internet is owned by:
(a) A world-wide governing body
(b) The United States government
(c) Large organisations
(d) No single organisation

3 The following statement is true about the Internet:

(a) Viruses can be easily downloaded
(b) It contains a lot of inaccurate information
(c) There are many sites that promote pornography and religious and racial propaganda
(d) All of the above

4 TCP/IP is a protocol suite that was designed to be used with:

(a) Apple computers
(b) All computers
(c) IBM-compatible computers (i.e. PCs)
(d) None of the above

5 The following is not a browser:

(a) Google
(b) Microsoft Internet Explorer
(c) Netscape Navigator
(d) Mozilla Firefox

6 You can do the following with browsers:

(a) View hundreds of millions of web pages all over the world
(b) Send and receive e-mail
(c) Participate in on-line conferences
(d) All of the above

7 The IP address of a computer on the Internet consists of:

(a) 4 bits
(b) 8 bits
(c) 16 bits
(d) 32 bits

8 To upload a file means to:

(a) Move your file from your diskette to the hard drive
(b) Copy information from a web site to your hard drive
(c) Send files from your computer to other computers on the Internet
(d) None of the above

9 Which of the following would you use to create web pages?

(a) HTML
(b) FTP
(c) HTTP
(d) TCP/IP

## Short answer questions



1 Many individuals and organisations are connected to the Internet.

(a) What is the Internet?
(b) List the hardware requirements needed to connect to the Internet.

2 Explain the term 'Internet Service Provider'.

3 List and explain THREE types of communication links that may be used to get an Internet connection.

4 What is an IP address and why is it necessary?

5 Define the terms:

(a) Protocol
(b) TCP/IP
(c) Router

6 List the four main types of services available on the Internet.

7 List the different types of modems and explain how they differ.

8 Many people now use e-mail for sending letters.

(a) What is e-mail?
(b) List THREE advantages and TWO disadvantages of e-mail over normal mail.
(c) Why does a user need to have a password to access and send e-mail?
(d) Give TWO advantages of using e-mail as opposed to using a phone.

9 Define the following:

(a) Mail server
(b) Mail client

10 What is the difference between a mailing list and a newsgroup?

11 List and explain THREE different methods of chatting.

12 Explain the following:

(a) FTP
(b) Terminal emulation services

13 What is the difference between the Internet and the World Wide Web?

14 Explain the following:

(a) Hypertext
(b) Hypermedia
(c) Hyperlink
(d) HTTP
(e) HTML

15 (a) What is a search engine?
(b) Give the names of THREE popular search engines.
(c) Explain how information can be found using a search engine of your choice.

16 (a) What is a browser?
(b) Give the names of TWO browsers.
(c) List the main features of a browser.

17 Give TWO examples of how a browser may be used for:
(a) Business purposes
(b) Personal use

18 Explain the difference between uploading and downloading.

19 With the aid of examples, explain what URLs are.

20 How does an intranet differ from the Internet?

21 What are some of the benefits that can be gained by a company that has set up an intranet?

22 Explain the term extranet.

23 Using an example, briefly explain how the Domain Name System operates.

## Crossword

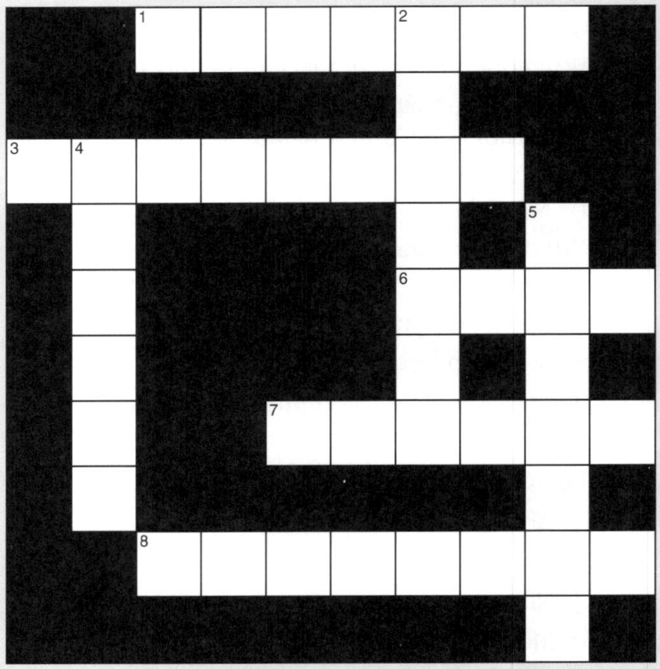


### Across

1 An area of storage allocated to you by a mailserver (7)

3 A set of rules that defines how computers interact or communicate with each other (8)

6 This topology connects the computers on the network through a central hub (4)

7 It runs the networking software that allow resources to be shared with other computers on the network (6)

8 The term used to describe the copying of a file from one computer on the Internet to a storage device on your computer (8)

### Down

2 Used to navigate the WWW (7)

4 A device or computer designed specifically for sending packets of data to their correct destination (6)

5 An interface that enables communication between two different networks (7)

# 8 Programming

## OBJECTIVES

At the end of this chapter you will be able to:

- Define the term 'computer program'
- Classify computer languages into generations
- Explain the steps in algorithm development
- Develop an algorithm
- Test and debug an algorithm
- Produce a trace table for a given problem
- Explain the difference between the operations of an interpreter and a compiler

We are faced with problems every day, from the time we get out of bed in the morning until the time we fall asleep at night. A problem is any task that requires a solution. The problem may be simple or complex. In order to come up with a solution we must:

1. Have a clear understanding of the problem.
2. Determine what we need to help solve the problem.
3. Decide what results we want to achieve.
4. Consider different ways to achieve our result and select the best one.

Let's look at a picture that depicts a neighbourhood in which a house and a school are located (Figure 8.1).

We can come up with a step-by-step sequence of instructions to get from the house to the school. For example:

1. Enter the car
2. Turn right into the road when safe to do so
3. Drive forward to the stop sign
4. Stop the car
5. Turn left onto the main street when safe to do so
6. Drive forward to the traffic light
7. Turn left on the signal of the traffic light
8. Drive forward to the school
9. Turn right into the car park when safe to do so
10. Park the car
11. Exit the car

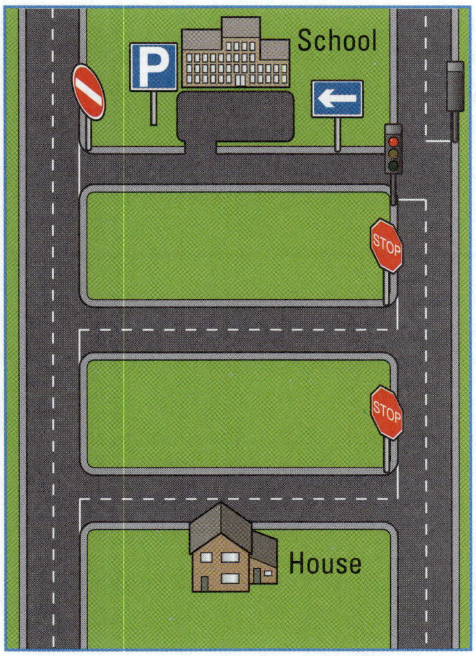


*Figure 8.1*

This problem, and its solution, is from the real world; computers can also solve problems using a similar logic.

A computer program is a series of coded instructions for the computer to obey in order to solve a problem. The computer executes these instructions (obeys the instructions) when told to do so by the user. The number of these instructions varies, depending on the complexity of the problem.

An **algorithm** is a sequence of instructions which, if followed, produces a solution to the given problem. At the end of each instruction, there is no question as to what needs to be done next, and the instructions eventually come to an end. An algorithm is written using special rules and statements.

A **pseudocode** is an algorithm that models or resembles the real programming language of the computer. It cannot be executed by the computer.

Algorithms, pseudocode and computer programs are written using the specific rules and statements of the particular computer language being used, much like grammar rules in the English language. The specific rules for writing in the particular computer language is known as **syntax**

# Generations of computer languages

Computer languages can be classified according to whether they are low level or high level.

Low level languages are machine dependent. Different brands of computer use different program codes.

The program code written for one brand of CPU will not run on another brand of CPU as codes are written with the internal operations and architecture of a particular CPU in mind.

High level languages are independent of the machine. They are not specifically designed for any one brand of computer.

Many computer languages have been developed and evolved over the years. They can be classified according to the following generations.

## First generation (1GL) – low level language

**Machine language** is written using 1s and 0s, i.e. binary code. This is the internal language of computers as you have seen in Chapter 5. It is the only instruction that the CPU understands and can obey or execute directly without having to translate it. The physical workings of computers rely on this system. An example of **machine code** is:

```
1101 1101    1011 1011
1110 0001    1100 0111
0010 1110    1011 0011
```

### Characteristics of 1GL

- Fastest to execute because it is already in the language that the computer can understand
- Difficult to decipher (requires the aid of a reference manual to decipher the meaning of each code)
- Easy to make mistakes in the sequence of 1s and 0s; replacing a 1 for a 0 can result in the wrong command/instruction being executed
- Time consuming/tedious to write
- Machine dependent
- Programming becomes more difficult as the complexity of the program increases

## Second generation language (2GL) – low level language

**Assembly language** is written using mnemonic codes, short codes that suggest their meaning and are therefore easier to remember. These codes represent operations, addresses that relate to main memory, and storage registers of the computer. Typical codes might be: LDA, STO, ADD, NOP, etc.

An example of a program code to add and store two numbers would be:

| | | |
|---|---|---|
| LDA | A, 20 | *load accumulator A with the value 20* |
| ADD | A, 10 | *add the value 10 to accumulator A* |
| STO | B, A | *store contents of accumulator A into storage register B* |
| NOP | | *no operation (stop here)* |

### Characteristics of 2GL

- Easier to write than machine language
- As with machine language, assembly language is machine dependent

## Third generation (3GL) – high level language

This generation of languages was designed so that it is even easier for humans to understand.

### Characteristics of 3GL

- It uses English words and symbols, and is therefore even easier to write
- It is machine independent

*Table 1*
*Some examples of third generation languages*

| Language | Example |
| --- | --- |
| **Pascal**<br>Designed to be used in teaching programming, and in business programs.<br><br>Pascal was developed by Niklaus Wirth, a Swiss computer scientist in 1970, and is named after Blaise Pascal, the 17th-century mathematician who invented the mechanical calculator. | PROGRAM Addition (Input, Output);<br>VAR<br>    Num1, Num2, Sum: Integer;<br>BEGIN<br>    READLN (Num1, Num2);<br>    Sum := Num1 + Num2<br>END |
| **BASIC – *B*eginner's *A*ll-purpose *S*ymbolic *I*nstruction *C*ode**<br>Designed for beginners to use | 10 INPUT Num1<br>20 INPUT Num2<br>30 Sum 3 Num1&Num2<br>40 PRINT Sum |
| **C** – developed by Bell Laboratories in the USA (now AT&T)<br>Used for both high and low level programming. | #INCLUDE <STDIO.H> MAIN ( )<br>{<br>INT Num1, Num2, Sum;<br>Read (Num1, Num2);<br>Sum = Num1 + Num2;<br>Printf (Sum);<br>} |
| **FORTRAN** – ***FOR***mulator ***TRAN***slator<br>Designed for use by engineers and scientists for complex mathematical calculations | c Program to find the sum of 2 numbers<br>INTEGER Num1, Num2, Sum<br>READ (10, 20) Num1, Num2<br>10 Format (14, 14)<br>Sum = Num1 + Num2<br>Print, Sum<br>Stop<br>End |

**COBOL** – **CO**mmon **B**usiness **O**riented **L**anguage

In business, finance and administrative systems, used to manipulate large databases,files and business applications. Can be a tedious language to write.

```
IDENTIFICATION DIVISION.
PROGRAM-ID. SUM OF TWO NUMBERS.
ENVIRONMENT DIVISION.

DATA DIVISION.
WORKING-STORAGE SECTION.
01 Num1    PIC 99 VALUE ZEROS.
01 Num2    PIC 99 VALUE ZEROS.
01 Sum     PIC 999 VALUE ZEROS.

PROCEDURE DIVISION.
DISPLAY "Enter First Number:" WITH NO
ADVANCING
ACCEPT Num1
DISPLAY "Enter Second Number:" WITH NO
ADVANCING
ACCEPT Num2
ADD Num1, Num2 GIVING Sum
DISPLAY "Sum is =", Sum
END-PERFORM.
STOP RUN.
```

### *Did you know?*

The standard international unit of pressure in physics – Pa, or pascal – was also named after Blaise Pascal.

## Fourth generation (4GL) – high level language

### Characteristics of 4GL

- Designed for the development of commercial business software
- Uses English-like statements that are very user friendly, hence programs are easier to write
- This reduces the time taken to write programs
- It also reduces the cost of software development
- Fourth generation languages contain a built in 'function wizard' to assist the user in solving problems

4GL languages fall into the following categories:

- Database query languages, e.g. SQL (Structured Query Language)
- Report generators, e.g. Oracle Report, RPG-II, RPG-III, RPG-IV (Report Program Generator)
- Data manipulation, analysis and reporting languages, e.g. Focus
- Data stream languages, e.g. Iris Explorer
- Screen painters and generators, e.g. Oracle Forms
- GUI (graphical user interface) creators, e.g. Visual Basic

Here is an example of SQL programming code:

```
USE STOCKLIST
SELECT ALL Items WHERE
Price > $10.00
```

## Fifth generation Languages (5GL) – high level language

5GLs are designed to build specific programs that help the computer solve specific problems. They are essentially 4GLs with a knowledge base. The programmer only needs to be concerned with the problem and the constraints or conditions to be met for that particular problem. The main difference between 4GLs and 5GLs is that 4GLs are designed to build specific programs while 5GLs are designed to make the computer solve the problem for you: all codes for the 5GLs are automatically generated.

A 5GL program is written by specifying certain parameters and constraints. It uses a visual or graphical development interface to create a program that is usually compiled with a 3GL or 4GL programming language compiler (a program used to convert the program language to machine code). 5GLs are used mainly in artificial intelligence.

Examples of 5GLs are OPS5 (Official Production System), Prolog (Logical Programming) and Mercury.

Here is an example of Prolog programming language:

| | |
|---|---|
| *dog(sparkie).* | (The program code "Sparkie is a dog") |
| *?- dog(sparkie).* | (Question asked "Is Sparkie a dog?") |
| *yes.* | (The program returns yes) |
| *?- dog(spot).* | (Question asked "Is Spot a dog?") |
| *no.* | (The program returns no.) |

You must remember that, in reality, the computer does not understand Pascal or any of the high level languages. Computers work in machine code or machine language, as we saw earlier. A **compiler** or **interpreter** converts the programs into the machine language of the computer you are using, the language that that computer understands. Only then can the program be executed.

## Program development – steps in algorithm development

As we saw at the start of the chapter, we can approach a problem by going through a set of steps. In computing, we do the following:

1 Define the problem
2 Analyse the problem
3 Develop an algorithm/method of solving the problem
4 Write a computer program corresponding to the algorithm
5 Test and debug the program
6 Document the program (a written explanation of how the program works and how to use it).

## Step 1 – defining the problem

In defining the problem there must be no ambiguity. The problem should be clear and concise and have only one meaning.

Examples of unambiguous problems are:

- Calculating the price of an item after a 10% discount
- Converting a temperature from °C to °F
- Computing the average rainfall for the month of May in a certain place.

## Step 2 – analysing the problem

In order to write a program to accomplish a certain task you must analyse the task as a sequence of instructions that can be performed by the computer.

These instructions can be divided into three main parts: Input and Storage instructions, Processing instructions and Output instructions.

### Exercise 1

1 What is an algorithm?
2 Explain the difference between fourth generation languages and fifth generation languages.
3 List THREE characteristics of first generation languages.
4 What is the difference between assembly language and machine language?
5 A programmer wishes to write a program in a low level language rather than a high level language. Explain why she would want to do this. List TWO advantages of using low level languages and two disadvantages.

## Input and Storage instructions

These instructions allow information or data to be accepted by the computer. The input is information that is needed by the computer to solve the problem. Words such as 'Enter', 'Input' and 'Read' within problem statements usually indicate what data the computer requires.

### Example 1

*What are the input and storage instuctions here?*

1. *Read the price of an item and calculate the discount of 10%.*
2. *Enter the name and year of birth of a person and calculate the person's age.*
3. *Input the length of a side of a square tile and find the area.*

Let's analyse these instructions to determine the inputs and what we need to store.

1. read and store the price of an item
2. enter the name and year of birth of a person
3. input the length of the side of a square tile

## Processing instructions

These instructions manipulate the input data. They involve calculations, that is, mathematical operations (e.g. addition, subtraction, multiplication and division), repeating instructions, selecting instructions and comparison instructions. They also include commands and constructs.

A **command** is a word that instructs the computer what must be done to accomplish a specific task. Commands are specific to a particular programming language: for example, WRITE, PRINT, READ, INPUT, etc.

```
IF a < 10 THEN
       READ Num
ENDIF
```

A **construct** is a group of instructions that work together with commands to accomplish a specific task. An example is the 'IF-THEN' construct:

Problem statements that contain the words 'calculate', 'compute', 'convert', 'add', 'sum', 'subtract', 'minus', 'multiply', 'divide', 'percentage', 'average', indicate what needs to be done. Problem statements can also imply what needs to be processed by looking at what results are required for output; for example: 'Print the **area** of the room'.

### Example 2

*What are the processing instructions here?*

1. *Read the price of an item and calculate the new price after a 10% discount.*
2. *Enter a temperature in degrees Celsius and convert it to degrees Fahrenheit.*
3. *Input the name and year of birth and compute and print the age of a person.*

Let's analyse these instructions to determine what we need to process.

1. calculate the new price after a 10% discount
2. convert it to degrees Fahrenheit
3. compute the age of a person

### *Repeat statements and comparison statements*

These are the repeating instructions and comparison instructions mentioned above.

- *Comparison/selection/decision statements* involve determining whether a condition is true or false in order to perform a set of instructions.
  For example:
  *Read the weekly hours worked by an employee. If the hours worked are greater than 40, then calculate overtime salary at 1.5 times the standard hourly rate of $8.50, for those hours over 40.*
  The condition that is checked is the number of hours worked to determine if it is more than 40.
- *Repeat statements/loopings/iterations* are used when a problem has to be done a number of times.
  For example:
  *Read the marks for three subjects, English, Maths and Spanish, for each student; find the average mark of each student in a class of 15, over the three subjects.*
  The process of finding the average for the three subjects has to be repeated 15 times.

## Output instructions

These instructions allow information to be displayed on the screen. Problem statements that include key words like 'print', 'output', 'display', 'return' and 'write' indicate what data should be output to the screen.

### Example 3

*What are the output statements here?*

1 *Enter the name and year of birth of a person and compute and display the age of the person.*

2 *Write an algorithm to print a conversion table of degrees Celsius to degrees Fahrenheit, 10 °C to 20 °C inclusive.*

Let's analyse these instructions to determine what we need to output.

1 display the age of the person

2 print a conversion table

Let's analyse a few problems.

### Example 4

Write a program to enter the base and height of a triangle and find and print the area.

| Input & Storage | Processing | Output |
|---|---|---|
| Base<br>Height | Calculate Area<br>Area = (Base * Height)/2 | Area |

### Example 5

Write a program to read the temperature in degrees Celsius (°C) and convert it to degrees Fahrenheit (F) where F = 32 + (9C/5). Output the temperature in degrees Celsius and Fahrenheit.

| Input & Storage | Processing | Output |
|---|---|---|
| C | Calculate Fahrenheit<br>F = 32 + (9C/5) | C<br>F |

### Example 6

Write a program to *read* the answer to the sum 10 * 12. (The answer is 120.) Return the comment "Correct" if the answer is right and "Incorrect" if the answer is wrong.

| Input & Storage | Processing | Output |
|---|---|---|
| Answer | If Answer = 120 then print "Correct" otherwise print "Incorrect" | "Correct" or "Incorrect" |

### Example 7

Write a program that reads the result of 10 games played by a team and find the percentage of games won by the team. Output the percentage games won.

| Input & Storage | Processing | Output |
|---|---|---|
| GameResult | • Repeat 10 times<br>Read GameResult add 1 to TotalWins if Game Result is a "Win"<br>• PercentageWins = (TotalWins/10)*100 | PercentageWins |

### Example 8

A school has a house system implemented. Points are awarded to a house based on the performance of its members. 1st place – 4 points, 2nd place – 3 points, 3rd place – 2 points, 4th place – 1 point, and last place – no points awarded. Read the names of 10 members of the Aripo house and the place they came in the events; calculate and print the total points awarded to the house.

| Input & Storage | Processing | Output |
|---|---|---|
| Name | • Repeat 10 times | Total |
| Place | • Check Place<br>If Place = 1 then add 4 to Total<br>If Place = 2 then add 3 to Total<br>If Place = 3 then add 2 to Total<br>If Place = 4 then add 1 to Total | |

## Exercise 2

Analyse the following problems by dividing them into input and storage, processing and output.

1. Write a program to enter an individual's year of birth and the current year and calculate and return the individual's age.
2. Write a program to enter a number, double the number, and output the result.
3. A box can hold one and a half dozen cans of tomatoes. Read the number of boxes and the price of a can of tomatoes; calculate and print the total cost of all the cans of tomatoes.
4. Write a program to accept four numbers and produce an output of their sum, average and product.
5. Write a program to read a month in the year and print 'This is the month of the rights of the child' if the month entered is 'October'.
6. Persons under 18 are not allowed in at 'Shutters Night Club'. Write a program to read a person's age if it is under 18, and output 'Underage person'.
7. Students are awarded extra credit points depending on how they perform in their coursework; if they make over 80 they are given a bonus credit point. Read the student course mark and add one bonus point to the total credit points if the student's mark is over 80. Print the students' total credit points.
8. Write a program to input a number N. If the number is greater than 50 subtract 10 from the number, otherwise multiply the number by 2 and add 5. Print the number and the result.
9. Three football teams are awarded points based on matches they played. Read the team, the team total and whether it won, drew or lost the match and print the team total. Award the points as follows: 2 – win, 1 – drawn, 0 – lost, to the teams' total points.
10. Write a program to determine the average age and height of students in a class of 35. Read the age and height of each student and print the averages.
11. A computer technician works for $50.00 an hour at his regular paying job of 40 hours a week. If he takes on private jobs he charges $150.00 an hour for his work. Write a program to read the number of private jobs he has this week and the number of hours it takes him to perform the jobs. Calculate the total amount of money earned by the technician for the week.
12. To enter a theme park children under 12 pay $3.00, children over 12 and adults pay $7.00 and babies 2 years and under pay $0.00. Input the number of persons entering the park. Read whether a person entering the park is an adult, child or baby and calculate the total revenue earned by the park for that day.

# Step 3 – developing an algorithm

Once you have analysed the problem the next step is to develop an algorithm. In doing this you need to take account of several factors.

## Constants

This is the data that does not change but remains the same during the execution of the program. For example, pi is 3.14159 or 22/7 – this value does not change; or 15% VAT, or the name of a person, 'Jack', are constants.

There are two types of constants:

- **Numeric constants** are simply numbers: integers and whole numbers with fractions (called real or floating point numbers, see Chapter 5), e.g. 39, –6, 3.25. The value of a numeric constant is the actual number.
- **String constants/character strings** are a set of characters or text enclosed in single or double quotation marks, e.g. 'James', "SUM =", 'Average', etc. The value of a string constant is the characters without the quotation marks.

## Variables

In the memory of a computer are storage cells (or bytes), each of which has a unique address. Data occupy these storage locations rather like the way people occupy houses. A person living in a particular house can be located by their surname or house number; similarly, memory locations are given names that allow the computer to locate the relevant data easily. It is easier to refer to the data by name.

During the execution of the program, instructions may cause the contents in these memory locations to change or vary, hence the term **variable**. Variable names should always be meaningful: they should convey the meaning of what is being stored.

There are two types of variables: numeric and string variables.

**Numeric variables** are used to store numbers only. **String variables** are used to store a set, or string, of characters. Look at this example:

*Storage Locations*

| Jack | 160 | 13 | 78 |
|---|---|---|---|
| **Firstname** | **Height** | **Age** | **Marks** |

*Variable Names*

Notice that you cannot store the name 'Jack' in the storage location for age.

## Writing instructions

### Data input and storage instructions

These instructions accept data that is entered into the computer and store the value in the location with the given variable names.

Commands used to input data are READ or INPUT.

Syntax: READ < Variable name >, < Variable name >

Example: READ Name, Score

### Prompting instructions

Prompting statements are used along with input statements to request or notify the user to enter data into the computer. These statements are usually displayed on the screen. Prompting instructions usually precede input instructions.

Commands used to prompt the user are PRINT or WRITE.

Syntax: PRINT <String>

Example: PRINT "Enter student name"

### Example 9

*(a) Let's look at the question from Example 4:*

*Write a program to enter the base and height of a triangle and find and print the area.*

The inputs were base and height.

```
PRINT "Enter the Base,
Height of the triangle"
READ Base, Height
```

Or

```
PRINT "Enter the Base"
READ Base
PRINT "Enter the Height"
READ Height
```

*(b) Look at the question from Example 5:*

*Write a program to read the temperature in degrees Celsius (°C) and convert it to degrees Fahrenheit (F) where $F = 32 + (9C/5)$. Output the temperature in degrees Celsius and Fahrenheit.*

```
PRINT "Enter temperature in Celsius (C)"
READ C
```

*(c) Look at the question from Example 6:*

*Write a program to read the answer to the sum 10 * 12. (The answer is 120.) Return the comment "Correct" if the answer is right and "Incorrect" if the answer is wrong.*

```
PRINT "Enter the answer for the problem 10 * 12 ="
READ Answer
```

*(d) Look at the question from Example 7:*

*Write a program that reads the result of 10 games played by a team and find the percentage of games won by the team. Output the percentage of games won.*

```
PRINT "Enter game results (Results)"
READ Results
```

## Exercise 3

The following questions will allow you to practise writing prompting, input and storage instructions. The first question has been answered for you.

**1** Write an instruction to read N.

*Answer:*

```
PRINT "Enter a value for N"
READ N
```

**2** Write an instruction to enter the length and width of a pool.

**3** Write an instruction to read the height and weight of an individual.

**4** Write an instruction to read the names of students, their school houses and the places they came in a sporting event.

**5** Write an instruction to read a time.

**6** $\frac{+b-c(c+d)}{a}$ : write an instruction to enter values for *a*, *b*, *c* and *d*.

**7** Write an instruction to input the price of a textbook and the percentage discount given.

**8** Write an instruction to enter the size (length and width) of a wall and the size of tile (length and width) used to cover the wall.

### *Output instructions*

These instructions display/output data that is in the computer's memory.

Commands used to output data are PRINT or WRITE. You can output string variables and numeric variables as follows.

Syntax: PRINT <Variable name>, <Variable name>

Example:

```
PRINT Name, Score    Jane Doe, 78
PRINT Percentage     15
```

The value of a variable is printed, for example, 'Jane Doe' and '78' are printed.

### Outputting a string constant

When a string constant is printed, the exact characters within the quotation marks are printed.

Syntax: PRINT "String"

Example:

```
PRINT "Carlos is my name."   Carlos is my name.
PRINT "Time"                 Time
PRINT "Sum = 3 + 4"          Sum = 3 + 4
```

### Outputting a string constant and a variable

It may become necessary to output a label for a variable to identify what is being printed.

For example, if $4.35 is printed by itself, you may not know what it means unless a descriptor or label goes along with it, such as:

The total cost is: $4.35

Syntax: PRINT "String", <Variable>

Example: Print "The total cost is:", Cost

## Exercise 4

Write output instructions for the following problems.

1 Write an algorithm to display 'My name is Carla'.

2 Write an algorithm to output the number of adults and children on a flight, appropriately labelled.

3 Write an algorithm to output 'Warning: Read all labels before washing'.

4 Write an algorithm to output the message 'At times like this, who needs enemies'.

5 Write an algorithm to read a time and output the message: 'At a time like this', time, 'who needs enemies'.

6 Write an instruction to print the average score of 25 students, and the name and mark of the person receiving the highest mark.

7 Print the name of an item, cost of the item, the price inclusive of the VAT, the discount, and the final price of the item.

8 Write an algorithm to read the name and amount on a cheque and display this information.

9 Input and output the following information: the name, age and sex of a person, appropriately labelled.

10 Print the principal, rate, time and interest for a loan.

## Calculations

The mathematical operators for addition (+), subtraction (–), multiplication (*) and division (/) are used in writing calculation statements. The equal sign in a calculation statement is known as the **assignment symbol**. Variables are assigned the results of the calculation.

For example:

A = B + C

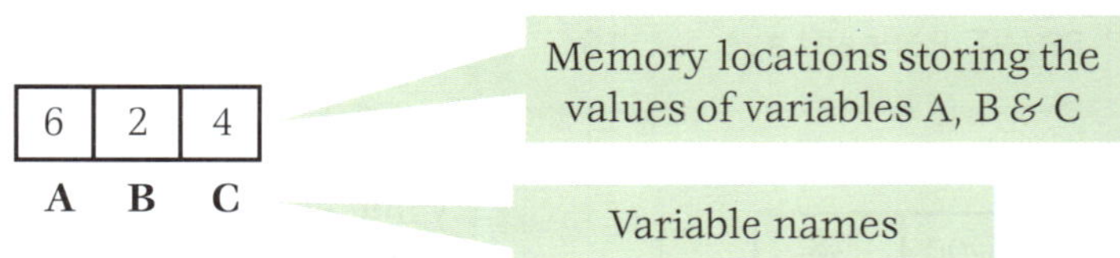


In this statement the variable A is assigned the result of the calculation of B + C, so that the memory location A will hold the result of the calculation performed on the variables B and C.

Syntax: <Variable> = <actual calculation>

Examples:

Area = (Base * Height)/2

F = 32+(9C/5)

PercentageWins = TotalWins/10

Calculation statements are always written with a variable being assigned the value of a calculation, rather than a calculation being assigned a variable.

Incorrect syntax: <actual calculation> = <Variable>

Incorrect example: (Base * Height)/2 = Area

## Exercise 5

Write calculation instructions for the following problems.

1 Enter the length and width of a pool and calculate and print the length of rope needed to cord off the pool.

2 Input the price of a textbook. Calculate and print the total cost of the book after 15% VAT is added.

3 Pipes are laid by an oil company. If the company has to lay down 3 km of pipes and each pipe is 25 metres long, calculate and print the number of pipes needed to cover the distance.

4 Enter the size of a wall in square metres, to be laid between two columns. If the area of one brick is 0.6 $m^2$, calculate and print the number of bricks required to build the wall.

5 Read the cost of a meal at a restaurant. If a 10% service charge were added to the bill, write an algorithm to calculate and return the total amount on the bill.

6 Write a program to read the temperature in degrees Celsius (°C) and convert it to degrees Fahrenheit (F) where F = 32+(9C/5). Output the temperature in degrees Celsius and Fahrenheit.

7 $\frac{+\ b-c(c+d)}{a}$ Write an instruction to enter values for $a$, $b$, $c$ and $d$ and compute and print the result of the equation.

8 Write an instruction to enter the size (length and width) of a wall and the size of tile (length and width) in square metres used to cover the wall. Estimate the number of tiles needed to cover the wall, adding 10% more tiles to cover for breakage. Print the size of the wall, the size of tiles used and the total number of blocks needed, inclusive of number of tiles added to cover breakage.

9 Read the height in inches and weight in pounds of an individual and compute and print their BMI (body mass index). BMI = ((weight/height)/height) * 703.

10 A carpenter is paid a contract fee of $2000.00 for 3 days work. He hires 3 workers who work for the 3 days at $75.00 a day. Calculate and print the amount of money paid to each worker, the total paid to all workers and the amount the carpenter is left with.

## Comparison/selection/decision statements

It sometimes becomes necessary when processing data to compare the value of a variable to the value of another variable, or to compare the value of a variable to that of a constant.

The following relational operators are used to make such comparisons.

A **condition** is an expression that when evaluated gives either a TRUE or a FALSE. This expression is called a **Boolean** expression. These conditions use the relational operators between two variables, or between a variable and a constant.

*Table 8.2*

| Relational operator | Meaning |
|---|---|
| = | Equal to |
| < >, # | Not equal to |
| > | Greater than |
| < | Less than |
| > = | Greater than or equal to |
| < = | Less than or equal to |

Examples:

Boys in Class > = 35

Number of Boys < > Number of Girls

## The IF-THEN construct

The IF-THEN construct contains a condition which is tested before an action can be undertaken. If the condition holds true, then the action is taken. Otherwise, the instruction statements between IF-THEN and ENDIF are not taken but are ignored.

Syntax:

IF < condition > THEN

< Action to be taken if condition is true >

(that is, instruction statements that would be performed if the conditions are met)

ENDIF

### Example 10

*A company gives out bonuses based on the amount of income generated by their sales representatives per month. Once the income is greater than $5000.00, a bonus of 10% of the generated income is given to the employees. Read the income generated and print the bonus.*

The decision to give a bonus is based on the amount of income the sales representative generates.

Input/read the Income Generated.

The action to be taken is the calculation and printing of the bonus.

Only if the Income Generated is greater than $5000.00 is the bonus calculated.

***Case 1***

We must be aware of where the PRINT statement is placed. If it is placed within the IF-THEN-ENDIF construct, *only* if the income generated is greater than $5000.00 is the bonus printed.

```
PRINT “Enter the Income-Generated”
READ Income-Generated
IF Income-Generated > $5000.00 THEN
      Bonus = Income-Generated * 10%
      PRINT “Bonus”, Bonus
ENDIF
```

***Case 2***

In this case, the PRINT statement is placed outside the IF-THEN-ENDIF construct. So the word Bonus is printed regardless of whether the bonus is actually calculated or not.

```
PRINT “Enter the Income-Generated”
READ Income-Generated
IF Income-Generated > $5000.00 THEN
      Bonus = Income-Generated * 10%
ENDIF
PRINT “Bonus”, Bonus
```

### *Initialising a variable*

It may sometimes be necessary or wise to **initialise** a variable, that is, to give the variable a starting or initial value.

A variable is assigned to a position in memory that is not used. That position may nevertheless have data stored there (from some previous operation); this data therefore needs to be erased by setting an initial value for the variable.

In Case 2 in Example 10, since the bonus is printed regardless of whether the employee generates an income > $5000.00, it is necessary to void the memory location where the variable is assigned, and initialise it to $0.00. In this way, a figure will be printed along with the word Bonus, and not the data that was stored from a previous operation.

Variable **Bonus** is assigned a position in memory that is not used, but contains data 98474 from a previous operation

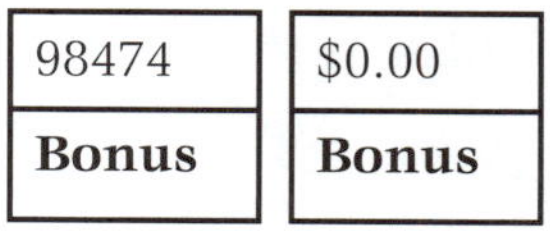


Data is erased by initialising the variable to $0.00 which erases the previous value

***Case 3***

In Case 3, if the income generated is less than or equal to $5000.00 and no bonus is calculated then the bonus printed will be $0.00. This is because the figure has previously been stored in memory.

```
Bonus = $0.00
PRINT "Enter the Income-Generated"
READ Income-Generated
IF Income-Generated > $5000.00 THEN
       Bonus = Income-Generated * 10%
ENDIF
PRINT "Bonus", Bonus
```

### Example 11

*A car rental firm leases its cars for $250.00 per day. The manager give a discount based on the number of days that the car is rented. If the rental period is greater than or equal to 7 days then a 25% discount is given. Read the rental period and print the discount given.*

Input the rental period

The decision is based on the length of time the car is rented.

The action is to calculate the discount to be given for the rental period.

Only if the car is rented for 7 days or more is the discount calculated.

```
PRINT "Enter car Rental Period"
READ Rental Period
IF Rental Period >= 7 THEN
       Discount = ($250.00 * Rental Period) * 25%
ENDIF
PRINT "Discount", Discount
```

## The IF-THEN-ELSE construct

The IF-THEN-ELSE construct contains two parts: the THEN part and an ELSE part. The condition is tested before an action can be undertaken. If the condition holds TRUE, the THEN action is taken, otherwise the ELSE action is taken if the condition is FALSE.

Indentation is used for readability, so that you can see at a glance the structure of the construct – especially which statements belong to the THEN part, and which belong to the ELSE part.

Syntax:

IF <Condition> THEN

        <THEN part: Action to be taken if condition is TRUE>

ELSE

        <ELSE part: Action to be taken if condition is FALSE>

ENDIF

### Example 12

*A company gives out bonuses based on the amount of income generated by their sales representatives per month. Once the income is greater than $5000.00 then a bonus of 10% of the generated income is payable; otherwise the bonus is 3% of the generated income. Read the income generated and print the bonus.*

```
PRINT "Enter Income-Generated"
READ Income-Generated
IF Income-Generated > $5000.00 THEN
        Bonus = Income-Generated * 10%
ELSE
        Bonus = Income-Generated * 3%
ENDIF
PRINT "Bonus", Bonus
```

## Boolean operators

When selection is based upon one or more expressions/decisions being TRUE or FALSE, it is possible to combine the expressions/decisions together using the Boolean operators AND or OR.

- If the AND operator is used *both* conditions must be met, in order for the *total* expression to be true or false.
- If the OR operator is used, *either* condition must be met, in order for the *total* expression to be true or false.

### Example 13

*A club plays cricket only on Sundays, and only if it is not raining. Read the day and the weather and print 'Game on' if it is a suitable day for playing.*

What happens with each of the two operators? Let's try some algorithms.

***With the AND operator***

Both conditions must be met for the expression to be true and 'Game on' is printed. If either condition is not met, such as the day is not 'Sunday' or the weather is 'Rain', then the action (printing 'Game on') is not taken.

```
PRINT "Enter the Day and the Weather"
READ Day, Weather
IF Day = "Sunday" AND Weather = "No Rain" THEN
     PRINT "Game on"
ENDIF
```

***With the OR operator***

In this case, if either condition is true then the action is taken. So, if the day is 'Sunday', regardless of the weather, the game is on. If the weather is 'No Rain', regardless of the day, the game is on.

```
PRINT "Enter the Day and the Weather"
READ Day, Weather
IF Day = "Sunday" OR Weather = "No Rain" THEN
     PRINT "Game on"
ENDIF
```

In this case the game would always takes place on a Sunday regardless of the weather; the game would also be played any other day of the week, as long as there is no rain. The only time the game is not played is if it is any of the days Monday to Saturday, and it is raining on that particular day. But, note that this is not exactly what the club wants. So, only the AND operator works to meet the conditions set out by the club.

The AND operator is also used to limit values within a particular range.

### Example 14

*A company gives out bonuses based on the amount of income generated by their sales representatives per month. Once the income is greater than $5000.00 and less than or equal to $8000.00 then a bonus of 10% of the generated income is given to the employee. Read the generated income and print the bonus.*

```
PRINT "Enter Income-Generated"
READ Income-Generated
IF (Income-Generated >= $5000.00) AND (Income-Generated <= $8000.00) THEN
     Bonus = Income-Generated * 10%
ENDIF
PRINT "Bonus", Bonus
```

## Nested selections

IF statements embedded one within another are said to be nested. For every IF-THEN statement there must be an ENDIF.

Syntax:

IF < Condition 1 > THEN

< Action to be taken if condition 1 is true >

ELSE

IF < Condition 2 > THEN

< Action to be taken if condition 2 is met >

ELSE

IF < Condition 3 > THEN

< Action to be taken if condition 3 is met >

ELSE

< Action to be taken if conditions 1 to 3 are not met >

ENDIF

ENDIF

ENDIF

If the first condition is not met the second condition is checked, if the first and second conditions are not met then the third condition is checked, and so on.

### Example 15

*A company gives out bonuses based on the amount of income generated by their sales representatives per month. Once the income generated is greater than or equal to $10,000.00 a bonus of 20% is given. If the income generated is greater than or equal to $8000.00 but less than $10,000.00 a bonus of 15% is given. If the income generated is greater than or equal to $5000.00 but less than $8000.00 a bonus of 10% is given. If the income generated is less than $5000.00 then a 3% bonus is given. Read the income generated and print the bonus.*

```
PRINT "Enter Income-Generated"
READ Income-Generated
IF (Income-Generated >= $10,000.00) THEN
        Bonus = Income-Generated * 20%
ELSE
IF (Income-Generated >= $8000.00) AND (Income-Generated
< $10,000.00) THEN
        Bonus = Income-Generated * 15%
ELSE
IF (Income-Generated >= $5000.00) AND (Income-Generated
< $8000.00) THEN
        Bonus = Income-Generated * 10%
ELSE
        Bonus = Income-Generated * 3%
ENDIF
ENDIF
ENDIF
PRINT "Bonus", Bonus
```

## Exercise 6

Using the IF-THEN and IF-THEN-ELSE construct write instructions for the following problems.

**1** Write an algorithm to read the number of days a person has been using a demo and display the message "Time Up" if the number of days exceeds 12.

**2** A video club rents videos for three days. Write an algorithm to read the date borrowed and the present date; calculate the number of days borrowed. If the number of days borrowed exceeds three days compute the number of days overdue and the overdue charge. Use a rate of $1.50 for every day overdue or part thereof.

**3** Read the weather; if the weather is sunny output 'Good day for the beach'.

**4** Read the present date, appointment date, time, place and contact name. If the appointment date is equal to the present date, display the appointment information appropriately labelled.

**5** Read N; if N is greater than 100 then subtract 50 from N, otherwise multiply N by 3.

**6** A club plays cricket only on Sundays and only if it is not raining. Read the day and the weather and output 'Game on' if the weather is good and the day is Sunday, or 'Play suspended' if it is Sunday and it is raining.

**7** Write an algorithm to read the name of the student and the value of the student's mark. Print the name of the student and the appropriate grade based on the following grading scheme.

80 or more A

Less than 80 but more than or equal to 65 B

Less than 65 but more than or equal to 50 C

Less than 50 but more than or equal to 35 D

Less than 35 F

**8** Write an algorithm which reads three values, for $a$, $b$ and $c$, and prints the roots of the quadratic equation $ax^2 + bx + c = 0$. The roots are given by $\frac{-b+\sqrt{b^2-4ac}}{2a}$ and $\frac{-b-\sqrt{b^2-4ac}}{2a}$ provided that $b - 4ac < 0$ and $a <> 0$.

**9** Write an algorithm to read the withdrawal amount from a savings account. Determine if there are sufficient funds in the account, and whether the daily withdrawal limit has been exceeded. Output, appropriately labelled, 'Not enough funds' and 'daily withdrawal limit exceeded'.

**10** Read the height in inches and weight in pounds of an individual, and compute and print their BMI (body mass index). BMI = ((weight/height)/height) * 703. If the BMI is less than 18.5, output 'You are underweight'; if the BMI is between 18.6 and 24.9, output 'Your weight is normal'; if the BMI is between 25 and 29.9, output 'You are overweight'; if the BMI is greater than 30, output 'Your health is at risk, you are in the obese category'.

## Repeat statements/looping/counting/iterations

It is often necessary to repeat certain parts of a program a number of times. One way of doing this would be to write that part of the program as many times as needed. This is impractical, however, as it would make the program lengthy. In addition, in some cases the number of times the section of code needs to be repeated is not known beforehand.

Two of the methods used to repeat sections of instructions/codes are the FOR construct and the WHILE construct.

You need to keep track of how many times the instructions are repeated. Counting or **iteration** involves increasing the value of a counter variable by a fixed number (this can be any value, such as 1, 2, 5, etc.) every time the instructions are repeated. This counter can be part of a condition for stopping the instructions from repeating when the value of the counter becomes equal to a certain value.

### *Counting*

Syntax:

<Counter variable> = <Counter variable> + 1

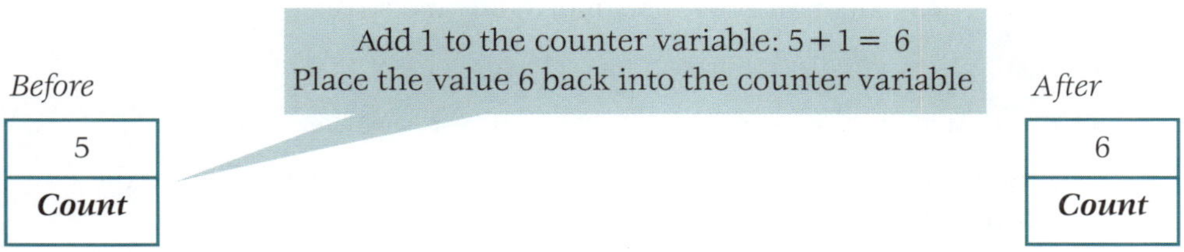


This example simply states that 1 is added to the value of the counter variable and the result is placed back into the counter variable. The counter variable must be initialised before the instructions are carried out. It is usually set to 0; this is often, but not always, the case. The choice of name for the counter variable can reflect what is being counted: in the case below, NumofCars for the number of cars.

### Example 16

*A car rental firm leases its cars; read a car registration number and count the car. Print the number of cars.*

(a)

```
PRINT "Enter a car number"
Counter = 0
READ Car number
Counter = Counter + 1
PRINT Counter
```

(b)

```
PRINT "Enter a car number"
NumofCars = 0
READ Car number
NumofCars = NumofCars + 1
PRINT NumofCars
```

In these two examples the variable name 'Counter' and the variable name 'NumofCars' are used to keep track of the number of cars where 'Car Number' is the car's registration number.

It may become necessary to keep track of more than one item. In this case two counter variables are needed.

> *Note:* You can use any abbreviation or word as a variable name to convey the meaning of what is being stored.

### Example 17

*A car rental firm leases its cars; read the car registration number and count the car. If the car is a station wagon also count the number of station wagons. Print the number of cars and the number of station wagons.*

```
PRINT "Enter a Car Registration Number and Car Type"
NumofCars = 0
NumStationWagon = 0
READ Car Number, Car Type
IF Car Type = "Station Wagon" THEN
        NumStationWagon = NumStationWagon + 1
ENDIF
NumofCars = NumofCars + 1
PRINT "Number of Cars", NumofCars
PRINT "Number of Station Wagons", NumStationWagon
```

## Cumulative totals

It often becomes necessary to keep adding values to a current total to get a new total. For example, you may want to keep track of the total runs made by various batsmen on a cricket team:

batsman 1: **23**; batsman 2: **67**; batsman 3: **90**, and so on.

Syntax:

<Cumulative Total> = <Cumulative Total> + <Variable>

It is important to initialise the Cumulative Total variable to 0 before the values are added.

### Example 18

*A car rental firm leases its cars; read the number of cars leased in one day and add it to the numbers of cars leased. Print the total number of cars leased.*

```
PRINT "Enter the number of cars leased in one day"
TotalCars = 0
READ CarsLeased
TotalCars = TotalCars + CarsLeased
PRINT "Total Number of Cars Leased:", TotalCars
```

## Loops

When a group of statements/instructions are repeated it is called a loop. There are two types of loops.

- A **finite loop** is where the number of times a repetition is to be made is known.
- An **indefinite loop** is where the instructions are repeated an unspecified number of times.
  Iteration is repeating a set of instructions over and over. One execution of a set of statements in a loop is called an **iterate**.
  A sentinel or terminal value is required to cause the program to exit the loop. A **sentinel value** is a lookout value such that if the data being entered ever becomes equal to the sentinel value, the computer exits the loop. The sentinel value must not be one of the values in the list of data to be processed. Either the user can input this value, or the computer can be programmed so that a certain condition can be met, triggering the end of the loop.

For example, if a number of student ages in a class is to be read and the number of students is not known, a particular value can be entered to indicate the end of the list. This value could be 0 or 199 since none of the students in the class would have an age of 0 or 199. These values are sentinel/terminal values since they indicate the end of the list.

## The FOR construct

In this construct the loop is controlled by a counter which increases each time the set of instructions is executed. This construct is used when the number of times a set of instructions has to be repeated is known.

Syntax:

FOR < Variable > = < Beginning value > TO < Ending value > DO

    < Action to be repeated >

ENDFOR

or

FOR < Variable > = < Beginning value > TO < Ending value > STEP < incremental value > DO

    < Action to be repeated >

ENDFOR

Example:

FOR Counter = 1 TO 4 DO

    < Action to be repeated >

ENDFOR

> *Note:* the variable in the FOR construct is a counter variable which keeps track of the number of times the loop is executed.

When this statement is executed, the counter variable is initially set to the beginning value, in this case, 1. After the execution of the instructions between the FOR and the ENDFOR, the counter variable is increased by 1. The instructions are repeated and the counter variable increases until it becomes equal to the Ending value, in this case, 4. So the instructions are repeated four times.

### Example 19

*A car rental firm leases 4 cars in one day. Read the number of days for lease of each car and calculate the total rent paid to the firm if a car is leased for $250.00. Print the total rent paid to the rental firm.*

```
Total Rent = 0
FOR Counter = 1 TO 4 DO
      PRINT "Enter the number for days for
        lease"
      READ NoofDays
      Rent = NoofDays * $250.00
      Total Rent = Total Rent + Rent
ENDFOR
PRINT "Total rent paid to firm", Total Rent
```

The STEP clause allows you to increase the counter by the increment value every time the instructions are repeated, until it becomes equal to or exceeds the ending value. It is often used when we want to print tables.

### Example 20

*Print a table to find the square and cube of numbers 1 to 10.*

- In this case Number becomes set to the initial value 1.
- The first time through the loop, Square becomes equal to Number * Number which is 1 * 1 and Cube becomes equal to Number * Number * Number which is 1 * 1 * 1.
- Then the Number, Square and Cube are printed.

```
Print "Number", "Square", "Cube"
FOR Number = 1 TO 10 DO
      Square = Number * Number
      Cube = Number * Number * Number
      Print Number, Square, Cube
ENDFOR
```

- The second time through the loop, Number becomes set to 2 and the Square and Cube are calculated and printed.
- This continues until Number becomes equal to the ending value, which is 10.

### Example 21

*Print a table to find the square and cube of all even numbers between 2 and 20 inclusive.*

```
Print "Number", "Square", "Cube"
FOR Number = 2 TO 20 STEP 2 DO
        Square = Number * Number
        Cube = Number * Number * Number
        Print Number, Square, Cube
ENDFOR
```

- In this case Number becomes set to the initial value 2.
- The first time through the loop Square becomes equal to Number * Number which is 2 * 2 and Cube becomes equal to Number * Number * Number which is 2 * 2 * 2.
- Then the Number, Square and Cube are printed.
- The second time through the loop Number becomes set to 4 as the STEP clause increases the value of the Number by 2 every time it goes through the loop. The Square and Cube are calculated and printed.
- This continues until Number becomes equal to the ending value, which is 20.

### Example 22

*Calculate the sum of all the odd numbers between 1 and 20. Print the total.*

The statements that make up the body of the FOR loop can consist of other constructs such as the IF-THEN, and IF-THEN-ELSE constructs.

```
Sum = 0
FOR Oddnumber = 1 TO 20 STEP 2 DO
        Sum = Sum + Oddnumber
ENDFOR
PRINT Sum
```

### Example 23

*A company gives out bonuses based on the amount of income generated by their sales representatives per month. Once the income generated is greater than or equal to $10,000.00 a bonus of 20% is given. If the income generated is greater than or equal to $8000.00 but less than $10,000.00 a bonus of 15% is given. If the income generated is greater than or equal to $5000.00 but less than $8000.00 a bonus of 10% is given. If the income generated is less than $5000.00 then a 3% bonus is given to the employee. Write an algorithm to read 10 employees' numbers, their income generated, and determine the bonuses of 10 employees. Print the employee number, income generated and the bonus earned by the employee.*

```
Print "EMPLOYEE NUMBER", "INCOME GENERATED", "BONUS"
FOR NumEmployees = 1 TO 10 DO
        PRINT "Enter Employee Number, Income- Generated"
        READ Employee Number, Income-Generated
        IF (Income-Generated >= $10,000.00) THEN
                Bonus = Income-Generated * 20%
        ELSE
        IF (Income-Generated >= $8000.00) AND (Income-
            Generated < $10,000.00) THEN
                Bonus = Income-Generated * 15%
        ELSE
        IF (Income-Generated >= $5000.00) AND (Income-
            Generated < $8000.00) THEN
                Bonus = Income-Generated * 10%
        ELSE
                Bonus = Income-Generated * 3%
        ENDIF
        ENDIF
        ENDIF
        PRINT Employee Number, Income-Generated, Bonus
ENDFOR
```

The FOR loop can be used to find the maximum and minimum values in a set of numbers.

### Example 24

*Write an algorithm to read 25 numbers and print the lowest.*

You need to choose an initial value for Lowest so that any number entered would be lower than that value. You cannot choose 0 (zero) as an initial value for Lowest as of the 25 numbers entered it may not be the lowest value. The variable 'Count' is chosen as the variable counter to keep track of the number of times the instructions are executed.

```
Lowest = 999999
FOR Count = 1 TO 25 DO
        PRINT "Enter a number"
        READ Number
        IF Number < Lowest THEN
        Lowest = Number
        ENDIF
ENDFOR
PRINT "The lowest number entered is:", Lowest
```

## Exercise 7

Using the FOR construct write instructions for each of the following problems.

1. Write a program that reads the result of 10 games played by a team and finds the percentage of games won by the team. Output the percentage games won.
2. Write an algorithm to enter 10 numbers and output the highest and lowest numbers appropriately labelled.
3. Write an algorithm which finds the total of the numbers 10 to 25 and print the total.
4. Write an algorithm to compute the following expression:

   $Y1 = 2(2-x^2)$ and $Y2 = 2-(2-x^2)$ using values −4 to +4 for the value of $x$. Print $x$, Y1 and Y2.
5. An airline does not charge for babies 2 years and under; it charges half price for children 2 to 12 years and the full price for persons above 12 years. Read the airfare and the age of the person; calculate and print the total amount paid by a family of five.
6. A school has a house system implemented. Points are awarded to a house based on the performance of its members: 1st place – 4 points, 2nd place – 3 points, 3rd place – 2 points, 4th place – 1 point and last place – no points awarded. For 10 members of the Aripo house read the place they came in the events; calculate and print the total awarded to the house.
7. Print a five-times multiplication table for numbers 1 through 20.
8. Write an algorithm to input an integer N. Find and output the value generated when 2 is raised to the power N, where N is between 0 and 10.
9. Write an algorithm to input a country and exchange rate of the country's currency against the US dollar. Output a table showing the amount of US dollars and the equivalent amount of the country's currency, for 1 to 20 US dollars.
10. Write an algorithm to output the sum of all the even numbers in the range 2 to 40.
11. Write a program that accepts a positive integer and prints all numbers from the given number down to 1 inclusive.

## The WHILE construct

In the WHILE construct the computer executes a set of statements/instructions repeatedly for as long as a given condition is true. When you do not know beforehand how many times statements within a loop are to be repeated, use the WHILE construct.

- In the WHILE construct the condition is tested; if it is true the instructions within the WHILE and ENDWHILE are executed until the condition becomes false and the loop is then exited.
- Statements/instructions before the WHILE construct are carried out once. The while loop is executed until the condition becomes false, which forces the loop to stop. Then the statements after the ENDWHILE are carried out once.
- If, after carrying out the instructions before the loop, the condition in the WHILE loop is tested and is false, the computer skips the instructions within the WHILE loop and continues with the statements after the ENDWHILE.

- The trigger that causes the loop to stop is a value that is entered for the input data. This value is read in within the loop and it is called a **dummy value**, a **terminating value** or sentinel value. It must not be one of the values in the list of data to be processed. For example, when calculating the average age of students in a class, a dummy value could be 999, since no one in the class will be 999 years old. This value signals the end of the data to be entered.
  Syntax:
  WHILE <Condition> DO
  <Action to be taken if condition is true>
  ENDWHILE

## Example 25

*Write an algorithm to enter the age and count the number of students in a class. Calculate the average age of the group of students if the data is terminated by the value 999. Print the number of students in the class and the average age of the students.*

```
PRINT "Enter the student's age"
READ Age
Count = 0
WHILE Age <> 999 DO
        Total = Total + Age
        Count = Count + 1
        PRINT "Enter the student's age"
        READ Age
ENDWHILE
Average = Total/Count
PRINT "Number of students:", Count
PRINT "Average ages of students:", Average
```

The statements that make up the body of the WHILE loop can consist of other constructs such as the IF-THEN, and IF-THEN-ELSE constructs.

## Example 26

*Write an algorithm to read a set of numbers terminated by 0; print the number of positive and the number of negative numbers.*

```
Negative = 0
Positive = 0
PRINT "Enter a number"
READ Number
WHILE Number <> 0 DO
        IF Number > 0 THEN
                Positive = Positive + 1
        ELSE
                Negative = Negative + 1
        ENDIF
        PRINT "Enter a number"
        READ Number
ENDWHILE
PRINT "Number of Negative Numbers", Negative
PRINT "Number of Positive Numbers", Positive
```

The WHILE loop can be used to find the maximum and minimum values in a series of numbers.

> *Note:* the highest number is initialised to 0 so that any number entered is higher than that value. Each number entered must be checked against the previous one.

## Example 27

*Write an algorithm to read a set of numbers terminated by 0 and print the highest number.*

```
Highest = 0
PRINT "Enter a number"
READ Number
WHILE Number <> 0 DO
        IF Number > Highest THEN
                Highest = Number
        ENDIF
        PRINT "Enter a number"
        READ Number
ENDWHILE
PRINT "The highest number entered is:", Highest
```

## Exercise 8

Using the WHILE construct write instructions for each of the following problems.

1 Persons working for an income between $20,000 and $30,000 dollars per annum pay an income tax of $12,000 per annum. Persons working for an income of between $30,000 and $40,000 per annum pay an income tax of $15,000 per annum. Read the employee number and income, and calculate the total tax paid by employees. Data is terminated by employee number 000.

2 Enter the marks of students terminated by 999. Find and print the average and the highest mark.

3 A resident person leaving their country is required to pay a departure tax of $100.00. However, if the person is a visitor to the country, an additional $20.00 must be paid. Read in the passenger number, terminated by 0, and whether the passenger is a visitor or resident. Write an algorithm to calculate the total amount of tax collected for the day.

4 A company gives out bonuses based on the amount of income generated by their sales representatives per month. Once the income is greater than $5000.00, a bonus of 10% of the generated income is added to the sales representative's salary of $4000.00. Write an algorithm to input the sales representative's number and income generated; calculate the bonus, and salary plus bonus. Data is terminated by entering the value 000 for the sales representative number.

5 Write an algorithm to find and print the mean of a list of positive integers. The number of integers is not known in advance. The procedure is terminated by the value 0.

6 A car rental firm leases its cars for $250.00 per day. The manager gives a discount based on the number of days that the car is rented. If the rental period is greater than or equal to 7 days then a 25% discount is given. Read a car number and the rental period, and calculate the total amount earned by the car rental firm after discounts, if the number of cars rented is not known in advance. The process is terminated by car number 0.

7 A supermarket is keeping track of the amount in stock of an item. Write an algorithm to keep track of how many of the items remain at the end of the day if the initial quantity was 210. Input the quantity bought at each purchase; calculate the total amount sold and the quantity remaining, if the number of sales and quantity purchased is not known in advance. Terminate the data by entering 0 for quantity.

8 Write an algorithm to accept a list of positive integers. Each sub-list of non-zero integers is terminated by a zero. Each time a zero is read, output the sum of the non-zero integers. The data is terminated by –1. Indicate the number of non-zero integers and the number of sub-lists.

9 Write an algorithm to input integers until a sentinel value of 0 is entered; print the sum of all the positive numbers entered and the sum of all negative numbers entered. The number of positives and negatives must also be printed.

10 Write an algorithm to accept a number of integers until a sentinel value of 0 is reached. The algorithm must print each pair of consecutive numbers where the first number is larger than the second. For example: if the inputs are 1, 3, 2, 4, 5, 2, –1, 0 and 0, the output would be "3, 2" and "5, 2" and "2, –1".

## Step 4 – writing a computer program corresponding to the algorithm

After developing an algorithm or method of solving the problem, the next step is to write a computer program corresponding to the algorithm, using programming language. Converting the algorithm to the programming language requires the use of the specific syntax of that programming language.

After the program is written it must be tested and debugged. Algorithms can also be tested and debugged.

# Step 5 – Testing and debugging the program

Once an algorithm or a program is developed or written, the next stage is to check that the algorithm or program is doing what it was designed to do, and is doing so correctly.

There are two types of testing:

- Manual testing/dry running
- Computer testing.

## Manual testing/dry running

**Tracing** is a technique that allows the user to detect any **logic errors** in the program or algorithm. Also called **dry-running** or **desk-checking**, tracing involves executing the program *manually* by using input values for variables and recording what takes place after each instruction is executed.

A **trace table** is a table completed upon manual execution of an algorithm or program to determine what the program is doing. The first action when creating a trace table is to write down all the variables found in the algorithm as headings, as well as the heading 'OUTPUT' to represent what is printed.

### Example 28

*What is printed by the following algorithms?*

(a)

```
Count = 0
WHILE Count < = 10 DO
        Count = Count + 2
        PRINT Count
ENDWHILE
```

| Count | OUTPUT | |
|---|---|---|
| 0 | | Count is set as 0; Count < 10 |
| 2 | 2 | 2 is added to Count and 2 is printed; Count < 10 |
| 4 | 4 | 2 is added to Count and 4 is printed; Count < 10 |
| 6 | 6 | 2 is added to Count and 6 is printed; Count < 10 |
| 8 | 8 | 2 is added to Count and 8 is printed; Count < 10 |
| 10 | 10 | 2 is added to Count and 10 is printed; Count not less than 10 so the loop is exited. |

(b)

```
FOR Kg = 1 TO 5 DO
        Lb = Kg * 2.2
        PRINT Kg, Lb
ENDFOR
```

| Kg | Lb | OUTPUT |
|---|---|---|
| 1 | 2.2 | 1, 2.2 |
| 2 | 4.4 | 2, 4.4 |
| 3 | 6.6 | 3, 6.6 |
| 4 | 8.8 | 4, 8.8 |
| 5 | 11 | 5, 11 |

(c)

```
A = 3
B = 5
C = 6
D = B * A
E = C + B
IF E > D THEN
        A = E
ELSE
        A = D
ENDIF
PRINT A, B, C, D, E
```

| A | B | C | D | E | OUTPUT |
|---|---|---|---|---|---|
| 3 | 5 | 6 | 15 | 11 | |
| 15 | | | | | 15, 5, 6, 15, 11 |

At the end of the program the values for B, C, D and E do not change.



## Exercise 9

**1** What is printed by the following?

```
R = 5
S = 6
IF S > 5 THEN
        T = S * R
ELSE
        T = S/R
ENDIF
PRINT T
```

**2** What is printed by the following?

```
S = 25
N = 1
WHILE N < 12 DO
        S = S – N
        PRINT S
        N = N + 2
ENDWHILE
```

**3** Using numbers 5, 20, 25, 30, –1 for Num and 2, 4, 4, 3 for Rate respectively, what is printed by the following algorithm?

```
READ Num
WHILE Num >= 0 DO
        READ Rate
        Value = Num *
          Rate/100
        PRINT Rate,
          Num, Value
        READ Num
ENDWHILE
```

**4** What is printed by the following algorithm if N = 4?

```
READ N
IF N < 3 THEN
        G = 1
        F = 2
ELSE
        F = 1
        G = 2
ENDIF
FOR J = 1 TO N DO
        H = F + G
        F = G
        G = H
        PRINT H
ENDFOR
```

**5** What is printed by the algorithm?

```
For X = 1 to 6 DO
        R = X
        WHILE R >= 1 DO
              PRINT R
              R = R – 1
ENDWHILE
ENDFOR
```

**6** What is printed by the following algorithm if Num is 10?

```
READ Num
FOR Count = Num to 1
   STEP –2 DO
        Sum = Count +
        Num
        PRINT Sum
ENDFOR
```

**7** What is printed by the following algorithm if B = 5 and C = 4?

```
READ B, C
A = B
B = C
C = A
D = B + C
E = E * C
F = D – B
A = D
B = E
C = F
PRINT A, B, C, D, E, F
```

**8** What is printed by the following algorithm?

```
X = 1
WHILE X <= 8 DO
        Y = 2X + (X *
          X) – 4
        PRINT Y
        X = X + 2
ENDWHILE
```

**9** What is printed by the following algorithm?

```
Sum = 0
N = 25
WHILE N < 40 DO
        Sum = Sum + N
        PRINT N, Sum
        N = N + 4
ENDWHILE
```

## Exercise 9

10 What is printed by the following algorithm?

```
FOR X = 1 TO 2 DO
    FOR Y = 1 to
        10 DO
      PRINT Y
    ENDFOR
```

11 What is printed by the following algorithm?

```
R = 1
S = 4
WHILE R <> S DO
  READ Num1, Num2
  IF Num1 > Num2 THEN
  Print Num2, Num1
  ELSE
  Print Num1, Num2
  ENDIF
  READ Num1, Num2
  R = R + 1
ENDWHILE
```

## Computer testing

Computer testing involves running the program using test data to discover any errors in the program. There are three types of errors: syntax, logic and runtime errors.

- **Syntax error** is an error in the grammar of the programming language.
- **Logic error** is an error in reasoning, such as the incorrect sequencing of instructions, and flawed comparisons and selection statements.
  One of these errors within a program is known as a **bug**. The process of finding and correcting these errors is called **debugging**. Tracing is an invaluable tool used in debugging a program or algorithm.
  In the process of debugging a program or algorithm, test data is used to verify that the program is doing what it is supposed to. The program should be tested using suitable test data. If you test using only meaningful data within a well-defined range, you would be assuming that only valid data will be used in the program. The data used must be chosen to deal with all eventualities and should include extreme data – data outside the range as well as data within the range.
  For example:

```
Highest = 0
PRINT "Enter a number"
READ Number
WHILE Number <> 0 DO
        IF Number > Highest THEN
        Highest = Number
        ENDIF
        PRINT "Enter a number"
        READ Number
ENDWHILE
PRINT "The highest number entered is:", Highest
```

  Testing this program with data 2, 3, 0, 8, 1 would cause 3 to be printed as the highest number: once 0 is entered, the program would stop and you would not be able to enter any numbers after entering 0.
  However, testing this program with –2, –8, –14, –1, 0 would cause –1 to be printed.
- **Runtime errors** are errors that occur after the program has been tested and debugged; they occur during the execution or running of the program. One of the reasons these errors can occur is if the program is stuck in an infinite loop. Since some computers set limits for how long your program is allowed to run, a runtime error may occur if the loop continues up to the time limit allowed.

During the computer testing process the program is executed or run. This involves converting from the programming language to the language the computer understands, namely machine language or machine code.

The program written in the specific programming language is known as the **source code**. This source code is translated into **object code** by a compiler or an interpreter. Object code can be the same as or similar to machine or executable code.

The execution of a program occurs in two distinct steps, as follows.

### *In the case of an interpreter*

The interpreter translates the source code to machine code; the machine code is executed (Figure 8.2).

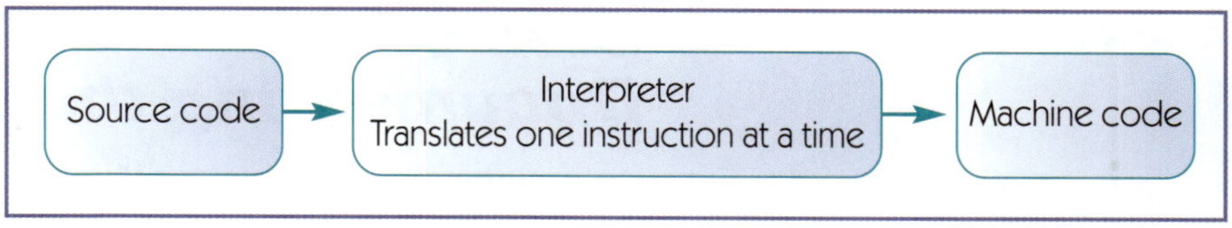


*Figure 8.2*
*An interpreter*

An interpreter translates and executes one instruction at a time as it is encountered. The machine codes are not saved after execution.

#### *Advantages*

- It translates one instruction at a time, therefore it uses a minimum amount of the computer's memory.
- It is also helpful in the debugging process, as the interpreter can relate error messages to the instruction being executed.

#### *Disadvantage*

The interpreter takes longer to run a program as time is spent interpreting the source code every time the program needs to be run.

### *In the case of a compiler*

A compiler translates the entire program (source code) to machine code, then the code is executed. The translated codes are known as object codes and are saved as a file on disk. The object code (machine code) stored on disk has an EXE file name extension. It is then loaded or linked (stored in memory) and executed (Figure 8.3). The code to be executed by the computer (the one stored in the computer's memory) is called executable code and is still also known as machine code. Unlike the translator, the compiler flags all the errors in the program by creating a list of errors, hence the programmer must return to the source code and fix the errors.

*Figure 8.3*
*A compiler*

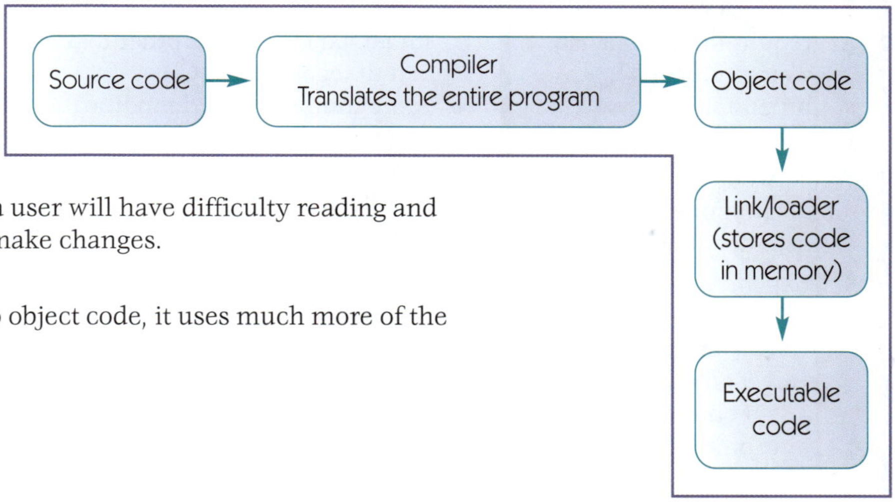


#### *Advantages*

- It can be executed faster than when using an interpreter, as the object codes are saved and can be run at any time.
- Object codes are harder for a user to change than the source code. The object code is machine language and therefore a user will have difficulty reading and interpreting the code in order to make changes.

#### *Disadvantage*

As the entire program is translated to object code, it uses much more of the computer's memory.

# Step 6 – Documenting the program

Documentation is a written explanation of how the program works and how to use it. There are two types of documentation; user documentation and technical documentation.

## User documentation/user guides

This documentation is written to explain to the user how to use the program. It is written in plain English and not in the technical programming language of technical documentation. It includes:

- Hardware requirements
- How to install the program
- How to run the program
- How to enter data
- What the output looks like
- How to use any menus
- Special features of the program
- Error messages and advice on how to correct them (troubleshoot any errors).

## Technical documentation

This documentation is for use by the programmer. It includes information on the program itself, i.e. technical aspects of how it works. Some of the reasons for technical documentation include:

- The programmer needs to understand what was written a few weeks or even months before, when writing a long program.
- Extremely large programs are written in teams, where certain teams write particular sections of the program code. Each team needs to understand what the other teams have written so that the whole thing can fit together.
- A program may need modification in time to come. It may need to be revised to fit a new situation, or corrected for a logic error that may have shown up after using extreme data. On many occasions these modifications are not done by the original programmer; the new programmer will need to be able to read and understand the written program.

Technical documentation includes:

- The problem that the program is intended to solve (purpose of the program)
- The algorithm
- The program code/listing with its internal documentation (see below)
- Test data and results produced by the program
- Data and file structures
- Structure and flow diagrams which show the relationships between the program modules.

Internal documentation within the program code/listing includes:

- Indentation and spacing (these assist in the readability of the program, so that sections of code can be easily identified)
- Explanatory remarks (comments)
- Suitable variable names (which can be associated with what is being stored so that further explanation is not needed).

### Exercise 10

1. A programmer is asked to modify a program that has been in use by a company for a few years. However, there is no technical documentation for the program. List some of the problems that might result from this.
2. List FOUR of the requirements of a good user guide for a program.
3. Explain the difference between technical documentation and user documentation.
4. Explain the difference between an interpreter and a compiler. Discuss why a programmer might choose to use an interpreter rather than a compiler.
5. What does it mean to debug a program?
6. List the THREE types of programming errors and explain what they are.

# Summary

1 An algorithm is a sequence of instructions which if followed produces a solution to a given problem.

2 A pseudocode is an algorithm that models or resembles real programming language syntax.

3 A computer program is a series of coded instructions for the computer to obey in order to solve a problem.

4 Computer programs are written using specific rules and statements of the particular computer language of the program, known as syntax.

5 There are two levels of programming languages, low level and high level. High level languages are machine independent; they are not specifically designed for any one brand of computer. Low level languages are machine dependent and are designed for only one type of computer.

6 Programs written in high level languages must be compiled or translated before they are executed by the computer.

7 There are five generations of computer programming languages.

8 Program development is made up of six basic steps: defining the problem; analysing the problem; developing an algorithm/method of solving the problem; writing a computer program corresponding to the algorithm; testing and debugging the program; documenting the program.

9 Programming instructions can be divided into three main types: Input and Storage instructions, Processing instructions and Output instructions.

10 A command is a word that instructs the computer what must be done to accomplish a specific task.

11 A construct is a group of instructions that work together with commands to accomplish a specific task.

12 Data that does not change but remains the same during the execution of the program is called a constant; if it changes during the execution of the program it is called variable.

13 When you know how many times statements within a loop are to be repeated, the FOR construct is used.

14 In the WHILE construct, the computer executes a set of statements/instructions repeatedly for as long as a given condition is true. When you do not know beforehand how many times statements within a loop are to be repeated, the WHILE construct is used.

15 Tracing is a technique that allows the user to detect any logic errors in the program or algorithm.

16 A syntax error is an error in the grammar of the programming language.

17 A logic error is an error in reasoning, such as the incorrect sequencing of instructions and flawed comparisons and selection statements.

18 Runtime errors occur during the execution or running of a program, after the program has been tested and debugged.

19 A program written in a specific programming language is known as source code. This source code is translated into machine language with the use of a compiler or an interpreter.

20 Documentation written to explain to the user how to use a program is known as user documentation/user guide.

21 Documentation for use by a programmer is known as technical documentation.

# 9 System security and computer crimes

## OBJECTIVES

At the end of this chapter you will be able to:

- Define 'data integrity'
- List some of the ways data could lose integrity
- Define 'data security'
- Describe different methods of securing data
- Explain 'data encryption'
- Define 'computer virus'
- Describe different types of computer virus
- List ways computer viruses are spread
- List ways to prevent computer systems from getting a virus
- Explain 'data privacy'
- List some rules of the UK Data Protection Act of 1998 concerning the storage of personal data
- Explain the term 'computer surveillance'
- Define 'spyware'
- Explain what a computer crime is
- Define 'software piracy'
- Describe different types of software piracy
- Define 'hacking' and list some reasons for hacking
- Explain what Internet fraud is
- Describe some different types of Internet fraud
- Explain the term 'industrial espionage'

The increasing use of computers, along with the expansion of the Internet and the many services available on it, have resulted in new types of crimes and new methods of perpetrating old crimes. In an effort to reduce the levels of computer crimes, governments, companies and organisations continuously have to find new methods of dealing with system security. System security concerns the protection of hardware, software and data.

## Data integrity and security

The area of data integrity and data security is becoming more and more important, due to the increased use of computers and the expansion of the Internet and world wide web applications. **Data integrity** concerns the consistency, accuracy and reliability of data. Data is said to have integrity if it is accurate and complete when it enters a system and does not become inaccurate after further processing. The goal of integrity is to protect against data becoming corrupted – being changed, deleted or substituted without authorisation. Data integrity can be compromised in a number of ways:

- Human error (e.g. inaccurate data entry, accidental deletion, accidental changing of data)
- Natural disasters such as fires, floods and earthquakes
- Worms and viruses
- Hardware malfunctions
- Fraud
- Malicious deletion or changing of data.

**Data security** concerns protecting data from unauthorised access and is one of the methods used to ensure data integrity. Data can be secured using both physical and software safeguards.

### Physical data security

Physical safeguards deal with the protection of hardware and software from accidental or malicious damage, destruction or theft. Depending on the sensitivity of the data stored, a combination of the following methods may be used.

1 *Only allowing authorised personnel access to computer facilities*: The goal is to limit physical contact with the computer system. This is necessary to eliminate equipment theft, media theft, console or network access and physical destruction of media or equipment. One or a combination of the following methods may enforce this:
   - Locks
   - Security guards
   - Burglar alarms
   - Monitoring system using video cameras
   - Biometric scans
   - Electronic doors that can only be opened using passwords or magnetic cards.

2 *Outer structural security*: This entails reinforcements to doors, windows, walls and roofs to make the building where data is stored more secure. It makes no sense installing expensive locks on fragile doors and windows; for this reason structural security needs to look at many interlinked factors to ensure maximum physical protection.
3 *Storing data in a fireproof safe or cabinet*: This may protect data even when a fire destroys most of a room or building.
4 *Storing data in another building or in another location*: This is physical data backup, which maintains data security in the event of natural disasters (earthquakes, floods), fire, theft of equipment and media, or unauthorised or accidental changing of data in the main system.
5 *Distributing work to a number of employees instead of just one*: In this way no one employee has access to all the data.
6 If data storage is more long-term it is known as **archiving**, a form of physical data backup involving the removal of inactive files from the computer. These files are no longer in use or have not been accessed for a long time, but may yet be needed at some future date. They are stored in devices such as magnetic tape, microfiche or CD-R and can be retrieved if necessary.

## Software-based data security

Software safeguards are another equally important method of protecting data. Data will never be fully secure unless both the physical safeguards and software safeguards are in place.

Some of the most common software safeguards are:

1 *Passwords for the system*: A password is a combination of characters used to control access to computers. In a password system a user has to enter a password or PIN (Personal Identification Number) to gain access to the computer system.
2 *Passwords for individual files or folders*: Multiple levels of passwords can provide entry to different levels of information in a database or other computer storage system. For example, in a company, everyone may have a password to gain access to the company's network. However, not everyone may be permitted to access all the different data stored on the network. This is because some files or folders may contain sensitive or highly confidential information and are not available to everyone. To gain access to some of these files or folders another password may be needed. Other levels of passwords may also be included depending on the sensitivity of the data.
3 *Audit trails or access logs*: Security software programs can audit computer use by providing a comprehensive record of all the network or system activity, including who is accessing what data, when, and how often. This may be necessary if there is an initially unidentifiable breach of security, and you want to 'zero in' on the individuals who may have used the network during a specific period of time.
4 **Encryption**: This is encoding (scrambling) data during storage or transmission so that it cannot be understood by someone who does not have the **encryption key** or software to convert it back to its original form. A key is a randomly generated set of characters that is used to encrypt/decrypt data. A mathematical algorithm determines the way an encryptor (the program that encrypts the text) alters the original communication, to produce enciphered (scrambled) text. This is a very effective method of preventing unauthorised persons from stealing, reading or changing data. Consider this very simple method of encrypting, substituting another character for every character in the character set. Table 1 gives the actual code and the coded character for some characters in the character set.

*Figure 9.1 Biometric scanning*

| Actual character | Coded character | Actual character | Coded character |
|---|---|---|---|
| A | R | O | A |
| B | S | P | @ |
| C | Q | Q | + |
| D | N | R | P |
| E | L | S | H |
| F | U | T | $ |
| G | # | U | J |
| H | ! | V | M |
| I | Z | W | K |
| J | B | X | % |
| K | T | Y | ; |
| L | Space | Z | Y |
| M | C | . | F |
| N | W | Space | G |

*Table 1*
*A simple code for encrypting messages*

Using effective encryption techniques, sensitive valuable information can be protected against organised criminals, malicious hackers, or spies from other companies or countries. Encryption is used to secure data such as credit card numbers, bank account information, health information and even personal correspondence that is transmitted over the Internet. Encryption is one of the most effective methods of securing data against **electronic eavesdropping**: the tapping of a data transmission line to access data being transmitted. Two of the most popular data encryption schemes are PGP (Pretty Good Privacy) and DES (Data Encryption Standard).

Using our made-up code the encrypted message @PZMRQ;GZHGZC@AP$RW$F means 'PRIVACY IS IMPORTANT.' when decrypted.

Do you think you can write a program to encrypt and decrypt data quickly?

**5** **Firewall:** This is a program, a hardware device or a combination of both that filters the information coming in through your computer system's or network's connection to the Internet. It prevents unauthorised users from gaining access. A firewall can also perform audit and alarm functions that record all access attempts to and from a network. Two popular firewall software packages are BlackICE Defender and Zone Alarm. Firewalls can protect systems from:

- *Remote login*: This is when someone is able to connect to your computer and control it in some form, ranging from being able to view or access your files to actually running programs on your computer.
- *Spam* (electronic junk mail): By gaining access to a list of e-mail addresses, a person can send unwanted spam to thousands of users.
- *E-mail bomb*: This is when someone sends you the same e-mail hundreds of thousands of times until your e-mail system cannot accept any more messages.
- *Viruses*: More information on these below.

6 **Anti-virus software** is a special type of software used to remove or inactivate known viruses from a computer's hard disk, floppy disk or memory stick. It scans the different storage media looking for known viruses; if viruses are found they are either removed or quarantined. These programs can also scan incoming and outgoing e-mail messages to ensure they do not contain infected data. Anti-virus software should be updated via the Internet regularly. Failure to do this may render your software ineffective against new viruses which are created all the time, and which may pose serious risks to your computer system. Typical anti-virus software includes: Norton AntiVirus, McAfee Virus Scan and AVG.

### Did you know?

Did you know that the use of encryption can be traced as far back as ancient Babylonian merchants who used an intaglio? This was a piece of flat stone carved into a collage of images and writing, and was the equivalent of what today we call a 'digital signature'. Buyers knew that a particular intaglio belonged to a particular trader, since only he had the intaglio to produce that exact signature. Traders therefore used the intaglio to identify themselves when making transactions.

## More about worms and viruses

Worms and viruses are two types of programs that may cause destruction to data and software. Worms and viruses differ in the way they spread and how they function. However, many people simply refer to both by the term 'computer virus'.

A **worm** is a program that uses computer networks and security holes (weakness in a security system) to repeatedly copy itself into a computer's memory or onto a magnetic disk, until no more space is left. A copy of the worm scans the network looking for another machine that has a specific security hole, and then starts to replicate itself again. For example, a worm known as 'Code Red' replicated itself over 250 000 times in about nine hours on 19 July 2001, causing traffic on the Internet to slow down considerably.

*Figure 9.2 Anti-virus software packages*

A **virus** is a program purposefully written by someone to activate itself unknown to the victim and destroy or corrupt data. A virus must attach itself to some other program or document in order to be executed (executed here means 'started up'). Viruses are one of the main threats to a computer system and have caused many businesses to lose millions of dollars due to corrupted data, lost data and computer 'downtime' (times when your computers are unusable).

Some common types of viruses are:

- *File virus*: These are viruses that infect program files. The viruses attach themselves to executable program files and are started each time the program is run. For example, a virus may attach itself to a word processing program. Each time the word processing program is run the virus also runs.
- *E-mail virus*: This type of virus comes as either an attachment to an e-mail or as the e-mail itself. It usually spreads by automatically mailing itself to everyone on the address book of its victim. For example, in March 1999 the Melissa virus replicated itself so many times and so quickly that it forced Microsoft and a number of large companies to completely turn off their e-mail systems until the virus could be contained. The ILOVEYOU virus in the year 2000 had the same effect.
- *Trojan horses*: A Trojan horse is a computer program that places destructive code in programs such as games. When the user runs the game the hidden code runs in the background, usually unknown to the user; it erases either their entire hard disk or some programs on the disk.
- *Boot-sector virus*: The boot sector is part of the operating system; it holds a small program telling the computer how to load the rest of the operating system when the computer is started up. A boot-sector virus corrupts or replaces the instructions in the boot sector, thereby preventing the operating system from loading properly and the computer from booting or powering up.

### How viruses are spread

Viruses are usually spread by:

- Downloading infected programs and files from the Internet
- Opening infected files received through e-mails
- Booting the computer with an infected disk in the disk drive
- Using a storage medium such as a floppy disk, tape or CD that contains infected files.

### Prevention of and protection against viruses

You need to be continually aware of the possibility of viruses entering your system. Some of the signs that may indicate that your system has a virus are:

- Weird or obscene messages
- Garbled information
- Incorrect document contents
- Missing files or folders
- Your application crashes or hangs when opening documents.

To help prevent this happening:

1. Install an anti-virus software package on your computer system.
2. Do not use storage media from other computers in your computer. If you have to use them, make sure you run a virus scan first to remove any viruses.
3. Do not open any e-mail attachments that contain an executable file: these have file extensions such as .exe, .com and .vbs.
4. If you are using Microsoft applications, ensure that the Macro Virus Protection is enabled.
5. Use an operating system such as UNIX which has security features that protect computers from many of the traditional viruses.

## Data privacy

Many businesses, government bodies and other organisations hold information on individuals. Information given to these bodies is given for a specific purpose. In many cases the information is personal to the individual (e.g. their name, address, age, sex and telephone number) and can be valuable to any number of organisations, not least commercial organisations that want to approach you directly to offer a product or service. The ease with which data stored on databases can be accessed, cross-referenced and transmitted from one computer to the next in a LAN, WAN or over the Internet emphasises the need for data privacy laws. In many countries where there are no data protection laws, companies may be inclined to sell copies of their databases to other companies. The result is that personal or private information can now be used for purposes for which it was not intended.

This raises numerous questions about an individual's right to privacy. Privacy in this context refers to the right of individuals to determine what information is stored about them and how that information will be used. The privacy act of 1984 in the United States requires that all data stored about an individual must be accurate and used only for the purpose for which it was collected. The act also states that organisations must allow individuals to view whatever data is stored about them, and can request that it be amended if it is not correct.

In the United Kingdom the Data Protection Act of 1998 ensures that any organisation, company or governmental body storing information on individuals abides by the following rules:

- Data held must be relevant, adequate and not more than is required.
- Data must not be used for any purpose other than that for which it was intended.
- Data must be updated to maintain its integrity.
- Data must be protected from unauthorised access and use.
- Individuals have the right to check data held about them.
- Data must not be kept longer than necessary.
- Data must not be transferred to countries which do not have adequate data protection laws.

Many Caribbean countries have recognised the need for such legislation and are swiftly moving in the same direction as the United States and the United Kingdom. For example, the Ministry of Public Administration and Information in Trinidad & Tobago published the *Draft National Policy on Data Protection* for comment in November 2004. The data protection policy applies to all personal information collected, used or disclosed by private sector and public sector organisations in the course of commercial or government-related activity. The main points in the draft policy are:

- Organisations must seek the consent of individuals prior to collecting, using or disclosing their personal information
- Organisations must ensure that there are security safeguards to protect personal information; these must be appropriate to the sensitivity of the information
- Individuals have the right to access personal information about themselves held by an organisation and have it amended, if necessary.

## Computer surveillance

Computer surveillance can involve accessing the storage mechanism of an individual's computer, or monitoring an individual's operation of a computer, in most cases without their knowledge. Computer surveillance can be achieved by both hardware and software methods.

One hardware method of computer surveillance is **keylogging** or keystroke logging. A hardware keylogger is a device that plugs in between your keyboard and your computer. Once plugged in, all data entered via the keyboard is stored in the keylogger's memory.

The software method of computer surveillance involves the use of **spyware** This type of software, which is usually secretly installed on a computer, covertly monitors the user's actions without his or her knowledge. It can save its findings locally or transmit them to someone else. Spyware software can be categorised as surveillance spyware and advertising spyware.

Surveillance spyware includes software keyloggers, screen captures devices and Trojan horses. This type of software can be used by:

- Law enforcement and intelligence agencies to solve and/or prevent crimes
- Corporations and companies to monitor the use of their computer resources
- Criminals to acquire passwords and credit card numbers
- Private investigators hired to spy on individuals or organisations
- Government agencies to spy on citizens
- Parents to monitor their children's use of the computer.

> **Did you know?**
>
> Did you know that many companies use spyware to monitor their company resources? Employers use spyware to increase security, improve employee productivity and reduce information leaks. However, many employees and trade unions believe that the use of spyware to monitor individuals' computer use infringes on privacy rights. Employers counter by saying they have a right to protect their business from potential employee idleness, fraud and misbehaviour. Discuss this issue with classmates. In companies where spyware is being used, should the employees be informed?

Advertising spyware, also known as adware, is used to gather personal information about computer users or to show advertisements. Some advertising spyware records information such as e-mail addresses, web browsing history, online shopping habits, passwords and other personal information. Advertising spyware is usually bundled with freeware or shareware, when the unsuspecting user downloads it from the Internet. Freebies like screen savers, emoticons and clip art will sometimes have spyware hiding in them.

Spyware can be legal or illegal. For example, law enforcement officials can use spyware legally after obtaining the relevant legal permission. However, it is illegal for a person to install software on another person's computer without that person's specific permission.

## Computer crimes

A computer crime occurs when a computer is used in some way to perform an illegal activity. This could take place in a number of ways, including software piracy, hacking and Internet fraud such as telemarketing schemes, investment schemes and many others. For example, a computer crime may occur if a person in an organisation (not a hacker) makes changes to information in a computer without authorisation, for personal benefit or for malicious reasons. Many computer crimes are committed by disgruntled employees who sometimes want to get even with their employer.

### Software piracy

Software piracy is the unauthorised copying, use or selling of software that is copyrighted. Some of the main types of software piracy are:

- *Licensed-user duplication for unlicensed users*: If someone buys a new computer from a reputable company, within the overall price of the computer they usually also pay for copyrighted software present on that specific machine. A private purchaser of a computer is therefore simultaneously buying a single-user licence for the software on that machine. Licensed-user piracy occurs when the user make copies of the machine's software and distributes or sells it to other individuals or companies.
  Another common example of this is if a company purchases a software package for use on say 20 machines, but ends up installing the software in more than 20 machines. All of the computers in excess of the 20 the licence was granted for are therefore using pirated software, since the licence was a limited one.
- *Pre-installed software*: Software piracy can also occur when, for example, a computer store uses a copy of a software package that was licensed for use on one computer, but installs it in many computers.
- *Internet piracy*: Some web sites allow individuals to download unauthorised copies of software.
- *Counterfeiting*: This occurs when individuals or companies make illegal copies of software and package it to look like the original packaging from the manufacturer.

You may wonder what is wrong with software piracy. The main answer is that it is an infringement of ownership rights. It is the theft of the work and effort of another individual or company. The owner therefore loses potential revenue as a result of piracy, just as if someone were to steal your hard-earned money by picking your pocket on the street. Pirated software is therefore simply theft, and using it is morally wrong. Some of the other reasons why pirated software should not be used are:

- Pirated software may not contain all the elements and documentation of the program, causing problems for the user.
- Pirated software may not have the upgrade options often provided as an add-on (e.g. with an encryption key) in legitimate software.
- Pirated software may have viruses that can be harmful to your hard drive or network.
- Pirated software is simply illegal – most countries have laws against software piracy; individuals convicted of this crime can pay hefty fines or even be jailed.

All software is copyright – the person or company who wrote it always retains the right to decide whether it can be copied or not. But it is not always illegal to copy and distribute such software.

For example, **public domain** software can be copied as many times as you like. Software is in the public domain when it is put on web sites for free distribution, with the consent of the copyright owner. One popular public domain program is Adobe Reader, available from www.adobe.com.

There is also 'freeware' software available at specialist web sites such as www.download.com. Once again, this software is copyright, but you are nevertheless allowed to copy it as many times as you like for personal use. In this case the owners distribute it for free out of a spirit of co-operation, or perhaps to promote themselves as a software writer.

*Figure 9.3 As technology makes advances some criminals try to take advantage of it in the most invasive way – by hacking.*

### *Hacking*

Hacking is the unauthorised accessing of a computer system; the individual who does this is referred to as a **hacker**. Hackers are usually excellent computer programmers. Many hackers are young men who hack into systems just for the challenge or as a prank. Although this may seem harmless, it can cause considerable damage and is illegal in many countries. The more criminally minded hackers access computer systems for one or more reasons:

- To steal important and highly confidential information
- To copy computer programs illegally
- To alter data
- To destroy data either by deleting it or installing a virus to destroy or corrupt it
- To transfer money from one bank account to another using electronic funds transfer (EFT).

Some of the most common methods hackers use to gain access to computers are:

- Impersonation – pretending to be someone who is a legitimate user
- Brute force attacks – trying every possible combination of characters to find the password
- Remote login – using the flaws in operating systems to find a back door that allows a hacker to connect to a remote computer and control it.

### *Internet fraud*

The term 'Internet fraud' refers generally to any type of fraud scheme that uses one or more components of the Internet – such as chat rooms, e-mail, message boards or web sites – to present fraudulent offers to prospective victims, and conduct fraudulent transactions.
Some major types of Internet fraud are:

- *Telemarketing schemes online*: Telemarketing is the buying and selling of products over the Internet. Companies or individuals set up virtual shops/malls on web sites that users can access to view items on sale. These businesses purport to offer high-value items that are likely to attract many consumers, since the items are usually offered for sale at very reduced prices. Internet fraud occurs when the company or an individual bills the customer for the purchase, collects the money and then does not deliver the items purchased, or delivers a product that is substandard and far less valuable than what was promised.
- *Credit card fraud*: This is a slight variation on the above scheme. The fraud involves setting up temporary bogus businesses on the Internet. These businesses lure individuals into giving their credit card numbers in order to steal their money. A common method is to send e-mails pretending to be from a major bank. These messages direct you to a bogus web site which asks you to type in your bank details, thereby allowing the fraudster to steal your money.
- *Business opportunity/'work-at-home' schemes online*: There are many fraudulent schemes which use the Internet to advertise business opportunities that supposedly allow individuals to get rich or earn large sums of money working at home. These schemes typically require individuals to pay for information and material to start the business, but then fail to deliver the materials or information.

### *Industrial espionage*

Industrial espionage is when confidential information from within companies and other commercial organisations is obtained by spying, in an effort to gain some advantage, to the detriment of the body being spied on. It is illegal in most countries. Such information may be anything from the design of a new gadget, to a list of unpublished prices of a new product or products, to a list of senior employees' names and addresses.

The spies on the ground are usually employees (especially those who are still with the company but on the verge of leaving it) or on-site contractors. Companies that are victims of industrial espionage attacks may suffer financial losses as a result of the usefulness of the information to those spying – for example, if a competitor adjusts its prices in line with those of its victim, thereby gaining some of their customers. Companies may also have to contend with legal fees in the case of litigation, and diminished public trust if an attack is publicised.

In June 2005 an industrial espionage ring was broken by Israeli police. The perpetrators of the crime hired a private programmer to custom-create a Trojan horse virus which was then planted on a rival company's PCs. The Trojan horse virus allowed the perpetrators to access PCs remotely and gather confidential commercial information, such as the amount of money bid by the company for lucrative commercial contracts. The investigation implicated car importers, cell-phone providers and many other companies. The overall losses amounted to hundreds of millions of dollars. Victims said they lost competitive bids and thousands of customers because of the spying.

# Summary

1 Data integrity concerns the consistency, accuracy and reliability of data. It can be compromised by human error (e.g. inaccurate data entry, accidental deletion or changing of data), natural disasters (e.g. fires, floods and earthquakes), viruses, hardware malfunctions, fraud and malicious deletion or changing of data.

2 Data security concerns the safety of data and is one of the methods used to ensure data integrity. It consists of physical safeguards, which deal with the protection of hardware and software from accidental or malicious damage, destruction or theft, and software safeguards, which deal with the protection of software and data theft, corruption or destruction.

3 Hardware protection methods include: using locks, security guards, burglar alarms, monitoring systems, biometric scans; using doors that require passwords or magnetic cards; storing data in a fireproof safe; storing data in another building; distributing work to a number of employees.

4 Software protection methods include: using passwords for the system, and passwords for the files or folders; using audit trails; using encryption; adding anti-virus software; using firewalls.

5 A virus is a deliberately written program which activates itself unknown to the user and destroys or corrupts data. A worm is similar to a virus; it copies itself repeatedly, using up memory or disk space to crash a computer. There are four main types of virus: viruses that infect program files, e-mail viruses, Trojan horses and boot-sector viruses.

6 Viruses are usually spread by downloading infected programs and files from the Internet, opening infected files received through e-mails, or using a storage medium that contains infected files. They are contained using anti-virus software, avoiding opening programs with certain extensions, and avoiding using unknown storage media in your machine.

7 Computer surveillance can involve accessing or 'reading' the storage mechanism of an individual's computer, or monitoring an individual's operation of a computer, in most cases without their knowledge.

8 Spyware is a type of software which is usually secretly installed on a computer and covertly monitors the user's actions without his or her knowledge. It may save its findings locally or transmit them to someone else.

9 Data privacy refers to the right of individuals to determine what information is stored about them and how that information will be used.

10 Computer fraud is using a computer in some way to commit a dishonest act by obtaining an advantage or causing the loss of something of value. This can take place in any number of ways, including: hacking; e-mail hoaxes; auction, investment and retail schemes; falsely claiming to be expert on a certain subject area.

11 Software piracy is the unauthorised copying, use or sale of software that is copyrighted and is not public domain software or freeware. Some of the main types of software piracy are: licensed-user duplication for unlicensed users; pre-installed piracy in a store; Internet piracy; counterfeiting.

12 Hacking is the unauthorised accessing of a computer system to access, copy, steal, corrupt or destroy data; the individual who does this is referred to as a hacker.

13 Internet fraud refers generally to any type of fraud scheme that uses one or more components of the Internet – such as chat rooms, e-mail, message boards or web sites – to present fraudulent offers to prospective victims, to conduct fraudulent transactions or to transmit the proceeds of these.

14 Industrial espionage is when secret commercial information about companies, organisations and even governments is obtained by spying in an effort to gain an advantage over a competitor.

# Exercise

## Fill in the blanks.

1 ______________________________ concerns the consistency, accuracy and reliability of data.

2 __________________________________ is one of the most effective methods of securing data from electronic eavesdropping.

3 __________________________________ is used to scan your personal computer hard disk for known viruses and remove them once they are found.

4 A program, a hardware device or a combination of both, that filters the information coming in through the Internet connection to your computer system or network is called a ____________________.

5 A ___________________________ is a program written by someone that activates itself unknown to the user and destroys or corrupts data.

6 ______________________________ refers to the rights of individuals to determine what information is stored about them and how that information will be used.

7 The unauthorised copying, use or selling of software that is copyrighted is known as ____________________.

8 A person who accesses a computer system without authorisation is called a ______________________.

9 ______________________________ is using the computer in some way to commit a dishonest act by obtaining an advantage or causing loss of something of value.

10 ________________________________ refers generally to any type of fraud or scheme that uses one or more components of the Internet.

## True or False?

1 Data integrity and security mean the same thing. T ❑ F ❑

2 Distributing work to a number of employees instead of just one is a physical safeguard method of securing data. T ❑ F ❑

3 Passwords for files and folders can be used to protect data. T ❑ F ❑

4 Encryption is not a very effective method of protecting data during storage or transmission. T ❑ F ❑

5 A firewall can consist of software, hardware or a combination of both of these. T ❑ F ❑

6 Viruses can cause businesses to lose millions of dollars. T ❑ F ❑

7 Viruses cannot be spread through e-mails. T ❑ F ❑

8 In many countries individuals are legally entitled to determine what information is stored about them and how that information will be used. T ❑ F ❑

9 Software piracy is not morally wrong. T ❑ F ❑

10 When you purchase copyright software it belongs to you and you can make copies to give to your friends. T ❑ F ❑

11 Hacking is the unauthorised accessing of a computer system. T ❑ F ❑

12 Internet fraud occurs mainly through telemarketing. T ❑ F ❑

## Multiple choice

1 Data integrity concerns:
(a) Consistency of data
(b) Accuracy of data
(c) Reliability of data
(d) All of the above

2 Data integrity can be compromised by:
(a) Human error
(b) Natural disaster
(c) Viruses
(d) All of the above

3 Which of the following is not a physical safeguard method used to secure data?
(a) Biometric scans
(b) Anti-virus programs
(c) Security guards
(d) Fireproof safe

4 Which of the following is not a software safeguard method used to secure data?
(a) Passwords for the system
(b) Audit trails
(c) Encryption
(d) The operating system

5 Which of the following is not a computer virus?
(a) Worm
(b) Trojan horse
(c) E-mail virus
(d) McAfee

6 A computer virus is not spread by:
(a) Downloading infected files from the Internet
(b) Opening infected files received through e-mails
(c) Placing infected disks one on top of the other
(d) Using infected storage media that contracted infected files

7 You can protect your computer against viruses by:
(a) Installing an anti-virus package on your computer system
(b) Not using storage media from other computers in your computer system
(c) Not opening e-mail attachments that contain any executable files with the extension exe, com or vbs.
(d) All of the above

8 Which one of the following is not a type of software piracy?
   (a) Internet piracy
   (b) Copying freeware
   (c) Counterfeiting
   (d) Licensed-user duplication for unlicensed users.

9 A criminally minded hacker may access my computer system to:
   (a) Install anti-virus software
   (b) Steal important and highly confidential information
   (c) Inform companies of security loopholes in their system
   (d) Play games

## Short answer questions

1 Explain the term 'data integrity'.

2 List SIX ways in which data integrity can be compromised.

3 Explain the term 'data security'.

4 Distinguish between data integrity and data security.

5 Describe FOUR hardware methods used to protect data.

6 Describe FOUR software methods used to protect data.

7 (a) Define the term 'computer virus'.
   (b) Briefly describe FOUR types of computer viruses.
   (c) List FOUR methods that can be used to prevent and protect against viruses.

8 (a) Explain the term 'data privacy'.
   (b) List FIVE rules of the UK Data Protection Act of 1998 concerning the storing of information about individuals.

9 (a) Define the term 'software piracy'.
   (b) Describe FOUR types of software piracy.
   (c) Do you feel someone should be jailed or fined if found guilty of software piracy?

10 (a) Define the term 'hacking'.
   (b) List FIVE reasons why people may hack.
   (c) List THREE methods used to gain illegal access to a computer.

11 (a) What is computer fraud?
   (b) Explain the term 'Internet fraud'.
   (c) Briefly describe FOUR types of Internet fraud.

## Crossword

### Across

1 A piece of software, hardware or both that is used to prevent unauthorised access to a computer network. (8)

3 The unauthorised accessing of a computer system. (7)

6 A type of software used to protect computer systems from viruses. (9)

7 Another name for electronic junk mail. (4)

### Down

2 A method used to encode data during storage or transmission (10)

4 It refers to the right of individuals to determine what information is stored about them and how that information will be used. (7)

5 A small piece of software that uses computer networks and security holes to replicate itself. (5)

# 10 Word processing

## OBJECTIVES

At the end of this chapter you will be able to:

- Define 'word processing' and 'word processor'
- List the elements in a Word window
- Understand the purpose and function of various keys on the keyboard
- Create, save, retrieve and print documents
- Apply formatting functions:
  - Changing fonts
  - Superscript and subscript
  - Line spacing
  - Text justification
  - Bulleted or numbered lists
- Perform editing and text-proofing functions in preparing a document:
  - Use the search-and-replace function, redo and undo functions
  - Do spelling and grammar checks
  - Use the copy, cut and paste functions
- Apply page layouts:
  - Page numbering, tabs, page breaks
  - Paper size and orientation
  - Margins
  - Inserting headers, footers, footnotes and endnotes
- Use the mail-merge facilities of a word processor
- Insert columns into a document
- Insert tables into a document
- Insert graphics into a document
- Import files (text, graphics, tables) into a document

Word processing is the preparation of documents such as letters, reports, memos, books or any other type of correspondence. A word processor is an application package or program that allows you to edit, print and save these documents for use at a later date. A word processor also includes many other capabilities – such as the ability to copy and move text, find and replace specific words and phrases, delete, edit and format documents, and print documents.

Popular word processors include Microsoft Word, Lotus Word Pro and Word Perfect. All these word processors contain similar functions. For practical reasons the particular operations described in this chapter feature Microsoft Word and its functions. 'Word' is part of the Microsoft Office package, currently the most popular integrated software package available.

Fundamentally, a word processor package on a computer allows you to enter text and make changes to that text without having to retype the entire document from scratch, as would be the case with a typewriter. You can save the document on disk and retrieve it at a later date, even if it is not yet complete. A word processor also allows you to perform complex formatting features that cannot be done on a typewriter.

## Starting Word

***To start Word using the Start button on the task bar:***

1. Select **Programs** from the **Start** menu
2. When the **Programs** menu appears select **Microsoft Word**, or select **Microsoft Word** from the **Microsoft Office** menu.

The Word window appears as shown in Figure 10.1.

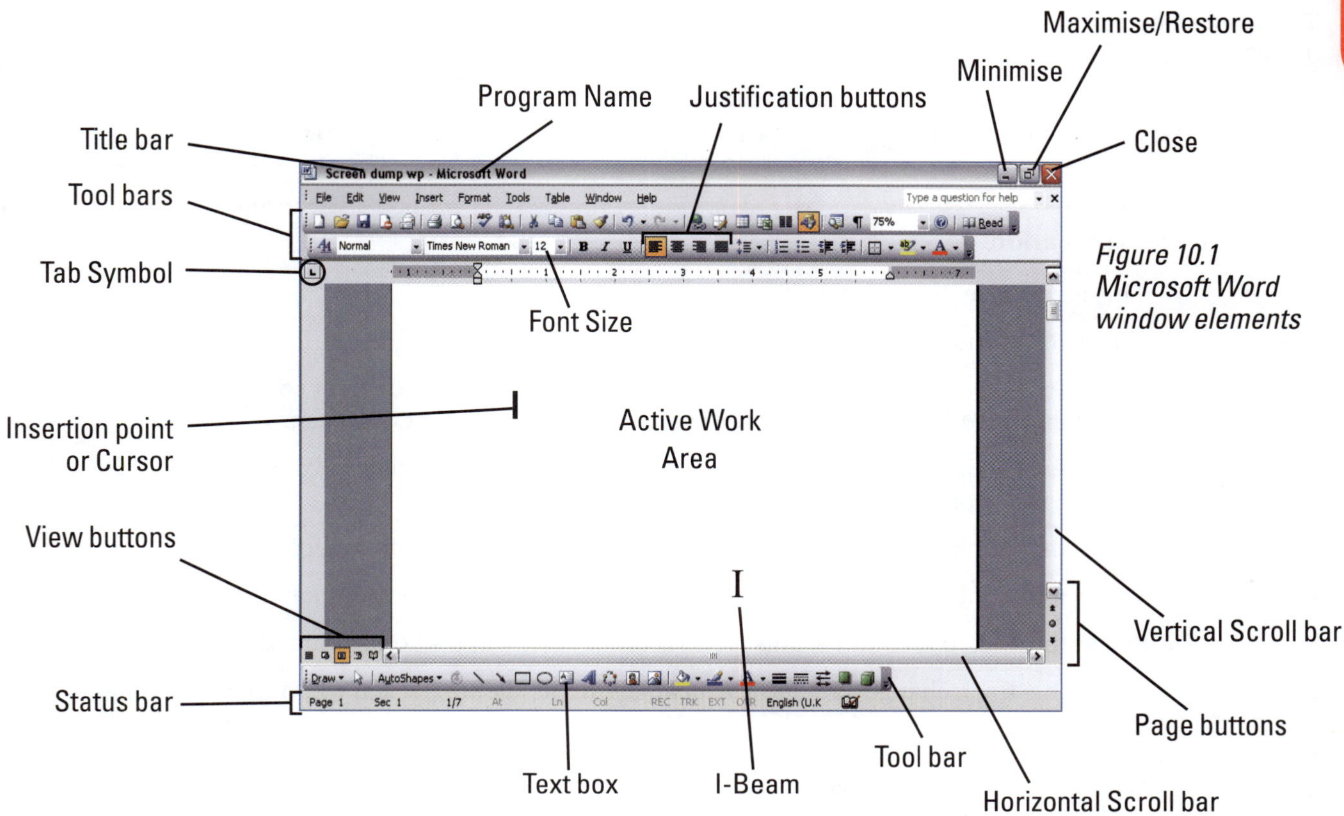


*Figure 10.1 Microsoft Word window elements*

*Table 1 Key elements of the Word window*

| Element | Function |
|---|---|
| Title bar | Displays the document name, the program name, as well as the Minimise, Restore and Close buttons |
| Menu bar | Contains nine drop-down menus; each menu has a list of commands |
| Standard toolbar | Contains buttons that are shortcuts for many common Word commands |
| Formatting toolbar | Contains buttons that are shortcuts for formatting a document. Usually one or two bars are shown. Right-clicking on these allows you to add or remove further toolbars, such as the drawing toolbar |
| Ruler | Shows the margins, the tab setting and the indents |
| Insertion point or cursor | A flashing vertical line, which indicates the position where the next character will be inserted |
| I-beam or mouse pointer | This allows you to move to a specific position where the next character will be inserted: Position the I-beam where you want the character to be inserted and click on the left mouse button. The beam converts to a pointed arrow when you move it into the margin |
| Vertical scroll bars | Allow you to scroll up or down a document |
| Horizontal scroll bars | Allow you to scroll from left to right or vice versa in a document |
| Page buttons | Allow you to move up or down a document a page at a time |

## Status bar

This is located at the bottom of the document window (Figure 10.2) and displays information shown in Table 2.

*Figure 10.2*
*The status bar*

| Element | Explanation |
|---|---|
| Page | This is the page displayed on the screen |
| Sec | Shows the section of the document displayed on the screen |
| 1/6 | Indicates the page number displayed and the total pages the document contains. The example shows that page 1 is displayed on the screen and the document has 6 pages |
| At | Indicates the distance from the top of the page to the insertion point. Example: At 1" indicates that the insertion point is one inch from the top of the page. |
| Ln | Shows the number of lines from the top of the page to the insertion point |
| Col | Shows the number of characters from the left margin to the insertion point, including spaces |
| REC | Shows the 'macro recorder' status. The recorder is off when REC is dimmed |
| TRK | Shows the 'track changes' status. The changes are not being tracked when TRK is dimmed |
| EXT | Shows the 'extend selection' status. The extended selection is turned off when EXT is dimmed |
| OVR | Shows the 'typeover' status. You are in insertion mode when the OVR is dimmed. Double clicking on OVR will turn on the typeover mode |

*Table 2*
*Elements of the status bar*

## The keyboard

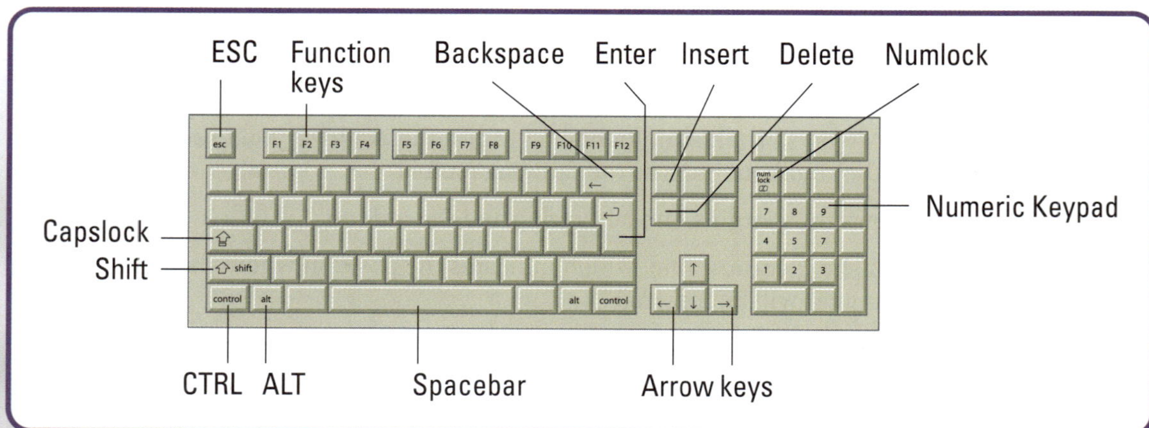


*Figure 10.3*
*A computer keyboard*

*Table 3*
*Elements of the keyboard*

| Key | Function |
|---|---|
| Enter | Moves the insertion point to the next line |
| Spacebar | Moves the insertion point one space to the right |
| Caps Lock | Toggles between upper case and lower case. Pressing this key causes the 'Caps Lock' indicator light on the keyboard to light and any letter that is typed will be displayed in upper case. |
| Esc | Pressing this key immediately after an action takes you out of, or cancels, that action |
| Shift | This key is used along with other keys to allow second-function commands. For example, if the computer is not in 'Caps Lock' mode, you can get a capital letter by holding down the Shift key and pressing the desired letter. |
| Backspace | Deletes the character to the left of the insertion point |
| Delete | Deletes the character to the right of the insertion point |
| Insert | Toggles between **insert mode** and **overtype mode**. The insert mode (the default mode), allows you to enter extra characters at the insertion point. In the overtype mode new characters being typed erase the characters that were previously there. |
| Num Lock | Toggles between a numeric keypad and directional keys that allow you to move text or the cursor around |
| Function keys | Function keys labelled F1 to F12 perform different functions depending on the program being used |

## Entering text

Once Microsoft Word has been started a new document is automatically opened. You can begin typing immediately in the active work area of the window. This work-space will contain what you type or draw. The window displays a typing area similar to that of a clean sheet of paper. The document will be set up with **default settings** – a number of features have been preset such as page size, margin size, line spacing and font style and size.

### *Word wrap*

Word wrap is one such default setting; it is an important feature you should know about. Word wrap allows text to move automatically to the next line without you needing to press the Enter key. When words approach the right margin, if the last word is too long to fit on the line, it automatically moves to the next line.

You should therefore use the Enter key only when:

- You want to create blank lines
- You have reached the end of a line you want to keep short in appearance
- You have reached the end of a paragraph.

Figure 10.4
View buttons

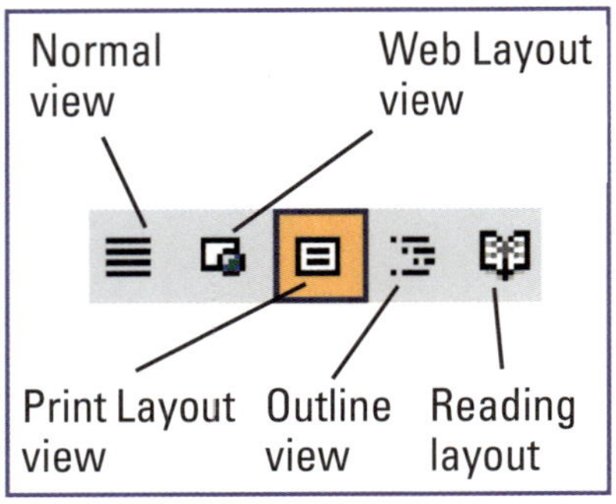


## Different views of a document

Microsoft Word allows you several different ways to view a document. These views include Normal, Web Layout, Print Layout, Outline and Reading Layout. You can access them by selecting the desired view from the **View** menu, or by clicking the appropriate view button on the bottom left-hand corner of the document window. The icons are shown in Figure 10.4.

- *Normal View*: In this view the layout of each page of the document is simplified to enable you to enter text quickly. In this layout you can type, edit and format your documents. It displays the document with all its formatting.
- *Print Layout/Page Layout View*: In this layout you can create, edit and format your documents. It allows you to see how text and graphics are placed on the paper you may print the document on, since it shows the edges of the 'paper'. You can therefore adjust the position of text and graphics quite precisely on the page. This view displays the document fully formatted and shows how it would look if it were to be printed out on paper.
- *Outline View*: This view shows the structure of a document. The extra symbols and indentation that appear in Outline View are not printed. This view enables you to make adjustments quickly to the structure of a document. For example, you can shift headings and text up or down by clicking on the up or down arrows.
- *Web Layout/Online Layout View*: This view enables you to look at a document as a web page to see what it would look like before it is published on the Internet.
- *Reading Layout*: This view enables you to view the document with minimum eye strain and with tools optimised for reading. It is designed to make reading documents on the screen more comfortable. In this mode, Word removes distracting screen elements, such as extraneous toolbars. Word also uses your computer's screen resolution settings to resize the document for optimum readability.

## Saving a document

Saving a document onto a backing storage device makes it available for editing and printing at a later date. A document temporarily resides in the computer's RAM memory as you work. If the computer is switched off, or there is power failure, all the work you have done since the last time the document was saved would be lost. It is therefore important to save your document to backing storage regularly to avoid losing data.

### Saving a document for the first time

1. Choose the **Save As** or **Save** command from the **File** menu or click on the **Save** icon. When either of these commands is used to save a document for the first time, the 'Save As' dialogue box appears (Figure 10.5).
2. Select the location where you want to save the document by selecting from the drop down menu of the 'Save in' box.
3. Type a name for the new document in the 'File Name' or 'Save As' box.
4. Select the kind of file type you want to save the document as by selecting a file type from the 'Save as type' box.
5. Click the **Save** button.

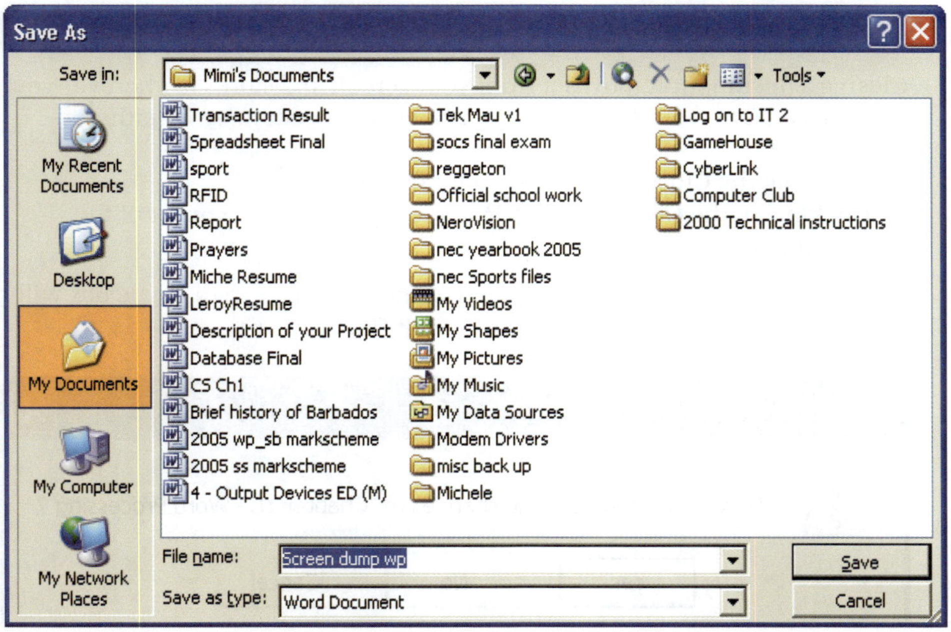


*Figure 10.5*
*'Save As' dialogue box*

## Saving a document that you have previously saved

Once you have saved a document, you can use the Save function to save further changes to it.

1 Selecting **Save** from the **File** menu or clicking on the **Save** icon will save the document in its current format.
2 Selecting the **Save As** function is another option; the 'Save As' dialogue box appears. You can either save changes to the previously saved document using its previously saved name, or make another copy of the document by saving it under another name and/or storing it in another location.

## Saving a document to a diskette in drive A

1 Insert the diskette into drive A.
2 Select **Save As** from the **File** menu. The 'Save As' dialogue box appears (Figure 10.5).
3 Click on the down arrow in the drop-down box labelled 'Save in'.
4 Select '3½ Floppy (A:)'.
5 In the box labelled 'File name' type in a name for the document.
6 Click on the **Save** button.

> **Shortcut**
> Click on the diskette icon on the standard toolbar to save a document for the first time or to save changes to a document that has already been saved.

## File names

File names can have a length of up to 255 characters and contain letters, numbers and other characters. However, file names cannot contain the following symbols: ?, /, \, >, <, *, ", : or ;. It is a good rule to choose file names that are meaningful to you, since they give an idea of what the contents of the file are.

## Closing a document

Closing a document removes it from your screen and stores it wherever you have placed it on your hard drive. You can close a document by either:

- Selecting the **Close** option from the **File** menu; or
- Clicking on the **Close** button at the top right-hand corner of the document window.

If you try closing a changed document without saving it, a dialogue box will appear to give you an opportunity to save it (Figure 10.6).

Remember that if you do not save your work or changes that you made to a document it will not be available to you to use again!

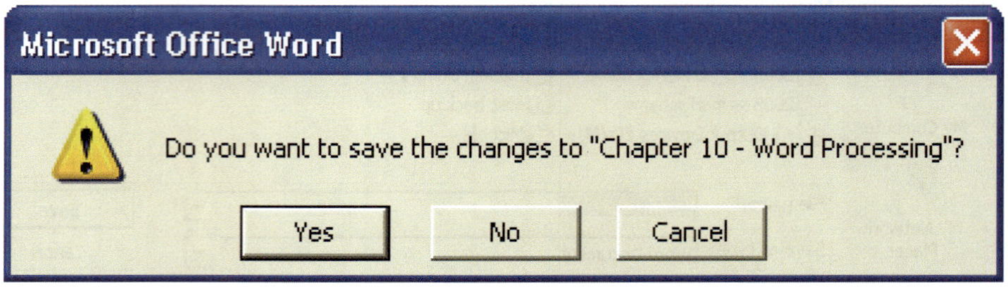


*Figure 10.6*
*Opportunity to save*

## Opening a document

When you need to work with an existing document, you have to open it first. Opening a document places a copy of the original in your word processor window. The original is left intact in its location in backup storage.

### *Retrieving a document*

1. Select **Open** from the **File** menu; or
2. Click the **Open** icon on the toolbar.
3. The 'Open' dialogue box appears (Figure 10.7). Using the 'Look in' box, select the location where the file is stored.
4. When the list of files/folders is displayed, you can either:
   - Type the name of the file you want to open in the 'File name' box and click **Open**; or
   - Double-click on the name of the desired file.

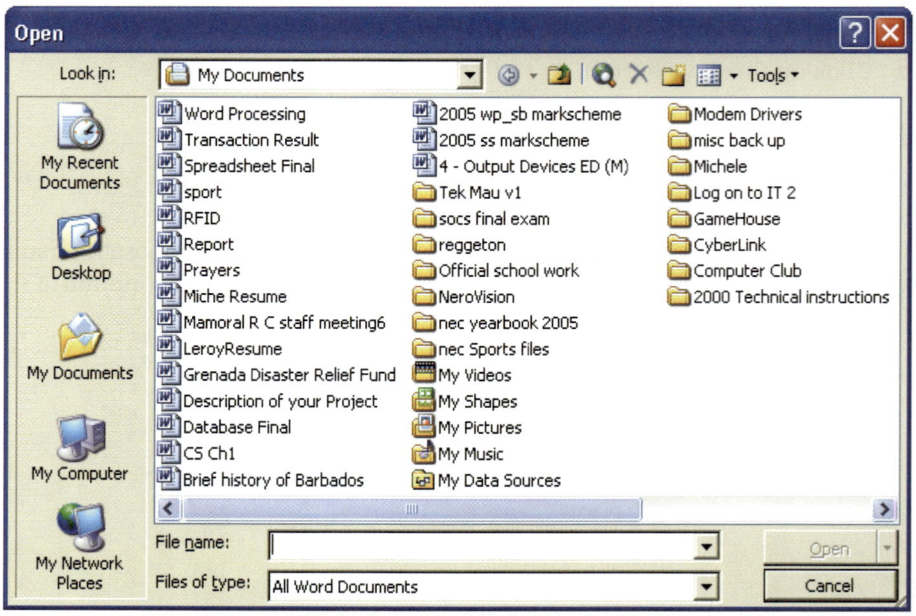


*Figure 10.7*
*'Open' dialogue box*

## Printing a document

Printing a document allows you to produce a hard copy of your work.

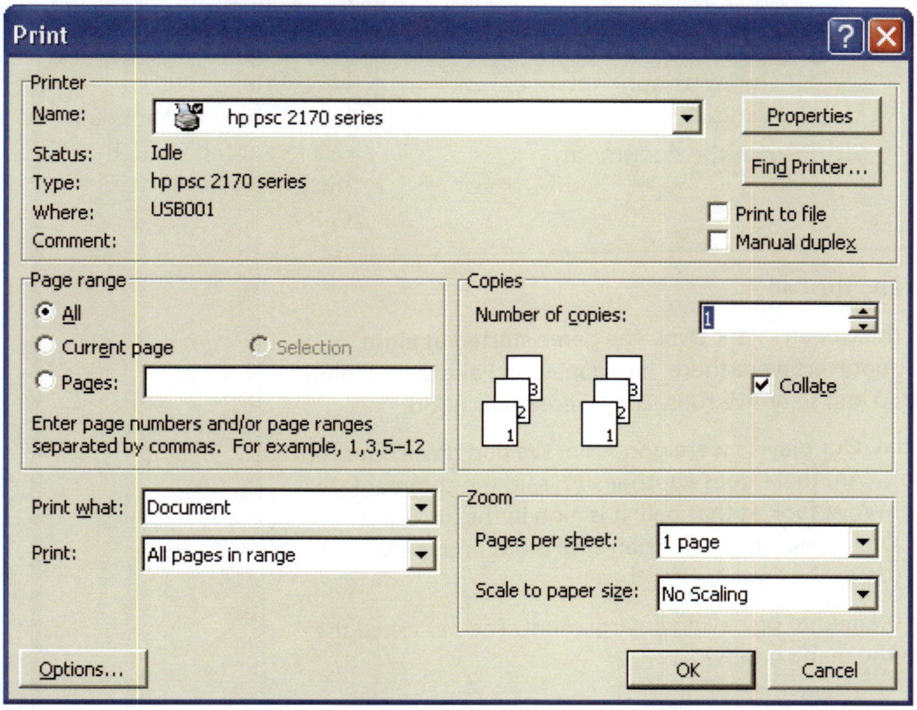


*Figure 10.8*
*'Print' dialogue box*

> **Note:** In your school, ask your teacher for permission before you attempt printing.

> ***Shortcut***
> Click on the **Printer** icon on the toolbar to print the entire document. Note also that the keystroke Ctrl + P opens up the 'Print' dialogue box.

## Using the print option from the menu bar

1 Select **Print** from the **File** menu. The 'Print' dialogue box appears (Figure 10.8).

2 Make the appropriate selections (such as number of copies, pages).

3 Click the **OK** button to start printing.

### Exercise 1

***Short answer questions***

1 What is the function of a word processor?

2 List the different ways of viewing a document in Microsoft Word.

3 What is the 'word wrap' feature and why is it useful?

4 Why do you need to save a previously saved document after making changes to it?

5 Explain the difference between typeover mode and insert mode.

## Activity 1

1 On your computer, double-click on the word processing icon (Microsoft Word icon) to open the application.

2 Type the following document as accurately as possible.

(a) Save the document as 'The Argument' on a diskette.

(b) Print the document.

(c) Close the document.

(d) Retrieve the document.

(e) Resave the document as 'Cricket at the Oval' in the 'My Document' folder.

The Argument between the Bat and the Ball

It was a bright and sunny day at the Queen's Park Oval. The game started at eight o'clock. Brian Lara's family and supporters were there. It began, with Pakistan winning the toss. They made three hundred and sixty-five runs. They were really good.

Then it was West Indies time to bat. Our players were good too. We had three hundred runs when Brian Lara came to bat. "Ah, there goes another six", said the commentator. "Brian Lara is absolutely brilliant! Wow, look at that ball; it is high in the air. But a Pakistani player is right under it. Oh no! He caught it. Brian Lara is out and the West Indies team is down. What a sad day at the Oval."

Meanwhile, the ball and the bat seemed to be having an argument. The bat asked the ball, "Why did you have to fall in the man's hands?"

"Not me, it was your fault. It was you who sent me there."

"If you did watch what going on we would never lose."

"You old crooked bat, I'm not playing with you again." And so they left the oval and so did I, very unhappy.

Jeremy Taylor

Std. 5

Cunapo R.C., Sangre Grande, Trinidad

# Editing and proofing text

There are many features in a word processor that permit quick changes to a document which would be difficult and tedious to perform manually. Some of these features, such as deleting text using the Delete and the Backspace key, and inserting and typing over text using the Insert key, have already been discussed. Other editing features include:

- Cutting, copying and pasting
- Finding and replacing text.

## Cut, copy and paste

The **cut** function allows you to select and remove an item from a document – such as a character, a word, a line of text, or a picture – and place it in the clipboard. This item can then be inserted anywhere, and as many times as you want, in any open document. This process is called **pasting**. For example, you can cut and paste a table or graph created in the Microsoft Excel application into a Microsoft Word document.

The copy function places a copy of an item selected onto the clipboard: the original item stays exactly where it was to start with. Meanwhile the copy on the clipboard can then be inserted anywhere and as many times as you like in any open document.

The **clipboard** is a temporary storage location in memory where cut or copied text or graphics are placed. The items remain on the clipboard until you cut or copy a new item. The items can be copied from the clipboard into different areas of the document or into another document or even another program, as many times as you like. The clipboard can store up to 24 items.

To use the cut or copy feature the item must first be selected. There are many ways to select items. For example:

- you can use the menu bar to select an entire document
- you could use the mouse by itself, or together with other keys.

### Selecting text using the mouse

1. Position the mouse pointer in front of the first character of the block of text to be selected.
2. Hold down the left mouse button and drag the mouse over the text you want to select. The area becomes highlighted; release the mouse button at the end of the block of text.

### Selecting an entire document using the menu

1. Choose **Select All** from the **Edit** menu. The entire document becomes highlighted.

### Other methods of selecting text

*Table 4*

| Method | Result |
|---|---|
| Position the I-beam on a word and double-click | Selects the word |
| Hold down the control key and click on a sentence | Selects the sentence |
| Triple-click on a paragraph | Selects the paragraph |

### To cut and paste (moving text)

1. Select the block of text to be cut.
2. Select **Cut** from the **Edit** menu or click the **Cut** icon.
3. Click in the position where you want the removed text to be placed. This can be anywhere in the same document or in another opened document.
4. Select **Paste** from the **Edit** menu or click the **Paste** icon.

### To copy and paste

1. Select the block of text you want to copy.
2. Select **Copy** from the **Edit** menu or click on the **Copy** icon.
3. Click in the position where you want the copied text to be placed. This can be anywhere in the same document or within another opened document.
4. Select **Paste** from the **Edit** menu or click the **Paste** icon.

## Find and Replace

The **Find function** allows you to search a document for a particular word or string of characters that you may want to change or edit.

1 Select **Find** from the **Edit** menu.
2 Enter the word or phrase in the 'Find What' box.
3 Select **Find Next**.

Meanwhile the **Replace function** allows you to search for a word or string of characters and replace it with another word or string of characters.

1 Select **Replace** from the **Edit** menu (Figure 10.9).
2 Enter the word or phrase you wish to replace in the 'Find what' box.
3 Enter the word or phrase you wish to replace it with in the 'Replace with' box.
4 Click the **Find Next** button to find the first (and subsequent) occurrence of the word or phrase.
5 Click the **Replace** button to replace the word or phrase.

### Did you know?

If you want to replace the word every time it appears in the document, you can simply click the **Replace All** button.

### Activity 2

1 Retrieve the document 'Honesty is the Best Policy' from the companion CD-ROM.
2 Find and replace all occurrences of the word 'girls' with 'boys'.
3 Save the document.

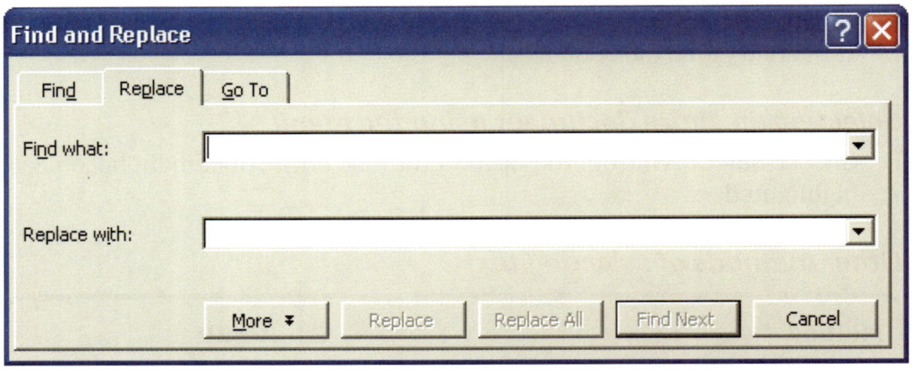


*Figure 10.9*
*'Find and Replace' dialogue box*

## Spelling and grammar checks

Spelling and grammatical errors undermine the look of a document, whether it is a professional letter or your school assignment. To help create a more accurate and professional-looking document, you can use your word processor's spelling and grammar check facility.

Words that are misspelt or not recognisable by Word are highlighted by underlining the word with a jagged red line. If the spellchecker believes it has spotted an incorrectly spelled word, it will display a list of possible suggestions in a suggestion box, from which you can choose an alternative.

When Microsoft Word spots a phrase or sentence that contradicts grammatical rules, or when there is inaccurate spacing between characters, the text is identified using a green jagged underline. The grammar checker displays possible grammatical errors and correction suggestions. You could choose to Ignore the suggestions or Change and accept the suggestions.

### Did you know?

Most computers use American spelling and grammar as default. This can be changed to other common examples, such as UK English, using the 'Spelling and Grammar' dialogue box under the **Tools** menu (click on **Options** in this box).

### *Proofing a document using the menu*

1 Position the I-beam at the point of the document where you would like to start the spelling and grammar check.
2 Select **Spelling and Grammar** from the **Tools** menu or click on the **Spelling and Grammar** icon . Or, press the function 7 (F7) key to activate the checker.

3 If there is a spelling error or a grammatical error the 'Spelling and Grammar' dialogue box is displayed (Figure 10.10). This box will show some possible suggestions in a 'Suggestions' box. You can choose any of the options displayed, or choose to ignore them (Table 5).

*Table 5*
*The Spelling and Grammar dialogue box offers you several options*

| | |
|---|---|
| Ignore Once | If you do not want to change the word or this occurrence of the word |
| Ignore All | If you do not want to change any and all occurrences of the word throughout the document |
| Change | Click on the appropriate word in the 'Suggestions' box and click the **Change** button |
| Change All | If you want to change all occurrences of the word in the document |
| Add to Dictionary | If the computer has detected a word that it does not recognise and which is not in the computer's dictionary, you can choose to add the word to the dictionary. Note that this word will be marked as 'incorrect' to start with. |

**Did you know?**

The spelling and grammar check is not exhaustive – it does not know every word in English or every possible grammatical construction. It is therefore not a substitute for your own knowledge of the language, but rather a general guide or helper. Use your own knowledge and good sense, therefore, before you accept what the checker tells you.

After making all the changes, the message 'The Spelling and grammar check is complete' is displayed.

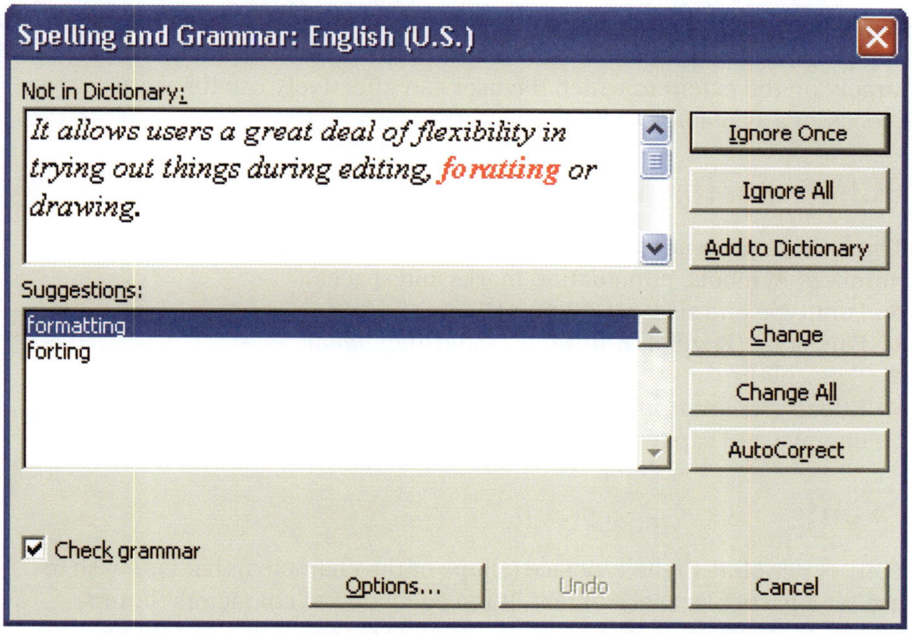


*Figure 10.10*
*'Spelling and Grammar' dialogue box*

## Undo and Redo

The Undo and Redo function allows you to undo mistakes or changes made during editing, formatting or drawing. For example, if you intentionally or unintentionally change a document, the changes can be reversed using the **Undo** button. Actions are usually reversed right after you complete the action – that is the point at which you are most likely to change your mind. However, you can undo more than one previous action. A list of the most recent actions that can be undone is displayed when the arrow next to the **Undo** button in the standard tool bar is clicked. You can scroll down to undo as many of these recent actions as you wish.

Meanwhile the **Redo** button allows you to undo an undo: that is, if you later decide you did actually want to stick with the change you originally made.

## Activity 3

1 Retrieve the document 'Crime in Schools' from the companion CD.

2 Add the following text to the end of the document:

> Many students have difficulty dealing with their problems and may exhibit poor behavioural responses to situations. Guidance counsellors are needed in the present system to help students deal with some of their problems.

3 Insert the heading 'Crime in Schools'.

4 Spell-check the document.

5 Save the document as 'A solution to crime'.

## Activity 4

1 Retrieve the document 'Honesty is the Best Policy'.

2 Spell-check the document.

# Formatting

Changing the appearance of the text in a document is called formatting. The impact created on the reader of your document is greatly dependent on the appearance of your document. The final appearance of a document depends largely on the extent to which the user can effectively use the word processor's available formatting features.

## Character formatting

The following are attributes that can be applied to characters (i.e. letters, numbers, symbols, punctuation marks and spaces):

- Font type and size, e.g. 12-point Times
- Font style (Regular, **Boldface**, <u>Underline</u>, *Italic*)
- Font colour
- Effects (strikethrough, superscript, subscript, shadow, outline, emboss, engrave and caps)

## Font

**Font type** refers to the typeface (shape of the character) that you wish to use for a particular piece of text. It is a collection of characters (letters, numbers, symbols, punctuation marks and spaces) with a consistent appearance. For example:

| | |
|---|---|
| Times New Roman | Times New Roman |
| Lucida Handwriting | *Lucida Handwriting* |
| Script MT Bold | ***Script MT Bold*** |
| Old English Text MT | Old English Text MT |
| Impact | **Impact** |
| Wingdings | ♦✱■♑♎✱■♑⬩ |

**Font size** is measured in units called points; this refers to the height of a character, where one point is $^{1}/_{72}$ of an inch. Therefore when you choose a font size of 72 points your characters will be one inch in height, when printed. The larger the point size the larger the font.

**Font style** changes the way the text appears. It includes Plain text, Bold (B), Italic (I), Underline (U), as well as many others or a combination of styles.

### To change the font type, style and size

1. Select **Font** from the **Format** menu. The 'Font' dialogue box will appear.
2. The top part of the Font tab window is divided into three sections: Font, Font style and Size (Figure 10.11).
   - To select the required font type, use the scroll bar under the Font heading and select the desired font.
   - To select the required style select from the options available.
   - To select the required size use the scroll bar in the 'Size' box and select the desired size: 8, 9, 10, 11, 12, etc.

   You can see a preview of the options selected in the preview box at the bottom of the 'Font' window.

   Many of the options, such as font type, style and font size, are available on the formatting toolbar.

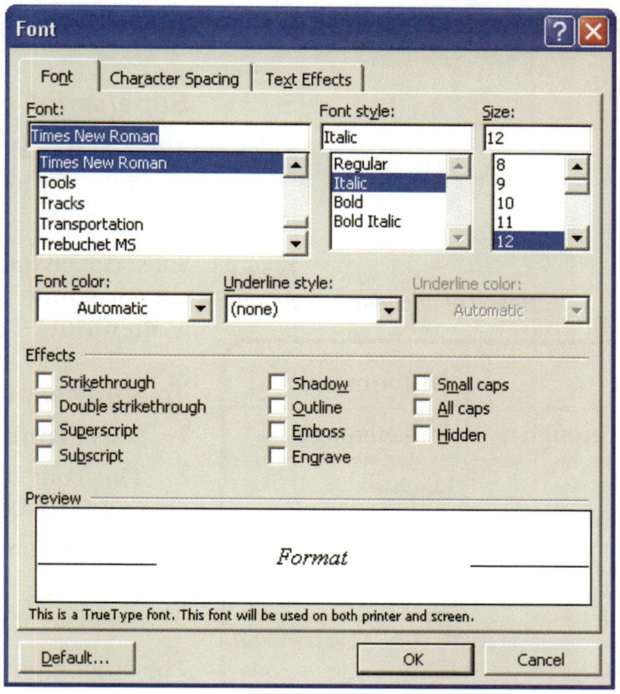


*Figure 10.11*
*'Font' dialogue box*

### To change the font type using the Formatting toolbar

1. Click on the arrow next to the displayed font type. A list of available font styles will appear (Figure 10.12). Select the desired style.

### To change the font size using the Formatting toolbar

1. Click on the arrow next to the displayed font size. A list of available font sizes will appear (Figure 10.13). Select the desired size by clicking on the number.

> ***Did you know?***
> If a desired size is not displayed you can type the number in the font size box and press the enter key.

### To change the font style using the Formatting toolbar

1. Click **B** *I* U for bold face (B), italic (I) or underline (U) as required.

### To change the font colour using the Formatting toolbar

1. Click on the down arrow next to the **Font Colour** button (a font colour box appears, Figure 10.14).
2. Click on the colour you want.

*Figure 10.12*
*Font types*

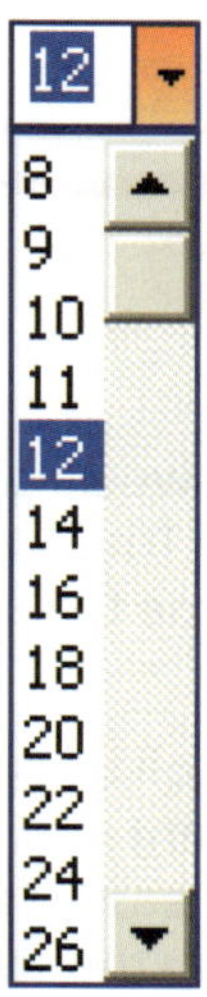


*Figure 10.13*
*Font sizes*

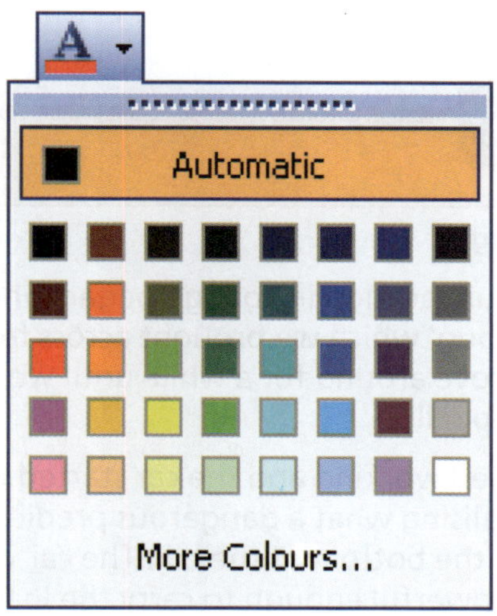


*Figure 10.14*
*Font colour box*

## Applying effects

### *Superscript and subscript*

A superscript character is one that is raised above the normal line. For example, $3^{rd}$, 100 °C, $4x^2$ have the characters rd, 0 and 2 raised above the normal line and are superscript characters.

Subscript characters are placed below the normal line. For example, the chemical representation of water is $H_2O$ or a number in base 2 can be written $1101_2$. The number 2 in each of these cases is a subscript character.

*Table 6*
*Result of applying font effects*

| Effect | Outcome |
|---|---|
| Strikethrough | Strikethrough |
| Double strikethrough | Double strikethrough |
| Shadow | Shadow |
| Outline | Outline |
| Emboss | Emboss |
| Engrave | Engrave |

### *To apply superscript and subscript*

1. Select **Font** from the **Format** menu.
2. The 'Font' dialogue box appears. Check the superscript or subscript box in the effects section and click the **OK** button.
3. Type the character you want to format as superscript or subscript.
4. To change back to normal typing mode, you need to go back to the 'Font' dialogue box and uncheck the superscript or subscript box.

The other effects can be applied by checking the appropriate box in the same way as for superscript and subscript. The outcome of applying the following format effects is shown in Table 6.

## Change case (upper case or lower case)

On occasion it may become necessary to change portions of typed text, for example, from lower case (common letters) to upper case (capital letters) and vice versa. This can be done easily using the Change Case function.

### *To change case*

1. Select the text.
2. Select **Change Case** from the **Format** menu. The 'Change Case' dialogue box appears (Figure 10.15).
3. Check the **Upper case** or **Lower case** radio button.
4. Click **OK**.

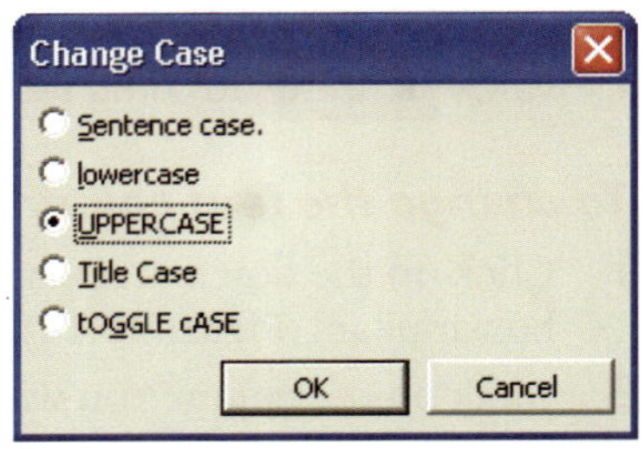


*Figure 10.15*
*'Change Case' dialogue box*

## Activity 5

**A car ride in Tobago**

Our first day of our vacation in Tobago began when we all piled into my mum's car. The car was a little blue 'bug' which we brought across from Trinidad to Tobago on board the Panorama. We drove around for a while until we came to Fort George, which was at the top of a very steep hill.

The engine stopped working and the car started to roll backwards. Foolishly we kids were all excited not realising what a dangerous predicament we were in. The car eventually came to a stop at the bottom of the hill. The car was easily restarted; apparently the engine was not powerful enough to carry the load up the steep incline. We all came out of the vehicle and walked up to the fort while my mum drove up the hill. It was an adventure I would never forget. Halfway up the hill the car started to have engine trouble.

## Activity 5 cont.

1 Type the document as shown above. The number of words per line may differ, but do not worry about this, just keep the paragraph structure.
2 Delete the heading.
3 Copy and paste the second-last sentence of the second paragraph as the new heading.
4 Bold and centre the heading.
5 Change the heading to uppercase.
6 Cut and paste the last sentence of the second paragraph to the beginning of the second paragraph.
7 Change the colour of the word 'Tobago' throughout the document, to blue.
8 Change the font of the words 'Fort George' in the first paragraph.
9 Underline and italicise the word 'Panorama'.

## Paragraph formatting

A paragraph in Microsoft Word can be any amount of characters. It can include text, graphics, objects (e.g. charts), blank lines and other items followed by the paragraph mark. The paragraph mark can only be seen by clicking on the **Show/Hide** button ¶ in the standard toolbar. The paragraph mark appears each time the Enter key is pressed and hence a new paragraph is created. A document can therefore have a number of paragraphs.

The **Show/Hide** button on the standard tool bar allows you to display all formatting marks such as white spaces and other markers not normally visible in the normal document.

## Line spacing

Line spacing is the distance between lines of text. The spacing between the lines of text is also relative to the size of the font on a line. The larger the font size the larger the line spacing. Appropriate line spacing improves the appearance and readability of a document. The line spacing available is 'single', 'double', '1.5', 'at least', 'exactly' and 'multiple'. The default line spacing for Microsoft Word is single. It may be necessary to change the line spacing, depending on the nature of a document.

### *Changing line spacing*

1 Place the insertion point in a paragraph or select multiple paragraphs.
2 Select **Paragraph** from the **Format** menu.
3 The 'Paragraph' dialogue box appears (Figure 10.16).
4 Select the required spacing by selecting the option from the line spacing box.

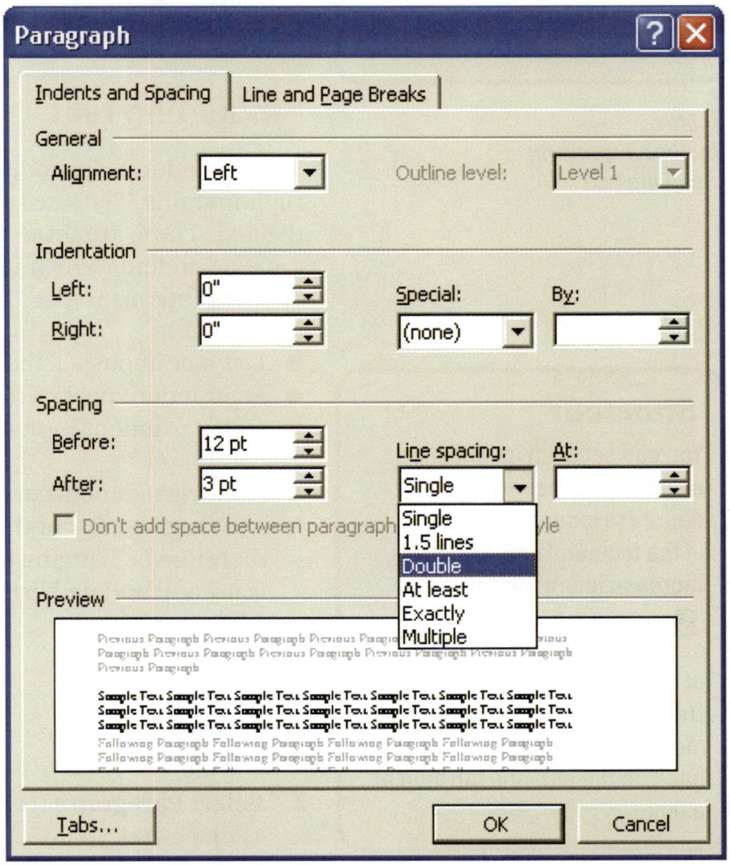


*Figure 10.16 'Paragraph' dialogue box*

> **Shortcut**
> You can choose the desired spacing as shown in Figure 10.17 from the formatting toolbar. Place the insertion point in a paragraph or select multiple paragraphs.

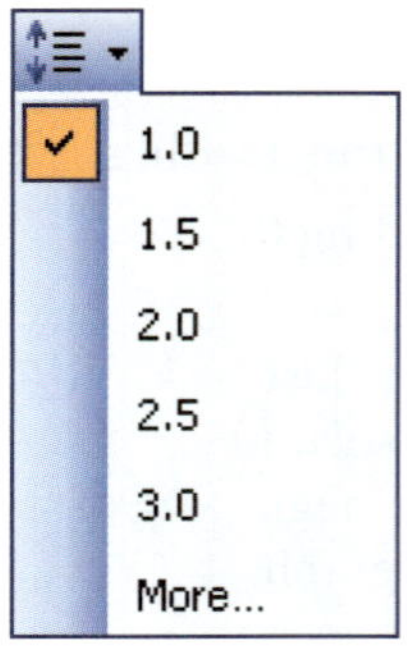


Figure 10.17
Line spacing dropdown box

| Spacing | Symbol |
|---|---|
| Single | |
| 1.5 Space | |
| Double | |

Table 7
Line spacing icons on Format toolbar

## Justification

This is the process of aligning a block of text, paragraph or entire document within the text margins or frame borders. The default setting for Microsoft Word is left justification. Text can also be right, centre or fully justified.

- *Left justification (alignment)* means that the text is flush on the left margin (text at the right margin is uneven).
- *Right justification (alignment)* means that text is flush with the right margin (text at the left margin is uneven).
- *Centre alignment* means that the text is centred along the middle of the document or frame.
- *Fully justified/Left and Right justification (alignment)* mean that the text is flush with both left and right margins.

> **Shortcut**
> To justify text, select the text and click on the appropriate button in the Formatting toolbar, as shown in Table 8.

| Justification | Button |
|---|---|
| Left justification | |
| Centre justification | |
| Right justification | |
| Full justification | |

Table 8
Toolbar buttons for justifying text

### To change the justification using the menu

1. Select the text.
2. Select **Paragraph** from the **Format** menu. The 'Paragraph' dialogue box will appear.

Select the alignment from the Alignment box by clicking on the down arrow and choosing the desired alignment (Left, Centre, Right and Full).

## Indenting text

You can indent a line or a paragraph by pushing them away from the left or right margins. The size of an indent is the distance between the margins and the text. There are three indent settings: the left indent, the right indent and a special indent (which includes First line/Hanging). The default setting for all three indents is zero. This means that a paragraph would initially have no indentation.

- *Left* indent pushes the paragraph away from the left margin.
- *Right* indent pushes the paragraph away from the right margin.
- *First line* indent is one in which the first line is shorter than the rest of the paragraph.
- *Hanging* indent occurs when the first line of a paragraph is left indented less than the rest of the lines in the paragraph. The first line will therefore be hanging to the left of the rest of the lines in the paragraph. It is used in bulleted lists, numbered lists, numbered paragraphs and bibliographies.

> **Shortcut**
> You can set a left indent using the increase and decrease indent buttons in the toolbar. The **Increase indent** button moves the left indent marker to the right, a distance of one tab stop at a time. The **Decrease indent** button moves the left indent marker back (to the left) one tab stop at a time.

### To indent text

1. Place the insertion point in a paragraph or select the required paragraphs.
2. Select **Paragraph** from the **Format** menu. The 'Paragraph' dialogue box is displayed.

3 Specify the indentations in the right, left and or special indent boxes. The preview box at the bottom will show the effect of the changes on the text.

4 Click **OK** when you are finished.

The indent settings are maintained when each new paragraph is started by pressing the enter key.

## Activity 6

1 Type out the document shown below. The number of words per line may differ, but keep the paragraph structure.

(a) Centre the first two lines of the document.

(b) Change the font size of the first two lines of the document to a size larger than the rest of the document.

(c) Change the first line of the document to upper case.

(d) Change the font type of the second line of the document to Black Chancery.

(e) Place a blank line between the first two lines of the document and the date.

(f) Indent the first line of the first paragraph.

(g) Create a bulleted list for the type of forms to be used, that is the Cash-List Form and the Fund Raising Form.

(h) Use boldface for the words 'Cash-List Form', 'Fund Raising Form', 'Approved Budget 2005/2006', 'Quantity', 'Items' and 'Cost'.

(i) Underline and italicise the words 'Items Approved'.

(j) Double space the approved items.

(k) Check for spelling errors.

(l) Save the document as 'New Record-Keeping Practices'.

THE PANORAMA COMPANY

Wine and Cheese Club

26th January 2005

The Manager,

Wine and Cheese Club

As new members of the executive, we have decided that in order to promote transparency and proper accounting and record keeping, the following systems must be implemented.

Cash-List Form – This form will be used to record all petty cash transactions.

Fund Raising Form – This form will be used to inform the executive of all fund raising details.

Approved Budget 2005/2006

The items listed below have been approved for the 2005/2006 budget.

Items Approved:

| Quantity | Items | Cost |
|---|---|---|
| 2 dozen | Wine glasses | $84 |
| 4 dozen boxes | Chocolates | $400 |
| 6 cases | Wine | $6000 |
| 2 dozen | Tee-Shirts | $1600 |
| 2 dozen | Cutlery items | $500 |

If there are any questions concerning the new forms please contact the assistant treasurer. We look forward to your continued support.

____________________

Treasurer

2 Type out the following and save to a single file called 'Practising Effects':

(a) 40 °C

(b) $3^3 \times 4^4 = y$

(c) $Fe^{2+}$ ions

(d) $2P + 5Cl_2 \rightarrow 2PCl_5$

(e) $Ca(OH)_2 + 2HCl \rightarrow CaCl_2 + 2H_2O$

(f) $2Fe_2O_2 + 3C \rightarrow 4Fe + 3CO_2\uparrow$

(g) $3X^3 - 4X^2 + 2X - 2 = Y$

## Bullets and numbering

Bullets and numbers can be added to already typed text or to text that is being typed. Several different styles of bullets and numbering are available.

*Examples of numbering*:

| | | | |
|---|---|---|---|
| 1. Monday | I. Monday | (a) Monday | A. Monday |
| 2. Tuesday | II. Tuesday | (b) Tuesday | B. Tuesday |
| 3. Wednesday | III. Wednesday | (c) Wednesday | C. Wednesday |

*Examples of bullets*:

| | | | |
|---|---|---|---|
| • Monday | ❖ Monday | ○ Monday | ◇ Monday |
| • Tuesday | ❖ Tuesday | ○ Tuesday | ◇ Tuesday |
| • Wednesday | ❖ Wednesday | ○ Wednesday | ◇ Wednesday |

**Shortcut**

You can use the Formatting toolbar to add bullets or numbers to a list. Select the text and click on the numbers button to add numbers, or click on the bullet button to add bullets. Note that the last bulleted or numbered style is displayed when the numbers or bullets button is selected.

### *Adding bullets or numbers to a list*

1. Select the list you want to add bullets or numbers to.
2. Select **Bullets and Numbering** from the **Format** menu. The 'Bullets and Numbering' dialogue box appears.
3. Choose the appropriate tab, **Bulleted** or **Numbered**.
4. Select the desired bullet or numbering style.
5. Click **OK**.

### *To remove bullets or numbers from a list*

1. Select the numbered or bulleted list.
2. Click the **Bullet** or **Numbering** button to deselect or turn off the bullets or numbering.

# Page layout

## Paper size and page orientation

You may want to select the paper size and page orientation (portrait or landscape) of your document before you begin to type in it.

### *Selecting the paper size and page orientation*

1. Select **Page Setup** from the **File** menu. The 'Page Setup' dialogue box will appear.
2. Select the **Paper** tab. The 'Paper Size' dialogue box is displayed (Figure 10.18). This contains three options, Paper size, Paper source and Preview.

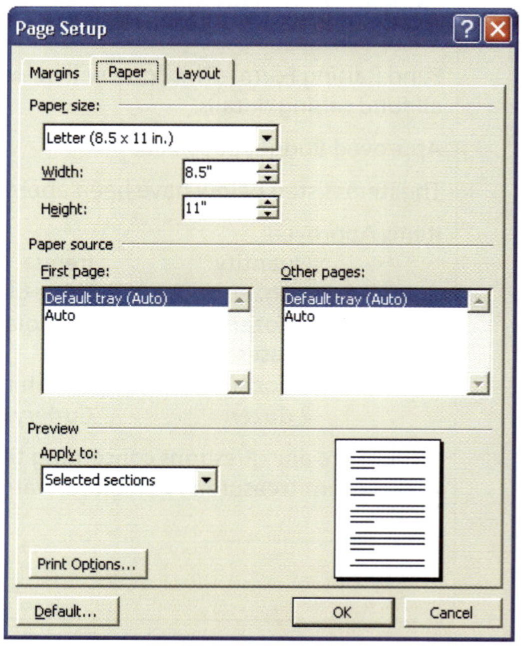


*Figure 10.18 'Page Setup' dialogue box*

3 Select a paper size from the pull-down list provided in the 'Paper Size' dialogue box or type in a width and height in the respective boxes for a custom size.

4 To select the page orientation, select the **Margins** tab (Figure 10.19) and click on the **Portrait** (vertical) or **Landscape** (horizontal) boxes.

5 Click **OK**.

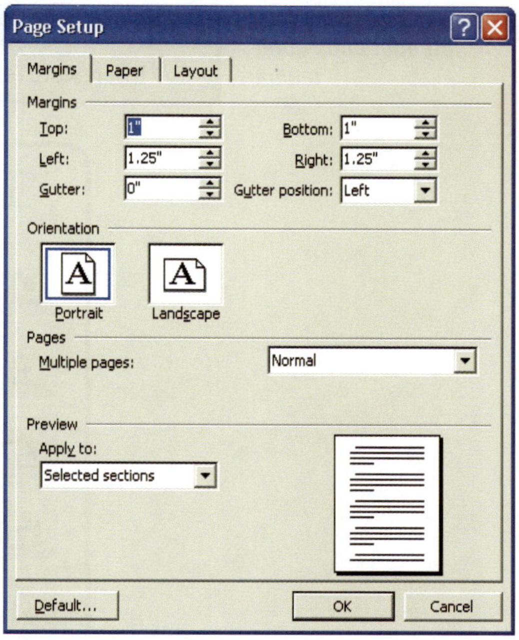


*Figure 10.19*
*Selecting page orientation*

## Margins

Margins are the blank areas around the work area of a sheet of paper, or the distance between the text and the edge of paper. There are four margins: top, bottom, left, right. Then there is the **gutter margin**, the space allotted for binding. This is necessary so that work will not be hidden if the document is bound, i.e. made into a booklet or book. A blank document in Microsoft Word has a default setting of 1 inch for the top and bottom margins, 1.25 inches for the left and right margins, and 0 inches for gutter. These default settings can be changed for the entire document or part of a document.

*To change margins*

1 Select **Page Setup** from the **File**. The 'Page Setup' dialogue box appears.
This contains four options: Margins, Orientation, Pages and Preview.
The 'Margins' tab dialogue box displays the default values for the top, bottom, left, right and gutter margins.

2 These values can be changed by selecting the up arrow to increase the size or the down arrow to decrease the size of the respective margins, or by typing in the values.

3 As the values are changed a preview of how the document will change appears in the preview section.

4 You can change the margins for the whole document or from a particular point by selecting **Whole document** or **This point forward** in the 'Apply to:' section of the dialogue box.

### Activity 7

1 Retrieve the document 'New Record Keeping Practices' you created earlier.

2 Change the left and right margins to 1.5 inches.

3 Change the line spacing in the document to 1.5.

## Headers and footers

A **header** or **footer** is text or graphics that appears in the top or bottom margins of every page of a document. The header appears in the top margin and the footer appears in the bottom margin. Headers and footers are normally used to print information such as the title of a document or chapter name and/or author name, page numbers, current date and time, letterheads and company logos. A different header and footer can be used for odd and even pages. The first page of a document can also have a different header and footer from the rest of the document.

*Figure 10.20 'Header and Footer' toolbar*

| | |
|---|---|
| Insert AutoText | A dropdown list box from which predefined text can be automatically inserted |
| | Inserts the page number |
| | Inserts the total number of pages in the document |
| | Formats the page numbers |
| | Inserts the current date |
| | Inserts the current time |
| | Page setup |
| | Shows/Hides the text in the document |
| | Switches between the header and footer |
| | Links to the previous header or footer |
| | Shows the previous header or footer |
| | Shows the next header or footer |

*Table 9 Functions in the 'Header and Footer' toolbar*

### Creating a header and footer

1 Select **Header and Footer** from the **View** menu. The Header textbox (Figure 10.21) and the Header and Footer toolbar appear (Figure 10.20).

You can type in the header in the Header textbox. Click on the **Switch between Header and Footer** button for the Footer box to appear. Type in the footer. On screen, the text or graphics typed is displayed dimmed.

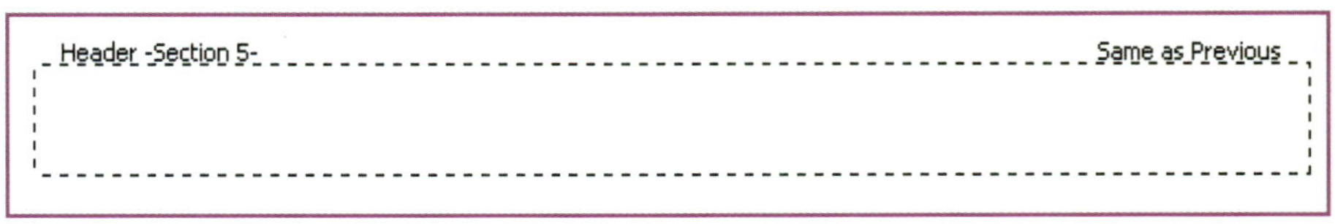


*Figure 10.21 Header text box*

### To delete a header or footer

1 Place the insertion point somewhere on a page where the header or footer appears.

2 Select **Header and Footer** from the **View** menu.

3 Select the Header or Footer text you want to delete.

4 Press **Backspace** or press **Delete**.

5 Click the **Close** button on the Header and Footer toolbar to return to the document.

## Footnotes and endnotes

You may want to insert a reference mark – such as a number, character or combination of characters – in the main body of your text, to indicate that additional information is provided elsewhere in the document to explain or expand on a word, a sentence or text. The reference is placed in a section of the document called a footnote or endnote.

A **footnote** is placed at the end of the page containing the reference mark. It is usually positioned in the footer section of the page, below the text. Footnotes are usually used to expand the text and give detailed comments or explanations.

An **endnote** is placed at the end of the document or the end of a section. Endnotes are often used for citing sources, for example indicating another book that was used as a reference for the document you are writing.

By default, Microsoft Word places footnotes at the end of each page and endnotes at the end of the document.

### *To insert a footnote or an endnote*

1. Place the insertion point at the relevant section (that is, where the reference mark will be placed).
2. Choose **Reference** from the **Insert** menu.
3. Select **Footnote**. The 'Footnote and Endnote' dialogue box will appear (Figure 10.22).
4. In the Location section of the box choose either **Footnotes** or **Endnotes** by clicking the radio buttons.
5. Select where you want to place the footnote or endnote.
6. Select the character (a number or custom mark/symbol) that will become your reference mark from the Format section of the box.
7. If the reference mark is a number, select the starting number and whether you want to continue the numbering from the previous pages, or restart the numbering for each page or section.
8. Click the **Insert** button.

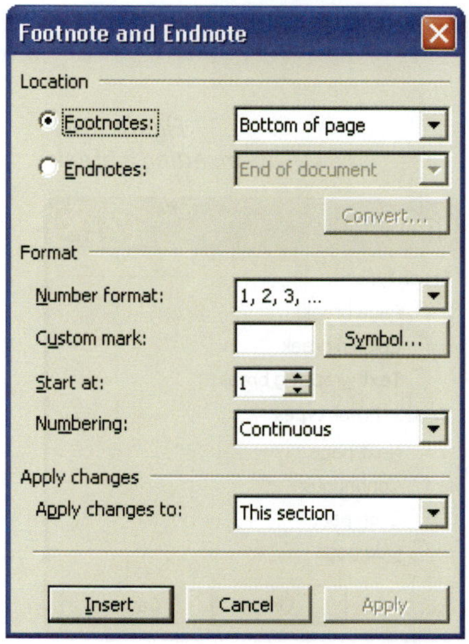


*Figure 10.22 'Footnote and Endnote' dialogue box*

### *To delete a footnote or an endnote*

Delete the reference mark, not the text in the note. Microsoft Word automatically renumbers the notes accordingly.

## Page numbering

You will often want to number the pages of a document when it becomes longer than a few pages. Page numbers can be placed automatically on each page by using the **Insert** menu, or the page number option in **Headers and Footers.**

### *Inserting page numbers from the Insert menu*

1. Select **Page Numbers** from the **Insert** menu. The 'Page Number' dialogue box appears (Figure 10.23 on page 172).
2. Select the position where you want the number displayed – at the top of the page or bottom of the page.
3. Select the alignment from the list provided, such as left, right, centre.
4. You can check or uncheck the **Show number on first page** box.
5. Click **OK**.

## Inserting page numbers using the Header and Footer toolbar

1. Select **Headers and Footers** from the **View** menu. The Header and Footer textbox and toolbar is displayed.
2. In the Header or Footer textbox, position the insertion point where you would like to place the number.
3. Click on the **Insert Page Number** button from the Header and Footer toolbar.
4. Click **Close**.

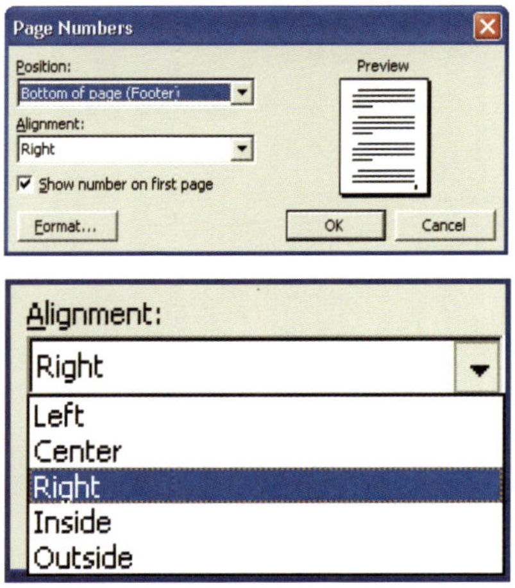


*Figure 10.23*
*Page number options*

## Page breaks

Microsoft Word automatically determines the end of a page depending on the paper size selected. These automatic page breaks, which are called **soft page breaks**, can be seen as a single dotted line at the end of a page when you view the document in Normal View. In Page Layout view, you literally see the end of the page.

Despite this automatic function, you may still choose to insert a page break before the actual end of a page – for example, when you want to finish a section half-way down a page and start a new section immediately on the next page. This type of page break is called a **hard page break** and, once inserted, is seen as a solid horizontal line marked 'page break'.

*Figure 10.24*
*Inserting a break*

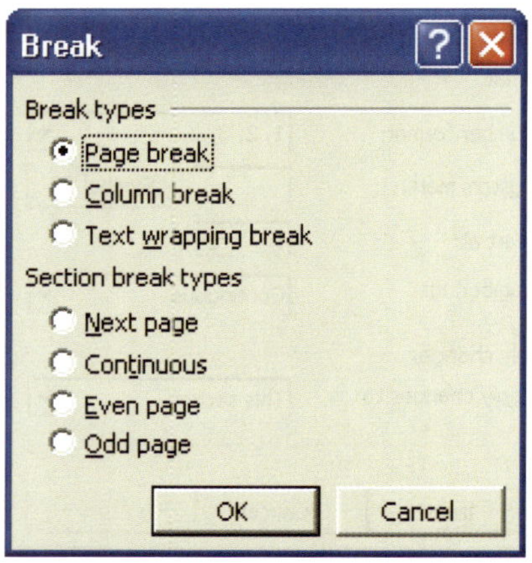


## Inserting a hard page break

1. Position the insertion point where you would like to end the page.
2. Select **Break** from the **Insert** menu. The 'Break' dialogue box appears (Figure 10.24).
3. Check the **Page Break** button.
4. Click on **OK**.

## Deleting a hard page break

1. Ensure the **Show/Hide** button in the toolbar is in the 'on' position.
2. The page break will be displayed as a solid line, plus the words 'page break'.
3. Select the line and press the **Delete** key.

## Activity 8

1. Retrieve the document 'Art' from your Companion CD.
2. Move the article 'What is Art?' above the article 'Ancient Art'.
3. Centre and embolden each article heading.
4. Insert a header 'The Artist Newsletter – Volume 1, Number 2'.
5. Right align and italicise the header.
6. Insert automatic page numbering at the bottom centre of each page.
7. Double-space each article.
8. Change the left margin to 2" and all other margins to 1".
9. Insert the following footnote to refer to 'Paleolithic period' in the article 'Ancient Art'. Use this reference mark: α

   'The Paleolithic period refers to the second part of the Stone Age, beginning about 750 000 to 500 000 years BC, and lasting until the end of the last ice age, about 8500 years BC.'
10. Spell-check the document.
11. Fully justify the paragraphs of the document.
12. Change the font size of each article to 16 points.
13. Save the document as 'Art Newsletter'.

## Tabs

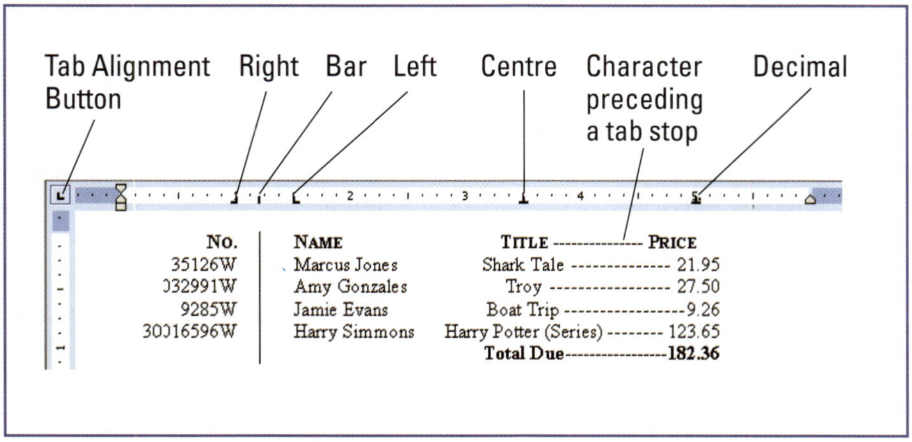


*Figure 10.25 Setting tabs using the Ruler*

Tab stops are used to place text or numbers at predetermined positions in a document. This is a helpful feature that allows you to spread text or figures across a page evenly. The default tab position is 1.27 centimetres (or 0.5 inches). This means that every time the Tab key is pressed the cursor moves 1.27 centimetres (or 0.5 inches).

Tabs can be used for creating simple tabular-style documents or tables within a document. However, they are not an alternative to proper tables. You can also specify a particular character such as a full stop or a dash to precede a tab stop. Microsoft Word offers five types of Tab stops (Figure 10.25).

| Tab | Function |
|---|---|
| Left | The text starts and is aligned at the tab stop |
| Right | Text ends at the tab stop |
| Centre | Text is centred under the tab stop |
| Decimal | Lines up the decimal point in numbers in a column at the tab stop |
| Bar | Creates a thin vertical line at the tab stop |

*Table 10 Tabs*

### Setting tab stops using the ruler

1 Click on the **Tab Alignment** button at the extreme left of the ruler until the desired icon is displayed. . Click on the ruler where you want to place a tab stop for the paragraph.

### To remove or move a tab stop

1 Select the paragraph(s) that contains the tab stop markers you want to remove or change.

2 Drag the tab stop marker off the ruler to remove it; or

3 Drag the tab stop to the left or right to change its position.

**Did you know?**

More precise tab stops can be set using the **Tab** command in the **Format** menu.

### To set tabs using the 'Tabs' dialogue box

1 Choose **Tabs** from the **Format** menu. The 'Tabs' dialogue box appears.

2 Type in or select the tab position you want in the default tab stop position box.

3 Click **Set**.

4 After setting all the tabs click **OK**.

The tab stops set can be used for the entire document or it can be changed for each paragraph or tables within the document.

### To clear tab stops

1 In the 'Tabs' dialogue box, select the tab and click on **Clear** to select one at a time or click on **Clear All** to remove all the tabs.

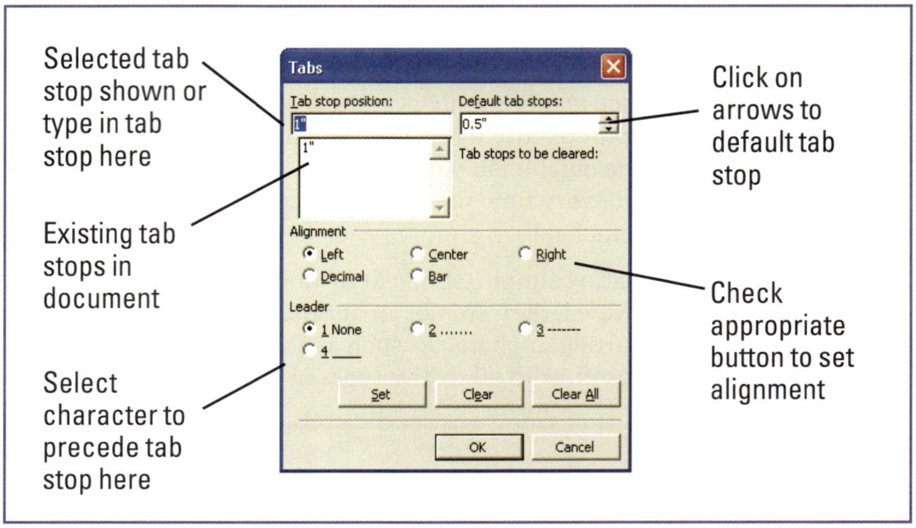


*Figure 10.26 'Tabs' dialogue box*

## Activity 9

1 Type the following menu, setting a centre tab at 1.5" and a decimal tab with dots leader (...) at 4".

2 Centre the heading.

3 Change the font to Bookman Old Style.

4 Change the font size to 14 points.

*Breakfast Special*

*Bake and Shark . . . . . . . . . . . . . . .$5.00*
*Bake and Saltfish . . . . . . . . . . . . . .$3.50*
*Egg and Toast . . . . . . . . . . . . . . . . .$2.00*
*Cowheel Soup . . . . . . . . . . . . . . .$11.25*
*Tea . . . . . . . . . . . . . . . . . . . . . . . .$1.50*
*Coffee . . . . . . . . . . . . . . . . . . . . . .$2.00*
*Juice . . . . . . . . . . . . . . . . . . . . . . .$3.00*

5 Below is a list of five students with their corresponding student number, name, weight (kg), height (cm) and age.

111, Tricia Bridgemohan, 40.5,110.5,16

112, Kizzy Joe-Johnson, 45.2, 180.3,15

113, Phillip McIsaac, 50.6, 141.0,17

114, Dwane Philips, 49.3, 150.2,16

115, Richard Williamson, 66.0, 195.3,18

(a) Type out the data in a tabular format with the given headings, using appropriate tabs.

(b) Separate each column with a vertical line.

(c) Boldface and underline each heading.

## Drawing a line

In Microsoft Word you can also draw objects, the simplest of which is a line. A line is treated as an object and can therefore be moved. Note on the other hand that underlining is associated with text and cannot be moved by itself. It has to be moved with the accompanying text.

### Drawing lines

1. Display the Drawing toolbar – right-click on any of the displayed toolbars and select **Drawing**.
2. Click on **AutoShapes**.
3. Select **Lines**.
4. Click on the **Line** button.
5. In your document, move the indicator to the desired starting position for your line.
6. Click, hold and drag the mouse button to make the line, in any direction you wish.
7. Click off the line to deselect.

A Drawing Canvas in which you are to perform your drawing may appear after selecting the **Line** button. If you do not want to draw within this designated area, press the Esc key to remove the Drawing Canvas. You can then continue, moving your indicator to the desired position and drawing as you wish.

## Mail merge

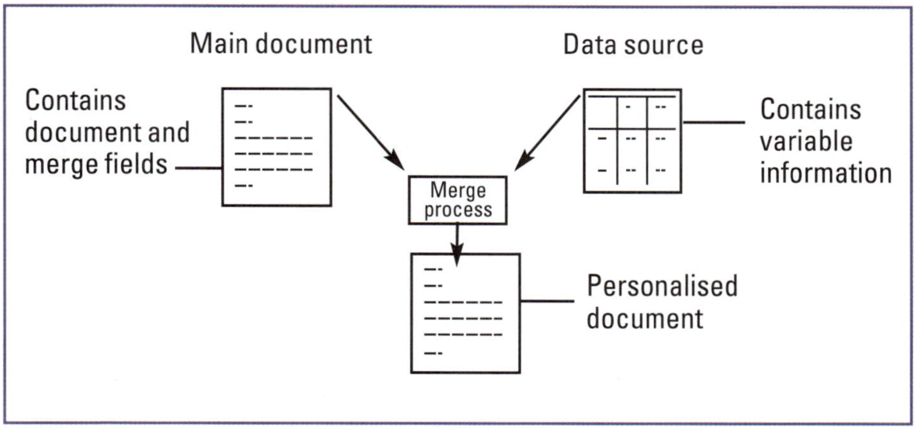


*Figure 10.27*
*Diagram of mail merge*

The **mail merge** feature in Microsoft Word 2003 is significantly different from Microsoft Word 2000. In this section we will look at the 2003 version. Using the mail merge feature, you can produce large volumes of personalised letters, mailing labels, memos and e-mails without having to type each one individually for each recipient. For example, many companies send standard letters to customers in which the body of the letter is the same but the name, address and a few pieces of additional information may be different. This type of multi-recipient correspondence can be produced easily using mail merge. Merging requires the use of two files: a main document (primary file) and a data source (secondary file). Data from the data source is inserted into the main document to produce personalised documents. Figure 10.27 shows the merging process.

- The main document (or primary file) contains the letter or other document that is meant for each recipient. It also contains the merge fields, which are positioned at the points where the information from the data source is to be inserted. When the mail merge begins, the merge fields are replaced with the information from the data source.
- The **data source** (or secondary file) contains the personalised information that would vary in each document, such as names and addresses of individuals. The data source can be an existing data source, or you can create a new data source by using the 'Mail Merge Helper'.

The information stored in the data source is organised in the form of a table. The first row, known as the header row, contains the merge fields. A **merge field** is the name of a data item that will be stored in the data source and later be merged into the main document. Some common field names are Title, Firstname, Address, Phoneno, etc. When creating merge fields, you must ensure that each merge field:

- is unique
- begins with a letter
- contains no more than 40 characters
- does not contain any blank spaces (for Microsoft Word 2000)

Each row after the header row contains the information that is unique to each document, and is known as a data record. The collection of data records is called a **data file**.

## Creating a main document

> If you want to find out more about this topic you could look up the related animations and activities on your companion CD-ROM.

You can create a main document before you access the 'Mail Merge Wizard Task Pane'. The areas designated to hold the data that will be unique to each recipient could be indicated as blank spaces, or by typing dummy field names enclosed in double angle-brackets, e.g. < < Name > >. This is necessary so that the field codes will be inserted in the correct positions, even though the actual codes will not be available to be inserted into the main document until you have created the data source document.

The following are steps to create a mail merge document:

1. Decide on the type of document you are going to create, e.g. letter, e-mail message, label, envelope, directory.
2. Decide on the starting document: either use the current active document or open a document from storage.
3. Change the document layout if necessary (for envelopes and labels only).
4. Decide on the recipients: decide what data source to use, i.e. whether to create it or to use an existing one.

## Creating the data source

1. Select **Letters and Mailings** from the **Tools** menu.
2. Select **Mail Merge**. (The 'Mail Merge' Wizard Task Pane appears, as shown in Figure 10.28.) The task pane appears on the right side of the Word document window and allows you to choose from available options to perform your task.
3. Select the starting document. Choose the appropriate option by clicking on the radio button (Figure 10.29).
   - **Use the current document** allows you to use the current active/open document.
   - **Start from a template** allows you to choose one of the Word templates to use to create your letter.
   - **Start from existing document** allows you to choose an existing file to work with.
4. Click on **Next: Select recipients** at the bottom of the task pane. The Select recipients Task Pane appears (Figure 10.30).
5. Choose **Type a new list**; this allows you to create a new listing. Then click **Create**.
6. The 'New Address List' dialogue box appears (Figure 10.31). Microsoft Word has some predefined fields. You can choose to use these fields, or, delete them and add your own (Figure 10.32).

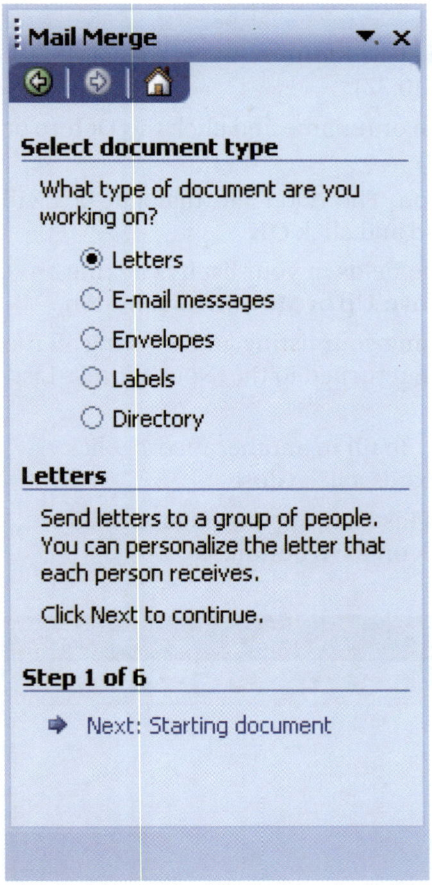


Figure 10.28

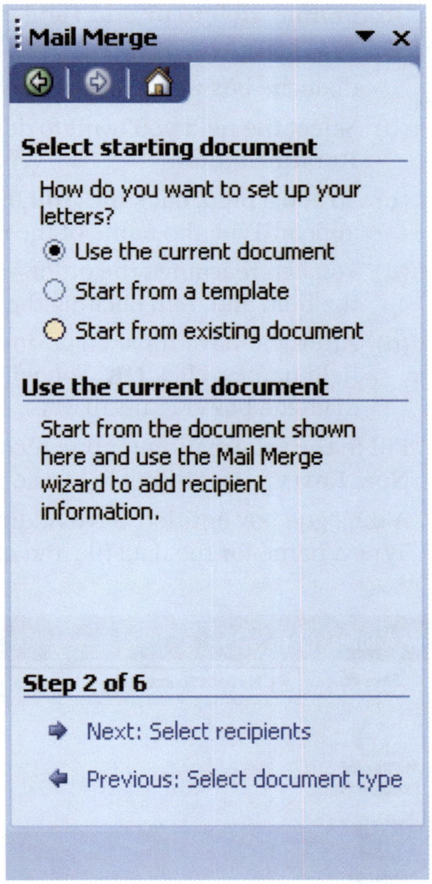


Figure 10.29

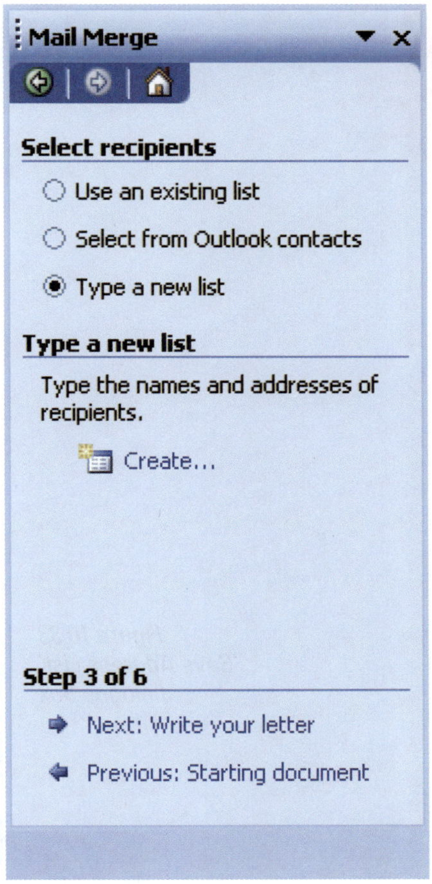


Figure 10.30

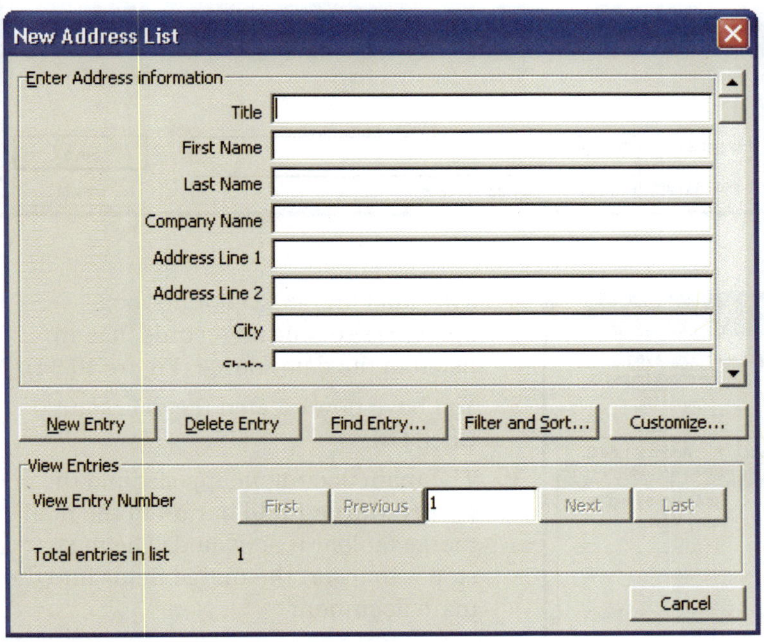


Figure 10.31
'New Address List' dialogue box

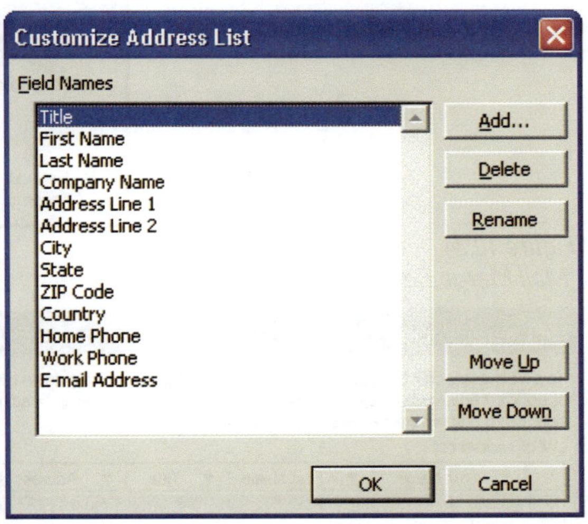


Figure 10.32
'Customize Address List' box

### To rename, delete or add fields

(a) Choose the **Customize** button. The 'Customize Address List' dialogue box will appear (Figure 10.32).

(b) Select the field you want to delete or rename and click the **Delete** or **Rename** button.

(c) To add a field, click the **Add** button. The 'Add Field' dialogue box will appear. Type the name of the field and click **OK**.

(d) You can rearrange the order of the fields in your list by clicking on the field and then clicking the **Move Up** or **Move Down** button.

(e) After you have finished customising your listing and entering all the field names, click **OK**. You will be returned to the 'New Address List' dialogue box (Figure 10.31).

6 Fill in the information for one record. To fill in another record, click **New Entry**. After filling in all the records, click **Close**.

7 A dialogue box entitled 'Save Address List' will appear (Figure 10.33). Type a name for the data file and click on **Save** button.

*Figure 10.33 'Save Address List' dialogue box*

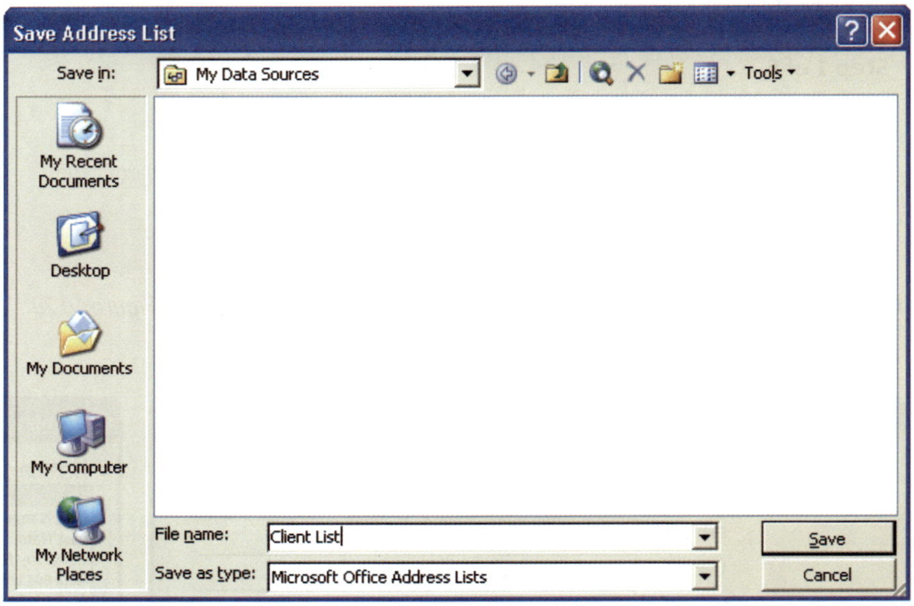


*Figure 10.34 'Mail Merge Recipients' box*

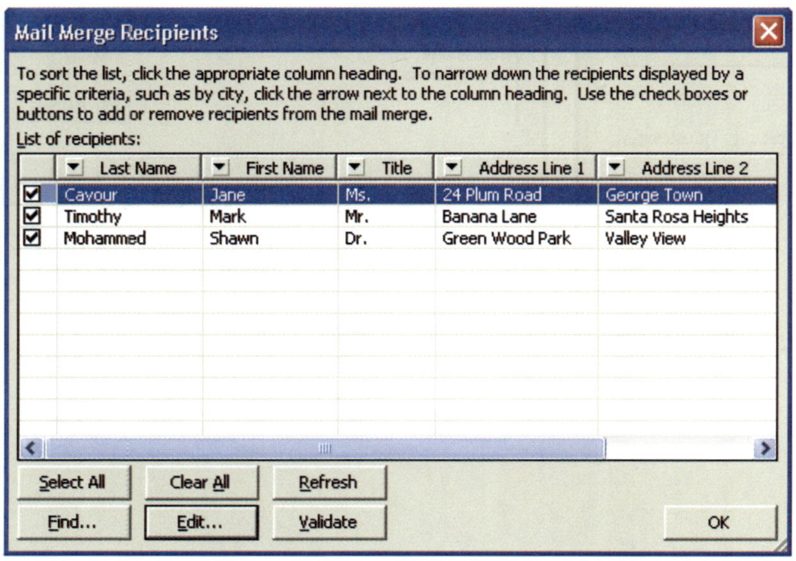


8 The 'Mail Merge Recipients' box appears, showing all records that are listed in the data source (Figure 10.34).

9 You have now created the data source. Click **OK**.

10 The main document appears and the **Insert Merge Field** button in the mail merge toolbar is activated. The next step is to insert the merge fields into the main document.

*Figure 10.35*
*Mail Merge toolbar*

The Mail Merge toolbar (Figure 10.35) becomes available at this point in the mail merge process. However, it can also be accessed by:

- Selecting **Toolbars** from the **View** menu and then clicking on **Mail Merge**
- Selecting **Letters and Mailings** from the **Tools** menu and then selecting **Show Mail Merge Toolbar**
- Right-clicking in the grey/blue area at the top of the document window (next to the toolbars) and selecting **Mail Merge**.

The symbols and their meanings in this toolbar are described in Table 11.

*Table 11*
*Functions of the Mail Merge toolbar*

| Button | Function |
|---|---|
| | Main document setup – allows you to select the type of document you want to create |
| | Opens the Data source or secondary document |
| | Opens a listing of the mail merge recipients |
| | Inserts an address block |
| | Inserts a greeting line |
| | Inserts the merge fields |
| Insert Word Field | Inserts Word Fields |
| | The Merge Data button allows you to view the merged document before printing or merging. |
| 1 | Allows you to move through the records, from the first record, previous records, displays the current record, next record, first record and last record. |
| | Check for errors |
| | Merge to a new document |
| | Merge to the printer |
| | Merge to e-mail |
| | Merge to fax |

Figure 10.36
'Insert Merge Field' dialogue box

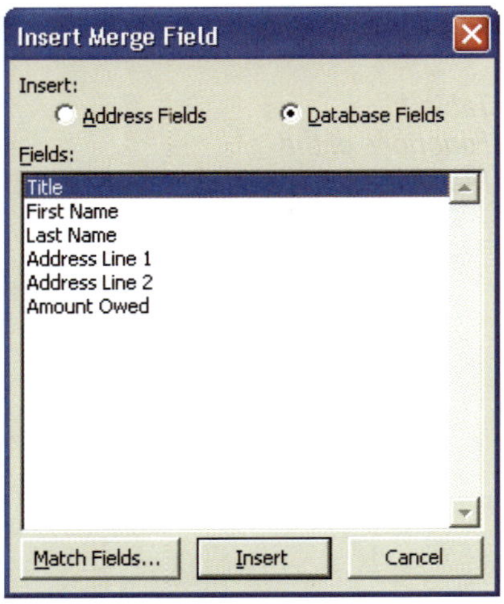


### Inserting the merge fields

1 Position your insertion point where the first merge field is to be inserted into the document.

2 Click on the **Insert Merge Field** button. The 'Insert Merge Field' dialogue box appears (Figure 10.36).

3 Select the desired field and click the **Insert** button. The field appears in the position you indicated (Figure 10.37).

4 Place all the other fields in their respective positions.

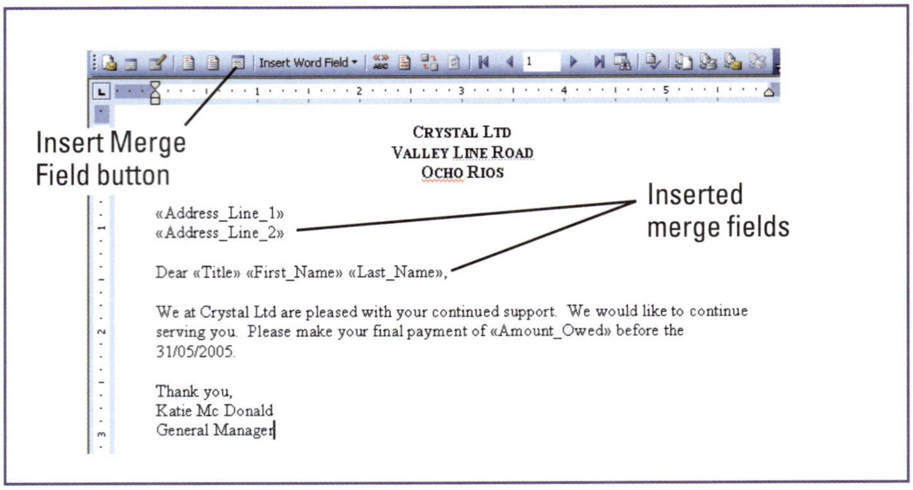


*Figure 10.37 Inserting the merge fields in their correct positions*

## Updating the data source

Once you have created a data source, you can make changes to it later.

1 Display the Mail Merge toolbar.

2 Click on the **Open Data Source** button. The Mail Merge toolbar becomes active.

3 Click on the **Mail Merge Recipients** button. The 'Mail Merge Recipients' dialogue box appears.

4 Select **Edit**.

5 The 'Address List' dialogue box appears. Choose **Customize** and follow the instructions to rename, delete and add fields, as you wish.

### *Deleting a record*

1 Click on the **Mail Merge Recipients** button. The 'Mail Merge Recipients' dialogue box appears.

2 (a) Uncheck the boxes to remove the records from the mail merge, or

(b) click the **Edit** button, select the record to be deleted from the 'Address List' dialogue box and click **Delete Entry**.

### *Editing a record*

1 Click on the **Mail Merge Recipients** button. The 'Mail Merge Recipients' dialogue box appears.

2 Click on the **Edit** button.

3 Select the record to be edited and select the data item; insert, change or replace the existing data as you wish.

## Activity 10

Patients of the Diamond Valley Clinic are sent letters to remind them of their appointment date and what they are required to bring with them.

> Diamond Valley Clinic
> 28 Diamond Boulevard
> Cape Town
>
> <Title> <First Name> <Last Name>
> <Address Line 1>
> <Address Line 2>
>
> Dear <Title> <Last Name>,
>
> This is to remind you of your appointment with us at <time> on <appointment date>. This is a follow-up of your last visit on <date of last visit>. Please bring this letter when you arrive at the Medical Out-Patient Consultant No. 3. You will be attended to by Dr. <Doctor>.
>
> Please bring a sample of <sample>.
>
> Yours respectfully,
>
> ________________
>
> Clinic Administrator

1 Type in this document to be used in a mail merge and save it to a file called 'Appointment Reminders'.

2 Indent the name and address of the clinic to 4 inches.

3 Create a secondary document, called 'Patients', using the following data as a basis:

| | |
|---|---|
| Title | Mr |
| Patient First Name | Martin |
| Patient Surname | Jades |
| Patient Address | 65 Pine Drive, Mavewood Park |
| Time | 9.30 am |
| Appointment Date | 1/6/05 |
| Date of Last Visit | 2/1/05 |
| Doctor | James Mahabir |
| Sample | Urine |
| | |
| Title | Ms |
| Patient First Name | Leselle |
| Patient Surname | Kotes |
| Patient Address | Banana Bread Lane, Diamond Village |
| Time | 2.00 pm |
| Appointment Date | 10/6/05 |
| Date of Last Visit | 22/3/05 |
| Doctor | James Mahabir |
| Sample | Stool |

4 Add three records of your own to the data file.

5 Delete the 'Patient First Name' field from the data file.

6 Merge the two files to produce the personalised letters to be sent to patients.

7 Save the letters to a file called 'Appointment Letters'.

## Newspaper columns

Text columns are a very useful feature when you want to produce newsletters, newspaper-style documents, indexes or any text that needs to be in continuous columns. When the first column is filled at the bottom of the page, the text continues in the next column at the top of the page. Figure 10.38 shows a page divided into two sections. The first section has one column and the second section has two columns. When the first column is completed in the second section, the insertion point goes to the start of the second column.

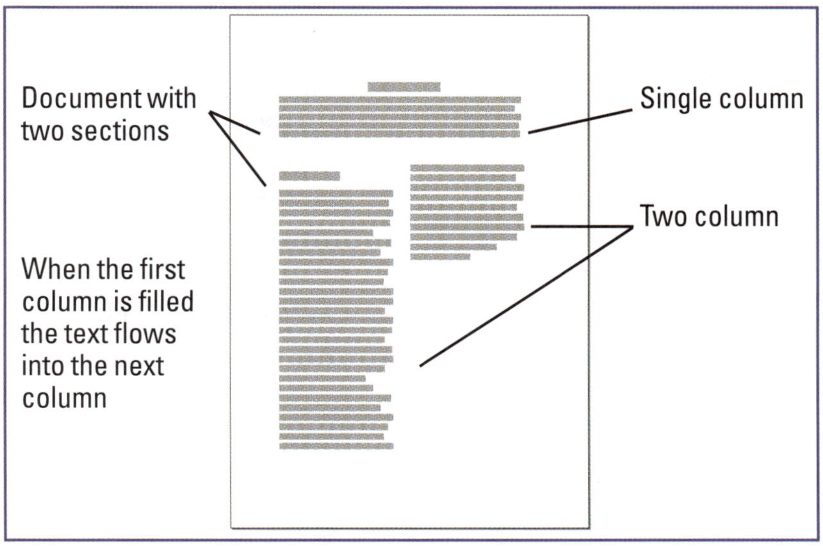


*Figure 10.38*
*Document with several columns*

Newspaper columns can be created by using the **Columns** icon in the toolbar or from the **Format** menu.

*Figure 10.39*
*'Columns' dialogue box*

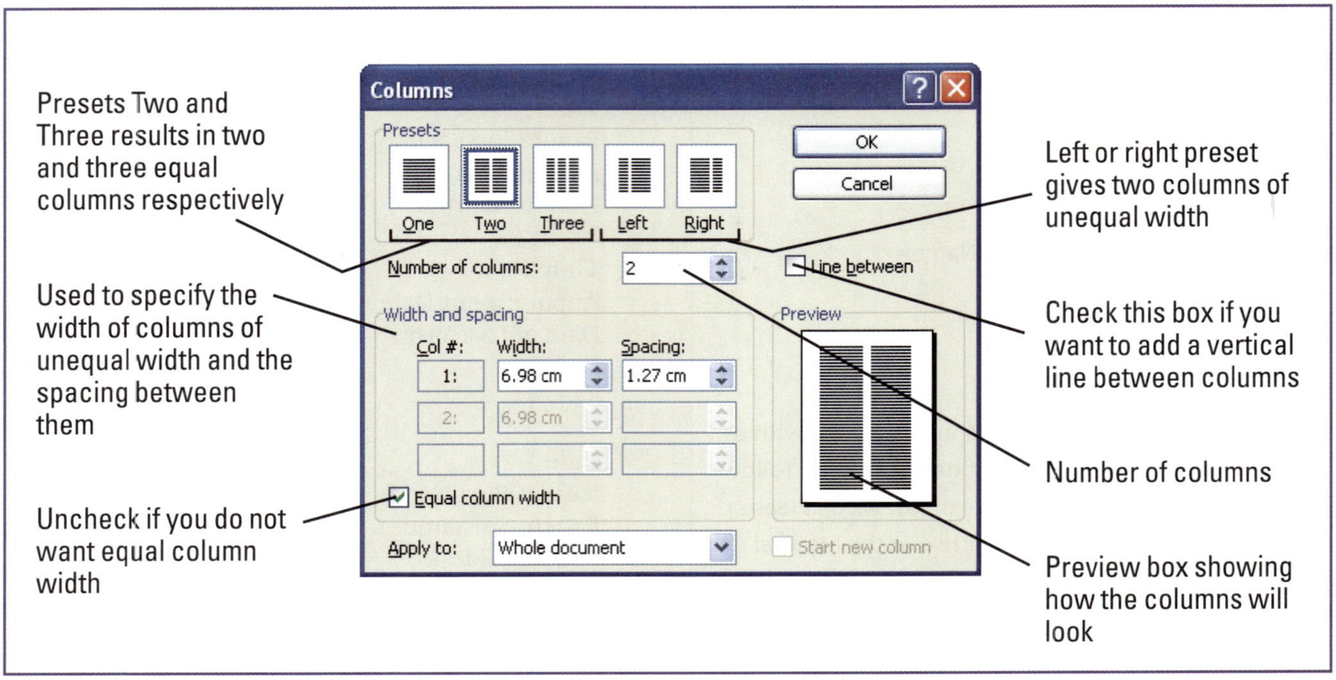


## Shortcut

You can also insert columns by using the Columns button in the standard toolbar. Clicking on this button produces a drop-down set of icons, which you drag across to select the number of columns required. These columns would all be of equal width. However, note that the width of a column and the spacing between columns cannot be changed when the Columns button is used.

### *Creating columns using the Format menu*

1. Select **Columns** from the **Format** menu. The 'Columns' dialogue box will appear.
2. Select the number of columns required by clicking on one of the presets; or move to the 'Number of columns' section and use the up-arrow to increase the number of columns or the down-arrow to decrease the number of columns.
3. The 'Width and spacing' section allows you to specify the width of each column and the spacing between them. A preview of the selections made can be seen in the 'Preview' section.
4. The 'Apply to' box lets you choose between formatting the entire document, or formatting it just from a specified point.

## Column break

The position in a column where the text ends and the next column starts is called a **column break**. If a document has two columns and you reach a particular point in the first column where you would like to finish and start the next column, you can insert a column break.

### *To insert a column break*

1. Position the insertion point where you want to end the column.
2. Select **Break** from the **Insert** menu. The 'Break' dialogue box appears.
3. Check the **Column break** radio button.
4. Click **OK**.

## Activity 11

The Royal Bank of Grenada produces a newsletter called *Bank News*. The articles shown below are to be part of the next newsletter. You will create the document by doing the following:

1. Type out the articles for the document, as shown opposite.
2. Insert a title-heading, "Bank News", at least 24-point text.
3. Centre and embolden the heading. Ensure that it uses a large font.
4. Use a bold font and capital letters for the title of each article, at least 18-point text.
5. Use at least 14-point text for the body of each article.
6. Double line-space each article.
7. Change the left and right margins to 1.5 inches and the top and bottom margins to 1.25 inches.
8. Format the document using two newspaper-style columns. The title-heading should not be part of any column.
9. Insert the following header into every page of the document:

   **Bank News, Volume 3, Number 8**
10. Insert the page number into the footer. Centre the page number.
11. Fully justify each article.
12. Correct all spelling and any grammatical errors in the document.
13. Save the document as 'Bank News'.

Here are the articles for the newsletter:

Staff Departures

The bank would like to express its sincere appreciation to the following for their services, which will be sadly missed:

Mr Frank Jackson, Accounts Development Officer, West Cape branch, has resigned his position with effect from 27 July 2005. Mr Jackson was employed at the bank continuously over the last seven years.

Miss Janet Jebodsingh, Regional Manager, Wester Isle, has resigned her position with effect from 11 June 2005. Miss Jebodsingh served the bank for eleven years.

New Staff

The bank would like to welcome the following new employees:

Mrs Laura Ellison has been employed as a computer programmer in the M.I.S. department at headquarters, and will take up her position on 23 August 2005.

Mr Alton Royal has been employed as teller in the South Wiscombe branch, and will take up his position on 10 August 2005.

Staff Promotions

The bank would like to congratulate Sheena MacDonald, currently Junior Accounts Supervisor at headquarters, on being promoted to the position of Accounting Supervisor for West Cape branch. Miss MacDonald will move to the branch on 3 September 2005.

Training News: Seminar on Money Laundering

The Bank's Inspection Department will be conducting a seminar for supervisors between $10^{th}$ and $14^{th}$ October 2005, at the training centre at headquarters. The seminar is designed to empower all staff with the necessary skills to spot, report and explain possible cases of money laundering occurring in customers' accounts.

Supervisors attending the seminar will conduct knowledge-sharing presentations at their respective branches upon their return.

Sport News

The Bank's Annual Sports and Family Fun Day, 2005, will be held at the Centre of Excellence at headquarters, on 25 July 2005, from 10:00 am. All branches are asked to elect their team captains and start making preparations for this grand annual event. There will be events for the entire family, such as games, team sports, music, and of course, the barbecue. Branches of the bank will distribute tickets nearer the time of the event.

# Tables

Tables are very useful for displaying numerical and statistical data within a document and can also be useful for keeping text aligned. They are one way of enhancing the presentation of data within documents.

A table is made up of three components: rows, columns and cells.

- A row runs horizontally
- A column runs vertically
- A cell is an individual 'box' in the table, in which you place data. It is at the intersection of a row and a column.
  Information can be inserted in the table by placing the insertion point in the appropriate cell and typing.
  Tables can be inserted into a document by using the menu, or by using the table button in the menu bar.

## Inserting a table using the menu bar

1 Click on **Insert** in the **Table** menu.

2 Select **Table**. The 'Insert Table' dialogue box appears (Figure 10.40).

3 Make the appropriate selections and click **OK**.

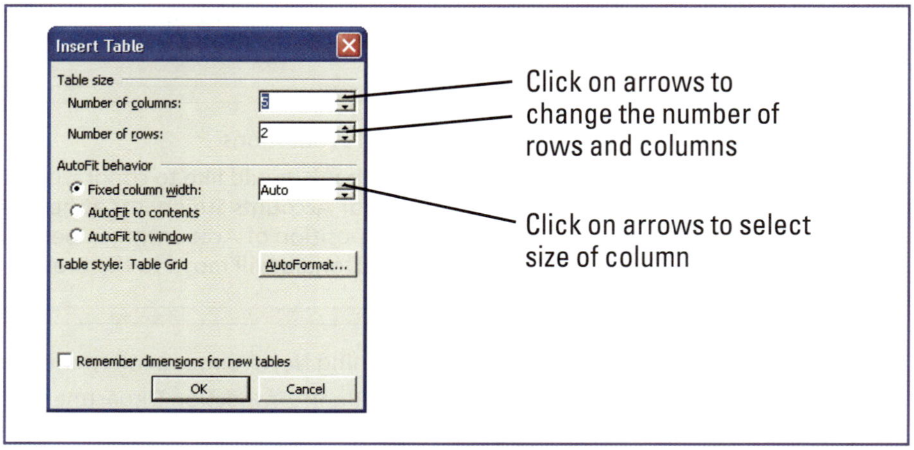


*Figure 10.40 'Insert Table' dialogue box*

## Inserting a table using the Table button from the standard toolbar

1 Place the insertion point at the location where you want to insert the table.

2 Click the **Insert Table** button on the toolbar.

3 Drag the mouse down to select the number of rows and then right to select the number of columns. A highlighted grid of the number of rows and columns is displayed as you are selecting (Figure 10.41).

4 Release the mouse button; the table will be inserted in the document.

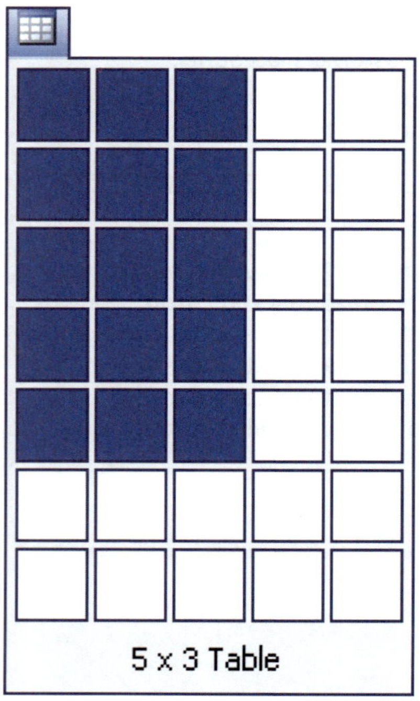


*Figure 10.41*

## Adding rows and columns in a table

1 Place the insertion point in the row or column next to where you would like to insert the new row or column.

2 Select **Insert** from the **Table** menu. A drop-down list with the following options appears: Columns to the left, Columns to the right, Rows above, Rows below and Cells.

3 Clicking on the desired option places the new row or column in the position relative to the selected row or column.

### Deleting a row or column

1. Place the insertion point in the row or column you would like to delete.
2. Select **Delete** from the **Table** menu. A drop-down list with the following options appears: Table, Column, Row, Cells.
3. Select the desired option.

### Drawing a table using the Tables and Borders toolbar

You can draw tables using the Tables and Borders toolbar.

### Displaying the Tables and Borders toolbar

1. Select **Toolbars** from the **View** menu.
2. Click on **Tables and Borders** from the drop-down list.
3. The Tables and Borders toolbar is displayed (Figure 10.42).

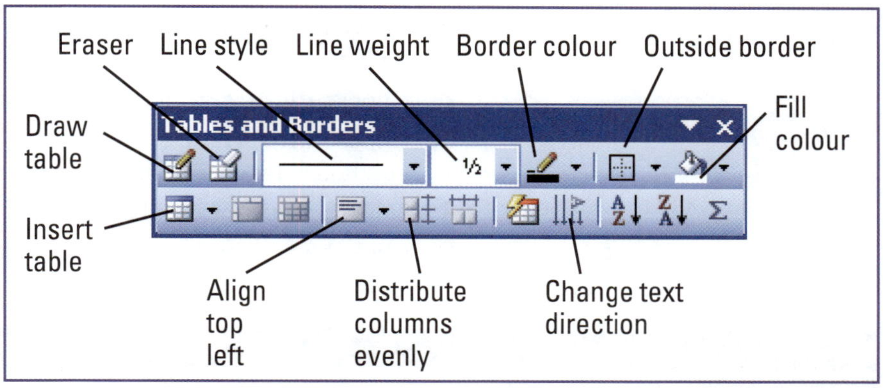


*Figure 10.42 Tables and Borders toolbar*

### Drawing the table

1. Click on the **Draw Table** button (the table-and-pencil icon).
2. Change the line weight if necessary, that is, the line thickness. (Click on the line weight drop-down arrow.)
3. The mouse pointer is displayed as a pencil. At the insertion point, press and hold the mouse button. Drag the pencil to draw tables and add lines.

### Deleting lines

In the latest versions of Microsoft Word you can easily delete individual lines within tables.

1. Click on the **Eraser** button on the toolbar. The pointer becomes an eraser.
2. Click on the line to be erased.

## Activity 12

1. Here is a list of some foods we typically eat and the approximate amount of energy we get from them, measured in kilojoules.
   - A portion of fish 363
   - A portion of potatoes 129
   - One boiled egg 380
   - A slice of bread and butter 180
   - One peanut 25
   - One carrot 85

   (a) Create a table with two rows and two columns.

   (b) Put the information above into the table under the headings 'Food' and 'Energy'.
2. Information about the planets in the solar system is listed opposite, in the following order: Planet, Diameter (km), Distance from the Sun (millions of km) and length of year.

   Mercury, 4840, 58, 88 Earth days
   Venus, 12 200, 108, 225 Earth days
   Earth, 12 800, 150, 365 Earth days
   Mars, 6750, 228, 687 Earth days
   Jupiter, 143 000, 778, 12 Earth years
   Saturn, 121 000, 1430, 29 Earth years
   Uranus, 47 200, 2870, 84 Earth days
   Neptune, 44 600, 4500, 154 Earth years
   Pluto, 6000, 5900, 248 Earth years

   (a) Create a table with two rows and four columns.

   (b) Put the information above into the table under headings in the appropriate columns.

   (c) Centre justify the data in the second and third columns.

# Inserting graphics

Graphics are another way of enhancing the presentation of a document. Microsoft Word provides a wide selection of **clip art** which can be inserted into documents. You can also scan drawings or photos using a scanner, or download graphics from a digital camera or the Internet, saving these to a graphics file that can be inserted into documents.

## Inserting a graphic into a document

1. Place the I-beam to the left of the point where you want the graphic displayed.
2. Choose **Picture** from the **Insert** menu.
3. Choose **Clip Art**. The 'Microsoft Clip Organizer' appears (Figure 10.43). Or choose **From File** if the graphic is stored in a file.
4. Select a picture from the various categories provided.
5. Click the picture once then click on **Insert** to insert the graphic in the document.

*Figure 10.43*
*Microsoft Clip Organizer*

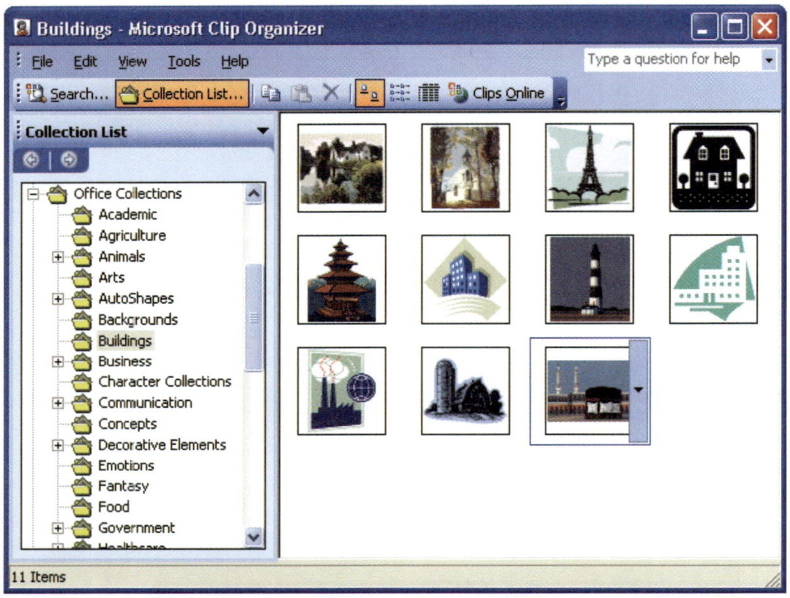


If you are not happy with the position and/or size of the graphic, both can be changed relatively easily.

## Resizing a graphic

1. Click once on the graphic. The graphic is displayed with eight selection handles around it (Figure 10.44). Placing the mouse pointer on the selection handles changes the mouse pointer to a double-headed arrow (vertical, horizontal or diagonal).

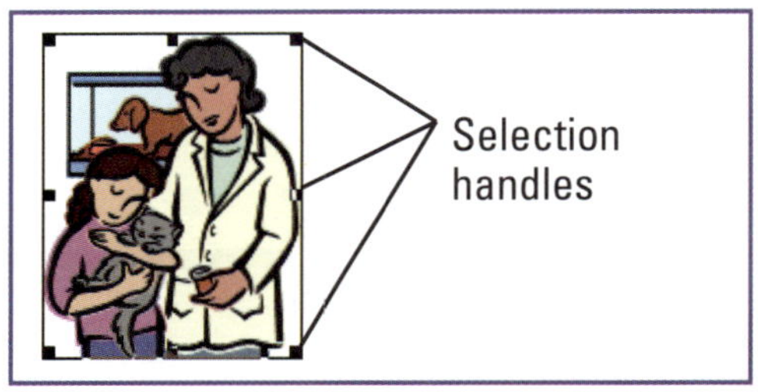


*Figure 10.44*

2. To reduce or enlarge the graphic proportionately:
   (a) Click on any of the corner handles (the mouse pointer becomes diagonal double-headed arrows).
   (b) Drag away from the centre of the graphic to enlarge.
   (c) Drag towards the centre of the graphic to reduce.

## To change the position of the graphic

1. Place the mouse pointer anywhere within the graphic except on any of the eight handles.
2. Click and hold down the left mouse button within the handles until a small square appears on the tail of the pointer.
3. The graphic can then be dragged to the desired position.

When a graphic is placed in a document, by default the text is placed at the top and bottom of the graphic. However, it may be necessary – especially in the case of newsletters, newspapers and magazines – to have the text flow or wrap around the graphic, to save space and enhance presentation (Figure 10.45).

### Wrapping text around a graphic

1. Position the pointer where the graphic is to be inserted; insert the graphic.
2. Size the graphic proportionately.
3. Choose **Picture** from the **Format** menu. The 'Format Picture' dialogue box appears.
4. Select the **Layout** tab.
5. Select the required wrapping style.
6. Click **OK**.

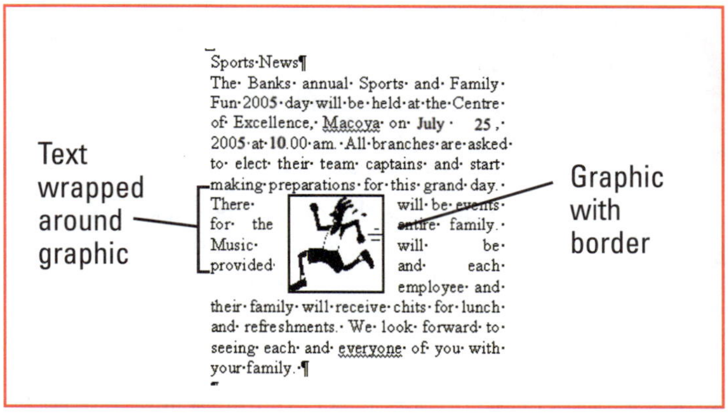


*Figure 10.45*
*Text can be wrapped round a graphic*

### Inserting a border around a graphic

1. Click once on the picture to select the picture.
2. Choose **Picture** from the **Format** menu. The 'Format Picture' dialogue box appears.
3. Choose the **Color and Lines** tab.
4. From the Line section choose the line style, colour and weight.
5. Click **OK**.

## Inserting symbols and special characters

In a number of cases you may be required to prepare documents that need symbols that do not appear as keys on the keyboard. For example, π, ÷, α and √‾ are all symbols that might be part of a document. These can be found in the 'Symbol' dialogue box as shown in Figure 10.46. These symbols and characters are easily inserted in a document.

### To insert a symbol/special character

1. Position the insertion point where you want the symbol/special character inserted.
2. Choose **Symbol** from the **Insert** menu. The 'Symbol' dialogue box appears (Figure 10.46).
3. Select the desired symbol.
4. Click on **Insert**.

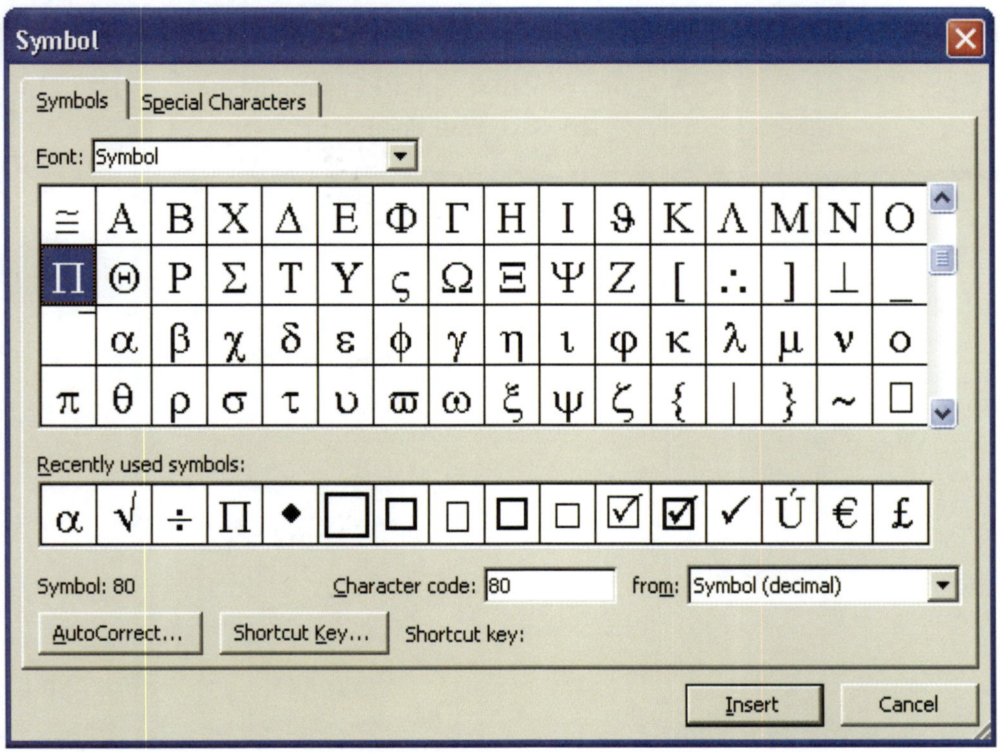


*Figure 10.46*

## Activity 13

**1** Enter the following text and save it as 'Math Notes'.

> 1. Acceleration is the rate of increase of velocity. If $v$ is velocity, and $a$ is the acceleration of an object at time $t$, then:
>
>    $v$ = Ú $a$ dt
>
> 2. The angle between two lines where O is the origin and A and B are points, one on each line passing through O, each point being 1 unit of distance from O.
>
>    $|AO| = 1$
>
>    A has coordinates $(p_1, m_1, n_1)$
>
>    B has coordinates $(p_2, m_2, n_2)$
>
>    Therefore $(AB)^2 =$
>    $(p_2 - p_1)^2 + (m_2 - m_1)^2 + (n_2 - n_1)^2$
>    = Â$p_1{}^2$ + Â$p_2{}^2$ – 2Â$p_1p_2$

(a) Insert the heading 'Vectors'.

(b) Italicise the coordinates p, m and n.

(c) Change the numbering to bullets.

**2** Create the following table.

| Traditional | Arcade | Puzzles |
|---|---|---|
| Solitaire | Pacman | Big Money |
| Chess | Ping Pong | Mah-jong |
| Scrabble | AstroPop | Bejeweled |
| Hang man | Heavy Weapon | Mummy Maze |

(a) Bold and centre the headings.

(b) Autofit to the contents of the table.

(c) Insert a column to the right of the Puzzles column and insert the heading 'Word'.

(d) Enter the following data for the Word column: Bookworm, Psychobabble, Text twist, Typer Shark

**3** Retrieve the document 'Art Newsletter' that you saved earlier.

(a) Insert a title for the document 'Art is Life'.

(b) Centre and boldface the title and increase the font size to a size larger than in the rest of the document, including the subheadings.

(c) Change the line spacing to 1.5.

(d) Centre the header in a smaller font than is used elsewhere in the document.

(e) Except for the title of the document, format the rest of the document in two fully justified newspaper columns.

(f) Remove the page numbering from the first page.

(g) Insert an appropriate graphic of your choice, within the article 'What is Art' with square text wrapping.

(h) Save your document.

# Summary

1 A word processor is an application package that allows you to prepare letters, reports, memos, books or any other type of correspondence. Once created, these documents can be saved to be worked on later or printed.

2 Word-wrapping: when entering text, you do not have to worry about where the end of each line comes. The word-wrapping feature allows you to move automatically to a new line. You only need to press the Enter key if the line is a short line, or to move to a new paragraph.

3 A word processor contains many editing and proofing features that enable users to make changes to a document quickly and easily. Some of the editing features are:

- Delete (characters, words and blocks of text can easily be deleted)
- Insert (characters, words and blocks of text can easily be inserted)
- Cut, Copy and Paste (characters, words and blocks of text can be removed or copied from one part of a document and placed in another part of the same document or in another document that is currently on the desktop)
- Find and Replace text (you can search for a word or string of characters and replace it with another word or string of characters)
- You can check a document for correctness by using tools such as the spelling and grammar checkers.

4 Formatting determines the final appearance of a document. Formatting can be carried out at three levels – character, paragraph and page.

5 Characters can be formatted using:

- Font type (Times New Roman, Old English, etc.)
- size (height of a character)
- font style (regular, boldface, underline, italic)
- font colour
- special effects (superscript, subscript, strikethrough, shadow, outline, emboss, engrave, caps).

6 Paragraph formatting includes:

- Line spacing (distance between lines)
- justification (alignment of a block of text according to the margins: e.g. left, centre, right and full justification)
- indenting (pushing a line or paragraph in or out from the left or right margin).

7 Pages can be formatted by adjusting the margins and by including headers and footers (text or graphical items that appear at the top or bottom of every page of a document) and page numbers.

8 An endnote is placed at the end of the document or the end of a section and a footnote is placed at the end of a page. They give additional information to explain, expand on or make reference to a word, sentence or text within the document, using reference marks.

9 A document can be displayed using any number of columns, for example to produce newsletters and newspaper-style documents.

10 Tables can be inserted into a document to display statistical and numerical data.

11 The mail merge feature allows you to produce a large number of personalised letters, mailing labels and memos without having to type each one individually. Mail merging requires two files:

- The main document or primary document contains the letter or other material meant for each recipient, and also contains the merge fields, which are positioned where information from the data source should be placed.
- The data source or secondary document contains the personalised information needed to complete the main document.

# Questions

## Fill in the blanks

Text or graphics that appears on the top and bottom margins of every page of a document is called ________ and ________. The ______ appears in the bottom margin and the _______ appears in the top margin. A _____ is placed at the end of the document or the end of a section and a _______ is placed at the end of a page. They give additional information to explain, comment on or give reference to a word, sentence or text within the document with the use of ________ ______.

## Multiple choice

**1** From which menu would you be able to find Columns?

(a) File
(b) Edit
(c) Insert
(d) Format

**2** Which of the following is not considered a formatting feature?

(a) Font style
(b) Redo and Undo
(c) Font size
(d) Underline

**3** Which of the following is involved in creating a document?

(a) Saving and storing
(b) Entering text
(c) Formatting text
(d) All of the above

**4** The sequence of actions that allows you to double underline a piece of text in your document is:

(a) Edit, Insert, Underline, Double
(b) Format, Paragraph, Underline, Double
(c) Format, Font, Underline style, Double
(d) Format, Font, Spacing, Underline style, Double

**5** The difference between copy and paste and cut and paste is:

(a) Cutting moves the text to where you want it to appear and also leaves a copy in the original position.
(b) Copying moves the text to where you want it to appear; cutting does not.
(c) Copying leaves a copy of the text in the original position; cutting deletes it from its original position.
(d) Cutting leaves a copy of the text in the original position; copying deletes it from its original position.

**6** Footnotes refer to and expand on text within a document; they are placed:

(a) At the end of the document
(b) In the top margin of the document
(c) At the bottom of the section
(d) At the end of a page

**7** Mail merge allows you to create multiple copies of a single document such as a letter, so that it is partly personalised for a number of different recipients. You need to have a main document and:

(a) A secondary data file
(b) A primary document
(c) A primary file source
(d) A merged letter

**8** Which menu would most likely allow you to adjust your line spacing?

(a) Edit
(b) File
(c) Format
(d) Insert

**9** Which key allows you to type over text?

(a) Backspace
(b) Insert
(c) Caps Lock
(d) Num Lock

**10** Which of the following is not a type of tab?

(a) Full Justify
(b) Decimal
(c) Right
(d) Left

## Crossword

### Across

1 A feature that will allow you to go automatically to the next line without pressing the enter key (2 words) (8)

7 Used to place text or numbers in predetermined position in a document (4)

8 A reference to text in the document and is placed at the end of a document (7)

9 Removes text from its original position (3)

### Down

2 The unit used to measure the size of a character (6)

3 The process of creating personalised mailing letters for a number of individuals (2 words) (9)

4 Text that appears at the bottom of every page (6)

5 A page break that is inserted before the actual end of the page (4)

6 Another word for typeface (4)

## Short answer questions

1 Explain what is mail merge and state ONE way in which a small tee-shirt supply company can use mail merge.

2 Give TWO advantages of using a word processor over a traditional typewriter.

3 Name THREE important features that a word processor provides for a newspaper journalist.

4 Name THREE features of a word processor that allow you to present information that is difficult or impossible to do manually or using a traditional typewriter.

5 Give TWO ways in which word processing software can be used by individuals in the following jobs:

(a) Teacher

(b) Musician

(c) Construction worker

(d) Policeman

(e) Caterer

## True or False?

1 You can reverse an undo action by clicking Redo. T ❑ F ❑

2 You cannot ignore a suggestion given by Word to say you should correct a spelling error. T ❑ F ❑

3 When the OVR on the status bar is dimmed it indicates that you can type over the text. T ❑ F ❑

4 You can only view a document in two views: Print Layout View and Outline View. T ❑ F ❑

5 When you select text the area becomes highlighted. T ❑ F ❑

6 The default setting for page margins can be changed. T ❑ F ❑

7 To move text from one place to another you need to copy and paste. T ❑ F ❑

8 Endnotes are placed at the end of a page. T ❑ F ❑

9 Page numbering can be placed in the header or footer area of a document. T ❑ F ❑

10 There are a number of ways in which text can be wrapped around a graphic. T ❑ F ❑

# 11 Spreadsheets

## OBJECTIVES

At the end of this chapter you will be able to:

- Define a spreadsheet
- Give examples of where spreadsheets can be used
- Identify elements of the Excel application window
- State what is meant by a row, column, cell, label, value, formula and range
- Navigate to specified locations within a spreadsheet
- Format a worksheet
  - Align cells
  - Change orientation of cells
  - Resize columns/rows
  - Format values as currency with decimal values
- Perform editing
  - Edit and delete contents of cells
  - Insert and delete rows/columns
  - Copy/move data
  - Insert/delete/rename worksheets
- Develop formulae using different arithmetic operators (+, –, *, / and ^) to create worksheets
- Use functions to create a worksheet (SUM, MIN, MAX, IF, COUNT, TODAY(), NOW())
- Use absolute and relative cell addressing
- Sort data
- Select records using the AutoFilter and Advanced Filter menu options
- Use spreadsheet data to produce charts (e.g. column charts and pie charts)
- Use the options in the 'Print' dialogue box to print a worksheet.

A spreadsheet package is an application package that enables you to carry out numerical work easily and flexibly. The name derives from the way in which the package lets you display or *spread* out number data on a computerised *sheet*. It is a way of showing how numerical data items relate to each other.

A spreadsheet enables you to store not only numerical data but also **formulae** to carry out operations on the numerical data. These formulae are applied to the data in the sheet whenever you make a change to it. So if you change any data values, the entire worksheet is automatically re-calculated, updating other numbers as necessary. Automatic re-calculation is one of the most important features of a spreadsheet. The ability to represent the numerical data quickly and easily in one of many graphical forms (such as pie charts, bar graphs, histograms, etc.) is another important advantage.

A spreadsheet package is a flexible modelling tool that can be used in any job that involves repetitive numerical calculations. This is because it allows you to obtain quickly answers to what are called 'what-if scenarios'. Suppose your cricket club wants to predict the income it would earn from fundraisers based on last year's income. Using a spreadsheet program such as Excel you can set up the appropriate model and then test various assumptions. For example, 'What if the raffle sales increased by 10%?' or 'What if the Bar-B-Que sale made 15% less?' Some other examples of where spreadsheets can be used are:

- Statistics – e.g. finding averages or calculating the standard deviation
- Loan calculations
- Financial plans – e.g. budgeting
- Stock-keeping in a supermarket
- Payrolls
- Company accounts
- Keeping accounts in a club
- Preparing end-of-term school reports

> **Software note**
> Most of the features of Microsoft Excel 2003 are exactly the same as Excel 2000.

### Features of Excel equivalent or similar to Word

Excel is one of the applications in the Microsoft office suite. As such, many of the operations are the same for all the applications. In Excel, all the basic commands such as Open, New, Close, Save and Save As, work in the same way as they do in Word. The only difference to note is that when you save an Excel file it is given the file extension **.xls**.

Other features which are similar are Spell Check, Find and Replace, Page Setup for margins, Page Orientation and many of the formatting features.

## Starting Excel

Excel is started in much the same way as any other program. If the Windows desktop includes a Microsoft Office Excel 2003 shortcut icon, you can start Excel by double-clicking on this icon. Excel can also be started using the following steps:

1. Click **Start**, then **All Programs** (**Programs** in Win 98).
2. Select **Microsoft Office** then **Microsoft Office Excel 2003**.

## The Excel application window

The initial Excel application window includes the following elements:

- *Title bar*: This displays the name of the program, as well as the name of the current **workbook** if it has been saved. (If the workbook has not been saved, it is identified by a number; for example, 'Book1'.)
- *Menu bar*: A horizontal bar usually seen at the top of a **worksheet** with key words that represent menus.
- *Vertical/horizontal scroll bars*: These are used to scroll the workbook window vertically/horizontally through a worksheet.
- *Worksheet tabs*: These identify the various worksheets in a workbook, and allow you to move from one worksheet to another. Worksheets are therefore sub-parts of workbooks.
- *Status bar*: This displays helpful information as you use the program. The 'Ready' indicator that currently appears lets you know that the program is ready for data input.
- *Standard/Formatting toolbars*: These display a number of shortcut buttons and boxes for performing common Excel operations. When you point to one of these buttons or boxes, the name of the button/box appears in a small window (**ScreenTip**) next to the mouse pointer.
- *Name box*: This identifies the active cell.
- *Formula bar*: This displays the contents of the active cell, if any.
- *'Getting Started' task pane* (not available in Excel 2000): This displays options for accessing Microsoft Office Online, a web site for users of Microsoft Office products, as well as options for opening an existing workbook file and for creating a new workbook. The program includes several other task panes. Each pane includes options for performing a specific task (for example, inserting a picture into a worksheet).
- *Workbook window*: This window, which occupies the majority of the screen, displays an Excel workbook.

A workbook initially contains three worksheets, which are saved in a single file. A spreadsheet can be thought of as an electronic version of an accountant's columnar pad. It is a large grid divided into rows and columns. The rows run from left to right and are numbered, while the columns run up and down and are lettered. Since an entire Excel worksheet contains 256 columns and 65 536 rows, only a small part appears in this window at one time. A typical screen display may contain 25 rows and 12 columns. Figure 11.1 shows a typical screen display. The intersection of a row and a column is called a **cell**. Each cell in the spreadsheet can be identified by its **cell address** or **cell reference**. The cell reference is simply the column position and the row position combined. For example, the address F6 means that the cell is in column F and row 6. Notice that cell D3 is currently surrounded by a border. This border, or **cell pointer**, identifies the **active cell**; that is, the cell in which any information entered from the keyboard will be stored.

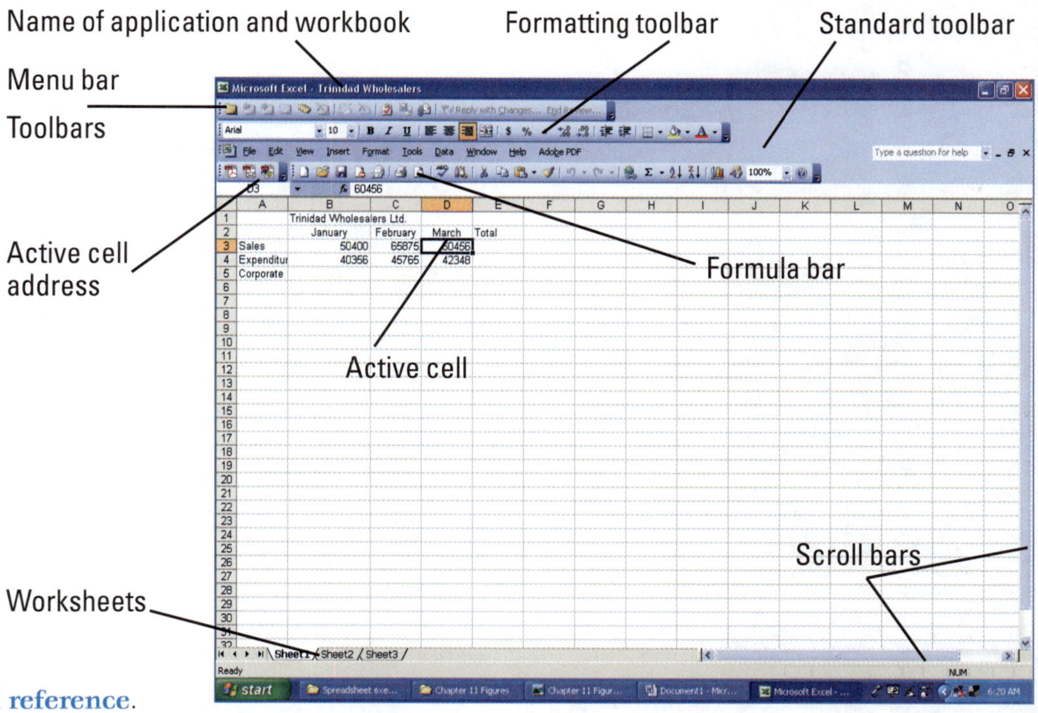


*Figure 11.1*
*Some elements of an Excel window*

## Basic concepts

A cell can contain one of three types of information: label (text), value (number) or formulae.

- A **label** can be used as a title or heading to describe an aspect of the worksheet. It can contain any string of characters (letters or numbers) but must only start with a character that does not indicate a formula or number. A label cannot be used in a calculation.
- A **value** is a piece of data that can be used in a calculation.
- A formula is an instruction to perform operations on values. Depending on the package you are using, a formula must start with one of these special symbols: +, −, @, = to identify it as a formula. All formulae in Excel start with an equal sign (=).

## Navigating around worksheets

| | |
|---|---|
| Mouse click | Click any cell with your mouse |
| Cursor keys on keyboard | Use the cursor keys to move in the direction of the arrow one cell at a time |
| Enter | Moves one cell down |
| Tab | Moves one cell to the right |
| CTRL + HOME | Moves back to cell A1 |
| HOME | Moves to the first cell in a row |
| CTRL + END | Moves to the last cell in the worksheet |
| CTRL + PgDown | Moves to the next worksheet in the workbook |
| CTRL + PgUp | Moves to the previous worksheet in the workbook |
| F5 | To a designated cell |

# Entering data

Before data can be placed in a cell, the cell must be selected. You can do this by simply moving the cursor to it and clicking the left mouse button or by using the arrow keys. Notice that when you type data, it is displayed in the entry line of the formula bar as well as in the cell itself as it is being entered. The data enters the cell when keys such as the Enter key or arrow keys are pressed.

Once you start entering data the formula bar buttons (Cancel and Enter) are activated (Figure 11.2).

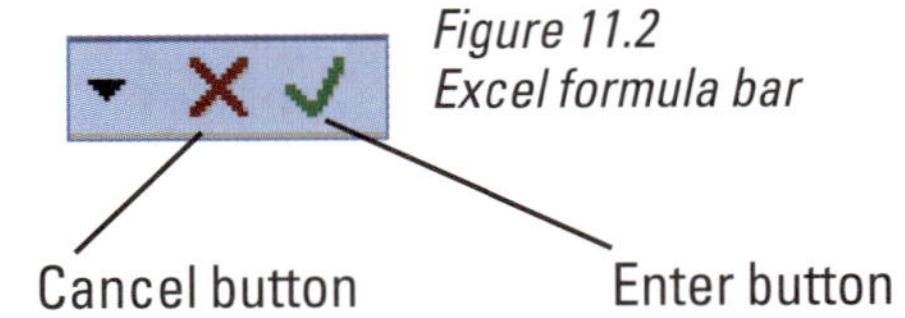


*Figure 11.2 Excel formula bar*

After you have typed all you require into a cell you need to confirm the data entry: that is, definitively say that this data should stay in this cell. There are various ways of doing this. One way is to click on the **Enter** formula bar button. If you make a mistake while you are entering data click the **Cancel** button on the formula bar to discard the entry and clear the cell. This will also switch off the formula bar buttons. Alternatively, press the ESC key on the keyboard.

## Confirming data entry

We see from above that the Enter button on the formula bar will confirm entry, but there are alternative methods. The method used will depend upon where you wish to type next. Table 1 summarises the different methods of confirming data entry and where the position of the active cell will move to.

| Method of confirming entry | Position of active cells |
|---|---|
| Enter button on formula bar | Active cells remain the same |
| Enter key on keyboard | Cell below original becomes active |
| Tab key on keyboard | Cell to right of original becomes active |
| One of four cursor keys on keyboard | Cell in direction of cursor key becomes active |
| Click any other cell in worksheet (do not use this method when entering formulae) | New cell clicked becomes the active cell |

*Table 1*
*Methods of confirming data entry*

## Default text formatting

Excel applies the following defaults to text:

- Text is automatically left aligned; 'text' includes a string of numerical characters which include hyphens or spaces, such as telephone numbers.
- Numbers are automatically right aligned.
- Text is 10-point Arial by default. If you type text that exceeds the width of a column it will appear to flow into the next cell if that cell is empty. If the next cell is not empty the text that does not fit into the cell will be hidden.

### Activity 1

Create the worksheet shown in Figure 11.3 as follows:

1. Select cell B1 and enter the label "Trinidad Wholesalers Ltd".
2. Select cells B2 to D2 one at a time and enter the labels "January", "February" and "March" respectively. Select cells A3 and A4 and enter the labels "Sales" and "Expenditure".
3. Select the appropriate cells and enter the values as shown in the worksheet.
4. Save the worksheet as 'Sales'.

*Figure 11.3*
*Sample worksheet for Activity 1*

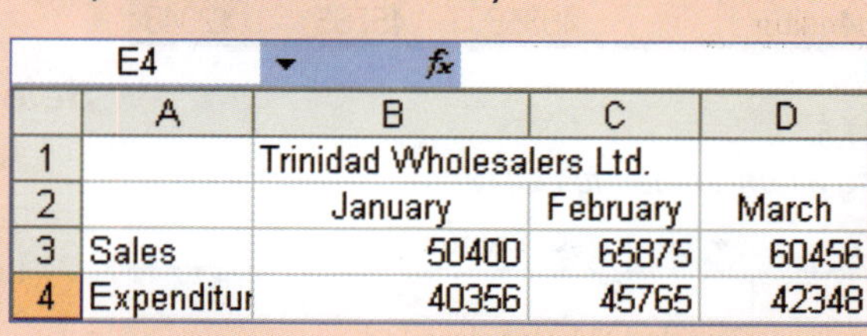
E4

| | A | B | C | D |
|---|---|---|---|---|
| 1 | | Trinidad Wholesalers Ltd. | | |
| 2 | | January | February | March |
| 3 | Sales | 50400 | 65875 | 60456 |
| 4 | Expenditur | 40356 | 45765 | 42348 |

### *To retrieve a worksheet from a floppy disk or hard disk*

1. Pull down the **File** menu.
2. Select **Open**. The 'Open' dialogue box appears.

   Choose the appropriate location where the document is stored – e.g. hard disk (C:), 3.5-in floppy (A:) – from the drop-down list in the 'Look in' window.
3. Double-click the icon of the selected worksheet or click the icon once and then click **Open**.

## Exercise 1

1. What is the name of the spreadsheet package you are using?
2. Define the following terms:
   - (a) Cell
   - (b) Cell reference
   - (c) Label
   - (d) Value
   - (e) Formula
3. (a) What is the default alignment for text and numbers in Excel?
   - (b) What is the default font type and size in Excel?
   - (c) What happens to text that exceeds the width of a cell?
   - (d) List THREE features of Excel which make it a very useful package.
4. Look at the worksheet in Figure 11.3.
   - (a) How many rows and columns are there in the figure?
   - (b) What is the content of cell C4?
   - (c) What is the address of the selected cell?
5. Besides the examples listed in the chapter, give TWO additional situations where you think a spreadsheet may be used. Give reasons for your answers.

*Figure 11.4*
*Selecting a range of cells*

A1 | fx

| | A | B | C | D |
|---|---|---|---|---|
| 1 | | Trinidad Wholesalers Ltd. | | |
| 2 | | January | February | March |
| 3 | Sales | 50400 | 65875 | 60456 |
| 4 | Expenditur | 40356 | 45765 | 42348 |

*Figure 11.5*
*Selecting a non-adjoining cell range*

C2 | fx February

| | A | B | C | D |
|---|---|---|---|---|
| 1 | | Trinidad Wholesalers Ltd. | | |
| 2 | | January | February | March |
| 3 | Sales | 50400 | 65875 | 60456 |
| 4 | Expenditur | 40356 | 45765 | 42348 |

## Ranges

A range can be a cell or a group of adjoining cells treated as a unit. A range can be represented by the address of the first cell and last cell in a group of continuous cells. For example, in Figure 11.4 the cells A1:D4 represent a range. To select a range of cells, click on the first cell and then drag down to the last cell.

### *Selecting a non-adjoining cell range*

1. Select the first range (e.g. A2:A4).
2. To select the non-adjoining cell range, hold down the CTRL key and select the second range (e.g. C2:C4).

This feature comes in very handy when selecting data to create graphs. Figure 11.5 shows non-adjoining cell ranges selected.

After entering the data, notice that the numbers move to the right of the cells (they are right aligned) and the labels (text) move to the left (they are left aligned). These alignments occur automatically (by default), but can be changed. You can change the alignment of a cell or range of cells as follows.

### Changing the alignment of a cell or range of cells

1 Select the cell or range of cells.

2 Pull down the **Format** menu and select **Cells**. The 'Format Cells' dialogue box appears as shown in Figure 6.

3 Select the **Alignment** tab.

4 Select the required alignment (e.g. left, centre, right) from the 'Horizontal' combo box.

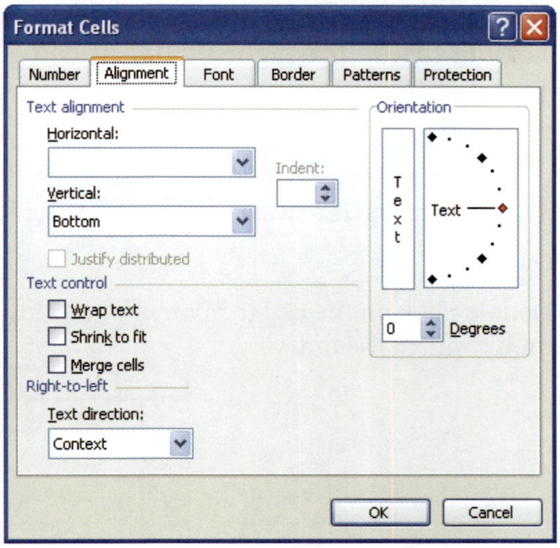


*Figure 11.6*
*'Format Cells' dialogue box*

### Changing the orientation of a cell or range of cells

1 Select the cell or range of cells.

2 Pull down the **Format** menu and select **Cells**. The 'Format Cells' dialogue box appears.

3 Select the **Alignment** tab.

4 Click on the dots in the orientation pane to get the number of degrees you want the data angled at, or click the arrow keys in the 'Degrees' combo box.

**Shortcut**

You can justify the contents of a cell or range of cells by highlighting the cell or range of cells and clicking one of the Align buttons in the toolbar, such as left, centre or right.

## Wrapping text

The 'Wrap text' option allows a label which is more than one word and which exceeds the width of a cell to move to another line in the same cell. For example, the label in cell B1 in Figure 11.7 is wrapped.

### To wrap text in a cell

1 Select the cell or range of cells.

2 Pull down the **Format** menu and select **Cells**. The 'Format Cells' dialogue box appears.

3 Select the **Alignment** tab.

4 Check the **Wrap text** box in the Text control pane.

5 Click **OK**.

## Basic editing

If you make a mistake when entering data into a cell, you can easily change the data or remove it entirely. The procedure is as follows.

### To delete the contents of a cell

1 Select the cell which has the data you wish to delete.

2 Press the **Delete** key on the keyboard.

Or:

Select **Clear** from the **Edit** menu, then select **All**.

## Activity 2

Create the spreadsheet shown in Figure 11.4. You are required to:

1. Change the contents of cell B3 from 50400 to 54000. Perform the edit within the cell.
2. Centre align all the values.
3. Change the orientation of the labels in cells B2, C2 and D2 to 45 degrees.
4. Wrap the label in cell B1.

### *How it is done*

1. Double-click on cell B3. The cursor appears in the cell. Edit the number.
2. Select the range B3 to D4. Use either the centre align shortcut icon on the formatting toolbar or the Format menu method.
3. Select the range B2 to D2. From the **Format** menu select **Cells**. The 'Format Cells' dialogue box appears.
4. Click on the 'Alignment' tab. Click the up-arrow in the degrees box in the orientation pane until you reach 45 degrees. Click **OK**.
5. Select the cell B1. The 'Format Cells' dialogue box appears.
6. Click on the **Alignment** tab. Check the **Wrap text** box in the Text control pane. Click **OK**.

Figure 11.7 shows the result of the activity.

### *Changing the contents of a cell by editing inside the formula bar or cell*

1. Click once in the cell requiring the edit.
2. Click inside the text in the formula bar (a cursor or insertion point appears in the formula bar). Edit the contents.
3. Confirm the entry using any of the methods outlined earlier.

Or:

Double-click on the cell to open it for editing and edit directly in the cell, then confirm the entry.

F4 ▾ fx

| | A | B | C | D |
|---|---|---|---|---|
| 1 | | Trinidad Wholesalers Ltd. | | |
| 2 | | January | February | March |
| 3 | Sales | 50400 | 65875 | 60456 |
| 4 | Expenditur | 40356 | 45765 | 42348 |

*Figure 11.7 Sample worksheet for Activity 2*

## Inserting and deleting rows and columns

A row or column can be inserted between existing rows or columns. You can also delete rows and columns.

### *To insert a row*

1. Click on a cell in the row below the row where you want the new row to go.
2. Pull down the **Insert** menu and select **Rows**.

### *To insert a column*

1. Click on a cell in a column to the right of the column where you want the new column to go.
2. Pull down the **Insert** menu and select **Columns**.

If you wish to insert more than one row or column, for step 1 select the exact number of rows or columns you require and then carry out step 2.

### *To delete a row or column*

1. Click on a cell in the row or column that you want to delete.
2. Pull down the **Edit** menu and select **Delete**.
3. Check the **Entire row** or the **Entire column** radio button.

Or:

1. Select the whole row(s)/column(s) you wish to delete.
2. From the **Edit** menu select **Delete**.

### Right-click method for inserting rows and columns

1. Select the whole row(s) or column(s) to the right, or below, of where you want to enter the new one.
2. Right-click anywhere in the selected area.
3. The 'Insert' drop-down menu shown in Figure 11.8 appears. Select **Entire row** or **Entire column** as desired.

To delete a row or column, follow the same procedure as above and click **Entire row** or **Entire column** when the 'Delete' dialogue box appears.

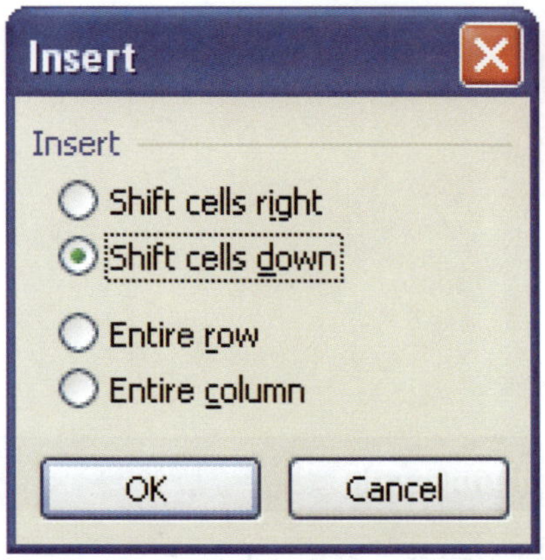


*Figure 11.8*
*'Insert' drop-down menu*

# Formatting

Using formatting, you can control the appearance of cells and of the worksheet in general. We have already looked at one aspect of formatting – the alignment of the contents of cells. We will now look at other aspects of formatting.

## Resizing columns/rows

Columns and rows may be resized in various ways.

### Resizing with click and drag

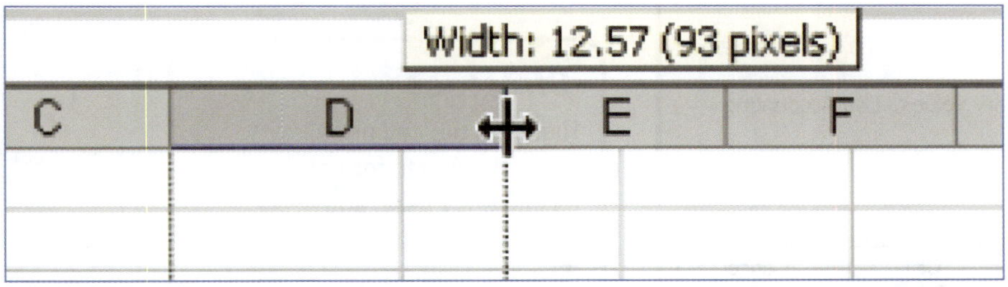


*Figure 11.9*
*Resizing a column with click and drag*

The height of each row and width of each column in a worksheet can be adjusted using the mouse. When the mouse pointer is moved between the row and column headings it changes shape to a two-way arrow as shown in Figure 11.9. When the two-way arrow appears, click and drag to the desired position. For example, to increase or decrease the width of column D, click between the D and E column heading and drag either to the right or left to the position you require.

### Resizing with autofit

To **autofit** a column, double-click the right boundary of the column heading. To autofit a row, double-click on the lower boundary of the row heading. Excel then 'looks' at all the entries in the column/row and will resize the column/row to match the width/height of the longest/tallest entry.

### Resizing using the Format menu

From the **Format** menu select **Column** (or Row), then select **Width** (or **Height**). When the 'Column Width' dialogue box appears (Figure 11.10), enter an exact measurement. *Only a value between 0 and 255 will be accepted.*

*Figure 11.10*
*'Column Width' dialogue box*

## Formatting numbers

Another aspect of formatting concerns the way in which numbers are represented. For instance, some standard formats are:

- *General*: if you want no specific number format
- *Number*: used for general display of numbers (decimal places and negative)
- *Currency*: used to represent monetary values (e.g. $589.54)
- *Accounting*: for lining up currency symbols and decimal points

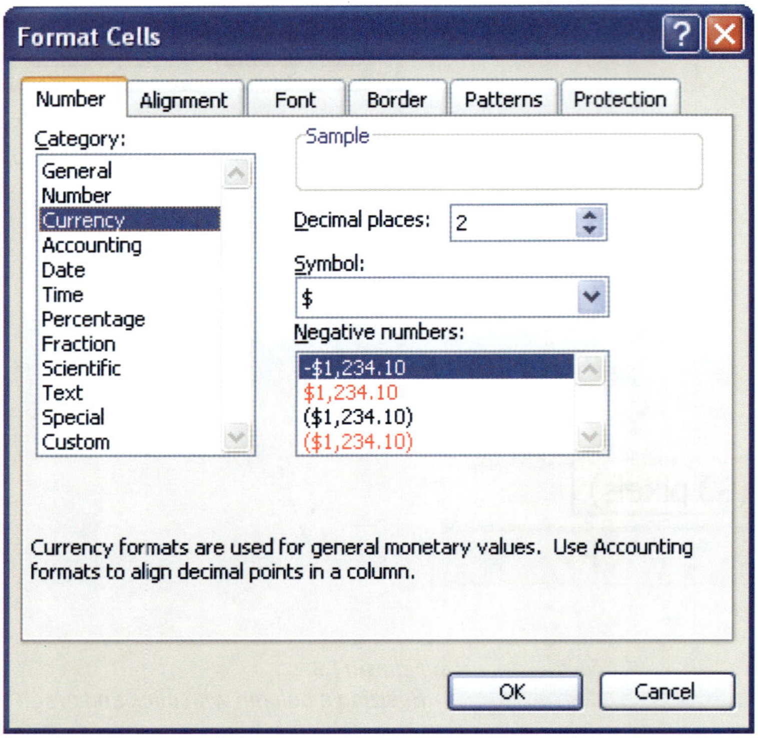


*Figure 11.11*
*The 'Format Cells' dialogue box*

### *To format the worksheet for currency data*

1. Highlight the cell or range to be formatted.
2. Pull down the **Format** menu and select **Cells**. The 'Format Cells' dialogue box appears.
3. Select the **Number** tab, then select **Currency** from the displayed list of categories as shown in Figure 11.11.
4. Choose the number of decimal places and the currency symbol you want to use. Click **OK**.

**Shortcut**

Highlight the cell or cells that you want to format as currency data, and click the Currency icon ($) in the toolbar.

**Note:**

- When you Copy, and then use the Paste command, the data remains on the clipboard so you can repeat the paste many times. The cell containing the original data will have a broken line around it indicating that the data is still on the clipboard. To get rid of the broken lines around the cell containing the original data *and* remove the data from the clipboard, press the ESC key.
- When you use the Cut command when moving data, or if you use the Enter key to paste data you have copied, you will find that you can only paste once as the data does not remain on the clipboard. To paste again you will have to copy or cut again.

# Editing

## Copying data

It is possible to copy data from cell(s) to cell(s) within a worksheet, across to a different worksheet or even to a different workbook. This can be achieved using one of several methods.

### Cut, Copy and Paste commands

The Cut, Copy and Paste commands can be used as with other Windows programs (e.g. Microsoft Word).

1. Select the cell(s) containing the data you wish to copy or move.
2. Select the **Cut** or **Copy** command (from the **Edit** menu or on the toolbar).
3. Click in the cell where you wish to copy or move the data to.
4. Either select the **Paste** command or press the **Enter** key.

### Fill down

1 Select the cell that has the data you wish to copy.
2 Click on the bottom right hand corner of the cell (fill handle) as shown in Figure 11.12 and drag down or across as desired. The value in the first cell will be copied to all the cells selected.

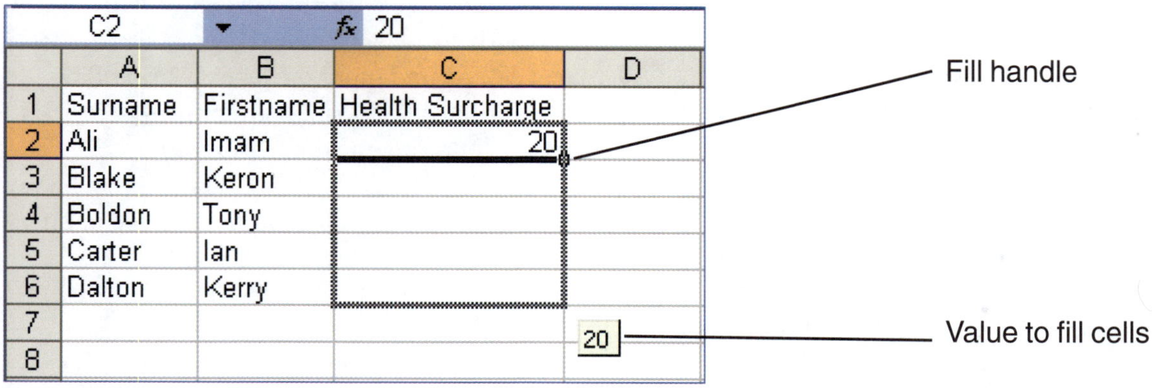


*Figure 11.12*
*Spreadsheet with cells selected to be filled using the fill handle*

# Working with worksheets

By default each new workbook is provided with three worksheets (Sheet 1, Sheet 2 and Sheet 3) of which the active worksheet is always white. These sheets allow you to keep varied and large amounts of information together in one workbook. To move from worksheet to worksheet, click on the worksheet tab for the worksheet you require, at the bottom of the screen.

## Inserting, deleting, renaming worksheets

Right-click one of the worksheet tabs and then select the command you require from the drop-down menu shown in Figure 11.13. Any inserted worksheet will be given a default name, e.g. Sheet 4. Selecting **Rename** allows you to change the name of the worksheet. Figure 11.14 shows Sheet 1 renamed as '1st Quarter Report'.

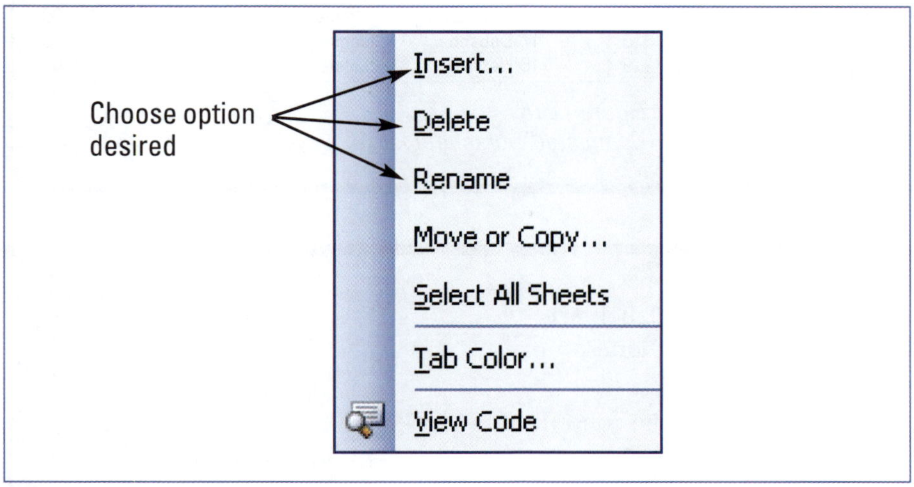


*Figure 11.13*
*Worksheet drop-down menu*

*Figure 11.14*
*Renamed worksheet*

## Activity 3

| | A | B | C | D |
|---|---|---|---|---|
| 1 | Surname | Firstname | Position | |
| 2 | Abbot | John | Supervisor | |
| 3 | Alexis | Mark | Carpenter | |
| 4 | Brown | Kerry | Carpenter | |
| 5 | Berch | Tom | Mason | |
| 6 | Cameron-E | Phillip | Labourer | |
| 7 | Hugh-Baile | Shane | Mason | |
| 8 | Dobson | Jonny | Labourer | |
| 9 | Henry | Lelsie | Labourer | |

*Figure 11.15 Worksheet for Activity 3*

Create the worksheet shown in Figure 11.15.

1. Insert the details of a new employee between rows 4 and 5: Surname – McLoclanding, First name – Johnathan, Position – Mason.
2. Insert a column to the left of column A.
3. Type the label "Worker ID" in cell A1.
4. Input the following worker ID numbers for the nine workers. Starting from the first worker: 10, 11, 12, 13, 14, 15, 16, 17, 18.
5. Resize all columns to make all the data visible.
6. Insert the label "Health Surcharge" in cell E1.
7. Input the value 20 for each worker in the Health Surcharge column.
8. Format the Health Surcharge values as currency.
9. Delete row 4.
10. Change the name of the worksheet to 'Salary'.
11. Save the worksheet as 'Payroll'.

### *How it is done*

1. Place the cursor anywhere in row 5. Click the **Insert** menu and select rows or right-click the mouse and select **Insert**. Check the **Entire row** radio button in the 'Insert' dialogue box. Enter the data in the appropriate cells.
2. Select any cell in column A. Click the **Insert** menu and select **Column** or right-click the mouse and select **Insert**. Check the **Entire column** radio button in the 'Insert' dialogue box.
3. Select cell A1 and input the label "Worker ID".
4. Select cell A2. Type 10 and press **Enter**. Continue entering the other Worker ID numbers.
5. Place the cursor between column B and column C. Double-click the mouse.
6. Select cell E1. Type in the label "Health Surcharge".
7. Select cell E2 and enter the number 20. Using the fill handle at the bottom left corner of the cell, drag to fill the cells for each worker.
8. Select the range E2 to E10. Click on the dollar sign ($) in the formatting toolbar or click **Format menu/Cells/Number/Currency**.
9. Select the entire row. Click **Edit menu/Delete**. Or:
   Select any cell in row 4. Click **Edit menu/Delete/Entire row**.
10. Right-click Sheet 1. Select **Rename**. Type "Salary".

Figure 11.16 shows the completed worksheet.

| | A | B | C | D | E |
|---|---|---|---|---|---|
| 1 | Worker ID | Surname | Firstname | Position | Health Surcharge |
| 2 | 10 | Abbot | John | Supervisor | $20.00 |
| 3 | 11 | Alexis | Mark | Carpenter | $20.00 |
| 4 | 13 | Mc Locla nding | Johnathan | Mason | $20.00 |
| 5 | 14 | Berch | Tom | Mason | $20.00 |
| 6 | 15 | Cameron-Brown | Phillip | Labourer | $20.00 |
| 7 | 16 | Hugh-Bailey | Shane | Mason | $20.00 |
| 8 | 17 | Dobson | Jonny | Labourer | $20.00 |
| 9 | 18 | Henry | Lelsie | Labourer | $20.00 |

*Figure 11.16*
*Completed worksheet for Activity 3*

## Exercise 2

1. Define the term 'range'.
2. Explain what you understand by the term 'formatting'.
3. Retrieve the worksheet 'Payroll', which was shown in Figure 11.16.
   (a) Insert an empty row above row 1.
   (b) Type the label "Ace Construction Company" in cell B1.
   (c) Change the contents of cell B5 to "McLocland".
   (d) Change the orientation of the labels in cells A2 to F2 to 45 degrees.
   (e) Insert a column between columns D and E.
   (f) Type the label "NIS".
   (g) Type the value 80 in cell E3.
   (h) Fill in the NIS value of 80 for each worker.
   (i) Format all monetary values to currency.
   (j) Rename the worksheet as 'Paysheet'.

# Formulae

Formulae are used to perform calculations using data contained in the cells and to display the results. Some of the features of a formula are:

- A formula is entered in the cell in which the result is to be displayed
- A formula begins with an equal sign ( = )
- A formula includes **arguments** (such as cell references, text or numbers) and **operators**. Operators are mathematical symbols that are used in formulae. Examples of operators used in formulae include:

| | | | |
|---|---|---|---|
| Addition | + | Division | / |
| Subtraction | – | Exponentiation | ^ (raising to a power) |
| Multiplication | * | | |

After a formula has been confirmed in a cell only the calculation result will be displayed in that cell; the formula will be displayed in the formula bar. If you double-click on a cell containing a formula the full formula will be displayed and will be ready for you to edit.

## BODMAS rule

An expression in a formula in a spreadsheet package follows the same order of precedence as for normal arithmetic. This means that whatever is within brackets is performed first, followed by exponentiation, then multiplication and/or division, and then addition and/or subtraction.

Figure 11.17(a) shows examples of various formulae on the values in the range A3 to B7. Figure 11.17(b) shows the results of applying the formulae.

*Figure 11.17 (a) Examples of various formulae*

C3 | fx =A3 +B3

| | A | B | C |
|---|---|---|---|
| 1 | Various Formulae | | |
| 2 | | | |
| 3 | 25 | 2 | =A3 +B3 |
| 4 | 25 | 2 | =A4-B4 |
| 5 | 25 | 2 | =A5*B5 |
| 6 | 25 | 2 | =A6/B6 |
| 7 | 25 | 2 | =A7^B7 |

*Figure 11.17 (b) Results of applying various formulae*

| | A | B | C |
|---|---|---|---|
| 1 | Various Formulae | | |
| 2 | | | |
| 3 | 25 | 2 | 27 |
| 4 | 25 | 2 | 23 |
| 5 | 25 | 2 | 50 |
| 6 | 25 | 2 | 12.5 |
| 7 | 25 | 2 | 625 |

## Activity 4

The worksheet in Figure 11.18 shows the sales and expenditure for the first quarter of 2005 for the Optimum Trading Company. You are required to calculate:

1. The profit before tax for each month
2. The tax on the profit which is set at 15%
3. The profit after tax
4. The percentage of profit (profit %) made each month
5. The total for sales, expenditure, profit before tax, tax, profit after tax and profit percentage
6. Format the range B5:F8 as currency and G5:G8 as %.

### *How it is done*

1. Select cell D5 and type the formula = B5–C5. Copy this formula to cells D6 and D7.
2. Select cell E5 and type the formula = .15*D5. Copy this formula to cells E6 and E7.
3. Select cell F5 and type the formula = D5–E5. Copy this formula to cells F6 and F7.
4. Select cell G5 and type the formula = F5/B5. Copy this formula to cells G6 and G7.
5. Select cell B8 and type the formula = B5 + B6 + B7. Copy the formula to cells C8, D8, E8, F8 and G8.
6. (a) Select the range B5:F8.
   (b) From the **Format** menu select **Cells/Number/Currency**.
   Or:
   Select the dollar sign ($) from the formatting toolbar.
   (c) Select the range G5:G8.
   (d) Select **Format/cells/number/percentage**.
   Or:
   Select the percentage (%) sign from the formatting toolbar.

Figure 11.18 shows the formulae used to create the worksheet.

| | A | B | C | D | E | F | G |
|---|---|---|---|---|---|---|---|
| 1 | | | | Optimum Trading Company | | | |
| 2 | Quarterly Sales Report | | | | | | |
| 3 | | | | | | | |
| 4 | | Sales | Expenditure | Profit before Tax | Tax (15%) | Profit after Tax | Profit % |
| 5 | January | 456852 | 154275 | =B5-C5 | =0.15*D5 | =D5-E5 | =F5/B5 |
| 6 | February | 654587 | 256478 | | | | |
| 7 | March | 554587 | 268975 | | | | |
| 8 | Corporate | =B5+B6+B7 | | | | | |
| 9 | | | | | | | |

*Figure 11.18*
*Worksheet showing formulae for Activity 4*

It is important to note that the formula includes the *cell addresses* and not the values that are currently in the cells. If you type the values themselves, the re-calculation feature of the spreadsheet package would not work. For example, typing the formula = 456852 + 654587 + 554587 in cell B8 would give the correct answer for the 'Corporate' sales but the re-calculation feature would not work. If any of the values in the cells were changed, the total in cell B8 would remain the same. If the value in cell B5 were changed from 456852 to 556852, the formula = 456852 + 654587 + 554587 in cell B8 would remain unchanged which would result in the wrong total for the new value in cell B5. However, when we use cell addresses in a formula, any changes to the content of a cell that forms part of a formula results in immediate adjustments to any cell that depends on the value that was changed.

| | A | B | C | D | E | F | G |
|---|---|---|---|---|---|---|---|
| 1 | | | | Optimum Trading Company | | | |
| 2 | Quarterly Sales Report | | | | | | |
| 3 | | | | | | | |
| 4 | | Sales | Expenditure | Profit before Tax | Tax (15%) | Profit after Tax | Profit % |
| 5 | January | $ 456,852.00 | $154,275.00 | $302,577.00 | $ 45,386.55 | $257,190.45 | 56% |
| 6 | February | $ 654,587.00 | $256,478.00 | $398,109.00 | $ 59,716.35 | $338,392.65 | 52% |
| 7 | March | $ 554,587.00 | $268,975.00 | $285,612.00 | $ 42,841.80 | $242,770.20 | 44% |

*Figure 11.19*
*Completed worksheet for Activity 4*

If you want to find out more about this topic you could look up the related animations and activities on your companion CD-ROM.

## *Did you know?*

Notice that to calculate the formula for the percent profit in cell G5 of Figure 11.18 we did not write the formula as:

= F5/B5 * 100

as you would do in mathematics. If you did this the result would be expressed in the cell just as a number without a percentage symbol. If you format it to percent at this point it would be multiplied by 100. Therefore when you write your formula to calculate percentages you must remember to leave the formula expressed just as a fraction and not multiply by 100.

## Exercise 3

1 (a) Create the spreadsheet shown in Figure 11.20.

(b) Insert a row between row 1 and row 2 and insert the label "First Quarter Sales" in cell D2.

(c) Insert the label "Total" in cell E3.

(d) Find the total sales for each branch for each month.

(e) Find the Corporate total for each month for all branches.

(f) Centre align the labels January, February and March.

(g) Format the range B3:E8 as currency.

(h) Save the worksheet as 'Home Makers'.

*Figure 11.20 Worksheet for question 1*

| | A | B | C | D | E |
|---|---|---|---|---|---|
| 1 | | Home Makers | Furniture Store | | |
| 2 | | January | February | March | |
| 3 | North | 26500 | 22442 | 23456 | |
| 4 | South | 45600 | 23246 | 67543 | |
| 5 | Central | 34568 | 29687 | 46578 | |
| 6 | East | 78540 | 98755 | 65981 | |
| 7 | West | 53546 | 94786 | 65847 | |
| 8 | Corporate | | | | |

2 (a) Create the worksheet shown in Figure 11.21.

(b) Insert a blank column between column A and column B.

(c) Insert the label "Profit" in cell A5.

(d) Insert the label "Total" in cell F2.

(e) Calculate the total sales and total expenditure.

(f) Calculate the profit for each month and the total profit.

(g) Format all values with currency.

(h) Save the worksheet as 'Trinidad Wholesalers'.

| | A | B | C | D |
|---|---|---|---|---|
| 1 | | Trinidad Wholesalers Ltd. | | |
| 2 | | January | February | March |
| 3 | Sales | 50400 | 65875 | 60456 |
| 4 | Expenditure | 40356 | 45765 | 42348 |

*Figure 11.21 Worksheet for question 2*

3 Create the worksheet shown in Figure 11.22.

(a) Insert the label "Total" in cell E4.

(b) Calculate the Total for each item.

(c) Insert the label "VAT" in cell F4.

(d) Calculate VAT on each item at 15%.

(e) Calculate the final cost of each item.

(f) Insert a label "Total cost" in an appropriate cell and calculate the total cost of all the items.

(g) In an appropriate cell calculate a discount of 20% of the Total cost.

(h) In an appropriate cell calculate the amount the customer has to pay.

| | A | B | C | D | E | F |
|---|---|---|---|---|---|---|
| 1 | | | Triple Point Stationery Supplies | | | |
| 2 | Purchase Order | | Order No: 125 | | | |
| 3 | | | | | | |
| 4 | Item | Unit | Unit Price | Quantity | | |
| 5 | Erasers | Box | 8.99 | 5 | | |
| 6 | Pencils | Box | 9.6 | 20 | | |
| 7 | Pens | Box | 18 | 15 | | |
| 8 | Paper | Box | 250 | 3 | | |
| 9 | Markers | Box | 60 | 8 | | |

*Figure 11.22 Worksheet for question 3*

4 Create a spreadsheet to calculate the percentage change in sales for each month and the total for the period January to March 2004 and the same period in 2005 (Figure 11.23).

| | 2004 | 2005<br>Percentage change (%) |
|---|---|---|
| January | $254781 | $547869 |
| February | $652457 | $654785 |
| March | $547896 | $745895 |
| Total | | |

*Figure 11.23 Spreadsheet for question 4*

# Functions

There are easier and faster methods to find the total of a group of cells. The SUM function could accomplish the same task as the formula we used in Activity 4 to calculate the total sales for the first quarter. A **function** is a *predefined* formula in Excel that can automatically calculate results, perform worksheet actions or assist with decision making based on the information provided in your worksheet. Functions fall into several categories including:

- *Math*: This category includes functions for computing totals, square roots, tangents, etc.
- *Statistical*: This category includes functions for computing averages, maximums, minimums, etc.
- *Financial*: This category includes functions for computing loan repayments, rates of return, depreciation, etc.
- *Date and Time*: This category includes functions for computing the number of days in a specific date interval, the number of hours in a specific time interval, etc.

## The SUM function

The SUM function starts with an equals (=) sign, followed by the word 'SUM', an open bracket, the arguments and a closing bracket. An argument is the information passed to a function, on which it operates. The general form of the SUM function is as follows:

$$=\underbrace{\text{Sum}}_{\text{Function}}(\underbrace{\text{first cell:last cell}}_{\text{Arguments}})$$

The worksheet in Figure 11.20 shows the first-quarter sales figures for the five branches of Home Makers Furniture Store in North, South, Central, East and West branches. To find the total sales for the North branch for the period January to March, we need to find the total of cells B5, C5 and D5. The formula would be =B5+C5+D5 or, using the SUM function, the formula to put into cell E5 will be =SUM(B5:D5). Whenever we want to add up the values of a column or row of continuous cells, we can use the SUM function. Every time cell E5 is highlighted, the content box will show the formula.

If we wanted to find the total for the South branch for the period January to March, we would now have to go to cell E5 and type out another formula. The formula would be =B6+C6+D6 or =SUM(B6:D6). The formula to calculate the total for the Central branch would be =SUM(B7:D7) and for the East branch would be =SUM(B8:D8) and for the West branch it would be =SUM(B9:D9). Notice that the formula is almost the same for each branch except that the cell addresses are different. So instead of making us type out five different formulae, the package lets us copy the original formula to the other cells. The structure of the formula remains the same, but the addresses of the cells used in the formula will change relative to the position of the formula. This feature is called **relative cell addressing**.

### AutoSum button

Another method of easily summing a row or column of cells is to use the AutoSum button. To use AutoSum either:

1. Click in the cell where you want the result to appear: in this case, the first vacant cell under the five cells we are summing (B10).
2. Click the **AutoSum** button [Σ].

3 Check the formula entered by Excel, to ensure that the correct range of cells has been chosen. If an incorrect range of cells has been selected by Excel, simply click and drag to select the correct range.
4 Confirm the entry.

Or:

1 Select the range of cells to be added and also the cell where you wish to place the formula. In this case it will be cells B5:B10 as shown in Figure 11.24.
2 Click the **AutoSum** button. In this case the formula is entered and confirmed automatically.

*Figure 11.24 Worksheet showing the use of AutoSum*

| | A | B | C | D | E |
|---|---|---|---|---|---|
| 1 | | | | Home Makers Furniture Store | |
| 2 | | | | | |
| 3 | | First Quarter Report | | | |
| 4 | | January | February | March | |
| 5 | North | 26500 | 22442 | 23456 | |
| 6 | South | 45600 | 23246 | 67543 | |
| 7 | Central | 34568 | 29687 | 46578 | |
| 8 | East | 78540 | 98755 | 65981 | |
| 9 | West | 53546 | 94786 | 65847 | |
| 10 | Corporate | | | | |

### *The Insert Function button*

1 Click in the cell where you want the result to appear. Using the worksheet in Figure 11.24, this is the first vacant cell under the five cells we are summing (B10).
2 Click the **Insert Function** button on the formula bar. The 'Insert Function' dialogue box appears as shown in Figure 11.25.
3 Select the **SUM** function from the 'Insert Function' dialogue box and click **OK**. The 'Arguments' dialogue box appears.
4 Check that the correct cell range is selected for summing. Here the range B5:B9 should be displayed.

If an incorrect range has been selected, move the 'Functions Arguments' dialogue box out of the way if necessary, select the correct range with your mouse, and then click **OK** on the dialogue box.

The resulting formula will appear identical to the formula constructed by the previous methods.

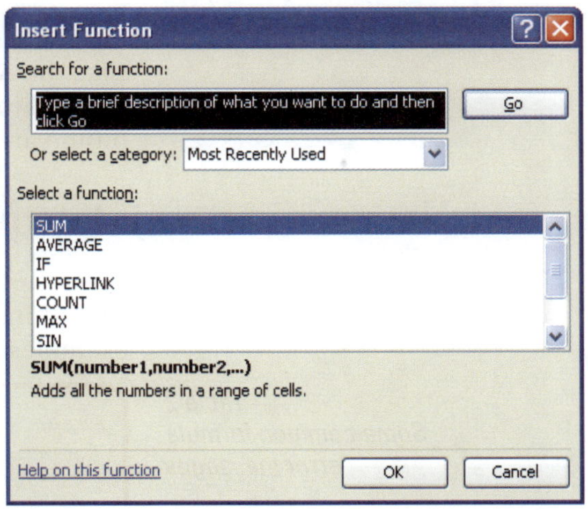


*Figure 11.25 'Insert Function' dialogue box*

### *AutoSumming many columns/rows at once*

If you have a table of data you can sum all the columns and rows at once. To do this:

1 Select all the rows and columns of data *and* one blank cell under each column and to the right of each row.
2 Click the **AutoSum** button.

Each column and row will now contain the correct formula to sum the cells above in the case of columns and to the left in the case of rows.

## Other functions

### AVERAGE function

The **AVERAGE** function is used to find the mean of a set of values. The general form of the function is =AVERAGE(first cell:last cell). For example, if you want to find the average of the range A2 to A9, the formula would be =AVERAGE(A2:A9). It can be entered into a worksheet either manually or by expanding the AutoSum button and by selecting the AVERAGE option in the list that appears.

### MAX function

The **MAX** (maximum) function is used to find the largest value in a set of values in a row or column. The general form of the maximum function is =MAX(first cell:last cell). For example, if you want to find the largest value in the range A2 to A9, the formula would be =MAX(A2:A9).

### MIN function

The **MIN** (minimum) function is used to find the smallest value in a set of values in a row or column. The general form of the minimum function is =MIN(first cell:last cell). For example, if you want to find the lowest value in the range A2 to A9, the formula would be =MIN(A2:A9).

### Count function

The **COUNT** function returns the number of entries in its argument list that represent numbers. For example, if you wanted to count the amount of number values in the range A2 to A9 the formula would be =COUNT(A2:A9). The COUNT function does not count blank cells or labels.

Like the AVERAGE function, the MAX, MIN and COUNT functions can be entered into a worksheet either manually or by expanding the AutoSum button and selecting the appropriate option in the list that appears.

## Interpreting formula error messages

Error messages will appear when you use incorrect syntax or try to do something that prevents Excel from calculating the formula. Some common examples are shown in Table 2.

*Table 2*
*Some common formula error messages*

| | |
|---|---|
| ##### | Means that the column is not wide enough to display the value. Use any of the methods described earlier to widen the column to allow the value to display. |
| #DIV/0! | Formula is attempting to divide by zero. Check the values of the cell in the formula. |
| #NAME? | Excel does not recognise text in a formula. Check the spelling of your function or check that a name exists. |
| CIRCULAR | The formula is referencing itself. The cell reference containing the formula is also part of the formula. |
| #VALUE! | Occurs when the wrong type of operand or argument is used. |

In Excel 2003, whenever an error message appears you will also see a green marker in the top left of the cell. If you click on the cell to select it an information symbol will appear. Click on this symbol to display a drop-down menu which offers you many choices, including a 'Help on this error' option which will take you to a help file explaining the message error in detail.

## Activity 5

Retrieve the worksheet 'Home Makers'.

1 Change the label "First Quarter Report" to "First Quarter Sales Report".

2 Insert the label "Expenditure" in cell F4.

3 Enter the following expenditure for each branch.

| ***Branch*** | ***Expenditure*** |
|---|---|
| North | 25000 |
| South | 32056 |
| Central | 30123 |
| East | 54345 |
| West | 45632 |

4 Calculate the following:

(a) The amount of tax paid if the profit is taxed at 15%

(b) The after-tax profit

(c) The corporate totals for every column

(d) The greatest after-tax profit, i.e. which store performed best?

(e) The lowest after-tax profit, i.e. which store performed worst?

(f) The mean after-tax profit across all the stores

(g) The amount of branches processed.

5 Format all monetary values as currency.

### *How it is done*

1 Retrieve the worksheet 'Home Makers'.

2 Select cell B3. Change "First Quarter Sales" to "First Quarter Sales Report".

3 Select F4. Enter the label "Expenditure".

4 Enter the expenditure data in the appropriate cells.

5 Select cell G4. Enter the label "Profit before tax".

6 Change the width of the cell to accommodate the label.

7 Select cell G5. Enter the formula = E5-F5. Copy the formula down to G9.

8 Select cell H4. Enter the label "Tax on Profit" and change the column width.

9 Select cell H5. Enter the formula = G5*.15. Copy the formula down to H9.

10 Select cell I4. Enter the label "Profit after Tax" and change the column width.

11 Select cell I5. Enter the formula =G5-H5. Copy the formula down to I9.

12 Select cell B10. Enter the formula =Sum(B5:B9). Copy the formula across to I10.

13 Highlight or mark off the range B5 to I10. Change the number format to currency.

14 Select cell A13. Enter the label "Maximum Profit".

15 Select cell B13. Enter the formula =Max(I5:I9).

16 Select cell A14. Enter the label "Minimum Profit".

17 Select cell B14. Enter the formula =Min(I5:I9).

18 Select cell A15. Enter the label "Average Profit".

19 Select cell B15. Enter the formula =Average(I5:I9).

20 Select cell A16. Enter the label "Branches Processed".

21 Select Cell B16. Enter the formula =Count(I5:I9).

22 Highlight B13 to B15. Change the number format to currency.

23 Save the worksheet.

After completing steps 1 to 23 the worksheet should look like Figure 11.26.

*Figure 11.26*
*Worksheet after Activity 5 is complete*

B16 =COUNT(I5:I9)

| | A | B | C | D | E | F | G | H | I |
|---|---|---|---|---|---|---|---|---|---|
| 1 | | | | Home Makers Furniture Store | | | | | |
| 2 | | | | | | | | | |
| 3 | | First Quarter Sales Report | | | | | | | |
| 4 | | January | February | March | Total | Expenditure | Profit before tax | Tax on Profit | Profit after Tax |
| 5 | North | $ 26,500.00 | $ 22,442.00 | $ 23,456.00 | $ 72,398.00 | $ 25,000.00 | $ 47,398.00 | $ 7,109.70 | $ 40,288.30 |
| 6 | South | $ 45,600.00 | $ 23,246.00 | $ 67,543.00 | $136,389.00 | $ 32,056.00 | $ 104,333.00 | $15,649.95 | $ 88,683.05 |
| 7 | Central | $ 34,568.00 | $ 29,687.00 | $ 46,578.00 | $110,833.00 | $ 30,123.00 | $ 80,710.00 | $12,106.50 | $ 68,603.50 |
| 8 | East | $ 78,540.00 | $ 98,755.00 | $ 65,981.00 | $243,276.00 | $ 54,345.00 | $ 188,931.00 | $28,339.65 | $ 160,591.35 |
| 9 | West | $ 53,546.00 | $ 94,786.00 | $ 65,847.00 | $214,179.00 | $ 45,632.00 | $ 168,547.00 | $25,282.05 | $ 143,264.95 |
| 10 | Corporate | $238,754.00 | $ 268,916.00 | $269,405.00 | $777,075.00 | $ 187,156.00 | $ 589,919.00 | $88,487.85 | $ 501,431.15 |
| 11 | | | | | | | | | |
| 12 | | | | | | | | | |
| 13 | Maximum Profit | $160,591.35 | | | | | | | |
| 14 | Minimum Profit | $ 40,288.30 | | | | | | | |
| 15 | Average Profit | $100,286.23 | | | | | | | |
| 16 | Branches Processed | 5 | | | | | | | |

## Exercise 4

1 (a) Define a function.

(b) List FOUR categories of functions.

2 Give the general form and an example of the following functions: SUM, AVERAGE, MAXIMUM, MINIMUM and COUNT.

3 The following table shows the gross pay for some employees of R and R Enterprises Limited.

| Employee | Anderson K | Henry P | Joseph A | Jack M |
|---|---|---|---|---|
| Salary | $15 000 | $16 575 | $14 356 | $18 675 |

Each employee has to pay a Health Surcharge (HSCH) of $120.00, National Insurance (NIS) of $150.00 and income tax based on how much is earned.

Income tax is calculated on the gross salary as follows:

Create a spreadsheet to calculate the net pay for each employee using the information opposite. Format the worksheet appropriately.

*Income tax table*

| Income | Rate |
|---|---|
| < $5000 | 5 % |
| > = $5000 and < $10 000 | 10% |
| > = $10 000 and < $15 000 | 15% |
| > = $15 000 and < $20 000 | 20% |
| > = $20 000 | 25% |

4 *Table A*

| | A | B | C | D | E | F |
|---|---|---|---|---|---|---|
| 1 | Premier Services | | | | | |
| 2 | Sales Team Salaries | January 2005 | | | | |
| 3 | | | | | | |
| 4 | Surname | Firstname | Sales | Basic Salary | Commission | Net Salary |
| 5 | Ramesar | Randal | $35457 | $3500 | | |
| 6 | Mohammed | Aneesa | $75654 | $3500 | | |
| 7 | Dean | Melissa | $18000 | $3500 | | |
| 8 | Brown | Kerry | $67594 | $3500 | | |

Table A shows the name, sales and basic salary for some employees of Premier Services. Each employee is given a commission based on sales shown in Table B.

Calculate the Net salary for each employee.

| Sales | Commission |
|---|---|
| < $20 000 | 2% |
| > = $20 000 and < $30 000 | 3% |
| > = $30 000 and < $ 50 000 | 4% |
| > =$50 000 | 6% |

*Table B*

# Absolute cell references

As we saw earlier, you can copy a formula to other cell(s) in a row or column and let Excel change the formula relative to the position of the cell(s) (relative cell reference). However, there are situations where you do *not* want Excel to adjust the cell references when a formula is copied from one location to another. To prevent the cell references in a formula from changing, place a dollar ($) sign before and after the column. These are called **absolute cell references**. In Figure 11.28 the values of $B$1 and $B$2 remain unchanged no matter where they are copied or moved in the worksheet.

## Activity 6

| | A | B | C | D | E |
|---|---|---|---|---|---|
| 1 | MARK UP | 20% | | | |
| 2 | VAT | 15% | | | |
| 3 | | | | | |
| 4 | Item | Cost price | Marked-up price | Vat | Final Selling price |
| 5 | Hat | $20.00 | | | |
| 6 | Shirt | $75.00 | | | |
| 7 | Pants | $235.00 | | | |
| 8 | Jersey | $145.00 | | | |
| 9 | Shoes | $225.00 | | | |

*Figure 11.27*
*Data for calculating a final selling price*

*Figure 11.28*
*Calculation of the final selling price*

| | A | B | C | D | E |
|---|---|---|---|---|---|
| 1 | MARK UP | 20% | | | |
| 2 | VAT | 15% | | | |
| 3 | | | | | |
| 4 | Item | Cost price | Marked-up | Vat | Final Selling price |
| 5 | Hat | $20.00 | $24.00 | $3.60 | $27.60 |
| 6 | Shirt | $75.00 | $90.00 | $13.50 | $103.50 |
| 7 | Pants | $235.00 | $282.00 | $42.30 | $324.30 |
| 8 | Jersey | $145.00 | $174.00 | $26.10 | $200.10 |
| 9 | Shoes | $225.00 | $270.00 | $40.50 | $310.50 |

A store-owner would like to build a worksheet to calculate the final selling price of each item in his store. He first adds a markup of 20% to the cost price, to produce something called the marked-up price. He then adds on 15% VAT to the marked-up price to get the final selling price.

### *How it is done*

The values for markup and VAT are placed at the top of the worksheet, so that they can be easily changed.

1. Enter the data as shown in Figure 11.27.
2. Move to cell C5. Type the formula =B5+ (B5* $B$1).
3. Copy the formula to cells C6, C7, C8 and C9.
4. Move to cell D5. Type the formula =C5 * $B$2.
5. Copy the formula to cells D6, D7, D8 and D9.
6. Move to cell E5. Type the formula =C5 + D5.
7. Copy the formula to cells E6, E7, E8 and E9.

Figure 11.28 shows the completed worksheet.

## Reference to cells in other worksheets

Sometimes you may wish to refer to a cell in another worksheet when writing a formula. The general formula is:

=worksheetname! cellreference

For example, if you want to use the value of cell D12 from the worksheet 'Shares' in Figure 29(a) in cell B5 in the worksheet 'Assets' as shown in Figure 29(b), the formula will be =Shares!D12.

| | A | B | C | D |
|---|---|---|---|---|
| 1 | Company | Amt.Share | Current Price | Current Value |
| 2 | | | | |
| 3 | BBX | 290 | $ 25.00 | $ 7,250.00 |
| 4 | SBD | 235 | $ 15.25 | $ 3,583.75 |
| 5 | NTL | 1000 | $ 11.47 | $11,470.00 |
| 6 | CSQ | 700 | $ 12.80 | $ 8,960.00 |
| 7 | RPO | 100 | $ 62.40 | $ 6,240.00 |
| 8 | DHK | 1820 | $ 27.00 | $49,140.00 |
| 9 | LKT | 700 | $ 19.00 | $13,300.00 |
| 10 | | | | $99,943.75 |
| 11 | | | | |
| 12 | Total | | | $99,943.75 |

*Figure 11.29 (a)*
*Shares Worksheet*

B5 =Shares!D12

| | A | B |
|---|---|---|
| 1 | Assets | 2005 |
| 2 | Top Money market | $ 72,988.07 |
| 3 | Zenith Bank | $ 130,607.03 |
| 4 | Bonds | $ 64,000.00 |
| 5 | Shares | $ 99,943.75 |
| 6 | Total | $ 367,538.85 |
| 7 | | |

*Figure 11.29 (b)*
*Assets Worksheet*

# Sorting

To sort means to arrange in order. A typical spreadsheet package enables you to sort data (text or numbers) into ascending or descending order. If you do not specify an ordering, the rows and columns are sorted in ascending order (lowest to highest). This means the lowest is at the top of the sheet and the highest is at the bottom. The opposite holds for descending order.

Data can be sorted in a number of ways. For example, a teacher who enters the names of students and end-of-term marks for five subjects can sort the column of names into alphabetical order, with the students' marks being moved accordingly as well. The teacher could also create a worksheet to rank the students according to a particular subject, again with a corresponding movement of all the other rows.

When sorting a list of data, most spreadsheet packages use the following guidelines:

- Rows with blank cells are placed at the bottom of the sorted list
- Hidden rows are not moved
- Numbers used as text are sorted before text alone.

### *To sort a column by a single criterion*

1. Select a cell in the column you wish to sort.
2. Pull down the **Data** menu and select **Sort**.
3. In the 'Sort by' box, select the primary column by which you want your data sorted.
4. Check the **Ascending** or **Descending** radio button. If the column has a header row, for example 'Title', check the **Header row** radio button.
5. Click **OK**.

## Sorting using multiple criteria

You may need to sort the data in a worksheet by more than one field. For example, a book store may want to sort all their books by author's name. The owner may then want to sort each author's books alphabetically by title. The sorting procedure for a multiple sort is exactly the same as that for a single criterion, except that after the first criterion is selected you then move down to a second sort field and add additional sort criteria.

### *To sort by multiple criteria*

1. Select a cell in the column you wish to sort.
2. Pull down the **Data** menu and select **Sort**.
3. In the 'Sort by' box, select the primary column by which you want your data sorted.
4. Check the **Ascending** or **Descending** radio button.
5. In the first 'Then by' box, select the secondary column by which you want to arrange your data.
6. Check its **Ascending** or **Descending** radio button.
7. If you wish to sort a third column, repeat steps 5 to 6 with the next 'Then by' box.
8. Click **OK**.

**Shortcut**

You can sort data by selecting a cell in the column you want to sort and then clicking either the **Sort Ascending** [A↓Z] or **Sort Descending** [Z↓A] button in the toolbar.

## Exercise 5

1 Use examples to explain the difference between relative and absolute addressing.

2 (a) Define sorting.

(b) What are the advantages of sorting a worksheet?

3 The worksheet in Figure 11.30 shows a listing of books from a supplier to the Small Book Store. Do the following:

(a) Create the worksheet.

(b) Sort it into ascending order of classification.

(c) Re-sort the worksheet in descending order by author and then by title.

(d) Add a column to calculate the total cost for each title. (Total cost = No. of copies * Unit cost).

(e) Sort the worksheet in descending order of total cost.

*Figure 11.30 Book list*

| | A | B | C | D | E | F |
|---|---|---|---|---|---|---|
| 1 | | | The Small Book Store | | | |
| 2 | | | | | | |
| 3 | Author Surname | Author First Name | Title | Classification | No. of Copies | Unit Cost |
| 4 | Brown | James | Back to Godhead | Religious | 12 | $ 50.00 |
| 5 | Jaira | Khadine | Eagle and the Falcon | Thriller | 4 | $ 65.00 |
| 6 | Lucas | Gary | Dracula | Horror | 15 | $ 85.00 |
| 7 | Jaira | Khadine | Apocalypse | Thriller | 24 | $ 51.00 |
| 8 | Lucas | Gary | Lost Forever | Thriller | 6 | $ 45.00 |
| 9 | Mars | Gary | Star Chase | Science Fiction | 8 | $ 59.00 |
| 10 | Brown | James | Faith Healers | Religious | 21 | $ 85.00 |
| 11 | Lucas | Gary | Bad Omens | Horror | 16 | $ 66.00 |
| 12 | Richards | Jenifer | Outer Planet Experience | Science Fiction | 25 | $ 48.00 |
| 13 | Mohammed | Afzal | In Touch with God | Religious | 31 | $ 54.00 |
| 14 | Lucas | Gary | The Dark Side | Horror | 8 | $ 38.00 |
| 15 | | | | | | |

# Filtering records

Filtering a worksheet displays records that contain a certain value or that meet a set of criteria. The two methods used for filtering records in Excel are AutoFilter and Advanced Filter.

## AutoFilter

**Note:** Before a worksheet can be filtered it must have column labels.

AutoFilter allows the selection of records based on one criterion. For example, from the worksheet in Figure 11.30, you can select all the books classified as 'Horror'.

### Using the AutoFilter command

Using the worksheet in Figure 11.30, select all the religious books.

1 Select the range to be filtered. Select A3:F14.

2 Select from the **Data** menu **Filter/AutoFilter**. A drop-down list arrow appears in the cell of each column label as shown in Figure 11.31.

3 Click on the drop-down list arrow in the cell with column label "Classification". A list of the different values (Religious, Science Fiction, etc.) contained in that column is displayed.

4 Select the desired criterion, in this case 'Religious'.

*Figure 11.31 Book store worksheet using AutoFilter*

| | A | B | C | D | E | F |
|---|---|---|---|---|---|---|
| 1 | | | The Small Book Store | | | |
| 2 | | | | | | |
| 3 | Author Surna | Author First Name | Title | Classification | No. of Copi | Unit Co |
| 4 | Brown | James | Back to Godhead | Religious | 12 | $ 50.00 |
| 5 | Jaira | Khadine | Eagle and the Falcon | Thriller | 4 | $ 65.00 |
| 6 | Lucas | Gary | Dracula | Horror | 15 | $ 85.00 |
| 7 | Jaira | Khadine | Apocalypse | Thriller | 24 | $ 51.00 |
| 8 | Lucas | Gary | Lost Forever | Thriller | 6 | $ 45.00 |
| 9 | Mars | Gary | Star Chase | Science Fiction | 8 | $ 59.00 |
| 10 | Brown | James | Faith Healers | Religious | 21 | $ 85.00 |
| 11 | Lucas | Gary | Bad Omens | Horror | 16 | $ 66.00 |
| 12 | Richards | Jenifer | Outer Planet Experience | Science Fiction | 25 | $ 48.00 |
| 13 | Mohammed | Afzal | In Touch with God | Religious | 31 | $ 54.00 |
| 14 | Lucas | Gary | The Dark Side | Horror | 8 | $ 38.00 |

All the records containing the classification 'Religious' will be displayed as shown in Figure 11.32.

*Figure 11.32 List of all religious books*

| | A | B | C | D | E | F |
|---|---|---|---|---|---|---|
| 1 | | | The Small Book Store | | | |
| 2 | | | | | | |
| 3 | Author Surnan | Author First Nan | Title | Classification | No. of Copi | Unit Co |
| 4 | Brown | James | Back to Godhead | Religious | 12 | $ 50.00 |
| 10 | Brown | James | Faith Healers | Religious | 21 | $ 85.00 |
| 13 | Mohammed | Afzal | In Touch with God | Religious | 31 | $ 54.00 |
| 15 | | | | | | |

## Advanced filter

Sometimes you may want to select records based on more than one criterion. For example, using the spreadsheet in Figure 11.30, if you would like to select all the books that are written by the author Lucas and are classified as horror you would need to use an advanced filter.

### *Performing an advanced filter*

1. Select **Filter/Advanced Filter** from the **Data** menu. The 'Advanced Filter' dialogue box appears as shown in Figure 11.33.
2. The first step is to specify the 'List range'. This is the range you would like to perform the advanced filter on. Excel automatically selects this area and displays it in the 'List range' combo box. If you would like to change the range selected, click on the 'collapse button' on the right side within the combo box. The 'List range' combo box will be displayed alone, the other options become hidden. Type in or drag the mouse over the area desired. The range will be displayed in the combo box. Click on the collapse button again to see the entire 'Advanced filter' dialogue box.
3. The second step involves the selection of the criteria range. This refers to the different criteria you are going to use to select the records. For example, using the worksheet in Figure 11.30 you can select records by using the criteria author surname (e.g. Lucas), classification (e.g. Horror), No. of copies (e.g. >10). To select the criteria range you need to move to another part of the worksheet and type in or copy and paste the column labels and the criteria you wish to use to select the records. The cells A17 to C18 in Figure 11.34 shows the criteria range for selecting records in that worksheet.
4. Finally, you can
   - filter the worksheet in place: the selected records will be displayed and the other records will be hidden, or
   - copy the selected records to another location within the worksheet.

   To filter the worksheet in place click **OK**. To place the selected records in another location check the radio button **Copy to** in the 'Advanced Filter' dialogue box. A third combo box appears in the 'Advanced Filter' dialogue box. Select a cell in the area of the worksheet where you would like to place the selected records and click **OK**. The selected records will be displayed.

If you want to find out more about this topic you could look up the related animations and activities on your companion CD-ROM.

## Activity 7

Using the worksheet named 'Book Store' shown in Figure 11.30, select the records of all the books by the author 'Lucas', classification 'Horror' and 'No. of copies' greater than ten (10).

### *How it is done*

1 From the **Data** menu select **Filter/Advanced Filter**. The 'Advanced Filter' dialogue box appears as shown in Figure 11.33.

2 Excel selects the list range 'Sheet 1!$A$17:$C$18' and places it in the 'List range' combo box.

3 To enter the criteria range select the following cells and enter the corresponding values: A17 – "Author Surname", B17 – "Classification", C17 – "No. of Copies", A18 – "Lucas", B18 – "Horror", C18 – ">10".

4 To filter the list in place click **OK**. The results are shown in Figure 11.34.

5 To copy the records to another location within the spreadsheet, check the **Copy to another location** radio button in the 'Advanced Filter' dialogue box. Excel selects a location to copy the records to. In this example Excel selects the range A19 to F19 as shown in Figure 11.33. The selected records are shown in Figure 11.35.

*Figure 11.33 The 'Advanced Filter' dialogue box*

*Figure 11.34 Records selected when the list is filtered in place*

| | A | B | C | D | E | F |
|---|---|---|---|---|---|---|
| 1 | | | The Small Book Store | | | |
| 2 | | | | | | |
| 3 | Author Surname | Author First Name | Title | Classification | No. of Copies | Unit Cost |
| 6 | Lucas | Gary | Dracula | Horror | 15 | $ 85.00 |
| 11 | Lucas | Gary | Bad Omens | Horror | 16 | $ 66.00 |
| 15 | | | | | | |
| 16 | | | | | | |
| 17 | Author Surname | Classification | No. of Copies | | | |
| 18 | Lucas | Horror | >10 | | | |

*Figure 11.35 Selected records copied to another location*

| | A | B | C | D | E | F |
|---|---|---|---|---|---|---|
| 1 | | | The Small Book Store | | | |
| 2 | | | | | | |
| 3 | Author Surname | Author First Name | Title | Classification | No. of Copies | Unit Cost |
| 4 | Brown | James | Back to Godhead | Religious | 12 | $ 50.00 |
| 5 | Jaira | Khadine | Eagle and the Falcon | Thriller | 4 | $ 65.00 |
| 6 | Lucas | Gary | Dracula | Horror | 15 | $ 85.00 |
| 7 | Jaira | Khadine | Apocalypse | Thriller | 24 | $ 51.00 |
| 8 | Lucas | Gary | Lost Forever | Thriller | 6 | $ 45.00 |
| 9 | Mars | Gary | Star Chase | Science Fiction | 8 | $ 59.00 |
| 10 | Brown | James | Faith Healers | Religious | 21 | $ 85.00 |
| 11 | Lucas | Gary | Bad Omens | Horror | 16 | $ 66.00 |
| 12 | Richards | Jenifer | Outer Planet Experience | Science Fiction | 25 | $ 48.00 |
| 13 | Mohammed | Afzal | In Touch with God | Religious | 31 | $ 54.00 |
| 14 | Lucas | Gary | The Dark Side | Horror | 8 | $ 38.00 |
| 15 | | | | | | |
| 16 | | | | | | |
| 17 | Author First Name | Classification | No. of Copies | | | |
| 18 | Gary | Horror | >10 | | | |
| 19 | Author Surname | Author First Name | Title | Classification | No. of Copies | Unit Cost |
| 20 | Lucas | Gary | Dracula | Horror | 15 | $ 85.00 |
| 21 | Lucas | Gary | Bad Omens | Horror | 16 | $ 66.00 |
| 22 | | | | | | |

## Creating graphs and charts

The ability to convert worksheet data into one of many graphical forms is a very important feature of any spreadsheet package. Graphs and charts are very useful because they can simplify numerical data that may otherwise be confusing. They make the data easier to interpret. They grab your attention almost instantly and allow information to be assimilated quickly. Therefore charts can be important tools for data analysis and the presentation of data.

The first step in creating a chart is to select the data values you want to place in it. A spreadsheet package enables you to plot any row or column of data against any other row or column of data. For example, if you want to represent the first-quarter sales for the months of January to March for the five branches of the Home Makers Furniture Store for the values shown in Figure 11.26, you need to select the range B5:D9.

After selecting the data values, you need to select a type of chart that is relevant to the situation. The type of chart you choose depends on the type of data you have and how you want to represent it. Some charts are best for representing certain types of data. For example, the data that represents sales of different branches of a company over a period may be displayed using a column graph. Data that represents portions of a whole might best be represented using a pie chart.

If any values in the data selected are changed after the chart has been created, the changes are immediately reflected in the chart. Also, more data can be inserted between the first and last rows or columns. These changes will also be automatically included in the chart. Before creating a chart, make yourself familiar with the elements of a chart. Figure 11.36 shows a completed chart for the first-quarter sales of the Home Makers Furniture Store.

*Figure 11.36 Sales chart with its elements named*

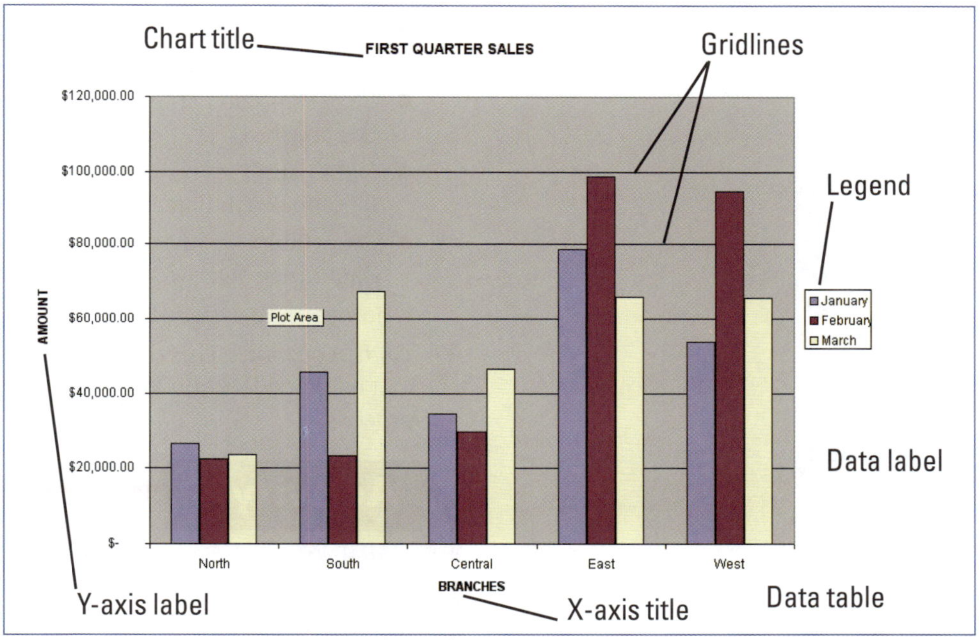


### Chart elements

- **Axes**: the vertical and horizontal lines against which data is plotted. The X-axis is referred to as the **category axis** and the Y-axis is known as the **value axis**.
- **Data range**: The data selected to create the chart.
- **Series**: The row or column headings that make up the range of values from the worksheet that is used to create the graph.
- *Titles*: There are three titles: for the chart, category axis and value axis. They are lines of text used to describe the chart elements.
- *Gridlines*: Incremental lines that may appear along each axis; they help you to read values from the graph more easily.
- *Legend*: A cross-reference showing how each series is represented in the chart, i.e. a key.
- *Data labels*: The actual value, percentage or name of a bar or segment of a chart.
- *Data table*: The range of values, included at the bottom of the chart, that is used to chart the graph.

### *Creating a chart in Excel using the Chart Wizard*

Creating a chart using Excel's Chart Wizard is a very simple process. After selecting the data, click the **Chart Wizard** icon [ ] on the toolbar. The Wizard then guides you towards the final chart by means of four steps, each with its own dialogue box.

1 *'Chart Type'*: From this dialogue box you can select the type of chart that you want: standard or custom, each with many alternatives. Select a chart type that is suited for your presentation and click **Next**.

2 *'Chart Source Data'*: This dialogue box has two tabs, labelled 'Data Range' and 'Series'. From the 'Data Range' tab, you can display a representation of the graph and the data range that was used. You can change the appearance of the chart by changing the 'Series in' selection from columns to rows or vice versa. The 'Series' tab enables you to add or remove a series. When you are ready, click **Next**.

3 *'Chart options'*: This dialogue box has six tabs:

- Titles – you can type a chart title, and titles for the category (X) axis and value (Y) axis
- Axes – you can specify how the axes are labelled
- Gridlines – you can choose whether or not to include major and minor gridlines for the axes
- Legend – you can include a legend and select a position to place it in the chart
- Data Labels – you can include the values, percentage value and/or label for each data element
- Data Table – you can choose whether or not to show in the chart the data range that was used to create it.

When you are satisfied with the settings shown in each tab, click **Next**.

4 *'Chart Location'*: This dialogue box enables you to select where the chart will be placed. When you have done that, click **Finish** to complete the process.

## Activity 8

Using the worksheet in Figure 11.37, create a column graph to show the first-quarter sales for Home Makers Furniture Store.

*Figure 11.37 Worksheet to form the basis of a graph*

| | A | B | C | D | E |
|---|---|---|---|---|---|
| 1 | | | Home Makers Furniture Store | | |
| | | | | | |
| 2 | | January | February | March | Total |
| 3 | North | $26,500.00 | $22,442.00 | $23,456.00 | $72,398.00 |
| 4 | South | $45,600.00 | $23,246.00 | $67,543.00 | $136,389.00 |
| 5 | Central | $34,568.00 | $29,687.00 | $46,578.00 | $110,833.00 |
| 6 | East | $78,540.00 | $98,755.00 | $65,981.00 | $243,276.00 |
| 7 | West | $53,546.00 | $94,786.00 | $65,847.00 | $214,179.00 |
| 8 | Corporate | $238,754.00 | $268,916.00 | $269,405.00 | $777,075.00 |

## Activity 8 continued

***How it is done***

1. Select the range B3 to D7.
2. Click on the **Chart Wizard** icon.
3. From the 'Chart type' list on the 'Standard Types' tab, select **Column**; and from the 'Chart sub-type' options select the first sub-type. Click **Next**.
4. Check the **Columns** radio button. Click **Next**.
5. For each tab, do as follows:
   - *Titles*: In the 'Chart title' field, type "FIRST QUARTER SALES".

     In the 'Category (X) axis' field, type "Branches".

     In the 'Value (Y) axis' field, type "Amount".
   - *Axes*: Ensure the 'Category (X) axis' and the 'Value (Y) axis' boxes are checked, and check the **Automatic** radio button.
   - *Gridlines*: Check **Value (Y) axis: Major gridlines**.
   - *Legend*: Check the **Placement: Right** radio button.
   - *Data Labels*: Check the **None** radio button.
   - *Data Table*: Check the **Show data table** box. (You may leave the box unchecked if you don't want to show the data table.)

     Click **Next**.
6. Leave the chart as an object in Sheet 1. Click **Finish**.

   The chart created by this process is shown in Figure 11.36.

## Activity 9

Using the worksheet in Figure 11.37, create a graph to compare the total sales for the four branches.

***How it is done***

1. Select columns A3 to A7 and E3 to E7. These can be copied to another part of the worksheet and then selected; or you can simply select A3 to A7 and then hold down the Ctrl key and select E3 to E7.
2. Click on the **Chart Wizard** icon.
3. With the **Standard Types** tab displayed, select **Column** from the 'Chart type' box. Then select the second chart from the 'Chart sub-type' box. Click **Next**.
4. Select the **Series** tab. Type "Total Sales" in the 'Name' field. Click **Next**.
5. On the **Titles** tab:

   (a) In the 'Chart title' field, type "First Quarter Total Sales".

   (b) In the 'Category (X) axis' field, type "Branches".

   (c) In the 'Value (Y) axis' field, type "Amount".

   (d) On the **Data Labels** tab, check the **Show value** button.

   Click **Next**.
6. Click **Finish**.

   The graph produced should look like Figure 11.38.

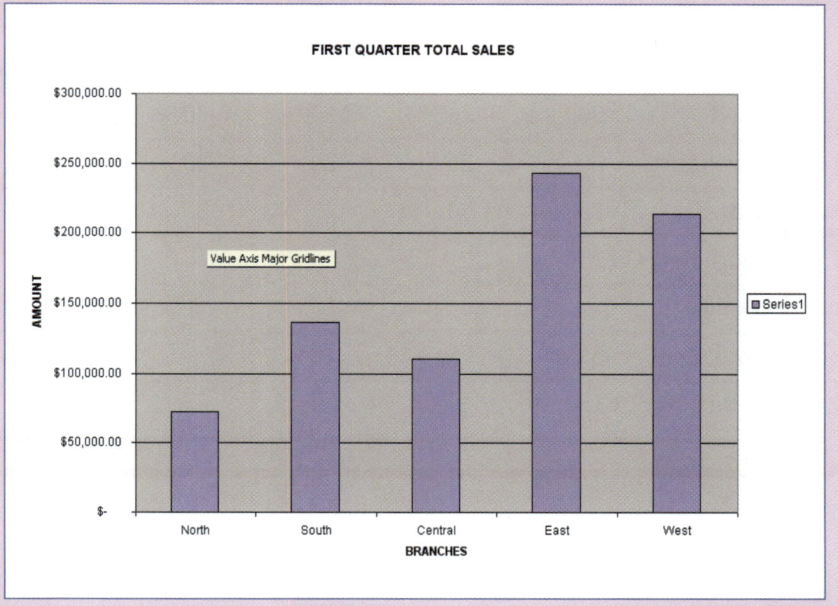


*Figure 11.38*
*A graph of total sales*

## Activity 10

### *To create a pie chart*

The data represented in Figure 11.38 can also easily be represented as a pie chart. The steps are as follows:

1 Select columns A3 to A7 and E3 to E7.

2 Click on the **Chart Wizard** icon.

3 With the **Standard Types** tab displayed, select **Pie** from the 'Chart type' box. Then select the first chart from the 'Chart sub-type' box. Click **Next**.

4 Select the **Series** tab. Type "Total Sales" in the 'Name' field. Click **Next**.

5 On the **Titles** tab:

- In the 'Chart title' field, type "First Quarter Total Sales". (There are no other options available in this tab.)
- On the **Data Labels** tab, check the **Percentage** button.

Click **Next**.

6 Click **Finish**.

The pie chart produced should look like Figure 11.39.

*Figure 11.39 A pie chart of total sales*

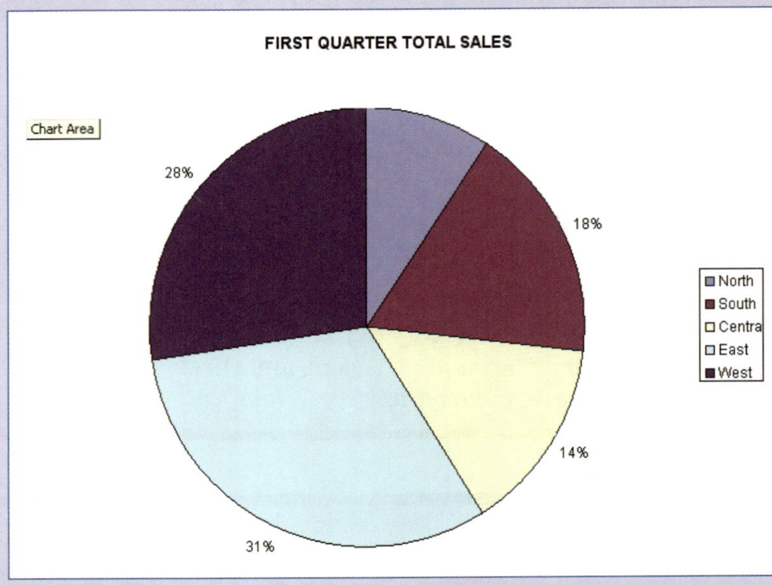


## Exercise 6

1 Table 3 shows the money spent by a student on different items over a four week period.

(a) Calculate the total amount of money spent on each item over the four weeks.

(b) Create a pie chart showing the total amount spent on each item. The pie chart should display the percentage spent on each item.

| ITEMS | WEEK 1 | WEEK 2 | WEEK 3 | WEEK 4 | TOTAL |
|---|---|---|---|---|---|
| Food | 200 | 245 | 180 | 80 | |
| Stationery | 50 | 25 | 20 | 40 | |
| Travel | 25 | 30 | 25 | 35 | |
| Clothes | 150 | | | | |
| Medical | | | 125 | | |
| Books | 50 | 75 | | | |
| Other | 120 | 45 | 85 | 65 | |

*Table 3*

## Exercise 6 continued

2 Table 4 shows the cost of three types of juices, the quantity sold over a four week period and the expenses of the Fresh Juice Stall. You are required to create a spreadsheet to calculate:

(a) the income earned for each week

(b) the profit/loss for each week

(c) the total amount of each type of juice sold over the four week period.

(d) Create an appropriately labelled column graph showing the total amount of each juice sold over the four weeks.

| | Fresh Juice Stall | | | | | |
|---|---|---|---|---|---|---|
| **Juices** | **Cost** | | | | | |
| Orange | $5 | | | | | |
| Melon | $7 | | | | | |
| Pineapple | $8 | | | | | |
| | | | | | | |
| | Orange | Melon | Pineapple | Income | Expenses | Profit/Loss |
| WEEK 1 | 124 | 21 | 65 | | $120 | |
| WEEK 2 | 135 | 80 | 45 | | $250 | |
| WEEK 3 | 154 | 56 | 84 | | $165 | |
| WEEK 4 | 110 | 85 | 94 | | $155 | |

*Table 4*

## The IF function

The IF function tests a condition that is either true or false. The general form of the function is as follows:

Function Condition Instructions

**= IF (logical_test, value_if_true, value_if _false)**

When the function is executed, the first instruction (the second argument) is executed if the condition tested is true, and the second instruction (the third argument) is executed if the condition tested is false. Either instruction can be text, a number, a formula, a function or a cell address. If the instruction is a formula, function or cell address, the result, and not the instruction itself, will be displayed.

For instance, consider the function =IF(F5>=50000,10,8). If the value in cell F5 is greater than or equal to 50000, the function will return the value 10. If the value is less than 50000, the function will return the value 8. The following logical operators can be used in the IF function:

| **Operator** | **Meaning** |
|---|---|
| > | Greater than |
| = | Equal to |
| > = | Greater than or equal to |
| < | Less than |
| < = | Less than or equal to |
| < > | Not equal to |

## Activity 11

The First Trinidad National Bank pays a yearly interest of 8% on fixed-deposit balances less than or equal to $50 000, and 10% on fixed-deposit balances greater than $50 000. The interest earned is then added to the customer's balance at the beginning of the year to give the final balance.

The worksheet in Figure 11.40 shows some customers and their balances. The function =IF(C4< =50000,8%,10%) in cell D4 compares the value in cell C4 to see if it is less than or equal to 50 000. Since the value is 45 000, the condition is true, so the value 8% is returned. However, if the value in cell C4 had been greater than 50 000, the value 10% would have been returned, as is the case for D5, D6 and D8.

In Figure 11.41, we have decided not to show the interest rate explicitly, but just the result of using it to calculate the interest earned. Look at the new formula for D4 at the top of the figure. The value in cell C4 is checked to see if it is less than or equal to 50 000. If the condition is true, the value in cell C4 is multiplied by .08 and if the condition is false it is multiplied by .10.

| | A | B | C | D | E | F |
|---|---|---|---|---|---|---|
| 1 | | | Zenith Bank | | | |
| 2 | | | | | | |
| 3 | First Name | Surname | Starting Ba | Interest Ra | Interest Earned | Final Balance |
| 4 | Larry | Adams | 45000 | 8% | $ 3,600.00 | $ 48,600.00 |
| 5 | Marie | Balfour | 69569 | 10% | $ 6,956.90 | $ 76,525.90 |
| 6 | James | Chin-Fat | 84254 | 10% | $ 8,425.40 | $ 92,679.40 |
| 7 | Harry | Doodnath | 35789 | 8% | $ 2,863.12 | $ 38,652.12 |
| 8 | Krishna | Singh | 55467 | 10% | $ 5,546.70 | $ 61,013.70 |

*Figure 11.40 Banking worksheet, showing the interest rate explicitly*

D4 =IF(C4<=50000,C4*0.08,C4*0.1)

| | A | B | C | D | E |
|---|---|---|---|---|---|
| 1 | | | Zenith Bank | | |
| 2 | | | | | |
| 3 | First Name | Surname | Starting Balance | Interest Earned | Final Balance |
| 4 | Larry | Adams | 45000 | $ 3,600.00 | $48,600.00 |
| 5 | Marie | Balfour | 69569 | $ 6,956.90 | $76,525.90 |
| 6 | James | Chin-Fat | 84254 | $ 8,425.40 | $92,679.40 |
| 7 | Harry | Doodnath | 35789 | $ 2,863.12 | $38,652.12 |
| 8 | Krishna | Singh | 55467 | $ 5,546.70 | $61,013.70 |

*Figure 11.41 Banking worksheet without an explicit interest rate*

## Nested IF statement

As you have seen, the IF statement can return one value if the condition is true or another value if the condition is false. The IF statement can also be used in situations where there are several conditions to be tested. For example, the worksheet in Figure 11.42 shows the identification number, first name, surname, marks for four subjects, total and average marks for student in a class. Students are awarded grades based on the average mark. The grades awarded for each range are:

| Average mark | Grade |
|---|---|
| > =80 | A |
| > =65 and < 80 | B |
| > =55 and < 65 | C |
| > =50 and < 55 | D |
| < 50 | F (fail) |

To award grades we need to write a formula using several IF (nested IF) statements. In cell J2 we write the formula:

=IF(I2 > =80,"A",IF(I2 > =65,"B",IF(I2 > =55,"C",IF(I2 > =50,"D","F")))).

The formula is then copied to the other cells in the column.

J2 fx =IF(I2>=80,"A",IF(I2>=65,"B",IF(I2>=55,"C",IF(I2>=50,"D","F"))))

| | A | B | C | D | E | F | G | H | I | J |
|---|---|---|---|---|---|---|---|---|---|---|
| 1 | Student ID | First Name | Surname | Subject1 | Subject2 | Subject3 | Subject4 | Total | Average | Grade |
| 2 | 1245 | Jim | Brown | 90 | 85 | 65 | 80 | 320 | 80 | A |
| 3 | 1246 | Harry | Baker | 85 | 82 | 76 | 68 | 311 | 77.75 | B |
| 4 | 1247 | Joanne | Cameron | 45 | 35 | 50 | 38 | 168 | 42 | F |
| 5 | 1248 | Gloria | Carrington | 52 | 68 | 65 | 55 | 240 | 60 | C |
| 6 | 1249 | Eric | Diaz | 75 | 45 | 45 | 40 | 205 | 51.25 | D |
| 7 | 1250 | George | Dominic | 76 | 80 | 86 | 91 | 333 | 83.25 | A |
| 8 | 1251 | Bud | Homer | 65 | 87 | 46 | 75 | 273 | 68.25 | B |
| 9 | 1252 | Neil | Jupiter | 68 | 56 | 58 | 40 | 222 | 55.5 | C |

*Figure 11.42 Nested IF statements*

## Exercise 7

1. Create the worksheet shown in Figure 11.41.
   (a) Insert five additional customers and their starting balances.
   (b) Sort the worksheet on customer name in descending order of surname.
   (c) A 15% tax is charged on interest earned IF the customer is under 55 years of age. Insert a column with the heading "Age" and insert ages varying from 20 years to 70 years for each client on the spreadsheet. Calculate the tax, if any, on the interest.
   (d) Calculate the interest after tax.
   (e) Calculate the final balance (starting balance + interest after tax).
2. Create the worksheet shown in Figure 11.42.
   (a) Format the average mark as percent.
   (b) Insert a row above row 1.
   (c) Type the label "Form Class 4s".
   (d) Type in the label "comment" in cell K2.
   (e) Write an IF statement in column K to insert a comment based on the grades obtained using the following conditions:

      A – Very good

      B – Good

      C – Fair

      D – Try harder

      F – Much more effort needed

# Finding a record in a list

Searching for records in a list using a single criterion or multiple criteria can be done easily and quickly with a spreadsheet package. The search can be done using the same operators that are used in the IF function. If a search is done using multiple criteria then all the criteria must be met before a record matching all the criteria is displayed. If there is no match, the data form will display the current record.

### *To find a record in a list*

1. Click a cell in the list you want to search.
2. Pull down the **Data** menu and select **Form**. The 'Form' dialogue box appears.
3. Click the **Criteria** button. (The fields in the dialogue box are cleared.)
4. Click the dialogue-box field corresponding to the worksheet column you want to search.
5. Type the condition (e.g. Smith, >500, < =75, < >200, etc.).
6. If you want to use more than one criterion, repeat steps 4 and 5.
7. Click **Find Next** to display the next record that matches the criteria, or **Find Prev** to find the previous record that matches them.

# Date function

When entering a date into a cell, Excel will accept various different formats. Some of the formats are:

15-5-2005
15-5-05
15-May
15-May-05

### To store dates in a particular format

1. Enter a date into an empty cell and confirm entry.
2. Select the cell with the date.
3. Click on the **Format** menu and select **Cells**. The 'Format Cells' dialogue box appears.
4. Select **Date** from the **Numbers** tab.
5. Select the date format required from the 'Type' window.

Excel has a number of functions that aid in computations involving dates. Some of the functions are:

**TODAY() :** Gives today's date in date format (e.g. 15/04/2005)

**NOW()** : Gives today's date and time (e.g. 15/04/2005 11:45)

Because dates (and times) are stored as numbers, they can be used in calculations. For example, it is easy to work out the number of days between two dates. Consider the following example.

A video club rent videos to their customers for a down payment of $3.00 and a daily rental of $2.00. The amount a customer pays is found by calculating the number of days from the day borrowed to the present day, multiplied by the daily rental.

*Figure 11.43(a)*

H2 | fx =TODAY()

| | A | B | C | D | E | F | G | H | I | J |
|---|---|---|---|---|---|---|---|---|---|---|
| 1 | Member Number | First Name | Surname | Movie Borrowed | Date Borrowed | Cost per Day | Down Payment | Date Returned | Number of days | Cost |
| 2 | 10 | Brian | Dyal | Kings | 4/2/2005 | $ 2.00 | $ 3.00 | 10/2/2005 | 183 | $366.00 |
| 3 | | | | | | | | | | |

I2 | fx =H2-E2

| | A | B | C | D | E | F | G | H | I | J |
|---|---|---|---|---|---|---|---|---|---|---|
| 1 | Member Number | First Name | Surname | Movie Borrowed | Date Borrowed | Cost per Day | Down Payment | Date Returned | Number of days | Cost |
| 2 | 10 | Brian | Dyal | Kings | 4/2/2005 | $ 2.00 | $ 3.00 | 10/2/2005 | 183 | $366.00 |
| 3 | | | | | | | | | | |

*Figure 11.43(b)*

To get the present date the function =TODAY() is entered in cell H2 (Figure 11.43(a)).

To get the number of days the video was rented type the formula =(H2-E2) in cell I2 (Figure 11.43(b)).

To calculate the cost enter the formula =I2*F2 in cell J2.

## Exercise 8

Journey Car Rentals rent three types of cars at the rates shown in Table 5. A customer renting a car has to make a down payment of $200. If the car is returned in good condition the customer is refunded the $200 otherwise the customer loses the down payment.

Rental charge is calculated by multiplying the number of days rented by the daily charge. Using the present date on the computer as the date returned, create a spreadsheet to calculate the amount paid by the various customers in Table 5.

*Table 5*

| | A | B | C | D | E | | | |
|---|---|---|---|---|---|---|---|---|
| 1 | Journey Car Rentals | | | | | | | |
| 2 | Rate per day | | | | | | | |
| 3 | Class A | $400 | | | | | | |
| | | | | | | | | |
| 4 | Class B | $300 | | | | | | |
| 5 | Class C | $200 | | | | | | |
| 6 | | | | | | | | |
| 7 | Customer | DP# | Class | Date Rented | Down payment | Date Returned | Condition Returned | Amount Paid |
| 8 | Jacob J | 26548 | A | 11/08/05 | $200 | | Good | |
| 9 | Hobson D | 43577 | A | 13/08/05 | $200 | | Bad | |
| 10 | Clarke G | 24576 | C | 15/09/05 | $200 | | Bad | |
| 11 | Jupiter V | 34571 | B | 15/10/05 | $200 | | Good | |

# Printing a worksheet

Printing allows you to get a hardcopy of your worksheet. There are two main ways you can get data from your worksheet to the printer: by clicking the **Print** button on the standard toolbar or using the menu.

Clicking on the **Print** button sends your document directly to the printer. Your document will be printed using the default settings. Using the menu gives you many more options, such as the ability to select the range of pages, the number of copies and the print settings.

### *To print a worksheet*

1. Pull down the **File** menu and select **Print**.
2. Make appropriate selections when the 'Print' dialogue box appears as shown in Figure 11.44.
3. To change the paper size and orientation of print (portrait or landscape), click the **Properties** button in the dialogue box.

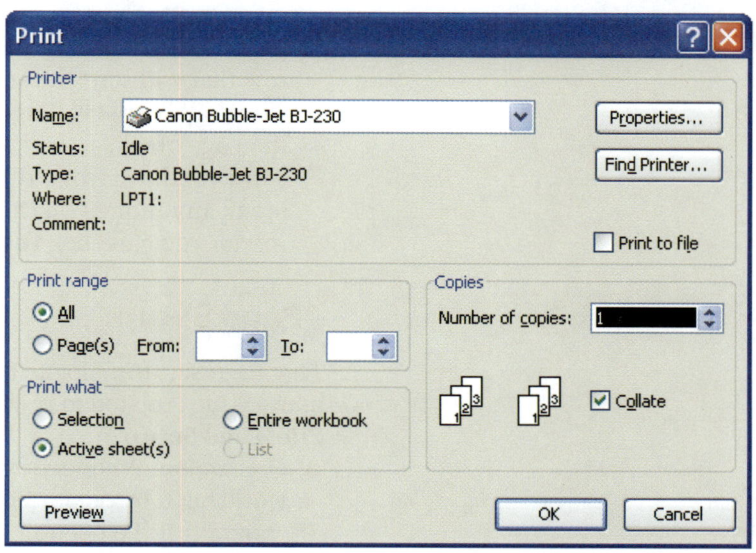


*Figure 11.44*
*The 'Print' dialogue box*

## Elements of the 'Print' dialogue box

- *Printer Name combo box*: Displays the name of the default printer. If more than one printer is available, when you decide to print, click the **Printer Name** combo box and select the desired printer from the list.
- *Print range*: Depending on the size of your worksheet you can print all the pages or just a partial range of pages.
- *Print what section*: Allows you to print a part of the worksheet, the active worksheets (the worksheet that is displaying in the background) or the entire workbook.
- *Number of copies*: Using the arrows you can set the number of copies to be printed.
- *Properties*: This button allows you to configure or change some of the properties related to the selected printer.

## Print Preview

Print Preview allows you to preview your worksheet before the actual printing. It opens a special window that presents the document as it would appear when it is printed. The 'Print View' dialogue box as shown in Figure 45 allows you to have an idea of what your worksheet would look like on a piece of paper. You can preview your worksheet by clicking the **Print Preview** button from the standard toolbar, the **File** menu, or the 'Print' dialogue box.

In Microsoft Excel, the 'Print Preview' window is not just used to preview the printed document. There are other options you can choose.

Home Makers Furniture Store

First Quarter Sales Report

| | January | February | March | Total | Expenditure |
|---|---|---|---|---|---|
| North | $ 26,500.00 | $ 22,442.00 | $ 23,456.00 | $ 72,398.00 | $ 25,000.00 |
| South | $ 45,600.00 | $ 23,246.00 | $ 67,543.00 | $136,389.00 | $ 32,056.00 |
| Central | $ 34,568.00 | $ 29,687.00 | $ 46,578.00 | $110,833.00 | $ 30,123.00 |
| East | $ 78,540.00 | $ 98,755.00 | $ 65,981.00 | $243,276.00 | $ 54,345.00 |
| West | $ 53,546.00 | $ 94,786.00 | $ 65,847.00 | $214,179.00 | $ 45,632.00 |
| Corporate | $238,754.00 | $ 268,916.00 | $269,405.00 | $777,075.00 | $ 187,156.00 |

| | |
|---|---|
| Maximum Profit | $160,591.35 |
| Minimum Profit | $ 40,288.30 |
| Average Profit | $100,286.23 |
| Branches Processed | 5 |

*Figure 11.45*
*The 'Print Preview' dialogue box*

### *'Print Preview' dialogue box configuration options*

- The **Page Break Preview** feature allows you to tell the printer where you want each page to start. Microsoft Excel allows you to start a new page *anywhere* on the worksheet. To set your own page end, first click the row that will start the subsequent page. Then on the main menu, you would click **Insert/Page Break**. You should notice a line that points to the page break.

  After you have worked with the page break, or if you don't need the page break any more, you can remove it. To remove a page break, on the main menu, you can click **Insert/Remove Page Break**.

## Page Setup

The 'Page Setup' dialogue box allows you to specially configure and control many issues related to printing. To access it on the main menu, click **File/Page Setup**.

- *Orientation*: Whenever you ask Microsoft Excel to print the contents of a worksheet, by default it prints the document vertically; this is called 'portrait'. If the document or the section to be printed is wider than taller, you can change the orientation to 'landscape'.

- *Scaling*:By default, the printed document will adjust itself to 100% fitting, that is, a ratio of 1:1 page width to height. To change any of these settings, use the appropriate arrow button in the 'Scaling' section. The options are 'Adjust To', 'Fits To' and 'Page(s) Wide By'.
- *Paper size*: By default, the paper size is set to 'Letter', which represents 8.5 by 11 inches paper. The 'Paper Size' combo box allows you to select a different size from the list.
- *Print Quality*: The result of printing depends on your printer. If your printer allows more configuration, click the 'Print Quality' combo box and select a different setting.
- Within the 'Page Setup' dialogue box, the **Print** button calls the 'Print' dialogue box as shown in Figure 11.44. If you want to take a look at the printed result before actually printing, click the **Print Preview** button.
- *Margins*: The 'Margins' property page allows you to control all four margin sections of a document. You can also create one or two special sections for the title or the lower areas of the printed paper; these are the Header and the Footer sections.
  By default, a document prints starting at the top left corner of the paper. This may look awkward if your document contains just one section or a chart. Therefore the 'Margins' property page allows you to centre the content of the worksheet horizontally and/or vertically. This is done using the **Horizontally** or the **Vertically** check box in the 'Center On Page' section.
  The 'Header/Footer' property page of the 'Page Setup' dialogue box allows you to set and configure some of the items you would like to display in the top and bottom sections of the printed document. To configure one of the sections, you can click either the **Custom Header** or the **Custom Footer** buttons. The Custom Header button calls the 'Header' dialogue box. The Custom Footer button calls the 'Footer' dialogue box. Both dialogue boxes look alike.
  Just remember that whatever you input in any of the boxes will be repeated on every sheet, as in Word.
- The **Sheet** tab in the 'Page setup' dialogue box allows you to print part or all of the worksheet (Figure 11.46).

Since most of the buttons are not very explicit, whenever you want to find what a button is used for, you can right-click it and click 'What's This'.

*Figure 11.46*
*The sheet tab of the 'Page Setup' dialogue box*

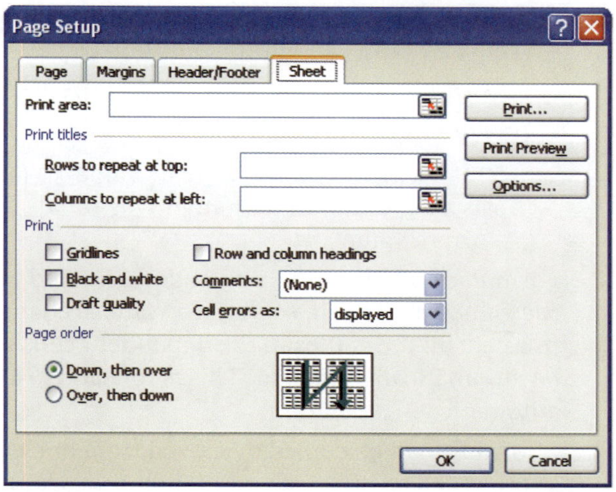


The 'Print area' text box allows you to select an area of your worksheet for printing. To use it, click its selection button [ ]. This would shrink the 'Page Setup' dialogue box, allowing you to make a selection of the area you want to print. After setting the desired area, you can click the selection button to restore the 'Page Setup' dialogue box.

The **Sheet** tab allows you to set or select a row or range of rows to display on top of every printed sheet. If you know the row or range of rows you want to use, you can just type it in the 'Rows to repeat at top' text box, but the safest way to configure it is to click the selection button [ ], then click any cell in the desired row or click the desired cells. In either case, the whole row or rows will be selected.

The 'Columns to repeat at left' text box is used like the previous box except that, this time, it would display a particular column on the left side of each printed sheet.

If you want to print the gridlines, in the 'Print' section, click the **Gridlines** check box.

If you want to display the column and row headers on your printed paper, click the **Row and column headings** check box.

## Summary

1 A spreadsheet package is an application package that can be used for any job that involves repetitive numerical calculations. It is a large grid divided into rows and columns. The intersection of a row and a column is called a cell. Each cell is identified by its cell reference (column and row position). A cell can hold one of three kinds of information: label (text), value (number) or formula.

2 Formulae are used to perform operations on numbers. A formula must start with an equal (=) sign, which is followed by numbers, different operators or cell references that are part of the calculation. Excel also contains built-in functions for performing calculations, including:

- =SUM(First cell:Last cell). Finds the sum of a row or column of numbers.
- =MAX(First cell:Last cell). Finds the maximum value in a row or column of numbers.
- =MIN(First cell:Last cell). Finds the minimum value in a row or column of numbers.
- =AVERAGE(First cell:Last cell). Finds the mean of a row or column of numbers.
- =IF(logical_test, value_if_true, value_if_false). Tests a condition that is either true or false and returns a value.

3 Formulae usually contain cell addresses and not the values in the cell, so that if a value is changed in a cell, all the values in the dependent cells will be automatically updated. This is referred to as automatic re-calculation.

4 A formula can be copied or moved from one cell to another cell or range of cells. When the formula is moved, all cell references in the formula change with respect to the formula's new cell location. This is called relative cell addressing. However, it may be necessary to move or copy a formula but keep the cell reference in the formula fixed. This is done using absolute cell referencing.

5 Most of the editing features available in a word processor are also available in Excel – for example, 'Delete', 'Cut', 'Copy', 'Paste', 'Find' and 'Replace'.

6 Formatting enables you to control the appearance of cells and the worksheet in general. Commands that control the formatting can be triggered from the toolbar or from the Format pull-down menu. Formatting includes:

- Alignment of cells (left-, centre- or right-justified)
- Representation of numbers (general, number, currency, accounting)
- Changing the column width, row height, font size and style and including borders and patterns.

7 A group of continuous cells that form a square or a rectangle is called a range of cells and is identified by the addresses of the first and last cells. You can use a single command to affect a range of cells. For example, a range of cells can be formatted for currency, or the contents of the cells can all be centre-justified, by selecting the range and using one command.

8 A spreadsheet enables data to be sorted in ascending or descending order according to the content of one or more fields.

9 Excel enables users to convert worksheet data easily into a wide range of graphs. Simply select the data range that you want to use to create the graph and then follow the steps using the Chart Wizard.

10 Worksheets can be printed using the printer icon in the standard menu or using Print in the File menu.

## Questions

1 A student receives an allowance of $100.00 a week. The table shows how he spends the money each day.

*How a student spends his allowance*

| | Monday | Tuesday | Wednesday | Thursday | Friday |
|---|---|---|---|---|---|
| Travelling | 4 | 4 | 4 | 4 | 4 |
| Lunch | 2 | 3 | 2 | 4 | 6 |
| Snacks | 0 | 2 | 1 | 2 | 2 |
| Games World | 0 | 0 | 5 | 0 | 10 |

Create a worksheet to:

(a) Calculate the total money spent each day of the week

(b) Calculate the total money spent on each item for the week

(c) Calculate his total expenses for the week

(d) Calculate the amount left from his allowance.

(e) Format the worksheet with $ signs.

(f) Centre all headings.

(g) Save the worksheet as 'Allowance'.

2 Currency conversion: the rates of exchange against the United States (US) dollar for some islands in the Caribbean in 2005 were as follows:

US $1 = TT $6.30 (Trinidad & Tobago dollars)

US $1 = BDS $1.99 (Barbados dollars)

US $1 = EC $2.25 (Eastern Caribbean currency)

US $1 = J$24 (Jamaica dollars)

Create a spreadsheet to convert the following amounts of Trinidad and Tobago dollars – 1, 5, 10, 20, 30, 40, 50, 60, 70, 80, 90, 100 – to Barbados, Eastern Caribbean and Jamaican dollars. Save the worksheet as 'Currency'.

3 Calculate the square, square root, cube, and the cube minus twice the number itself, for each of the following numbers – 1, 5, 7, 9, 12, 16, 20, 25, 36, 40, 64, 80.

(a) Format the square root to two decimal places.

(b) Centre all labels and numbers.

(c) Add three numbers of your own to the table.

(d) Save the worksheet as 'Numbers'.

4 The Super Stationery Store is in receivership. The receiver has to value each piece of furniture and equipment for sale, and has decided that the furniture and equipment should be depreciated at 10% for each year on the reducing balance. The names of the furniture and equipment, their quantity and their initial cost are listed in Figure 11.47.

Create a worksheet to:

(a) Calculate the initial total cost of the items.

(b) Calculate the value of each item after depreciation for each year up to the year 2005.

(c) Calculate the total value of all the items for each year up to the year 2005.

(d) Format the worksheet with $ to two decimal places.

(e) Centre all headings.

(f) Sort the data in the year 2005 column in descending order.

(g) Save the worksheet as 'Depreciation'.

5 The worksheet in Figure 11.48 shows the item code, name, quantity and unit price for seven different items bought from LowPrice Retailers. A discount of 12% is given on all purchases.

(a) Calculate the total cost of each item.

(b) Calculate the discount for each item.

(c) Calculate the discounted price of each item.

(d) Centre-justify all headings.

(e) Modify the numbers in the Unit Price, Cost, Discount and Discounted Price columns to show dollar ($) values and two decimal places.

(f) Save the worksheet as 'Purchases'.

*Figure 11.47 The receiver's worksheet for the Super Stationery Store*

| | A | B | C | D | E | F | G | H |
|---|---|---|---|---|---|---|---|---|
| 1 | | | Super Stationary Store | | | | | |
| 2 | | | | | | | | |
| 3 | Item | Initial Price | Quantity | Initial Total Cost | 2002 | 2003 | 2004 | 2005 |
| 4 | Desk Chairs | 850 | 4 | | | | | |
| 5 | Desks | 1500 | 3 | | | | | |
| 6 | Fans | 250 | 5 | | | | | |
| 7 | Filing Cabinets | 1200 | 3 | | | | | |
| 8 | Photocopiers | 4500 | 2 | | | | | |
| 9 | Display Cupboards | 2500 | 4 | | | | | |
| 10 | Computers | 8500 | 2 | | | | | |
| 11 | | | | | | | | |

*Figure 11.48 Worksheet for items bought from LowPrice Retailers*

| | A | B | C | D | E | F | G |
|---|---|---|---|---|---|---|---|
| 1 | | | | LowPrice Retailers | | | |
| 2 | | | | | | | |
| 3 | Item Code | Name | Quantity | Unit Cost | Cost | Discount | Discounted Price |
| 4 | AA123 | Under arm Deodorant | 24 | 15 | | | |
| 5 | AA128 | Superior Colonge | 15 | 65 | | | |
| 6 | AB200 | Dew Drop Perfume | 20 | 95 | | | |
| 7 | AC456 | Gloss Powder | 56 | 24 | | | |
| 8 | CD231 | Nail Polish | 65 | 10 | | | |
| 9 | CF145 | Mouth Wash | 50 | 35 | | | |
| 10 | MN767 | Dental Floss | 96 | 8 | | | |

*Figure 11.49 Student marks in six subjects*

| | A | B | C | D | E | F | G | H | I |
|---|---|---|---|---|---|---|---|---|---|
| 1 | | | | RB College Barbados | | | | | |
| 2 | | | | | | | | | |
| 3 | | | Form 3.1 | Mark | Sheet | | | | |
| 4 | Names | Maths | Biology | Chemistry | Physics | English | History | Total | Average |
| 5 | Victoria Bishop | 67 | 76 | 45 | 55 | 23 | 45 | | |
| 6 | Renee Eastman | 76 | 42 | 45 | 57 | 45 | 78 | | |
| 7 | Ravi Omar | 58 | 67 | 42 | 61 | 65 | 65 | | |
| 8 | Melissa Cardinal | 79 | 56 | 67 | 84 | 56 | 68 | | |
| 9 | Donny Seepersad | 87 | 43 | 64 | 83 | 76 | 84 | | |
| 10 | Gary Fredricks | 65 | 67 | 38 | 76 | 62 | 67 | | |
| 11 | Shimona Vaughn | 61 | 65 | 56 | 65 | 45 | 71 | | |
| 12 | | | | | | | | | |
| 13 | Subject | Highest mark | Lowest mark | | | | | | |
| 14 | Maths | | | | | | | | |
| 15 | Biology | | | | | | | | |
| 16 | Chemistry | | | | | | | | |
| 17 | Physics | | | | | | | | |
| 18 | English | | | | | | | | |

**6** The Zenith Oil Company has four oil-producing districts. The manager of the company wants to forecast the profit that it will make for the last quarter of the year, based on the present production levels, operating cost and price of a barrel of oil.

The price of oil is presently quoted as US$30.00 a barrel. The operating cost per barrel of oil is US$8.00. The table shows the number of barrels of oil produced for each month in each district.

(a) Create a spreadsheet to calculate the operating cost and profit for each district for each month.

(b) Calculate the total expected production cost for the period October to December.

(c) Calculate the total projected profit.

(d) What will be the projected profits if a barrel of oil drops to US$25.00 and then to US$20.00?

(e) Create a chart to display the total oil production for each district.

(f) Create a chart to compare the projected profits from the three rates (US$30, US$25 and US$20) per barrel of oil.

| District | October production | November production | December production |
|---|---|---|---|
| 1 | 2300 | 2500 | 2400 |
| 2 | 3500 | 3500 | 3500 |
| 3 | 4300 | 4200 | 4000 |
| 4 | 1500 | 1800 | 2400 |

*Barrels of oil produced by the Zenith Oil Company*

**7** Figure 11.49 shows the names of students and their marks in six subjects. Enter the data into a worksheet as shown.

Complete the worksheet by carrying out the following tasks:

(a) Enter a blank row between row 3 and row 4.

(b) Calculate the total marks obtained by each student.

(c) Calculate the average mark for each student.

(d) Using a built-in function, extract the highest (maximum) mark and lowest (minimum) mark for each subject.

(e) Calculate and display the mean mark for the class, correct to two decimal places.

(f) Centre all headings.

(g) Delete Melissa Cardinal and all her data from the worksheet.

(h) Insert the name and marks for this student into the worksheet:

Ishana Jyoti, Maths 75, Chemistry 85, English 71, Biology 80, Physics 60.

(i) Move to an appropriate part of the worksheet and extract the highest total and lowest total.

(j) Save the worksheet as 'School report'.

8 The Superior Car Company sells five different models of foreign used cars: the Vx5, Chameleon, Rhino, Speed Star and Pinnacle. The advertised car price is called the showroom price. The buyer also has to pay a 20% government tax on the showroom price and a fixed licence fee of $15 000. The final price is the price on the road. The table shows how many of each model the company sold for the month of June:

| Model | Quantity | Showroom Price |
|---|---|---|
| Chameleon | 5 | $25 550 |
| Pinnacle | 7 | $20 500 |
| Rhino | 4 | $45 500 |
| Speed Star | 9 | $17 850 |
| Vx5 | 3 | $50 450 |

*Cars sold by the Superior Car Company*

The manager of the company wants to know the following information:

(a) The tax paid on each model of car
(b) The price including tax for each model
(c) The cost of each car on the road
(d) The total monthly sales value ($) for each model
(e) The average price of a car on the road
(f) The maximum sales total among the different models
(g) The minimum sales total among the different models
(h) On a graph, the comparative total monthly sales for each model.

Design and appropriately format a worksheet to show this information.

9 The Repeaters' College is a full-time school for students wishing to repeat their CSEC examination in various subject areas. The college has the following fee structure for each academic term:

Registration fee – $50.00

Cost per subject – $650.00

Lab fees per Lab subject – $100.00

For each student a total fee is calculated based on the registration fee, the number of subjects for which the student registers and the additional fee for each Lab subject. However, a student doing five or more subjects gets a 10% reduction in the total fee. A student is allowed three payments to complete the total payment of fees. The owners of the college need to know how much money each student has to pay, how much is received and how much is outstanding.

(a) Create a worksheet to satisfy the requests of the owners, using the data in the table.
(b) Format the worksheet as follows:
- Centre all labels and values
- Set the discount given, total fees and balance to two decimal places
- Set total fees, payments and balance to currency.

(c) Edit the worksheet as follows:
- Delete all information pertaining to Ian Sobers
- Insert the names of two students of your choice along with the number of subjects and Lab subjects for which they wish to register
- Sort the worksheet on name in descending order.

(d) Save the worksheet as 'Payments'.
(e) Select all the students who are doing three or fewer subjects.
(f) Change the Lab fee from $100 to $150 and the Subject fee from $650 to $675.
(g) What is the maximum fee paid?
(h) What is the minimum fee paid?
(i) What is the average number of subjects being taken by students in the school?

*Subjects taken by Repeaters' College students*

| Student's name | Total number of subjects | Number of Lab Subjects |
|---|---|---|
| Carter, Daryl | 4 | 1 |
| Ali, Feroze | 6 | 3 |
| Brown, Michelle | 3 | 1 |
| Simmons, Pat | 5 | 2 |
| Simmons, Brandon | 7 | 3 |
| Foster, James | 3 | 1 |
| Maharaj, Rudy | 4 | 2 |
| Sobers, Ian | 5 | 2 |
| Roberts, Carl | 6 | 3 |
| Taylor, Petal | 5 | 2 |

**10** The owner of a small contracting firm has 12 employees, divided into two categories: skilled and unskilled. Each worker is contracted to work a 40-hour week at a set rate, and for any time worked above 40 hours is paid an overtime rate of 1.5 times the regular rate. The set rate for an unskilled worker is $20 per hour and a skilled worker gets $30 per hour. The rates of pay are subject to change over time. The names of the employees, category and total number of hours worked for four weeks for the month of July 2005 are shown in the table.

(a) Create a worksheet that will show, for each employee, the employee's name, category, weekly number of hours worked and weekly salary. It should also include the total number of hours worked and the total salary for *all* the employees for the month.

(b) Calculate and display:

- The average weekly salary
- The minimum salary for the week
- The maximum salary for the week.

(c) Format the salary with '$' and two decimal places.

(d) Format the worksheet so that all column labels are centre-justified.

(e) Sort the spreadsheet on name in ascending order.

(f) Select all the unskilled workers who work more than 200 hours for the four weeks.

(g) Save the spreadsheet as 'July wages'.

(h) Delete all information pertaining to Richard Bobart.

(i) Add the following data to the worksheet:

Employee – Wesley Taylor

Category – unskille

Hours worked – week 1: 50; week 2: 60; week 3: 45; week 4: 40.

(j) Change the rate of pay for unskilled workers from $20 to $25 and for skilled workers from $30 to $40.

(k) Save the worksheet as 'July wages1'.

(l) Prepare an appropriately labelled bar graph to show the total weekly wages for the four weeks. Save the graph as 'Wage1'.

(m) Prepare an appropriately labelled pie chart to show the total number of hours worked for each week for the month of July. Save the chart as 'Hours'.

| **Employee** | **Category** | **Hours worked** | | | |
|---|---|---|---|---|---|
| | | *Week1* | *Week2* | *Week3* | *Week4* |
| Jason Agard | Skilled | 45 | 56 | 45 | 40 |
| Ralf Brown | Skilled | 56 | 45 | 50 | 68 |
| Anslem Douglas | Skilled | 40 | 45 | 40 | 55 |
| Brian Despot | Skilled | 40 | 40 | 45 | 56 |
| Larry James | Unskilled | 40 | 40 | 56 | 60 |
| Rolston Granger | Unskilled | 35 | 40 | 67 | 40 |
| Rudy Maraj | Unskilled | 40 | 55 | 43 | 55 |
| Gerry Parker | Unskilled | 56 | 45 | 76 | 45 |
| Richard Bobart | Unskilled | 65 | 45 | 45 | 57 |
| Luke Thompson | Unskilled | 70 | 45 | 34 | 45 |
| Moses Fredricks | Unskilled | 30 | 40 | 56 | 35 |
| Vernon Johnson | Unskilled | 40 | 40 | 64 | 62 |

# 12 Databases

## OBJECTIVES

At the end of this chapter you will be able to:

- Define the terms 'database' and 'database package'
- List situations in which databases would be useful
- List the similarities and differences between a manual and a computerised database
- Define the terms table, record, field, query, form and report
- Create a database using Microsoft Access
- Create a table in Design view
- Enter, delete and edit records in a table
- Create a form using a wizard and edit the design
- Create and run queries to select, update, append and delete
- Create a report using the wizard and edit the design

A **database** is an organised collection of related data. Data on any subject matter can be stored in a database. It can be used to store information on students, patients in a doctor's or dentist's office, music or video collections, stock in a supermarket, employee records, information on various countries ... almost anything. **Database management** is the process by which information is organised and stored on a computer in such a way that there is efficient retrieval, updating and manipulation of the data. A **database package** is a piece of software used to create and manage a computerised database. Using a computerised database is far more flexible than using a manual one. Information can be organised, retrieved, collated, displayed and printed much more easily this way.

## Manual databases

Understanding how a manual database is set up will help you to understand how computerised databases are set up. A manual database is much like a filing cabinet in which you might keep all related information on a particular subject. Consider a filing cabinet at a doctor's office in which one drawer of the cabinet contains information on patients, another drawer contains information on employees, and another information on stocks and suppliers. In the drawer that contains the patients' information there is a folder containing patient records, such as information on medication prescribed to them. To find this information, the doctor opens the appropriate drawer, extracts the appropriate folder and reads through the documents one by one until she finds the one she wants. Things become difficult when the doctor tries to relate the medicines prescribed to each patient (in one drawer) to the supplies needed of that medicine (another drawer). These two concepts are related, and updating the records requires work on files in two different drawers. Manual databases therefore present many problems including:

- Finding records can be a time-consuming process
- Files and folders can be easily misplaced if they are not filed properly
- These databases require large amounts of physical storage space
- Cross-referencing information between files is difficult
- Accessing information from another location (e.g. another office) is difficult.

# Computerised databases

A computerised database allows you to create and manage your database much more efficiently and effectively than a manual database. It can summarise data, sort data, select data and answer ad hoc requests for specific information. A database that links together logically related data stored in several files or tables is known as a **relational database**. Database packages have many built-in features that allow you to manipulate your data and extract information using a number of objects. An **object** is an option you can select and manipulate. These objects include tables, forms, queries, reports, macros and modules. We will look at some of these objects fully in the course of this chapter.

### Advantages of a computerised database

- Information can be accessed quickly and easily with little probability of it being lost.
- Related files can be linked together – once one is updated the related file(s) will also automatically be updated.
- Information need not be duplicated: it can be stored only once and accessed in several different ways.
- It is easy to update or change records, and their structure, in computerised databases.
- Data being entered can be easily validated, thereby preventing mistakes on entry (for example, the computer can tell you that you are entering an impossible date, such as '13' for the month).
- It is easy to store backup copies of the database 'offsite'.

### Disadvantages of a computerised database

- Computer breakdown can cause files to become inaccessible or corrupted.
- It is easy to copy or steal files unless the files are stored and protected carefully.
- Database operators require training, which may take some time.

## Basic concepts

- A **database file** is the entire database.
- A **table** is a basic unit of a database and contains data on a specific topic, e.g. *all* the personal information about *all* the members of a video club.
- A table **record** consists of a group of related fields containing information pertaining to *one* person, place or thing, e.g. *all* the personal information about *one* member of a video club. Tables therefore have multiple records.
- A **field** is an area within a record reserved for one very specific piece of data, e.g. the *address* of *one* video club member. Tables therefore have multiple fields.
- **Data** is the information that is held in the table fields.
- A **field definition** is the attributes that describe a field. It consists of a field *name*, data *type*, and other attributes such as field description, field size/width, etc. (Table 1). A field definition determines the kind of work that can be performed with the field; for example, you can define a field to hold numbers or text. A field with numbers can allow you to perform calculations on those numbers.

| Field Name | Field or Data Type | Field Size/Field Width |
|---|---|---|
| **Name** (e.g. Mathew Johnson) | Text | 25 |
| **Sex** (e.g. M) | Text | 1 |
| **Date of Birth** (e.g. 22/03/90) | Date/Time | |
| **Address** (e.g. 23 Guiaco Street) | Text | 50 |
| **Date of Visit** (e.g. 11/03/05) | Date/Time | |

*Table 1*
*An example of a database record*



## Creating a database using Microsoft Access (Office XP)

Unlike spreadsheet or word processing documents, database documents have to be named before you start work on them.

1 Click on the **Start** button.

2 Click on **Programs**.

3 Select **Microsoft Access**. The 'Microsoft Access' window appears, as shown in Figure 12.1 with the 'task pane' on the right of the window.

The task pane gives you the option to:

- Create a database from scratch
- Use a template
- Open an existing database.

*Figure 12.1*
*The Access window*

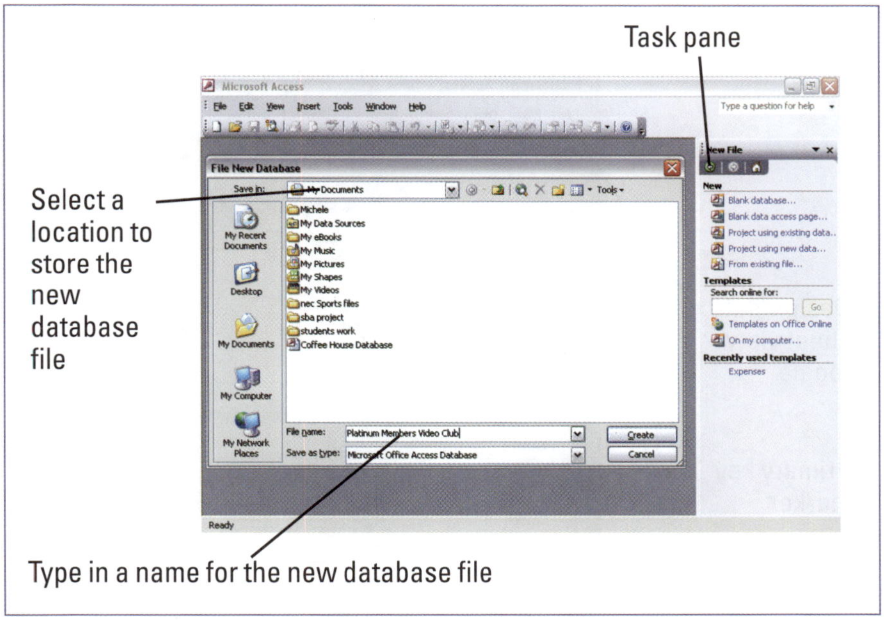


### Creating a new database from scratch

1 Click **Blank Access Database** on the task pane.

2 Give your database a name by clicking in the 'File name' box and typing a name.

3 Specify a location by selecting from the options available in the 'Save in' box.

4 Then click **Create** to create and save the database. Notice that the database window opens, as shown in Figure 12.2.

All the **objects** of the database are organised in the database window. The database window opens on the default setting from which tables can be created. This setting also displays all the tables in the database.

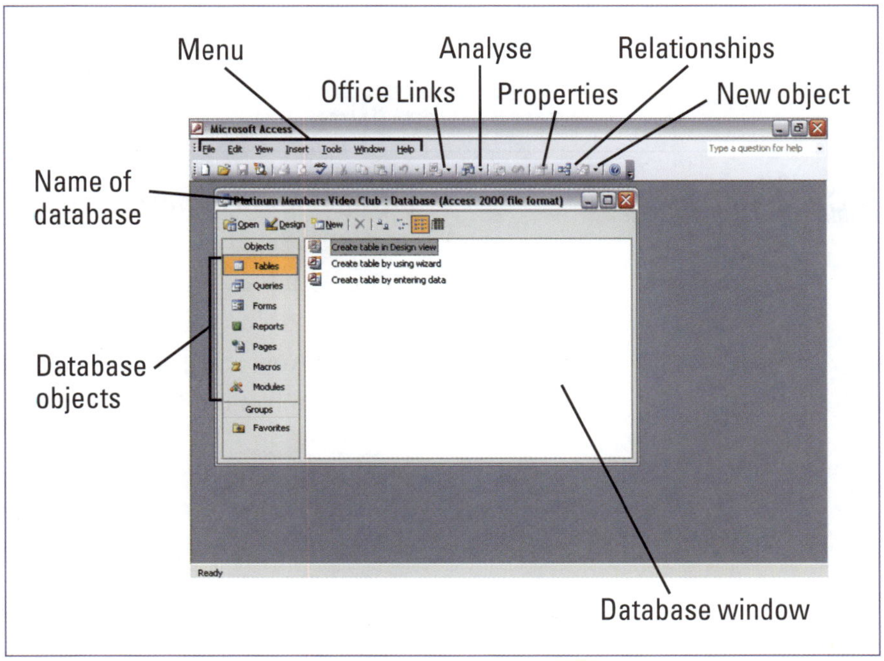


*Figure 12.2*
*The Database window*

## Creating tables

A table stores data about a specific topic. Creating separate tables for each topic allows you to store the data only once, hence limiting data entry errors and data duplication. It also increases the efficiency of the database.

Tables can be created using any of the following three options:

- **Datasheet view:** Data is entered into a datasheet grid, which consists of rows and columns labelled 'Field 1', 'Field 2', 'Field 3', etc. The data type is determined by Access, based on the data that is entered.
- **Design view:** This option allows you to create a database from scratch. It allows you to define the fields in the database and set all the attributes of that field.
- **Table Wizard:** The Table Wizard walks you through a four-step process that is easy to follow. However, the table produced may not meet your exact requirements. This method is the easiest and fastest way of creating a table.

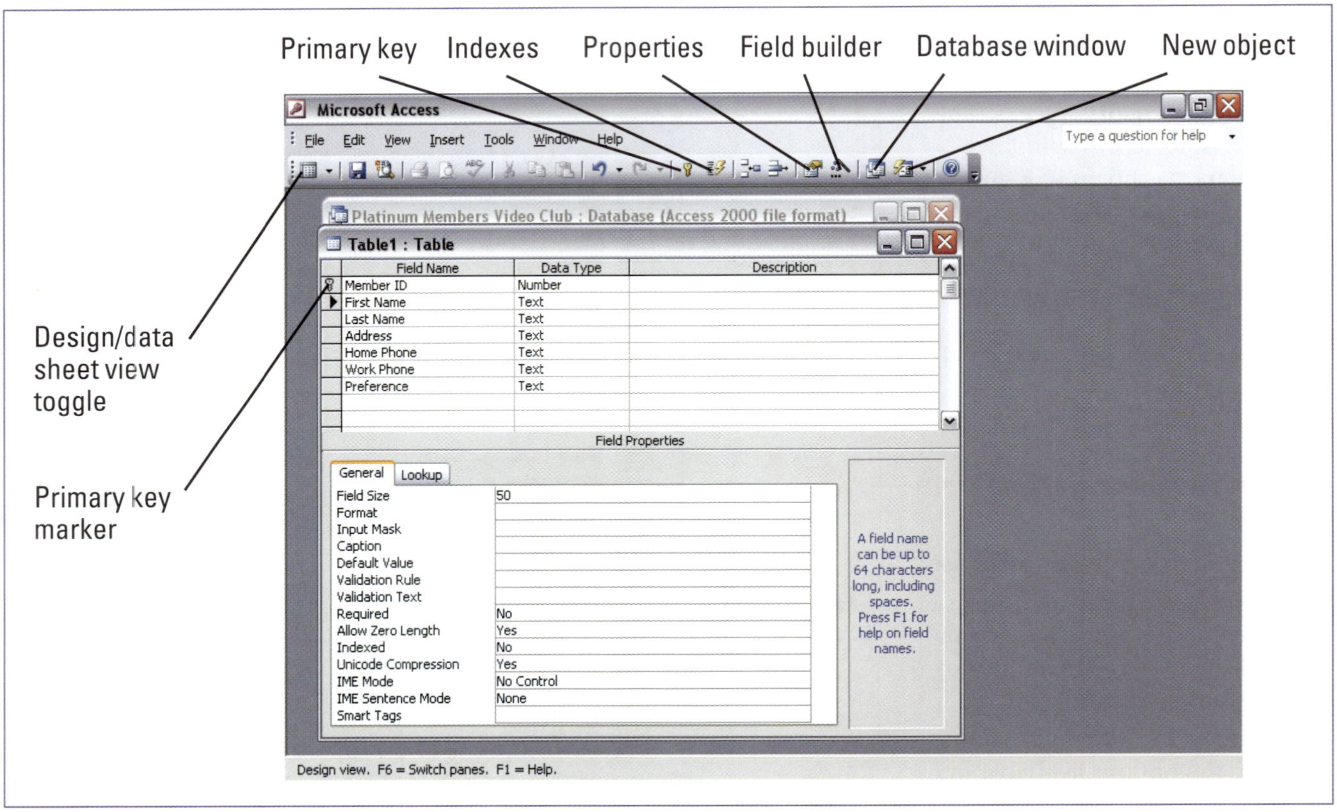


*Figure 12.3*
*Table window in Access*

### Creating a table in design view

1. Open the database.
2. Click on **Tables** (Figure 12.2).
3. Double-click on **Create table in Design View**, or
   Click on **New** and select **Design View**.
4. Define each of the fields in your table (Figure 12.3). This is called 'table definition':
   - Enter the field name in the 'Field Name' column (note: these field names become the headings for your table).
   - Select the appropriate data type for that field in the 'Data Type' column.
   - Enter text in the 'Description' column. This describes the data that will be entered in this field. (This field is optional.)

The 'Data Type' column enables you to select an appropriate data type from a drop-down list. When you have selected a data type, the 'Field Properties' pane appears at the bottom of the window. Access provides default field properties that are suitable for many applications, but you can change these if necessary. Table 2 lists the various data types and an explanation of the data types.

*Table 2*
*Data types and their explanation*

| Data type | Explanation |
|---|---|
| Number | Can store only a number, decimal point, and a plus or minus sign. Number data type can be used in calculations |
| Text | Stores alphabetic, alphanumeric, numeric and special characters. A text field can store up to 255 characters. Calculations cannot be performed on numbers stored in text fields |
| Memo | Stores lengthy text such as notes and description up to 65 536 characters in length |
| Date/Time | Stores several different formats of date and/or time |
| Currency | Used to store currency values. This data type prevents rounding off during calculations |
| AutoNumber | Stores a unique sequential or random number which is inserted when a record is added |
| Yes/No | Allows the storage of data that can have only two possible values: Yes/No, True/False or On/Off. Example: In an Employee database to say whether an employee is a union member or not the field name 'Union Member' could have a Yes/No data type in which the the check box could be ticked if the employee is a union member and not checked if the employee is not a union member. |
| OLE Object | Used to store embedded objects such as word processing and spreadsheet documents, pictures and sound |
| Hyperlink | Can store a URL (website address) or a path to a file Example: http://www.checkout.com C:\MyDocuments\mydatabase.mbd |
| Lookup Wizard | Selecting this data type starts a wizard which allows you to choose a value from another table or select a value from a list of values in combo box |

5 Select suitable properties for that field from 'Field Properties' in the bottom pane. A description of each of the field properties is given below.

6 Choose **Save** or **Save As** to save the table within the current database.

7 Type the name of the table and click **OK** (Figure 12.4).

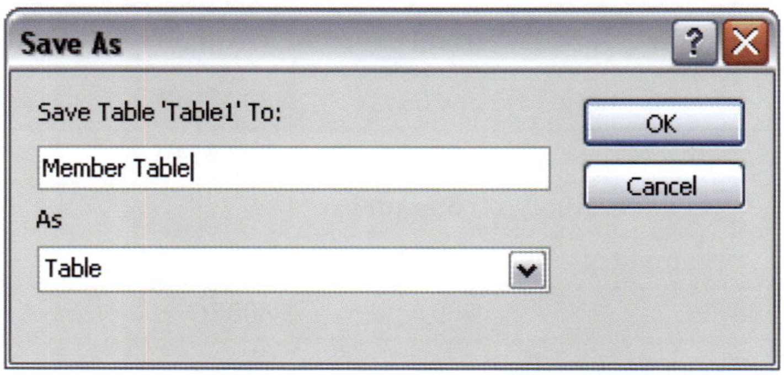


*Figure 12.4*
*'Save As' dialogue box for table*

# Properties

Properties determine how a field is stored, works and is displayed. Access automatically assigns default field properties to each field, depending on the data type. The default field properties are sufficient for many databases but you can change them if necessary. Some field properties enable you to restrict data that is entered into a field, and this may increase the efficiency and accuracy of data entry.

The following is a list of field properties and their explanations.

## Field Size

This property specifies the number of characters you want the field to have. It is usually applied to text or number fields. This should cater for the longest data that would be entered into this field.

- **Text Field Size:** The default is usually 50 characters for text fields; however, up to 255 characters can be entered. Limiting the number of characters being entered can save disk space or even prevent data entry errors.
- **Numeric Field Size:** There are a few options available for the field size for numbers (Table 3).

*Table 3 Numeric field size options*

| Numeric Field Size | Explanation |
|---|---|
| Byte | A positive integer between 0 and 255 |
| Integer | Positive and negative integers between -32768 and 32768 |
| Long Integer (default) | Larger positive and negative integers between approx. –2 billion (–2,147,483,648) and approx. 2 billion (2,147,483,647) |
| Single | A single-precision floating-point value with about 7 digits of accuracy |
| Double | A double-precision floating-point value with about 15 digits of accuracy |
| Replication ID | A special value known as a Globally Unique Identifier (GUID). It is used only with database replication |
| Decimal | A decimal number up to 28 digits in accuracy |

## Format

This (optional) property determines the way the field is displayed or printed.

- **Text and Memo Format:** this property conforms the data entered in the field to a specified format (Table 4).

*Table 4 Text and memo format*

| Format | Data | Display | Symbol | Explanation |
|---|---|---|---|---|
| @@@-@@@@ | 8976543 | 897-6543 | @ | Indicates a required space or character |
| @@@-@@@& | 897654 | 897-654 | & | Indicates an optional character or space |
| < COMPUTER | computer | < | | Converts the text to lowercase |
| > computer | COMPUTER | > | | Converts the text to uppercase |
| @\EC | 800 | 800EC | \ | Adds characters to the end |
| @;"Not Yet Rated" | PG | PG | | |
| @;"Not Yet Rated" | (blank) | Not Yet Rated | | |

- **Number format:** This property allows a selection from a drop-down menu or values can be displayed according to different assigned formats (Table 5).

*Table 5*
*Number format*

| Format | Data | Display | Explanation |
|---|---|---|---|
| ###,##0.00 | 476839.99 | 476,839.99 | # is a placeholder that displays a digit or nothing if there is none<br>0 is a placeholder that displays a digit or 0 if there is nothing |
| $###,##0.00 | 0 | $0.00 | |
| ###.00% | .055 | 5.5% | % multiplies the number by 100 and adds a percentage sign |

- **Date format:** This property displays the date and time in an appropriate format. The various formats can be selected from the drop-down menu or values can be displayed according to different assigned formats (Table 6).

*Table 6*
*Date formats*

| Format | Display | Explanation |
|---|---|---|
| dddd"," mmmm d"," yyyy | Friday, March 3, 2005 | dddd, mmmm, and yyyy prints the full names of the day, month and year. Note: what is enclosed in quotation marks is printed as it is. |
| ddd"," mmm"." d"," yy | Fri, Mar. 3, 05 | ddd, mmm, and yy prints the first three letters of the day, month and the last two digits of the year. |
| dddd "is a sunny day" | Friday is a sunny day | |
| h:n:s: AM/PM | 3:15:00 PM | 'n' is used to represent minutes rather than 'm', so as not to confuse minutes with months. |

- **Currency format:** The various formats can be selected from the drop-down menu.
- **Input Mask**
  This only works with text and date fields. It enables you to define a character string to act as a template so that data entered is formatted in a specific way. It is similar to the format property but displays the data on the datasheet before the data is entered. The Input Mask Wizard takes you through the steps easily.

*Table 7*
*Input mask format*

| Format | Explanation |
|---|---|
| 0 | A digit 0 through 9 without the + or – sign |
| 9 | A digit or space |
| # | A digit with +/- sign |
| A | A letter or digit |
| a | A letter |
| L | A Letter |
| C | Any character or space |
| & | Any character or space |
| < | Converts letters to lower case |
| > | Converts letters to upper case |
| ! | Displays from left to right |
| \ | Displays the next character |

- **Caption:** This is a label other than the field name that can be used in forms and reports
- **Default Value**
  This value is automatically entered in a field in each record of the table.
- **Validation Rule**
  This specifies the condition that limits the values that can be entered into the field or the requirements that must be met. For example '< > 0' the value must not be equal to 0.
- **Validation Text**
  A message you may want displayed if the validation rule is not met.
- **Required**
  If the record is selected but no value is inserted in this field, the record will be rejected and an error message is displayed.
- **Allow zero length**
  This allows a text or memo field to be filled with blanks or with a string of zero length.
- **Indexed**
  Creating indexes on a field allows tables to be sorted and searched faster.

### *Adding a field between two rows*

1. Open the table in Design view.
2. Select the row above which you want the new field to be inserted.
3. Choose **Rows** from the **Insert** menu.

A blank row appears for you to type in the new field name, data type and description (optional).

### *Deleting a field*

1. Open the table in Design view.
2. Select the row to be deleted.
3. Press the **Delete** key or select **Delete** from the **Edit** menu.

# Setting a primary key

A **primary key** is a selected field or fields in a table that uniquely identifies a record. An index is created when a primary key is set; this speeds up the operations of the database.

## Characteristics of a primary key

*Note:* A primary key need not be defined, but it is usually a good idea.

A primary key:

- Is not allowed to be null values (i.e. leaving a field blank indicates that there is no value for that field), it must always have a unique value
- Speeds up data storage and retrieval and the running of queries
- Sorts records according to the values in the field
- Enables a relationship between tables so that they can be joined.

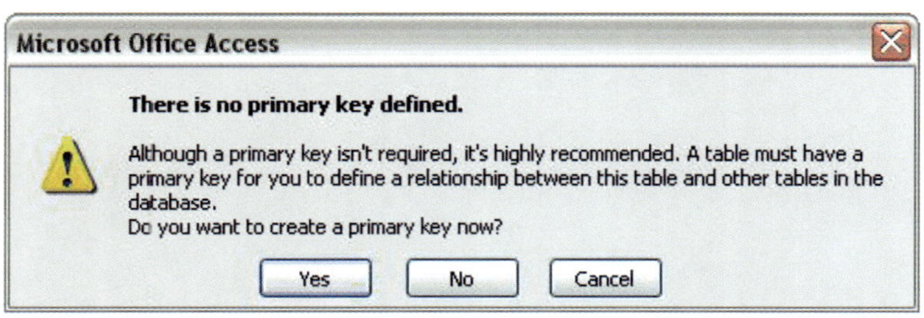


If you do not select a primary key while building your database table structure, the message on the left would appear.

If **Yes** is selected, Access adds an 'AutoNumber' field to your table and sets it as the Primary Key. If **No** is selected, the table is saved without a primary key being defined.

### *Defining a primary key*

1. Open the table in Design view.
2. Select the field you want to define as the primary key.
3. Select the Primary Key icon on the toolbar or choose **Primary Key** from the **Edit** menu.

### *Deselecting a primary key*

1. Open the table in Design view.
2. Select **Primary Key** from the **Edit** menu, or click on the Primary Key icon.

## Exercise 1

### *Multiple choice*

1. The following are all objects in a database except
   (a) Text
   (b) Form
   (c) Report
   (d) Table
2. An organised collection of related records is a:
   (a) Cell
   (b) Table
   (c) Field
   (d) Report
3. All of the following are advantages of a computerised database except:
   (a) Once one file is updated all other files will automatically be updated if they are linked together
   (b) Information can be stored just once and accessed in several different ways
   (c) It requires training to use the system
   (d) It is easy to update or change the record structure
4. All of the following are problems associated with manual databases except:
   (a) Folders are easily misplaced
   (b) Large amounts of storage space are required to store files
   (c) Cross-referencing information from different files is difficult
   (d) Retrieval of simple information is relatively fast and easy
5. An area within a table reserved for a specific piece of data is called a:
   (a) Field
   (b) Record
   (c) Cell
   (d) Query
6. Which of the following can be used as a primary key?
   (a) Make
   (b) Order date
   (c) Serial Number
   (d) Purchase date
7. Which of the following is not a characteristic of a primary key?
   (a) Enables you to establish relationships between tables
   (b) Can have duplicate values
   (c) Is automatically indexed
   (d) Speeds data retrieval
8. A field such as Item Price is considered ________ data type.
   (a) Currency
   (b) Text
   (c) Autonumber
   (d) Number

### *Short answer questions*

1. Define the following terms.
   (a) Table
   (b) Record
   (c) Field
   (d) File
2. Define the term 'database'.
3. What is a relational database?
4. What is a database package?
5. What are the functions of a primary key field?
6. What are field properties?
7. List THREE field properties and explain their purpose.

## Activity 1

Tackle the following practical activities on your computer. There are some suggested solutions to start you off.

1 A wholesaler of appliances would like to change over from a manual method of stock keeping to a computerised method. Create a database called 'Tropical Appliances Wholesalers' to keep track of their stock using the structure below.

| Field Name | Data Type | Description |
|---|---|---|
| Appliance | Text | Type of appliance |
| Manufacturer | Text | The manufacturer of the appliance |
| Model | Text | The model of appliance |
| Serial Number | Number | A 5-digit unique serial number for the appliance |
| Price | Currency | Appliance's selling price |

(a) Set the serial number as the primary key.

(b) Set appropriate field sizes for the text data types.

(c) Save the table as 'Appliance Table'.

### *How it is done*

#### *Create the 'Tropical Appliances Wholesalers' database*

*1* Open the Access program.

*2* Click **Blank Access Database** on the task pane.

*3* Give your database a name by clicking in the 'File Name' box and typing a name.

*4* Specify a location by selecting from the options available in the 'Save in' box.

Then click **Create**, to create and save the database.

*5* Click on **Tables**.

*6* Double-click on **Create table in Design View** or click on **New** and select **Design View**.

*7* Place the cursor in the 'Field Name' column in the first row.

*8* Type "Appliance" into the column.

*9* Move to the 'Data Type' column. The default data type 'Text' will be displayed. To select a different field type, click on the down-arrow in the 'Data Type' box; a drop-down list will appear. Select the appropriate data type.

*10* Click in the 'Description' column and type "Type of Appliance". This describes the data that will be entered in this field.

*11* Move to the second row and enter the field name, data type and description for the second field.

*12* Do the same for the remaining fields.

#### *Setting the primary key*

*1* Click anywhere in the 'Serial No' row.

*2* Click on the Primary Key icon on the toolbar, or select **Primary Key** from the **Edit** menu.

#### *Save the table structure*

*1* Once all the fields are complete, select **Save** or **Save As** from the **File** menu to save the table within the current database.

*2* Type the name "Appliance Table" in the 'Save As' dialogue box and click the **OK** button.

2 Retrieve the 'Tropical Appliances Wholesalers' database you created in the previous exercise.

(a) Change the field sizes for the following fields:

| Field Name | Data Type |
|---|---|
| Appliance | 25 |
| Manufacturer | 30 |
| Model | 15 |
| Serial Number | Long Integer |
| Price | |

(b) Format the Serial Number to accept a 5-digit number.

Include a caption for each field.

| Field Name | Caption |
|---|---|
| Appliance | Appliance Name |
| Manufacturer | Manufacturer Name |
| Model | Model Number |
| Serial Number | SN |
| Price | Item Price |

### *How it is done*

#### *Change the field sizes for the fields*

*1* Display the 'Appliance Table' in Design view.

*2* Click anywhere in the 'Appliance' row. The 'Field Properties' pane will be displayed.

*3* Click on the 'Field Size' box; delete "50" and type "25".

*4* Do the same for the remaining fields.

## Activity 1 continued



*Format the Serial Number to accept a 5-digit number*

*1* Display the 'Appliance Table' in Design view.

*2* Click anywhere in the 'Appliance' row. The 'Field Properties' pane will be displayed.

*3* In the 'Format' box type "00000" where the 0 is a placeholder that displays the digit or 0 if there is nothing.

*Include a caption for each field*

*1* Display the 'Appliance Table' in Design view.

*2* Click anywhere in the 'Appliance' row. The 'Field Properties' pane will be displayed.

*3* In the 'Caption' box type "Appliance Name".

*4* Do the same for the remaining fields.

3 Retrieve the 'Tropical Appliances Wholesalers' database you created in the previous exercise.

(a) Create another table to hold the client information with the structure as shown below.

(b) Set Client ID as the primary key.

(c) Save this table as 'Client Records'

| Field Name | Data Type | Description | Field Size | Caption |
|---|---|---|---|---|
| Client ID | Autonumber | A unique number for the client | | Client Identification Number |
| Client Name | Text | The name of the person who makes the purchase | 30 | Client |
| Business Name | Text | The name of the Client's business | 30 | Company |
| Address | Text | Address of the Client's business | 50 | Company Address |
| Phone | Number | A 7-digit phone number | Long Integer | Telephone Number |
| Date of Last Order | Date/Time | Date of last purchase from Tropical Appliances Wholesalers | | Last Order Date |

4 A company that makes and sells quilts receives orders from various clients. The company wants to enter their orders into a database. Create a database called 'Quilts Incorp' using the structure given.

(a) Set the order number as the primary key.

(b) Format the order number to contain two digits followed by a dash followed by the remaining digits, e.g. 26-3359.

(c) Format the Date/Time field of the Order Date to Medium date.

(d) Format the Date/Time field of the Supply date to yyyy“,” dddd d“,”F mmmm.

(e) Save the table as 'Order Table'.

| Field Name | Data Type | Description | Field Size |
|---|---|---|---|
| Order Number | Number | A unique 6-digit number given to customer for that particular order | Long Integer |
| Order Date | Date/Time | Date the order was placed | |
| Supply Date | Date/Time | Date for the order to be shipped to customer | |
| Customer FName | Text | Customer's first name | 15 |
| Customer LName | Text | Customer's last name | 20 |
| Customer Phone | Number | A 7-digit phone number for customer | Long Integer |
| Delivery Address | Text | The address to which the order is to be delivered | 50 |

## Activity 1 continued

| | | | |
|---|---|---|---|
| Design Type | Text | A 6-character alphanumeric code that indicates the type of quilt design | 6 |
| King | Number | Number of King size quilts ordered | Integer |
| Queen | Number | Number of Queen size quilts ordered | Integer |
| Full | Number | Number of full size quilts ordered | Integer |
| Twin | Number | Number of twin size quilts ordered | Integer |

# Entering records into a table

### Adding records

1 In the database window, click on **Tables** under **Objects** on the left side of the screen (which shows all the tables in the database).

2 Select the table you wish to enter records into.

3 Click **Open** or double-click on the table (*Note*: the Datasheet view table contains the field names at the top of the individual columns.)

4 Type in the data in the respective columns. New records can be added to the table in the Datasheet view in the new record row denoted by the asterisk (*) (Figure 12.5). You can also move to an empty record by clicking on the **New record** button at the bottom of the datasheet window.

*Figure 12.5*
*Adding records*

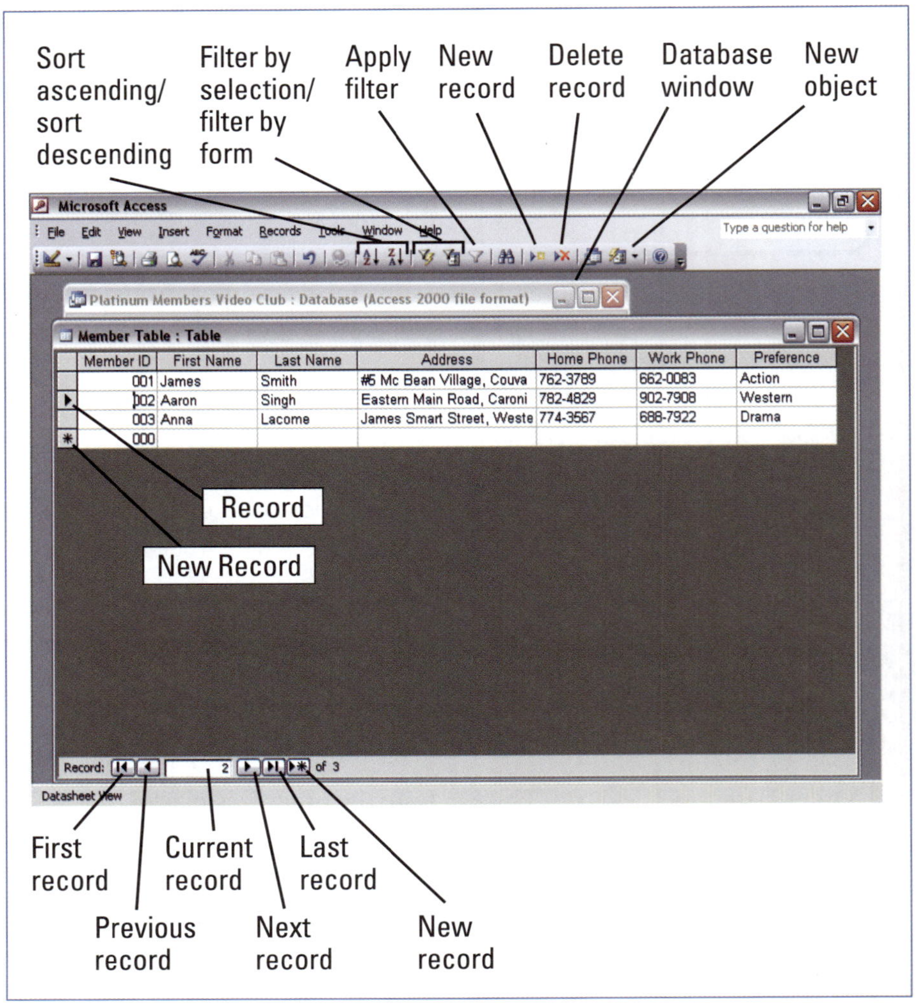


### Deleting a record

1 Open the table in Datasheet view.

2 Select the record to be deleted by placing the cursor in any field of the 'Record' row.

3 Select **Delete** from the **Edit** menu or click on the **Delete Record** icon. You can also press the Delete key on your keyboard. *Note*: A message appears to inform you that a record is about to be deleted.

### Editing a record

1 Open the table in Datasheet view.

2 Select the field of the record to be edited and make the necessary changes.

### Copying data from one field to the next

If the same data has to be repeated in another record you may need to use the Copy feature to copy data from one field to the next.

1 Open the table in Datasheet view.

2 Select the data in the field to be copied.

3 Choose **Copy** from the **Edit** menu or click on the Copy icon.

4 Click where you want the data copied and choose **Paste** from the **Edit** menu or click the Paste icon.

### Copying a table and its data

1 From the database window select the table to be copied.

2 Choose **Copy** from the **Edit** menu or click the Copy icon.

3 Click in the white space of the database window.

4 Choose **Paste** from the **Edit** menu or click the **Paste** icon. A 'Paste Table As' dialogue box appears (Figure 12.6).

5 Select the **Structure and Data** option.

6 Type a name for the table in the 'Table Name' box and click **OK**.

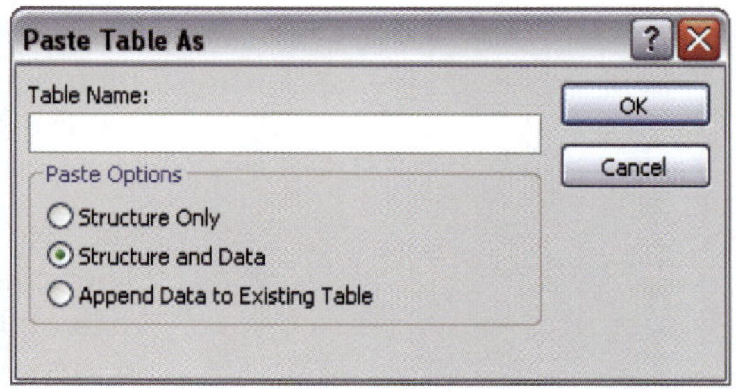


*Figure 12.6 The 'Paste Table As' dialogue box*

### Copying data from one table to another existing table

1 From the database window select the table to be copied.

2 Choose **Copy** from the **Edit** menu or click the Copy icon.

3 Click in the white space of the database window.

4 Choose **Paste** from the **Edit** menu or click the Paste icon. A 'Paste Table As' dialogue box appears.

5 Select the **Append Data to Existing Table** option.

6 Type the name of the existing table that you want to add the data to in the 'Table Name' box and click **OK**.

## Activity 2

1 Retrieve the 'Tropical Appliances Wholesalers' database that you created in Activity 1.

(a) Add a new field in the 'Appliance Table' called Client ID with the following data types and description:

| Field Name | Data Type | Description |
|---|---|---|
| Client ID | Number | The ID number of the client who purchases the appliance |

(b) Add a new field to the Appliance Table with the following attributes:

Field name – Sold

Data Type – Yes/No

2 Retrieve the 'Quilts Incorp' database that you created in Activity 1 and perform the following instructions.

(a) Open the Order Table in design view and change the field name of the Supply Date field to Shipping Date.

(b) Insert a row after the Customer Phone field name.

(c) Add a new field 'Client Address' to the Order Table.

(d) Set the data type, description and the field size for this field as follows:

Data type – Text

Description – The address of the client

Field size – 50

(e) Delete the field 'Delivery Address' as deliveries are no longer made, clients collect their orders.

(f) Save the table.

# Designing a database

In designing a database some important questions must be asked such as:

- What is the purpose of the database?
- What questions do you want the database to answer?
- What reports do you want to produce?
- How do you want the database sorted?

## Example: a video club database

Platinum Members Video Club, owned and operated by Kaycee Kylock, has been in business for two years. Due to increased membership Kaycee has decided to computerise her records to make the business more efficient. Membership is free and at present Kaycee has 500 members. She maintains an inventory of 5500 VCR movies and 2500 DVDs.

Kaycee has assigned each member a unique 3-digit member ID, and has an index card for each member. The card contains information such as member's ID, name, address and phone numbers for home and work. Kaycee keeps a note of what type of movies the member prefers under the category 'preference'.

She also keeps a set of index cards of her VCR and DVD movie inventory. The index cards contain a host of information: the movie ID (a unique 5-digit alphanumeric), whether it is a VCR or DVD, the movie title, the lead actors/actresses, the category (Family, SciFi, Adventure, Drama, Western, etc.), the rating (G, PG, PG13, R), its condition (good, average, need to replace), date rented, duration rented.

*Figure 12.7*
*Record tables*

Fields | Data

| Member record | |
|---|---|
| Member ID: | **123** |
| First Name: | **Mark** |
| Last Name: | **Smith** |
| Address: | **23 Adventist Street, Arima** |
| Home Phone: | **646-5689** |
| Work Phone: | **662-3542** |
| Preference: | **Westerns** |

| Movie record | |
|---|---|
| Movie ID: | **W0231** |
| Type: | **VCR** |
| Movie Title: | **Unforgiven** |
| Lead Actors: | **Clint Eastwood** |
| Category: | **Western** |
| Rating: | **PG 13** |
| Condition: | **Good** |
| Date Rented: | **05/03/05** |
| Duration: | **1 week** |

Customers are allowed to rent up to five movies at a time. Movies can be rented for one day ($2.00), two days ($3.00) or a week ($6.00). A $1.00 late fee is charged if movies are not returned on time.

When a movie is rented the movie card is placed together with the member card. When the movie is returned the date on the movie card is checked and a late fee is calculated if the movie was returned late.

In this case the owner of the video club may want data on any number of things, such as:

- How many of her movies are out on loan
- Which members have overdue movies or movies that are more than a certain number of days late
- How many movies the club has in each category.

In this section we will be creating a database that can answer these kinds of questions.

## Grouping related data and identifying fields

In creating the database Kaycee needs to group all related data to form separate records, much like the card index files she currently uses. The most important factors in her database are the video club members, and then the movies they rent. It is therefore logical that the member information is grouped together and the movie information is grouped together. After grouping the data into these two different tables, individual fields need to be identified. Then, she will want to find a way of linking the two tables, so that she knows, for example, which member is renting which movie.

Within the Member table and the Movie table, the entries may be as in Figure 12.7.

## Understanding relationships between groups of data

To retrieve data from both tables there must be a relationship between them. The two tables must be linked by a field common to both tables. In this case the member ID can be placed in the movie table in order to pull up what movies that particular member has borrowed. The table entries may look like this:

| Movie ID | Movie Title | Category | Member ID |
|---|---|---|---|
| W0231 | Unforgiven | Western | 123 |
| T0287 | SAW | Thriller | 123 |
| D0026 | The Graduate | Drama | 123 |

There are three types of relationships:

- **One-to-many relationship:** One record or entity in a table or file is linked to many records/entities in another table/file. For example, one member can borrow many movies (Figure 12.8).

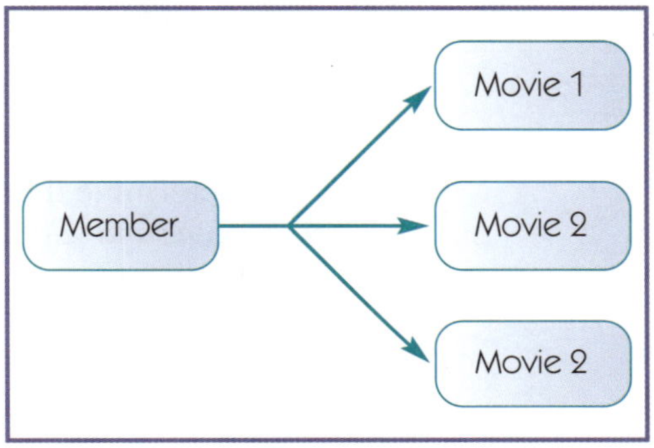


*Figure 12.8*
*A one-to-many relationship*

- **Many-to-many relationship**: Many records/entities in the primary file/table are linked to many records/entities in another file/table through a common entity. For example, a movie can have many actors and an actor can act in many movies (Figure 12.9).

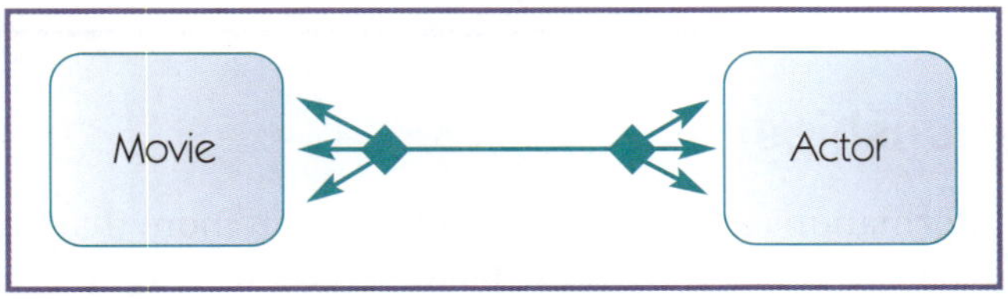


*Figure 12.9*
*A many-to-many relationship*

Imagine that Kaycee expands her database later so that members can ask about all the films the club owns in which a certain actor or actress has appeared. In this case, the database would now also contain many-to-many relationships.

- **One-to-one relationship**: This is where one record or entity in a primary table or file is linked to exactly one record/entity in another file/table (Figure 12.10).
  For example, a movie cannot be loaned to more than one person at the same time, so movie-to-person is a one-to-one relationship.

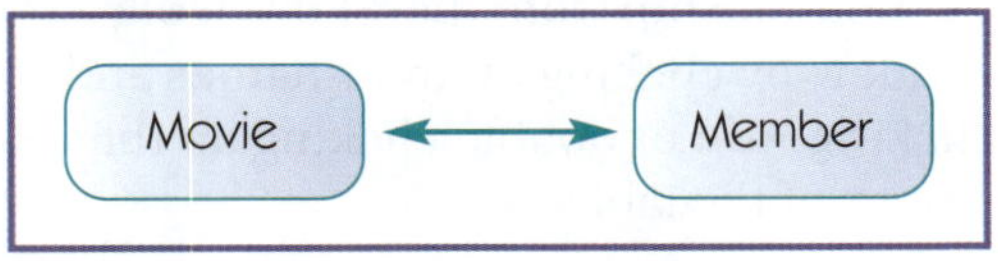


*Figure 12.10*
*A one-to-one relationship*

The steps required to design a database can be summarised in Table 8.

*Table 8*
*Steps required to design a database*

| Step | Purpose |
|---|---|
| 1 | Determine the goal of the database. This will help you determine the needs for your database.<br>Example: Your goal is to keep track of the books rented from your library. What do you need to know to accomplish this? |
| 2 | Analyse your goal to determine your needs, and wants, exactly. Make a list of statements to further define the problem.<br>Example:<br>I need to know who borrowed a particular book.<br>I want to know what is the most borrowed book.<br>I want to know how many copies of a particular book we have. |
| 3 | Determine the data items you need to store to meet your needs and wants. Make a list of relevant data items that will assist in reaching your goal. |
| 4 | Design your tables. Group related data items (books, library members). This will allow you to define your tables/files. |
| 5 | Determine the field names and data types. Decide on a *field name and data type* for each data item and how the item is to be stored.<br>Example: Storing the name of a person, the two field names 'First Name' and 'Last Name' will have a data type of 'Text'. |
| 6 | Determine how the tables will be related.<br>Create a relationship between the two tables that will allow them to link so that information can be cross-referenced. The two tables must therefore have a field in common. |

## Creating relationships

The duplication of information caused by repeating fields in more than one table can be prevented by linking fields in the tables to establish a relationship.

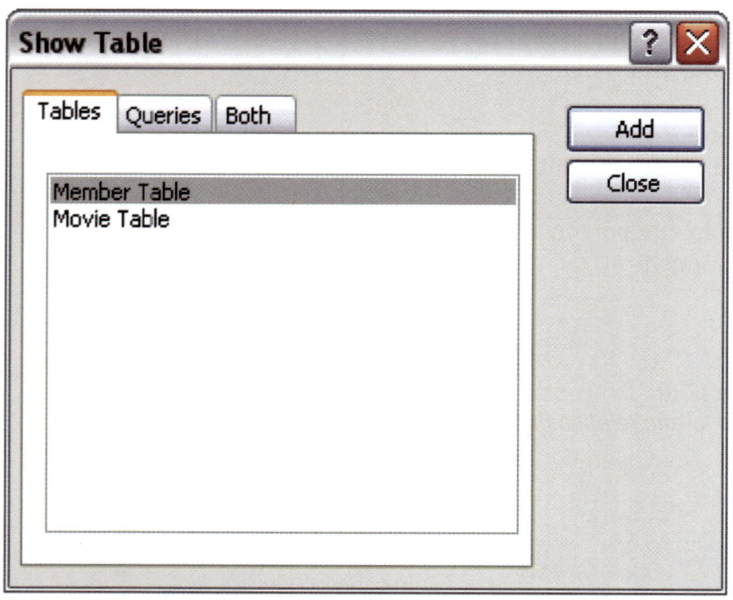


### *To link two tables*

1. Click the **Relationships** button on the toolbar. The 'Show Table' window will appear (Figure 12.11).
2. If the 'Show Table' window does not appear, click the **Show Table** icon on the toolbar.
3. Select the tables you would like to include in the relationship from the 'Show Table' window by clicking on their names and clicking **Add** or double-clicking on the names of the tables.
4. Click **Close** after you have finished adding all the tables.

*Figure 12.11*
*'Show Table' window*

5 To link fields from two different tables, click and drag the field from one table to the corresponding field in the other table and release the mouse button. The 'Edit Relationships' window appears.

6 This window allows you to select different fields to link if necessary. You can also select the option to **Enforce Referential Integrity**. Enforcing referential integrity ensures that a value entered in one field of a linked table (related table) matches an existing value in the related field of the primary table.

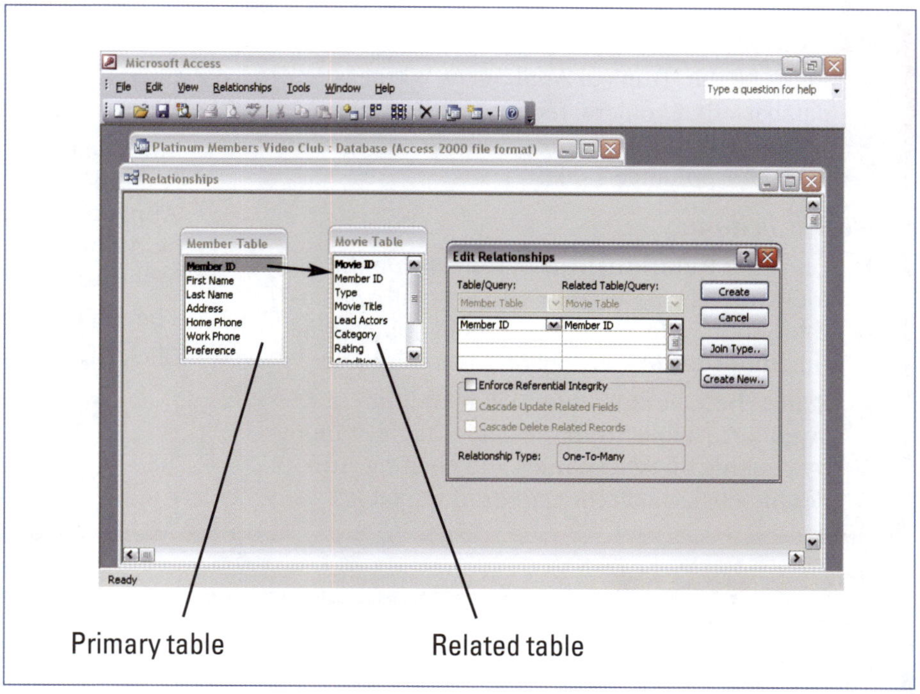


*Figure 12.12*
*'Relationships' window*

7 If the **Cascade Update Related Fields** box is checked, changing a primary key value in the primary table automatically updates the matching value in all related records.

8 If the **Cascade Delete Related Records** box is checked, deleting a record in the primary table deletes any related records in the related table.

9 Click **Create** to create the link. A line connecting the two fields in the relationship window appears:

- A one-to-one relationship is represented by a straight line.
- A one-to-many relationship is represented by 1 and the infinity (∞) symbol on a line (Figure 12.13). The symbol indicates which table has what relationship to the other.

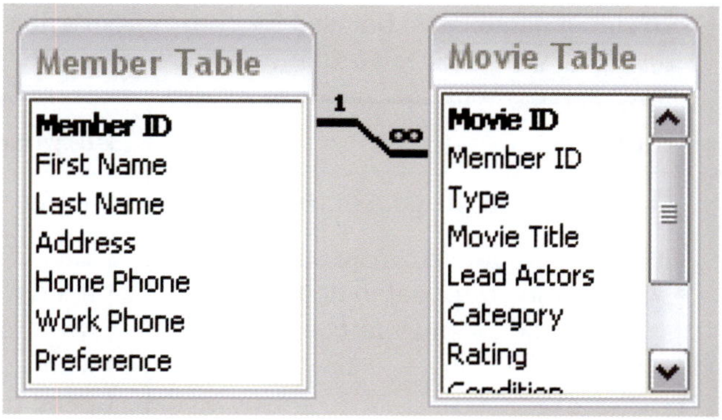


*Figure 12.13*
*One-to-many relationship between tables*

10 Expand and collapse indicators appear in the datasheet of a relational table, allowing you to view the sub-datasheets matching the information from the other table (Figure 12.14).

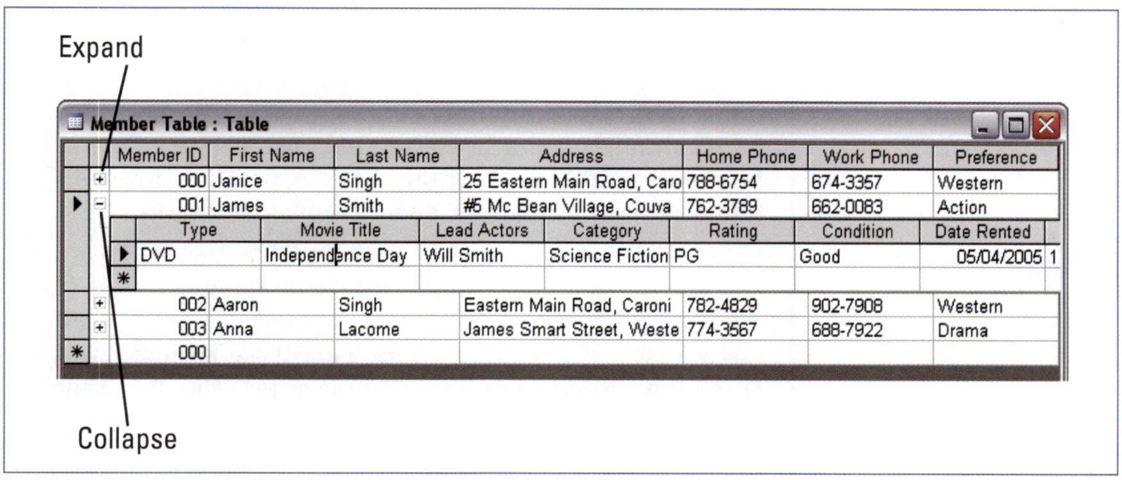


*Figure 12.14*
*Table showing expand and collapse buttons*

## Activity 3

1 Retrieve the 'Tropical Appliances Wholesalers' database that you created in Activity 1. Set a relationship between the 'Client Records' table and the Appliance Table.

### *How it is done*

1 Click the **Relationships** button on the toolbar. The 'Show Table' window will appear. If the 'Show Table' window does not appear click the **Show Table** icon on the toolbar.

2 Select the 'Client Records' table and the 'Appliance Table' from the 'Show Table' window by clicking on their names and clicking **Add**, or double-clicking on the names of the tables.

3 Click **Close** after you have finished adding all the tables.

4 Link the Client ID field from the 'Client Records' table to the Client ID from the 'Appliance Table' by clicking and dragging the field from one table to the corresponding field in the other table and release the mouse button.

5 The 'Edit Relationships' window will appear.

6 Click **Create** to link the two tables.

## Exercise 2

### *Planning databases*

This is an exercise in designing databases, by determining the fields needed, grouping the related fields and deciding on the relationships:

### Example

Design a database to be used by your school's librarian to keep track of the library's collection and members/borrowers.

| **Step** | **Purpose** |
|---|---|
| **1** Determine the goal of the database | Your goal is to keep track of the books rented from your library. |
| **2** Analyse your goal to determine your needs, and wants,exactly. | I need to know who borrowed a particular book.<br>I want to know what is the most borrowed book.<br>I want to know how many copies of a particular book we have.<br>I need to know what books are overdue.<br>I need to know how many days overdue is a particular book.<br>I need to know when a particular book is due to be returned |
| **3** Determine the data items you need to store to meet your needs and wants. | Book number, Title, Author, ISBN number, Date Due, Date Borrowed, Number Borrower's Name, Borrower's Address, Phone Number Borrower's Class, Subject (e.g. Science), Category (e.g. Fiction, Non Fiction), Borrower's ID |
| **4** Design your tables | Group related data items (books, library members).<br>**Book Table will contain** Book Number, Title, Author, ISBN number, Subject, Category, Date Due, Date Borrowed<br>**Borrower's Table will contain** Borrower's ID, Borrower's Name, Borrower's Address, Phone Number, Borrower's Class. |
| **5** Determine the field names how and data types. | Decide on a *field name and data type* for each data item and the item is to be stored. **Book Table** Book Number – Text, Title – Text, Author – Text, ISBN number – Number, Subject – Text, Category – Text, Date Due – Date/Time, Date Borrowed – Date/Time. **Borrower's Table** Borrower ID – Number, Name - Text, Address – Text, Phone – Number, Class – Text. |
| **6** Determine how the tables will be related. | **Borrower ID** can link the two tables, therefore it must be included in the Book Table to be able to determine who borrowed a particular book. |

## Exercise 2 continued

1 Design a database to keep track of Dwayne Haze's music collection. As he frequently loans his friends his CDs he also needs to keep track of who has what CD.

2 A caterer has decided to computerise her business; she needs to keep track of her orders and the clients she services. Design a database to accomplish this.

3 Tiffs Flight Attendant Services owns a number of vehicles that are used to chauffeur its employees to and from work. Two flight attendants can share a vehicle, depending on the flight they are scheduled to work on and the area in which they live. Design a database that would keep track of the flight attendants, the vehicle pickups and the flight attendants' work schedule.

> ***Hint:***
> *You may require three tables, one for the flight attendants information, one for the work schedule and one for the vehicles.*

4 An independent dealer of used cars, Joshua Bane, owns a used car business in a small town. Joshua imports vehicles from Japan and sells them to customers. Joshua has six sales persons working for him to whom he gives a commission based on the number of sales generated by the individual per month. He want to keep track of his stock and his sales, as well as the employee who sold the vehicle. Design a database to help Joshua accomplish this.

> ***Hint:***
> *You can use two or more tables, depending on whether you want to keep track of who bought the vehicles.*

5 A Job Placement Company is looking to computerise their manual database. Clients usually approach the company for help in finding jobs, for which a small fee is charged. Information such as skill, personal information, available work hours, references and other relevant information on each client is kept. The organisation receives a list of available job openings from various firms, which they keep on file. These files are updated regularly as the post may become filled by means other than the Job Placement Company. A listing of clients and their skills is matched to the available jobs. Once the client is accepted for a job, an additional sum is paid to the organisation. You are required to design a database for the Job Placement Company.

### *Crossword*

**Across**

1 The type of value/data that would be entered into a field (2 words) (8)

3 A name given to a field (2 words) (9)

5 A type of relationship which selects a number of records from one table that is related to a record in another table (3 words) (9)

6 Sets the number of characters needed by a field (2 words) (9)

**Down**

2 A field that uniquely identifies a record (2 words) (10)

4 Allows faster sorts and searches on a database (7)

### *Short answer questions*

1 Explain the purpose of field validation rules.

2 Explain, giving examples, how input masks are used to format data.

3 List THREE characteristics of primary keys.

4 Give TWO examples of how text and memos can be formatted.

5 What is the difference between the integer field size and the long integer field size?

6 List FIVE field attributes or field properties and explain their purpose.

# Indexing and sorting data

## Sorting a table

If you close and reopen a datasheet, the records will appear to be sorted in ascending order according to the values in the 'Primary Key' field.

If a primary key was not selected the records would be displayed in the order that they were entered.

If you want to find out more about this topic you could look up the related animations and activities on your companion CD-ROM.

### Sorting data on a single field

1. Click in the desired field (in any record or on the Field Name at the top).
2. Select **Sort** from the **Records** menu and choose **Sort Ascending (AZ)** or **Sort Descending (ZA)** from the submenu that appears, or click the Sort Ascending (AZ) or Sort Descending (ZA) icons.

### Sorting on multiple fields

It may become necessary to sort the data in the table on more than one field; for example, sorting on surname and then on first name or sorting by form and then by the student's surname in that form. You can use **Advanced Filter Sort** to accomplish this.

1. Select **Filter** from the **Records** menu (a submenu appears).
2. Select **Advanced Filter/Sort**. The filter window opens, the top part of this window contains the table to be sorted, the bottom part contains a grid to select the fields you would like to sort (Figure 12.15).
3. Click in the first box in the 'Field' row and select the field you would like to sort on from the drop-down menu.
4. Click in the 'Sort' row and select the order of the sort, whether Ascending or Descending.
5. Similarly, select the other fields to sort.
6. Choose **Apply Filter/Sort** from the **Filter** menu or click the Apply Filter icon on the toolbar.

*Figure 12.15*
*Table filter window*

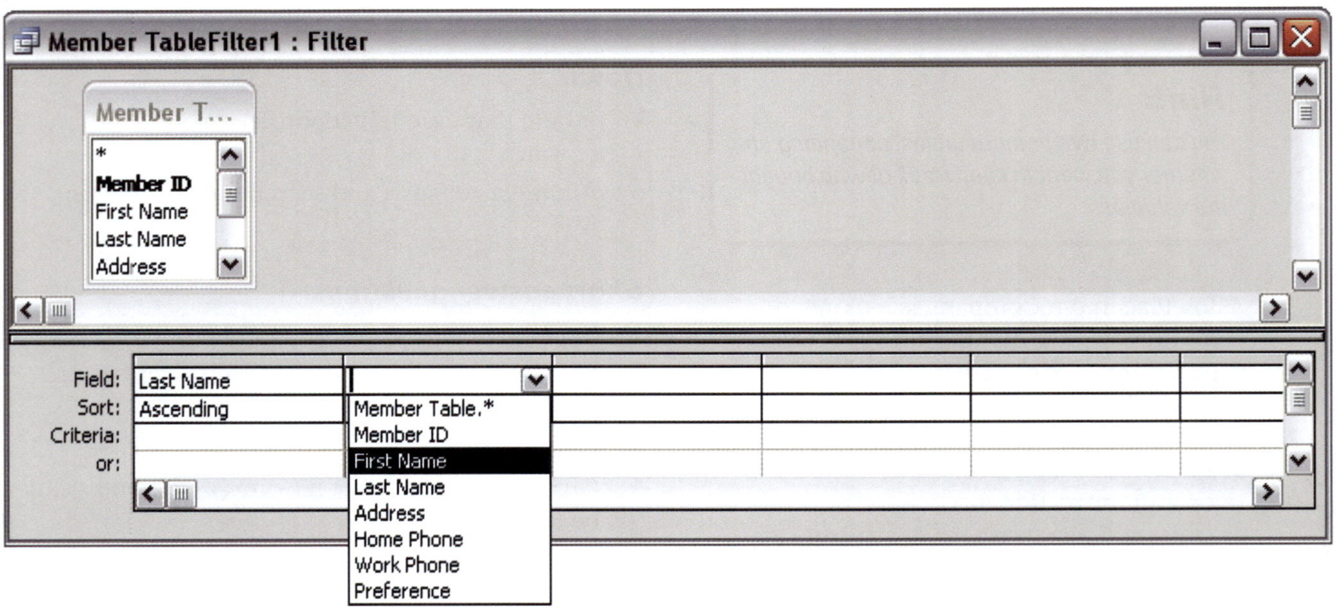

## Indexing

Records can be found and sorted faster using an index. Similar to the index in a book, Access uses indexes to find data by looking up the location of the data in the index.

An index can be created on a single field or on multiple fields. It is a table that has two columns:

- one stores a sorted list of values of the field or fields being indexed
- the other stores pointers to the data values that are stored in specific columns of the table. These pointers provide the location of each record in the table.

You should consider indexing fields that are searched and sorted frequently. The primary key field is automatically indexed. A multiple field index can be created if you search or sort on two or more fields at a time, for example if you sort on both Last Name and First Name fields.

### *Creating an index*

1. Open the database in Design view.
2. Select the field on which you want to set an index.
3. Choose **Indexes** from the **View** menu or click on the **Indexes** icon .
4. You can also click on the **Indexed** box in the 'Field properties' for that specific field.
5. Choose the one of the following options:
   - **Yes (Duplicates OK)** – this creates an index on a selected field
   - **Yes (No Duplicates)** – creates a unique index for the selected field and prevents you from entering duplicate values in the field.
6. Save the changes to the table.

### *Creating a named index*

1. Open the database in Design view.
2. Select the field on which you want to set an index.
3. Choose **Indexes** from the **View** menu or click on the Indexes icon on the toolbar (Figure 12.16).
4. Type the name of the index in the 'Index Name' column.
5. Select the field on which you want to place the index from the drop-down menu in the 'Field Name' column.
6. Select the order of sort from the 'Sort Order' column.
7. Close the 'Indexes' dialogue box.
8. Save the changes to the table design.

### *Deleting an index*

1. Open the table in Design view.
2. Choose **Indexes** from the **View** menu or click on the **Indexes** icon on the toolbar.
3. Select the row selector for the index you want to delete.
4. Click the **Delete Row** icon on the toolbar or press the Delete key on the keyboard.
5. Save the table.

*Figure 12.16*
*Index window*

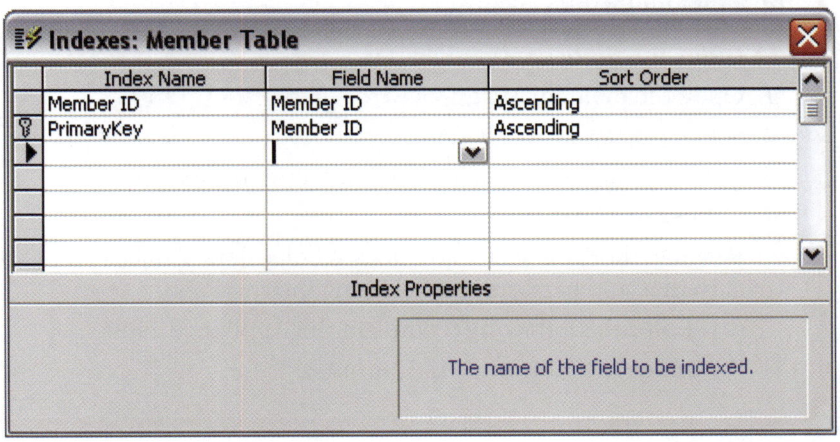

## Activity 4

**1** Retrieve the 'Platinum Member Video Club' database from your companion CD.

(a) Add the following data to the 'New Members' table.

(b) Index the table on Member ID.

| New Members | | | | | | | |
|---|---|---|---|---|---|---|---|
| **Member ID** | **First Name** | **Last Name** | **Address** | **City** | **Home Phone** | **Work Phone** | **Preference** |
| 007 | Jason | Kanhai | Peter Trace, Palmiste Village | Chagg Town | 687-9046 | 567-4884 | Horror |
| 008 | Michelle | Lee | #4 Erin Road | Arima | 644-6822 | 663-0987 | Documentary |
| 009 | Devon | Amoraso | 11 Mc Bean Main Road | Couva | 772-0011 | 624-9908 | Classics |
| 010 | Ethan | Nagra | Beckham Road, Smart Village | St. Helena | 764-9034 | 622-0090 | Science Fiction |
| 011 | Jack | Grant | #56 Extention Road, Gulf View | Gulf City | 722-8484 | | Comedy |

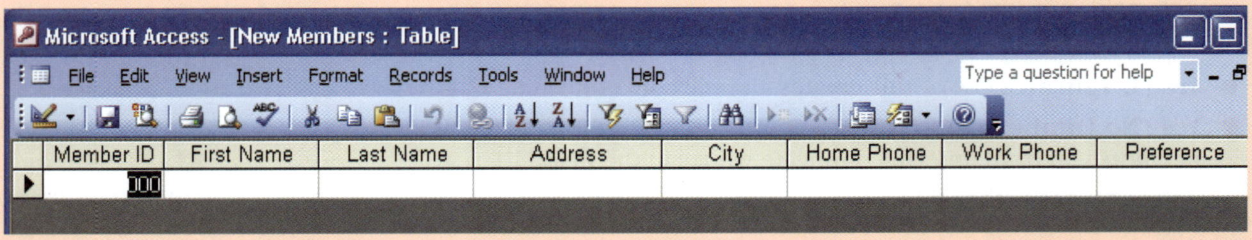


*Figure 12.17*
*New Members table headings*

### *How it is done*

#### *(a) Enter the records*

*1* Open the Platinum Member Video Club database window.
*2* Select the 'New Members' table.
*3* Click **Open**.
*4* The 'Datasheet View' window appears with the field names as shown in Figure 12.17.
*5* Type "007" under Member ID.
*6* Press the Tab key to move to the next column.
*7* Type the name "Jason" in the 'First Name' column.
*8* Continue to enter the data for the first record in the appropriate columns.
*9* Press **Enter** or use the mouse to move to the next row.
*10* Enter all records one by one.

#### *(b) Index the table on Member ID*

*1* Open the table in Design view.
*2* Select the 'Member ID' field.
*3* In the 'Field Properties' pane click on the **Indexed** box.
*4* Choose **Yes (No Duplicates)**.

**2** Retrieve the 'Tropical Appliances Wholesalers' database that you created in the earlier activities and perform the following instructions.

(a) Enter the following records in the Appliance Table.

(b) Index the table on Serial Number.

## Activity 4 continued



| Appliance | Manufacturer | Model | Serial Number | Price | Client ID | Sold |
|---|---|---|---|---|---|---|
| Refrigerator | G.E. | R424 | 82736 | $3500 | 8 | Yes |
| Stove | Consol | S789 | 45622 | $1999 | | No |
| Microwave | Sharp | M008 | 12312 | $999 | 6 | Yes |
| Refrigerator | Samsung | R324 | 22245 | $10500 | 6 | Yes |
| Washing Machine | Samsung | W212 | 56324 | $3000 | | No |
| Washing Machine | Consol | W786 | 33233 | $1495 | | No |
| Stove | Atlas | S001 | 09876 | $850 | | No |
| Convection Oven | Mabe | O332 | 32109 | $350 | 5 | Yes |

(c) Open the table in Design view and add a new field name called 'Description' whose attributes are text and field size 50.

(d) Format this new field to display "Description not available" if no data is entered.

(e) Enter the following records in the 'Client Record' table.

| Client ID | Client Name | Business Name | Address | Phone | Date of Last Order |
|---|---|---|---|---|---|
| 1 | John, Mark | S and M Appliances | James Smart Village, Tobago | 663-9862 | 10/2/03 |
| 2 | Ali, Devon | Ali's Furniture Store | Oren Road, Christ Church, Barbados | 465-3820 | 20/12/04 |
| 3 | Mohammed, Amy | Couva District Appliance Centre | Eastern Main Road, Couva | 661-0048 | 2/1/05 |
| 4 | Alexander, Ramond | Home Needs Wares | Maggie Road, Valley View, St. Lucia | 398-0874 | 30/3/05 |
| 5 | Blake, Karen | Blake Appliance Store | #44 Eastern Main Road, Sangre Grande, Trinidad | 668-0025 | 7/8/04 |
| 6 | Alexander, Leslie | LesAlex Home Centre | Baxter Street, Grand Cayman Island, Grand Cayman | 849-1829 | 3/11/04 |
| 7 | Singh, Ryan | Drive Through Buyers | 34 Fredrick Street, Port of Spain, Trinidad | 622-1904 | 28/1/05 |
| 8 | Singh, Rhyan | Market Centre | Mango Street, Caynan Bonacord, Tobago | 639-6620 | 28/11/04 |
| 9 | Gomez, Evon | Center City Appliance Centre | #67 Navet Road, St. Michael, Barbados | 490-8383 | 5/1/05 |

(f) Sort the Appliance Table according to Price in descending order.

(g) Index the Appliance Table on Manufacturer followed by Appliance in ascending order.

(h) Index the 'Client Records' table on Client Name in ascending order.

## Activity 4 continued

3 Retrieve the 'Quilts Incorp' database that you created in the earlier activities and perform the following instructions.

(a) Enter the following records in the 'Order' table.

| Order Number | Order Date | Shipping Date | Customer FName | Customer LName | Customer Phone | Address | Design Type | King | Queen | Full | Twin |
|---|---|---|---|---|---|---|---|---|---|---|---|
| 100111 | 1/3/05 | 8/3/05 | Liz | Massey | 664-0938 | Orange Grove, Belair, Trincity | MP3905 | 4 | 6 | 2 | 5 |
| 100112 | 1/3/05 | 15/3/05 | Mary-Ann | Mohammed | 668-5733 | Breadfruit Lane, Santa Rosa | SUN289 | 1 | 8 | 1 | 1 |
| 100113 | 12/3/05 | 24/3/05 | Jacque | Simmons | 668-8390 | Sangre Chiquito, Sangre Grande | MP3887 | 2 | 2 | 12 | 2 |
| 100114 | 13/3/05 | 14/3/05 | David | Carter | 691-yate | #43 Devon Lane, Mount Dor, Mount Hope | GR0290 | 3 | 1 | 7 | 0 |
| 100115 | 17/3/05 | 7/4/05 | Ann-Marie | Waldross | 660-3322 | Eastern Main Road, Princes Town | FR0090 | 5 | 7 | 8 | 8 |
| 100116 | 2/3/05 | 12/3/05 | Jennifer | Ramdass | 622-7809 | #11 St. Vincent Street, Port of Spain | SE5643 | 1 | 6 | 224 | 2 |
| 100117 | 31/3/05 | 31/4/05 | Lee | Chan | 621-4682 | Amber Road, Valley View | SE5643 | 0 | 45 | 75 | 9 |
| 100118 | 1/4/05 | 3/4/05 | Radha | Singh | 720-5920 | Peninton Ave. Guaico | FR0090 | 0 | 2 | 50 | 1 |
| 100119 | 3/4/05 | 3/4/05 | Romaine | Singh | 698-2201 | Hights of Aripo Road, Wallafield | SE5643 | 2 | 5 | 25 | 25 |
| 100120 | 6/4/05 | 16/4/05 | Darlia | Smith | 758-2201 | Common Main Road, Grand Rivera | DRY278 | 5 | 5 | 5 | 5 |
| 100121 | 8/3/05 | 20/3/05 | Brian | Mohammed | 654-2340 | LP79 Toco Main Road, Toco | SUN289 | 11 | 12 | 0 | 0 |

(b) Create a table in the 'Quilts Incorp' database called 'Prospective Customers' with the following structure.

| Field Name | Data Type | Description | Field Size |
|---|---|---|---|
| Customer FName | Text | Customer's first name | 15 |
| Customer LName | Text | Customer's last name | 20 |
| Customer Phone | Text | Telephone contact for customer | 8 |
| Address | Text | Customer's Address | 50 |

(c) Enter the following data into the 'Prospective Customers' table of the 'Quilts Incorp' database.

| Customer Lname | Customer FName | Address | Customer Phone |
|---|---|---|---|
| John | Mark | James Smart Village, Sangre Chiquito | 663-9862 |
| Ali | Devon | Oren Road, Best Village, Point-a-Pierre | 665-3820 |
| Jessie | James | Novel Street, Little Dove Company, Diamond Vale | 897-6654 |

## Queries

A **query** selects records from one or more tables, based on specific criteria. This resulting set of records can be viewed and analysed and sorted. The resulting collection of records is called a **dynaset** (dynamic subset). As the original tables are updated the dynaset is also updated when the query is run again.

There are several types of queries:

- **Select query** – which extracts data from tables based on a criterion or specified value.
- **Action queries**:
  - **Update query** – which makes changes to a group of records, or all records in one or more tables.
  - **Append query** – adds a group of records from one or more tables to the end of one or more other tables. The tables do not need to have the same number of fields for the tables to be merged. For example, if Table1 has seven fields and Table2 has four that are similar to those in Table1, and you want to append Table2 to Table1, the records will merge minus the three additional extra fields from Table1.
  - **Delete query** – deletes a group of records from one or more tables.
  - **Make table query** – creates a new table from all or some of the fields of data in one or more tables. These queries are useful for creating tables to export to other databases or to other documents.
- **Crosstab query** – calculates and restructures data to make it easier to analyse.

### Select Queries

#### *Creating a query in Design view*

1. Click on **Queries** under **Objects** on the left side of the screen.
2. Double-click **Create query in Design view** or click on the **New** button (the 'New Query' dialogue box appears, Figure 12.18) and select **Design View** then click **OK**.
3. Select tables and existing queries from the 'Show Table' dialogue box (Figure 12.19).

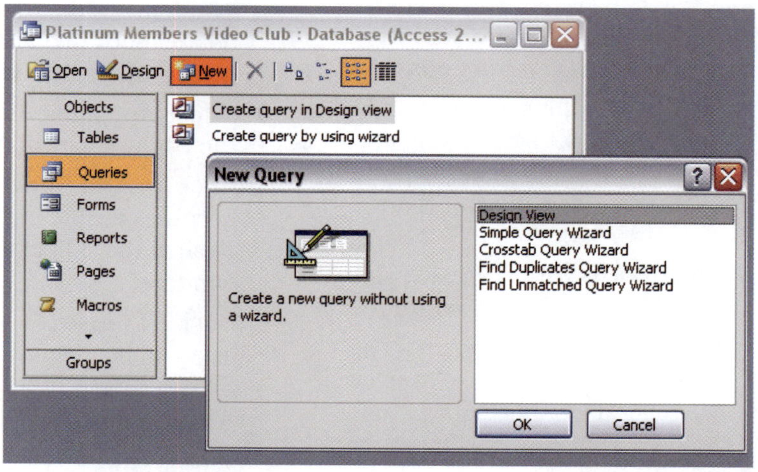


*Figure 12.18*
*The 'New Query' dialogue box*

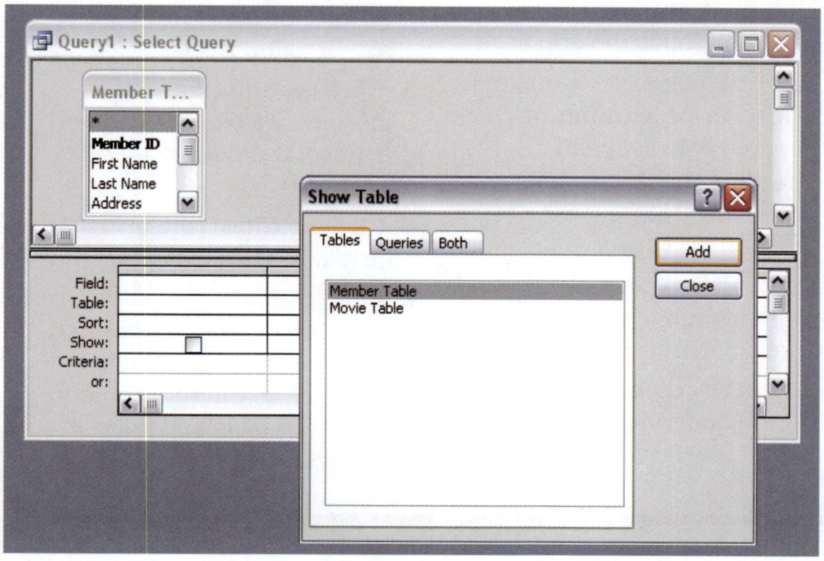


*Figure 12.19*
*The 'Show Table' dialogue box*

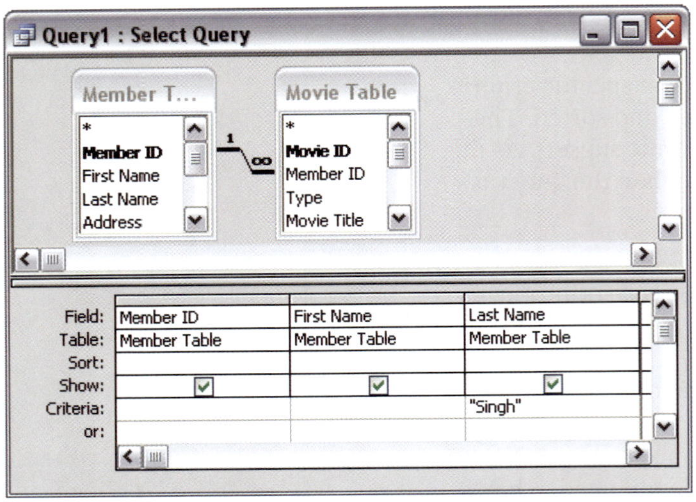


*Figure 12.20*
*Adding fields to the query grid*

4 Click **Tables** and **Queries** and click the **Add** button to add tables or existing queries to the new query. Click **Close**.

5 Add fields for the tables to the query grid by double-clicking on the field name in the table boxes, or select the field from the 'Field row' drop-down menus (Figure 12.20).

6 Specify the sort order if necessary.

7 Enter the criteria for the query in the 'Criteria' row of the specified field. A criterion can contain values or expressions. Expressions can be equated to formulae much like those found in Excel. The Expression Builder can be used to write a formula/expression (see pages 260–261).

8 After selecting all the fields and entering the criteria click the **Run** icon [ ! ] on the toolbar.

9 Save the query by clicking the **Save** button.

## Activity 5

1 Retrieve the 'Tropical Appliances Wholesalers' database that you created earlier and perform the following instructions.

(a) Create a query to show all the serial numbers of the appliances where the price is greater than $3000.

(b) Create a query to select all clients who ordered refrigerators.

(c) Create a query to select all clients whose last purchase was more than a year ago.

(d) Create a query to select all the appliances that have been sold and the names of the clients to whom they were sold.

### *How it is done*

#### *(a) Show all the serial numbers of the appliances where the price is greater than $3000*

*1* Click on **Queries** in the 'Tropical Appliances Wholesalers' database window.

*2* Click on **New**.

*3* Select **Design View** from the 'New Query' dialogue box or double-click on **Create a new query in Design view**.

*4* Select 'Appliance Table' from the 'Show Table' dialogue box.

*5* Click on **Add** (the table becomes visible in the upper pane of the 'Select Query' window).

*6* Click on **Close** (the query grid will be displayed).

*7* Click on the arrow in the first column of the 'Field' row and select **Appliance**, or double-click on **Appliance** in the table box above the grid.

*8* Move to the next column and select **Serial Number** or double-click on **Serial Number** in the table box above the grid.

*9* Move to the next column and select **Price** or double-click on **Price** in the table box above the grid.

*10* Enter the criterion " >3000" for the query in the 'Criteria' row of the 'Price' field.

*11* Click the **Run** icon on the toolbar.

*12* Save the query by clicking the **Save** button.

#### *(b) Create a query to select all clients who ordered refrigerators*

*1* Click on the **Queries** in the 'Tropical Appliances Wholesalers' database window.

*2* Click on **New**.

*3* Select **Design View** from the 'New Query' dialogue box or double-click on **Create a new query in Design view**.

*4* Select **Appliance Table** and **Client Records** from the 'Show Table' dialogue box.

*5* Click on **Add** (the tables become visible in the upper pane of the 'Select Query' window).

*6* Click on **Close** (the query grid will be displayed).

*7* Link the two tables if they are not already linked, click and drag the Client ID from one table to the Client ID field in the other table and release the mouse button. A line

## Activity 5 continued

connecting the two fields is displayed (Figure 12.21).

*8* Fill out the query grid.

*9* Enter the criterion "Refrigerator" for the query in the 'Criteria' row of the 'Appliance' field.

*10* Click the Run icon on the toolbar.

**2** Retrieve the 'Quilts Incorp' database that you created earlier and perform the following instructions.

(a) Create a query to select all customers who placed an order for quilts on 16/04/05.

(b) Create a query to select all customers who ordered more than five king size quilts.

(c) Create a query to select the design type of all full size quilts.

(d) Create a query to select all orders that are to be supplied between 1/5/05 and 15/5/05.

*Figure 12.21*
*Linked tables and query*

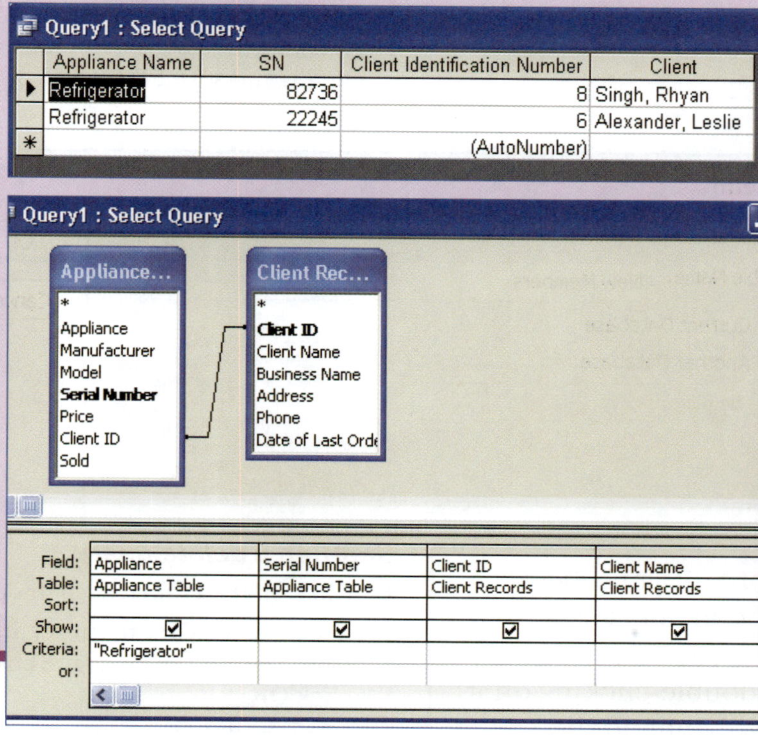


## Action Queries

### *Creating an update query*

1. Click on the **Queries** tab under **Objects** on the left side of the screen.
2. Double-click **Create query in Design view** or click on the **New** button (the 'New Query' dialogue box appears) and select **Design View** then click **OK**.
3. Click the **Tables** and **Queries** tabs and click the **Add** button to add tables or existing queries to the new query. Click **Close**.
4. Select **Update Query** from the **Query** drop-down menu on the toolbar (Figure 12.22).
5. Select the field to update by double-clicking on the field.
6. In the 'Update To' row enter the data you want to update the field to. The Expression Builder (see pages 260–261) can also be used to enter a formula or expression in the 'Update To' row.

*Figure 12.22*
*Query drop-down menu*

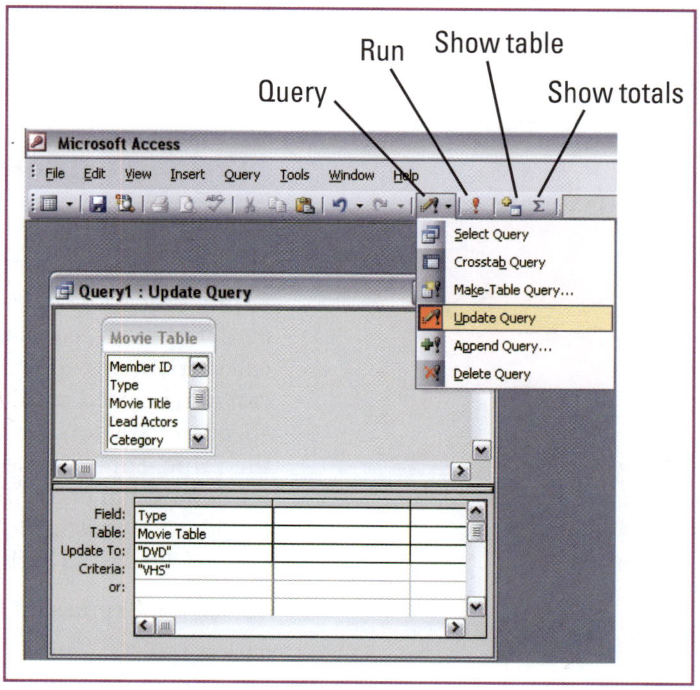


> *Note:* If you save an update query, every time you run the query by double-clicking on it, it will update the records to the table.

### Creating an append query

1. Click on the **Queries** tab under **Objects** on the left side of the screen.
2. Double-click **Create query in Design view** or click on the **New** button (the 'New Query' dialogue box appears) and select **Design View** then click **OK**.
3. Click the **Tables** and **Queries** tabs and click the **Add** button to add the table you want to append. Click **Close**.
4. Select **Append Query** from the **Query** drop-down menu on the toolbar.
5. Click the down-arrow in the 'Append' dialogue box that appears (Figure 12.23) and select the name of the table to which you want to add the records.
6. Add fields to the query grid that would be added to the appended table.
7. Click the **Run** icon on the toolbar or select **Run** from the **Query** menu.

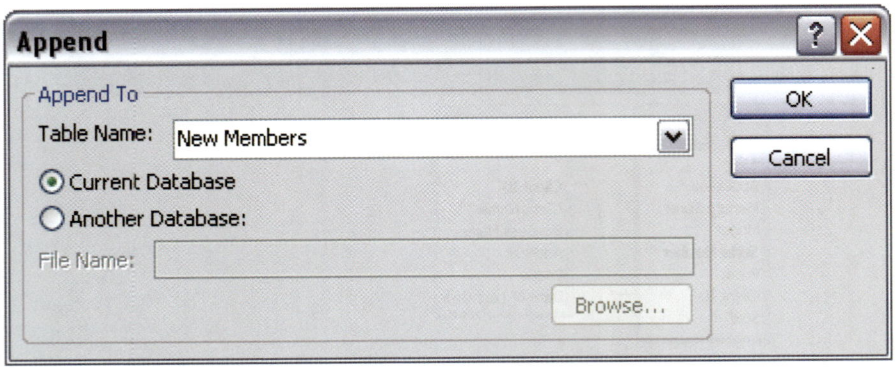


*Figure 12.23*
*'Append' dialogue box*

> *Note:* If you save an append query, every time you run the query by double-clicking on it, it will append the records to the table.

### Creating a delete query

1. Click on the **Queries** tab under **Objects** on the left side of the screen.
2. Double-click **Create query in Design view** or click on the **New** button (the 'New Query' dialogue box appears) and select **Design View** then click **OK**.
3. Click the **Tables** and **Queries** tabs and click the **Add** button to add the table you want to delete from. Click **Close**.
4. Select **Delete Query** from the **Query** drop-down menu on the toolbar.
5. Add fields to the query grid, and complete the criteria similar to the select query.
6. Select **Where** from the drop-down list in the 'Delete' row of the field.
7. Enter the criteria for the query in the 'Criteria' row of the field.
8. Run and save the query.

## Writing expressions

You can use the Expression Builder to write an expression or formula for a criterion.

Expressions can consist of identifiers (field names), operators (+, −, *, / etc.), functions, constants and values. An expression is used to perform a calculation, provide criteria for a query and also retrieve a value. Wildcards can also be used within expressions. They are symbols that can be used to specify characters where you do not know the value of or only know part of the value. For example when a wildcard is used to search a particular field for names that end with 'son' many combinations of the word such as Davidson, Jamison, Johnson may be retrieved. Table 9 shows examples of expressions using both operators and wildcards.

To use the Expression Builder select the **Build** icon from the toolbar.

The 'Expression Builder' dialogue box appears. The box consists of a top pane and three bottom panes (Figure 12.24).

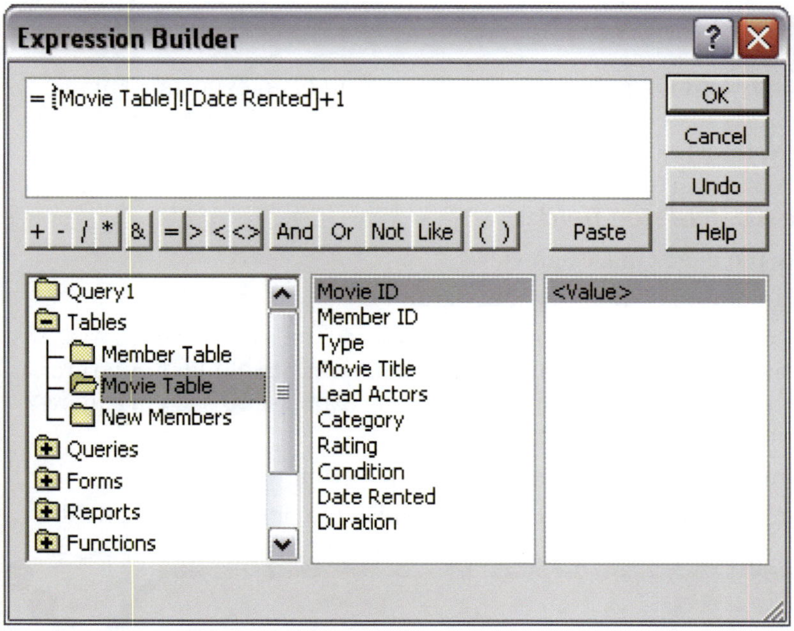


*Figure 12.24*
*'Expression Builder' dialogue box*

| Examples of wildcards/operators | Symbol | Explanation |
|---|---|---|
| ?aren | Wildcard ? or _ (underscore) | Takes the place of a single character, therefore in this example it finds any word where the first letter can be anything but the remaining letters are 'aren'. |
| *Arima<br>( )<br>J*<br><br>B*n | Wildcard * or % | A wildcard that represents any number of characters.<br>Words ending in Arima.<br>Words beginning with J.<br>Words beginning with B and ending with n. |
| < 500 | Relational operators<br>>, <, > =, < =, =, < > | Values less than 500. |
| > = $5000.00 AND < $8000.00<br>"Smith" OR "Singh"<br>BETWEEN #04/05/05# AND #18/05/05# | Boolean operators – AND, OR, NOT, BETWEEN | |
| = [DateReturned] –[DateBorrowed]<br>= [UnitPrice]*[Quantity] *[Discount] | | Calculates the difference between the two values.<br>Calculates the discount on a quantity of items. |

*Table 9*
*Wild cards and expression operators*

## Using the Expression Builder

1. Double-click on the **Tables** folder and select the table that contains the field or fields that will be part of your formula.
2. Double-click on the field/fields that would be part of your expression or formula.
3. Select any relational or Boolean operator and use them to build your expression.
4. Click **OK** when you are finished building your expression or formula.
5. Run and save your query.

## Calculated fields

A **calculated field** is a new field where the result of an expression or formula that is created is displayed. The Expression Builder can be used to build the expression/formula.

### *To create a calculated field*

1. Display the query in Design view.
2. Select an empty field in the query grid.
3. Type a new field name followed by a colon (:), followed by the expression, which can be built using the Expression Builder or written using the field names that form part of the expression, each in square brackets along with the relevant operators.

   For example: Overdue:[Daysoverdue] * [Overduerate]
4. Click in the **Show** box of the field to display the new calculated field.

## Activity 6

1 Retrieve the 'Tropical Appliances Wholesalers' database that you created in the earlier activities and perform the following instructions.

(a) Create a query to change all Consol manufacturers in the 'Appliance Table' to G.E.

(b) Create a query to increase all the prices in the 'Appliance Table' by $100.00.

(c) Create a query to calculate the VAT of 15% of all appliances.

(d) All Serial Numbers of the appliances are off by one due to a data entry error. Update the serial numbers in the 'Appliance Table' by adding one to the serial number.

***How it is done***

***(a) Create a query to change all Consol manufacturers in the 'Appliance Table' to G.E.***

*1* Use an update query to change all Consol manufactures in the 'Appliance Table' to G.E.

*2* Add the 'Appliance Table' to the query grid.

*3* Pull down the **Query** menu and select **Update Query**.

*4* Add the 'Manufacturer' field to the query grid.

*5* In the 'Update To' row of the 'Manufacturer' field type **"G.E."** : include the double quotes.

*6* Save and run the query.

***(b) Create a query to increase all the prices in the 'Appliance Table' by $100.00.***

*1* Add the 'Appliance Table' to the query grid.

*2* Pull down the **Query** menu and select **Update Query**.

*3* Add the 'Price' field to the query grid.

*4* In the 'Update To' row of the 'Price' field type "[Price]+100".

*5* Save the query.

***(c) Create a query to calculate the VAT of 15% of all appliances***

*1* Add the 'Appliance Table' to the query grid.

*2* Select the fields to be displayed.

*3* Click in the next empty column in the 'Field' row.

*4* Type "VAT:[Price]*[0.15]"

*5* Save the query.

2 Retrieve the 'Quilts Incorp' database that you created in an earlier activity and perform the following instructions.

(a) Append the 'Prospective Customers' table to the 'Orders Table'.

(b) Delete all orders where the order amount is >=50 for all Full sizes of quilts.

## Including totals in a query

You can modify a query to include summary or statistical information. Table 10 shows some examples.

| Function | Explanation |
|---|---|
| Sum | Calculates the total of all the values in a field |
| Avg | Finds the average of all the values in a field |
| Min | Finds the lowest value in a field |
| Max | Finds the highest value in a field |
| Count | Finds the number of values in a field, ignoring the null values |
| StDev | Calculates the standard deviation of all the values in a field |
| Var | Calculates the variance of all the values in a field |
| First | Finds the first value in a field |
| Last | Finds the last value in a field |

*Table 10 Functions*

*Figure 12.25*
*Totals in a Query*

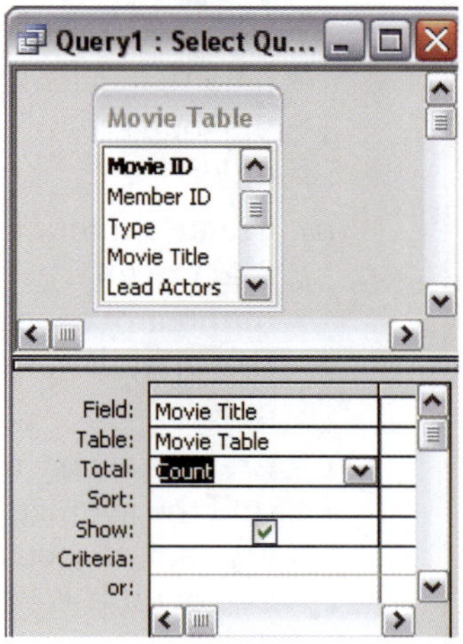


### To include totals in a query

1. Display the query in Design view.
2. Click on the **Totals** icon (Σ) on the toolbar or select **Totals** from the **View** menu.
3. Select the field/fields on which you want to find the totals (Figure 12.25).
4. Click on the drop-down arrow of the field/fields and select the function you want to perform.
5. Run and save your query.

*Figure 12.26*
*New Query window with Find Duplicates Query Wizard highlighted*

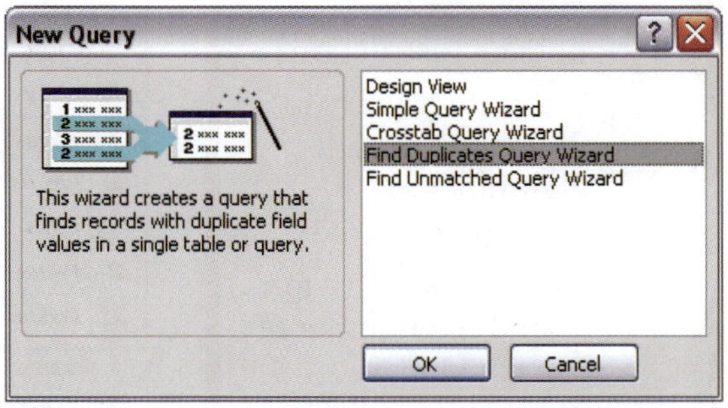


## Find duplicate queries

This displays the records with duplicate values for one or more specified fields. It filters out the records with duplicates in a specified field.

### To find duplicates

1. Click the **New** button in the 'Queries' database window.
2. Select **Find Duplicates Query Wizard** from the 'New Query' window and click **OK** (Figure 12.26).
3. Choose the table or query on which you want to find the duplicates and click the **Next** button (Figure 12.27).
4. Select the field/fields that may contain the duplicates by clicking on the **>** or **>>** buttons to move the fields from the 'Available Fields' pane to the 'Duplicate-value Fields' list and click **Next**.

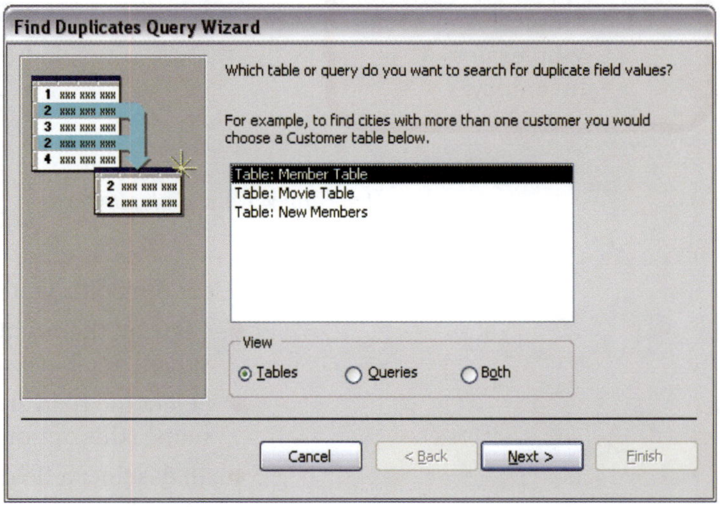


*Figure 12.27*
*Find Duplicates Query Wizard window*

## Activity 7

1 Retrieve the 'Quilts Incorp' database that you created earlier and perform the following instructions.

(a) Quilts are sold for $199.00 – King, $150.00 – Queen, $99.00 – Full, $56.00 – Twin. Create a calculated field that calculates the total cost of the order.

(b) Create a query to find the total number of each size of quilt ordered.

(c) Create a query to find the average number of each size of quilt ordered.

2 Retrieve the 'Tropical Appliances Wholesalers' database that you created earlier and perform the following instructions.

(a) Create a query to find the total number of appliances sold.

(b) Create a query to find the number of each kind of appliance in the Tropical Appliances Wholesalers inventory.

5 Select additional fields if necessary to be displayed and click **Next**.

6 Give your query a name and click the **Finish** button.

7 Your query should be displayed (Figure 12.28).

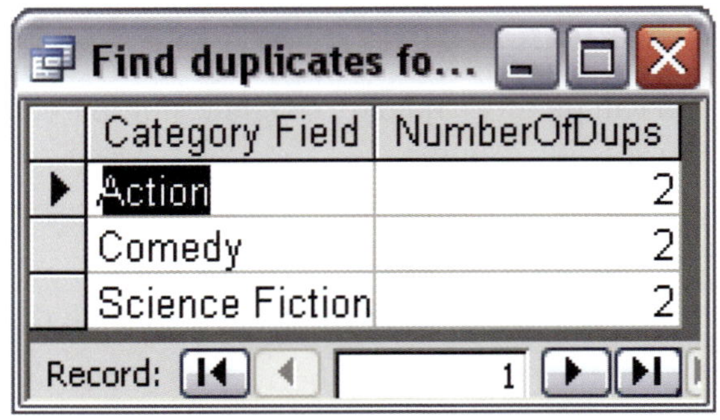


*Figure 12.28*
*The 'Find duplicates' query*

# Forms

A **form** is a graphical representation of a table. It allows you to create a more aesthetically pleasing display for data entry. You can add, update and delete records in the table from the form. A form can have a different name from the table but they both manipulate the same data in the same way. If a record is changed in the form it is also changed in the table.

## *Creating a form using the wizard*

This the the quickest and easiest method for creating a form for data entry.

1 In the database window click on the **Forms** tab under **Objects** on the left side of the screen.

2 Double-click on **Create Form Using Wizard**. The 'Form Wizard' window appears (Figure 12.29).

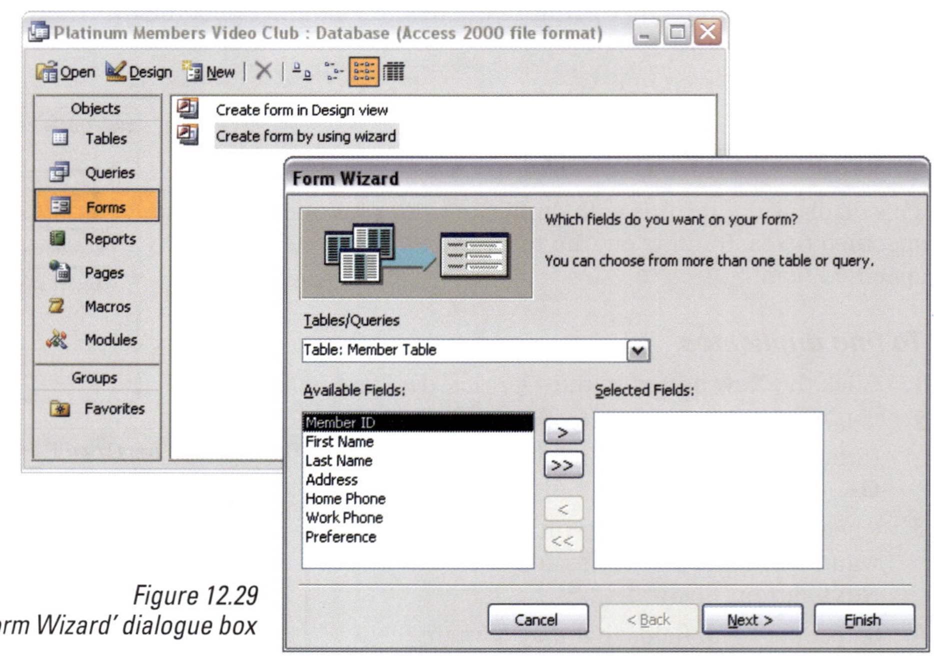


*Figure 12.29*
*The 'Form Wizard' dialogue box*

3 Select the fields you want to view on your form:

- Click on the **>>** button (this will select all the fields from the specified table or query)
- Select the field and click on the **>** button or double-click on the field name (this option will select only certain fields)
- To deselect a field click on either the **<<** or **<** button.

4 Click **Next**, and select the layout you would like for your form.

5 Click **Next**, and select the style for your form.

6 Clicking **Next** on the style options brings you to the final option screen where you give your form a title or accept the default title for the form.

7 Click the **Finish** button.

The new form appears in the database window and will be ready for data entry (Figure 12.30). If the form is not open, double-click on the name of the form in the database window.

One record at a time is displayed. You can scroll through the records by using the record selection buttons at the bottom of the form.

*Figure 12.30*
*Member Table form*

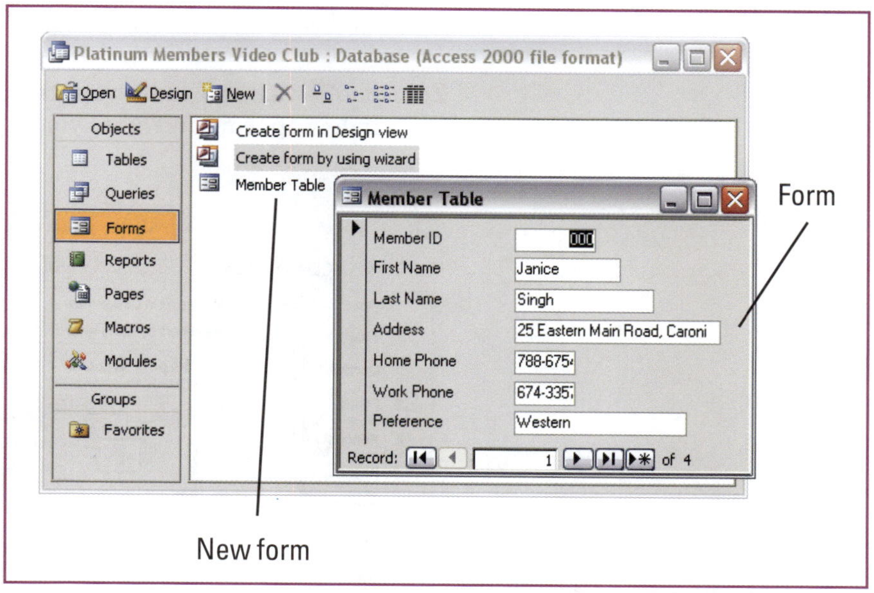


## Modifying the design of the form

To modify aspects of the form, open the form in Design view.

1 If the form is already open select **Design View** from the **View** menu.

2 If the form is not open, select the form and click on the **Design** icon.

3 This layout allows you to adjust the width of the data entry fields. Access sets the width of the field to a default size which may not be wide enough to display the data and hence needs to be adjusted. Place the mouse at the edge of the field box so that the cursor changes to a double-headed arrow. Hold and drag the mouse to adjust the width.

4 To return to the Data Entry view, select **Form View** from the **View** menu. The design changes that were made can be seen in the 'Form' view (Figure 12.31).

*Figure 12.31*
*The Form view, showing changes*

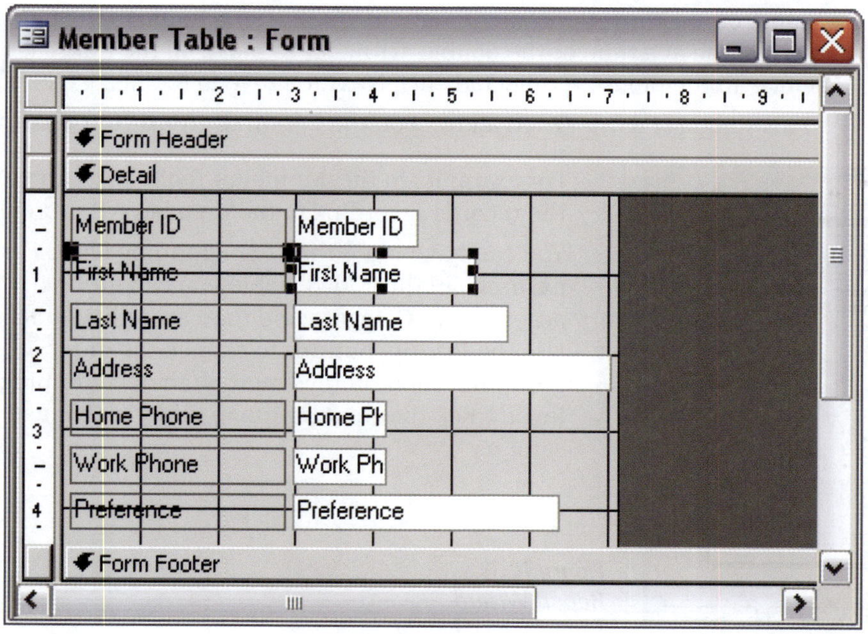


## Activity 8

1 Retrieve the 'Quilts Incorp' database that you created earlier and perform the following instructions.

(a) Create a form to enter the Orders for Quilts Incorp.

(b) Create a form to enter the Prospective Customers for Quilts Incorp.

2 Retrieve the 'Tropical Appliances Wholesalers' database that you created earlier and perform the following instructions.

(a) Create a form to enter the records for the 'Appliance Table'.

(b) Create a form to enter the 'Clients Records'.

# Reports

**Reports** organise and group information from tables or queries and format the data in a way suitable for online viewing or for printing from the database.

## *Creating a report using the wizard*

This the the quickest and easiest method for creating a report.

1 In the database window click on **Reports** tab under **Objects** on the left side of the screen.

2 Double-click on **Create report by using wizard**. The 'Report Wizard' window appears and takes you through a series of options (Figure 12.32).

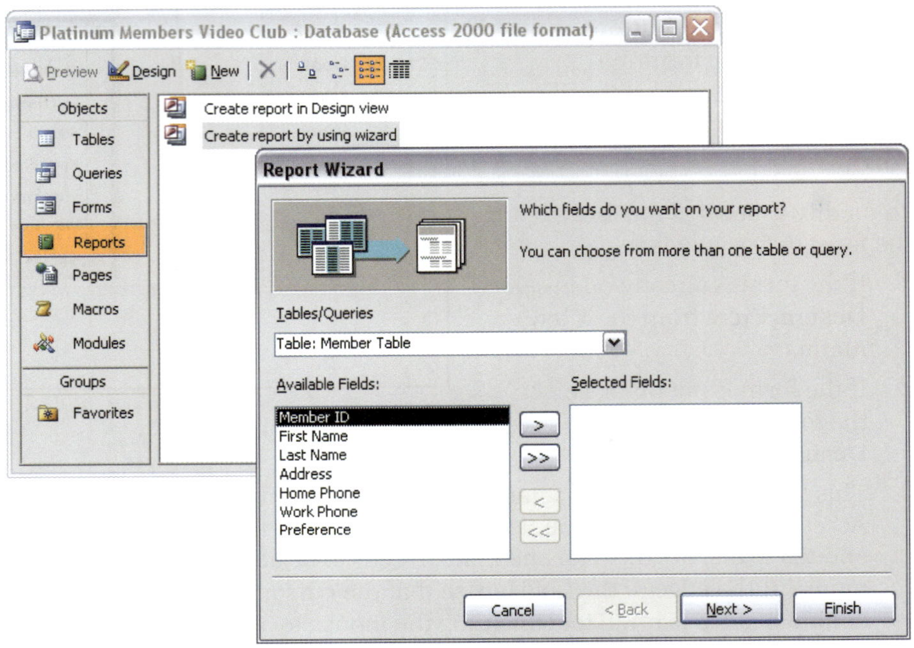


*Figure 12.32*
*The 'Report Wizard' dialogue box*

3 Select the tables or queries that contain the fields you want displayed in the report by transferring them from the 'Available Fields' window to the 'Selected Fields' window. This can be done by double-clicking on the field name or clicking on the single right arrow button **>** to move the fields across one at a time or the double arrow **>>** to move all the fields at once. Once all the fields are selected click **Next** to move to the next screen.

4 This screen (Figure 12.33) allows you the option to group your records.

For example, in the 'Members Table' you can group the records according to the members' Preferences.

You can have more than one grouping level. For example, in the 'Movie' table you can group according to Category and then according to Rating. Use the Priority buttons to change the order of the grouping when there is more than one grouping level. Click the **Next** button to move to the next screen.

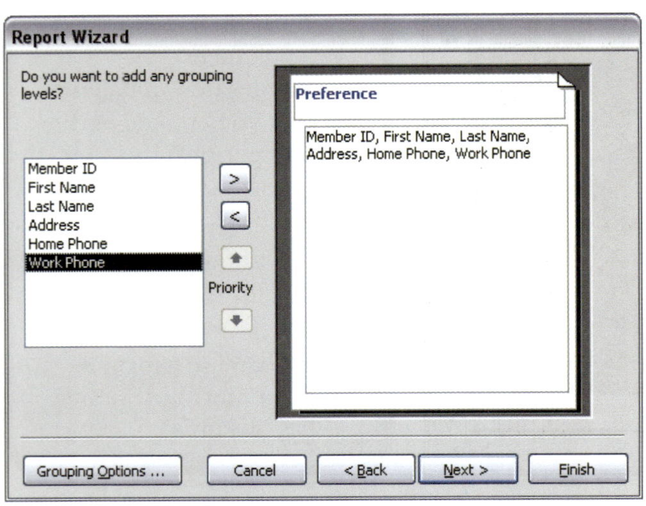


*Figure 12.33*
*Report Wizard*
*Preference window*

5 The 'Sort Order' dialogue box appears (Figure 12.34). If the records are to be sorted, you can set the sort order here.You can sort up to four fields in either ascending or descending order. Select the fields to sort and click the **A–Z** sort button to choose from ascending or descending order. Click the **Next** button to move to the next screen.

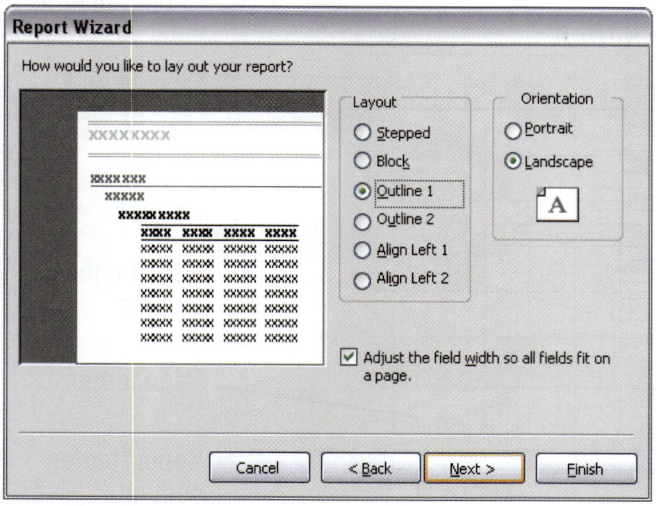


*Figure 12.35*
*Report Wizard Layout window*

6 Select a layout and page orientation for the report (Figure 12.35) and click **Next** to move to the next screen.

7 Select the style for your report (Figure 12.36). This option allows you to choose the colour, font and graphic style for your report. Click **Next** to move to the final screen.

8 This screen (Figure 12.37) allows you to give your report a name and select whether to open it in Print Preview or Design View. The default is Print Preview. Click the **Finish** button to create the report.

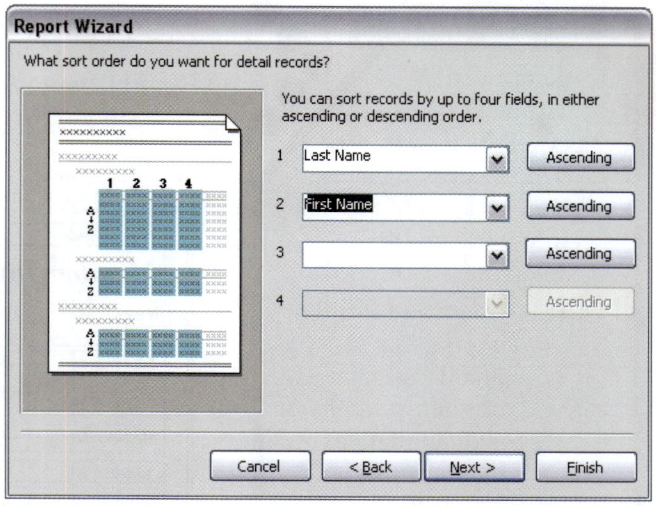


*Figure 12.34*
*Report Wizard sort window*

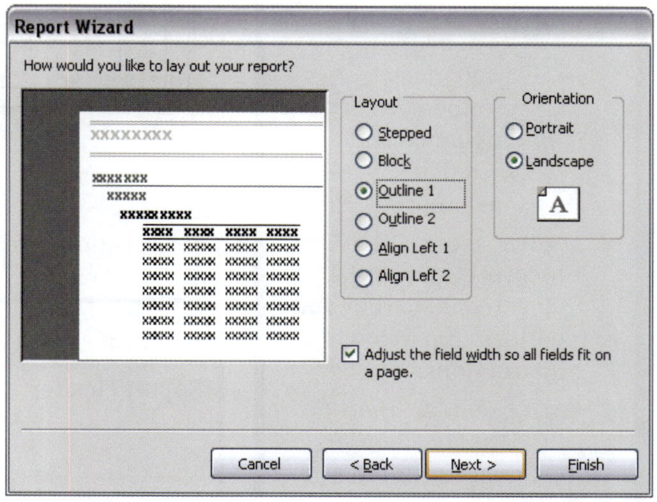


*Figure 12.36*
*Report Wizard style window*

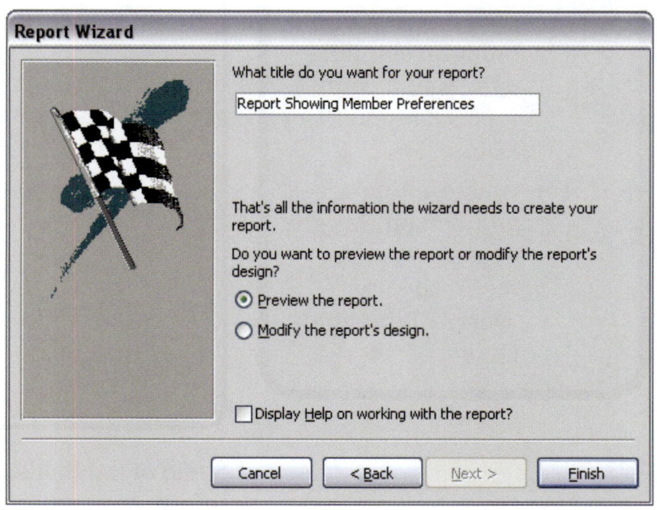


*Figure 12.37*
*Report Wizard title window*

## Activity 9

1 Retrieve the 'Tropical Appliances Wholesalers' database that you created earlier and perform the following instructions.

(a) Create a report that lists the appliances, models, serial numbers and prices of all appliances that have not yet been sold.

(b) Create a report that lists all the customers who have bought appliances, grouped on appliance and sorted on customer's name.

2 Retrieve the 'Quilts Incorp' database that you created earlier and perform the following instructions.

(a) Create a report to display all orders placed, sorted on OrderDate.

(b) Create a report to display all orders sorted in ascending order on shipping date. Name your report 'Shipping Dates'.

(c) Create a report grouped on Design Type. Give your report the title 'Design Types for Quilts'.

## Modifying the layout of the report

A report layout is divided into sections (Figure 12.38).

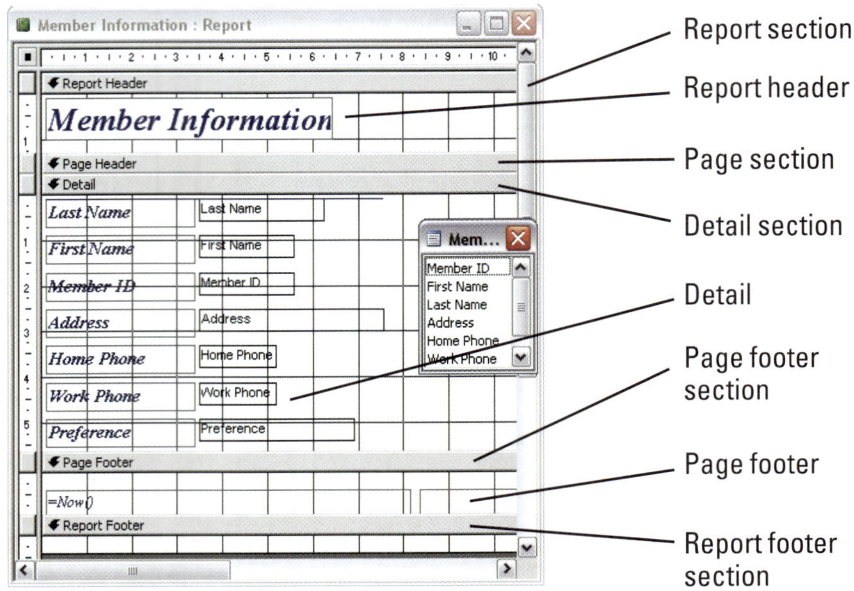


*Figure 12.38 A Report*

These sections are listed in Table 11.

| Section | Description |
|---|---|
| Report Header | This section is at the beginning of the report. It usually contains the name of the report and describes the information listed in it. |
| Page Header | Appears just after the report header. It displays the column headings (field names) and page numbers. |
| Group Header and Group Footer | If records are sorted into groups based on a common value, a group header is placed at the start of each group and a group footer after the last record in the group. |
| Details Section | This section contains the primary information of the report. It contains data for each record. |
| Report Footer | Appears at the bottom of the last page of the report, before the page footer on that page. It holds summary information, such as the number of records, grand totals, etc. |
| Page Footer | Last item on each page of the report. It could contain a page number or other descriptive information. |

*Table 11*

Some of the fields may need to be resized so that all the information will show and nothing will be cut off. The process is similar to that in the Forms Design View. You can resize the field boxes, change the font and font colour and so on.

If you return to the Print View, you should see the changes in the design that you have made.

# Summary

1 A database is an organised collection of related data.

2 Database management is the process by which information is organised and stored on the computer is such a manner that there is efficient retrieval, updating and manipulation of the data so that persons requiring the information will receive it in a timely manner.

3 A database package is a piece of software that enables the user to organise and store related data together so that specific pieces of information can be retrieved quickly and easily.

4 Manual databases have many problems associated with them such as misplacing of files, difficulty cross-referencing data, requires large storage space and the length of time spent finding records.

5 A database file is the entire database.

6 A table is a basic unit of a database and contains data on a specific topic. Tables may contain multiple fields.

7 A field is an area within a table reserved for a specific piece of data.

8 A record consists of a group of related fields containing information pertaining to one person, place or thing.

9 Data is the information that is held in the field.

10 A field definition is the attributes that describe a field.

11 Tables/files can have one of three kinds of relationships to each other:

- One-to-many relationship, where one record/entity in one table is linked to many records/entities in another file/table.
- Many-to-many relationship, where many records/entities in one table are linked to many records/entities in another file through a common entity.
- One-to-one relationship, where one record/entity is linked to exactly one record/entity in another file/table.

12 A primary key is a selected field or fields in a table that uniquely identifies a record.

13 Records can be found and sorted faster using an index. It is similar to the index in a book. Access uses indexes to find data by looking up the location of the data in the index.

14 A query selects records from one or more tables based on specific criteria. This resulting set of records can be viewed and analysed and sorted. The resulting collection of records is called a dynaset (dynamic subset). As the original tables are updated the dynaset is also updated when the query is run again.

15 A select query extracts data from tables based on a criterion or specified value.

16 An update query makes changes to a group of records, or all records in one or more tables.

17 An append query adds a group of records from one or more tables to the end of one or more other tables. The tables do not need to have the same number of fields for the tables to be merged. For example, if Table1 has seven fields and Table2 has four that are similar to those in Table1, and you want to append Table2 to Table1, the records will merge minus the three additional extra fields from Table1.

18 A delete query deletes a group of records from one or more tables.

19 A make table query creates a new table from all or some of the fields of data in one or more tables. These queries are useful for creating tables to export to other databases or to other documents.

20 A calculated field is a new field where the result of an expression or formula that is created is displayed.

21 A form is a graphical representation of a table. It allows you to create a more aesthetically pleasing display for data entry.

22 Reports organise and group information from tables or queries.They format the data in a way suitable for online viewing or for printing.

# Questions

## Short answer questions

1 List THREE capabilities of computerised databases.

2 What is a relational database?

3 What is a database package?

4 What is a database object? List FOUR of these objects.

5 Give TWO reasons for limiting the size of a field.

## Crossword

### Across

3 Extracts data from tables based on a criterion or specific value (6)

5 Adds groups of records from one or more tables to the end of one or more tables (6)

6 A database _______ is an entire database (4)

7 A group of related data belonging to one person, place or thing (6)

### Down

1 An area in a table reserved for a specific piece of data (5)

2 A graphically pleasing display for information for online viewing or to print data from the database (6)

4 Basic unit of a database (5)

6 A graphical representation of a table (4)

# 13 Integration of data

## OBJECTIVES

At the end of this chapter you will be able to:

- Create mail-merged documents using an Access or Excel table as the data source
- Integrate data and graphs from an Excel spreadsheet into a Word document
- Integrate reports and tables from an Access database into a Word document
- Export an Access database object to an Excel spreadsheet
- Import a spreadsheet to a database
- Tackle a sample SBA project involving data integration across all three applications

The previous three chapters dealt with Microsoft Word, Excel and Access, respectively a word processing program, spreadsheet program and database program. These applications form part of the Microsoft Office 2003 integrated package. As such, data can be copied or moved from one application to another quite easily. For example, we have looked at mail merge in Word and used the address fields to create the data table required to perform the mail merge. With an integrated package like Office 2003 we can also use a table created in Microsoft Excel or Microsoft Access to perform a mail merge. Other examples of integration include moving an Access table to Excel to analyse or produce charts, or publishing an Access report in Word to enhance a report.

## Mail merge (using an Access or Excel table as the data source)

In Chapter 10, mail merge was explained using a data source that was created in Word. Here the data source will be a table created in Access or Excel. The steps to mail merging are the same as outlined in Chapter 10, with the exception of selecting the data file.

### Step 1 – Selecting the document type

The first step in performing a mail merge is to select the document type. You can perform a mail merge using any of the document types shown in Figure 13.1.

1 For our purposes check the **Letters** radio button.
2 Click on **Next: Starting document** at the bottom of the dialogue box to move to the next step.

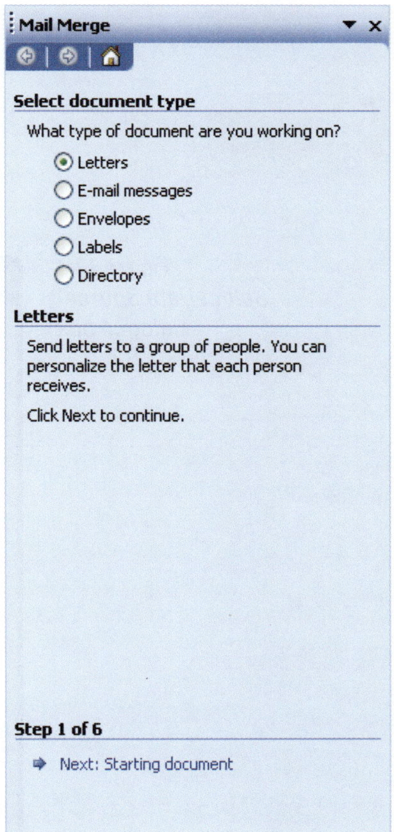


*Figure 13.1 'Select document type' dialogue box*

## Step 2 – Selecting the starting document

The ‘Select starting document’ dialogue box gives you three options to choose from to select the main document. You can:

- Use the current document
- Start from a template
- Start from an existing document.

1 Select the starting document by checking the appropriate radio button. Figure 13.2 shows the **Use the current document** option selected.

2 Click on **Next: Select recipients** at the bottom of the dialogue box to move to the next step.

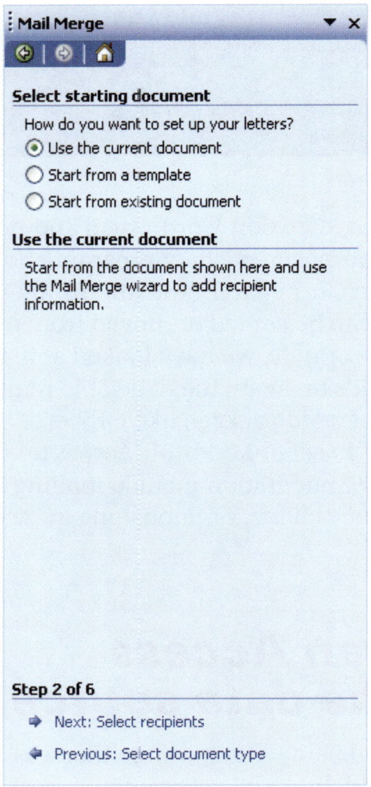


*Figure 13.2 ‘Select starting document’ dialogue box*

## Step 3 – Selecting recipients

In the ‘Select recipients’ dialogue box you have to indicate the location of the recipients (the data source).

1 Since our data file will be coming from Access or Excel you need to check the radio button for the option **Use an existing list** and then select **Browse** as shown in Figure 13.3.

2 The ‘Select Data Source’ dialogue box appears as shown in Figure 13.4. Select the location of the data source from the ‘Look in’ combo box. Select the data source and click **Open**.

**If the data source is from Access follow the instructions in step 3a, if it is from Excel follow the instructions in 3b.**

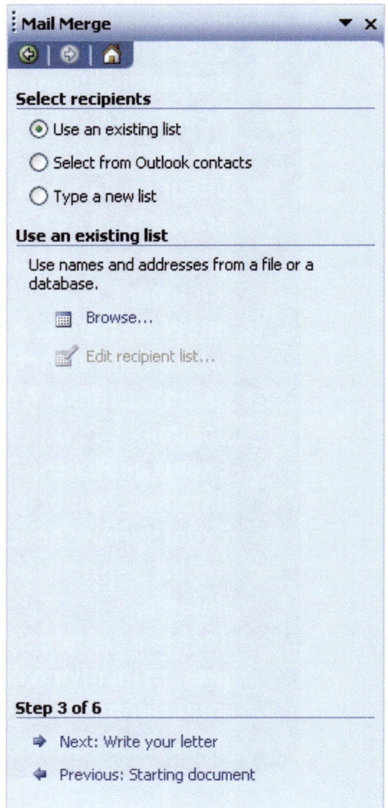


*Figure 13.3 ‘Select recipients’ dialogue box*

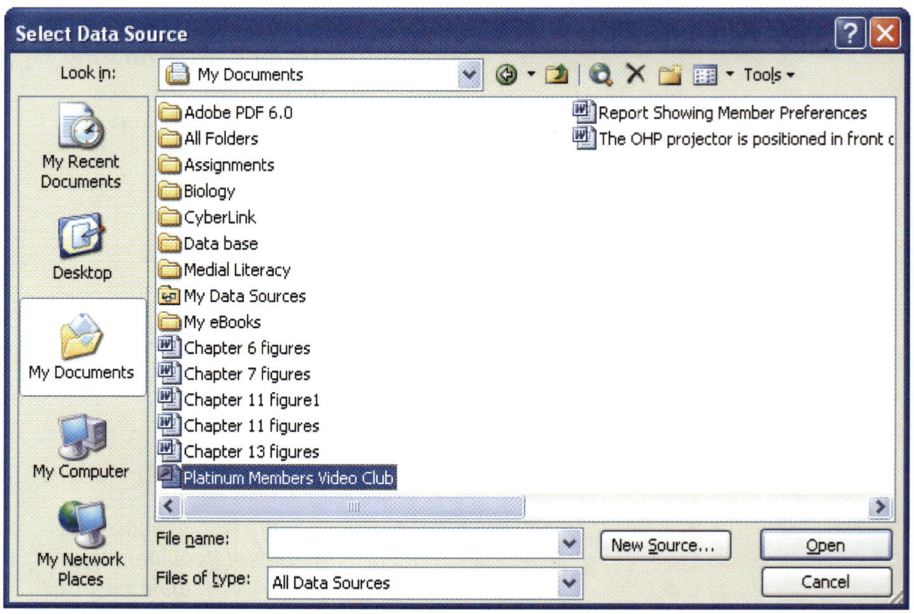


*Figure 13.4 ‘Select Data Source’ dialogue box*

**3a** *Using an Access table as the data source*: When the data source file is opened, the 'Select Table' dialogue box is displayed as shown in Figure 13.5.

- Select the table that will be used as the data source and click **OK**.

The 'Mail Merge Recipients' dialogue box displaying all the records in the table will be displayed as shown in Figure 13.6.

- Click **OK** to accept the records.

The 'Select recipients' mail merge dialogue box as shown in Figure 13.7 appears again, displaying the name of the table and the name of the database from which it is being taken.

- To continue the mail merge process click on **Next: Write your letter** to *go to step 4*.

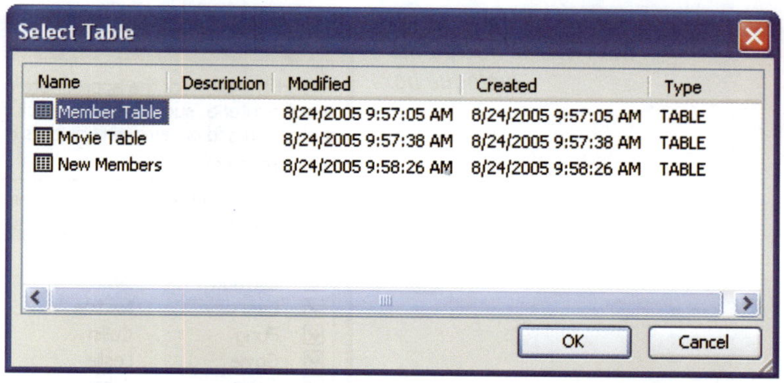


*Figure 13.5*
*'Select Table' dialogue box*

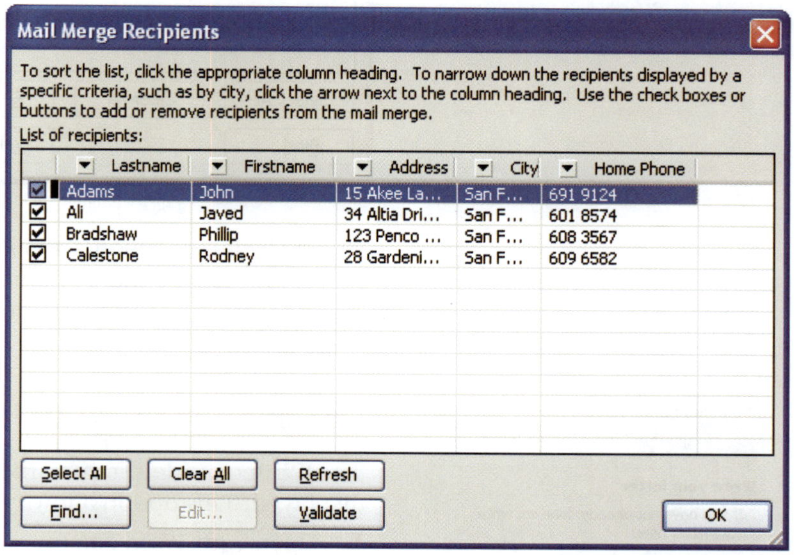


*Figure 13.6*
*'Mail Merge Recipients' dialogue box*

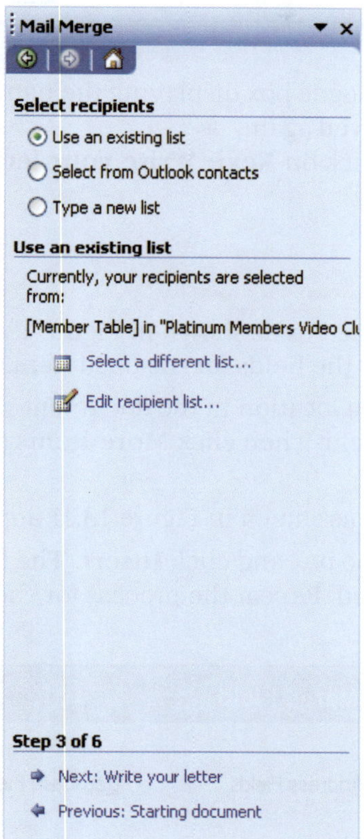


*Figure 13.7*
*'Select recipients' dialogue box with the name of the data source file listed*

**3b** *Using an Excel table as the data source*: When the data source file is opened, the 'Select Table' dialogue box as shown in Figure 13.8 is displayed.
This dialogue box displays all the sheets from the workbook selected.

- Select the sheet containing the data source and click **OK**.
  As in step 3a, the 'Mail Merge Recipients' dialogue box displaying all the records in the table is displayed as shown in Figure 13.9.
- Click **OK** to accept the data.

*Figure 13.8*
*'Select Table' dialogue box*

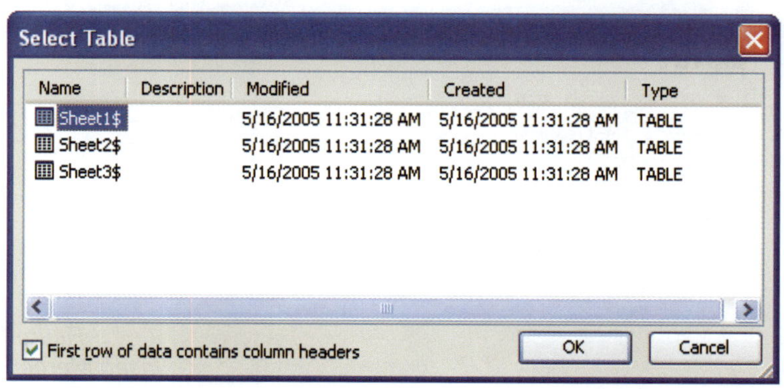

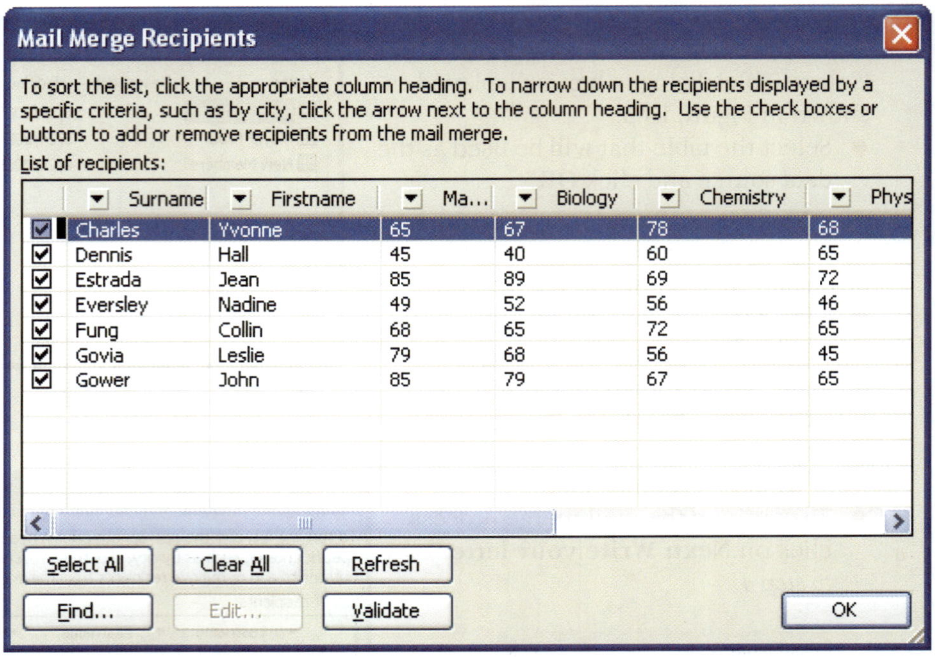


*Figure 13.9*
*'Mail Merge Recipients' dialogue box*

The 'Select recipients' mail merge dialogue box displaying the name of the worksheet and workbook is displayed again.

To continue the mail merge process click on **Next: Write your letter** to *go to step 4*.

## Step 4 – Write your letter

The 'Write your letter' mail merge dialogue box as shown in Figure 13.10 is displayed. This option allows you to view the fields for the document.

1 Open your Word document and click a location in the document where you would like to place a particular field. Then click **More items** (Figure 13.10).

The 'Insert Merge Field' dialogue box as shown in Figure 13.11 appears.

2 Select the field from the 'Fields' combo box and click **Insert**. The field will be inserted in the position selected. Repeat the process for each field.

3 When all the fields you require have been inserted, click **Next: Preview your letters**.

The 'Preview your letters' dialogue box appears as shown in Figure 13.12.

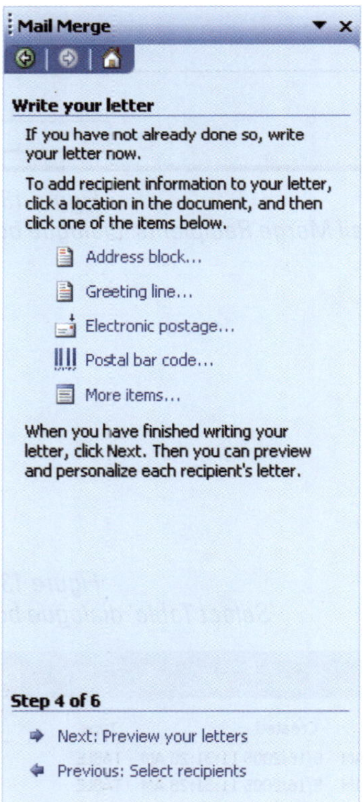


*Figure 13.10*
*'Write your letter' dialogue box*

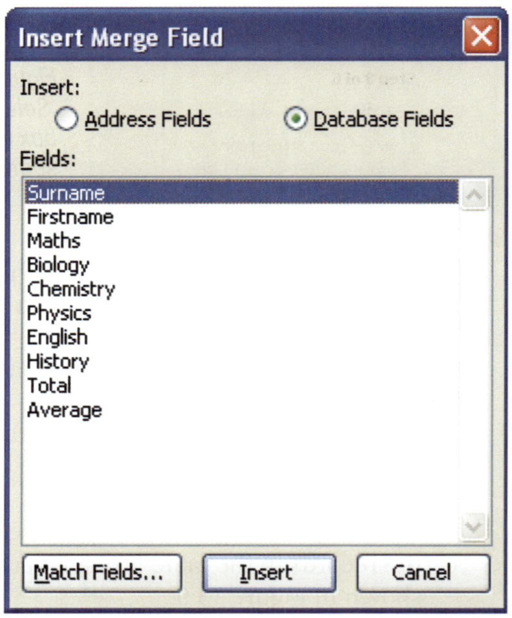


*Figure 13.11*
*'Insert Merge Field' dialogue box*

## Step 5 – Preview your letters

The 'Preview your letters' dialogue box allows you to preview the merged letters. At this point you can still make changes to the recipient list if you wish.

If you agree with the contents of the merged letters then click **Next: Complete the merge** to move to the next step.

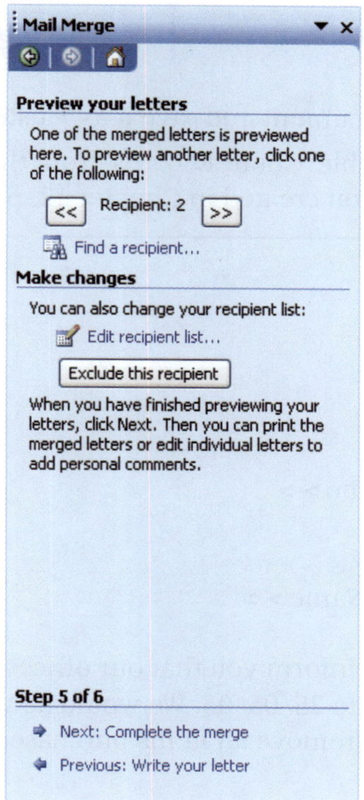


*Figure 13.12*
*'Preview your letters' dialogue box*

## Step 6 – Complete the merge

The 'Complete the merge' dialogue box as shown in Figure 13.13 appears.

1 To display all the merged letters click on **Edit individual letters**.

   The 'Merge to New Document' dialogue box appears as shown in Figure 13.14.

2 If you want to select all the records check the **All** radio button, otherwise input the appropriate range and click **OK**.

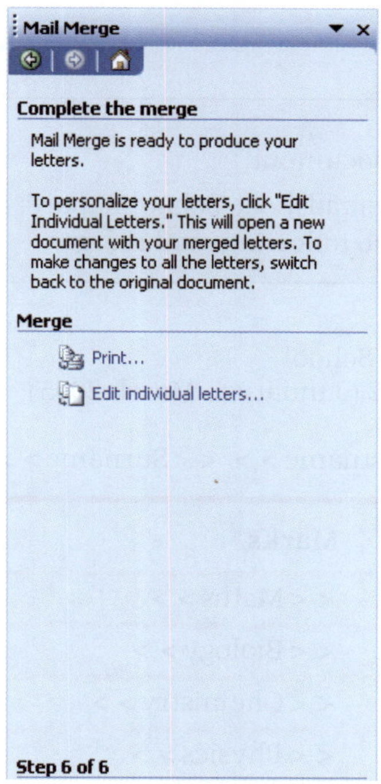


*Figure 13.13*
*'Complete the merge' dialogue box*

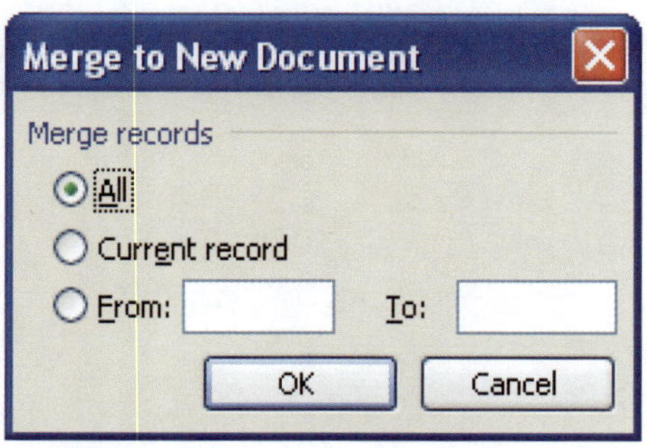


*Figure 13.14*
*'Merge to New Document' dialogue box*

## Activity 1

**1** (a) Type the following document and save it as 'Customers'.

(b) Using data from the table 'Client Records' from the database 'Tropical Appliances Wholesalers', which you created in Chapter 12, perform a mail merge.

12 Juniper Lane
St. James

12/05/05

< <Business Name> >
< <Address> >

Dear < <Client Name> >

We would like to inform you that our offices will be closed for stocktaking during the period 20/05/05 to 25/05/05. We would be very happy if you could make arrangements to remove all items purchased on < < Date of Last Order> >.

Yours truly,

Jonathan King
Sales Supervisor

**2** (a) Create the following document.

(b) Using data from the spreadsheet 'School Report', created in Chapter 11 perform the following mail merge.

Happy Hill High School
Report for Term 2 (January to March 2005)

Student : < <Firstname> > < <Surname> >

| **Subjects** | **Marks** |
|---|---|
| Mathematics | < <Maths> > |
| Biology | < <Biology> > |
| Chemistry | < <Chemistry> > |
| Physics | < <Physics> > |
| English | < <English> > |
| History | < <History> > |
| Total | < <Total> > |
| Average | < <Average> > |

Ann Margot
Class Teacher

# Integrating data and graphs from a spreadsheet into a word processing document

Many people have to write reports. For example, a teacher may have to write a report to the principal to show students' performance in her class. The principal may then have to write a report to show overall students' performances in the CSEC examinations. To make such a report more meaningful it may be necessary to include data and charts from a spreadsheet. Moving data and graphs from an Excel spreadsheet to a Word document involves copying, cutting and pasting.

## Copying data and charts/graphs from an Excel spreadsheet to a Word document

1. Open the Word document.
2. Open the Excel workbook.
3. Click the appropriate worksheet and select the data/chart required.
4. Select **Copy**.
5. Click the Word document on the task bar to make it active.
6. Position the cursor in the Word document where you would like to begin to insert the data or chart.
7. Click on the **Paste** icon or select **Paste** from the **Edit** menu.

## Activity 2

1. Type the following document and save it as 'CLASS REPORT'.
2. Copy and paste the data from the spreadsheet file 'Class Report' from your CD-ROM to the location specified in the letter.
3. Using the spreadsheet 'Class Report', create a column graph showing the average mark of each student.
4. Import the chart to the location specified in the letter to the Principal.
5. Save all changes made to the document.

The Principal
Happy Hill High School
25th March 2005

Dear Mr. John Bobb,

The following table shows the performance of students in my class for the different subject areas.

< < Paste spreadsheet table here > >

The average mark obtained by each student is represented as a chart for your convenience.

< < Paste chart here > >

Yours truly,
Darren Phillip
Class Teacher

# Integrating reports and tables from a database into a word processing document

Access objects such as tables, queries, reports and so on can also be published in a Word document.

### Publishing an Access object to a Word document

1 Open the Access file.
2 Click on the object.
3 Select the table, query, report, etc.
4 Click the **Tools** menu.
5 Select **Office Links**.
6 Select **Publish it with Microsoft Office Word**.

The object will be published in a new Word document. To move the object to the document you are working on, you can copy or cut it, and paste it. Figure 13.15 shows the selections involved in publishing the report 'Report Showing Member Preferences' from the 'Platinum' database.

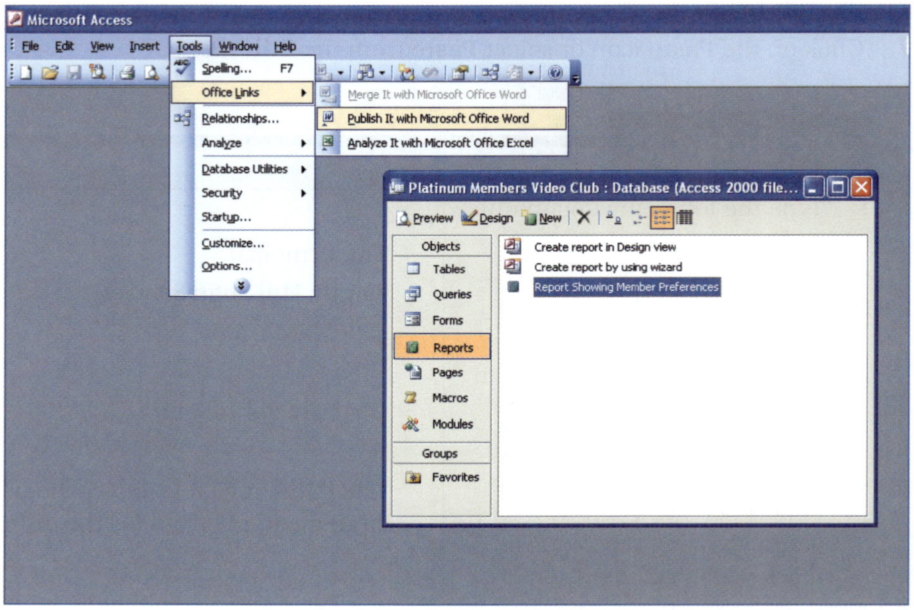


*Figure 13.15 Inserting a database report in a Word document*

## Activity 3

Publish the report 'Report Showing Member Preferences' from the Platinum database from Chapter 12 into a Word document. (The database can be found on your CD-ROM.)

# Exporting a database object to a spreadsheet

Data stored in tables in Access can be easily queried to extract information or produce reports. Sometimes, however, you may need to perform calculations on the data or represent the data graphically. Calculations can be carried out in Access but the process is much more difficult than in Excel. Therefore tables from an Access database can be copied to Excel to be worked on.

### Exporting an Access object to an Excel spreadsheet

1 Open the database file.
2 Click on the object.
3 Select the table, query, report, etc.

4 Click the **Tools** menu.

5 Select **Office Links**.

6 Select **Analyze It with Microsoft Office Excel**.

The object will be published in a new Excel worksheet. To move the object to the worksheet you are working on, you can copy or cut it, and paste it. Figure 13.16 shows the menu selections involved in publishing the table 'Member table' from the Platinum database.

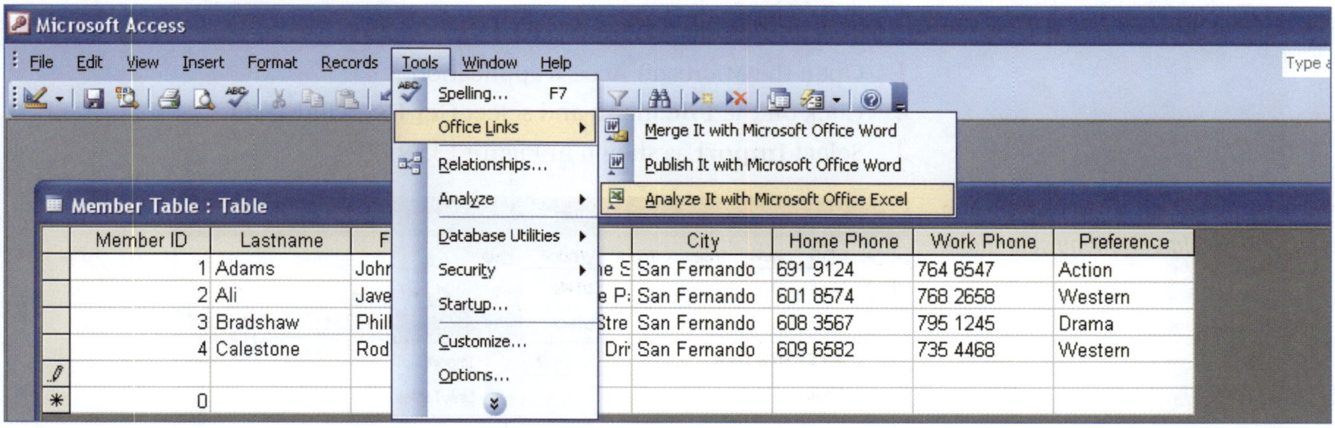


*Figure 13.16*
*Menu options to copy an Access table to Excel*

If you only want part of the table moved to the worksheet, select the contents and follow the steps outlined above. Figure 13.17 shows a section of a table selected; Figure 13.18 shows the result when it is pasted in Excel.

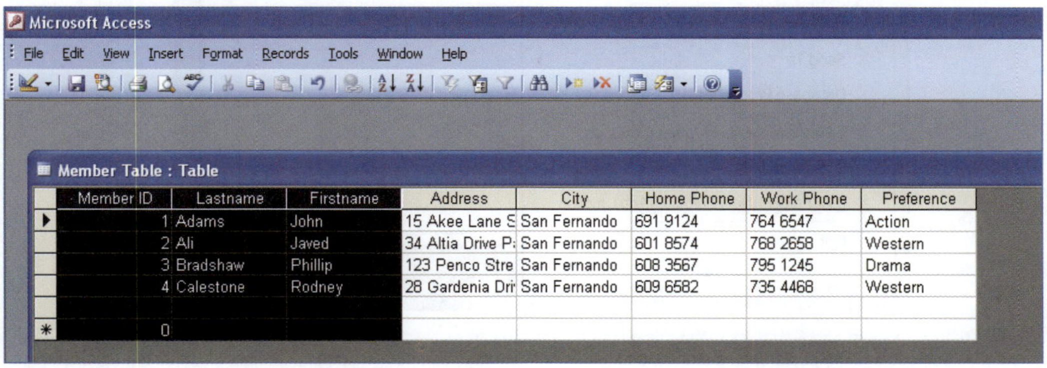


*Figure 13.17*
*Selecting the part of the table which you want to copy*

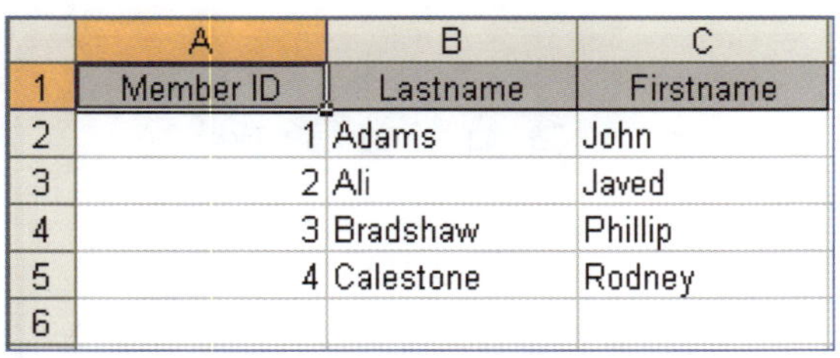


*Figure 13.18*
*Selection from Access table copied to Excel*

## Activity 4

1 (a) Import the table 'Member table' from the Platinum database stored on your CD-ROM to Excel.

(b) Save the worksheet as 'Members'.

# Importing a spreadsheet to a database

It is possible to convert an Excel table into an Access table. This may be necessary if you would like to perform more in-depth queries on your data. Note that the first row of the spreadsheet should contain the field names or row headings. The process is as follows.

### Step 1

1. Open the Microsoft Access application.
2. Click on the **File** menu and select **Get External Data**.
3. Select **Import** as shown in Figure 13.19.

*Figure 13.19*
*Import menu selections*

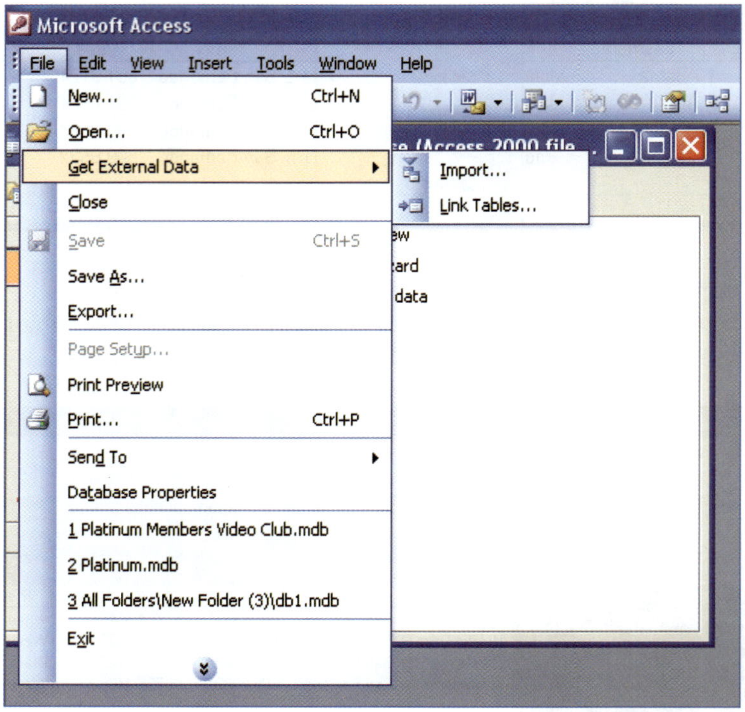


The 'Import' dialogue box appears as shown in Figure 13.20.

*Figure 13.20*
*The 'Import' dialogue box*

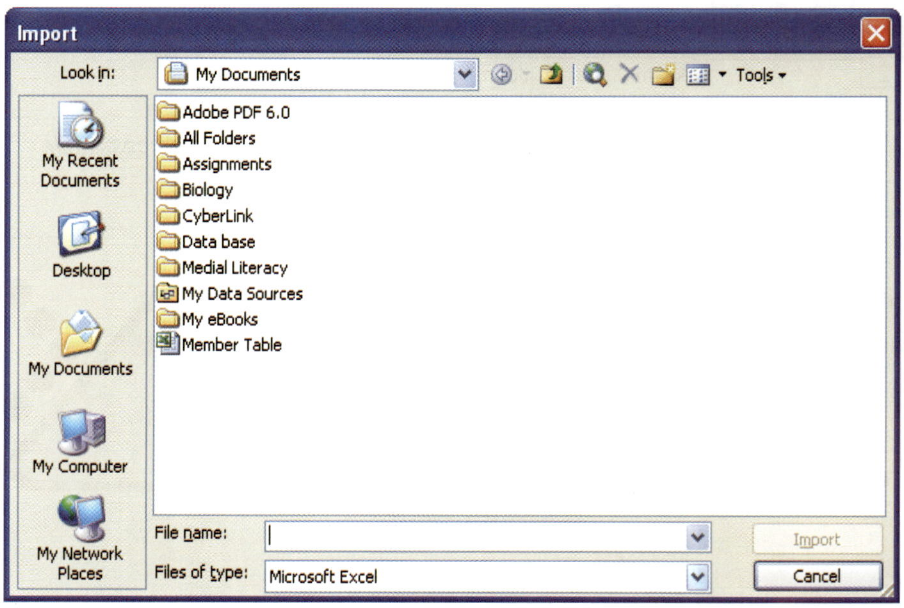

## Step 2

1 Select the location where the file is stored in the 'Look in' combo box.

2 Change the contents of the 'Files of type' combo box to 'Microsoft Excel'.

3 Click on **Import**. The 'Import Spreadsheet Wizard' dialogue box appears.

## Step 3

1 Check the **Show Worksheets** radio button.

2 Select the sheet that contains the data.

3 Click **Next**.

The worksheet will be displayed as shown in Figure 13.21 in the 'Import Spreadsheet Wizard' dialogue box.

## Step 4

Microsoft Access can use your column headings as field names for your table. Let the first row of your worksheet specify the column headings. If this is done then:

1 Check the **First Row Contains Column Headings** box (Figure 13.22).

2 Click **Next**.

## Step 5

You can store your data in a new table or in an existing table (Figure 13.23).

- To store the data in a new table check the **In a New Table** radio button.
- To store the data in an existing table check the **In an Existing Table** radio button and then select **Next**.

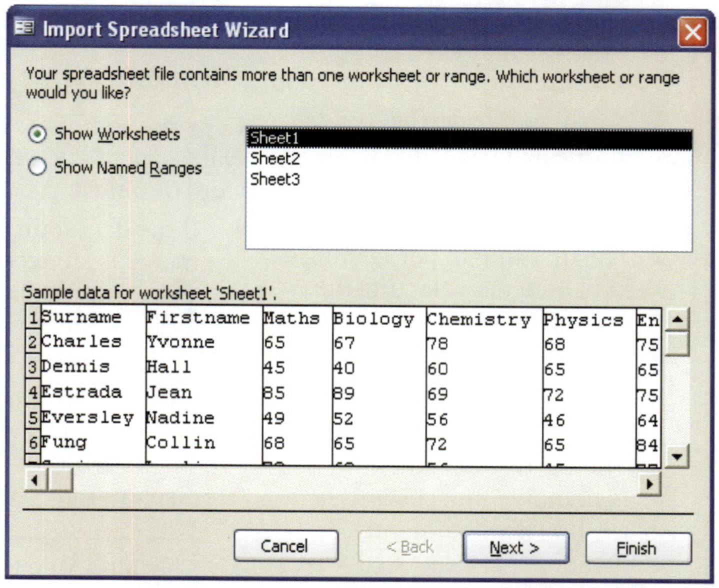


*Figure 13.21 'Import Spreadsheet Wizard' dialogue box*

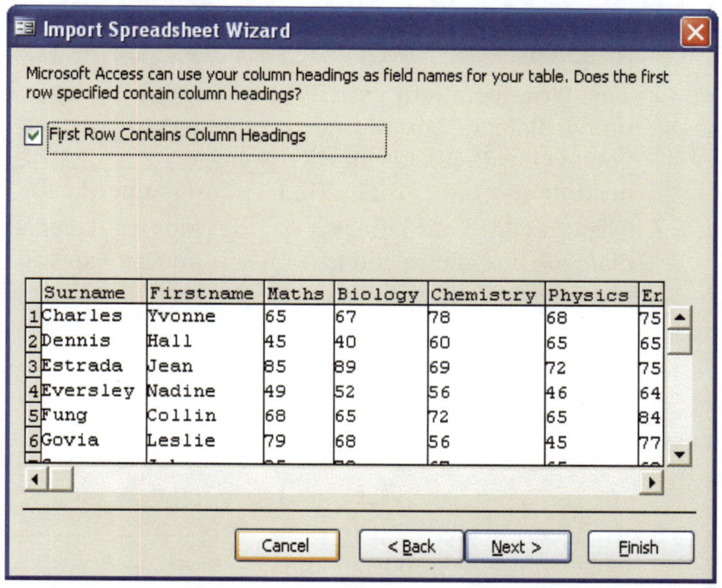


*Figure 13.22 Column headings window of Import Spreadsheet Wizard*

## Activity 5

1 (a) Create a database named 'Happy Hill school report'.

(b) Import the spreadsheet 'School Report' which is stored on the CD-ROM.

(c) Save the imported spreadsheet as a new table named 'Class report' in the database 'Happy Hill school report'.

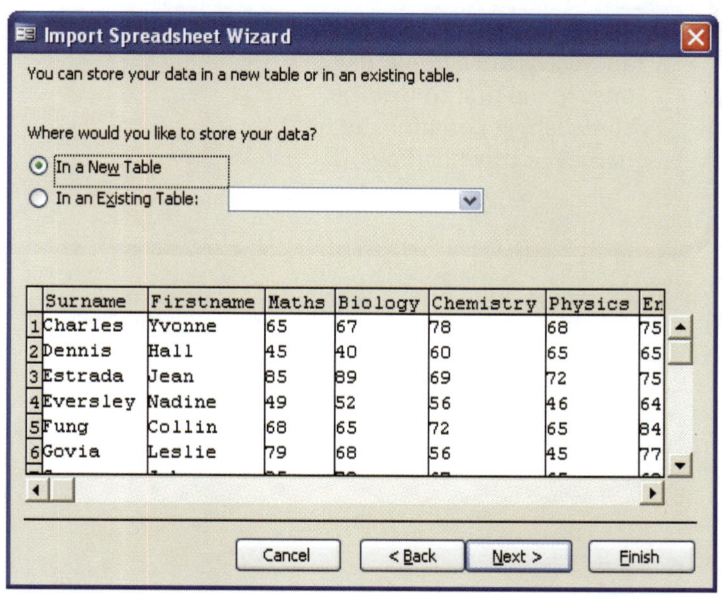


*Figure 13.23 Import Spreadsheet Wizard, storing data*

## Exercise 1

### True or False?

1 A mail merge can be performed with a table created in Access as the data source. T ❑ F ❑

2 The first step in performing a mail merge is selecting the document type. T ❑ F ❑

3 Labels cannot be used as a document type in a mail merge. T ❑ F ❑

4 The starting document in a mail merge must be an existing document only. T ❑ F ❑

5 The 'Select Recipients' dialogue box allows you to indicate the location of the recipients. T ❑ F ❑

6 The 'Write your letter' mail merge dialogue box allows you to view the fields for the document. T ❑ F ❑

7 The 'Preview your letters' dialogue box allows you to preview the merged letters. T ❑ F ❑

8 Moving data and graphs from an Excel spreadsheet to a Word document involves copying, cutting and pasting. T ❑ F ❑

9 An Access object such as a table cannot be imported into a Word document. T ❑ F ❑

10 To move an Excel table into an Access table you must ensure the first row of the spreadsheet contains the field names or row headings. T ❑ F ❑

### Fill in the blanks

Copy the sentences and fill in the blank spaces with an appropriate word or phrase.

1 If the data source of a mail merge is an Access table, the 'Select Table' dialogue box displays the ______________________.

2 If the data source of a mail merge is an Excel table, the 'Select Table' dialogue box displays the ______________________.

3 The 'Mail Merge Recipients' dialogue box displays all the ________________ in the table.

4 The 'Write your letter' mail merge dialogue box allows you to view the ________________ for the document.

5 Moving data and graphs from an Excel spreadsheet to a word document involves copying/cutting and ________________.

6 To convert an Excel table into an Access table, the first row of the spreadsheet should contain the ________________ or ______________________.

### Short answer questions

1 Describe the steps to perform a mail merge if the datafile is an Access table.

2 Describe the steps to perform a mail merge if the datafile is an Excel table.

3 Explain one reason for moving data and charts from an Excel spreadsheet to a Word document.

4 Explain the steps involved in importing a spreadsheet table or chart into a word processing document.

5 Describe the steps involved in publishing an Access object to a Word document.

6 (a) State ONE reason why you might want to export an Access table into Excel.

(b) Describe the steps involved in importing an Access table into Excel.

7 (a) Describe the process of importing an Excel table into an Access database.

(b) State ONE advantage of importing an Excel table into a database.

# Sample SBA project on data integration



Now you have seen how data can be copied or moved from one application to another, we will walk you through the solution for a sample SBA project. In this project many of the features you have learnt about in Chapters 10, 11 and 12, as well as in this chapter, will be used.

A completed SBA Project can be found on your companion CD-ROM.

## Description of your project

The IT Department of Tech Info Corporation, established in 2000, has decided to implement in January 2005 salary increases for its workers based on seniority, performance and qualifications. The Finance Department has decided to computerise this process and needs to do the following:

- Establish the present salaries of all workers
- Establish the increment each worker will receive based on his or her performance, seniority and qualifications
- Perform all the calculations necessary to work out the salary increases
- Send out letters to all the workers informing them of their salary increase
- Update all employee records with all the changes that were made
- Record on a printout any assumptions that were made.

## Spreadsheet section

At present increments are given to employees of rank 3 and above. Increments are fixed at 2% of their current salary. This increment is given every year after the first year of employment. The current salary plus the increments becomes their new salary.

Table 1 shows the current starting monthly salaries of employees:

*Table 1*

| Position held | Rank | Starting monthly salary |
|---|---|---|
| Data Processing Manager | 6 | 15000 |
| Database Administrator | 5 | 10000 |
| Network Administrator | 5 | 10000 |
| Systems Development Manager | 5 | 10000 |
| Business Analyst | 5 | 10000 |
| Operations Manager | 5 | 10000 |
| Systems Analyst | 4 | 8700 |
| Programmers | 3 | 8000 |
| Computer Operators | 2 | 5000 |
| Technical Support | 2 | 5000 |
| Data Control Clerks | 2 | 5000 |
| File Librarian | 1 | 3500 |
| Data Entry Operators | 1 | 3500 |

| Years of service | % increase |
|---|---|
| 5 | 7 |
| 4 | 5 |
| 3 | 3 |
| 2 | 2 |

*Table 2*

After a series of meetings the Board of Directors has decided to change the way the increment each worker receives on their salary is calculated each year. Instead of receiving fixed increments every year, increments are now to be based on seniority and rank.

A new agreement between the workers' union and the company states that employees will get their increments as of January 2005 according to the criteria listed in Table 2:

### You are required to:

**A** Using the data from Table 1 along with data you will make up, create a spreadsheet of no less than 25 employees showing their Employee ID, Name, Position, Rank, Starting Monthly Salary, Year of Entry, Years of Service. Each employee has a 3-digit employee ID number. Ensure that your data includes all the positions in the company along with a range of starting dates from the inception of the company.

Your spreadsheet should use labels appropriately, for example bear in mind that you may be asked to sort the spreadsheet on Employee Surname. The information should be easily interpretable.

**B** Create a spreadsheet to determine the annual salaries of employees over the years from their date of entry into the company to December 2004. Use currency format to display the salaries.

**C** Modify the spreadsheet to reflect the new agreement for 2005 salaries.

**D** Use appropriate formulae to determine the greatest and the least salary increase in 2005.

**E** Add the following two employees to the spreadsheet:

| Employee ID | Name | Position Held | Entry Year |
|---|---|---|---|
| 339 | Davanand Singh | Programmer | 2004 |
| 340 | Jessie Romero | Data Entry Operator | 2004 |

**F** Sort the data worksheet containing the 2005 yearly salaries on employee Surname, followed by First Name, in ascending order.

**G** Extract the records of ALL employees whose monthly salary is > = $8000.00 and who started working at the company in the year 2002 or after.

**H** Create a summary table to show the percentage of employees in each rank.

**I** Create a pie chart to show the percentage of employees in each rank. Your chart should be appropriately labelled.

**J** Create a graph to show the differences in the salaries between the old agreement in 2004 and the new agreement in 2005. Your graph should be appropriately labelled.

## Database section

Records are kept by the company of all existing employees and the state of their due salaries over the years. There are six ranks of employee. The salaries payable to each employee is dependent on his or her rank.

The company's database has two tables, one holding personal information on each employee, the other holding the history of the annual salary payment to each employee.

The 'Employee Information' table maintains the following information on each employee: employee ID, name, address, phone number, date of birth and gender. Each employee is also assigned a unique identification number for database recording purposes.

The 'Salary History' table holds information on employee ID, employee position, rank, year of entry, years of service, starting monthly salary and also maintains a history of the yearly payments. For example, Jane Doe was employed in 2000, so the company will maintain records for 2000, 2001, 2002, 2003, 2004 and 2005. These records will indicate what salaries were paid under the old agreement and what is due under the new agreement.

***You are required to:***

**A** Design and create a set of database tables which will meet with all the above criteria.

**B** Populate your database with the names and data used in your spreadsheet section. Include payment information from the year of entry for each employee.

**C** Delete the Surname and First Name field from the 'Salary History' table.

**D** Your database files should be created to be able to respond to the following queries. Test your database by running samples of the following queries.

(1) What are the names, addresses and phone numbers of all the Data Entry Operators?

(2) List all the employees who occupy positions above rank 4.

(3) List all employees and their salaries for 2005.

(4) What is the total sum of money that has been paid out in increments during the year 2003 by Tech Info Corporation?

(5) Create a query to determine the salaries for 2004 of all employees who entered the organisation before the year 2003.

Further test your database by performing the following operations on the database:

**E** Delete all the records related to Davanand Singh, Employee ID 339 who has now left the company.

**F** Prepare a report which must display the unique employee number, starting salary, rank and position held. For each employee the report should give information on the payment of salary (i.e. 2000 to 2005) from the year they started with the company. The salary information should be grouped by rank and sorted by employee number in ascending sequence.

## Word processing section

At the end of the year 2004 Tech Info Corporation has finished its salary adjustments for all its workers and is now ready to publish all the changes made to every worker.

***You are required to:***

**A** Send out letters to every employee notifying them of the change in salary increment structure for 2005 as compared to 2004, and what their new annual salary will be. Letters must be prepared on the company's letterhead containing the company's logo, address, phone/fax number, e-mail address and web site address.

**B** Every letter must contain the following information:
- The year the employee began to work in the company
- The rank that the employee holds
- The employee's starting monthly salary
- The percentage increase that was received up to the year 2004
- The percentage increase and new salary that the employee would be receiving at the beginning of 2005.
  - (a) Every letter has to be populated with the correct values as obtained from either the spreadsheet or database that you have already produced.
  - (b) The guidelines for writing the letter the employees will receive are as follows:
- The letter must begin with:

  Maria Brown
  The Chief Financial Officer
  Finance Department

  Dear ___________,

- Every letter should have the following footer in a smaller font than the rest of the document and in italics.

  ---

  © Tech Info Corporation
  Finance Department, 2004

- Include a space for the Chief Financial Officer's (CFO) signature.
  - (c) Using the mail merge facility, create letters to send out to all the employees.
  - (d) Make sure that the letters have been spell-checked and use appropriate grammar, i.e. that they are professional.
  - (e) Adjust the margin for each letter so that the top margin is 2 inches, in order to accommodate the letterhead, and the left margin is 1.5 inches and the bottom and right margins are 1 inch each.

**C** You are required to produce a financial report on the salary adjustments made, comparing 2004 and 2005 salaries.
- (a) The report must be addressed to the Board of Directors of Tech Info Corporation.
- (b) The report must inform the Board of Directors of the change in increments and how the new increments will be adjusted.
- (c) The report must give a brief reason for the change.
- (d) The graph from your spreadsheet showing the percentage of workers in each rank of the organisation, and the graph comparing the 2004 salaries to the 2005 salaries, should also be included.

# A solution to the project

## Spreadsheet section

### *Part A: Entering the data*

1 Open the spreadsheet program (Microsoft Excel).

2 Enter the headings in row 5 starting from column A: Employee ID, Surname, First Name, Position Held, Rank, Starting Monthly Salary, Year of Entry and Years of Service in sheet 1.

3 Enter data for 25 employees for each of the fields except Years of Service.

4 Enter in a cell above the table the label "Current Year" and in a cell next to the label the year "2004".

5 Enter the formula to calculate Years of Service where Years of Service = Current Year – Year of Entry. Use absolute referencing to refer to the cell holding the 'Current Year' value. Example: =$H$2–G6

6 Place the formula in the remaining cells below by filling down.

## Part B: Determining the annual salaries from 2000 to 2005

1 Copy Sheet 1 so as to create five more sheets for the years 2000–2004, by:
   (a) Selecting **Move or Copy Sheet** from the **Edit** menu. The 'Move or Copy Sheet' dialogue box will appear
   (b) Selecting the sheet to copy
   (c) Checking the **Create a Copy** box
   (d) Optional – you can rename the sheet by right-clicking on the sheet tab and choosing **Rename** from the pop-up menu.

2 Enter the headings "Current Year", and "2000", "2001", "2002", "2003", "2004", in their respective boxes on their respective sheets.

3 For each employee enter a formula to calculate the first year salary for that employee by multiplying the starting monthly salary by 12. Place the formula in the cell that indicates the year of entry for that employee. Example: = F6*12 where F6 contains the starting monthly salary of that employee.

4 Enter the formula to determine the salaries for the remaining years until 2004. This formula has two parts: (a) to determine the increment, (b) to determine the final salary by adding the salary to the increment.
   (a) To determine the increment:
      (i) Enter in a cell above the table the label "% Increment" and in a cell next to the label "2%".
      (ii) To do this you have to determine if the employee's rank is greater than or equal to 3. If it is, you multiply the previous year's monthly salary by 2% otherwise you multiply it by 0%. This requires you to use the IF function. Remember, the IF function is written in three parts:
      IF(Logical_Test,Value_If_True,Value_If_False)
         - The Logical_Test part determines if the employee's rank is greater than or equal to 3.
         - The Value_If_True part multiplies the employee's previous year's monthly salary by 2%.
         - The Value_If_False part multiplies the employee's previous year's monthly salary by 0%. Multiplying the employee's previous year's monthly salary by 0% will give $0.00 dollars as the increment.
           Example: IF(Rank > =3,%increment*previous year's monthly salary,0%*previous year's monthly salary)
           =IF($E$6 > =3,$F$2*J6,0%*J6) This calculates the increment.
   (b) To determine the final monthly salary add the salary to the increment: =(IF($E$6 > =3,$F$2*J6,0%*J6)+J6
   (c) Fill across to put the formula in the cells up to the year 2004 for that employee.
   (d) Repeat steps (a) to (c) for each employee.
   (e) Select all the salaries and place them in currency format by clicking the **Currency** $ button on the toolbar.

> *Note:* Absolute referencing is used for the 'Rank' and the '% Increment' as these values do not change as you fill across.

### Part C: Modifying the spreadsheet to reflect the new agreement for 2005

1 Add the heading 2005.

2 Enter the formula to calculate the 2005 salaries using the information provided.

This requires the use of the nested IF function:

=IF(celladdress>=2,M6*2%,IF(celladdress>=3,M6*3%,IF(celladdress>=4,M6*5%,M6*7%)))

In the example, the second IF statement is also the Value_if_False argument/part to the first IF statement.

Similarly, the third IF statement is the Value_if_False argument to the second IF statement.

For example, if the first Logical_Test (Years of Service>=2) is TRUE, the increment I8*2% is calculated.

If the first Logical_Test is FALSE, the second IF statement is evaluated, and so on.

A function can contain up to seven levels of nested functions.

=IF(Years of Service>=2,M6*2%,IF(Years of Service>=3,M6*3%,IF(Years of Service >=4,M6*5%,M6*7%)))

IF(H6>=2,M6*2%,IF(H6>=3,M6*3%,IF(H6>=4,M6*5%,M6*7%)))

To determine the 2005 salary by adding the 2004 salary to the increment

=(IF(H6>=2,M6*2%,IF(H6>=3,M6*3%,IF(H6>=4,M6*5%,M6*7%))))+M6

### Part D: To determine the greatest and least salary increase in 2005

1 Insert the heading "Salary Increase" next to the 2005 salary.

2 Enter the formula to determine the salary increase by subtracting the 2004 salary from the 2005 salary. Example: =N6–M6

3 Place the formula in the remaining cells by filling down.

4 Four cells below the table enter the labels "Greatest Increase" and "Least Increase".

5 Enter the formula for Greatest Increase. Example: =MAX(O6:O30)

6 Enter the formula for Least Increase. Example: =MIN(O6:O30)

### Part E: Add two new employee records

1 After the last employee record insert the given data for the two new employees Davanand Singh and Jessie Romero.

2 Insert the Rank and Entering Salary corresponding to their position.

3 Enter the formula to calculate their salary for the year of entry for the employees.

4 Enter the formula for the 2005 salary by filling down.

5 Recalculate the Greatest Increase and Least Increase by changing the range to include the two new employees.

**Remember:**

If you only select the column with the surname the surnames will sort and the rest of the table will remain the same.

### Part F: Sorting the worksheet on employee name

1 Select *all* the employee records including the headings, that is, from Employee ID to Salary Increase and from the first employee record to the last.

2 Select **Sort** from the **Data** menu.

3 In the 'Sort by' box select **Surname**. Ascending is the default sort order.
4 In the 'Then by' box select **First Name**.
5 In the 'My data range has' section of the dialogue box, make sure that a 'Header row' is selected. This indicates that your table has headings.
6 Click **OK**.

## Part G: Extracting records based on particular criteria

1 Two rows above the 'Entering Salary' heading copy the 'Entering Salary' heading.
2 Enter the criterion " >8000" below the heading you just copied.
3 Two rows above the 'Year of Entry' heading copy the 'Year of Entry' heading.
4 Enter the criterion " > =2002" below the heading you just copied.
5 Select all the employee records including the headings, that is, from Employee ID to Salary Increase and from the first employee record to the last.
6 Select **Filter** from the **Data** menu and then choose **Advanced Filter**. The 'Advanced Filter' dialogue box will appear.
7 Click the radio button **Copy to another location**.
8 The **Data Range** has already been selected when you selected all the employee records.
9 Click in the **Criteria Range** box and select the criteria that you placed above the table. Select the headings 'Entering Salary' to 'Year of Entry' as well as the values placed below these headings ' >8000' and ' > =2002'. The following range will appear in the Criteria Range box: $F$3:$G$4
10 Click in the **Copy to** box and a few rows below the table click in column A.
11 Click **OK**.

## Part H: Summary table to show percentage employees in each rank

1 Click on a new worksheet. If there are only two worksheets showing, select **Worksheet** from the **Insert** menu to insert a worksheet.
2 Create a table with the headings 'Rank', 'Number of Employees' and 'Percentage'.
3 Enter the ranks 1 to 6.
4 Enter the formula to calculate the number of employees using the COUNTIF function.
5 The COUNTIF function is divided into two parts:
=COUNTIF(Range,Criteria)
- The range is the list of employee ranks in Sheet2. Since this range does not change you need to use absolute referencing.
- The criterion is the rank that it is being checked against in the summary table. Example: =COUNTIF('Sheet2'!$E$6:$E$32,A5)

6 Enter the formula to find the total number of employees. Example: =SUM(B5:B10)
7 Enter the formula to calculate the percentage of employees in each rank; that is, the number of employees in a rank divided by the total number of employees. Then click on the percentage button on your toolbar. Example: =B5/$B$11. Remember you need to use absolute referencing so that the total number of employees does not change when you fill down.

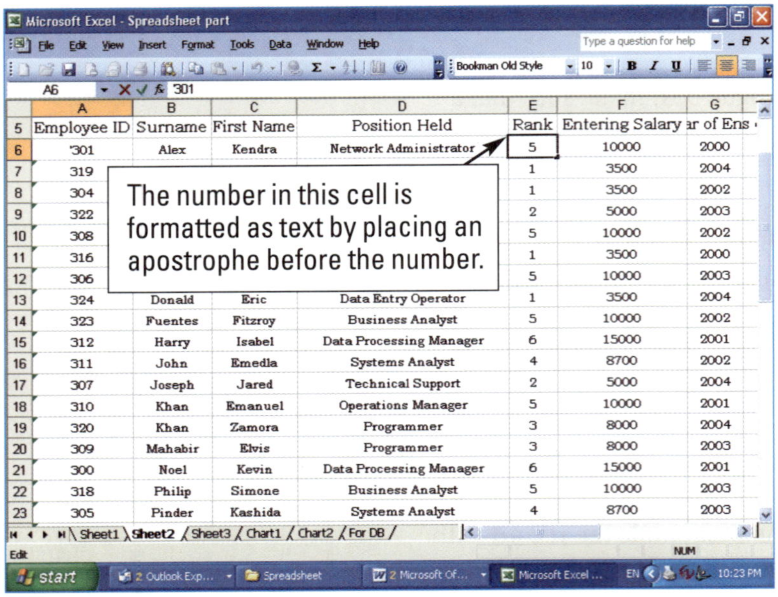


*Figure 13.24 Numbers formatted as text*

## Part I: Creating a pie chart to show the percentage of employees per rank

1. Since the ranks are numbers you need to format these numbers as text by placing an apostrophe before the number. Example: '5 (Figure 13.24).
2. Select the ranks and percentages by holding the Ctrl key.
3. Click the Chart Wizard button on the toolbar or select **Chart** from the **Insert** menu. The 'Chart Wizard' dialogue box will appear.
4. Select the type of chart **Pie** from the 'Standard Types' box and select the **Chart** sub-type.
5. Click the **Next** button.
6. The **Data Range** has already been selected. Click **Next** to continue to the next window.
7. Click the **Titles** tab and enter a title for your chart in the 'Chart Title' box.
8. Click the **Legend** tab and select the placement of the legend.
9. Click the **Data Labels** tab and check the **Percentage** box. Click the **Next** button to move to the next window.
10. Click the radio button **As a new sheet** to allow the chart to appear in a new sheet.

## Part J: Creating a graph to show the differences in the 2004 and 2005 salaries

1. Since the Employee IDs are numbers you need to format these numbers as text by placing an apostrophe before the number. Example: '301
2. You also need to format the headings 2004 and 2005 as text.
3. Select the Employee IDs, the 2004 and 2005 salaries of all the employees by holding the Ctrl key.
4. Click the Chart Wizard button on the toolbar or select **Chart** from the **Insert** menu. The 'Chart Wizard' dialogue box will appear.
5. Select the type of chart, **Bar** or **Column**, from the 'Standard Types' box and select the **Chart** sub-type.
6. Click the **Next** button.
7. The **Data Range** has already been selected. Click **Next** to continue to the next window.
8. Click the **Titles** tab and enter a title for your chart in the 'Chart Title' box.
9. Enter a title for the x-axis in the 'Category (x) axis' box.
10. Enter a title for the y-axis in the 'Value (y) axis' box.
11. Click the **Legend** tab and select the placement of the legend.
12. Click the **Next** button to move to the next window.
13. Click the radio button **As a new sheet** to allow the chart to appear in a new sheet.

## Database section

### Part A: Importing the spreadsheet data into the database

1 From the spreadsheet create a new worksheet by choosing **Worksheet** from the **Insert** menu.

*Optional:* You can rename the sheet by right-clicking on the sheet tab, choosing **Rename** from the pop-up menu and naming it 'For DB'.

2 Select the employee data from 'Sheet2' including all the headings.

(a) Click on the worksheet you created, that is, 'For DB'.

(b) Right-click on the first cell in the sheet –A1– and select **Paste special** from the pop-up menu. The 'Paste Special' dialogue box will appear.

(c) Click the radio button for **Values** from the 'Paste' section of the dialogue box.

3 Save and close the spreadsheet.

4 Open a blank database.

5 Select **Get External Data** from the **File** menu, then choose **Import**.

6 Choose the location of the file from the 'Look in' box.

7 From the **Files of type** select **Microsoft Excel**.

8 Select the Excel file and click the **Import** button.

9 Select the worksheet that contains the data for the database table – 'For DB'. Click the **Next** button.

10 Indicate by checking the box **First Row Contains Column Headings**. Click the **Next** button.

11 Click the radio button **In a New Table** to indicate where to store the data. Click the **Next** button.

12 *Optional*: You can further specify or modify information about each field; however, just click the **Next** button to move on to the next screen.

13 Click the radio button **Choose my own primary key** and select Employee ID as the primary key. Click the **Next** button.

14 In the 'Import to Table' box type the name "Salary History" and click the **Finish** button.

15 Open the 'Salary History' table in Design view and modify the data types, field sizes of all the fields, and format of salary to currency format.

### Part B: Creating the 'Employee Information' table

1 Open the database.

2 Click on the **Tables** objects tab.

3
- Double click on **Create table in Design view**, or
- Click on **New** and select **Design View**.

4 Define each of the fields in your table (table definition) – employee ID, name, address, phone number, date of birth and gender.

- Enter the field names in the 'Field Name' column (*Note:* these field names become the headings for your table).
- Select the appropriate data type for that field in the 'Data Type' column.
- Enter text in the 'Description' column. This describes the data that will be entered in this field. (This field is optional.)

## Part C: Deleting Surname and First Name fields from the 'Salary History' table

1. Open the 'Salary History' table in Design view.
2. Select the row(s) to be deleted.
3. Press the Delete key or select **Delete** from the **Edit** menu.

## Part D: Queries

**Query 1:** What are the names, addresses and phone numbers of all the Data Entry Operators?

1. Click on the **Queries** tab under **Objects** on the left side of the screen.
2. Double-click **Create query in Design view** or click on the **New** button (the 'New Query' dialogue box appears) and select **Design View** then click **OK**.
3. Select the 'Employee Information' and the 'Salary History' tables from the 'Show Table' dialogue box.
4. Click the **Tables** tabs and click the **Add** button to add the 'Employee Information' table and the 'Salary History' table. Click the **Close** button.
5. If the two tables are not linked on Employee ID, then link the two tables by dragging the Employee ID of the 'Employee Information' table to the Employee ID of the 'Salary History' table.
6. Add fields (Surname, First Name, Address and Phone Number) from the 'Employee Information' table and the field (Position Held) from the 'Salary History' table to the query grid by double-clicking on the field name in the table boxes, or select the field from the 'Field' row drop-down menus.
7. Enter the criterion 'Data Entry Operator' for the query in the 'Criteria' row of the 'Position Held' field.
8. After selecting all the fields and entering the criteria click the **Run** icon  on the toolbar.
9. Save the query by clicking the **Save** button and give the query the name 'Data Entry Operators qry'.

**Query 2:** List all the employees who occupy position above rank 4.

1. Repeat steps 1–5 from Query 1.
2. Add fields (Employee ID, Surname and First Name) from the 'Employee Information' table and the field (Rank) from the 'Salary History' table to the query grid by double-clicking on the field name in the table boxes, or select the field from the 'Field' row drop-down menus.
3. Enter the criterion " > 4" for the query in the 'Criteria' row of the 'Rank' field.
4. After selecting all the fields and entering the criteria click the **Run** icon on the toolbar.
5. Save the query by clicking the **Save** button and give the query the title 'Above Rank 4 qry'.

**Query 3:** List all employees and their salaries for 2005.

1. Repeat steps 1–5 from Query 1.
2. Add fields (Employee ID, Surname and First Name) from the 'Employee Information' table and the field (2005) from the 'Salary History' table to the query grid by double-clicking on the field name in the table boxes; or select the field from the 'Field' row drop-down menus.

3 After selecting all the fields and entering the criteria click the **Run** icon on the toolbar.

4 Save the query by clicking the **Save** button and give the query the title '2005 Salary qry'.

**Query 4:** What is the total sum of money that has been paid out in increments during the year 2003 by Tech Info Corporation?

- To perform this query you need first to determine what was the increment paid to each employee in 2003 by subtracting the 2002 salary from the 2003 salary.
- You need to find the grand total of all the employees' increments for the year 2003.

To perform the first step you need to perform a calculated query.

1 Repeat steps 1–4 from Query 1.

2 Click the **Tables** tab and click the **Add** button to add the 'Salary History' table. Click the **Close** button.

3 Add fields (Employee ID, 2002 and 2003) from the 'Salary History' table to the query grid by double-clicking on the field name in the table boxes; or select the field from the 'Field' row drop-down menus.

4 Select the next empty field in the query grid.

5 Type the new field name "Increment" followed by a colon (:).

6 Use the Expression Builder or write the formula using the field names that form part of the expression, each in square brackets along with the relevant operators. Example: Increment:[2003]–[2002]

7 Click in the **Show** box of the field to display the new calculated field.

8 After selecting all the fields and entering the criteria click the Run icon on the toolbar.

9 Save the query by clicking the **Save** button and give the query the title 'Employee Increments qry'.

To perform the second step you need to find the grand total of all the employees' increments.

1 Repeat steps 1–4 from Query 1.

2 Click the **Queries** tab and click the **Add** button to add the 'Employee Increments qry' query. Click the **Close** button.

3 Add the field (Increment) from the 'Employee Increments qry' query to the query grid by double-clicking on the field name in the table boxes; or select the field from the 'Field' row drop-down menus.

4 Click on the **Totals** icon (Σ) on the toolbar or select **Totals** from the **View** menu.

5 Click on the drop-down arrow of the 'Totals' row of the 'Increment' field and select the **SUM** function.

6 Run and save your query.

**Query 5:** Create a query to determine the salaries for 2004 of all employees who entered the organisation before the year 2003.

1 Repeat steps 1–5 from Query 1.

2 Add fields (Employee ID, Surname and First Name) from the 'Employee Information' table and the fields (Year of Entry and 2004) from the 'Salary History' table to the query grid by double-clicking on the field name in the table boxes; or select the field from the 'Field' row drop-down menus.

3 Enter the criterion "< 2003" for the query in the 'Criteria' row of the 'Year of Entry' field.

4 After selecting all the fields and entering the criteria click the Run icon on the toolbar.
5 Save the query by clicking the **Save** button and give the query the title '2004 Salaries qry'.

> *Note:* this must be done for each table separately.

### *Part E: Delete all the records related to Davanand Singh, Employee ID 339*

1 Repeat steps 1–5 from Query 1.
2 Select **Delete Query** from the **Query** drop-down menu on the toolbar.
3 Add field (Employee ID) from the 'Employee Information' table to the query grid by double-clicking on the field name in the table boxes; or select the field from the 'Field' row drop-down menus.
4 Select **Where** from the drop-down list in the 'Delete' row of the field.
5 Enter the criterion "339" for the query in the 'Criteria' row of the 'Employee ID' field.
6 After selecting all the fields and entering the criteria click the **Run** icon on the toolbar.
7 You do not need to save this query since, once the data is deleted, if the query is run again there will be no records to delete as the record has already been deleted.

> *Note:* you must delete Davanand's records from *both* tables.

You can also open the table, search for the record and click on the **Record selector** tab of the record to delete and click on the **Delete Record** button on the toolbar.

### *Part F: Creating the report*

1 Double-click on **Create report by using wizard**. The 'Report Wizard' window appears and takes you through a series of options.
2 Select the 'Salary History' table: it contains all the fields you want displayed in the report. Transfer the fields (Employee Number, Starting Salary, Rank, Position Held, Year of Entry and Salary Payments 2000–2005) from the 'Available Fields' window to the 'Selected Fields' window. This can be done by double-clicking on the field name or clicking on the single right arrow button > to move the fields across one at a time. Once all the fields are selected click **Next** to move to the next screen.
3 This screen allows you the option to group your records. Group the records according to the Rank.
4 Click the **Next** button to move to the next screen. The 'Sort Order' dialogue box appears. If the records are to be sorted, you can set the sort order here. Select the field 'Employee ID' to sort and click the **A-Z** sort button to choose from ascending order. Click **Next** to move to the next screen.
5 Select a layout and page orientation for the report and click **Next** to move to the next screen.
6 Select the style for your report. This option allows you to choose the colour, font and graphic style for your report. Click **Next** to move to the final screen.
7 This screen allows you to give your report a name, and select whether to open it in **Print Preview** or **Design View**. The default is Print Preview. Click the **Finish** button to create the report.

## Word processing section

### Part A: Creating a letterhead with the company's logo

1 Adjust the margin for each letter so that the top margin is 2 inches in order to accommodate the letterhead, the left margin is 1.5 inches and the bottom and right margins are 1 inch. To do this:

(a) Select **Page Setup** from the **File** menu.

(b) Click on the **Margins** tab and change the top margin to 2 inches, left margin to 1.5 inches and bottom and right margins to 1 inch.

2 Select **Header and Footer** from the **View** menu.

3 Move to the Header section and create your letterhead. Make the letterhead attractive, include:

- The name of the company in a larger font
- The address, phone/fax number, e-mail address and web site address
- The logo, which can be letters, a picture, a graphic or a symbol
- Borders and other formatting features.

### Part B: Creating the primary document and merging to a new document

Before you start you may need to check your database to ensure that all the fields required for the merge are in one table. If the data is in more than one table then you may need to create a query to hold all the information you need to use in the letter.

1 Create your main document by typing a suitable letter, using areas designated to hold the data by typing dummy field names enclosed in double angle-brackets, e.g. < < Name > >. This is necessary so that the field codes will be inserted in the correct positions. Include all necessary information that is required. Save your document.

2 Select **Letters and Mailings** from the **Tools** menu.

3 Select **Mail Merge**. The 'Mail Merge Wizard' task pane appears. The **task pane** appears on the right side of the Word document window and allows you to choose from available options to perform your task.

4 Check the **Letters** radio button and click on **Next: Starting document** at the bottom of the dialogue box to move to the next step.

5 Check the **Use the current document** option and click the **Next** button.

6 In the 'Select recipients' dialogue box you have to indicate the location of the recipients (data source). Since your data file will be coming from Access or Excel you need to check the radio button for the option **Use an existing list** and then select **Browse**.

7 Select the data source and click **Open**.

8 Select the table/query that will be used as the data source and click **OK**.

9 The 'Mail Merge Recipient' box appears, showing all records that are listed in the data source.

10 The main document appears and the **Insert Merge Field** button in the mail merge toolbar is activated. The next step is to insert the merge fields into the main document. Position your insertion point where the first merge field is to be inserted into the document.

11 Click on the **Insert Merge Field** button, the 'Insert Merge Field' dialogue box appears.

12 Select the desired field and click the **Insert** button. The field appears in the position you indicated.

13 Place all the other fields in their respective positions.

14 Once all the fields have been entered, click on the **Merge to a New Document** button. The individual mailing letters will be created in the new document.

15 Save both documents.

### *Part C: Produce a financial report on the salary adjustments*

- You can be creative in the design of your report: you can use the letterhead created earlier.
- Write the report, making sure that it is addressed to the Board of Directors of the company.
- Ensure that your report has a heading.
- Indicate who the report is coming from.
- The report must also be dated.

Insert the charts in the appropriate positions to do this:

1 Open the Word document (that is your report).

2 Open the Excel workbook containing your charts.

3 Click the appropriate worksheet and select the data/chart required.

4 Select **Copy**.

5 Click the Word document on the task bar to make it active.

6 Position the cursor in the Word document where you would like to begin to insert the data or chart.

7 Click on the Paste icon or select **Paste** from the **Edit** menu.

## Mark Scheme

### *Spreadsheet*

| **Criteria** | | **Marks** |
|---|---|---|
| Spreadsheet format/layout<br>Use appropriate format ($, %, etc.) and layout for spreadsheet which permits required information to be easily discerned | | **2** |
| Enter accurate salary for appropriate rank | | **1** |
| Use appropriate absolute references | | **1** |
| Enter formulae throughout worksheet | | |
| Formulae for calculating 2000–2004 salaries | 2 | |
| Formulae for 2005 salaries | 2 | |
| Formulae for max and min | 1 | |
| Formulae for summary sheet | 1 | |
| Use only some formulae correctly (2) | | **6** |
| Create summary table | | **2** |
| Entering two records Only 1 record entered (0) | | **1** |
| Extract records according to criteria | | **2** |
| Sort data in spreadsheet on surname | | **1** |
| Create graph correctly with appropriate labels | | |
| Accurate pie chart | 2 | |
| Accurate bar/column chart | 2 | **4** |
| TOTAL | | **20** |

| Criteria | Marks | |
|---|---|---|
| Importing table from spreadsheet | 1 | |
| Save as 'Salary History' | 1 | **2** |
| Good database file structure (both tables) | | |
| (no marks if adjusted only in one table) | | |
| All fields included | 1 | |
| Used appropriate field type/width | 1 | |
| Used appropriate indexes | 1 | **3** |
| Perform all stated queries | | |
| Data Entry Operators query | 1 | |
| Rank query | 1 | |
| 2005 salaries query | 1 | |
| Increments query | 3 | |
| 2004 salary query | 1 | **7** |
| Delete all stated records | | |
| (Records in one table deleted 1mark) | | **2** |
| Generation of report | | |
| Include all fields | 1 | |
| Used grouping order | 1 | |
| Used sorting order | 1 | |
| Appropriate title | 1 | **4** |
| Presentation | | |
| All parts required printouts submitted | 1 | |
| Candidate's database assignment was submitted in a coherent manner | 1 | **2** |
| **TOTAL** | | **20** |

| Criteria | Marks | |
|---|---|---|
| Creation of company letterhead | | |
| Attractive and effective design of company letterhead | 1 | |
| Company's name prominently displayed | 1 | |
| Company's logo | 1 | |
| All information included | 1 | **4** |
| Correct format of merged letters | | |
| All information included in primary document | 1 | |
| Use data source from the database or spreadsheet | 1 | |
| Use all required fields | 1 | **3** |
| Creation of appropriate main primary document | | |
| Insert merge fields in appropriate sections of primary document | 1 | |
| Correct merge (no change) | 1 | **2** |
| Header/Footer | | **2** |
| Setting appropriate margins | | **1** |
| Report | | |
| All information included in report | 3 | |
| Use at least two or more formatting features (e.g. bold, underline, etc.) | 2 | **5** |
| Importing files | | |
| Importing charts from spreadsheet | 2 | |
| Graphs/charts resized appropriately to fit in desired location | 1 | **3** |
| **TOTAL** | | **20** |

## Summary

1 A mail merge can be performed using an Access table or Excel table as the data source.

2 The steps involved in performing a mail merge using an Access or Excel table as the data source are:
- selecting the document type
- selecting the starting document
- selecting the recipients
- writing your letter
- previewing your letters
- completing the merge.

3 Data and graphs from an Excel spreadsheet can be moved to a Word document by selecting the required data or graph and cutting/copying and pasting into the Word document.

4 Access objects such as tables, queries and reports can be published in a Word document.

5 Tables from an Access database can be copied to Excel to be worked on.

6 A spreadsheet table can be imported into an Access table. This may be necessary if you would like to perform more in-depth queries on your data.

# 14 Careers in computing

## OBJECTIVES

At the end of this chapter you will be able to:

- List a number of careers available in the field of ICT
- State the job functions of different personnel in the computing field

Information and Communication Technology (ICT) has a significant impact on almost all facets of our daily lives. ICT is now used in our homes, our schools, health centres, banks and many other organisations in society. With changes in technology and the expansion of the ICT industry, new skills are now required in many of our institutions and workplaces, to design and develop new hardware and software systems and to incorporate new technologies. Every day the local newspapers in many Caribbean countries contain numerous advertisements aimed at finding people to fill the many jobs available in the computer field.

This chapter looks at the job descriptions of people in the Data Processing (ICT) departments of large organisations such as banks, insurance companies, government agencies and educational establishments. For smaller companies or organisations, the range of personnel will be much smaller, and the overlap in duties more extensive. We also look at some job descriptions for people who work in the ICT industry but who may not be part of an ICT department within a company.

## Jobs in an ICT department

### Information systems (ICT or data processing) manager

The ICT manager is responsible for planning, co-ordinating, managing and staffing the Information Systems department of a large organisation. The ICT manager plays an important role in defining the technological direction of the organisation. As such he/she must clearly understand the organisation's purpose and goals, and its unique data processing needs.

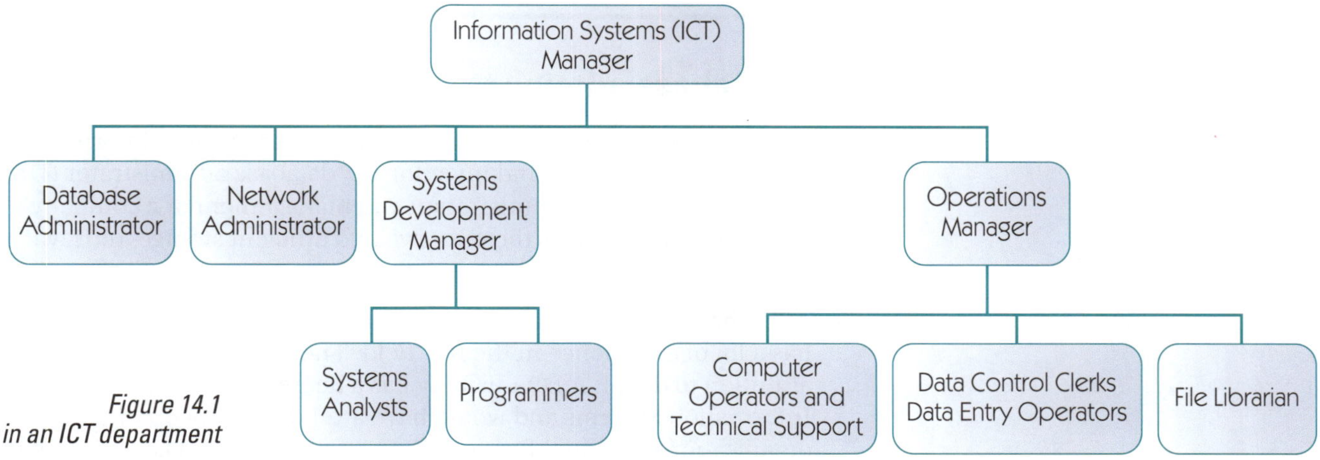


*Figure 14.1 Jobs in an ICT department*

An ICT manager must be aware of the latest developments in the ICT field and be able to chart the long-term vision, plans and policies of the way in which ICT can be used in the organisation.

Much of an ICT manager's time is spent reading reports on the system's performance and on developing strategies to improve it. A fair amount of time is also spent meeting users and members of other departments to discuss problems encountered with the system or new projects for computerisation. He/she is also responsible for preparing budget projections for the department, including the cost of new hardware and software for upgrades and the training of employees.

An ICT manager is usually someone who has been in the ICT field for a number of years and has considerable technical and managerial skills. Many ICT managers started off either as programmers or systems or business analysts and worked their way up. They must possess strong interpersonal skills, since a major part of the job is people-oriented. They should be good leaders and must be capable of motivating their staff to perform at their best as well as commanding the respect of other company executives.

People planning to seek a career in information systems management should pursue degree courses in computer studies, along with extra studies such as business administration and human resource management. Many information systems managers are now required also to possess a Master of Business Administration (MBA) degree with a strong emphasis on information technology along with other business courses.

### Summary of duties

- Plan, co-ordinate, manage and staff the data processing department
- Communicate with, motivate and lead a number of highly skilled people
- Be aware of the latest developments in the ICT field
- Read reports on the system's performance and develop strategies to improve it
- Meet users and members of other departments to discuss problems encountered with the system or new projects for computerisation
- Prepare budget projections for the department, including the cost of new hardware and software and the training of employees

## Database administrator

Many organisations have computer databases that store information on employees, customers and inventory. A database administrator (DBA) is responsible for the administration and management of a company's database. This involves the effective and efficient storage, retrieval, customisation and archiving of data.

A database administrator is usually someone who can think logically and has a lot of experience in the ICT field. They must also be able to pay close attention to detail. A DBA usually has a degree in Computer Studies or Information Systems and would have attended many other courses. In large organisations, the qualifications may also include a Masters Degree in Computer Science with an emphasis on database design,or an MBA.

### Summary of duties

- Interact with managers and users to ensure that the database is accomplishing what they need
- Meet with users to make modifications to the database whenever there are changes in the company's operation
- Ensure that the database is performing at its optimum at all times to meet the needs of its users
- Develop policies and procedures to ensure the security and integrity of the system
- Select and maintain database management software
- Co-ordinate database design
- Establish back-up and recovery procedure in case of failure or loss of data
- Establish a data dictionary that records company-wide data definitions and standards
- Co-ordinate the data collection and storage needs of users

## Systems development manager

A systems development manager is responsible for the development, implementation and maintenance of a company's computerised system. In companies with smaller information systems departments the systems development manager's job may be subsumed into that of the information systems manager.

### Summary of duties

- Manage teams of information systems personnel (systems analysts, engineers, programmers, technicians and others) to design, develop, implement, operate and administer computer software
- Oversee the professional development and training of personnel under his/her supervision

## Systems analyst

A systems analyst looks at the operations of a manual or computerised system in an organisation or company and tries to find solutions to specific end-user problems by implementing a new computerised system or upgrading an existing one. He/she is directly in charge of the development of the system from start to finish.

Before embarking on a project, the systems analyst must have a thorough understanding of the existing system. This is done by planning and conducting studies to determine if the existing system needs to be upgraded, or if a new system has to be put in place. The systems analyst then conducts a feasibility study and prepares a report giving:

- An analysis of the present system
- A proposal for a new or upgraded system (if required), including the hardware, software and personnel costs.

This study is presented to management, who will make the decision whether or not to continue with the project. If they approve, the analyst moves on to the next phase – designing the new system.

To accomplish this task, the analyst has to hold discussions with managers and users of the system to determine their exact needs. The input, output and processing specifications are worked out.

This leads to the implementation phase. The analyst can decide to purchase appropriate software if it is available or to direct a programming team to develop new software. If the programs are to be developed in-house, they are coded and tested to ensure they meet the needs of the users and management. If hardware has to be bought, the analyst is the person who makes recommendations and helps in the procurement.

After the programs have been fully tested and debugged, the system is then installed. The analyst has to ensure a smooth transition from the old system to the new. After the installation is complete, the systems analyst has to evaluate the performance of the system over a period of time to see if it is performing as expected.

The job of a systems analyst can be very demanding and challenging. To be able to perform the job competently requires skills in the following areas:

- *Analysis/problem solving*. A major part of the job depends on the ability of the individual to define problems and then to use a methodical and structured approach to solving them. The systems analyst must also be able to find and evaluate alternative solutions so that the best method is used to solve a particular problem.
- *Communication.* Good systems analysts must be able to express their thoughts clearly in speech and in writing. A significant part of the systems analysis process requires that they meet with users and managers to obtain information and make presentations.
- *Business.* Many systems analysts work in business organisations. Having a strong business background allows them to develop better systems, because they can see the wider uses and implications of their systems for the overall success and profitability of the company.

The educational backgrounds of systems analysts vary, but a degree in Computer Studies or equivalent is generally required.

### Summary of duties

- Plan and conduct studies to determine if the existing system needs to be upgraded or if a new system has to be put in place
- Hold discussions with managers and users of the system to determine their exact needs
- Gather facts about, and analyse the basic methods and procedures of, current information systems
- Design new systems, integrate existing procedures into new system specifications as required, and assist in the implementation of new designs
- Make recommendations for the procurement of hardware and software if necessary
- Test and debug the new system
- Create documentation for the system
- Assist in training employees to use the system
- Evaluate the performance of the system over a period of time to see if it performing as expected

## Programmer

Computer programmers are individuals whose main job function is programming. Programmers write programs according to specifications determined mainly by computer engineers or systems analysts. Besides writing new programs, programmers also update, repair, modify and expand existing programs.

Computer programmers can be classified into two categories, relating to the types of programs they develop. *Application programmers* write software to meet end-user requirements, and may produce applications such as payroll programs, science programs and word processing programs.

*Systems programmers* write systems software, such as programs to monitor and control peripheral devices. Regardless of the category of programmer, the job specifications are the same.

A programmer's job is usually very demanding. Programmers may regularly be called upon to work long hours and weekends in order to meet deadlines. The qualifications for this job vary between a diploma from a technical college and a degree from a university.

### Summary of duties

- Discuss program specifications with the systems analyst
- Write programs
- Test programs for correct operation and intended results
- Debug programs
- Document programs, i.e. produce system/program flowcharts and program listings (a list of variables used and an explanation of their purpose), details of data structures used (files, arrays, etc.), test data and expected output
- Update, repair, modify and expand existing programs

## Network administrator

Network administrators are responsible for the creation, administration and security of computer networks. The creation of a network starts with planning and designing, after which the hardware and software are installed. This is followed by a short period of testing to ensure that the network is functioning properly.

Once the installation problems have been solved, the network administrator starts to set up user accounts and arrangements for access, also ensuring that staff is trained to use the hardware and software that forms part of the network.

The network administrator also monitors the network's performance to ensure it is working at its optimum. In the event of users encountering problems, the network administrator is responsible for trouble shooting and solving problems. She/he is further responsible for creating security policies for the network and for ensuring compliance by its users. This includes regulating access to various computer files and enforcing rules on the changing of passwords.

Network administrators usually have a degree in computer studies along with some professional qualification in networking, for example Microsoft Certified Systems Engineer (MCSE) certification.

### Summary of duties

- Plan and design the network
- Oversee the installation of the network's hardware and software
- Test the network to ensure it is functioning properly
- Set up user accounts and arrangements for access
- Ensure that staff are trained to use the hardware and software that form part of the network
- Monitor the network's performance to ensure it is working at its optimum
- Troubleshoot and solve problems on the network
- Create security policies for the network
- Set up systems to ensure compliance by users of the network

## Operations manager

The operations manager is responsible for the overall operations of a computer department on a daily basis. In companies with small information systems departments the operations manager's job is sometimes performed by the information systems manager.

### Summary of duties

- Supervise the use and maintenance of equipment
- Supervise data reception and preparation
- Schedule processing activities
- Allocate duties to members under his/her charge
- Consult with the data processing manager on staff issues (problems, training and recruitment)

## Computer operator

A computer operator is responsible for monitoring and controlling computer hardware systems – especially mainframes – ensuring the efficient use of these devices. He/she is stationed in the computer room, and monitors and controls a computer system by operating the central console (the main terminal in a mainframe or mini-computer system, used by operators to give instructions to the operating system).

A computer operator usually acquires the skills needed for the work by on-the-job training. Additionally, ordinary level examination passes and a diploma from a technical institute may be required.

### Summary of duties

- Start up and shut down the system
- Respond to messages from system software and carry out the actions required
- Continuously observe the operations of the equipment, and report any faults to the supervisor

- Perform routine equipment maintenance, such as cleaning drive-heads
- Process jobs according to established procedures
- Load input and output units with materials such as tapes for tape drives and paper for printers
- Keep a log of matters such as machine performance, operating records and data processing supplies; maintain inventories and disk- and tape-library records

## Data control clerk

The data control clerk screens, edits and validates the input and output for a data processing unit. She/he also runs scheduled or requested jobs to provide clients with necessary data.

### Summary of duties

- Regulate workflow in accordance with operating schedules
- Be responsible for the receipt, safekeeping and retrieval of data, software, hardware and security items
- Distribute materials on request and follow up on overdue items
- Help with the destruction of information-system materials

## Data-entry operator

A data-entry operator enters data into a system in a form that is suitable for processing. The individual must have a general knowledge of data-entry machines and their operations and an ability to enter data at a rapid rate with very few errors.

### Summary of duties

- Transcribe data from a variety of source documents into the computer
- Keep records on the data transcribed
- Verify the data entered

## File librarian

A file librarian is responsible for keeping a company's data files and software organised and up to date.

### Summary of duties

- Maintain and protect the company's programs and data
- Catalogue and store magnetic tapes and disks
- Supply magnetic tapes and disks to authorised users
- Clean and inspect storage media
- Keep records of the disks and magnetic tapes stored

# Other jobs within the computer industry

## Data security analyst

Security problems have become more prevalent with the spread of networks, since skilled hackers from outside an organisation may find it easy to gain access to a company's network. A data security analyst looks after the protection of a company's computer-based information banks, and is responsible for keeping information safe from floods, fire, power outages, fraud, theft, invasion of privacy and viruses. A security analyst has constantly to analyse and assess the potential threats to a computer system.

The job entails working with different types of security software, including tools such as Nmap, which constantly scans the ports into the network from outside, and monitoring tools such as SpyNet. A security analyst also has to keep up to date with cryptographic tools and techniques, and with all the different types of security hardware and software. In-depth knowledge of operating systems such as Unix and Windows NT networking, especially in TCP/IP communications and firewall technologies, is also required.

The educational background needed by someone in this field depends on the sensitivity of the data and the complexity of the network. Having a degree in Computer Studies, along with extra certificates in networking such as Microsoft Certified Systems Engineer (MCSE) and CISCO courses, is a distinct advantage.

### Summary of duties

- Keep information safe from floods, fire, power outages, fraud, theft, invasion of privacy and viruses
- Analyse and assess the potential threats to a computer system
- Set up procedures to protect vulnerable information
- Develop, document and implement data security policies, standards and guidelines
- Identify and fix security vulnerabilities
- Work with different types of security software
- Ensure there are no security loopholes
- Conduct 'raids' on the system to try to expose security loopholes
- Keep up to date with cryptographic tools and techniques, and with all the different types of security hardware and software
- Have in-depth knowledge of operating systems and networking technology

## Computer consultant

A computer consultant is required to give an independent and objective opinion on how ICT can be used to meet the needs of an organisation. He/she is usually contracted for a short period of time to provide technical assistance to an organisation in areas such as systems analysis, design and programming, in the formation or upgrading of a data processing department. A computer consultant is required to upgrade his/her skills constantly and keep in touch with the latest technology in the field. He/she is usually someone with a lot of working experience in the field and usually has a first degree in Information Systems and Management, along with a masters degree in Computer Science or Business Administration.

**Summary of duties**

- Hold discussions with users to identify and clarify their information needs
- Identify and evaluate potential hardware and software
- Assist in the design, development and implementation of a company's computer system
- Assist in the development of programs, applications and documentation
- Develop training programmes for users

## Electronic data processing (EDP) auditor

EDP auditors ensure that all aspects of a company's information systems perform in the manner stated in the system design. EDP auditors provide information systems managers with expert opinions about the reliability of results and operations of computer systems. An individual interested in this job must have a logical and analytical approach to investigation, and the ability to pay close attention to detail. The individual usually has a lot of experience in the computer field and possesses a degree in Computing or Information Systems and Management.

**Summary of duties**

- Inspect programs, systems, operational procedures, documentation, control techniques, disaster plans, insurance protection and fire protection
- Use sample data to test the accuracy of computer programs and the control procedures that are built into them
- Check and report on the use of computing facilities
- Examine the input and output of programs for accuracy (an auditor will report any discrepancies to upper management)
- Make recommendations for changes to ensure system integrity and accuracy (these recommendations are frequently implemented by the data security analyst)

## Web-page designer

The world wide web (www) is growing at a tremendous rate and so too are the business activities that are transacted over it. To conduct business over the web, a company must advertise, which requires the building and maintenance of a web site. A web site consists of web pages. A web-page designer creates web pages containing information such as text and graphics. Web-site development is not as difficult a task as it once was, since there are now many packages available, such as Microsoft FrontPage, ColdFusion or Macromedia Dreamweaver, that make the task easier.

There are no formal qualifications for designing web sites, but a background in programming will help, since some developers choose to create their sites using HTML or Java languages directly. Any prior experience in graphic art would also definitely be an asset, as many people consider web-page design to be more an artistic field than an exercise in programming. Web-page designers frequently consult with graphic artists when developing web sites. A **webmaster** may be responsible for all of the above duties, with an added emphasis on maintenance, expansion and improvement of the existing web sites.

### Summary of duties

- Ensure that all the links on the site work and the site is easy to navigate
- Ensure the site contains the required information
- Develop a visually stimulating web site
- Run the web server software
- Find and install tools to create web content
- Maintain and improve existing web pages

## Computer engineer

Computer engineers are found at all levels of the computer industry. They design, develop, test and supervise the manufacture of components (such as new computer chips or circuit boards) and peripheral devices. If the company employing them is a large one, a different set of engineers will take care of the assembly and testing of new designs for overall effectiveness, cost, reliability and safety.

Some computer engineers working for hardware dealers or manufacturers are also responsible for maintaining and repairing computer hardware sold to clients.

### Summary of duties

- Design, develop, test and supervise the manufacture of components (such as new computer chips or circuit boards) and peripheral devices
- Assemble and test new designs for overall effectiveness, cost, reliability and safety
- Maintain and repair computer hardware sold to clients

## Computer sales representative

Sales representatives are important to any organisation, since they are the ones responsible for bringing in the company's profits. Computer sales representatives must have an understanding of the products they are selling, whether hardware, software or services. This is especially necessary in the case of hardware and software since the representative may often have to do demonstrations for customers. She/he also needs to stay abreast of the changing needs of clients and the new products that are available to satisfy their needs.

Depending on the company and product being sold, a sales representative may work in a display room, or visit the business premises of clients, or both. The qualifications for this job may be ordinary level passes and a good knowledge of computers, or specialised training in computer repairs and computer applications, or a degree in computers. A sales representative should have good communication skills, a pleasant personality and patience. They also need to have a shrewd business sense, since part of their earnings usually comes from commission on sales.

### Summary of duties

- Explain the specifications, functions and capabilities of hardware and/or software products to their company's customers
- Help customers to install new equipment
- Attend trade shows and seminars to keep abreast of the latest trends or products in the field
- Demonstrate equipment to clients

## Other ICT jobs

The computer games industry is rapidly expanding and has created a whole new range of jobs, including games programmer, games artist, games designer and games tester.

Others jobs available in the IT field include technical writer, ICT journalist, lecturer, trainer and e-commerce specialist.

As the ICT industry expands and computers become more ingrained in our society, ICT skills will continue to change but will be in greater demand.

## Summary

1 The ICT manager is responsible for planning, co-ordinating, managing and staffing the information systems department of a large organisation.

2 A database administrator (DBA) is responsible for the administration and management of a company's database.

3 A systems analyst looks at the operations of a manual or computerised system in an organisation or company and tries to find solutions to specific end-user problems by implementing a new computerised system or upgrading an existing one.

4 Programmers write programs according to specifications determined mainly by computer engineers or systems analysts. Besides writing new programs, programmers also update, repair, modify and expand existing programs.

5 Network administrators are responsible for the creation, administration and security of computer networks.

6 The operations manager is responsible for the overall operations of a computer department on a daily basis. In organisations with smaller information systems departments this function may be performed by the information systems manager.

7 A computer operator is responsible for monitoring and controlling computer hardware systems, especially mainframes, ensuring the efficient use of these devices. This is done through the central console (the main terminal in a mainframe or mini-computer system).

8 The data control clerk screens, edits and validates the input and output for a data-processing unit.

9 A data-entry operator enters data into a system in a form that is suitable for processing. The individual must have a general knowledge of data entry machines and their operations and an ability to enter data at a rapid rate with very few errors.

10 A file librarian is responsible for keeping a company's data files and software organised and up to date.

11 A data security analyst looks after the protection of a company's computer-based information banks, and is responsible for keeping information safe from floods, fire, power outages, fraud, theft, invasion of privacy and viruses.

12 A computer consultant provides technical assistance to an organisation in areas such as systems analysis, design and programming, in the formation or upgrading of a data processing department.

13 Electronic data processing (EDP) auditors ensure that all aspects of a company's information systems perform in the manner stated in the design.

14 A web-page designer creates web pages containing information such as text and graphics.

15 A webmaster may also create web pages, but focuses on maintenance, expansion and improvement of the existing web sites.

16 Computer engineers develop, test and supervise the manufacture of components (such as new computer chips or circuit boards) and peripheral devices.

17 Computer sales representatives market computer products and services.

# Questions

## Fill in the blanks

1 A ____________________ looks at the operations of a manual or computerised system in an organisation or company and tries to find solutions to specific end-user problems.

2 The ____________________ monitors and controls a computer system by operating the central console.

3 A ____________________ creates web pages which contain information such as text and graphics.

4 The ____________________ is responsible for planning, co-ordinating, managing and staffing of the Information Systems department of a large organisation.

5 A ____________________ is responsible for the administration and management of a company's database.

6 A ____________________designs, develops, tests and supervises the manufacture of components (such as new computer chips or circuit boards) and peripheral devices.

7 A ____________________ explains the specifications of the different hardware and software products sold by their company to customers.

8 The ____________________ screens, edits and validates the input and output for a data processing unit.

9 A ____________________ enters data into a system in a form that is suitable for processing.

10 A ____________________ is responsible for keeping a company's data files and software organised and up to date.

11 A ____________________ writes software to meet end-user requirements.

12 A ____________________ writes programs to monitor and control peripheral devices.

13 ____________________ are responsible for the creation, administration and security of computer networks.

14 A ____________________ looks after the protection of a company's computer-based information banks, and is responsible for keeping information safe from floods, fire, power outages, fraud, theft, invasion of privacy and viruses.

15 A ____________________ is contracted to provide technical assistance to an organisation in the formation or upgrading of a data processing department.

16 ____________________ ensure that all aspects of a company's information systems perform in the manner stated in the design.

## True or False?

1 The ICT manager plays an important role in the technological direction of the organisation. T ❑ F ❑

2 A database administrator is responsible for the effective and efficient storage, retrieval, customisation and archiving of data. T ❑ F ❑

3 A systems analyst selects and maintains database management software. T ❑ F ❑

4 A programmer plans and conducts studies to determine if the existing system needs to be upgraded or if a new system has to be put in place. T ❑ F ❑

5 Programmers update, repair, modify and expand existing programs. T ❑ F ❑

6 The network administrator oversees the installation of the network's hardware and software. T ❑ F ❑

7 The network administrator is responsible for creating security policies for the network and for ensuring compliance by its users. T ❑ F ❑

8 The operations manager supervises the use and maintenance of equipment. T ❑ F ❑

9 The computer operator can work from home. T ❑ F ❑

10 Performing routine equipment maintenance, such as cleaning drive-heads, is not one of the functions of a computer operator. T ❑ F ❑

11 A computer operator is responsible for transcribing data from a variety of source documents into the computer. T ❑ F ❑

12 A file librarian is responsible for transcribing data from a variety of source documents into the computer. T ❑ F ❑

13 A file librarian keeps records of the disks and magnetic tapes stored. T ❑ F ❑

14 A data security analyst conduct 'raids' on the system to try to expose security loopholes. T ❑ F ❑

15 A computer consultant holds discussions with users to identify and clarify their information needs. T ❑ F ❑

16 Electronic data processing auditors make recommendations for changes to ensure system integrity and accuracy. T ❑ F ❑

17 Experience in graphic art is never needed to become a good web-page designer. T ❑ F ❑

18 A webmaster may be responsible for the maintenance, expansion and improvement of existing web sites. T ❑ F ❑

19 Computer engineers are not responsible for maintaining and repairing computer hardware sold to clients. T ❑ F ❑

20 Computer sales representatives are only responsible for selling computer products and services. T ❑ F ❑

## Multiple choice

1 The ICT manager is responsible for:
(a) Preparing budget projections for the department
(b) Reading reports on the system's performance and developing strategies to improve it
(c) Planning, co-ordinating, managing and staffing of the Data Processing department
(d) All of the above

2 A database administrator:
(a) Interacts with managers and users to ensure that the database is accomplishing what they need
(b) Conducts a feasibility study
(c) Helps install new equipment
(d) Has in-depth knowledge of operating systems and networking technology

3 A systems analyst:
(a) Tests and debugs the new system
(b) Develops a visually stimulating web site
(c) Maintains and protects the company's programs and data
(d) Performs routine equipment maintenance, such as cleaning drive-heads

4 Computer programmers:
(a) Discuss program specifications with the systems analyst
(b) Write programs
(c) Test programs for correct operation and intended results
(d) All of the above

5 Network administrators are responsible for:
(a) Inspecting programs, systems, operational procedures, documentation, control techniques, disaster plans, insurance protection and fire protection
(b) Monitoring the network's performance to ensure it is working at its optimum
(c) Identifying and evaluating potential hardware and software
(d) All of the above

## Short answer questions

1 List THREE duties of a data processing (or ICT) manager.

2 Describe TWO job functions of each of the following:
(a) Operations manager
(b) Network administrator
(c) Database administrator

3 Distinguish between a systems programmer and an application programmer.

4 List FOUR duties of a systems analyst. What skills do you need to become a good systems analyst?

5 Why do companies that have confidential data stored in databases and accessed through a network need to have a data security analyst?

6 What skills must someone possess to become a web-page designer?

7 Use the WWW or any method available to you to find the job specifications of an e-commerce specialist.

# 15 Applications and implications of IT

## OBJECTIVES

At the end of this chapter you will be able to:

- State the main reasons why we collect, store and share information
- List some of the uses of computers and related technology in the fields of banking and business, education, engineering and manufacturing, artificial intelligence, law enforcement, medicine, entertainment and weather forecasting
- State the benefits and implications of the use of IT in these various fields; list some of the hardware and software required in these fields
- Explain the social effects of computers in areas such employment, communication, environment and employee health

## Collecting, storing and sharing information

Regardless of who we are and where we work, we collect, store and share information. Computers have made it easier for us to do this, both individually and within organisations large and small, public and private. We collect information because it is useful to us in some way. Information can be something as simple as a map from the Internet of a place we are going to visit. We store this information in order to be able to retrieve it or update it later – we save the map on our hard disk. Similarly, many situations require us to share information: a police department in one district may share information about suspected criminals with another department in another district. At a personal level, you may want your friends to have a copy of your map, so you share it with them by sending it to them as an e-mail attachment.

*Figure 15.1*
*Information collection, storage and sharing*

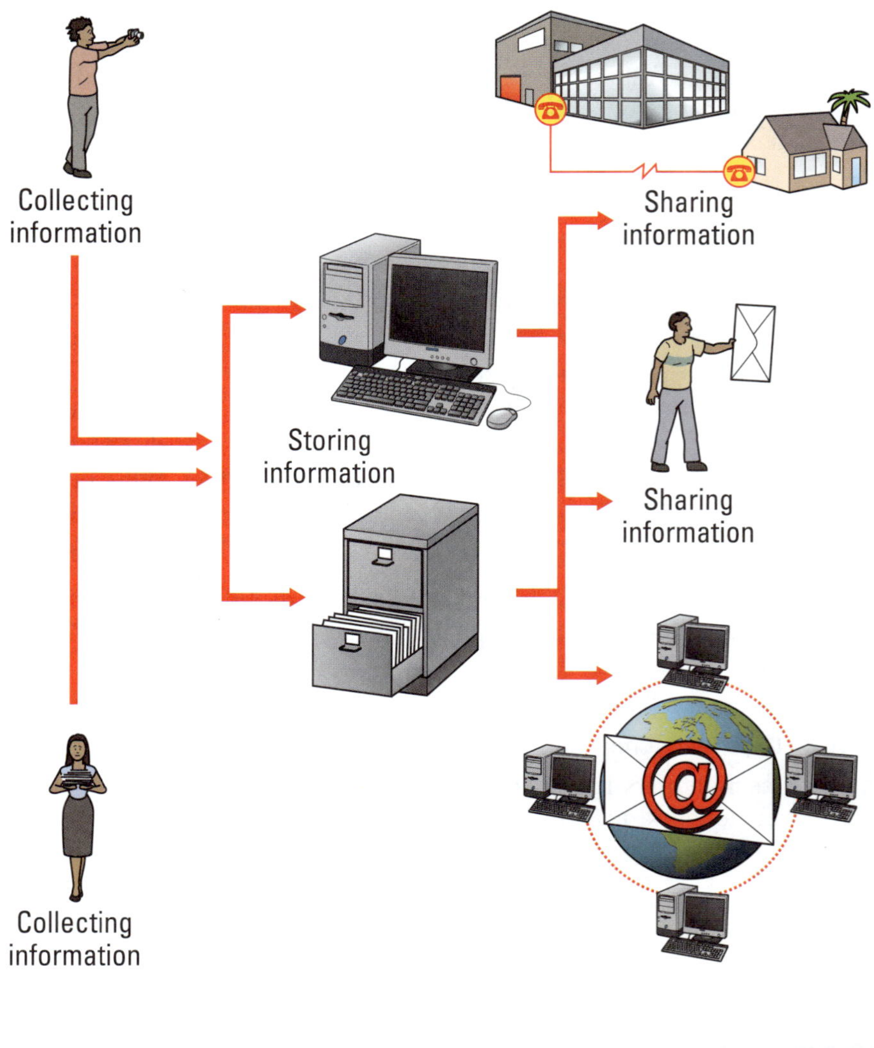

## Why we collect information

Information keeps us informed and is useful to us in a variety of circumstances. For example, a fisherman needs to be kept informed about the weather. This will help him decide whether to take his boat out or not. You may want to be kept informed about events in the election campaign in your country, so you listen to the radio and watch TV to gather information: this information will help you decide how to vote. Based on the information we receive, we can make suitable decisions. Information helps us to monitor, control and supervise systems, people and processes. If we do not have the information we need, suitable actions and decisions cannot be taken. Information often also has value and is therefore considered to be a commodity that can be sold and purchased.

In summary then, information is collected for four main purposes:

- To monitor, control and supervise systems, people and processes
- To be used as a commodity
- To be used in making tactical and strategic decisions
- To keep us informed.

Let us look at each of these in turn.

### *Monitoring, controlling and supervising systems, people and processes*

We need information in order to monitor, control and supervise systems, people and processes. For example, receiving information such as heart rate, blood pressure, sugar and cholesterol levels, allows a doctor to monitor her patient to determine whether he is improving or getting worse, and control the drugs that are then administered accordingly. If the patient needs to go to the operating theatre, information received from equipment in the theatre allows supervision of the operating procedure.

### *Information as a commodity*

Information can have a commercial value; in business, it constitutes a percentage of the cost of any product. For example, if you had to estimate the cost of building a bridge, the materials and the labour will take up a percentage of the cost. On top of this, the information about how to build the bridge, the technical information provided by the chief engineer, and the information contained in the design plans also constitute a percentage of the cost of building the bridge. Information, once it is considered useful, can therefore be bought and sold. A simple example would be a police officer paying for information from an informant.

### *Information for tactical and strategic decision-making*

All kinds of problems, challenges and circumstances arise in organisations or in individuals' lives. These necessitate decisions on how to deal with them. Organisations use information to come up with strategies that will place them in a more favourable position than before. At any time, a company or individual may need to come up with a plan on how to proceed (a tactical plan) given certain circumstances. For example, if you are about to build a house, you will need information about the design of the house, potential contractors and their past records in building, how to pass the safety inspection, and legal and financial matters. If problems arise during the construction of the house you must develop a plan of action based on the information you receive or collect.

### *Information to keep us informed*

Information is needed to keep us informed about a huge variety of things. In general, the more information we are able to store and have access to – whether it be about weather patterns, ancient civilisations, design and engineering techniques, or famous people's lives – the more informed we are about our world and the more likely we are to learn from what we know. The fact that we have these details stored somewhere may be of value to us at some future point in our lives.

## Why we store information

It serves little purpose if the information we collect cannot be stored. Imagine that we simply collect information, use it and discard it. If we need that same information again, we will need to collect it again, thereby wasting time and money. Thousands of years ago information was stored on the walls of caves and on stone tablets. Today we store information manually in files, in computerised databases, on diskettes, CDs, magnetic tape and other storage devices. We do this in order to:

- Refer to it when a decision has to be made or for confirmation of a fact
- Keep a backup in case the original data is lost or corrupted
- Analyse the information to come up with some interpretation, explanation or resolution of it
- Distribute the information to persons or systems that can make further use of it.

Stored information should be organised. Organising information makes it easy to retrieve it when we want it quickly, as we know exactly where it is. Computers – especially when used with specialist electronic databases – are highly efficient at organising information.

## Why we share information

Information that we have stored is often valuable to, and needed by, someone else. Over the years, people have found many different ways of sending information to others, such as the traditional mail service, word-of-mouth, the telephone and so on.

Information can be shared using manual files but there are numerous disadvantages to this. Manual files must first be organised (alphabetically, numerically or chronologically) and this is time-consuming work. Manual files can easily be misplaced; it is also difficult to distribute information manually when more than one group of persons require the same information at the same time.

Computer networks can offer a more efficient means of sharing this information. They allow several persons to use the same information from different places at the same time. Information can be easily updated from different sources since it can be stored in a central database and access to it can be made available to all computers on the network.

All modern computer networks contain tools for distributing information and the most obvious and popular of these is e-mail: a fast, efficient and cheap way of sharing information. It allows you to send the same information to a number of people at the same time and you can receive feedback or acknowledgement very soon after delivery of the message, by the same method.

## Exercise 1

### Short answer questions

1 Describe TWO reasons for collecting information.

2 Give TWO types of information that would be collected by:

(a) a school teacher

(b) a police officer

(c) a musician

(d) a doctor

(e) a meteorologist

Why would each of these professionals decide to collect this particular information?

3 Give THREE reasons why we need to store information.

4 Describe TWO methods by which information can be shared.

### Crossword

#### Across

5 Files that are not frequently used are ________ (8)

6 One of the fastest and cheapest ways of sharing information world wide (5)

#### Down

1 Certain decisions and plans that are made depend on the information received (8)

2 Information as something that can be bought or sold (9)

3 An efficient way of organising information (8)

4 The weatherman uses information to ________ the weather (7)

Computers and their related technology have become such an integral part of our daily lives that sometimes we barely notice their effect. They have had a major impact on the way we live, work and play. Even the most technophobe person is affected by computer technology and would live a drastically different life if this technology were removed from their lives. Computers impact both negatively and positively on our daily lives. We will now look at some of these applications and implications of information technology in greater detail.

# Computers in banking

Even when we undertake a seemingly very simple transaction, such as buying a few items from the grocery or supermarket, we interact with computers. The cashier may pass the barcode of the item over a barcode reader; you may then decide to pay using a debit card, credit card or cheque book. This scenario and many others in business and banking present many opportunities to use computer technology. Some of the hardware and software involved is listed in Table 1.

| Hardware requirement | Software requirement |
|---|---|
| Mainframe computer with networked terminals | Accounting and financial software |
| Printers (character, line and page)<br>– Character: for printing transactions on passbooks.<br>– Line: for printing duplicate copies and statements<br>– Laser: for printing reports | Database software |
| Cheque encoders and writers (MICR) | Word processing software for preparing documents |
| ATM machines | Security software (e.g. intrusion and forensics for detecting and tracing unauthorised access) |
| Magnetic card readers | Networking software for WAN |
| Currency counters | Video conferencing software |
| | Internet access software |
| | E-mail software |

*Table 1*
*Banking hardware and software*

In banking computers are used to:

- Process customer transactions (withdrawals, deposits, loans, bill payments)
- Process cheques
- Transfer funds (electronic fund transfer) from one account to another.

Let us look in detail at some of these computer functions in banking.

## Automated Teller Machines (ATM)

This machine, together with an ATM card (also known as a 'debit card'), allows you to perform a number of banking transactions, 24 hours a day. You can access your bank account to deposit and withdraw money, obtain balances, transfer funds and pay bills. The card contains a magnetic strip which holds a code to identify the card-holder's bank account, so that the holder can perform banking transactions. The card-holder enters a PIN (Personal Identification Number) to gain access to their account. ATMs can be found at a number of locations other than banks, such as supermarkets, airports, bus stations and shopping malls.

### *Using an ATM*

A customer must have an ATM card or debit card issued by a bank. This card has a magnetic strip at the back, which stores the customer's account number and name.

1 The customer inserts the card; the ATM reads the information from the strip and communicates with a central computer to access the customer's account.
2 A message appears on the ATM screen requesting that the customer enter her personal identification number (PIN).
3 The customer enters the PIN using the ATM's keypad.
4 If the PIN does not match the one stored in the computer's memory, the customer is given two chances to enter the information again. If the correct PIN is still not entered, the ATM keeps the card and the customer cannot carry out any further transactions.
5 If the PIN is correct, the computer asks the customer to select a transaction from a list displayed on the screen. In the case of a withdrawal or transfer of funds, the computer checks the customer's account to determine if sufficient funds are available for the transaction.
6 If sufficient funds are available, the transaction is processed and the account will be updated immediately to reflect it. The customer is issued a receipt showing the date, time, amount and type of transaction. The transaction will also be reflected on the customer's monthly statement.

*Figure 15.2 Using an ATM*

## Cheque processing

Millions of cheques are written every day all over the world. This method of payment, though decreasing in use, is still an important way of paying for goods and services.

- The amount of money to be paid to an individual or organisation is printed at the bottom of the cheque using a magnetic ink recognition (MICR) font. This money is normally deposited in the bank.
- If the cheque is presented at the bank where the cheque originated, payment can be received immediately. If both parties have accounts at the same branch the cheque is cashed and the accounts of both parties are updated.
- However, a cheque originating from a different bank is sent to a central clearing house. In the Caribbean, the Central Banks are responsible for this task. An MICR reader reads the information at the bottom of the cheque and the cheque is sorted according to its bank of origin. Payments between the different banks are made according to the value of cheques received. The cheques are then sent to the original banks, where the information is read into the main computer so that customers' accounts can be updated.

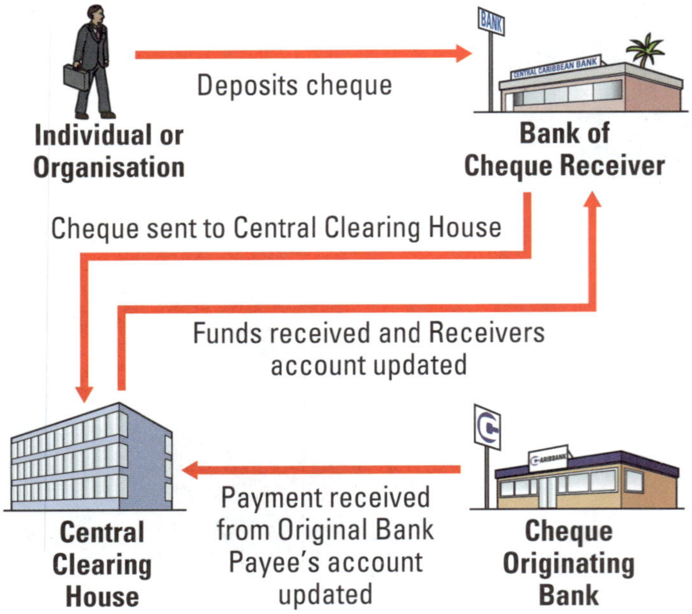


*Figure 15.3*
*A cheque being cleared*

## Credit cards

Credit cards are similar to debit cards. They give you access to funds in your credit account. When the card is 'swiped' in the store where you are purchasing goods, the card's magnetic strip is read and the information on the strip is transmitted to the credit card company. A check is performed to determine if sufficient funds are available for the purchase, before payment can be transferred to the merchant's account. If there is not enough money available, the transaction is denied or declined. The transaction is verified by the card-holder signing a receipt. Paying for an item in this way uses **Electronic Funds Transfer (EFT)**. The balances in both the merchant's account and your account are updated.

*Figure 15.4*
*A smart card*

## Smart cards

Smart cards contain wafer-thin memory chips embedded in the card. These chips can store more information than magnetic strip cards, and the information can be updated. Crucially, smart cards are more secure than debit or credit cards. The magnetic strips on the backs of the latter can be altered or forged, but this is much more difficult with a smart card chip.

These chips can hold information for cell phone accounts, debit and credit cards, or any other financial services. Eventually, smart cards may combine many functions, storing information about a person's driving history and their birth certificate or paper, for example, and could even be imprinted with the holder's voice, fingerprints and retinal scans, for identification purposes.

## Stored-value cards

Stored-value cards are cards that are reloadable or disposable and store a certain amount of money for a specific transaction. They include prepaid phone cards, prepaid debit cards and merchant gift cards. Stored-value cards are one of the most commonly available and fastest growing retail products. When they are passed through an appropriate reading system linked to a computer, they can be updated, for example to reflect the fact that you have purchased something using the card.

*Figure 15.5*
*A bank website*

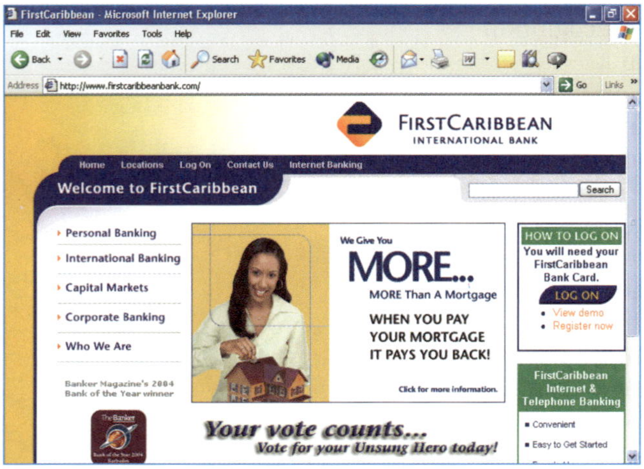


## Home or Internet banking

This form of banking gives you the convenience of doing transactions from home or anywhere there is Internet access. You can check your accounts, order cheque books, pay bills, transfer funds and even apply for loans via the Internet. The convenience associated with doing banking at home is appreciated by many customers.

# Computers in business

It is hard to imagine a modern business functioning without computers – they permeate every aspect of twenty-first century business life. Computers are used to create bills (invoices), monitor inventory (stock control), in point-of-sale systems (store checkouts), in accounting (profit and loss accounts), in marketing (promotion of merchandise), as well as in new developments such as e-commerce and telecommuting.

In this section we will look at some of the areas just mentioned. Meanwhile, some of the hardware and software commonly used by modern businesses is listed in Table 2.

### Did you know?

Every day we get closer to forming a cashless society where more and more persons are using EFT and Internet banking. Governments are implementing policies towards attaining this goal.



| Hardware requirement | Software requirement |
|---|---|
| POS terminals | Inventory software |
| Barcode readers | Payroll software |
| Mainframe or mini-computers with networked terminals and cash registers | Accounting and financial software |
| Printers (character, line, laser, thermal for printing statements, reports, bills) | Word processing software |
| Magnetic card readers (for the reading of credit cards, debit cards) | Video conferencing software |
| | Internet access software |
| | E-mail software |

*Table 2*

## Stock control

Most companies use the computer and its related technology to keep track of their stock inventory. For example, when an item is purchased in a store it is often swiped over a barcode reader. The reader sends a message to the stock computer to update the record of that particular item – decreasing the quantity in stock by one (point-of-sale systems).

The reverse occurs when items are added to stock and scanned by a reader in the warehouse. This system allows companies to set up their system to automatically re-order a quantity of an item. When the number of items sold diminishes to a point where the stock is at a low level – the designated re-order level – the system can warn the stock manager to re-order.

## E-commerce

**E-commerce** or electronic commerce consists of the buying, selling, marketing and servicing of products and services over computer networks. It also includes the transfer of funds in the buying process. There are two types of e-commerce:

- B2C or Business to Consumer (where businesses retail their supply goods and services over the Internet to individual private consumers), and
- B2B or Business to Business (where businesses supply other businesses with products and services that are required in the operations of that business).

In 2005, e-commerce accounted for close to 200 billion dollars in revenue for the world's economy. Many traditional companies have started adopting e-commerce as a secondary arm to their business, such as supermarkets in the

USA offering a home shopping service, while other companies have started up in the last few years purely as online businesses, such as online book and CD stores.

The advantages of e-commerce include:

- It allows companies to reach a wider market of potential customers, globally, via the company's web site. Similarly, potential buyers, whether individuals or companies, have the ability to source products and services from a wider range of potential suppliers, globally.
- The 'middle man', usually a physical store, is cut out of the buying process, so, in theory at least, prices should be cheaper.
- Shopping is easy and convenient this way: it can be done from the comfort of your own home or office. It is usually just a matter of: browsing items for sale on the web site, putting them in a 'virtual shopping basket' and going to the 'checkout' where you punch in your credit card details to pay for the item(s). The transaction is now complete: just sit back and wait for the items to be delivered.
- Automated computerised invoices, tied directly to the purchase made via the web site, mean fewer processing errors. This automation also helps with stock control and accounting. An e-commerce company can tie-in all its software to work in an integrated way, thus smoothing its operation.
- Companies have the ability to respond to customer demands, queries and comments: this can be done quickly, cheaply and easily, for example, via e-mail.

The disadvantages of e-commerce include:

- The lack of a 'customer facing' operation, i.e. a normal physical store, can reduce buyer confidence, especially when the customer would like to see the product they are considering buying, and have it explained to them in person.
- There is a perceived risk of fraud, and/or of data privacy being compromised: there have been documented cases of fake online stores being set up, which are simply a vehicle for stealing people's money. Consumers are therefore often wary of doing business over the Internet. Reputable e-commerce sites, though, use web servers that encrypt customer data (such as name, address, credit card number) when it is in transit between the customer's computer and their own.
- Although e-commerce web sites have the ability to reach a wide market, the number of business sites on the web increases daily and the probability of your site being visited may be reduced; traditional advertising may still be necessary, and costly.
- E-commerce has the potential to make small companies seem larger than they actually are and in some cases these companies are unable to handle the volume of orders received.
- There are significant cost and training issues associated with setting up e-commerce companies, such as the outlay on hardware and software, and the expense of training and/or recruiting computer-literate staff.

## Telecommuting

Technology has made it possible for individuals to stay at home and work, yet communicate with their offices using a combination of computer, modem, telephone, e-mail, teleconferencing and faxing. Telecommuting – also called teleworking – is just this type of employment: working from home and communicating with colleagues and customers using computer facilities. Telecommuting can be part-time (1–2 days per week) where workers can avoid the commute to and from the main office every day, and full-time (4–5 days per week) where the workers are part of 'virtual teams' who work from various, often changing, locations to perform the requirements of their business.

There are advantages and disadvantages to telecommuting, both for the employee and the employer.

Advantages of telecommuting to the employee:

- It reduces the time and cost of commuting to and from the worker's main office.
- It reduces stress, as there is no need to beat the early morning rush-hour to get to work, or to be exposed to regular office politics.
- It allows better organisation of personal time. If the employee is to work eight hours per day, there is a certain amount of flexibility as to when he or she decides to do so.
- There is less distraction from co-workers on the job.
- The full-time teleworker does not need to relocate to take on a new job – he or she can live virtually anywhere.

Advantages of telecommuting to the employer:

- In general there seems to be less absenteeism due to sick days: employees who may have been too sick to travel to work can sometimes do some work at home.
- Productivity may increase – employees may be more relaxed and concentrated in a home office, without the distractions of colleagues' chatter, and may therefore work harder.
- There is less expense in overheads, such as the need to rent a large office space.
- When recruiting, there is naturally an increased number of potential employees, since potential teleworkers are available all over the country.
- Work does not necessarily have to stop in extreme weather, for example, when hurricanes cause transport disruptions.

Disadvantages of telecommuting to the employee:

- There are potential distractions from family, neighbours and household chores; home life and work life may merge, benefiting neither.
- A teleworker may feel overly isolated from their employer, as there is less interaction with other workers.
- There is a possibility that either the employee may work excessive hours, since there isn't a clear 'going home' time, or the opposite, that motivation may reduce due to lack of supervision.
- The employee may be less aware of global changes that take place within the company, and therefore may feel less connected and loyal to the organisation.
- There may also be a fear that the employee can be overlooked for promotion or other benefits, as they are not a regular face seen at the office.

Disadvantages of telecommuting to the employer:

- Employee supervision is potentially the biggest disadvantage. For example, there may be difficulties contacting the employee, he or she could simply choose when to be available, and may become something of a 'law unto themselves'.
- Only certain kinds of work can be done well via telecommuting; many jobs still benefit from face-to-face contact between colleagues and customers in meetings.
- It may be more costly to set up an employee with all the equipment they would require at home, rather than the shared equipment that is used by several workers in a normal office.

## Exercise 2

1 Banks issue their customers with plastic cards, containing magnetic strips, that can be used to draw money from an ATM machine.

(a) Describe TWO items of information that can be stored on the magnetic strip.

(b) How can a bank customer use the card to draw money from the ATM?

(c) How does the bank prevent its customers from withdrawing more money than they have in their account?

2 (a) What is meant by the term 'e-commerce'?

(b) Decribe TWO advantages and TWO disadvantages of e-commerce.

3 (a) What is telecommuting?

(b) Name THREE pieces of hardware that you would need if you were to telecommute.

(c) Give THREE reasons why someone might want to telecommute.

(d) Give TWO reasons why their employer might agree to this.

(e) Describe TWO disadvantages of telecommuting.

# Computers in education

Computers are a major part of the global community because they can perform certain tasks more efficiently and effectively than humans. We now even use computers to assist with teaching and learning, since computers sometimes have the capacity to communicate information more effectively than humans – especially with the arrival of multimedia. Some of the hardware and software used in education is listed in Table 3.

| Hardware requirement | Software requirement |
|---|---|
| Computers (stand alone and networked) | Word processing for creating documents |
| Printers (laser, inkjet and sometimes character printers) | Web and video conferencing software |
| Devices for the learning disabled such as concept keyboards, voice synthesisers | CAI/CAL software for a variety of subjects and levels (simulations, drills and tutorials) |
| | Database software for managing student records |
| | Spreadsheet for grading students' marks |
| | CML (Computer Managed Learning) software which is used as an administrative tool for creating timetables, etc. |

*Table 3*

## CAA/CAL/CAI

These three acronyms represent computerised innovations that are helping to extend the educational options available to teachers and students alike. Let us look at them in turn.

### *Computer-Assisted Assessment (CAA)*

This is the use of computers to assist in the marking of examination scripts, such as multiple choice papers where you mark a box in pencil to indicate your preferred answer. An electronic reader sensitive to shading can assess which boxes have been marked, and give a score accordingly.

### Computer-Assisted Learning (CAL)/ Computer-Aided Instruction (CAI)

This is the use of computers and appropriate computer software to allow students to learn at their own pace, and/or to create a more interesting learning environment in which teaching material is presented.

There are three basic forms of CAL/CAI:

- *Drills and practices*: This is where students are repeatedly given a range of questions from a data bank, especially to practise skills and concepts that require repeated practice in order to become ingrained (such as vocabulary work, or mastering rules in mathematics). These questions will usually have an exact right or wrong answer, and are therefore very easy for the computer to mark.
- *Tutorials*: These are self-paced, self-instructional programs that guide the student through new material, acting as their tutor. Students can repeat a lesson as often as they like if they do not understand the material. The lessons can also be adjusted depending on the level of the student's competence – the tutorial may even test the student's competence at the outset, and adjust the tutorial scheme accordingly.
- *Simulations*: These use sound, text, video and graphics (multimedia) to demonstrate a realistic-looking and sounding outcome, based on a specific scenario. For example, a simulation may show you what happens when you mix two chemicals together in a test tube (e.g. bubbles, changes in colour, production of gas, etc.). Simulations therefore provide the opportunity for individuals to learn in a safe environment, without material wastage or high-risk situations. Note, though, that simulations can only produce sound and sight, not touch and smell.

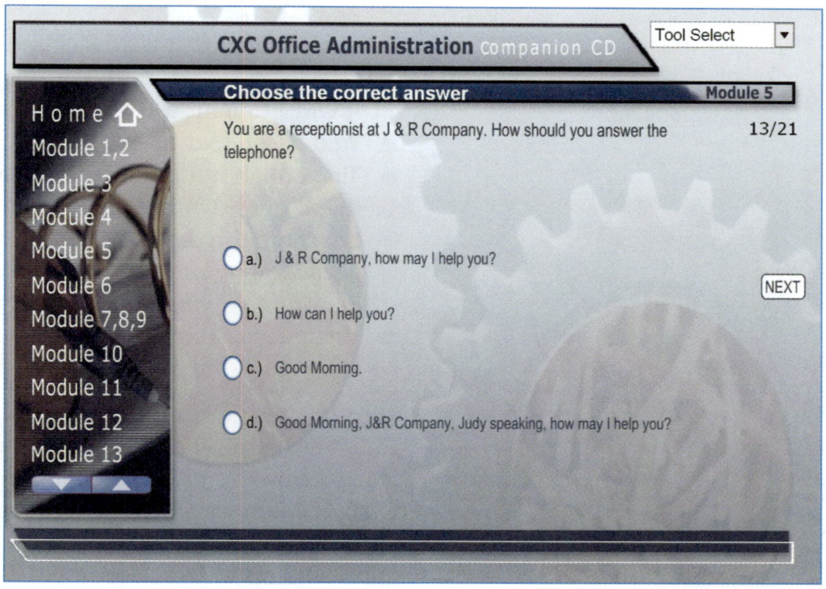


*Figure 15.6 Screenshot from the Longman Office Administration for CXC companion CD-ROM*

## CML/CMI

Computer Managed Learning (CML) and Computer Managed Instruction (CMI) are other tools used in education. However, unlike CAI and CAL, CML and CMI software is used as an administrative resource rather than an instructional one – to organise students' data and timetables, and in libraries to manage indexes.

## Referencing information

Computers are a popular means of sourcing information. Since information is knowledge, and knowledge is part of education, computers are inherently educational, especially when connected to the Internet.

For example, online libraries are becoming popular, as individuals can stay at home and access most of the information they need relatively quickly and easily. Through these libraries you can find information from books, magazines, journals, articles and newspapers around the world from both academic and commercial publishers. They range from subject-specific libraries, such as medical libraries or law libraries, to general libraries that cover a wide range of subject areas. Many require you to register and subscribe to their service by paying either a monthly or an annual fee, for example, Questia (www.questia.com). Once you are a member you are given a password and a user name that allows you access. Others do not charge a fee; however, for key books and articles your access may be limited to the abstracts and summaries.

Traditional encyclopaedias are now also available on CD-ROMs or online. The advantages of these are clear:

- They can be updated regularly; new information can be added.
- The electronic versions need less storage space than the printed encyclopaedia.

## Distance learning

Distance learning involves classes being conducted via the Internet, an extranet or intranet, satellite broadcasting, interactive television and CD-ROM. It includes:

- Web-based learning (WBL)
- Tele-collaboration, which means using global computer networks in a teaching/learning environment to connect students all over the world. Learners can collaborate or work together on projects through the use of e-mails, synchronised chat, threaded conversations and other forms of electronically mediated conversation
- Virtual classrooms, which is an online learning environment designed to carry out some of the roles of a physical school/classroom.

Many institutions are now conducting classes through distance learning. In the Caribbean, The University of the West Indies has its own distance learning programme conducted through the University of the West Indies Distance Education Centre (UWIDEC). Similarly, 'virtual schools' and 'virtual classrooms' (VCs) are used as a means of home schooling. You can apply and enrol in classes for your age group. The teaching environment provides training materials, newsgroups, annotation facilities and teleconferencing, all integrated into a single learning environment.

In some virtual classrooms students can follow the lecture from their computer. These schools offer support material and information for both students and parents. There are several projects to launch virtual classrooms in the Caribbean that are in various stages of development, such as VCOIN (Virtual Classroom Over the Internet) developed at Florida Atlantic University.

## Advantages of IT in education

- CAI and CAL use multimedia that make learning more interesting and interactive.
- Students can learn on their own and at their own pace even in the absence of a teacher.
- Feedback is immediate after answering the question or at the end of a simulation.
- An abundance of educational resources is available on CD-ROMs and on the Internet.
- Abstract concepts can often be explained more clearly with the use of multimedia.
- Dangerous experiments, experiments requiring expensive equipment and materials, and experiments that are difficult to perform, can be done through simulations.

- IT can assist the teacher in giving instructions to students where she may otherwise lack time, competence or resources.

### Disadvantages of IT in education

- It reduces face-to-face interaction with others.
- Computer Aided Instructions are set up in a pre-defined order; hence students can only follow in that order. This may sometimes be restrictive, not allowing for creative flow in lessons.

## Computers in engineering and manufacturing

In engineering and manufacturing computers are used to:

- Direct assembly line operations
- Perform simulations
- Design, draw and manipulate engineering, architectural, product, graphic and textile designs.

Some of the main hardware and software requirements are listed in Table 4.

| Hardware requirement | Software requirement |
|---|---|
| Robots | CAD and CADD software for design and draughting |
| Sensors | |
| Mainframes, mini and microcomputers | Specialised software to control machines |
| Printers and Plotters (for printing drawings) | CAE or Simulation software |
| Light pen and digitised tablets | |
| Monitors (high-resolution) | |

*Table 4*

### Computer Aided Design (CAD) and Computer Aided Design and Drafting (CADD)

This includes hardware and software to draw, manipulate and design such things as engineering and architectural designs, electronic products and even clothing designs. There are many types of CAD software; the one used depends on the specific kind of designing that is taking place. Adjustments, updates and duplications of designs can be easily done on the computer. CAD systems can allow designers to create three-dimensional (3D) objects that can be easily manipulated, rotated and viewed from many angles. The CAD package contains basic elements such as points, lines, circles, shapes and solids, from which all CAD drawings are constructed. Additionally, the computer keeps track of design dependencies, so that when a value is changed all other dependent values are automatically changed.

A high-resolution graphics monitor is needed to show the details of drawings done with a CAD package. The input devices needed for a CAD system include a mouse and a light pen or digitising tablet for drawing. Output devices such as a special printer or a plotter are needed for printing design specifications.

Some advantages of using CAD are:
- The length of time it takes to draw a design is reduced.
- It is easier to make changes or update the original design.
- Duplicates of the design are easy to produce, to distribute to various interested parties or other parts of the company.

## Computer Aided Manufacturing (CAM)

CAM systems are used to control manufacturing plant equipment and production equipment; for example in a car manufacturing plant or a factory that makes microprocessors for computers. CAM translates the design into the actual product, such as moulding a bottle or spoon. Many CAM systems use robots and sensors along with computers in the manufacturing process.

The advantages of CAM include:
- Faster production of parts and products, therefore meeting customer demand
- The ability to control and maintain the quality of the product better, so that it is produced more consistently.

*Figure 15.7*
*Computer aided manufacture*

## Computer Aided Engineering (CAE)

CAE systems analyse engineering designs, by simulating varying conditions to determine in advance whether the design is likely to work. For example, an aeroplane manufacturer might be able to simulate the forces of a hurricane wind on a plane wing using a CAE computer, or an engineer might be able to simulate the stresses applied to a bridge.

# Computers in Artificial Intelligence (AI)

AI has become one of the most innovative ways in which computers are used today.

In Artificial Intelligence computers are used to:
- Control robots
- Control systems and processes (through the use of sensors, temperature, air and water flow, pressure, light and other physical elements can be monitored)
- Produce voice recognition and synthesis systems
- Produce virtual reality and sensory capability systems
- Produce expert systems.

Some of the main hardware and software used in AI are listed in Table 5.

Table 5

| Hardware requirement | Software requirement |
|---|---|
| Robots | Software to control machinery such as robots, process, sensors |
| Sensors | Virtual reality software |
| Voice recognition and voice synthesis systems that include microphones and speakers | Voice recognition and voice synthesis software |
| Virtual Reality (VR) systems that include special clothing, head gear, data gloves, joysticks and handheld wands | Expert systems |

## Robotics

Robotics is the use of computer-controlled machines  in place of humans to perform repetitive and dangerous tasks. They are normally found in industry on assembly lines. For example, in the automotive industry robots are used for welding, paint spraying, assembling and loading. They are used to perform high precision tasks, which they can perform with fewer errors than humans. They do not get sick, complain or take strike action. Robots are also able to operate in extreme environments where it might be difficult or impossible for human beings to operate. They have been developed to perform specialised tasks. For example:

- Canadarm2 is a robot that plays a critical role in building and maintaining the International Space Station, currently under construction.
- Dante is a robot that enters active volcanoes to gather information about potential volcanic activity.
- Remotely operated vehicles (ROVs) are able to perform tasks such as searching for and recovering ship and plane wreckage, specialist scientific studies and the burial and repair of underground telecommunication cables.
- Other robots clean up hazardous waste sites and handle wastes that might be too dangerous for humans.

*Figure 15.8*
*An astronaut anchored to a foot restraint on the International Space Station's Canadarm2 robot*

## Control systems

Control systems use sensors to detect physical changes in the environment. Having gathered information, the sensors interface with software on the computer. The computer then tells an output device what to do, depending on the information given to it by the sensor. Sensors can detect changes in temperature, pressure, light, sound, pH, humidity, position and proximity of an object...the list goes on. For example, in some modern cars, light sensors turn headlights on automatically when the light intensity diminishes below a certain level. A similar thing occurs in street lamps.

## Process control

Process control is the automatic monitoring and control of a process by an instrument and computer programmed to respond appropriately by taking corrective measures, if necessary, in industrial settings such as chemical plants, steel mills and oil refineries.

The advantages of process control include the following:

- Data from the process can be stored and displayed so that changes over time can be seen.
- Safety can be ensured by sounding an alarm if necessary and shutting off the process.
- Product quality can be maintained.
- Employees can have better working conditions.
- Operating costs are lower because the system is efficient.

## Natural Language Processing (NLP)

The goal of NLP is to create computer systems that recognise, understand and process written and spoken language. In the future, they may benefit us enormously by making communication easier. NLP can include voice recognition and voice synthesis systems.

- *Voice recognition systems* process the spoken work and match it to a word stored in the computer's memory. If they match, the command or data being entered is accepted by the computer and processed. Simple commands can be used to control machines or even 'type' letters in a word processor. Voice recognition has made life easier for people with movement difficulties, such as the paralysed, who with suitable equipment can now operate a wheelchair, adjust lighting and even open doors using voice commands.
- *Voice synthesis systems* produce sounds resembling human speech. They convert written text to computer-generated speech (Text to Speech). They are used for computer-aided conversation by hearing- and speech-impaired persons, or for converting conversations or text written in one language into another.

Other applications of NLP include:

- Translation of one human language text into another. An online example that tries to do this is the Babel Fish translator, found at http://world.altavista.com
- Information retrieval and database queries. For example, the Grolier and Encarta encyclopaedias use NLP to find answers to users' questions.
- Grammar checking, for example, as found in Microsoft Word.

## Simulation of human sensory capabilities

This technology is available to varying degrees. Computer simulation of human sensory capabilities includes computers with the ability to see, hear, speak, feel (touch) and smell (detect odour). For example, some cars are fitted with sensors that detect how far you are from the edge of the road, or how close you are to another vehicle. The onboard computer can warn you about possible dangers.

*Virtual reality (VR) systems* include hardware and interactive graphics software which can replicate sensations that imitate the real world. You need special clothing, headgear and equipment to use VR systems, such as data gloves and joysticks. In these systems you can almost believe that you are in the actual situation because ultra-modern technologies are used to create a more physical sensation. For example, the fingertips of a data glove contain sensors that detect when the tip of a finger touches the sensor. The glove is tracked using a transmitter and a receiver; the information is fed into the computer which then renders a perfect replica of the position of the hand. The computer can then send 'tangible force feedback' to the glove – such as pressure, vibration and sound, creating a physical sensation.

Virtual reality systems are used to train military personnel, in medicine and in the space programme.

## Expert systems

These systems provide a vast knowledge database of information in specific fields such as medicine, mathematics, engineering, geology, computer science, business, law, defence and education. Expert systems or **knowledge-based systems** make decisions based on the results of questions put to the user; the program analyses input data and provides answers at the level of an expert in the particular field. By looking at various possibilities the computer makes the best informed decision. These systems perform the function of a human expert consultant in a particular field, providing support for decision making. They can also 'suggest' alternatives or other issues to be considered.

Expert systems consist of two parts: the **knowledge base** and the **inference engine**. The knowledge base contains a large volume of information in a particular field – for example, a medical expert system knowledge base contains a vast array of information about different types of diseases, symptoms and possible treatments. The inference engine complements the knowledge base: it analyses the input data using 'reasoning' methods, along with the knowledge base, to arrive at a conclusion. It also provides the user with an explanation of how it arrived at its conclusion, by showing the concepts that were used.

# Computers in law enforcement

Computers are now an integral part of law enforcement in all its aspects. National databases have been set up to hold information such as criminal records, profiles of wanted persons, data on stolen cars, fingerprints of convicted individuals and drivers who have had their licences suspended or revoked. These databases, such as the National Crime Information Center (NCIC) in the United States and the Police National Computer (PNC) in the United Kingdom, can be accessed by officers in law enforcement departments throughout the country.

*Figure 15.9 A data glove*

In law enforcement, computers are used to:

- Maintain criminal databases
- Examine forensic evidence
- Communicate with other departments and agencies
- Provide electronic surveillance
- Control traffic systems
- Provide assistance to officers through easy access to information
- Computerise many of the traditional office tasks.

Some of the key hardware and software involved in law enforcement is listed in Table 6.

| **Hardware requirement** | **Software requirement** |
| --- | --- |
| Robots (bomb detection and disarming) | Database management software |
| Security cameras and electronic surveillance equipment | Biometric identification software such as DNA, voice analysis, facial image identification and fingerprinting identification software |
| Biometric identification systems | |
| Scanners | Composite profiling software |
| Mainframes and microcomputers | Statistical analysis software |
| Printers | |

*Table 6*

## Security cameras

Security cameras can act as a visible deterrent to a criminal. Sometimes they are hidden in order to catch criminals in action. They can capture video footage of a crime in progress and the images can be used to identify the criminals. Most cameras today are linked to computer systems which can store and process the raw data.

## Biometric identification systems

Biometrics refers to the science of identifying an individual through their body characteristics, such as face geometry, hand geometry (e.g. fingerprints), iris or retinal scans, veins and voice patterns. All these forms of identification can be input into a computer system set up for security purposes. Two of the most commonly used methods are:

- *Fingerprints* obtained from a crime scene can be matched against a database of known criminals' fingerprints to identify a suspect. The complex patterns of the prints are stored and analysed by computer.
- *Computer-assisted facial image identification systems* use computers to identify a person from an image captured through a surveillance camera or photograph. There are three ways in which facial image identification is done, they are:
    1. Morphological comparison of facial features – 2D and 3D images are obtained and directly superimposed on a second image to see if they match
    2. Anthropometrical analysis – points are plotted on two images and distances and angles are measured to compare the images
    3. Face-to-face superimposition – anthropometrical points of one image are superimposed on the points of the second image to see if they match

All three methods are used together to identify a person. They can also be used to create an on-screen 'three-dimensional' facial reconstruction, based on the dimensions of the skull of a dead person, to show what an unidentified person might look like if they were alive.

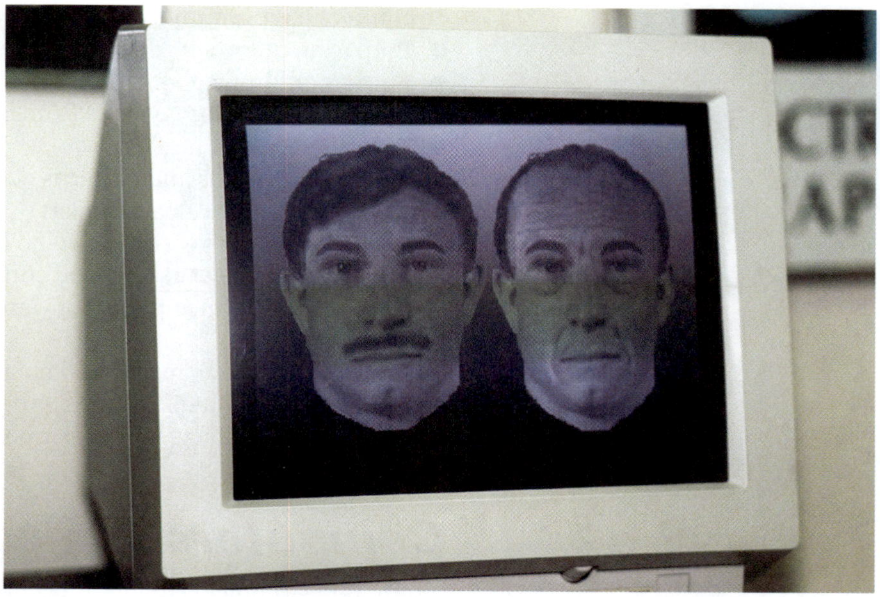

*Figure 15.10*
*Image built up by a facial image identification system*

## Profiling (computer composites)

Appropriate software can be used by the police to compose a picture of an alleged criminal based on the description of a witness. The picture can then be compared to those stored in the national databases. This method reduces the cost of police stations having a traditional composite artist and the sketch can easily be transmitted over the Internet to other police departments.

## Traffic control

Computerised traffic light systems control traffic flow using a specific sequence of lighting managed by the computer. These sequences are adjusted throughout the day, depending on the flow of traffic. The systems use a sensor in the road to detect traffic flow. They then process this raw data, adjusting traffic lights as necessary to promote the maximum flow of traffic at different times of the day. The data from the sensors is sent via wire-based or fibre-optic cables to the processing computer.

## Electronic surveillance

Wire taps, e-mail and online communication interception, location information (e.g. determining where you are from calls going to your cell phone) and communication analysis (e.g. monitoring when and where credit cards are used) are all forms of electronic surveillance. Such surveillance can help police track criminals' movements and activities.

## In-car computers

Many police patrol vehicles are now retrofitted with computers, allowing police officers to have an abundance of information at their finger tips. These computers are linked to the police local and national databases and allow police officers to make enquires about vehicle registration, drivers' licences and wanted criminals. They facilitate quick access to information. In the Caribbean a number of police vehicles are now retrofitted with these onboard computers.

Computers have a number of other functions in law enforcement, including:

- Preparing reports
- Equipment inventory
- Tracking the history of calls from a particular address
- Managing cases
- Identifying trends and patterns
- Carrying out statistical analysis
- Tracking parolees (criminals who have been released before the end of their jail term because of good conduct)
- Posting surveillance photos of wanted criminals and missing persons on the Internet
- Transmitting, exchanging and obtaining information from other police officers in other departments or other countries via the Internet
- Developing contacts with other police organisations.

## Computers in medicine

Computers are now virtually indispensable in the field of medicine. They can be used to:

- Monitor patients' vital signs
- Maintain databases of patients, diseases and drugs
- Aid in detecting and diagnosing diseases
- Assist in generating case-specific advice through the use of expert systems
- Help doctors to collaborate with colleagues and administer treatment over the Internet
- Perform research

Some of the key hardware and software requirements in medicine are listed in Table 7.

| Hardware requirement | Software requirement |
|---|---|
| Mainframes, micro and super computers (for performing research and diagnoses) | Database Management software |
| Sensors (heart rate, temperature, pressure) | Patient monitoring system software |
| Printers/plotters | Expert systems |
| Magnetic Resonance Imaging (MRI) systems | Imaging software |
| Computer Axial Tomography (CAT) scanning (X-ray tubes) | |
| Monitors (high-resolution) | |

*Table 7*

### Patients' records

Electronic patients' records help doctors provide medical care. Records of patients' health history, as well as their personal information, can be easily accessed if this information is computerised. This would be especially helpful where information about one patient exists in several different institutions. An extranet or central database could allow the patient's main doctor to access more complete information about the patient's treatment in several different institutions, thereby helping their analysis.

Most doctors' offices in the Caribbean still use manual databases to store information about their patients' diagnosis, symptoms and treatment. Computerised records can reduce the time spent looking for patient records in the case of an emergency. They can also make it easy for trends in diseases to be detected. However, potential challenges exist, such as maintaining the privacy of these records, how much access should be granted to health insurers, and what level of control should be given to patients regarding the content of their records.

## Patient monitoring systems

Patient monitoring systems help doctors monitor and treat patients – either at home or in hospital intensive care – by providing a 24-hour service which can reduce false alarms. These are computerised systems that monitor a person's vital signs, such as blood pressure, temperature and heart rate, using sensors attached to the patient. The system records the information at specific intervals and may sound an alert in the event of a dangerous abnormality in the readings.

## Computer-aided detection and computer-aided diagnosis

Both the following systems assist doctors in detecting or diagnosing abnormalities in the tissues of their patients.

- *Magnetic Resonance Imaging (MRI)* uses magnets to create two- and three-dimensional images of tissues such as the brain. The images are processed by computers for analysis by doctors. This helps to detect strokes, tumours, infections and even haemorrhages.
- *Computer Axial Tomography (CAT) scanning*: A CAT scanner is an X-ray tube that takes as many as 30 pictures per second as it rotates around the patient. The computer system reconstructs a three-dimensional view of parts of the patient's body from the pictures taken. This aids in the diagnosis of brain diseases, tumours and so on.

## Expert medical systems

This type of system analyses data and provides answers to questions in the field of medicine. It imitates the behaviour of a human adviser. Active knowledge systems use two or more items of patient data to generate case-specific advice.

The Quick Medical Reference (QMR) system (available from the Camdat Corporation) is a medical expert system that performs differential diagnosis in many areas of internal medicine. Other examples of expert systems are Mycin and Dentral.

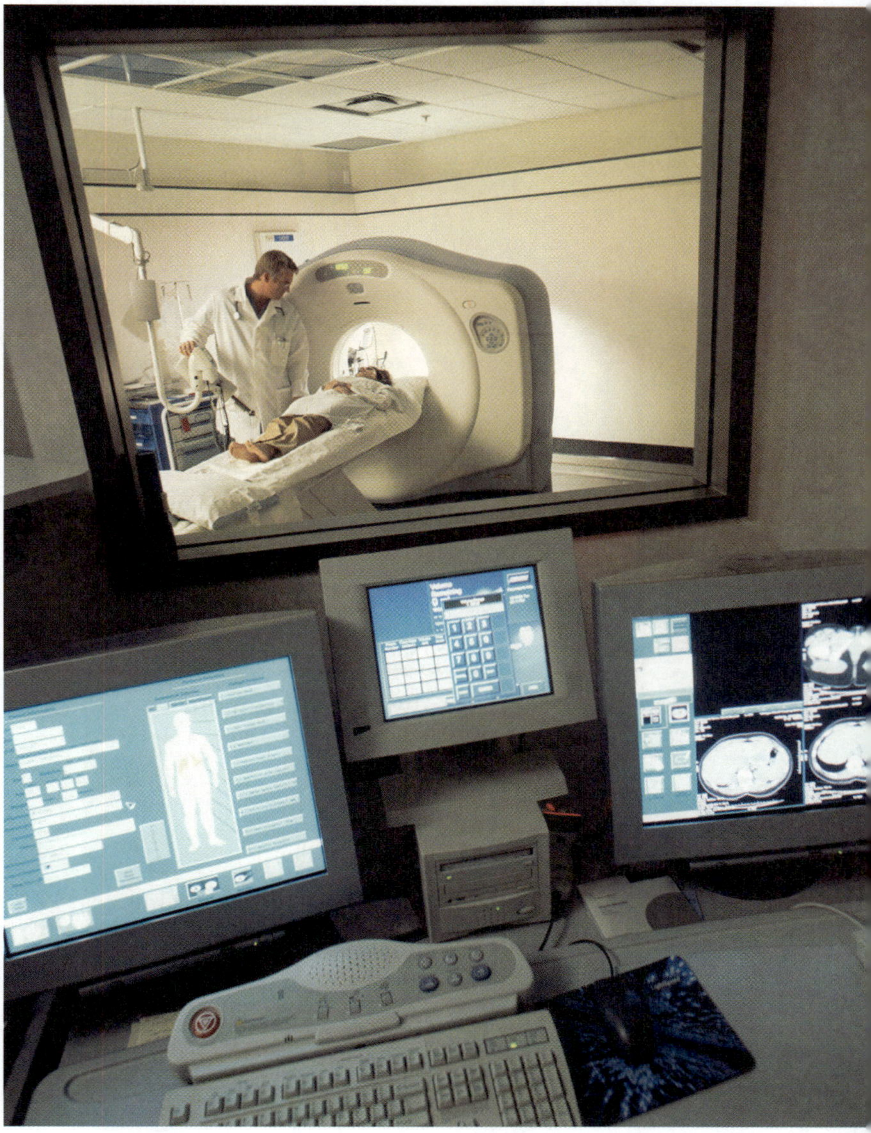

*Figure 15.11 MRI scan*

The advantages of an expert medical system are:

- It can support a doctor who is doubtful of his decision because of lack of knowledge or experience.
- Experts can use this system to arrive at a faster, more accurate conclusion.
- The theory behind the conclusion can be given.

Its disadvantages are:

- Instinct and common sense, which this system does not have, are often a good part of decision-making.
- The system cannot learn from its mistakes, unlike a real doctor.
- It could have disastrous effects if used by unqualified individuals.

### Practising medicine via the Internet

Doctors can use the Internet in any number of ways: to send information to patients; to send X-rays to other medical institutions; even to collaborate with colleagues on surgery 'live' in different parts of the world. Video and broadband connections may allow a specialist far away from the location of a surgical operation to give advice to the surgeon actually present, based on what the distant specialist is seeing on the computer screen.

Some doctors are now diagnosing patients' illnesses and prescribing medication online. However, potential legal problems may occur with this innovation, since it is not always clear who would be responsible if a patient were to worsen as a result of a poor web-based diagnosis. Many medical web sites contain disclaimers warning patients they must seek appropriate medical follow-up by meeting one-on-one with a real doctor.

## Computers in entertainment

Computers also feature heavily in the production, distribution and consumption of all forms of modern entertainment, from games to movies and music.

In entertainment computers are used to:

- Record, synthesise, edit and distribute music
- Create and play computer games
- Create animations and special effects in movies.

Table 8 lists some of the hardware and software requirements.

| **Hardware requirement** | **Software requirement** |
| --- | --- |
| Microcomputers | Music recording and editing software |
| Speakers | Animation software |
| Gaming consoles | Special effects software |
| Gaming wheel, joystick, game-pad | Actual games |
| Monitors (low- and high-resolution for graphics and animation) | Game editors used to create new levels in games |

*Table 8*

## Music and sound

The natural sounds of most musical instruments have been digitised into electronic versions and can now be played from a single instrument such as a keyboard. When the keyboard is connected to your computer you can record, play back and enhance music. The use of software to edit sound and music clips, and insert these clips into other pieces of music, is used extensively today. More and more music is being produced electronically in this way.

*Figure 15.12*
*A still shot from Matrix Revolutions*

Another application of computers in music is at the distribution and consumption end. It is now very fashionable to download popular music to cell phones and MP3 players from the Internet. This can be done legally for a relatively small transaction fee via various web sites, such as Apple's highly successful Music Store (www.apple.com/itunes/store). The convenience and choice available online – where you only buy the songs you actually want – contrasts with the traditional method of having to visit a real store and buy a complete ready-packaged CD.

## Movies and animation

Computers play a big part in the making of movie CGIs (Computer Generated Images) as featured in popular films such as *The Matrix*, *Star Wars*, *Finding Nemo*, *Terminator 2: Judgment Day* and *The Lord of the Rings* trilogy. Animations are now part of many popular movies; the old method of sketching on paper to create an animation is rapidly becoming defunct. Anima, a new method of animation, has also become popular in recent times. The Anima software allows persons without much computer skill to develop an animation from the beginning to final product. Developed at The Computer Graphics Research Group, the Anima II software allows you to develop an animation from an idea to the finished colour video product. This product can be observed and recorded in real time.

## Games

The gaming industry is another hugely successful entertainment arm of computing. Games for pure entertainment, or educational games known as 'edutainment', have become big business. The Nintendo, PlayStation I and II, X-Box and Game Boy (special computer game playing consoles) as well as computer games for the PC and the Mac, have become very popular, grossing millions of dollars every year.

*Figure 15.13*
*Game Boy*

# Computers in weather forecasting

Weather forecasting is the practice of trying to predict what the weather conditions will be like by measuring and observing the current weather conditions around the world.

In weather forecasting computers are used to:

- Gather and store data
- Analyse the data
- Display the data in an animated, easily digestible way.

| Hardware requirement | Software requirement |
|---|---|
| Supercomputers | Database software |
| Satellites | Statistical software |
| Doppler radar and other advanced radars | Weather Model forecasting software |
| Weather balloons | |
| Sensors (pressure, humidity, temperature) | |
| Plotters and printers (to print weather maps and charts) | |

*Table 9*

Data obtained from a variety of sensors and instruments is sent to a supercomputer to be logged and analysed. Supercomputers, along with a number of complex instruments, are used to predict weather conditions.

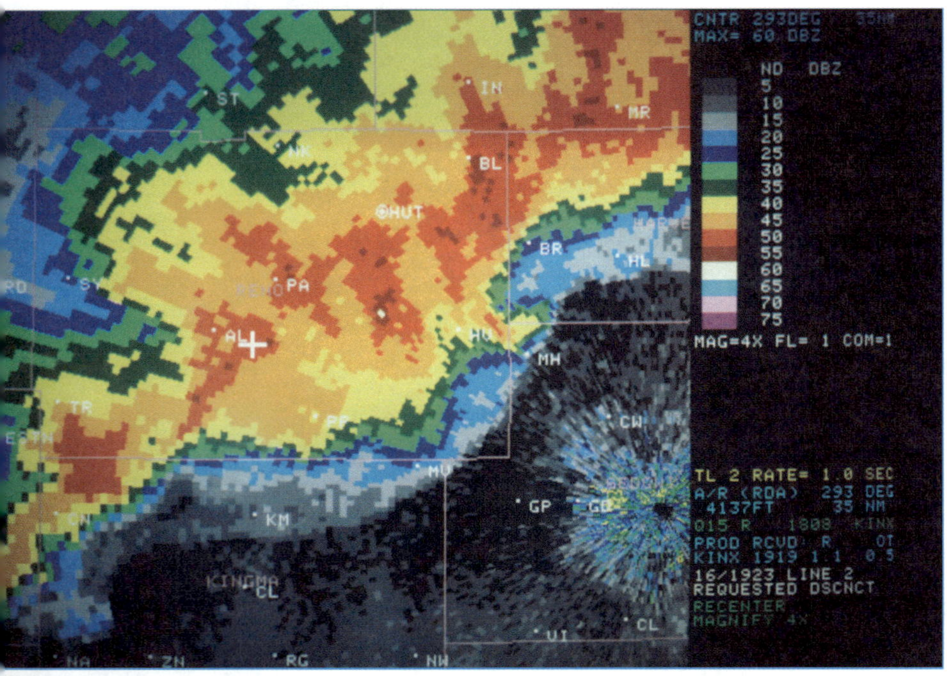


*Figure 15.14*
*Supercomputer showing a predicted weather pattern*

- Doppler radar gives the locations of storms. It also gives an indication of wind speeds, wind direction and precipitation.
- Weather balloons with radiosondes measure pressure, temperature and humidity in the air at many locations around the world. Radisondes are packages of light-weight measuring instruments that produce electrical signals that can be sent back to earth by radio.
- Satellites such as the GOES-8, orbiting high above the earth, take pictures to help create surface weather maps showing types of clouds and precipitation. These allow meteorologists to observe clouds across the entire globe.

The information gathered using these instruments, together with mathematical models, is used by the supercomputer to make predictions about the weather. The mathematical models are programs that contain complex mathematical equations. These try to predict weather conditions based on historical data. Even with the fastest computers, though, meteorologists cannot forecast day-to-day weather for more than a week ahead because elements of the weather may change quite radically.

Many new models are currently being developed. Some of these will help to forecast tropical features, such as hurricanes. Other models of the future will help to forecast smaller scale features, such as thunderstorms and severe weather outbreaks in fairly specific locations. Forecasters will be able to issue better and more timely warnings and advice. In the United States, the National Weather Service's National Centers for Environmental Predictions (NCEP) runs the computer models. All weather forecasters in the US rely on these models.

## Social effects of computers

Computers are very useful tools and we have seen that, in many ways, they are indispensable to our modern lives. Computers have both good and bad effects on our society; we will examine some of these in this section.

### Effects of computers on employment

Perhaps the area where computers have most greatly affected our lives is in the world of work. These effects are both good and bad.

#### *Loss of jobs*

Some jobs have become extinct with the advent of automation. Many jobs previously performed by humans are now being performed by computers or computer technology. Automated assembly lines (e.g. in car production plants) can perform many assembly jobs more efficiently and effectively then humans. As a result, significant job losses have occurred in production lines over the last two or three decades across the world.

Automation can also sometimes be used to replace humans where the jobs are boring, monotonous or dangerous. Dangerous or potentially hazardous jobs, such as the handling of chemicals, are now often done by robots instead of humans. In other cases, job losses have occurred because jobs previously requiring two or more persons to do them are now being done by just one person with a computer. Workers are being made redundant.

#### *Job creation*

Although there have been many job losses due to computerisation, there has also been job creation. The computer industry itself has created millions of new jobs across the world. Some jobs that have been created as a direct result of computerisation are in areas such as research, design, manufacturing, programming, maintenance, communication, education, consultation, marketing and security. Computerisation has resulted in the creation of high tech companies and jobs that require highly skilled workers. There is still a general shortage of workers for these types of high tech jobs.

Computerisation has also made jobs more accessible to the disabled person.

#### *Change in job skills*

With the introduction of computers into the workplace, many workers now need new skills or the upgrading of old ones. Many jobs now require basic computer knowledge; for example, office secretaries using typewriters are being asked to use computerised word processors and thus have to be retrained. Draughtsmen and architects are now required to produce their drawings and designs on computers using computer-aided design (CAD) packages.

### *Changes in work patterns*

Computers have also been changing the way people do their jobs. People can sit on a bus or in a café and work on their laptops. Teachers can send homework to absent students via e-mail, after normal school hours. A police officer can access and retrieve information from the computer in her police car, rather than go back to headquarters. Computers therefore allow us to work outside 'normal' working hours, and away from our 'normal' workplaces, i.e. telework or telecommute.

There may be consequences for family and social life as a result of this, both good and bad. It is now possible to choose when to work. If you are a teleworker you can juggle your work responsibilities with your family commitments, such as picking up your children from school. But it may not always be possible to have a full weekend off, dedicated to spending time with family and friends.

## Effects of computers on communication

Computers have allowed us to communicate almost instantaneously. We no longer use just telephones and mail, but also e-mail, which is both very cheap and very fast. E-mail has developed its own style of writing, a language all of its own with shortened words and symbols called 'emoticons'. This shortened form of English, a kind of jargon, aids quick communication in this computer age, but may have consequences in that traditional standards of grammar, spelling and punctuation are being eroded.

E-mail is also impersonal; using it we express ourselves in ways that we may not normally do in a face-to-face meeting. To some extent, relying on e-mail for communication, which can often occur where the parties communicating are far from each other, impedes the development of normal team-working relationships, since team members are literally faceless.

## Effects of computers on the environment

Technology has been blamed for polluting the environment. The use of solvents in the manufacturing of computers, and the disposal of old and used computer parts, can harm the environment, unless care is taken over this process. However, computers can have a positive impact on the environment by reducing levels of pollution. For example, if telecommuting becomes a big contributing force in how organisations run their operations, there will be fewer people commuting. This may contribute to a reduction in traffic pollution over time.

## The potential for overdependence on computers

The potential for overdependence on computers is a big issue. Computers can be used to manage critical systems in a power plant or an aircraft, to support the operations of large and small companies, transfer millions of dollars around the world and even assist a doctor performing a life-threatening operation. Despite all this, computers still fail – complete trustworthiness is so far elusive. For example, viruses can infect software and destroy data, with disastrous effects on individuals and organisations. Without a backup plan, companies, governments and other organisations affected by a computer failure for an extended length of time can cease to function properly.

# The effects of computers on employee health



Computer work is labour-intensive, requiring hours of repetitive work by the individual using the computer. Employees in this type of environment can suffer from a range of health problems known as computer work-related disorders.

## Repetitive strain injury (RSI)

There are two key types of **repetitive strain injury**. Tendonitis is where a tendon is inflamed, as a result of some repeated motion or stress on that tendon. Carpal tunnel syndrome (CTS) is an inflammation of the nerve that connects your forearm to the palm of your hand. Repeated or forceful bending of the wrist can cause CTS or tendonitis of the wrist. Symptoms of tendonitis of the wrist include extreme pain that extends from the forearm to the hand, along with tingling in the fingers. Symptoms of CTS include burning pains when the nerve is compressed, along with numbness and tingling in the thumb and first two fingers.

Excessive keying or mousing, bad posture and lack of rest are three key factors that may result in RSI.

### *Methods of preventing or reducing RSI*

- Take frequent breaks during any long computer session, roll your shoulders, exercise your hands and arms by shaking them and letting them hang loose.
- Type on the computer keyboard lightly, lifting your fingers up and down rather than moving your wrists.
- Position the mouse at the same height as your keyboard. When you slide the mouse around, move your entire arm and not just your wrist.

## Computer Vision Syndrome (CVS)

**Computer vision syndrome (CVS)** may cause any of the following conditions:

- sore, tired, burning, itching or dry eyes
- blurred or double vision
- headache or sore neck
- long-distance vision becoming blurred after prolonged staring at the monitor
- difficulty shifting focus between monitor and documents
- 'colour fringes' or 'after images' when you look away from the monitor
- difficulty focusing on the screen image
- increased sensitivity to light.

CVS is not thought to have any serious or long-term consequences, but it is nevertheless disruptive and unpleasant.

### *Methods of preventing or reducing CVS*

- Take a break of 5 to 10 minutes away from the computer every hour.
- Reduce glare and reflections from the computer screen – clean your screen and block out excessive sunlight and reflections from lamps.

- Adjust the contrast and brightness of the computer screen so that there is a high contrast between text on the screen and the screen background.
- Prevent eyestrain – the top of your screen needs to be at, or slightly below, eye level; find a comfortable distance between your eyes and the screen (usually eighteen to twenty-eight inches).
- Gently massage your eyes, cheeks, forehead, neck and upper back from time to time to keep blood flowing and muscles loose.

## Lower back pain

Lower back pain can be caused by bad posture or poorly designed or incorrectly assembled furniture or equipment.

### *Methods of preventing or reducing lower back pain*

- Use a firm, adjustable and comfortable chair. Adjust the chair height so that your thighs are horizontal, your feet are flat on the floor, and the backs of your knees are slightly higher than the seat of your chair. The back of the chair should support your lower back.
- Stretch your lower back now and then by standing up and pulling each knee to your chest, holding that position for a few seconds.
- Relax your shoulders. When you are keyboarding your upper arms and forearm should form a right angle, with your wrist and hand in roughly a straight line.
- Take short breaks (5 to 10 minutes per hour) – get up from your desk and walk around.

## Ergonomics

Ergonomics is a science that determines the best working conditions for humans who work with machines. Using these principles, manufacturers can incorporate features for comfort, efficiency and safety into computer furniture and equipment. For example:

- The curvature of a computer mouse may be designed to fit the average shape of the cup of a human hand.
- Desktop lamps can be designed to be flexible, with a bright and focused light that aids reading of printed computer documents.
- Computer keyboards are sometimes designed to arch in the middle. This is said to allow the human hand and arms to adopt a more natural, slightly angled, position when keying.

*Figure 15.15*
*An ergonomic keyboard*

# Summary


1 Information is collected for four main purposes: to monitor, control and supervise systems, people and processes; to be used as a commodity; to be used in making tactical and strategic decisions; to keep us generally informed.

2 We store information to make it easy to retrieve when we want to make a decision that is dependent on it; to manipulate it or analyse it or distribute it, at a time of our convenience; as a backup.

3 In banking we use computers when we withdraw cash from ATMs, use our debit cards and smart cards in stores, write and process cheques using MICR, use home or Internet banking, transfer funds by electronic funds transfer (EFT) and use stored-value cards.

4 In business we use computers in such areas as stock control and inventory, to set up or buy from e-commerce web sites, and in telecommuting or teleworking. There are advantages and disadvantages in buying from web sites. There are advantages and disadvantages to teleworking, both for the employer and the employee.

5 In education we use CAI and CAL tools to assist in teaching and learning, CAA tools to assist in assessment, and CML/CMI tools to administer resources. Computers are also used to find reference information (e.g. online libraries) and in distance learning. Using computers to assist teaching and learning has a major disadvantage in that it reduces face-to-face interaction between individuals.

6 We use computers in engineering and manufacturing for designing (CAD), drafting (CADD), manufacturing (CAM) and engineering (CAE).

7 Artificial intelligence (AI) has become one of the most innovative ways in which computers are used today, in such fields as robotics, process control, natural language processing (NLP), expert systems (e.g. in medicine) and virtual reality simulators.

8 Computers are used in law enforcement in areas such as: biometric identification systems; police car computers; national criminal intelligence databases; security cameras; profiling (computer facial composites); traffic control; electronic surveillance.

9 Computers are also used in medicine in areas such as: patients' records, patient monitoring, Magnetic Resonance Imaging (MRI scans), Computer Axial Tomography (CAT scans), expert medical systems, medicine via the Internet.

10 In the entertainment industry, computers are used to record, edit and distribute music, to write and play sophisticated games, and to produce special effects in the movies.

11 The social effects of computers are both positive and negative, and include: loss of jobs due to automation; the creation of many new jobs associated with computers; changes in job skills (necessitating retraining); changes in work patterns (times and places of work, telecommuting); changes in methods of communication (e-mail shorthand replacing face-to-face meetings); pollution of the environment unless hardware is properly disposed of; the potential for overdependence on computers.

12 Computers can have a negative impact on our health, the most common problems being repetitive strain injuries (RSI), such as tendonitis, where a tendon is inflamed, and carpal tunnel syndrome (CTS), an inflammation of the nerve connecting your forearm to the palm of your hand.

13 Computer vision syndrome (CVS) and lower back pain are other problems that can occur when using computers for extended periods of time. These can be tempered by using ergonomic equipment, such as appropriately designed keyboards and mouse, modern high-resolution screens, and chairs and desks designed specifically for computer work.


# Questions

## True or False?

1 Virtual reality is a form of artificial intelligence. T❑ F❑

2 A smart card stores information about your bank account on a magnetic strip. Your bank card is called a debit card. T❑ F❑

3 Educational gaming software is known as edutainment software. T❑ F❑

4 An individual cannot use CAI and CAL software at his/her own pace. T❑ F❑

5 Simulations allow you to perform dangerous experiments without risk to life or wastage of materials. T❑ F❑

6 Many special effects in movies are created using virtual reality. T❑ F❑

7 Biometrics is a form of traffic control. T❑ F❑

8 Human instinct is part of expert systems. T❑ F❑

## Multiple choice

1 Which of the following is not a health problem associated with extended use of the computer?
   (a) Back pain
   (b) CVS
   (c) RSI
   (d) High blood pressure

2 A factor that does not result in RSI is:
   (a) Sitting too close to the screen
   (b) Repetitive key strokes
   (c) Lack of rest and breaks between computer work
   (d) Bad posture

3 The following are disadvantages of using a medical expert system except:
   (a) Instinct and common sense are often a good part of decision-making, which this system does not have.
   (b) Experts can use this system to arrive at a faster, more accurate conclusion.
   (c) The system cannot learn from its mistakes, unlike a real doctor.
   (d) The system could have disastrous effects if used by unqualified individuals.

4 Information is collected for the purpose of:
   (a) Making tactical and strategic decisions
   (b) Monitoring, controlling and supervising systems, people and processes
   (c) Using it as a commodity
   (d) All of the above

5 In the police service, computers are used to do each of the following except:
   (a) Examine forensic evidence
   (b) Communicate with other departments and agencies
   (c) Design menus
   (d) Provide electronic surveillance

## Short answer questions

1 What do the following stand for?
   (a) CAE (b) CAL
   (c) CAI (d) AI
   (e) CML (f) ATM
   (g) NLP

2 (a) Explain the term 'expert system'.
   (b) List THREE fields in which expert systems are used.
   (c) State ONE advantage and ONE disadvantage of using expert systems.

3 Describe TWO applications of CAD and CADD.

4 Name TWO devices that can be used in CAM systems.

5 State FOUR ways in which computers and their related technology are used in medicine.

6 The Head of the English and Mathematics departments of a school are attempting to convince their staff to use CAI and CAL software. Explain the benefits and limitations of introducing such software.

7 Describe TWO applications of AI in our homes.

8 Your friend is ill but feels that waiting at the doctor's office is too time-consuming. She has found a web site where the doctor can diagnose illnesses online and prescribe medication. She wants to know more about this system. Discuss the benefits and implications of practising medicine via the Internet.

## Crossword

### Across

4 Allows you to perform banking transactions 24 hours a day (3)

6 An_____ system acts as a human adviser or consultant (6)

7 Is a feature used in making movies? (3)

### Down

1 Is a form of electronic surveillance? (2 words) (8)

2 Voice ______ systems produce sounds resembling human speech (9)

3 This card contains a memory chip that holds your banking transaction information (5)

5 Detects strokes and tumours (3)

# Glossary

## A

**absolute cell reference** A reference to a cell in a spreadsheet that remains unchanged if the formula that contains the reference is moved or copied to another cell.

**access point** A device attached to a LAN and containing a radio receiver, encryption and communications software. It translates computer signals into wireless signals, which it broadcasts to network interface cards (NICs) on the network.

**action query** A query that performs one or more actions when run, such as deleting records, updating records, creating tables and appending records to existing tables.

**active cell** The cell that is available for data entry.

**adaptor** *See graphics/video card*

**algorithm** A sequence of instructions which, if followed, produces a solution to the given problem.

**anti-virus software** A special type of software used to remove or inactivate known viruses from a computer's hard disk, floppy disk or memory stick.

**append query** Adds a group of records from one or more tables to the end of one or more other tables.

**archiving** A form of backup. Inactive files are removed from the computer and stored in case they need to be referenced at a later date.

**argument** Refers to cell references, text or numbers that are used in a formula.

**artificial intelligence** The science of attempting to develop machines that mimic human behaviours such as reasoning, learning, hearing, seeing and communicating.

**assembly language** A programming language written using mnemonic codes (short codes that suggest their meaning and are therefore easier to remember).

**assignment symbol** The equal sign in a calculation statement.

**autofit** Changing the width of a column to fit the width of the largest label or value in that column.

**axes** The vertical and horizontal lines against which data is plotted.

## B

**backbone** A single line or cable with nodes at different points.

**backup** A duplicate copy of a program, disk or data file.

**bandwidth** A measure of the volume of data that can be transmitted in a given time.

**barcode** A series of thick and thin bars representing data, and usually encoding an item number.

**base** The number of single digits denoting different values in a positional numeral system, including zero.

**binary number system** Consists of two digits, 0 and 1.

**biometric systems** Refers to the science of identifying an individual through their body characteristics such as face geometry and hand geometry (e.g. fingerprints), iris or retinal scans, vein and voice patterns.

**bistable device** A device that can function in one of only two positions.

**bit** The smallest unit of storage in a computer. It can be either a 0 or a 1.

**Bluetooth** A standard developed by a group of electronics manufacturers that allows any sort of electronic equipment (computers, digital video cameras, cell phones, PDAs, keyboards, etc.) to automatically make their own connections without wires, cables or any direct action from a user.

**Boolean expression** An expression or statement whose value can either be True or False when evaluated.

**Boolean operator** Words such as AND, OR and NOT used in expressions of logic.

**booting** Loading the operating system into memory.

**broadband channel** A transmission channel capable of transmitting large volumes of data at speeds of over 100 000 cps.

**browser** A program that enables you to find, retrieve, view and send hypertext and hypermedia documents over the world wide web.

**buffer** A temporary area holding data that is in transit from one device to another, so that neither device is delayed by the other.

**bug** An error within a program.

**byte** A combination of eight bits that has the storage power to represent one character.

## C

**cache memory** Very fast memory that the processor can access much more quickly than main memory or RAM.

CAD (**Computer Aided Design** or **Computer Aided Drafting**) The use of hardware and software for the drawing of engineering or architectural designs.

CAE (**Computer Aided Engineering**) The use of a computer to analyse engineering designs produced by CAD systems by simulating a variety of conditions to see if the design works.

**CAI (Computer Aided Instruction)** The use of a computer to help students acquire knowledge or further their knowledge in a particular subject area.

**CAL (Computer Assisted Learning)** The interactive use of computers for training and learning.

**calculated field** A new field where the result of an expression/formula that is created is displayed.

**CAM (Computer-Aided Manufacturing)** The use of a computer to control manufacturing plant and equipment in a production system.

**category axis** The X-axis of a chart.

**cell** The intersection of a row and a column in a spreadsheet, used to hold a label, value or formula.

**cell address** *See cell reference*

**cell pointer** Identifies the active cell.

**cell reference** The cell's (column, row) position.

**central processing unit (CPU)** *See processor*

**character** Can be a letter, a number, a symbol, a punctuation mark or a blank space.

**character printer** Prints one character at a time, much like a typewriter.

**character set** All the characters that a computer can store and process.

**chat room** A group of people with common interests communicating with one another interactively in real time.

**client** *See server*

**client/server** A network in which any computer can be designated as the server.

**clip art** A collection of icons, buttons, pictures and symbols used to represent common objects, processes and ideas that can be inserted into various documents.

**clipboard** A temporary storage area used to hold information cut or copied from a document.

**coaxial cable** A type of communications channel used to transmit voice, video and data.

**column break** The position in a column where the text ends and the next column starts.

**command** A word that instructs the computer what must be done to accomplish a specific task.

**compiler** A compiler translates the entire program (source code) to machine code, then the code is executed.

**computer** A programmable electronic device that processes data following a set of instructions to produce information, which it can output or store for future use.

**computer consultant** A person who is hired to give an independent and objective opinion on how ICT can be used to meet the needs of an organisation.

**computer engineer** An individual who maintains and troubleshoots computers and networks.

**computer operator** A person who monitors and controls a computer system by operating the central console.

**computer program** A series of coded instructions for the computer to obey in order to solve a problem.

**computer sales representative** A person who markets computer products and services.

**computer support technician** A person who performs tasks for the ongoing support of computer users.

**computer vision syndrome (CVS)** Eye and vision problems that occur due to prolonged use of the computer, characterised by eyestrain, headaches, blurred vision and eye irritation.

**concurrent processes** Processes running at the same time in a multitasked environment.

**condition** An expression that when evaluated either gives a TRUE or a FALSE.

**configuration** How computers on a network are connected together.

**constant** A value that never changes throughout the course of a running program.

**construct** A group of instructions that work together with commands to accomplish a specific task.

**continuous data** Data that can be measured and can be recorded at many different points.

**control system** A device or devices that controls and manages the behaviour of other devices through the use of sensors.

**crosstab query** Compresses the query results and displays them in a spreadsheet-like fashion.

**cut** Remove selected material from a document and copy it to the clipboard. *See paste*

**cylinder** All the tracks of the same number from all the metal disks that make up the hard disk, which can be read or written to at the same time.

## D

**data** All the raw facts and figures that a computer processes by following a set of instructions called a program.

**data capture** The first stage of getting data into the computer using various input devices.

**data communication** The transmission of data from one location to another for direct use or for further processing.

**data control clerk** A person who screens, edits and validates the input and output of a data processing unit.

**data entry operator** A person who enters data into a system in a form suitable for processing.

**data file** Same as data source.

**data integrity** Ensuring the accuracy and completeness of data when it enters a system and throughout its subsequent processing.

**data item** An individual piece of information stored in a field.

**data processing manager** The person responsible for the planning, coordinating, managing and staffing of a data processing department.

**data range** The data selected to create a chart.

**data security** The physical, hardware and software methods used to protect data.

**data security analyst** The person responsible for the protection of a company's computer-based information banks, and for keeping information safe from floods, fire, power outages, fraud, theft, invasion of privacy and viruses.

**data source** A file that contains the information or records that are required to be merged into a main document.

**database** An organised collection of structured data about a particular subject (person, place or thing).

**database administrator** The person responsible for the effective and efficient storage, retrieval, customisation and archiving of data.

**database file** The entire database.

**database management** The process by which information is organised and stored on a computer in such a way that there is efficient retrieval, updating and manipulation of the data.

**database package** A set of software that enables users to organise and store data so that specific items of information can be easily and quickly retrieved.

**debugging** The process of finding and correcting errors in a computer program.

**dedicated connection** A permanent connection to the Internet at all times.

**dedicated server** A server dedicated to a single function on a network.

**default settings** A preset number of features.

**delete query** Deletes a group of records from one or more tables.

**desk-checking/dry-running** Involves executing the program manually by using input values for variables and recording what takes place after each instruction is executed.

**desktop** The main screen in Windows where you can put files, folders and/or icons that act as shortcuts to various programs.

**digitising tablet /graphics tablet** An input board that allows you to enter drawings and sketches into the computer by detecting the position of a pointing device on its surface.

**direct access** Means that you can go directly to a specific piece of data without having to access any other data either before or after the data you want.

**directory** A collection of files or other (named) subdirectories, as part of a tree structure.

**discrete data** Data that can be counted.

**disk repair utility** A utility program that scans a hard disk or floppy disk for bad sectors (defective areas) and either makes repairs to these sectors, or marks the defective area so that the operating system will not store any data in that location.

**distance learning** Learning and education where the students and the instructor are in physically different locations, made possible through the use of technology such as the Internet, teleconferencing, videoconferencing and satellite.

**documentation** A written explanation of how the program works and how to use it.

**Domain Name System (DNS)** A distributed database system for translating a host computer name (such as 'a.b.com') to an IP address (such as '192.54.122.5') or vice-versa.

**download** Retrieve a file stored on another computer on the Internet.

**dry-running** *See desk-checking*

**dummy value** An input value that causes a loop to stop.

**dynaset** The resulting collection of records from a specific query.

## E

**e-commerce (electronic commerce)** The buying, selling, marketing and servicing of products and services over computer networks.

**EEPROM** A special type of ROM chip that can be erased and reprogrammed repeatedly by a user. It can be erased by exposing it to an electrical charge, which erases the entire chip.

**electronic data processing (EDP) auditor** The person responsible for ensuring that all aspects of a company's information systems perform in the manner stated in the system design.

**electronic eavesdropping** The tapping of a data transmission line to access data being transmitted.

**electronic funds transfer (EFT)** The movement of funds from one account to another electronically.

**e-mail** The sending and receiving of electronic messages (text, sound, video and graphics) using computers.

**e-mail address** A unique address used to identify persons sending and receiving e-mail.

**encrypting** Encoding (scrambling) data during storage or transmission so that it cannot be understood by someone who does not have the encryption key.

**encryption key** Software to convert encrypted data back to its original form.

**endnote** Text at the end of the document or section that cites the source or additional information pertaining to text within the document.

**EPROM** A type of ROM that can be erased and reprogrammed using special equipment.

**ergonomics** Determining the best working conditions for humans who work with machines.

**expert system** A program that analyses input data and provides answers at the level of an expert in a particular field.

**exponent** The power to which the base of a number is raised.

**extranet** Limited access to an organisation's intranet by people outside the organisation.

## F

**fibre optic** A communications channel consisting of hundreds of thousands of thin hair-like strands of glass that transmit pulsating beams of light.

**field** An area in a record reserved for a particular data item.

**field definition** The attributes that describe a field and determine how a field is stored, works and is displayed.

**field size** The maximum storage size allocated for a field.

**file defragmentation** Finding fragmented files and organising them back in a contiguous manner.

**file librarian** The person responsible for keeping all the data files and software organised and up to date in an enterprise.

**file transfer protocol (FTP)** A set of rules for transmitting stored files over the Internet, either by downloading or uploading.

**find duplicate query** Displays the records with duplicate values for one or more specified fields.

**find function** A search action that allows you to locate words, phrases or pieces of text within a document.

**finite loop** A loop where the instructions are repeated a specified number of times.

**firewall** A program or hardware device or combination of both that filters the information coming through the Internet connection into a computer system or network, to prevent unauthorised users from gaining access.

**folder** A directory.

**font** A particular typeface (shape of the character); a collection of characters (letters, numbers, symbols, punctuation marks and spaces) with a consistent appearance.

**font size** Refers to the height of a character measured in a unit called points where 1 point is $\frac{1}{72}$ of an inch.

**font style** Refers to whether the font is standard, bold or italic.

**footer** Text or graphic that appears in the bottom margin of every page of a document.

**footnote** Text at the bottom of a page that cites the source or additional information pertaining to information on the page.

**form** A method used to enter, view and print the information in a table other than in rows and columns.

**formula** Used to perform operations on numbers. It must start with an equals (=) sign, which is followed by numbers, different operators or cell references that are part of the calculation.

**full-duplex line** A transmission line that can simultaneously send and receive data.

**function** A predefined method of performing a specific task.

## G

**gateway** An interface that enables communication between two different networks.

**graphics/video card** or **adaptor** An electronic link between the computer's processor and the monitor; a circuit board that connects the processor to the monitor.

**gutter margin** A margin setting that allows additional space for binding.

## H

**hacking** Unauthorised access to a computer system.

**half-duplex line** A transmission line that can send and receive data but not simultaneously.

**handle** A made-up name that a person uses in a chat room.

**hard copy** Printed output from a computer.

**hard page break** A page break deliberately inserted before the end of a page.

**hardware** All the parts of the computer system you can see and touch.

**header** Text or graphic that appears in the top margin of every page of a document.

**high level language** Machine independent and not specifically designed for any one brand of computer.

**home or Internet banking** A form of banking which gives you the convenience of doing transactions from home or anywhere there is Internet access.

**hub** A common connection point for devices in a network.

**human readable** Output that can be read by human beings.

**hyperlink** An element in an electronic document that links to another place in the same document or to an entirely different document.

**hypermedia** Documents containing links to text, graphic, sound or video files.

**hypertext document** A document containing links to documents located on the same computer or on another computer on the Internet.

**Hypertext Markup Language (HTML)** A programming language used to create web pages.

**HyperText Transfer Protocol (HTTP)** A set of rules that controls how data travels between server and client.

## I

**icon** A pictorial object on your screen that represents files and activities with which you can work.

**image aspect ratio** Refers to the ratio of width to height of an image on the screen.

**impact printer** Printer that uses a number of metal hammers to strike an inked ribbon.

**indefinite loop** A loop where the instructions are repeated an unspecified number of times.

**index** A table containing two columns, one storing a sorted list of values in the field or fields being indexed, and the second storing pointers that give the location of each record in the table.

**inference engine** Part of an expert system that analyses input data using 'reasoning' methods, along with a knowledge base, to arrive at a conclusion.

**information systems manager** *See data processing manager*

**initialise** To give the variable a starting/initial value.

**ink jet printer** A printer that works by spraying ink through tiny nozzles to form characters and patterns on paper.

**input devices** Pieces of equipment that are used to put data into the computer.

**insert mode** A text entry mode where characters are inserted at the insertion point where the cursor appears and where characters are pushed to the right.

**instant messaging** A variation of IRC; it allows a user on the web to contact another user currently logged on and type a conversation.

**instruction register** Holds the instruction that is being processed.

**integrated circuit** A memory chip made up of millions of transistors and capacitors.

**Internet relay chat (IRC)** A real-time conference system that lets you talk with as many people as you like, grouped together on channels by topics, using text messages.

**Internet service provider (ISP)** A company that has a direct connection to the Internet and gives users access to it, usually for a fee.

**interpreter** An interpreter translates and executes one instruction at a time as it is encountered. The machine codes are not saved after execution.

**intranet** A micro-version of the Internet within a company or organisation.

**IP address (Internet Protocol address)** The unique address that identifies a computer on the Internet.

**iterate** Repeat a set of instructions over and over.

**iteration** One execution of a set of statements.

## J

**joystick** An input device that uses a lever to control movement of a cursor or graphic image.

**justification** The alignment of lines of text between the left and right margin of a document.

## K

**keylogging** A method used to record all the data entered via the keyboard.

**knowledge base** A database part of an expert system containing a large volume of information in a particular field.

**knowledge-based system** An expert system.

## L

**label** A title or heading to describe an aspect of the worksheet. It can contain any string of characters (letters or numbers) but must only start with a character that does not indicate a formula or number.

**LAN (Local Area Network)** A collection of computers in a building, department or school that can share peripherals, share information and communicate with each other on the Internet.

**language translator** Translates a program written by a programmer into machine language.

**latency time** The time it takes for the data to rotate under the read/write head of a disk.

**LCD (liquid crystal display)** A monitor which uses liquid crystals as part of the display.

**LCD panel** This multimedia projector is the size of a notebook and is placed directly on the surface of the overhead projector (OHP); it can be connected to devices just like the LCD projector.

**LCD projector** This multimedia projector has its own built-in lenses and light source and connects directly to computer, television, video/DVD player and video camcorder.

**light pen** A light-sensitive input device that detects the presence or absence of light on the display and is used to select an entry or indicate a position.

**line or bus topology** A network consisting of a single line or cable (also called the backbone) with nodes at different points. Servers, computers and other devices can be connected to any of the nodes on the line.

**line printer** Prints a line at a time using a limited number of characters. These printers do not print graphics.

**logic error** An error in reasoning, such as the incorrect sequencing of instructions, and flawed comparisons and selection statements.

**low level language** Machine dependent, different brands of computer use different codes.

## M

**machine code** The type of instruction that the computer's CPU can directly execute. Different types of computer have different machine-code languages.

**machine cycle** The sequence of instructions performed to execute one program instruction.

**machine language** Normally written using 1's and 0's, binary code.

**machine readable** Computer output that cannot be understood by humans.

**macro** Short program written to automate several steps in software, such as in database, spreadsheet and word-processing programs

**Magnetic Ink Character Recognition/Reader (MICR)** The use of magnetic ink, especially on cheques, to print and to detect special characters.

**magnetic strip reader** A device that reads the data contained in magnetic strips, such as those on the back of credit cards.

**mail client** A program that enables you to read and compose e-mail messages, send e-mail and access e-mail from the server.

**mail merge** The ability to produce a large number of personalised form letters, mailing labels and memos without having to type each one individually.

**mail server** A computer on the Internet that receives incoming messages and delivers outgoing messages.

**mailbox** The area of storage allocated to a registered user by a server to hold incoming messages.

**mailing list** A group of people using e-mail to communicate their views on common issues or interests.

**main memory** Holds data and instructions that the computer is processing at the time.

**make table query** Creates a new table from all or some of the fields of data in one or more tables.

**mantissa** The fractional part of a number written in standard form.

**many-to-many relationship** Where many records/entities in one table are linked to many records/entities in another table through a common entity.

**menu** A list of commands for program action from which you can choose.

**menu bar** An area, usually horizontal and near the top of a program's window, containing the names of menus relevant to the program's operation.

**merge field** The name of the data that will be stored in the data source and later be merged into the main document as part of a mail merge.

**microfiche** An output medium consisting of rectangular sheets of film. Highly compressed storage can be achieved using this method.

**microfilm** An output medium consisting of a roll of film.

**modem** Modulator/demodulator: a device to convert digital data from a computer into analogue form that can be passed along a telephone wire, and vice versa.

**modulation** The use of a rapidly oscillating waveform to transmit signals. Usually the amplitude of the wave represents the value of the signal being transmitted.

**monitor** The display unit (screen and controls) attached to your computer; also called the Visual Display Unit (VDU).

**mouse** A hand-controlled device that rolls across a flat surface and whose movement controls the action of a screen cursor.

**multi-access system** A system which allows a number of users with online terminals to interact with the same computer at the same time.

**multimedia chat** The use of microphone and/or web cam to communicate over the Internet.

**multimedia projector** A device to create and deliver dynamic presentations that include sound, photos, video, text and other moving graphics as well as other effects.

**multiprogramming** The ability of the computer to appear to run more than one program at the same time, although at a specific instant in time the CPU is dealing with only one instruction for one of the active programs.

**multitasking** A hardware device on a comuter that enables it to communicate over a network.

## N

**narrow-band** A communications channel, which can transmit data at slow speeds of between 10 to 30 characters per second (cps).

**natural language processing (NLP)** Computer systems that recognise, understand and process written and spoken language; includes voice recognition systems and voice synthesis systems.

**network** A group of two or more computers linked together so that they can share resources (hardware, software and peripherals) and communicate with each other.

**network administrator** The person responsible for the creation, administration and security of computer networks.

**network interface card (NIC)** A hardware device on a computer that enables it to communicate over a network.

**newsgroup** A group of people with common interests who communicate by posting messages and replies on the Internet.

**newsreader software** Software that allows you to read and post messages to newsgroups.

**non-impact printer** Printer in which the print head does not strike the paper.

**non-volatile** Cannot be easily changed.

**normalisation** The process of shifting the binary point and multiplying by a power of 2 in a binary fraction.

**numeric constant** A constant that represents an integer, real, complex or byte number.

**numeric variable** A variable that stores only numeric data.

## O

**object** An option you can select and manipulate; it include tables, forms, queries, reports, macros and modules.

**object code** Machine code produced by a compiler.

**one-to-many relationship** Where one record/entity in one table is linked to many records/entities in another file/table.

**one-to-one relationship** Where one record/entity is linked to exactly one record/entity in another file/table.

**online shopping** Buying goods and services over the Internet.

**online terminal** A device for entering or displaying data, which is connected to a computer system.

**operations manager** The person responsible for the overall operations of a computer department on a daily basis.

**operator** Mathematical symbols that are used in formulae.

**Optical Character Recognition (OCR)** The use of software and a scanner to read and recognise characters.

**Optical Mark Reader/Recognition (OMR)** A reader that detects the position of marks on a piece of paper.

**overtype mode** A text entry mode where the character to the right of the cursor is replaced by characters as you type.

## P

**packet** A group of bits transmitted as part of a data stream across the Internet, numbered so that the data stream can be reassembled when it arrives at the destination computer.

**page printer** Prints an entire page at a time.

**parity bit** An extra binary digit used to check for transmission errors, and appended to a binary word to make the total number of 1s odd (odd parity) or even (even parity).

**paste** Copy material from the clipboard into a document. *See cut*

**peer-to-peer network** A network in which computers can communicate directly with each other, so that each can be considered as both client and a server.

**peripheral** A device that is controlled or monitored by the CPU, usually for providing input or output facilities. They include keyboards, printers, speakers, mouse and hard drives.

**pixel** One of the many tiny illuminated dots that make up the picture on the monitor screen. Also known as picture element.

**plasma display** A monitor in which light is created by a plasma discharge from phosphors between two flat panels of glass.

**plotter** A device that draws by moving a pen, and is especially suited for line drawings and charts in conjunction with CAD packages.

**pointing device** Used by graphical operating systems (e.g. Windows) to show the motion of a pointer or cursor, and enable the control and selection of objects on the display.

**point-to-point protocol (PPP)** A protocol used to establish network-protocol-supporting links over telephone lines using modems.

**primary key** A selected field or fields in a table that uniquely identifies a record.

**printer** A device especially designed to produce a hard copy of computer output.

**process control** The use of digital computers to monitor external processes closely and take corrective action if necessary, in industries such as chemical plants, steel mills and oil refineries.

**processor** The 'brain' of the computer. It takes raw data and, following a set of instructions, converts it into information.

**program** A set of instructions to the computer to complete a task.

**program counter** A register which holds the address of the current instruction (the instruction being processed).

**programmer** A person who writes, tests, debugs, documents, updates, repairs, modifies and expands new or existing programs.

**programming language** A series of coded instructions for the computer to obey, written using the specific rules and statements.

**PROM** A type of ROM that can be programmed using special equipment; it can be written to, but only once.

**protocol** A set of rules and procedures controlling the transmission and reception of data so that different devices or computers can communicate with each other.

**pseudocode** An algorithm that models or resembles the real programming language syntax.

**public domain software** Free software available for public use on the Internet.

**puck** Mouse-like device moved over the surface of digitising tablet for drawing and sketching.

## Q

**query** A method used for storing and answering questions about information in a database.

## R

**radio frequency identification** A chip connected to a small antenna makes up the RFID transponder or RFID tag and uses radio waves as a means of identifying animals, persons and objects.

**random access memory (RAM)** A type of chip which holds data and instructions (programs) temporarily while processing is taking place using that data and program.

**range of cells** A group of continuous cells that forms a rectangle and is treated as a unit.

**read only memory (ROM)** A type of chip which holds data and instructions necessary for starting up the computer when it is switched on.

**record** A collection of related data about a specific subject.

**refresh rate** The number of times a second the image is repainted or refreshed on the screen.

**register** A temporary storage location that holds a single instruction or data item.

**relational database** A database that links together logically related data stored in several files or tables.

**relative cell addressing (reference)** A reference to a cell in a spreadsheet that changes with respect to its current position when the formula is moved or copied.

**remote network access** Transmitting data between computers using a satellite link.

**repetitive strain injury (RSI)** An injury that affects the tendons and nerves due to repeating the same movement continuously for extended lengths of time.

**replace function** Replaces all occurrences of a word or formatting within a document.

**report** To organise and group information from tables or queries to format the data for online viewing or to print the data from the database.

**resolution** The number of dots horizontally (w) and vertically (d) on a monitor screen, always specified in the form 'w × d'. It determines the clarity and sharpness of an image.

**robot** Computer-controlled machinery that includes functions such as locomotion, mobility, grasping and recognition.

**root drive** The base position of a disk.

**router** A specialised computer or a piece of electronic hardware designed to direct data efficiently towards its intended destination across a network.

**runtime errors** Errors occurring after the program has been tested and debugged during the execution or running of the program.

## S

**save** Store a document on a secondary storage device so that it can be made available for editing and printing at a later date.

**scanning device** Designed to scan pictures and text and translate them into a form that the computer can use.

**search engine** Software or a web site that enables you to find information quickly by typing in key words or phrases.

**search terms** The keywords or phrases you type into a browser to enable it to find the information you want.

**sector** The amount of data that can be read from or written to a disk by the computer in one read/write operation.

**seek time** How long it takes the read head to get to the right track on a disk.

**select query** Extracts data from tables based on a criterion or specified value.

**sensor** A device that measures physical quantities such as temperature, fluid flow, pressure, etc.

**sentinel value** *See dummy value*

**sequentially** Data is retrieved in the order in which it was stored.

**series** The row- or column-headings that make up the range of values from the worksheet that is used to create a graph.

**server** On a network, a computer running software that allows resources to be shared with the other computers (called clients).

**simplex line** A transmission line that can send or receive data but not do both.

**SLIP/PPP** Serial Line Internet Protocol/Point-to-Point Protocol: the rules that govern how a computer connects to the Internet.

**smart card** A card similar in shape and size to a credit card, but with an embedded microprocessor (a thin gold-coloured memory chip) having processing and storage capacity.

**soft copy** Output or temporary output refers to information displayed on a screen or in audio or voice form through speakers.

**soft page break** Moving from a completed to a new page automatically.

**software** A set of instructions (a program) that a computer needs to carry out its tasks.

**source code** Program written in the specific programming language.

**source document** Document on which data is first recorded before it is entered into the computer.

**speech synthesis/voice synthesis** The ability of a computer to produce sounds resembling human speech.

**spider** A program that searches the web looking for new pages to add to a search engine's database.

**spyware** Software that covertly monitors a user's actions without his/her knowledge and is capable of locally saving or transmitting those findings to someone else.

**star network** A network consisting of several computers and other devices connected to a central hub.

**stored-value cards** A card that is stacked with a certain amount of money or loyalty points and with each purchase a certain amount is deducted from the card.

**string constant** A sequence of characters/text that does not change during the running of a program.

**string variable** A variable that stores any kind of text information.

**stylus** A pointing device in the shape of a pen which allows you to make selections on the surface of a graphics/digitising tablet.

**subscript** Places characters below the normal line.

**superscript** Raises characters above the normal line.

**syntax** Specific rules and statements of that particular computer language.

**syntax error** A programming error caused by incorrect use, violating the rules governing the structure of the language.

**systems analyst** A person who studies the operations of a manual or computerised system and tries to find solutions to specific user problems by implementing a computerised system or upgrading an existing one.

**systems development manager** A person responsible for supervising the development of a new computer system or the maintenance of an existing system.

## T

**table** A basic unit of a database which contains data on a specific topic.

**TCP/IP (Transmission Control Protocol/ Internet Protocol)** A set of protocols used to transfer data from one computer to another over the Internet.

**telecommuting** Working at home instead of the office, and transmitting work over a communication network to the computer at the office.

**Telnet** A terminal emulation program that enables you to access data and programs from a host computer.

**terminating value** Same as sentinel value or dummy value.

**text-based chat** The use of text to communicate in a chat room.

**toggle key** A key, for example caps lock or insert, that switches back and forth between two modes or functions.

**topology** The way in which computers in a particular network are logically connected together.

**touch screen (touch terminal)** A device that enables you to input data by touching a screen with your finger or another object.

**trace table** A table of values that follows the effect of each line of program code on the variables being used within the program.

**tracing** A technique that allows the user to detect any logic errors in the program or algorithm.

**track** A set of numbered concentric rings on the surface of a disk.

**transmission time** The time taken to read the data from a disk and transmit it to the CPU.

**twisted pair** A communication channel consisting of two strands of twisted insulated copper wire.

## U

**Uniform Resource Locator (URL)** The address of an Internet file, usually in the format 'Protocol://Server/Path/ Filename'.

**update query** Makes changes to a group of records, or all records, in one or more tables based on specific criteria.

**upload** Send files to other computers on the Internet.

**user interface** The user-controllable part of the operating system which allows you to communicate, or interact, with it.

## V

**validation** Checking performed by the computer to ensure that data entered obeys the rules which apply to it.

**value** A piece of data that can be used in a calculation.

**value axis** The Y-axis of a chart.

**variable** A name that is given to represent a piece of data that can be changed/varied while the program is running.

**verification** Checking for accurate transcription of data entered.

**virtual reality system** Includes hardware and interactive graphics software which can replicate sensations that imitate the real world.

**virus** A program that activates itself, unknown to the user, and is capable of causing damage to your computer system.

**virus protection** *See anti-virus software*

**Visual Display Unit (VDU)** A monitor.

**voice recognition** The ability of a computer system to accept spoken words as input for processing.

**voice response systems** A set of digitised pre-recorded words, phrases, music, alarms or other sounds selected and played back based on selections made by the user.

**voice-band** A channel that can transmit data at a rate of 1000–8000 cps, e.g. a telephone line.

**volatile** Temporary and changeable.

## W

**WAN (wide area network)** A communications network that covers a wide geographical area such as a country.

**webcam** A small video camera connected to a computer.

**webcasting** The delivery of live or delayed sound or video broadcasts conducted over the World Wide Web.

**webinar** The conducting of a seminar or lecture via the World Wide Web.

**webmaster** A person who manages a web site.

**web portal** A web site that allow users to find information quickly and easily.

**web server** A computer that stores and makes available hypertext and hypermedia documents.

**window** A framed rectangular area on your display controlled by an executing program.

**word** The number of bits the computer can process in one operation.

**word length** The number of bits in a word.

**word wrap** A feature that enables you to complete a line of text and move automatically to a new line without pressing the 'Enter' key.

**workbook** Contains a number of worksheets.

**worksheet** The grid of rows and columns used by a spreadsheet program.

**worm** A program that uses computer networks and security holes (weaknesses in a security system) to repeatedly copy itself into a magnetic disk, until no more space is left.

# Index


A: drive *see* floppy disks
absolute cell references 211–12, 343
Access 235–68, 271–6, 278–82
*see also* databases
access points 85, 343
action queries 257, 343
active cells 193, 195, 343
adaptors 41, 343
ADSL (asymmetric digital subscriber line) 90
advanced filters 215
advanced search syntax 101
advertising spyware 144
AI *see* artificial intelligence
algorithms 107, 111–36, 343
alignment of cells 197
ALU (arithmetic and logic unit) 6
American Standard Code for Information Interchange (ASCII) 58–9
analytical skills 302
AND operator 122–3
animation 335
anti-virus software 141, 343
append queries 257, 260, 343
application programmers 303
application software 66–8
applications of IT 93–102, 312–37, 341–2
archiving 139, 343
arguments, formulae 203, 343
arithmetic and logic unit (ALU) 6
artificial intelligence (AI) 326–9, 343
ASCII Code 58–9
assembly language 108–9, 343
assignment symbols 118, 343
associations, files 75
asymmetric digital subscriber line (ADSL) 90
ATMs 316–17
attributes 234
audio input devices 21–3
audit trails 139
auditors 307
AutoFilter 214
autofit resizing 199, 343
Automated Teller Machines 316–17
AutoSum 206–7
Average function 208
axes, charts 217, 343

back pain 340
backup utility 77, 343
bandwidths 81, 343
banking applications 316–18
barcode readers 19, 20, 343
BASIC computer language 109
batch processing 71
BBS *see* bulletin board system
BCD *see* binary coded decimal
binary coded decimal (BCD) representation 57
binary numbers 50–4, 57, 60–1, 343
biometrics 23, 138, 139, 330–1, 343
bistable devices 50, 343
bits 28, 343
Bluetooth technology 86, 343
BODMAS rule 203–4
Boolean expressions/operators 119, 122–3, 343
boot-sector viruses 141
booting operating systems 68, 343
borders 187
Braille printers 46
broadband channels 81, 343
broadcasting 98
browsers 92, 343
buffers 69, 343
bugs 134, 343
bulletin board system (BBS) 96
bullets 168
bus topology LANs 84–5
business applications 319–22
business opportunity schemes 146
business skills 302
business-to-business (B2B) 319
business-to-consumer (B2C) 319
bytes 28, 343

C computer language 109
cable modems 90–1
cabled LANs 83–4
cache memory 26–7, 343
CAD *see* Computer Aided Design
CAE *see* Computer Aided Engineering
CAI *see* Computer Aided Instruction
CAL *see* Computer Assisted Learning
calculated fields 262, 343
calculations, algorithms 118–19
CAM *see* Computer Aided Manufacturing
cameras *see* digital cameras; security cameras
caption format 240
careers 299–311
carpal tunnel syndrome (CTS) 339
case, changing 164
CAT scanning *see* Computer Axial Tomography scanning
category axis 217, 343
cathode ray tube monitors 40–1
CD-R (Compact Disc-Recordable) 32, 33
CD-ROM (Compact Disc-Read Only Memory) 32, 33
CD-RW (Compact Disc-Re-Writable) 32, 33
cell addresses 193, 206, 343
cell pointers 193, 343
cell ranges 196–7
cell references 193, 211–12, 343
cells 184, 193, 197–8, 343
central processing unit (CPU) 5–6, 343
changing case 164
character printers 44–5, 343
character sets 58, 343
character strings 115
characters 28, 57–9, 162, 343
*see also* special characters
charts 217–21, 277, 290, 343–4
chat rooms 96, 343
chats 96–7
cheque processing 317–18
click and drag resizing 199
client/server network 83, 344
clients 82, 344
*see also* e-mail clients; mail clients
clip art 186, 344
clipboard 159, 344
closing documents 156
CMI (Computer Managed Instruction) 323
CML (Computer Managed Learning) 323
coaxial cabled LANs 84, 344
COBOL computer language 109–10
collecting information 312–15
columns 181–5, 193, 198–9, 212, 344
command-driven interface 71–2
commands 112, 344
communications 81–106, 338
Compact Disc... *see* CD...
comparison statements 112–13, 119
compilers 111, 135, 344
Computer Aided Design (CAD) 325–6, 343
Computer Aided Engineering (CAE) 326, 343
Computer Aided Instruction (CAI) 323, 343
Computer Aided Manufacturing (CAM) 326, 343
Computer Assisted Assessment (CAA) 322
Computer Assisted Learning (CAL) 323, 343
Computer Axial Tomography (CAT) scanning 333
computer consultants 306–7, 344
computer crimes 138, 144–6
computer engineers 308, 344
computer languages 107–11
Computer Managed Instruction (CMI) 323
Computer Managed Learning (CML) 323
computer operators 304–5, 344
computer output on microfilm/microfiche (COM) 47
computer programmers 303
computer programs 5, 131–6, 344, 348
*see also* programming
computer sales representatives 308–9, 344
computer vision syndrome (CVS) 339–40, 344
computers 4–13, 344
concurrent processes 70, 344
conditions 119, 344
confirming data entry 195
consoles 304
constants 115, 118, 344
constructs 112, 120–2, 127–30, 344
continuous data 50, 344
control systems 47, 313, 328, 344
control unit 5–6
copy function 158–9, 200–1, 245, 277
corrupted data 138
COUNT function 208
counting 125–6
CPU *see* central processing unit
credit cards 146, 318
crimes 138, 144–6
crosstab queries 257, 344
CRT monitors 40–1
CTS (carpal tunnel syndrome) 339
cumulative totals 126
currency format 200, 239
custom-written software 67–8
cut function 158–9, 200, 344
CVS *see* computer vision syndrome
cylinders 31, 344

data 4, 50–65, 234, 237, 245–8, 271–98, 344
collection 14
indexing/sorting 252–6
privacy 142–6
verification/validation 14
data capture 14, 344
data communications 81–102, 344
data control clerks 305, 344
data entry 194–9, 286–7
data entry operators 305, 344
data files 176, 344
data input instructions *see* input instructions
data integrity 138–42, 344
data processing jobs 299–305, 344
data range, charts 217, 344
data records 176
data security 138–42, 344
data security analysts 306, 344
data sources 175–80, 271–6, 344
database administrators 300–1, 344
database file 234, 344
database management 233, 344
databases 233–70, 271–85, 291–4, 344
SBA project 284–5, 291–4, 297
*see also* Access
datasheet view 236
date formats 224–5, 239
debit cards 316–17
debugging programs 132–5, 344
decimal/binary conversion 51–2, 54, 60–1
decision-making 313
decision statements 112–13, 119
dedicated connections 91, 344
dedicated servers 83, 344
default settings 153, 195–6, 344
defragmenting files 77, 345
delete query 257, 260, 344
deleting
cell contents 197
data sources 180
fields 240
footnotes/endnotes 171
hard page breaks 172
headers/footers 170
indexes 253
lines 185
merge fields 178
records 244, 294
rows/columns 185, 198–9
worksheets 201–2
deselecting primary key 241
design careers 307–8
design view 236, 257–9
desktop 72–4, 344
dial-up connections 91
digital cameras 22
Digital Versatile Disk *see* DVD
digital video cameras 23
digitising tablets 17, 344
direct access 29, 344
directories 75–6, 99, 344
discrete data 50, 344
disk repair utility 77, 344
diskettes *see* floppy disks
distance learning 93, 324, 345
DNS *see* Domain Name System
documentation of programs 136, 345
documents 154–61, 186, 271–2, 277–8
Domain Name System (DNS) 92–3, 345
dot matrix printers 44
downloading 90, 345
drawing 175, 185
dry running programs 132–3, 344
dummy value *see* sentinel value
duplex lines 82
DVD (Digital Versatile Disk) 33
dynasets 257, 345

e-commerce 319–20, 345
editing
cell contents 197–8
data sources 180
records 245
spreadsheets 200–1
text 158–62
EDP *see* electronic data processing
education applications 322–5
EEPROM *see* electrically erasable PROM
effects, applying 164

electrically erasable PROM
(EEPROM) 27, 33–4, 345
electronic data processing (EDP)
auditors 307, 345
electronic discussion forums 96–7
electronic eavesdropping 140, 345
Electronic Funds Transfer (EFT) 318,
345
electronic mail *see* e-mail
electronic organisers 9
electronic surveillance 331
e-mail 74, 94–5, 140–1, 345
embedded computers 9
employee effects of IT 321, 339–40
employer effects of IT 321
employment 320–2, 337, 339–40
*see also* jobs
encryption 139–40, 141, 345
endnotes 171, 345
engineering industry 308, 325–6
entertainment applications 334–5
entity relationships 247
environmental effects of IT 338
erasable programmable ROM
(EPROM) 27, 345
ergonomics 340, 345
error messages 208
errors in programs 134
Excel 192–282
*see also* spreadsheets
expand button 249
expert systems 329, 333–4, 345
Explorer 76–7
exponents 62, 345
exporting database objects 278–9
expression-writing 260–1
extensions 75
extranets 102, 345

facial image identification 330–1
fibre optic cabled LANs 84, 345
field definition 234, 345
fields 238, 240, 246, 262, 343, 345
data 245, 252
*see also* merge fields
fifth generation computers 10
fifth generation languages (5GL)
110–11
file defragmentation 77, 345
file librarians 305, 345
file management 70, 74–7
file names 155
file transfer protocol (FTP) 94, 345
filename protocols 100
fill handle 201
filtering records 214–16
find duplicate queries 263–4, 345
find function 160, 345
fingerprints 330
finite loops 126, 345
firewalls 140, 345
first generation computers 9
first generation language (1GL) 108
fixed hard disks 31, 35
fixed point representation 60–1
flash memory 33–6
flat-bed plotters 47
flat panel display 41
floating point numbers 62–3
floppy disks 29–30, 155, 196
folders 75–6, 345
fonts 162–4, 345
footers *see* headers and footers
footnotes 171, 345
FOR construct 127–9
formats 62–3, 238–40
formatting 29–30, 31, 162–8, 195–6,
199–200
forms 264–5, 345
formulae 192, 194, 203–5, 208, 343,
345
FORTRAN language 109
fourth generation computers 10
fourth generation language (4GL) 110
fraction conversions 60–1
fraud schemes online 146

FTP *see* file transfer protocol
full-duplex lines 82, 345
functions 206–10, 221–5, 345

games 335
gateways 86, 345
general-purpose software 66
grammar check 160–1
graphical user interface (GUI) 72–4
graphics 186–7
graphics card 41, 345
graphics tablet 17
graphs 217–21, 277, 290
grouping data 246–8
GUI (graphical user interface) 72–4
gutter margin 169, 345

hacking 145, 345
half-duplex lines 82, 345
hanging indents 166
hard copy output devices 40, 43–7,
345
hard disks 30–2, 35, 196
hard page breaks 172, 345
hardware requirements 5, 95, 316,
319, 322, 327, 330, 332, 334, 345
header row 176
headers and footers 169–70, 172, 227,
345
health effects of IT 339–40
Hertz, Heinrich Rudolf 5
high level computer languages
108–10, 345
home banking 318, 345
HTML *see* HyperText Markup
Language
HTTP *see* HyperText Transfer
Protocol
hubs 84, 345
human readable output 40, 345
human sensory capability
simulations 329
HyperText Markup Language
(HTML) 101, 346
HyperText Transfer Protocol (HTTP)
98, 346

icons 72, 346
ICT department jobs 299–305
identification systems 330–1
IF function 221–3
IF-THEN construct 120–1
IF-THEN-ELSE construct 122
image aspect ratio 42, 346
in-car computers 331
indenting text 166–7
indexing data 252–6, 346
industrial espionage 146
inference engine 329, 346
information 4, 312–15, 323–4
information systems managers
299–300, 346
initialising variables 121, 346
input devices 5, 14–25, 69, 346
input instructions 112, 116
input mask format 239
insert mode 153, 346
inserting
borders 187
fields 240
footnotes/endnotes 171
functions 207
graphics 186–7
merge fields 180, 274
page breaks 172
page numbers 171
rows/columns 198–9
symbols/special characters
187–8
tables 184
worksheets 201–2
instant messaging 97, 346
integer representation 54–7
integrated services digital network
(ISDN) 90
integrated software 66–7

integration of data 271–98
Internet 88–102, 146, 318–20, 334
Internet Explorer 74
Internet Protocol (IP) 91–3, 346
Internet relay chat (IRC) 97, 346
Internet service providers (ISPs) 91,
346
interpreters 111, 135, 346
intranets 102, 346
IP *see* Internet Protocol
ISDN (integrated services digital
network) 90
ISPs *see* Internet service providers
iterations 113, 125–6, 346

jobs 299–311, 337
*see also* employment
joysticks 16, 346
justification (text) 166, 346

keyboards 15, 152–3
keylogging 143, 346
keyword searching 100–1
knowledge-based systems 329, 346

labels 194, 346
language translators 77, 346
languages *see* computer languages
LANs *see* local area networks
laptops 7
law enforcement applications
329–32
LCD items 41–2, 346
letters 274–5
light pens 17, 346
line topology LANs 84–5, 346
lines 165–6, 175, 185
links 91, 248–9
Linux operating system 69
lists of records 223
local area networks (LANs) 82–6, 346
logic errors 134, 346
loopings 113, 125–6
loops 126–30
loss of jobs 337
low level computer languages
108–11, 346
lower back pain 340

machine cycles 5, 346
machine language/code 108, 346
machine readable output 40, 346
macros 67, 346
magnetic disks 29–32, 35
magnetic ink character recognition
(MICR) 18, 317, 346
Magnetic Resonance Imaging (MRI)
333
magnetic strip codes 20, 346
magnetic tapes 29, 35
mail clients 95, 346
mail merge 175–80, 271–6, 346
mail servers 95, 346
mailing lists 96, 347
main document 175, 176
main memory 6, 347
mainframes 8
make table query 257, 347
management careers 299–300, 301,
304
management functions 69–70, 74–7
mantissa 62, 347
manual databases 233
manual program testing 132–3
manufacturing applications 325–6
many-to-many relationships 247, 347
margins 169, 227
mark scheme 296–8
MAX function 208
medical applications 332–4
megabits 85
memory management 70
menu bar 157, 159, 160–1, 347
menu-driven interface 72
merge fields 176, 178, 180, 274, 347
merging mail 175–80, 271–6

mickey unit 16
MICR *see* magnetic ink character
recognition
microfiche/microfilm 47, 347
Microsoft Access *see* Access
Microsoft Excel *see* Excel
Microsoft Office *see* Access; Excel;
Word
Microsoft Word *see* Word
MIDI instruments 22
MIN function 208
minicomputers 8
modems 43, 89–91, 347
monitoring systems 313, 333
monitors 40–2, 347
mouse 16, 159, 347
movies 335
MRI *see* Magnetic Resonance
Imaging
MSDOS mode 71–2
multi-access systems 69, 347
multimedia chat 97, 347
multimedia projectors 42, 347
multiple criteria sorting 213
multiprocessing 70–1
multiprogramming/multitasking 70,
347
music 22, 335
My Computer window 73

named indexes 253
naming files 74–5
narrow-band channels 81, 347
narrowcasting 98
natural language processing (NLP)
328, 347
nested IF statement 222–3
nested selections 123–4
network administrators 303–4, 347
network interface cards (NICs) 83,
85, 347
networks 82–8, 314, 347
newsgroups 96, 347
newspaper columns 181–3
NICs *see* network interface cards
NLP *see* natural language processing
non-adjoining cell ranges 196
non-impact printers 45–6, 347
normalisation 62, 347
notebook computers 7
number formats 168, 200, 239
number systems 50–4, 62–3
numbering pages 171–2
numeric constants 115, 347
numeric field size 238
numeric variables 116, 347

object code 134–5, 347
objects 234, 278–9, 347
OCR 19, 347
Office *see* Access; Excel; Word
one-to-many relationships 247, 249,
347
one-to-one relationships 247, 249,
347
one's complement 55
online terminals 69, 347
opening documents 156
operating systems 68–77
operations managers 304, 347
operators 203, 221, 261, 347
optical character recognition 19, 347
optical disks 32–3, 35
optical mark reader (OMR) 18, 347
OR operator 122–3
orientation 168–9, 197, 226
Outlook Express 74
output devices 6, 40–9, 69
output instructions 113–14, 117–18
overtype mode 153, 347

packets 92, 347
page breaks 172
page layout 168–74
page numbering 171–2
page orientation 168–9

page printers 44, 45–6, 347
Page Setup 226–7
palmtop computers 9
paper size 168–9
paragraph formatting 165
parity bit 58, 60, 347
Pascal computer language 109
passwords 139
paste function 158–9, 200, 245, 347
path protocols 100
patients' records/monitoring
systems 332–3
peer-to-peer network 83, 347
peripherals 5, 14–17, 347
personal computers (PCs) 5, 7
phrase searching 100–1
physical data security 138–9
pie charts 220, 290
PIN number 316–17
pirated software 144–5
pixels 40, 347
plasma display monitors 41, 347
plotters 47, 347
point of sale (POS) system 19
point-to-point protocol (PPP) 91, 97,
347
pointing devices 15–17, 347
points, font size 162
primary file *see* main document
primary key 240–4, 348
primary storage 26–8
Print Preview 226
printers 44–6, 346, 348
printing 157, 225–7
privacy 142–6
problems 107, 111–15
process control 328, 348
processing 5–6, 71, 112–13
profiling 331
programmers 303, 348
programming 107–37, 348
programs 5, 131–6, 344, 348
projectors 42
PROM 27, 348
prompting instructions 116–17
proofing 158–62
protocols 91–4, 97–8, 100, 348
pseudocodes 107, 348
public domain software 145, 348
publishing Access objects 278
pucks 17

queries 257–64, 292–4, 348

radio frequency identification
(RFID) 19–20, 348
RAID storage system 32
random access memory (RAM) 26,
348
range of cells 196–7, 348
read only memory (ROM) 27, 348
real-time processing 71
recipients, mail merge 272–4
records 214–16, 223, 234–5, 244–5,
289, 294, 348
Redo button 161
referencing information 323–4
referential integrity 249
refresh rate 42, 348
registers 6, 348
relational databases 234, 348
*see also* databases
relationships 247–9
relative cell addressing 206, 348
remote controls 23
remote login 140
remote network access 91, 348
removable hard disks 31, 35
renaming 178, 201–2
repeat statements 112–13, 125–6
repetitive strain injury (RSI) 339, 348
replace function 160, 348
reports 266–8, 294, 348
representation of data 50–65
resizing 186, 199
resolutions 41, 348

right-click insertion method 199
robotics 47, 327, 348
ROM *see* read only memory
root drive 75, 348
routers 92, 348
rows 184–5, 193, 198–9, 240
RSI *see* repetitive strain injury
runtime errors 134, 348

sales representatives 308–9
sample project 283–98
saving documents 154–5, 348
SBA project 283–98
scanning devices 18–21, 348
screens *see* monitors
search engines 98, 348
searching the Internet 98–101, 348
second generation computers 10
second generation language (2GL)
108–9
secondary files *see* data sources
secondary storage devices 28–36
sectors 29, 348
security 70, 138–49, 306
security cameras 330
select queries 257, 348
selecting items 159, 196, 271–4
selection statements 112–13, 119,
123–4
SEM format *see* sign, exponent and
mantissa format
sensors 23, 47, 348
sentinel value 126–7, 130, 348
sequential storage 29, 348
serial line internet protocol 91, 348
series 217, 348
servers 82–3, 95, 100, 348
sharing information 312, 314
short message service (SMS) 97
Show/Hide button 165
sign and magnitude representation
54–5
sign, exponent and mantissa (SEM)
format 62–3
signed integers 54–7
simplex lines 82, 348
simulations 329
size 41, 162, 163
skills 302, 337
SLIP 91, 348
smart cards 21, 318, 348
SMS *see* short message service
social effects of computers 337–8
soft copy output devices 40–3, 348
soft page breaks 172, 348
software 5, 66–80, 348
AI requirements 327
application software 66–8
banking requirements 316
business requirements 319
data security 139–41
e-mail requirements 95
education requirements 322
entertainment requirements 334
Internet requirements 91–2
law enforcement requirements
330
medicine requirements 332
system software 68–71
weather forecasting 336
software piracy 144–5
sorting data 212–13, 252–6, 288–9
sound 22, 42–3, 335
source code 134–5, 348
source documents 14, 348
spam 140
speakers 42
special characters 187–8
speech synthesis 43, 348
spelling check 160–1
spiders 98, 348
spreadsheets 192–232, 271–84,
286–91, 296
spyware 143–4, 348
star topology LANs 84, 348
Start buttons 74, 150–1

status bar 152
stock control 319
storage 26–39, 50–65, 312, 314
storage instructions 112, 116
stored-value cards 318, 348
strategic decision-making 313
string constants 115, 118, 349
string variables 116, 349
stylus 17, 349
subscript 164, 349
SUM function 206–7
supercomputers 8, 336
superscript 164, 349
surveillance 143–4, 331
symbols 187–8
syntax 101, 107, 349
syntax errors 134, 349
systems 68–71, 303
systems analysts 301–2, 349
systems development managers 301,
349

tables 184–5, 257, 347, 349
copying 245
creating 236–7
definition 234
entering records 244–5
linking 248–9
mail merge 271–6
SBA project 289
sorting 252
tablet PCs 8
tabs 173–4
tactical decision-making 313
tailor-made software 67–8
task bar 74, 150–1
task management 70
TCP/IP suite 91–2, 349
technical documentation 136
telecommuting 320–2, 349
telemarketing schemes online 146
tendonitis 339
terminal emulation services (TES)
93–4
terminating value *see* sentinel value
TES (terminal emulation services)
93–4
testing programs 132–5
text
editing/proofing 158–62
entering 153
Excel formatting 195–6
field size property 238
indenting 166–7
justification 166
selecting 159
wrapping 187, 197
text-based chat 96–7, 349
text and memo format 238
thermal printers 45
third generation computers 10
third generation language (3GL)
109–10
time-sharing 71
toolbars 163, 179, 184, 185
topologies 84–5, 349
totals, queries 263
touch-sensitive screens 17, 349
touchpad mouse 16
trace tables 132–3, 349
tracing 132, 349
trackball mouse 16
tracks 29, 349
traffic control 331
transistors 10
Transmission Control Protocol *see*
TCP...
Trojan horses 141
twisted pair cabled LANs 83, 349
two's complement 55–7

Undo button 161
uniform resource locators (URLs) 99,
100, 349
update query 257, 259, 349
updating data sources 180

uploading 90, 349
USB drives 34–6
user documentation/guides 136
user interfaces 71–4, 349
utilities 77

validation 14, 349
value axis 217, 349
values 194, 349
variables 116, 118, 121, 349
verification 14, 349
video card 41
video club database example 246
video input devices 21–3
virtual reality (VR) systems 329, 349
viruses 77, 141–2, 349
visual display units (VDUs) 40–2, 349
voice-band channels 81, 349
voice recognition 21–2, 328, 349
voice response systems 43, 349
*Voyager* space probes 51

WANS (wide area networks) 86, 349
weather forecasting 336–7
web *see* world wide web
web browsers *see* browsers
web-page designers 307–8
web portals *see* search engines
webcasts 101, 349
webinars 101, 349
webmasters 308, 349
WHILE construct 129–30
wildcards 261
Windows 72–7
wireless [illegible]ication 82
wirele[illegible] 6
wizard[illegible]54–7
Word 15[illegible]–8
*see also* word processing
word length 28, 349
word processing 150–91, 277–8,
285–6, 295–6, 298
word wrap 153, 349
words 28, 349
work-at-home schemes online 146
work pattern changes 338
workbooks 193, 349
worksheets 193, 349
cell references 212
navigating 194
printing 225–7
retrieval 196
so[illegible]38–9
[illegible]with 201–2
[illegible]el
world[illegible]WWW) 98–102
worms 141-
wrapping text 1[illegible]97